Excel® PivotTables and PivotCharts

Your visual blueprint™ for creating dynamic spreadsheets

by Paul McFedries

WILEY

Wiley Publishing, Inc.

Excel® PivotTables and PivotCharts: Your visual blueprint™ for creating dynamic spreadsheets

Published by
Wiley Publishing, Inc.
111 River Street
Hoboken, NJ 07030-5774

Published simultaneously in Canada

Library of Congress Control Number: 2005937348

ISBN-13: 978-0-471-78489-0

ISBN-10: 0-471-78489-3

Manufactured in the United States of America

10 9 8 7 6 5 4 3 2 1

1K/SY/QS/QW/IN

Trademark Acknowledgments

Contact Us

For general information on our other products and services please contact our Customer Care Department within the U.S. at 800-762-2974, outside the U.S. at 317-572-3993, or fax 317-572-4002.

For technical support please visit www.wiley.com/techsupport.

Karlstejn Castle

Constructed between 1348 and 1357 by Czech king and Holy Roman Emperor Charles IV, Karlstejn Castle was built to safeguard the crown jewels and sacred relics of the Holy Roman Empire. Its spectacular Great Tower rises above the hillside, creating a fairy-tale landmark less than an hour outside Prague. Discover more about Czech castles and the sites of Prague in *Frommer's Best of Prague and the Czech Republic,* available wherever books are sold or at www.frommers.com.

Sales

Contact Wiley
at (800) 762-2974
or (317) 572-4002.

Praise For Visual Books...

"This is absolutely the best computer-related book I have ever bought. Thank you so much for this fantastic text. Simply the best computer book series I have ever seen. I will look for, recommend, and purchase more of the same."

—David E. Prince (NeoNome.com)

"I have several of your Visual books and they are the best I have ever used."

—Stanley Clark (Crawfordville, FL)

"I just want to let you know that I really enjoy all your books. I'm a strong visual learner. You really know how to get people addicted to learning! I'm a very satisfied Visual customer. Keep up the excellent work!"

—Helen Lee (Calgary, Alberta, Canada)

"I have several books from the Visual series and have always found them to be valuable resources."

—Stephen P. Miller (Ballston Spa, NY)

"This book is PERFECT for me — it's highly visual and gets right to the point. What I like most about it is that each page presents a new task that you can try verbatim or, alternatively, take the ideas and build your own examples. Also, this book isn't bogged down with trying to 'tell all' – it gets right to the point. This is an EXCELLENT, EXCELLENT, EXCELLENT book and I look forward to purchasing other books in the series."

—Tom Dierickx (Malta, IL)

"I have quite a few of your Visual books and have been very pleased with all of them. I love the way the lessons are presented!"

—Mary Jane Newman (Yorba Linda, CA)

"I am an avid fan of your Visual books. If I need to learn anything, I just buy one of your books and learn the topic in no time. Wonders! I have even trained my friends to give me Visual books as gifts."

—Illona Bergstrom (Aventura, FL)

"I just had to let you and your company know how great I think your books are. I just purchased my third Visual book (my first two are dog-eared now!) and, once again, your product has surpassed my expectations. The expertise, thought, and effort that go into each book are obvious, and I sincerely appreciate your efforts."

—Tracey Moore (Memphis, TN)

"Compliments to the chef!! Your books are extraordinary! Or, simply put, extra-ordinary, meaning way above the rest! THANK YOU THANK YOU THANK YOU! I buy them for friends, family, and colleagues."

—Christine J. Manfrin (Castle Rock, CO)

"I write to extend my thanks and appreciation for your books. They are clear, easy to follow, and straight to the point. Keep up the good work! I bought several of your books and they are just right! No regrets! I will always buy your books because they are the best."

—Seward Kollie (Dakar, Senegal)

"I am an avid purchaser and reader of the Visual series, and they are the greatest computer books I've seen. Thank you very much for the hard work, effort, and dedication that you put into this series."

—Alex Diaz (Las Vegas, NV)

July 05

Credits

Project Editor
Sarah Hellert

Acquisitions Editor
Jody Lefevere

Product Development Supervisor
Courtney Allen

Copy Editor
Tricia Liebig

Technical Editor
Namir Shammas

Editorial Manager
Robyn Siesky

Business Manager
Amy Knies

Media Development Specialist
Steve Kudirka

Manufacturing
Allan Conley
Linda Cook
Paul Gilchrist
Jennifer Guynn

Book Design
Kathie S. Rickard

Production Coordinator
Maridee V. Ennis

Layout
Joyce Haughey
Jennifer Heleine
LeAndra Hosier
Amanda Spagnuolo

Screen Artist
Jill A. Proll

Cover Illustration
Matthew Bell

Illustrator
Ronda David-Burroughs

Proofreader
Lisa Stiers

Quality Control
John Greenough

Indexer
Infodex Indexing Services, Inc.

Vice President and Executive Group Publisher
Richard Swadley

Vice President Publisher
Barry Pruett

Composition Director
Debbie Stailey

About the Author

Paul McFedries is the president of Logophilia Limited, a technical writing company. While now primarily a writer, Paul has worked as a programmer, consultant, and Web site developer. Paul has written over 40 books that have sold over three million copies worldwide. These books include the Wiley titles *Teach Yourself VISUALLY Windows XP, Second Edition*, *Top 100 Simplified Tips and Tricks for Windows XP, Second Edition*, and *Teach Yourself VISUALLY Computers, Fourth Edition*.

Author's Acknowledgments

I think you will find that the book you hold in your hands is an excellent learning tool. I am happy to have supplied the text that you will read, but the layout of the tasks, the accuracy of the spelling and grammar, and the veracity of the information are all the result of hard work performed by project editor Sarah Hellert, copy editor Tricia Liebig, and technical editor Namir Shammas. Thanks to all of you for your excellent work. My thanks, as well, to acquisitions editor Jody Lefevere for bringing me onboard.

TABLE OF CONTENTS

TABLE OF CONTENTS

HOW TO USE THIS BOOK

Excel PivotTables and Charts: Your visual blueprint for creating dynamic spreadsheets uses clear, descriptive examples to show you how to use Excel PivotTables and PivotCharts to analyze, summarize, and visualize large amounts of data. If you have never used a PivotTable or a PivotChart, this book will show you how powerful and useful they can be. As well, this book will give you step-by-step, visual guidance on how to create PivotTables and PivotCharts and how to customize them to suit your needs. If you are already familiar with Excel PivotTables and PivotCharts, you can use this book as a quick reference for almost anything you can do with Excel PivotTable and PivotCharts.

Who Needs This Book

This book is for experienced computer users who have never used Excel PivotTables and PivotCharts and are interested in finding out what these powerful Excel tools are all about, what they can do, and how they can enhance spreadsheet data analysis. This book is also for more experienced Excel PivotTables and PivotCharts users who want to take their understanding of these tools to a higher level by expanding their knowledge of the different features that Excel PivotTables and PivotCharts have to offer.

Book Organization

Excel PivotTables and PivotCharts: Your visual blueprint for creating dynamic spreadsheets has 11 chapters and 5 appendixes.

Chapter 1, "Understanding PivotTables," introduces you to PivotTables. You learn about data analysis, basic PivotTable concepts, the benefits, uses, and features of PivotTables, and the basics of PivotCharts.

In Chapter 2, you learn how to build a basic PivotTable from the data in an Excel list.

Chapter 3, "Manipulating Your PivotTable," takes you through a number of techniques for working with various parts of a PivotTable. Techniques such as selecting PivotTable items, removing fields from the PivotTable, and refreshing the PivotTable data will be used throughout the book. You also learn important tasks such as publishing a PivotTable to a Web page as well as printing and deleting PivotTables.

The topics in Chapter 4 all deal with changing the PivotTable view, and they include moving fields ("pivoting" the data), sorting PivotTable data, hiding PivotTable items, and grouping PivotTable data values.

In Chapter 5 you learn how to customize PivotTable field. You find out how to rename and field or item, format a PivotTable cell, apply numeric and date formats to PivotTable data, and more.

Chapter 6 takes you through a few PivotTable options, including applying an AutoFormat to an entire PivotTable, renaming a PivotTable, turning off grand totals, and protecting a PivotTable from changes.

Chapter 7, "Performing PivotTable Calculations," shows you how to work with a PivotTable's summary calculations. You learn how to change the calculation and how to convert the calculation to using the powerful difference, percentage, running total, and index summaries.

In Chapter 8, you learn how to create your own custom PivotTable calculations. You learn what custom calculations are, what you can do with them, and what limitations they have. From there, you find out how to create custom calculated fields and items and how to edit and manipulate these calculations.

In Chapter 9, you find out more about PivotCharts and you learn how to create them from existing PivotTables as well as from an Excel list. You also learn a number of PivotChart techniques, including how to change the chart type, change the series order, add titles, and how to print and delete PivotCharts.

Chapter 10, "Building More Advanced PivotTables," shows you how to create PivotTables from multiple consolidation ranges, from existing PivotTables, from external data, and from PivotTable data in a Web page.

In Chapter 11, you find out about online analytical processing (OLAP) and you learn how to create a PivotTable from an OLAP cube.

Appendix A tells you everything you need to know to build formulas for custom PivotTable calculations.

In Appendix B, you learn how to use Microsoft Query to work with external data that you can use in your PivotTables.

Appendix C shows you how to import data into Excel for use in a PivotTable. You learn how to import from a data source, an Access table, a Word table, a text file, a Web page, and an XML file.

Appendix D teaches you the basics of VBA that you need to know to use the various VBA scripts that are presented throughout the book to automate PivotTable tasks.

Appendix E presents a glossary of PivotTable and PivotChart terminology.

What You Need to Use This Book

For hardware, you will just need whatever is required by Office to work with Excel in the examples in this book. Several tasks show you how to use Excel with VBA, so you will need VBA for those tasks. Other tasks show how to use Excel with the Internet, so access to a site will be necessary. Many of the book's examples use data from the Northwind sample database that comes with Microsoft Access, so it would help if you have this database available. The other examples are available on the book's companion Web site — see the section "What's on the Web Site."

Windows Requirements

Windows 98, 2000, NT, ME, or XP

The Conventions in This Book

A number of styles have been used throughout *Excel PivotTables and Charts: Your visual blueprint for creating dynamic spreadsheets* to designate different types of information.

`Courier Font`

Indicates the use of PHP such as tags or attributes, scripting language code such as statements, operators, or functions, and code such as objects, methods, or properties.

Italics

Indicates a new term.

Numbered Steps

You must perform the instructions in numbered steps in order to successfully complete a section and achieve the final results.

Indented Text

Indented text tells you what the program does in response following a numbered step. For example, if you click a certain menu command, a dialog box may appear, or a window may open. Indented text after a step may also present another way to perform the step.

Notes

Notes give additional information. They may describe special conditions that may occur during an operation. They may warn you of a situation that you want to avoid, for example, the loss of data. A note may also cross reference a related area of the book. A cross reference may guide you to another chapter, or another section within the current chapter.

Icons

Icons are graphical representations within the text. They show you exactly what you need to click to perform a step.

Apply It

An Apply It section takes the code from the preceding task one step further. Apply It sections allow you to take full advantage of Excel PivotTables and Charts.

Extra

An Extra section provides additional information about the preceding task. Extra sections contain the inside information to make working with Excel PivotTables and PivotCharts easier and more efficient.

What's on the Web Site

The Web site www.wiley.com/go/pivottablesvb contains the sample files that you can use to work with the tasks in *Excel PivotTables and PivotCharts: Your visual blueprint for creating dynamic spreadsheets.*

Understanding Data Analysis

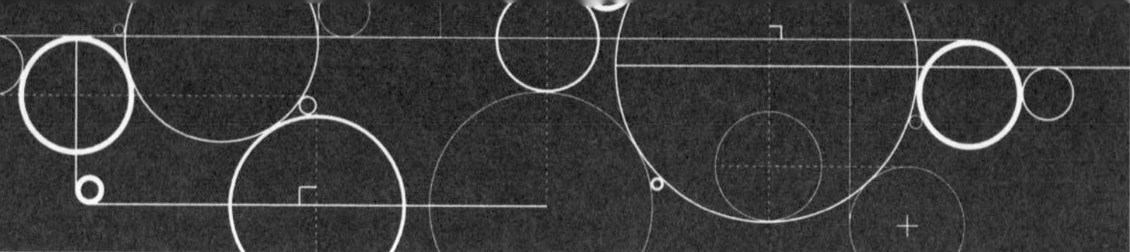

The PivotTables and PivotCharts that you learn about in this book are part of the larger category of *data analysis*. You can get the most out of these tools if you have a broader understanding of what data analysis is, what its benefits are, and what other tools are available to you.

Data analysis is the application of tools and techniques to organize, study, reach conclusions about, and sometimes also make predictions about, a specific collection of information. A sales manager might use data analysis to study the sales history of a product, determine the overall trend, and produce a forecast of future sales. A scientist might use data analysis to study experimental findings and determine the statistical significance of the results. A family might use data analysis to find the maximum mortgage they can afford or how much they must put aside each month to finance their retirement or their kids' education.

The point of data analysis is to understand information on some deeper, more meaningful level. By definition, raw data is a mere collection of facts that by themselves tell you little or nothing of any importance. To gain some understanding of the data, you must manipulate it in some meaningful way. This could be something as simple as taking the sum or average of a column of numbers, or as complex as a full-scale regression analysis to determine the underlying trend of a range of values. Both are examples of data analysis, and Excel offers a number of tools — from the straightforward to the sophisticated — to meet even the most demanding needs.

Data

The "data" part of data analysis is a collection of numbers, dates, and text that represents the raw information you have to work with. In Excel, this data resides inside a worksheet and you get it there in one of two ways: you enter it by hand or you import it from an external source. You can then either leave the data as a regular range, or you can convert it into a list for easier data manipulation.

Data Entry

In many data analysis situations, the required data must be entered into the worksheet manually. For example, if you want to determine a potential monthly mortgage payment, you must first enter values such as the current interest rate, the principal, and the term. Manual data entry is suitable for small projects only, because entering hundreds or even thousands of values is time-consuming and can lead to errors.

List

After you have your data in the worksheet, you can leave it as a regular range and still apply many data analysis techniques to the data. However, if you convert the range into a *list*, Excel treats the data as a simple flat-file database and enables you to apply a number of database-specific analysis techniques to the list. In Chapter 2, see the task "Create a List for a PivotTable Report."

Imported Data

Most data analysis projects involve large amounts of data, and the fastest and most accurate way to get that data onto a worksheet is to import it from a non-Excel data source. In the simplest scenario, you can copy the data — from a text file, a Word table, or an Access datasheet — and then paste it into a worksheet. However, most business and scientific data is stored in large databases, and Excel offers tools to import the data you need into your worksheet. See Appendixes B and C for more about these tools.

Data Models

In many cases, you perform data analysis on worksheet values by organizing those values into a *data model*, a collection of cells designed as a worksheet version of some real-world concept or scenario. The model includes not only the raw data, but also one or more cells that represent some analysis of the data. For example, a mortgage amortization model would have the mortgage data — interest rate, principal, and term — and also cells that calculate the payment, principal, and interest over the term. For such calculations, you use formulas and Excel's built-in functions, as described in Appendix A, "Building Formulas for PivotTables."

Formulas

A *formula* is a set of symbols and values that perform some kind of calculation and produce a result. All Excel formulas have the same general structure: an equals sign (=) followed by one or more *operands* — which can be a value, a cell reference, a range, a range name, or a function name — separated by one or more *operators* — the symbols that combine the operands in some way, such as the plus sign (+) and the multiplication sign (*). For example, the formula `=A1+A2` adds the values in cells A1 and A2.

Functions

A *function* is a predefined formula that is built into Excel. Each function takes one or more inputs — called *arguments*, such as numbers or cell references — and then returns a result. Excel offers hundreds of functions and you can use them to compute averages, determine the future value of an investment, compare values, and much more.

What-If Analysis

One of the most common data analysis techniques is *what-if analysis*, where you set up worksheet models to analyze hypothetical situations. The what-if part comes from the fact that these situations usually come in the form of a question: "What happens to the monthly payment if the interest rate goes up by 2 percent?" "What will the sales be if we increase the advertising budget by 10 percent?" Excel offers four what-if analysis tools: data tables, Goal Seek, Solver, and scenarios.

Data Tables

A *data table* is a range of cells where one column consists of a series of values, called *input cells*. You can then apply each of those inputs to a single formula, and Excel displays the results for each case. For example, you could use a data table to apply a series of interest rate values to a formula that calculates the monthly payment for a loan or mortgage.

Solver

You use Excel's Solver tool when you want to manipulate multiple formula components — called the *changing cells* — in such a way that the formula produces the optimal result. For example, you can use Solver to tackle the so-called *transportation problem*, where the goal is to minimize the cost of shipping goods from several product plants to various warehouses around the country.

Goal Seek

You use Excel's Goal Seek tool when you want to manipulate one formula component — called the *changing cell* — in such a way that the formula produces a specific result. For example, in a *break-even analysis*, you determine the number of units of a product that you must sell for the profit to be 0. Given a formula that calculates profit, you could use Goal Seek to determine the break-even point.

Scenarios

A *scenario* is a collection of input values that you plug into formulas within a model to produce a result. The idea is that you make up scenarios for various situations — for example, best-case, worst-case, and so on — and Excel's Scenario Manager saves each one. Later you can apply any of the saved scenarios, and Excel automatically applies all the input values to the model.

Introducing the PivotTable

Lists and external databases can contain hundreds or even thousands of records. Analyzing that much data can be a nightmare without the right kinds of tools. To help you, Excel offers a powerful data analysis tool called a *PivotTable*. This tool enables you to summarize hundreds of records in a concise tabular format. You can then manipulate the layout — or *pivot* — of the table to see different views of your data.

This book teaches you everything you need to know (and, indeed, just about everything there *is* to know) about PivotTables. You learn how to create them, edit them, pivot them, format them, calculate with them, and much more. You can get more out of the rest of the book if you take a few minutes now to get acquainted with some PivotTable background and basics.

Database Analysis

To understand pivot tables, you need to see how they fit in with Excel's other database-analysis features. Database analysis has three levels of complexity: lookup and retrieval, criteria and list functions, and multiple variables. As you move from one level to another, the need for PivotTables becomes apparent.

Lookup and Retrieval

The simplest level of database analysis involves the basic lookup and retrieval of information. For example, if you have a database that lists the company sales reps and their territory sales, you could use a data form (or even Excel Find feature) to search for a specific rep and to look up the sales in that rep's territory.

Criteria and List Functions

The next level of database analysis complexity involves more sophisticated lookup and retrieval systems in which you apply criteria to work with a subset of the data. You can then use this subset to apply subtotals and Excel's list functions (such as the `DSUM()` function, which sums those list cells that meet some specified criteria). For example, suppose that each sales territory is part of a larger region, and you want to know the total sales in the eastern region. You could either subtotal by region or set up your criteria to match all territories in the eastern region and use `DSUM()` to get the total. To get more specific information, such as total eastern region sales in the second quarter, you just add the appropriate conditions to your criteria.

Multiple Variables

The next level of database analysis applies a single question to multiple variables. For example, if the company in the preceding example has four regions, you might want to see separate totals for each region broken down by quarter. One solution would be to set up four different criteria and four different `DSUM()` functions. But what if there were a dozen regions? Or a hundred? Ideally, you need some way of summarizing the database information into a sales table that has a row for each region and a column for each quarter. This is exactly what PivotTables do and, as you see with Excel's PivotTable Wizard in the Chapter 2 task "Build a Basic PivotTable from an Excel List," you can create your own PivotTables with just a few mouse clicks.

What PivotTables Do

PivotTables help you analyze large amounts of data by performing three different operations: grouping the data into categories, summarizing the data using calculations, and filtering the data to show just the records you want to work with.

Grouping

A PivotTable is a powerful data analysis tool in part because it automatically groups large amounts of data into smaller, more manageable categories. For example, suppose you have a data source with a Region field where each cell contains one of four values: East, West, North, and South. The original data may contain thousands of records, but if you build your PivotTable using the Region field, the resulting table will have just four rows — one each for the four unique Region values in your data.

You can also create your own grouping after you have built your PivotTable. For example, if your data has a Country field, you could build the PivotTable to group together all the records that have the same Country value. When you have done that, you can further group the unique Country values into continents: North America, South America, Europe, and so on. See Chapter 4 to learn how to group PivotTable values.

Summarizing

In conjunction with grouping data according to the unique values in one or more fields, Excel also displays summary calculations for each group. The default calculation is Sum, which means for each group, Excel totals all the values in some specified field. For example, if your data has a Region field and a Sales field, a PivotTable could group the unique Region values and, for each one, display the total Sales. Excel has other summary calculations, including Count, Average, Maximum, Minimum, and Standard Deviation.

Even more powerful, a PivotTable can display summaries for one grouping broken down by another. For example, suppose your sales data also has a Product field. You could set up a PivotTable to show the total Sales for each Product, broken down by Region.

Filtering

A PivotTable also enables you to view just a subset of the data. For example, by default the PivotTable's groupings show all the unique values in the field. However, you can manipulate each grouping to hide those that you do not want to view; see the task "Hide Items in a Row or Column Field," in Chapter 4. Each PivotTable also comes with a page area — see the section "Explore PivotTable Features," later in this chapter — that enables you to apply a filter to the entire PivotTable. For example, suppose your sales data also includes a Customer field. By placing this field in the PivotTable's page area, you can filter the PivotTable report to show just the results for a single Customer.

PivotTable Limitations

PivotTables come with certain limitations and restrictions that you need to be familiar with. See the section "Explore PivotTable Features," later in this chapter, for explanations of the PivotTable terminology used here:

- The maximum number of column fields is 256. (Note that there is no maximum number of row fields.)
- The maximum number of page fields is 256.
- The maximum number of data fields is 256.
- The maximum number of items that can appear in a row field is 32,500. (If you are using a version of Excel prior to 2003, the maximum number is 8,000.)
- The maximum number of items that can appear in a column field is 32,500. (If you are using a version of Excel prior to 2003, the maximum number is 8,000.)
- The maximum number of items that can appear in a page field is 32,500. (If you are using a version of Excel prior to 2003, the maximum number is 8,000.)
- The size and number of PivotTables are limited by how much available memory your system has.

Learn PivotTable Benefits

If Excel comes with so many powerful data analysis tools and features, why do you need to learn how to build and work with PivotTables? The short answer is that PivotTables are a useful weapon to add to your data analysis arsenal. The long answer is that PivotTables are worth learning because they come with not just one or two, but a long list of benefits.

PivotTables are easy to build and maintain; PivotTables perform large and complex calculations amazingly fast; PivotTables are quickly and easily updated to account for new data; PivotTables are dynamic, so components can be easily moved, filtered, and added to; PivotTables are fully customizable so you can build each report the way you want; and, finally, PivotTables can use most of the formatting options that you can apply to regular Excel ranges and cells.

PivotTables Save Time

These days, we all have far too much to do and far too little time in which to do it. Computers are supposed to help us with this problem by reducing the amount of time we spend on routine tasks, such as adding up rows of numbers. Some computer features have the opposite effect — e-mail, for example, takes up increasing amounts of our time — but PivotTables are not one of them. The chore PivotTables are designed to replace — cross-tabulating massive amounts of data — is inherently time-consuming. But PivotTables, by virtue of being easy to use, lightning fast, and readily updated, reduce that time to a mere fraction of what it was, resulting in true time savings.

Easy

Perhaps the most important benefit of PivotTables is that they do not come with a daunting learning curve. After you understand the basic features, you can use the PivotTable Wizard to build a simple PivotTable report with as little as nine mouse clicks; see the section "Explore PivotTable Features," later in this chapter. Even the most complex PivotTables are not much harder to build because the Wizard takes you through everything step by step — in Chapter 2, see the task "Build a Basic PivotTable from an Excel List".

Fast

The average PivotTable must do quite a bit of work when it generates its report: it must analyze hundreds or even thousands of records, each of which may have a dozen or more fields, extract the unique values from one or more fields, calculate the data summary for each unique item, and then lay everything out on the worksheet. Amazingly, for all but the largest data sources, this entire process usually only takes a second or two.

Updateable

PivotTables are often used in situations where the original data changes. When that happens, the PivotTable can become out-of-date. However, each PivotTable "remembers" the original data upon which the report was based. This means that when a PivotTable is out-of-date, you do not need to re-create the report from scratch. Instead, you can run the Refresh Data command which instantly updates the PivotTable with the latest data. You can even set up your PivotTable to refresh its data automatically. For the details on refreshing PivotTables, see the task in Chapter 3 titled "Refresh PivotTable Data."

PivotTables Are Flexible

One of the traits that makes a PivotTable a powerful data analysis tool is its flexibility. For example, when you create a PivotTable, the resulting report is not set in stone. Instead, you can move components from one part of the PivotTable to another, filter the results, add and remove data, and more. Another aspect of the flexibility of PivotTables is their versatility, which means that you can create them from more than just Excel ranges and lists.

Dynamic

Every PivotTable is a dynamic creation that you can reconfigure to produce the kind of report you need. Specifically, most of the fields that you add to the PivotTable you can also move from one part of the report to another. This is called *pivoting* the data, and it causes Excel to reconfigure the PivotTable and recalculate the results. Excel produces the updated PivotTable immediately, so you can use this feature as needed, making PivotTables even more powerful and useful. In Chapter 4, see the task "Move a Field to a Different Area" to learn how to pivot data.

Manipulable

You can easily and quickly manipulate your PivotTable layout to get the results you are looking for. For example, you can always add new fields to any part of the PivotTable, usually with just a few mouse clicks, and you can easily remove any fields that you no longer need. Also, as you learned in the previous section, you can group and filter the PivotTable results to work with just the data you need.

Versatile

If you could create PivotTables only from an Excel range or list, then they would still be enormously useful. However, Excel has made PivotTables versatile enough to handle many other types of data. You can create them from Access tables, Word tables, text files, Web pages, XML data, and from tables in powerful database systems such as SQL Server and Online Analytical Processing (OLAP) servers. See Chapter 10 to build advanced PivotTables, and Chapter 11 to build a PivotTable from an OLAP Cube.

PivotTables Suit Your Needs

Although many of the PivotTables that you create will be for your own use, you will also likely find that you set up PivotTables for other people to view, either on-screen, on paper, or even on the Web; see the task in Chapter 3 titled "Publish a PivotTable to a Web Page." In these more public situations, you will usually want to set up your PivotTable so that it looks its best. To that end, Excel has given PivotTables a number of features that enable you to customize and format them as needed.

Customizing

Each PivotTable comes with a number of options that you can use to customize both the report as a whole and individual PivotTable components. For example, you can hide items, sort the data, and customize the report printout. You can also customize the calculations used in the report, either by changing to one of Excel's built-in calculations, or by defining custom calculations. For more about custom calculations, see Chapter 8.

Formatting

After you have the PivotTable result you want, you can spend time dressing up the report to make the data easier on the eyes. Fortunately, most of the cells in a PivotTable act as regular Excel cells. This means you can format them in the same way by changing the font, applying colors and borders, using numeric and date formats, and much more. See Chapter 5 to customize your PivotTable fields.

Survey PivotTable Uses

One of the keys to using Excel's data analysis tools is knowing which tool to use under which circumstances. If you want to glean one or two facts about your data, then a formula or two is often all you need. For more elaborate needs, especially ones where you need to build a worksheet version of some real-world concept, a data model is required. If you want to "interrogate" your data by plugging various values into a formula and comparing the results, a data table is best. If you are looking for a particular or optimal result, use Goal Seek for simple models or Solver for more complex models.

PivotTables, too, are best used only in certain scenarios. The situations where a PivotTable is your best data analysis tool — or, at least, a worthwhile one to consider — fall into three categories: the structure of the underlying data; the analysis you require; and your (or your manager's) reporting needs.

Data Structure

More than any other factor, the structure of your data determines whether a PivotTable is a good data analysis choice. Certain types of data simply cannot be analyzed in a PivotTable, while other data sets would produce largely useless results. In general, the best data structure for PivotTables is one where the data exists in a tabular format with consistent and repeated data, such as those found in databases of transactions. For more detailed information on setting up your data for a PivotTable report, see the section in Chapter 2 titled "Prepare Your Worksheet Data."

Tabular Data

Your data is a good candidate for a PivotTable analysis if it exists in tabular format. This means that the data is arranged in a row-and-column structure, with the same number of columns used in each row. If your data is scattered around the worksheet and cannot be rearranged into tabular format, you cannot build a PivotTable from it.

Consistent and Repeated Data

You should consider a PivotTable analysis if your tabular data also has consistent and repeated values. Consistent values means that each column contains the same type of data in the same format. For example, one column contains only customer names, another contains only order dates, and a third contains only invoice amounts. Repeated values means that at least one column contains only a limited number of values that repeat throughout the records. For example, a Region column may contain just four values — such as East, West, North, and South — that are repeated over hundreds or thousands of records.

Transactional Data

The perfect type of data to benefit from a PivotTable analysis is *transactional* data that records frequent, consistent exchanges of information. Common examples of transactional data include customer orders, accounts receivable, experiment results, inventory totals, product sales, survey answers, and production schedules. This transactional data creates the same data structure for each record, has consistent data, and has repeated values in at least one field, all of which make this kind of data ideal for a PivotTable approach.

Analysis Required

When deciding whether to build a PivotTable from your data, think about the type of analysis you require. What is your goal? What do you need to know? What secret do you suspect is hidden within all that data? Generally, building a PivotTable is a good idea if you are seeking one or more of the following as part of your analysis of the data: a list of unique values in a field; a summary of a large amount of data; relationships between two or more fields; and the trend of the data over time.

Unique Values

When faced with a huge amount of data, you may find that one of the first things you want from that data is a list of the unique values in some field. For example, in a database of thousands of orders, you may simply want to know which customers placed orders. The PivotTable is your best choice here because extracting a list of the unique values that occur in a field is one of the things that PivotTables do best.

Summary

Analyzing data often means summarizing it in some way: totaling it, counting it, finding the average or maximum value, and so on. Excel has worksheet functions, subtotals, and other tools for this kind of analysis, but none of them are suitable for summarizing large amounts of data, particularly if you want to view the results in a compact report. To do that, you must build a PivotTable.

Relationships

One of the biggest problems you face when confronted with a large data set is determining the relationships that exist between one field and another. Which customers are buying which products? How do product defects vary by manufacturing plant? PivotTables are ideal for this kind of analysis because they can break down the values in one field with respect to another. For example, you can display the total sales generated by each of your salespeople, and then break that down by customer, country, product, category, and so on.

Trends

If your data includes a field with date or time values, you may be interested to see how a particular field varies over time. This *trend analysis* can be extremely useful, and Excel has several powerful tools to help you see the trend. However, a PivotTable is an excellent choice if you want to summarize one field and break it down according to the date or time values. How do sales vary throughout the year? How do manufacturing defects vary throughout the day or week?

Reporting Needs

The final aspect to consider when deciding whether to analyze your data with a PivotTable is to determine what your reporting needs are. In other words, what do you want to end up with? Choose the PivotTable route if you want to end up with a report that is flexible and can easily handle frequent changes.

Flexibility

Build a PivotTable to analyze your data if you want the flexibility to change the report quickly and easily. If you need to switch the layout — for example, to switch from a vertical layout to a horizontal one — you can pivot any field with a click and drag of the mouse. If you need to view subsets of the results, you can filter the report based on the values in a particular field.

Frequent Changes

Choose a PivotTable if you think your underlying data will change frequently. You can easily update the PivotTable to use the latest data, so your report is always accurate and up to date. It is also easy to change the structure of the PivotTable — by adding a new field that has been inserted into the data — so you can always incorporate new data.

Explore PivotTable Features

You can get up to speed with PivotTables very quickly after you learn a few key concepts. You need to understand the features that make up a typical PivotTable, particularly the four areas — row, column, data, and page — to which you add fields from your data.

You also need to understand some important PivotTable terminology that you will encounter throughout this book, including terms such as *source data*, *pivot cache*, and *summary calculation*.

Ⓐ PAGE AREA

Displays a drop-down list that contains the unique values from a field. When you select a value from the list, Excel filters the PivotTable results to include only the records that match the selected value.

Ⓑ COLUMN AREA

Displays horizontally the unique values from a field in your data.

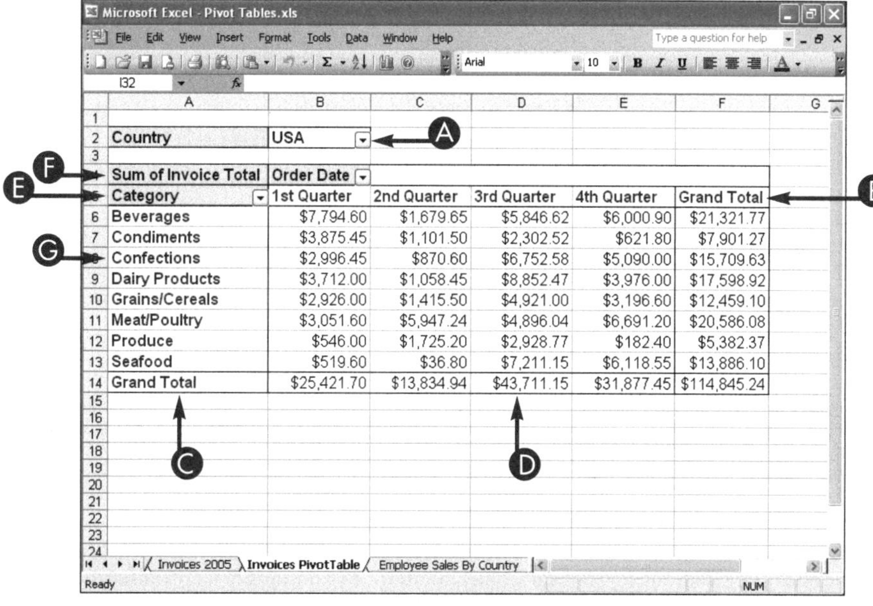

Sum of Invoice Total	Order Date				
Category	1st Quarter	2nd Quarter	3rd Quarter	4th Quarter	Grand Total
Beverages	$7,794.60	$1,679.65	$5,846.62	$6,000.90	$21,321.77
Condiments	$3,875.45	$1,101.50	$2,302.52	$621.80	$7,901.27
Confections	$2,996.45	$870.60	$6,752.58	$5,090.00	$15,709.63
Dairy Products	$3,712.00	$1,058.45	$8,852.47	$3,976.00	$17,598.92
Grains/Cereals	$2,926.00	$1,415.50	$4,921.00	$3,196.60	$12,459.10
Meat/Poultry	$3,051.60	$5,947.24	$4,896.04	$6,691.20	$20,586.08
Produce	$546.00	$1,725.20	$2,928.77	$182.40	$5,382.37
Seafood	$519.60	$36.80	$7,211.15	$6,118.55	$13,886.10
Grand Total	$25,421.70	$13,834.94	$43,711.15	$31,877.45	$114,845.24

Ⓒ ROW AREA

Displays vertically the unique values from a field in your data.

Ⓓ DATA AREA

Displays the results of the calculation that Excel applied to a numeric field in your data.

Ⓔ FIELD BUTTON

Identifies the field contained in the area. You also use the field button to move a field from one area to another.

Ⓖ FIELD ITEMS

The unique values for the field added to the particular area.

Ⓕ DATA FIELD BUTTON

Specifies both the calculation (such as Sum) and the field (such as Invoice Total) used in the data area.

PivotTable Glossary

PivotTables come with their own terminology, much of which may be unfamiliar to you, even if you have extensive experience with Excel. To learn PivotTables faster, you should understand not only the terms on the previous page, but also the words and phrases that appear in this glossary.

Source Data

The original data from which you built your PivotTable. The source data can be an Excel range or list, an Access table, a Word table, a text file, a Web page, an XML file, SQL Server data, or OLAP server data, among others.

External Data

Source data that comes from a non-Excel file or database. You can use Microsoft Query to import external data into your Excel worksheet; see Appendix B. Or you can use Excel's other data import tools; see Appendix C.

Pivot Cache

This is the source data that Excel keeps in memory to improve PivotTable performance.

Outer Field and Inner Field

When you have multiple fields in the row or column area — see the task in Chapter 3 titled "Add Multiple Fields to the Row or Column Area" — Excel places the fields either beside each other, in the row area, or one on top of the other, in the column area. In either case, the field that is closest to the data area is called the *inner field*, and the field that is furthest from the data area is called the *outer field*.

Drop Area

A region of the PivotTable onto which you can drop a field from the source data or from another area of the PivotTable. Excel displays each drop area with a blue border.

Pivot

To move a field from one drop area of the PivotTable to another.

Labels

The non-data area elements of the PivotTable. The labels include the field buttons, field items, and page area drop-down list.

Data

The calculated values that appear within the data area.

Summary Calculation

The mathematical operation that Excel applies to the values in a numeric field to yield the summary that appears in the data area. Excel offers 11 built-in summary calculations: Sum, Count, Average, Maximum, Minimum, Product, Count Numbers, Standard Deviation (sample), Standard Deviation (population), Variance (sample), and Variance (population); see Chapter 7. You can also create custom calculations; see Chapter 8.

Introducing the PivotChart

When you begin the process of building a PivotTable, Excel actually gives you a choice between building a PivotTable or a PivotChart. In basic terms, a PivotChart is to a PivotTable what a regular chart is to a range. That is, the former is a graphical representation of the latter. So the PivotChart enables you to visualize the PivotTable results by displaying the data area values in chart form.

However, it is also possible to say that a PivotChart is to a regular chart what a PivotTable is to a regular range. In other words, the PivotChart goes far beyond the capabilities of a simple chart because the PivotChart comes with most of the same features that make PivotTables so powerful: you can filter the results to see just the data you need, and you can pivot fields from one area of the PivotChart to another to get the layout you want. See Chapter 9 to learn how to create and work with PivotCharts.

PivotChart Concepts

As you might expect, PivotCharts have a number of elements in common with PivotTables, but there are also some key differences. The following items explain these differences and introduce you to some important PivotChart concepts.

Chart Categories (X-Axis)

Like a PivotTable, a PivotChart automatically groups large amounts of data into smaller, more manageable groups. For example, if you have data with a Category field containing values such as Beverages, Condiments, Confections, and so on, if you build your PivotChart using the Category field, the resulting chart will display one chart category (X-axis value) for each unique Category field value. This is the equivalent of a row field in a PivotTable.

Chart Data Series

Also, as with a PivotTable, you can break down your data in terms of a second field. For example, your data may have an Order Date field. If you add that field to the PivotChart, Excel creates one data series for each unique value in that field. This is the equivalent of a Column field in a PivotTable.

Chart Values (Y-Axis)

You can't have a PivotTable without a data field, and the same is true with a PivotChart. When you add a numeric field for the summary calculation, Excel displays the results as chart values (Y-axis). This is the equivalent of a data field in a PivotTable.

Filtering

Like a PivotTable, you can use the unique values in another field to filter the results that appear in the PivotChart. For example, if your source data has a Country field, you could add it to the PivotChart and use it to filter the chart results to show just those from a specific country. This is the equivalent of a page field in a PivotTable.

Dynamic PivotCharts

Perhaps the biggest difference between a PivotChart and a regular chart is that each PivotChart is a dynamic object that you can reconfigure as needed, just like a PivotTable. You can pivot fields from one area of the chart to another; you can add fields to different chart areas; and you can place multiple fields in any chart area.

Pros and Cons

PivotCharts have advantages and disadvantages, and understanding their strengths and weaknesses will help you decide when and if you should use them. On the positive side, a PivotChart is a powerful data analysis tool because it combines the strengths of Excel's charting capabilities — including most of the options available with regular charts — with the features of a PivotTable. Also, creating a basic PivotChart is just as easy as creating a PivotTable. In fact, if you already have a PivotTable, you can create the equivalent PivotChart with just a couple mouse clicks.

On the negative side, PivotCharts share the same caveats that come with regular charts, particularly the fact that if you do not choose the proper chart type or layout, your data will not be easily understood. Moreover, a PivotChart can quickly become extremely confusing when you have multiple category fields or data series fields. Finally, PivotCharts have inherent limitations that restrict the options and formatting you can apply. See the section in Chapter 9 titled "Understanding PivotChart Limitations."

PivotCharts carry over some of the same terminology that you saw earlier for PivotTables, including the concepts of the *page area*, *data area*, and *field button*. However, PivotCharts also use a number of unique terms such as *category axis* and *series axis* that you need to understand to get the most out of PivotCharts.

A PAGE AREA

Displays a drop-down list with unique values from a field that you use to filter the PivotChart data.

B CATEGORY ITEMS

The unique values from a field that define the chart's categories.

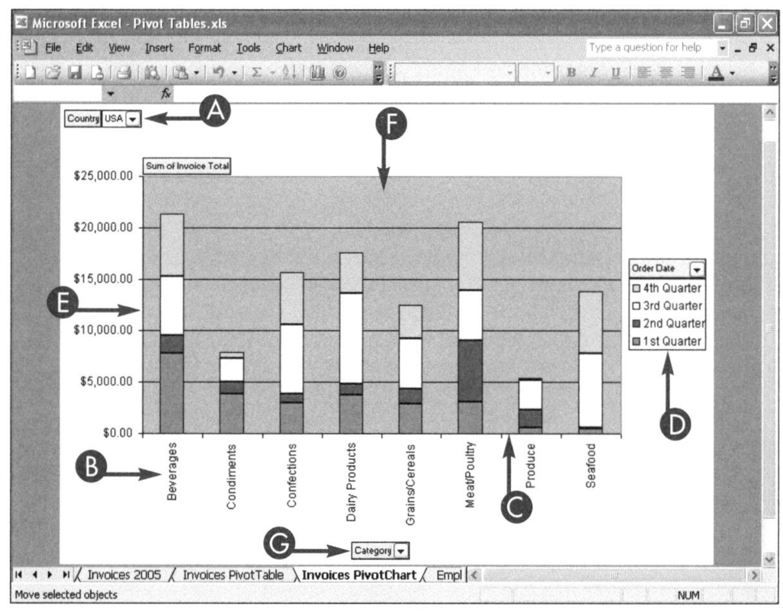

C CATEGORY AXIS

The chart axis (X-axis) that displays the category items.

D DATA SERIES ITEMS

The unique values from a field that define the chart's data series. The item names appear in the chart legend.

E SERIES AXIS

The chart axis (Y-axis) that displays the values of the data series items.

G FIELD BUTTON

Identifies the field contained in the area. You also use the field button to move a field from one area to another.

F DATA AREA

Displays the charted results of the calculation that Excel applied to a numeric field in your data.

Prepare Your Worksheet Data

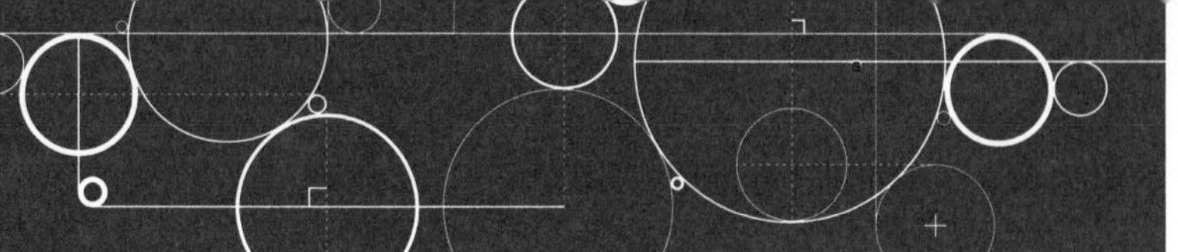

The most common method for building a PivotTable is to use data that exists in an Excel worksheet. You can make this task much easier by taking a few minutes to prepare your worksheet data for use in the PivotTable. Ensuring your data is properly prepared will also ensure that your PivotTable contains accurate and complete summaries of the data.

Preparing your worksheet data for use in a PivotTable is not difficult or time-consuming. At a minimum, you must ensure that the data is organized in a row-and-column format, with unique headings at the top of each column and accurate and consistent data — all numbers or all text — within each column. You also need to remove blank rows, turn off automatic subtotals, and format the data. In some cases, you may also need to add range names to the data, filter the data, and restructure the data so that worksheet labels appear within a column in the data. You may not need to perform all or even any of these tasks, but you should always ensure that your data is set up according to the guidelines you learn about in this task.

Organize Your Data

In the simplest case, Excel builds a PivotTable from worksheet data by finding the unique values in a specific column of data and *summarizing* — summing or counting — that data based on those unique values. For this to work properly, you need to ensure that your data is organized in such a way that Excel can find those unique values and compute accurate summaries.

Row-and-Column Format

You can perform some Excel tasks on data that is scattered here and there throughout a worksheet, but building a PivotTable is not one of them. To create a PivotTable, your data must be organized in a basic row-and-column format, where each column represents a particular aspect of the data, and each row represents an example of the data. For example, in a parts table, you might have columns for the part name, part number, and cost, and each row would display the name, number, and cost for an individual part.

Unique Column Headings

The first row in your data must contain the headings that identify each column. Excel uses these headings to generate the PivotTable field names, so the headings must be unique and they must reside in a single cell.

Incorporate Labels as Columns

Many worksheets use *labels* — cells that contain descriptive text — as headings to differentiate one section of the worksheet from another. For example, a parts table might have separate sections for each warehouse, and labels such as "East Warehouse" and "West Warehouse" off the side or above the appropriate section. Unfortunately, this setup prevents you from using the warehouse data as part of the PivotTable — in the page field, for example. To fix this, create a new column with a unique heading, such as "Warehouse," and copy the label value to each row in the section.

East Warehouse							
	Description	Number	Quantity	Cost	Total Cost	Retail	Gross Margin
	Gangley Pliers	D-178	5,700	$10.47	$59,679.00	$ 17.95	71.4%
	HCAB Washer	A-201	20,123	$ 0.12	$ 2,414.76	$ 0.25	108.3%
	Finley Sprocket	C-098	10,237	$ 1.57	$16,072.09	$ 2.95	87.9%
	6" Sonotube	B-111	860	$15.24	$13,106.40	$ 19.95	30.9%
West Warehouse							
	Description	**Number**	**Quantity**	**Cost**	**Total Cost**	**Retail**	**Gross Margin**
	Langstrom 7" Wrench	D-017	755	$18.69	$14,110.95	$ 27.95	49.5%
	Thompson Socket	C-321	5,893	$ 3.11	$18,327.23	$ 5.95	91.3%
	S-Joint	A-182	3,023	$ 6.85	$20,707.55	$ 9.95	45.3%
	LAMF Valve	B-047	6,734	$ 4.01	$27,003.34	$ 6.95	73.3%

Before

Warehouse	Description	Number	Quantity	Cost	Total Cost	Retail	Gross Margin
East	Gangley Pliers	D-178	5,700	$10.47	$59,679.00	$ 17.95	71.4%
East	HCAB Washer	A-201	20,123	$ 0.12	$ 2,414.76	$ 0.25	108.3%
East	Finley Sprocket	C-098	10,237	$ 1.57	$16,072.09	$ 2.95	87.9%
East	6" Sonotube	B-111	860	$15.24	$13,106.40	$ 19.95	30.9%
West	Langstrom 7" Wrench	D-017	755	$18.69	$14,110.95	$ 27.95	49.5%
West	Thompson Socket	C-321	5,893	$ 3.11	$18,327.23	$ 5.95	91.3%
West	S-Joint	A-182	3,023	$ 6.85	$20,707.55	$ 9.95	45.3%
West	LAMF Valve	B-047	6,734	$ 4.01	$27,003.34	$ 6.95	73.3%

After

Prepare Your Data

To get your data ready for PivotTable analysis, you may also need to run through a few more preparatory chores, including deleting blank rows, ensuring the data is consistent and accurate, and turning off subtotals and the AutoFilter feature.

Blank Rows

It is common to include one or more blank rows within a worksheet to space out the data and to separate different sections of the data. This may make the data easier to read, but it can cause problems when you build your PivotTable because Excel includes the blank rows in the PivotTable report. To avoid this, run through your data and delete any blank rows.

Consistent Data

It is important that each column contains consistent data. First, ensure that each column contains the same kind of data. For example, if the column is supposed to hold part numbers, make sure it does not contain part names, costs, or anything other than part numbers. Second, ensure that each column uses a consistent data type. For example, in a column of part names, be sure each value is text; in a column of costs, make sure each value is numeric.

Repeated Data

The power of the PivotTable lies in its ability to summarize huge amounts of data. That summarization occurs when Excel detects the unique values in a field, groups the records together based on those unique values, and then calculates the total (or whatever) of the values in a particular field. For this to work, at least one field must contain repeated data, preferably a relatively small number of repeated items.

Accurate Data

One of the most important concepts in data analysis is that your results are only as accurate as your data. This is sometimes referred to, whimsically, as GIGO: Garbage In, Garbage Out. PivotTables are no exception: you can be sure that the summaries displayed in the report are accurate only if you have made sure that the values used in the data field column are accurate. This applies to the other PivotTable fields, as well. For example, if you have a column that is supposed to contain just a certain set of values — North, South, East, and West — you need to check the column to make sure there are no typos or extraneous data items.

Automatic Subtotals

Excel PivotTables are designed to provide you with numeric summaries of your data: sums, counts, averages, and so on. Therefore, you do not need to use Excel's Automatic Subtotals feature within your data. In fact, Excel will not create a PivotTable from worksheet data that has subtotals displayed. Therefore, you should remove all subtotals from your data. Click inside the data, click Data→Subtotals, and then click Remove All.

Filtered Data

If you want to use only a subset of the worksheet data in your PivotTable, do not use Excel's AutoFilter feature. If you do, Excel will still use some or all the hidden rows in the PivotTable report, so your results will not be accurate. Instead, you need to use Excel's Advanced Filter feature and have the results copied to a different worksheet location. You can then use the copied data as the source for your PivotTable report.

Create a List for a PivotTable Report

You can make your PivotTable easier to maintain by converting the underlying worksheet data from a regular range to a list. In Excel, a list is a collection of related information with an organizational structure that makes it easy to add, edit, and sort data. In short, a list is a type of database where the data is organized into rows and columns; each column represents a database field, which is a single type of information, such as a name, address, or phone number; each row represents a database record, which is a collection of associated field values, such as the information for a specific contact. A list differs from a regular Excel range in that Excel offers a set of tools that makes it easier for you to add new records, delete existing records, sort and filter data, and more.

How does a list help you maintain your PivotTables? Using a regular range as the PivotTable source data works well when you insert or delete rows within the range. After the insertions or deletions, you can refresh the PivotTable and Excel automatically updates the report to reflect the changes. However, this does not work if you add new data to the bottom of the range, which is the most common scenario. In this case, you need to rebuild the PivotTable and specify the newly expanded range. You can avoid this extra step by converting your source data range into an Excel list. In this case, Excel keeps track of any new data added to the bottom of the list, so you can refresh your PivotTable at any time.

Create a List for a PivotTable Report

Note: This chapter uses the Orders.xls spreadsheet, available at www.wiley.com/go/pivottablesvb, or you can create your own sample database.

1. Click a cell within the range that you want to convert to a list.

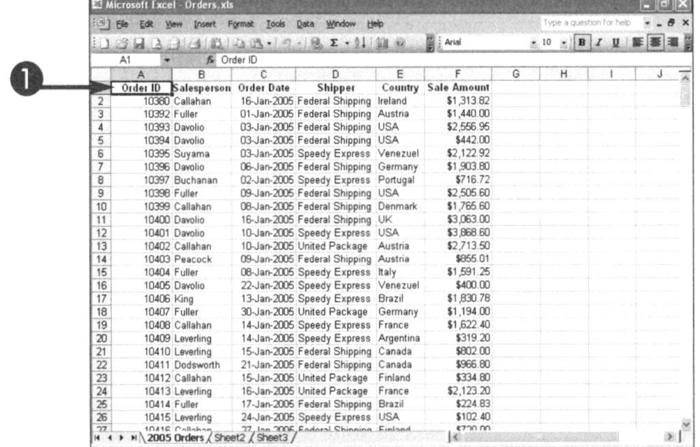

2. Click Data➔List➔Create List.

   You can also choose the Create List command by pressing Ctrl+L.

   The Create List dialog box appears.

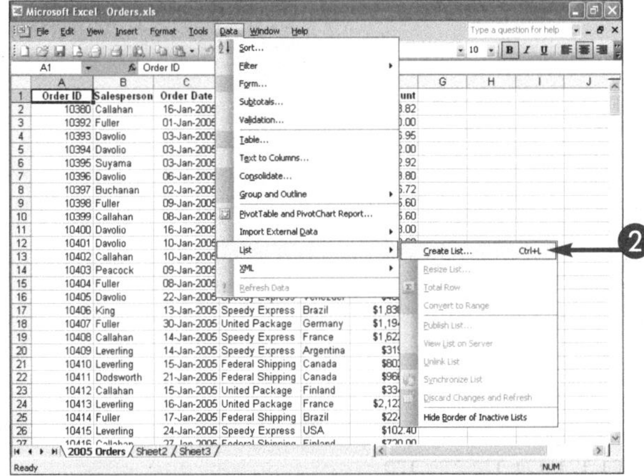

- Excel selects the range that it will convert to a list.

❸ To change the range, click here and then click and drag the mouse over the new range.

❹ Click OK.

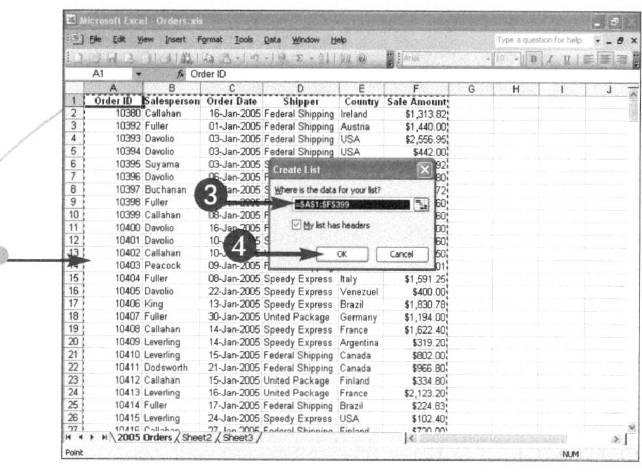

- Excel displays a border around the list.
- The List toolbar appears.
- The New Record item appears at the bottom of the list.

Note: If you do not see the New Record item, click any cell within the list.

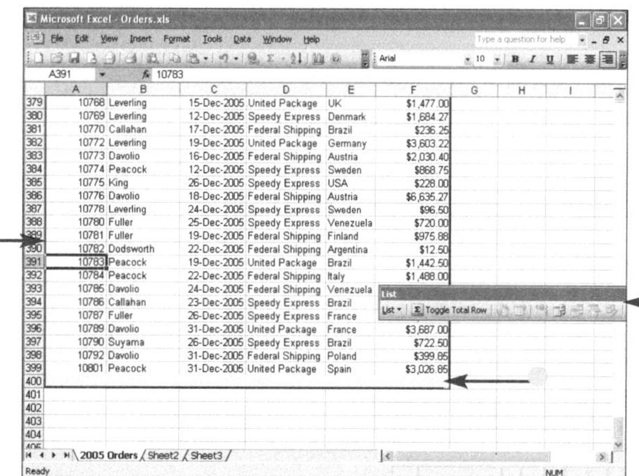

Extra

The New Record item is what makes lists so convenient for maintaining the source data for your PivotTable. To add a record to the list, click inside the list to display the New Record item, and then click the leftmost cell within the New Record row. Type your data for the first field and then press Tab to move to the second field. Excel displays a dialog box letting you know that you have inserted a row to your list; click OK. To avoid this dialog box in the future, select "Do not display this dialog again" (☐ changes to ☑). For the rest of the fields, type your data and press Tab to move to the next field.

After you have created a list, Excel offers a number of tools that enable you to easily maintain and work with the list. You will find these tools on the List toolbar, which you can display by clicking any cell within the list. For example, to add a record above the current record, click List→Insert→Row; to insert a new field in the list, click List→Insert→Column. You can also click List→Delete and then click either Row or Column to delete the current record or the current field. Finally, to convert the list back to a regular range, click List→Convert to Range.

Build a Basic PivotTable from an Excel List

If the data you want to cross-tabulate exists as an Excel range or list, you can use the PivotTable and PivotChart Wizard to easily build a PivotTable report based on your data. The wizard takes you step by step through the process of choosing the type of report you want, specifying the location of your source data, and then choosing the location of the resulting PivotTable.

The PivotTable and PivotChart Wizard has three main steps. In the first step, you choose whether you want a PivotTable or a PivotChart. In this task, you learn how to build a PivotTable. If you want to learn how to build a PivotChart instead, see Chapter 9. The first wizard step also enables you to specify the type of data source you are using. In this task, you learn how to build a PivotTable based on data in an Excel list or range, which is the simplest and most common type of data source. To learn how to build PivotTables from other types of data sources, see Chapters 10 and 11.

In the second step of the PivotTable and PivotChart Wizard, you specify the location of the list or range. If you choose a cell within the list or range in advance, the wizard automatically selects the surrounding list or range. Otherwise, you can click and drag with your mouse to select the data, or type the range address.

Finally, the third step of the wizard enables you to select a location for the new PivotTable report, and you can choose to place the PivotTable on either an existing worksheet or on a new worksheet.

Build a Basic PivotTable from an Excel List

1. Click a cell within the list or range that you want to use as the source data.
2. Click Data→PivotTable and PivotChart Report.

   The first PivotTable and PivotChart Wizard dialog box appears.

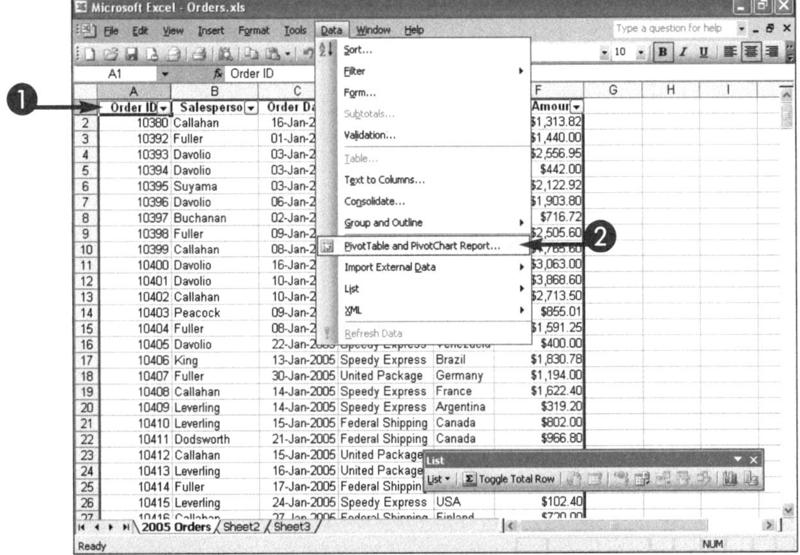

3. Select Microsoft Office Excel list or database.
4. Select PivotTable.
5. Click Next.

   The second PivotTable and PivotChart Wizard dialog box appears.

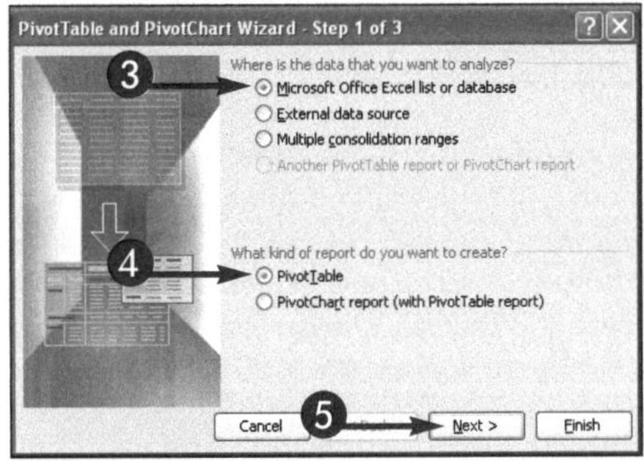

6. Ensure that the displayed range address is correct.

   - If the range address is incorrect, click the Collapse Dialog button and then click and drag with your mouse to select the range.

7. Click Next.

   The third PivotTable and PivotChart Wizard dialog box appears.

8. Select New worksheet to place the PivotTable on a new worksheet.

   - If you prefer to place the PivotTable on an existing worksheet, select Existing worksheet, click the Collapse Dialog button, and then click the worksheet and cell where you want the PivotTable to appear.

Note: To learn how to add fields directly from the wizard, see the task "Add Fields Using the PivotTable Wizard," later in this chapter

9. Click Finish.

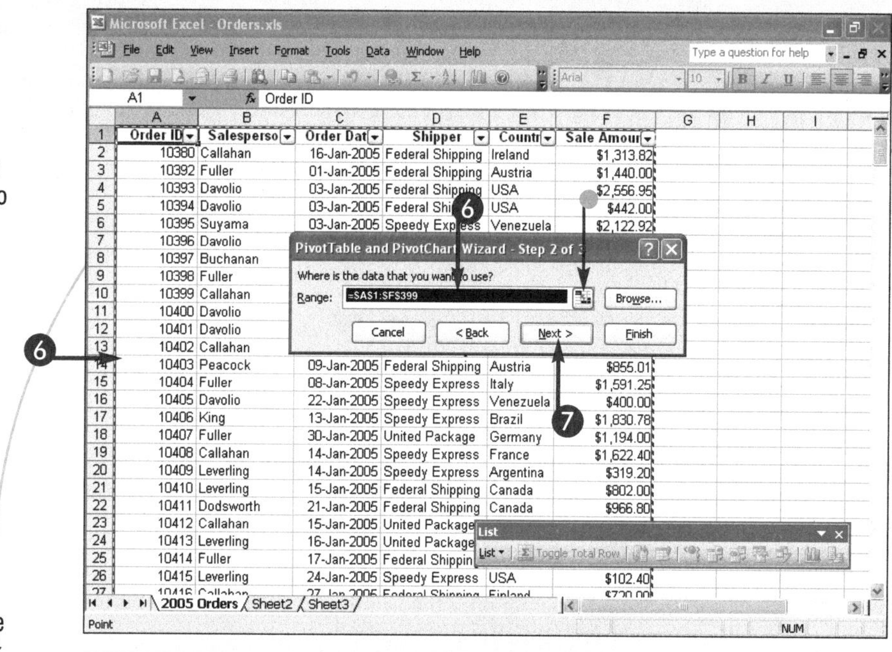

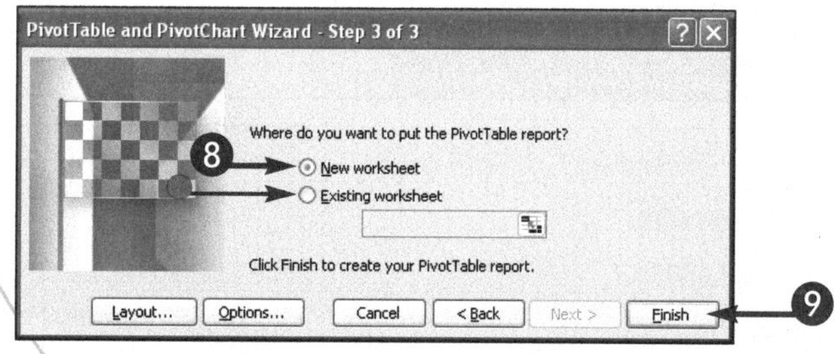

Apply It

It is not uncommon to have the source data for a PivotTable in one workbook and the PivotTable itself in a different workbook. In this case, in Step 6, you may prefer to type the range address in the Range text box. If so, then you need to specify not only the source data's range address, but also the workbook filename and the name of the worksheet that contains the range. Here is the general format to use:

```
'[WorkbookName.xls]SheetName'!RangeAddress
```

For example, suppose the source data resides in a workbook named Orders.xls, on a worksheet named Orders 2005, and in the range $A$1: $F$399. Here is the address you would type in the Range dialog box in Step 6:

```
'[Orders.xls]Orders 2005'!$A$1:$F$399
```

Build a Basic PivotTable from an Excel List (continued)

When you click Finish in the third PivotTable and PivotChart Wizard dialog box, Excel creates an empty PivotTable in a new worksheet or in the location you specified. The empty PivotTable displays four areas with the following labels: Drop Row Fields Here, Drop Column Fields Here, Drop Data Items Here, and Drop Page Fields Here. To complete the PivotTable, you must populate some or all of these areas with one or more fields from your data.

When you add a field to the row, column, or page area, Excel extracts the unique values from the field and displays them in the area. For example, if you add the Salesperson field to the row area, Excel displays the unique salesperson names as headings that run down the leftmost column of the PivotTable. Similarly, if you add the Shipper field to the column area, Excel displays the unique shipper names as headings that run across the top row of the PivotTable. Finally, if you add, say, the Country field to the page area, Excel displays the unique country names in a drop-down list above the PivotTable.

When you add a field to the data area, Excel performs calculations based on the numeric data in the field. The default calculation is sum, so if you add, for example, the Sale Amount field to the data area, Excel sums the Sale Amount values. How Excel calculates these sums depends on the fields you have added to the other areas. For example, if you add just the Salesperson field to the row area, Excel displays the sum of the Sale Amount values for each salesperson. You can also use other calculations such as Average and Count. See Chapter 8 to learn how to change the summary calculation.

Build a Basic PivotTable from an Excel List *(continued)*

- Excel creates the empty PivotTable.
- The PivotTable toolbar appears.
- The PivotTable Field List appears.

10 Click and drag a field from the PivotTable Field List and drop it inside the row area.

Excel displays the field's unique values in the PivotTable's row area.

- If you do not want Excel to display the unique values as you add non-data fields, click the Always Display Items button to turn off this feature.

11 Click and drag a numeric field from the PivotTable Field List and drop it inside the data area.

Excel displays the summary results in the PivotTable.

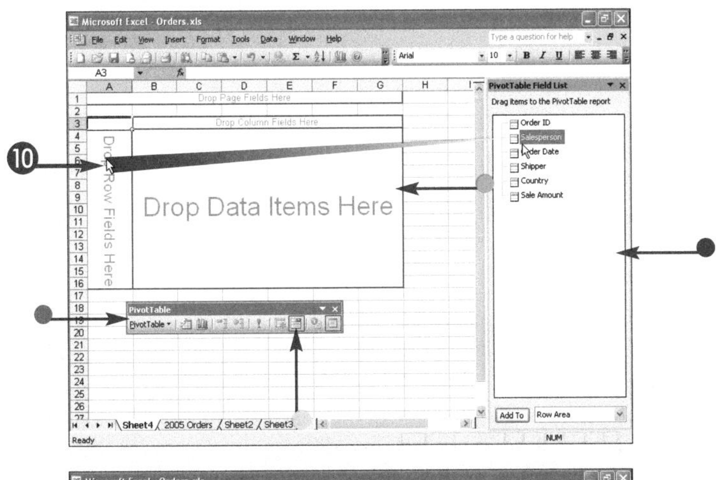

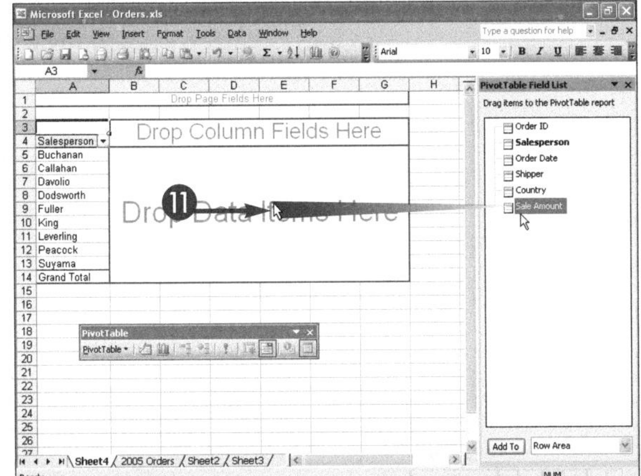

⑫ If required for your PivotTable, click and drag a field from the PivotTable Field List and drop it inside the column area.

Excel displays the field's unique values in the PivotTable's column area.

⑬ If required for your PivotTable, click and drag a field from the PivotTable Field List and drop it inside the page area.

Excel displays the field's unique values in the PivotTable's page drop-down list.

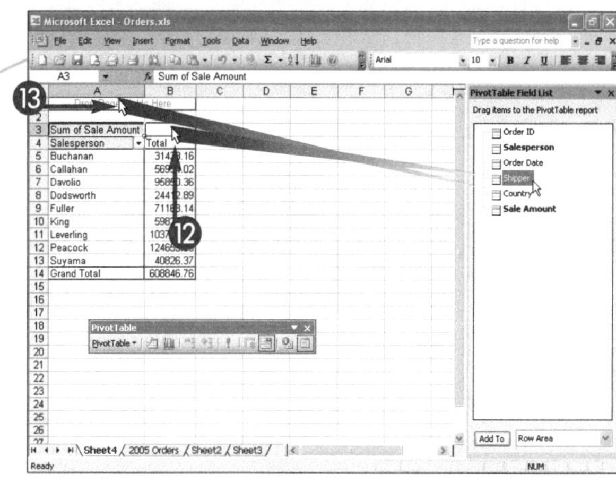

The basic PivotTable is complete.

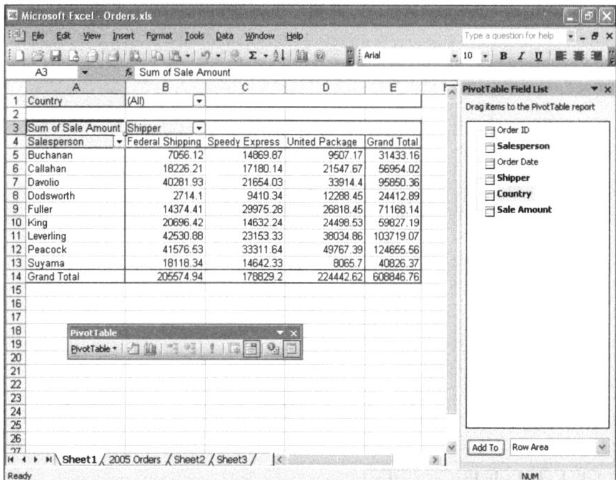

Extra

If you are not comfortable dragging items with the mouse, you can also add fields to the PivotTable using the PivotTable Field List. To begin, use the PivotTable Field List to click the field you want to add to the PivotTable. In the drop-down list at the bottom of the PivotTable Field List, click ▾ and then click the area of the PivotTable to which you want to add the field. Click Add To. Excel adds the field to the PivotTable area you selected.

Do not attempt to edit the values that Excel displays in the row, column, or data areas. These values are generated or calculated automatically based on the data in the source range or list. You can edit these results, but doing so does not change the source data, and any changes you make will be overwritten the next time you refresh the PivotTable, as described in Chapter 3. If you want to change the value of a PivotTable cell, you must change the corresponding value or values in the source range and then refresh the PivotTable.

Add Fields Using the PivotTable Wizard

In the previous task, you learned how to use the PivotTable Field List to add fields directly to the PivotTable's row, data, column, and page areas. However, there may be times when you prefer not to use the PivotTable Field List. For example, if you already have the task pane displayed, then the combination of the PivotTable Field List and task pane could take up more than half the screen. In this case, you might prefer to close the PivotTable Field List so that you can see more of your worksheet — in the PivotTable toolbar, click the Toolbar Close button (☒) to toggle the PivotTable Field List on and off. You can bypass the PivotTable Field List and use the PivotTable and PivotChart Wizard to set up your PivotTable fields.

The PivotTable and PivotChart Wizard has a Layout dialog box that enables you to add fields from your list or range to the PivotTable's row, data, column, and page areas. The Layout dialog box is divided into two sections. On the right you see buttons for the various fields in your range or list; on the left, you see a diagram of the PivotTable showing four sections that represent the four areas: Row, Data, Column, and Page. For each area that you want to include in your PivotTable, you click and drag a field button and then drop it inside the appropriate area. When you close the Layout dialog box and finish the PivotTable and PivotChart Wizard, your PivotTable will be complete.

Add Fields Using the PivotTable Wizard

1. Follow Steps 1 to 8 in the previous task.

   The third PivotTable and PivotChart Wizard dialog box appears.

2. Click Layout.

   The PivotTable and PivotChart Wizard Layout dialog box appears.

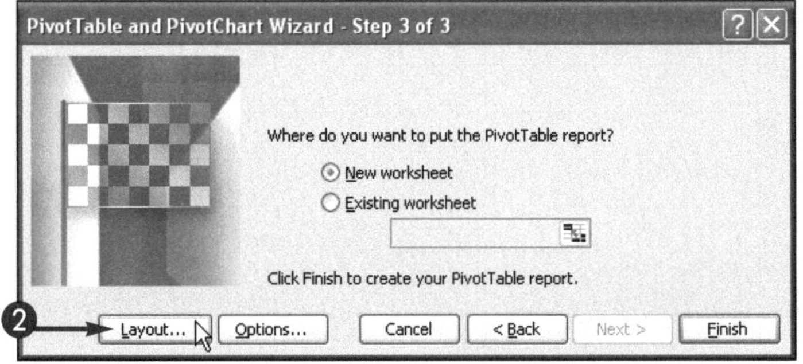

3. Click and drag one of the field buttons and drop it inside the Row section.
4. Click and drag a numeric field button and drop it inside the Data section.
5. If required for your PivotTable, click and drag a field button and drop it inside the Column section.
6. If required for your PivotTable, click and drag a field button and drop it inside the Page section.
7. Click OK to close the Layout dialog box.

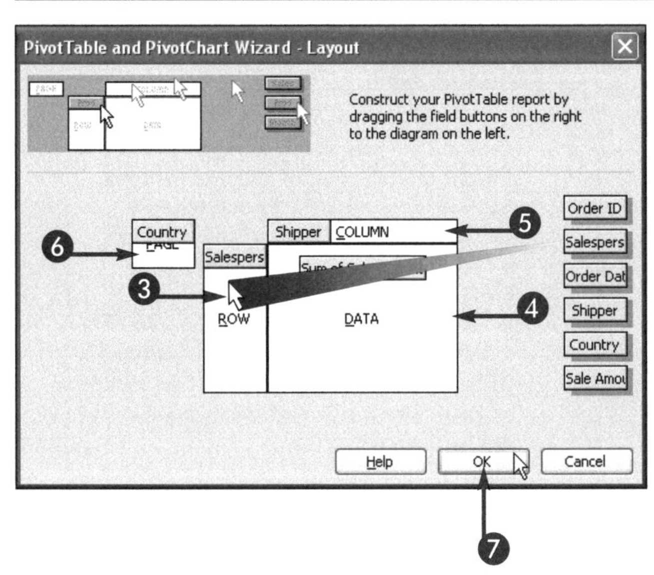

8 Click Finish to close the third PivotTable and PivotChart Wizard dialog box.

Excel creates the PivotTable.

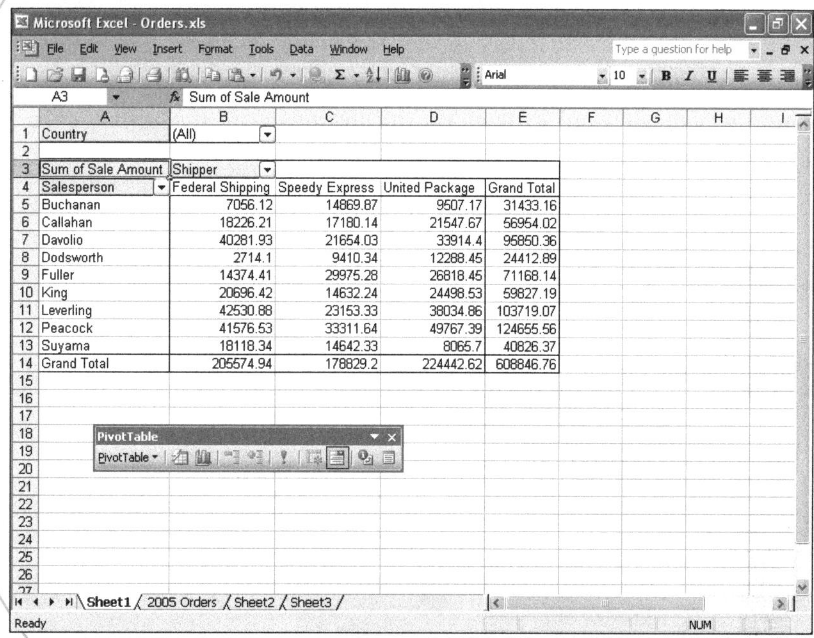

Microsoft Excel - Orders.xls
File Edit View Insert Format Tools Data Window Help
Type a question for help
Arial
A3
Sum of Sale Amount
Country (All)
Sum of Sale Amount Shipper
Salesperson Federal Shipping Speedy Express United Package Grand Total
Buchanan 7056.12 14869.87 9507.17 31433.16
Callahan 18226.21 17180.14 21547.67 56954.02
Davolio 40281.93 21654.03 33914.4 95850.36
Dodsworth 2714.1 9410.34 12288.45 24412.89
Fuller 14374.41 29975.28 26818.45 71168.14
King 20696.42 14632.24 24498.53 59827.19
Leverling 42530.88 23153.33 38034.86 103719.07
Peacock 41576.53 33311.64 49767.39 124655.56
Suyama 18118.34 14642.33 8065.7 40826.37
Grand Total 205574.94 178829.2 224442.62 608846.76
PivotTable
Sheet1 2005 Orders Sheet2 Sheet3
Ready
NUM

Extra

If you make a mistake when you are working within the PivotTable and PivotChart Wizard's Layout dialog box, you can easily fix the problem. If you added the wrong field button to the PivotTable diagram, click and drag the field button from the PivotTable diagram and then drop it outside of the PivotTable. Excel removes the field from the diagram. If you placed a field button in the wrong section of the PivotTable diagram, click and drag the field and drop it inside the correct section. If you have made a number of mistakes, click Cancel to shut down the Layout dialog box without saving your changes. When you are back in the third PivotTable and PivotChart Wizard dialog box, click Layout and start over again.

You can use the PivotTable and PivotChart Wizard's Layout dialog box to make changes to the PivotTable layout after you have created the report. In the PivotTable toolbar, click PivotTable→PivotTable Wizard. Excel displays the third PivotTable and PivotChart Wizard dialog box. Follow Steps 2 to 8 in this task, as well as the techniques in the previous tip, to make your layout changes.

Re-create an Existing PivotTable

The source data that underlies a PivotTable rarely remains static. You, or someone else, may add or delete records, edit the existing data, or add or delete fields. Therefore, you will need to update your PivotTable from time to time to reflect these changes. In most cases, particularly when you are using an Excel list as the source data, you need only refresh the PivotTable to incorporate any changes to the original data. See Chapter 3 to learn how to refresh an existing PivotTable.

However, you may find that in certain cases, refreshing the PivotTable does not incorporate all the changes that have been made to the source data. Similarly, you may have an important meeting or presentation coming up and you want to make sure that your PivotTable is using the most up-to-date information. In both situations, you can ensure that your PivotTable uses the latest source data by re-creating the PivotTable. This involves running the PivotTable and PivotChart Wizard on the existing PivotTable and using the wizard to select the updated range or list.

Re-create an Existing PivotTable

1. Click a cell within the existing PivotTable.
2. In the PivotTable toolbar, click PivotTable→PivotTable Wizard.

   You can also right-click any cell in the PivotTable and then click PivotTable Wizard from the menu that appears.

   The third PivotTable and PivotChart Wizard dialog box appears.

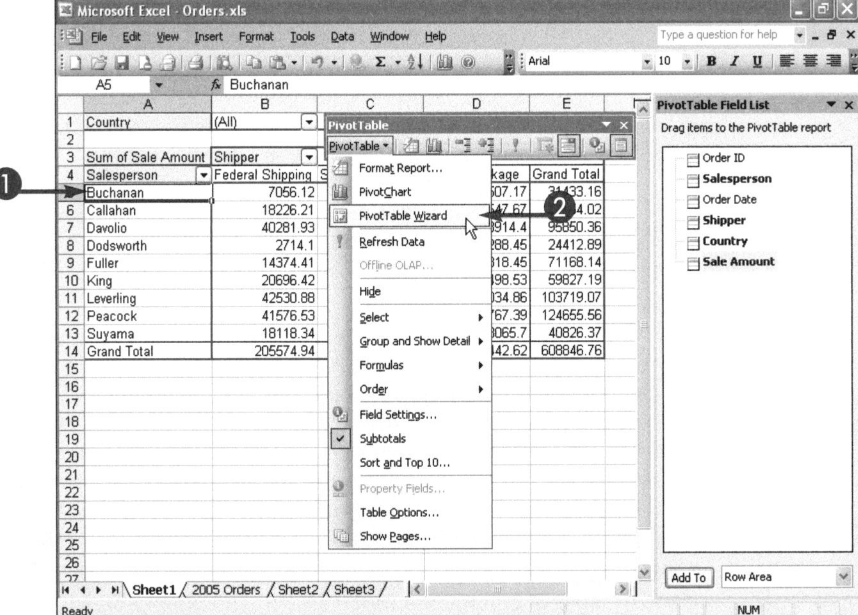

3. Click Back.

   The second PivotTable and PivotChart Wizard dialog box appears.

4. Click the Collapse Dialog button.
5. Click and drag with your mouse to select the updated range.
6. Click Finish.

   Excel re-creates the PivotTable.

   If any fields were removed from the source data, Excel removes those fields from the PivotTable and from the PivotTable Field List.

   If any fields were added to the source data, Excel adds those fields to the PivotTable Field List.

7. Use the PivotTable Field List to add any new fields to the PivotTable.

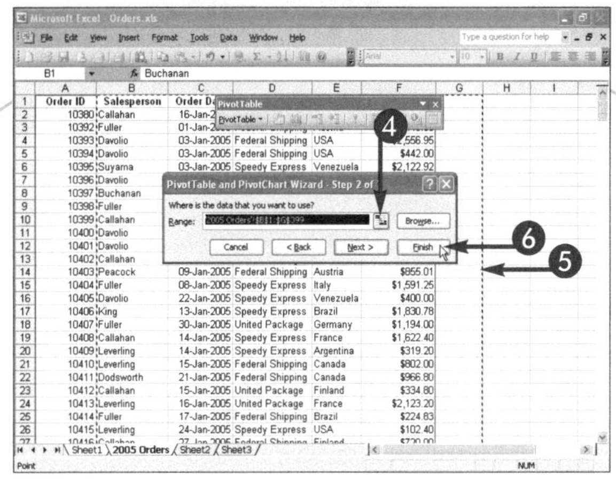

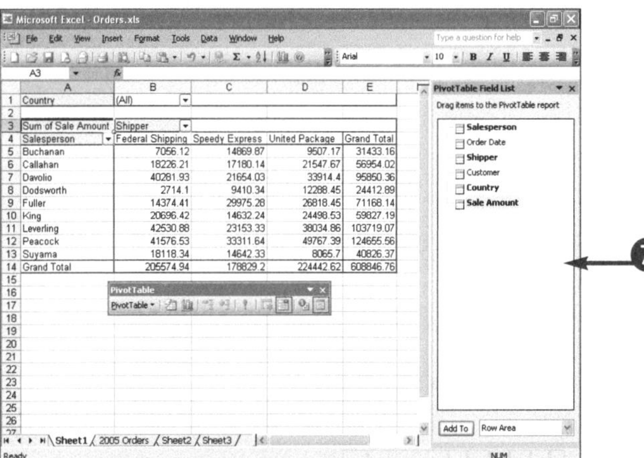

Apply It

When you run the PivotTable Wizard command on an existing PivotTable, the third PivotTable and PivotChart Wizard dialog box appears. To update your existing PivotTable, be sure to leave the Existing worksheet option activated and be sure that the range text box specifies the cell in the upper-left corner of your existing PivotTable. The upper-left corner of a PivotTable is the cell above the row area field button and to the left of the column area field button. In other words, you do not include the page area when specifying the upper-left corner.

On the other hand, there may be scenarios where you want to compare two PivotTable reports. For example, you might want to leave the existing PivotTable as is and create a second PivotTable that uses the updated source data. You could then examine the different results produced by the old and the new data. To do this, run Steps 1 and 2 in this task. In the third PivotTable and PivotChart Wizard dialog box, either select "New worksheet" or leave "Existing worksheet" selected, click the Collapse Dialog button, and then click the cell where you want the new PivotTable to appear. This will be the upper-left cell of the new PivotTable. Then follow Steps 3 to 5 in this task to create the new PivotTable.

Turn the PivotTable Toolbar On and Off

You can make your PivotTable chores quicker and easier by taking advantage of the buttons on the PivotTable toolbar. Most of these buttons give you one-click access to the most PivotTable features. You can also click the PivotTable button to display a list of commands available for your PivotTables.

Normally the PivotTable toolbar appears automatically when you create a PivotTable. When you click a cell outside the PivotTable, the PivotTable toolbar disappears, and it reappears when you click a cell within the PivotTable. However, you can also turn the PivotTable toolbar on and off by hand. For example, if your PivotTable report takes up all or most of the screen, you may prefer to turn off the PivotTable toolbar to prevent it from covering any data.

Here is a summary of the most useful PivotTable toolbar buttons; each button is described in more detail elsewhere in the book:

BUTTON	DESCRIPTION
	Displays the AutoFormat dialog box (Chapter 6)
	Creates a PivotChart (Chapter 9)
	Hides the detail in a group (Chapter 4)
	Shows the detail in a group (Chapter 4); shows the underlying detail for a field or data value (Chapter 3)
	Refreshes the PivotTable (Chapter 3)
	Includes hidden data in totals (Chapter 8)
	Displays unique field values as you add items to the PivotTable (Chapter 2)
	Displays the PivotTable Field dialog box (Chapter 5)
	Toggles the PivotTable Field List on and off (Chapter 2)

Turn the PivotTable Toolbar On and Off

TURN OFF THE PIVOTTABLE TOOLBAR

Note: This chapter uses the Orders.xls and PivotTables.xls spreadsheets, available at www.wiley.com/go/pivottablesvb, or you can create your own sample database.

1. Click the Toolbar Close button.

   You can also click View→Toolbars→PivotTable, or right-click any toolbar or menu and then click PivotTable.

   Excel turns off the PivotTable toolbar.

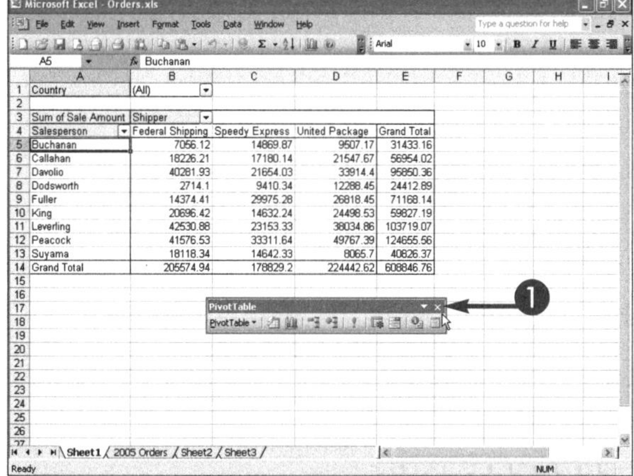

TURN ON THE PIVOTTABLE TOOLBAR

1. Click View→Toolbars→PivotTable.

   You can also right-click any toolbar or menu and then click PivotTable.

   Excel turns on the PivotTable toolbar.

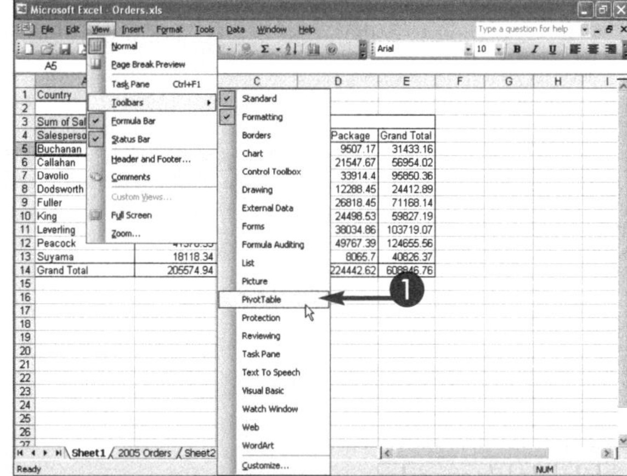

Customize the PivotTable Toolbar

The buttons on the default PivotTable toolbar are very useful, but you may find that you do not use some of them very often. For example, if you never group your PivotTable data, then you will never need the Hide Detail and Show Detail buttons; see Chapter 4. You can make the PivotTable toolbar easier to work with by removing those buttons you do not use.

On the other hand, there may be PivotTable features that you use quite often, but the PivotTable does not offer a button. For example, if you often use the PivotTable and PivotChart Wizard, you have to click PivotTable➔PivotTable Wizard to run it. You can save a click by adding a button for this command directly to the toolbar.

Here is a summary of the most useful extra PivotTable toolbar buttons that you can add; each button is described in more detail elsewhere in the book:

BUTTON	DESCRIPTION
	Ungroups PivotTable data (Chapter 4)
	Groups PivotTable data (Chapter 4)
	Starts the PivotTable and PivotChart Wizard (Chapter 2)
	Shows pages in separate worksheets (Chapter 4)
	Refreshes all PivotTables in the current workbook (Chapter 3)
	Automatically generates GETPIVOTDATA() formulas (Chapter 10)
	Displays properties associated with an OLAP cube (Chapter 11)

Customize the PivotTable Toolbar

REMOVE A BUTTON FROM THE PIVOTTABLE TOOLBAR

1. Click the Toolbar Options button to display the toolbar options.
2. Click Add or Remove Buttons➔PivotTable.

   Excel displays a list of all the available PivotTable toolbar buttons.
3. Click the button you want to remove from the toolbar.

   Excel removes the check mark from beside the button and updates the toolbar.
4. Click outside the list to close it.

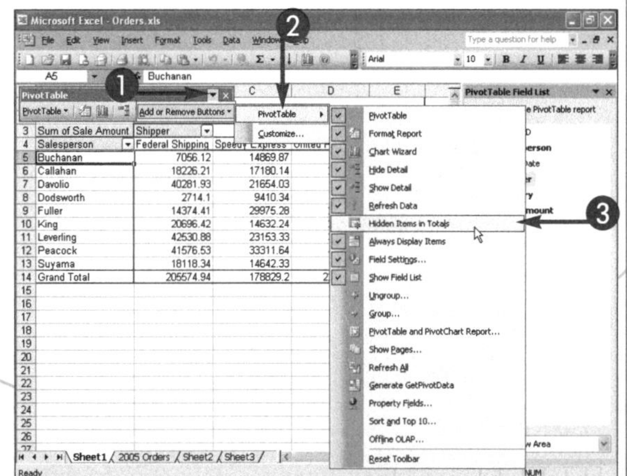

ADD A BUTTON TO THE PIVOTTABLE TOOLBAR

1. Click the Toolbar Options button to display the toolbar options.
2. Click Add or Remove Buttons➔PivotTable.

   Excel displays a list of all the available PivotTable toolbar buttons.
3. Click the button you want to add to the toolbar.

   Excel displays a check mark beside the button and updates the toolbar.
4. Click outside the list to close it.

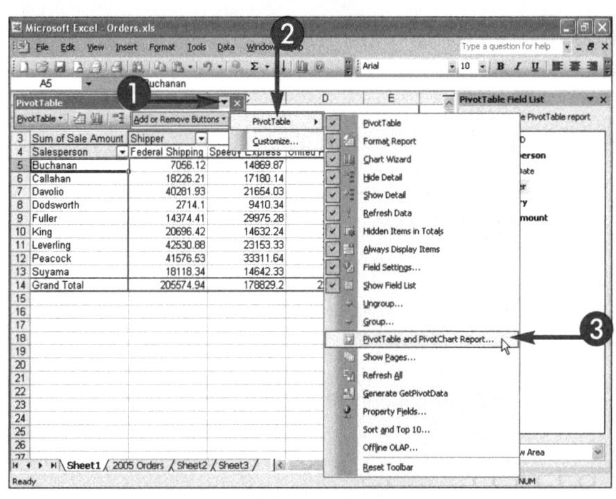

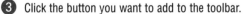

Select PivotTable Items

In many of the tasks in this book, you will apply formatting or settings to some or all of the PivotTable's cells, or you will perform some action on some or all of the PivotTable's cells. Before you can do any of this, however, you must first select the cell or cells you want to work with. You can speed up your PivotTable work considerably by becoming familiar with the various methods that Excel offers for selecting elements in a PivotTable report.

If you are familiar with Excel, then you probably already know the basic techniques for selecting cells. For example, you select a single cell by clicking it, and you select a range by dragging your mouse from the top-left corner of the range to the bottom-right corner. You can also select random cells by holding down Ctrl and clicking the cells you want. You can use all the standard techniques to select cells within a PivotTable report. However, Excel also offers several methods that are unique to PivotTables. For example, you can select one or more row or column fields, just the PivotTable labels, just the PivotTable data, or the entire table. Excel also offers handy toolbar buttons for most of these techniques, so you can customize the PivotTable toolbar for one-click access to PivotTable selection techniques.

Select PivotTable Items

SELECT A ROW OR COLUMN FIELD

1. For a column, move the mouse pointer just above the column label.

   The mouse pointer changes to a black, downward-pointing arrow.

   For a row, move the mouse pointer just to the left of the row label. The mouse pointer changes to a right-pointing arrow.

2. Click the mouse.

   Excel selects the column.

   From the keyboard, use the arrow keys to move the cursor into the label of the column or row.

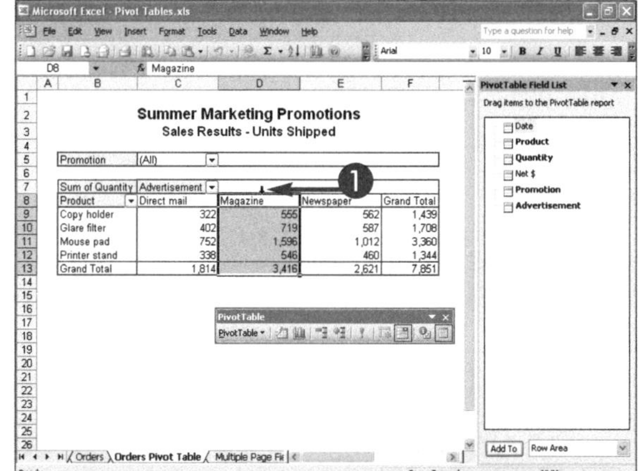

SELECT THE ENTIRE PIVOTTABLE

1. Click any cell within the PivotTable.

2. Click PivotTable→Select→Entire Table.

   You can also move the mouse pointer to the top or left edge of the upper-left PivotTable cell (the pointer changes to ⬇ or ➡) and then click.

   Excel selects the entire table.

   To select all the row and column fields, click any cell in a row or column field and then press Ctrl+Shift+8.

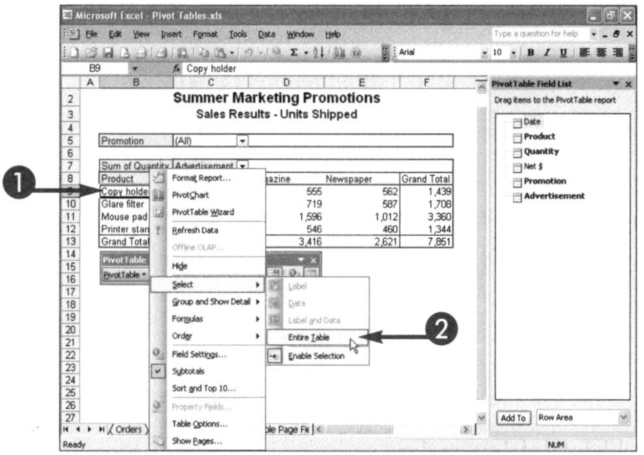

SELECT DATA ONLY

1. Select the entire PivotTable, as described on the previous page.
2. Click PivotTable➔Select➔Data.

   Excel selects just the PivotTable's data area.

   If you select a field instead of the entire table, click PivotTable➔Select➔Data to select just that field's data.

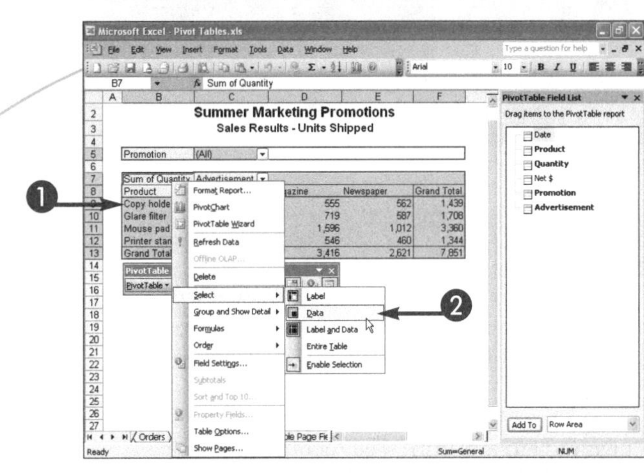

SELECT LABELS ONLY

1. Select the entire PivotTable, as described on the previous page.
2. Click PivotTable➔Select➔Label.

   Excel selects just the PivotTable's labels.

   If you select a field instead of the entire table, click PivotTable➔Select➔Label to select just that field's label.

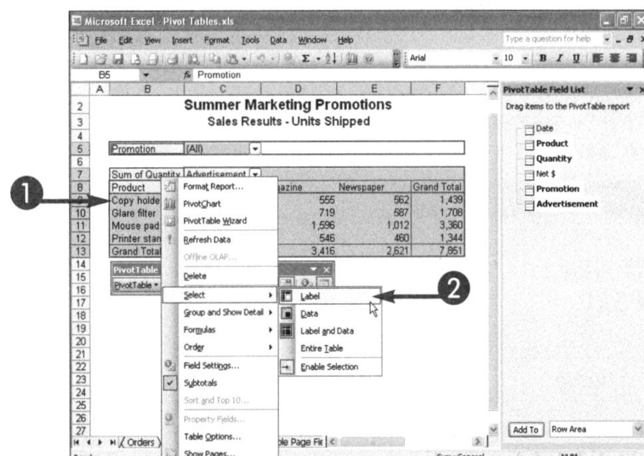

Extra

You can make your PivotTable selection chores even easier by incorporating one or more extra toolbar buttons on the PivotTable toolbar. Excel offers extra buttons for the Data, Label, and Label and Data commands that appear when you click PivotTable➔Select in the PivotTable toolbar.

Select View➔Toolbars➔Customize to display the Customize dialog box. Click the Commands tab and then click Data in the Categories list. Scroll down the Commands list until you see the following buttons:

BUTTON	DESCRIPTION
	Selects the PivotTable labels.
	Selects the PivotTable data.
	Selects a field's label and data when the field's label or data is currently selected.

Drag the button you want and drop it on the PivotTable toolbar. When you are finished, click Close to shut down the Customize dialog box.

Remove a PivotTable Field

After you have completed your PivotTable, the resulting report is not set in stone. You will see in Chapter 4 and in other parts of this book that you can change the PivotTable view, format the PivotTable cells, add custom calculations, and much more. You can also remove fields from the PivotTable report, as you learn in this task.

Removing a PivotTable field comes in handy when you want to work with a less detailed report. For example, suppose your PivotTable report shows the sum of sales data from four items in the Region field — East, Midwest, South, and West — that appear in the row area. This data is broken down by fiscal quarter, where each item in the Quarter field appears in the column area. If you decide you want to simplify the report to show just the total for each region, then you need to remove the Quarter field from the PivotTable.

Remove a field from a PivotTable only if you are sure you will not need the field again in the future. You can always add fields back into the PivotTable report, but deleting a field and then adding it back again is inefficient. If you only want to take a field out of the PivotTable report temporarily, consider hiding the field; see the task "Hide Items in a Row or Column Field," in Chapter 4.

Similarly, you do not need to go through the process of removing a field if you know that the field has been removed from the original data source. Instead, refresh the PivotTable and Excel will remove the deleted field for you automatically; see the task "Refresh PivotTable Data," later in this chapter.

Remove a PivotTable Field

REMOVE A FIELD FROM THE PIVOTTABLE REPORT

1. Click the button of the field you want to remove.
2. Drag the button outside of the PivotTable report.

   The mouse pointer changes to ☒.
3. Drop the button.

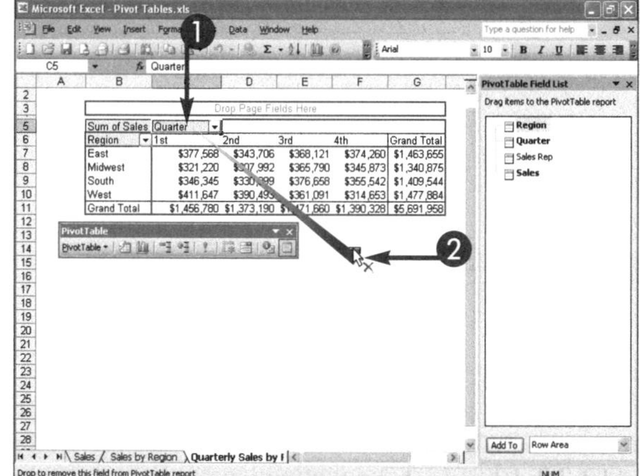

Excel removes the field from the PivotTable report.

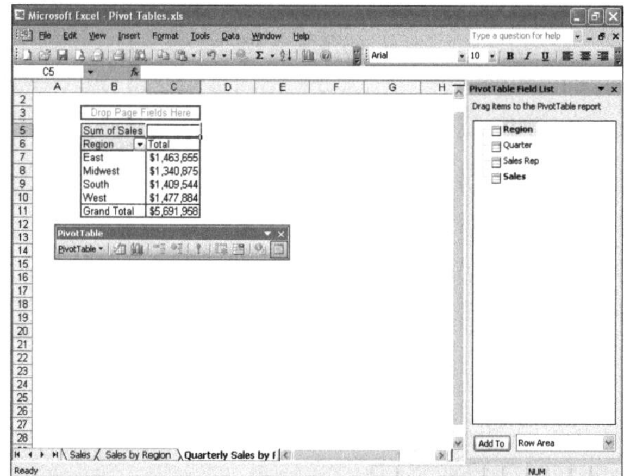

REMOVE A FIELD USING THE PIVOTTABLE WIZARD

1. Run the PivotTable and PivotChart Wizard and display the Layout dialog box.

Note: To learn how to display the Layout dialog box, see the task "Add Fields Using the PivotTable Wizard" in Chapter 2.

2. Click the button of the field you want to remove.

3. Drag the button outside of the PivotTable diagram.

   The mouse pointer changes to ![pointer].

4. Drop the button.

   Excel removes the field from the PivotTable diagram.

5. Click OK.

   Excel removes the field from the PivotTable report.

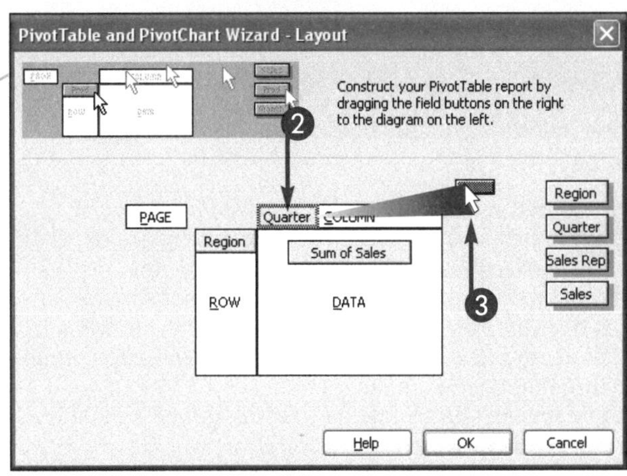

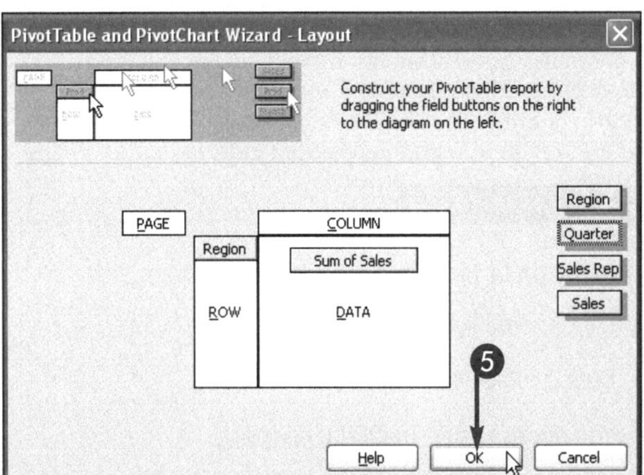

Apply It

Removing fields is particularly handy when you work with multiple fields in a single area, as described in the tasks "Add Multiple Fields to the Row or Column Area," "Add Multiple Fields to the Data Area," and "Add Multiple Fields to the Page Area," later in this chapter. If you find that a PivotTable with multiple fields in one area is too confusing or too cumbersome to manipulate, removing one or more of those fields can simplify the layout and help you get more out of your PivotTable.

It is worth noting here, as well, that you cannot delete part of a field. For example, if you have a Region field, you cannot delete the Midwest item. If you select a cell, row, or column within the PivotTable and press Delete, Excel displays an error message telling you that you cannot delete part of the PivotTable report. Again, it is possible to hide individual rows and columns within a PivotTable; see the task "Hide Items in a Row or Column Field" in Chapter 4.

Refresh PivotTable Data

Whether your PivotTable is based on financial results, survey responses, or a database of collectibles such as books or DVDs, the underlying data is probably not static. That is, the data changes over time as new results come in, new surveys are undertaken, and new items are added to the collection. You can ensure that the data analysis represented by the PivotTable remains up to date by refreshing the PivotTable, as shown in this task.

Refreshing the PivotTable means rebuilding the report using the most current version of the source data. However, this is not the same as running the PivotTable and PivotChart Wizard over again, as described in Chapter 2 in the task "Re-create an Existing PivotTable." Instead, when you refresh a PivotTable, Excel keeps the report layout as is and simply updates the data area calculations with the latest source data. Also, depending on the type of source data you are using, Excel will remove from the report any fields that have been deleted from the source data, and it will display in the PivotTable Field List any new fields that have been added to the source data.

Excel offers two methods for refreshing a PivotTable: manually and automatically. A manual refresh is one that you perform yourself, usually when you know that the source data has changed, or if you simply want to be sure that the latest data is reflected in your PivotTable report. An automatic refresh is one that Excel handles for you. For PivotTables based on Excel ranges or lists, you can tell Excel to refresh a PivotTable every time you open the workbook that contains the report.

Refresh PivotTable Data

REFRESH DATA MANUALLY

1. Click any cell inside the PivotTable.
2. Click the Refresh Data button.

   You can also select PivotTable→Refresh Data on the PivotTable toolbar. Alternatively, click Data→Refresh Data.

   To update every PivotTable in the current workbook, click the Refresh All button ( ) in the PivotTable toolbar; see the task "Customize the PivotTable Toolbar," earlier in this chapter, for more information.

   Excel updates the PivotTable data.

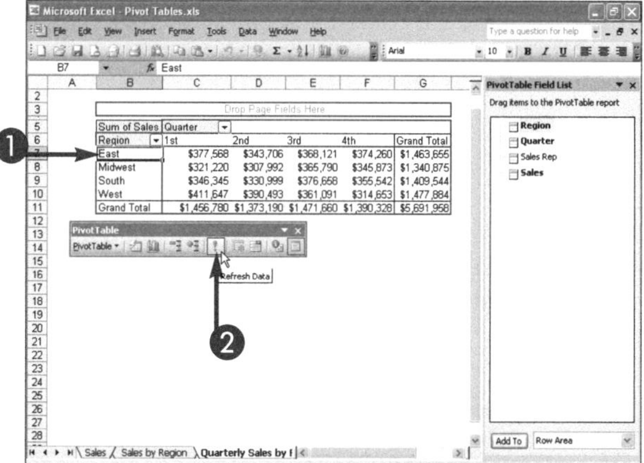

REFRESH DATA AUTOMATICALLY

1. Click any cell inside the PivotTable.
2. Click PivotTable→Table Options.

   The PivotTable Options dialog box appears.

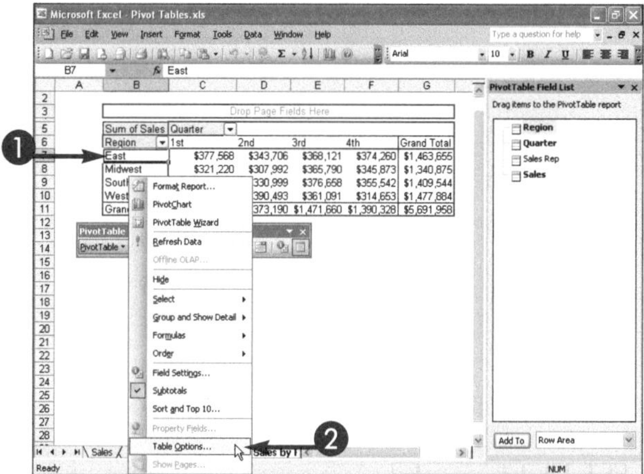

3 Select Refresh on open.

4 Click OK.

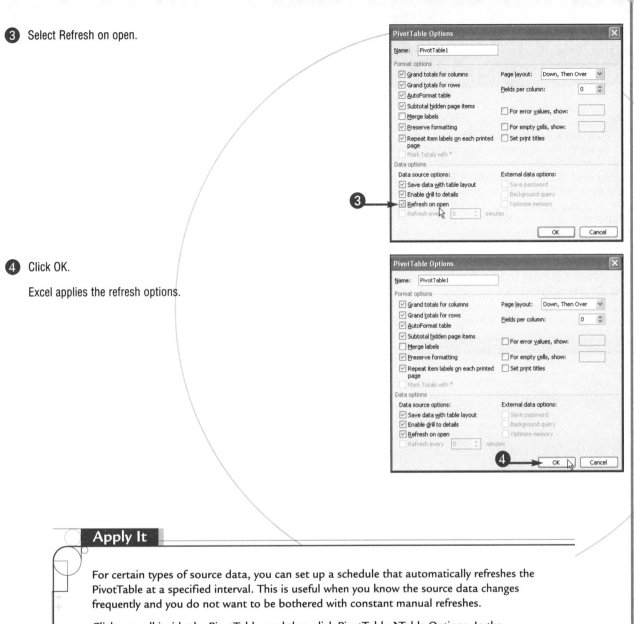

Excel applies the refresh options.

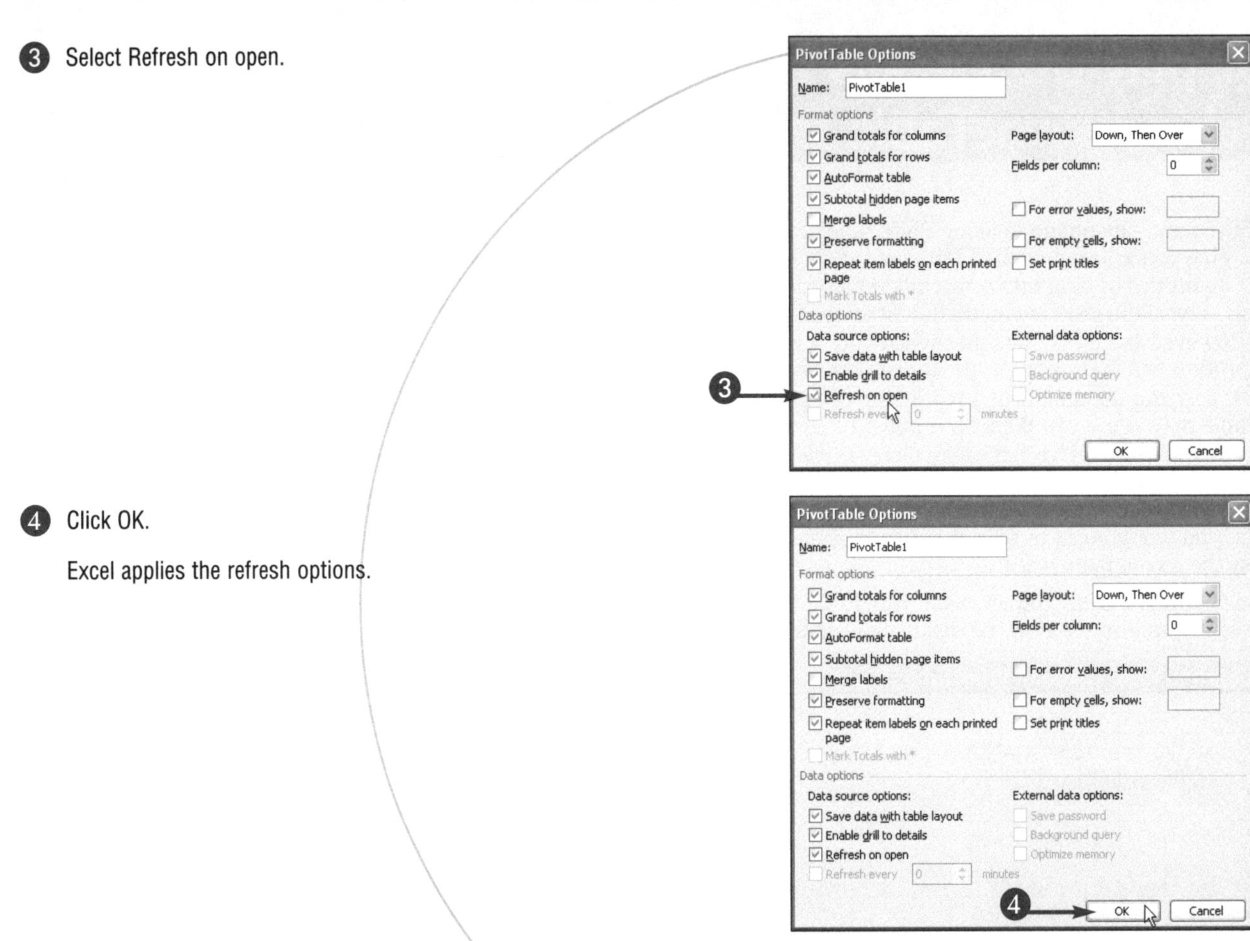

Apply It

For certain types of source data, you can set up a schedule that automatically refreshes the PivotTable at a specified interval. This is useful when you know the source data changes frequently and you do not want to be bothered with constant manual refreshes.

Click any cell inside the PivotTable, and then click PivotTable→Table Options. In the PivotTable Options dialog box, examine the "Refresh every" check box. If this check box is not enabled, it means your source data does not support automatic refreshing at preset intervals. For example, this check box is not enabled when you use an Excel range or list as the data source. However, for data that comes from other types of data sources, particularly external data, this check box is enabled. See Chapter 10 to learn how to build a PivotTable from data sources other than Excel ranges and lists. If you want to refresh the PivotTable automatically at a specified interval, select "Refresh every" (☐ changes to ☑), and then use the spin box (⬍) to specify the refresh interval, in minutes.

Note, however, that you might prefer not to have the source data updated too frequently. Depending on where the data resides and how much data you are working with, the refresh could take some time, which will slow down the rest of your work.

Display the Details Behind PivotTable Data

The main advantage to using PivotTables is that they give you an easy method for summarizing large quantities of data into a succinct report for data analysis. PivotTables show you the forest instead of the trees. However, there may be times when you need to see some of the trees that comprise the forest. For example, if you are studying the results of a marketing campaign, your PivotTable may show you the total number of mouse pads sold as a result of a direct marketing piece. However, what if you want to see the details underlying that number? If your source data contains hundreds or thousands of records, you would need to filter the data in some way to see just the records you want.

Fortunately, Excel gives you an easier way to do this by allowing you to directly view the details that underlie a specific data value. This is called *drilling down* to the details. When you drill down into a specific data value in a PivotTable, Excel returns to the source data, extracts the records that comprise the data value, and then displays the records in a new worksheet. For a PivotTable based on a range or list, this extraction takes but a second or two, depending on how many records there are in the source data.

This task shows you how easy it is to drill down into your PivotTable data. In fact, it is so easy and so useful, that many people find themselves frequently drilling down to peek behind the data. Unfortunately, because Excel creates a new worksheet each time, this often results in a workbook that is cluttered with many extra worksheets. Therefore, this task also shows you how to delete the detail worksheets.

Display the Details Behind PivotTable Data

1. Click the data value for which you want to view the underlying details.

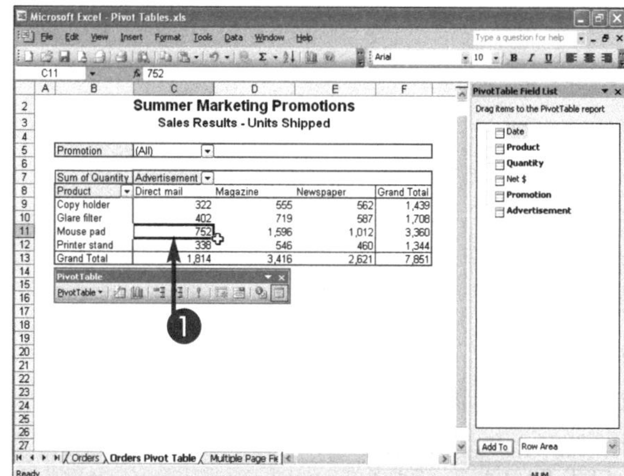

2. Click PivotTable→Group and Show Detail→Show Detail.

   You can also double-click the data value or click the Show Detail button () in the PivotTable toolbar.

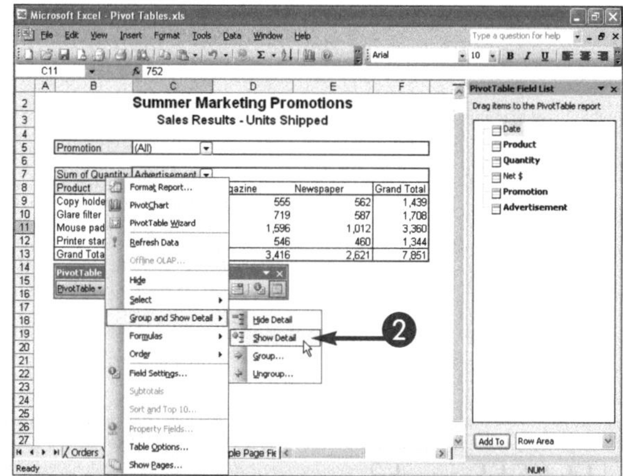

Excel displays the underlying data in a new worksheet.

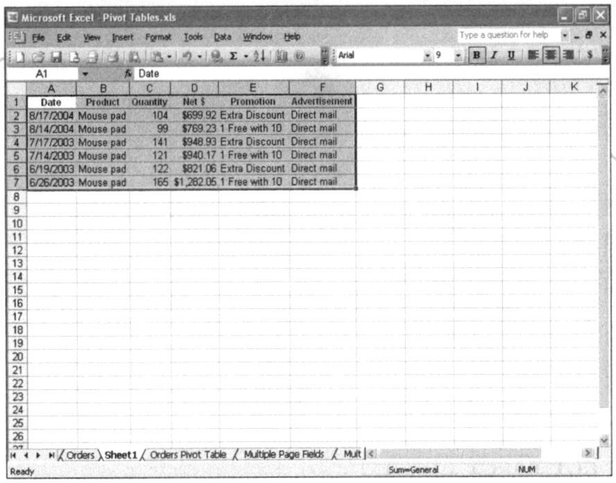

DELETE THE DETAIL WORKSHEET

1. Right-click the worksheet tab.
2. Click Delete.

   Excel displays a dialog box asking you to confirm the deletion.
3. Click Delete.

   Excel deletes the worksheet.

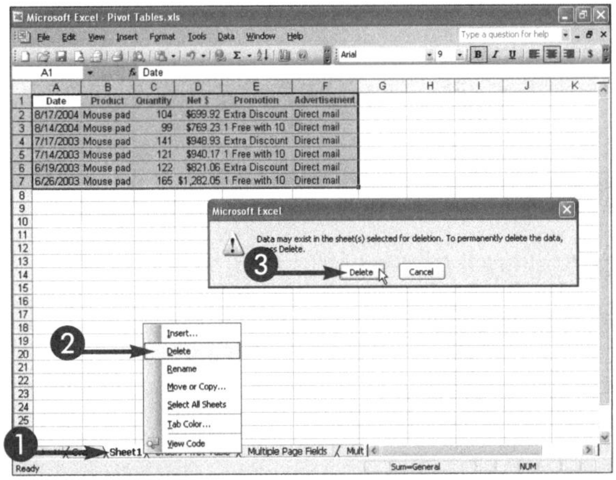

Extra

When you attempt to drill down to a data value's underlying details, Excel may display the error message "Cannot change this part of a PivotTable report." This error means that the feature that normally enables you to drill down has been turned off. To turn this feature back on, click PivotTable→Table Options to display the PivotTable Options dialog box. Select "Enable drill to details" (☐ changes to ☑), and then click OK.

The opposite situation occurs when you distribute the workbook containing the PivotTable and you do not want the other users drilling down and cluttering the workbook with detail worksheets. In this case, click PivotTable→Table Options to display the PivotTable Options dialog box, deselect "Enable drill to details" (☑ changes to ☐), and then click OK.

There may be times when you want to see all of a PivotTable's underlying source data. If the source data is a range or list in another worksheet, then you need only display that sheet. If the source data is not so readily available, however, then Excel gives you an easy way to view all the underlying data. Click the PivotTable's Grand Total cell and then click PivotTable→Group and Show Detail→Show Detail.

Create a Chart from PivotTable Data

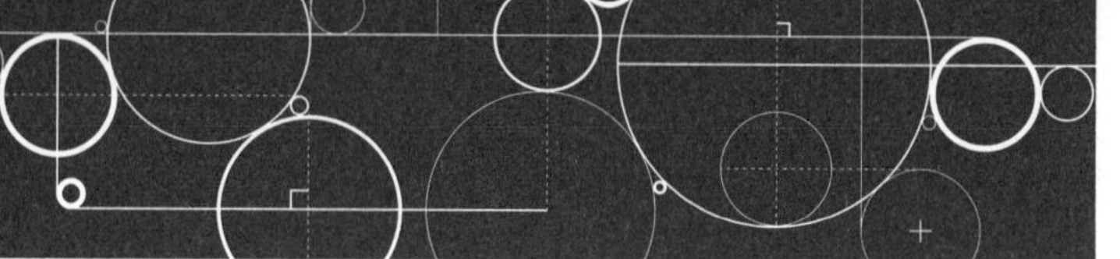

Excel charts are a great way to analyze data because they enable you to visualize the numbers and see the relationships between different aspects of the data. This is particularly useful in a PivotTable because it is often necessary to visualize the relationship between different columns or different rows. In Chapter 9, you learn how to create a PivotChart. However, if you just need a simple chart, or if you avoid the limitations that are inherent with a PivotChart, you can create a regular chart using the PivotTable data, as you learn in this task.

If you try to create a chart directly from a PivotTable, Excel will create a PivotChart. To create a regular chart from a PivotTable, you must first copy the PivotTable data that you want to graph, and then paste the data into another part of the worksheet. You can then build your chart using this copied data. In this case, you run through the various steps provided by the Chart Wizard to specify the chart type, chart options, and chart location.

Note, though, that this method produces a static chart. This means that if your PivotTable data changes, your chart does not change automatically. Instead, you need to re-create your chart from scratch. However, it is possible to create a dynamic chart that changes whenever your PivotTable does. See the tip on page 39 for details.

Create a Chart from PivotTable Data

CREATE A COPY OF THE PIVOTTABLE DATA

1. Select the PivotTable data you want to use for your chart.

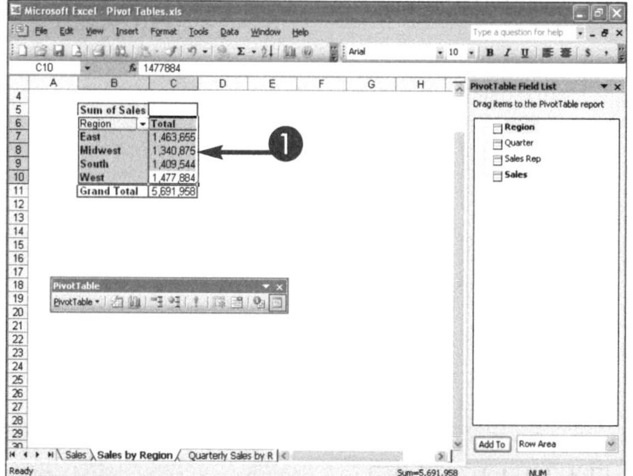

2. Click Edit→Copy.

You can also press Ctrl+C or click the Copy button (▯).

Excel copies the PivotTable data.

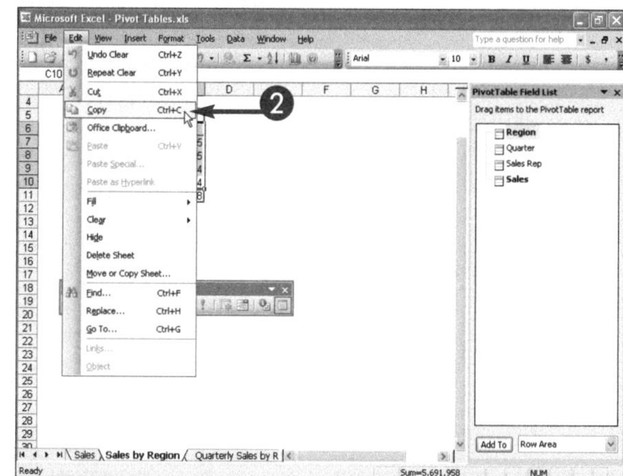

3. Click the cell where you want the copied data to appear.

4. Click Edit→Paste.

   You can also press Ctrl+V or click the Paste button ( ).

   Excel pastes the copied PivotTable data.

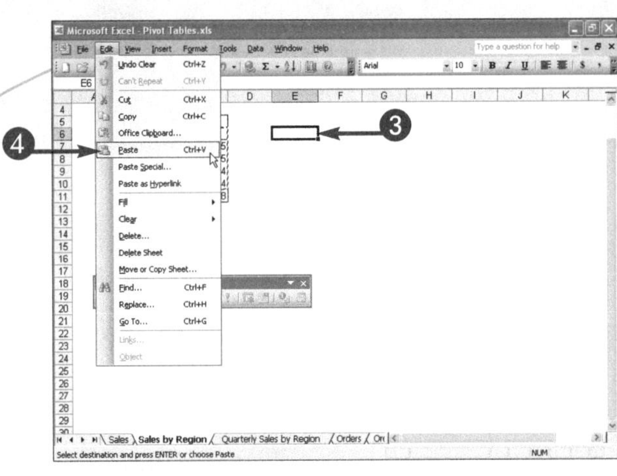

CREATE THE CHART

5. Select the copied data.

6. Click Insert→Chart.

   - You can also click the Chart Wizard button ( ).

   The Chart Wizard's first dialog box appears.

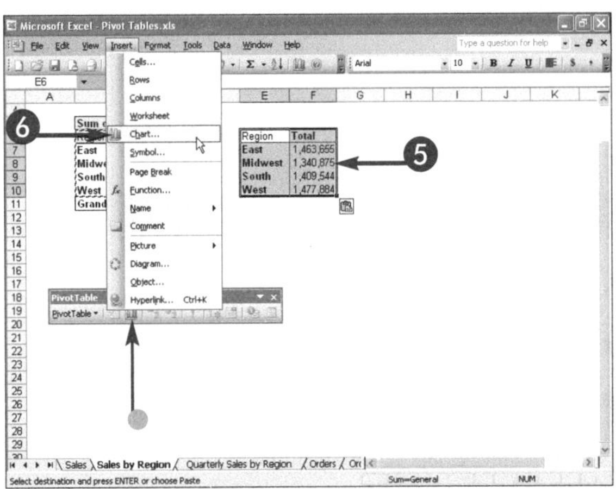

Extra

PivotTables often result in large workbooks because Excel must keep track of a great deal of extra information to keep the PivotTable performance acceptable. In Chapter 4, you learn how to pivot the data, which means moving a field to a different area of the PivotTable; see the task "Move a Field to a Different Area". To ensure that the recalculation involved in pivoting happens quickly and efficiently, Excel maintains a copy of the source data in a special memory area called the pivot cache.

When you copy a PivotTable and then paste it, Excel also pastes the pivot cache. This is wasteful because the pasted data does not and can not make use of the pivot cache. To avoid this, you should tell Excel to paste only the values from the PivotTable. To do this, follow the steps in the task "Convert a PivotTable to Regular Data," later in this chapter.

continued →

Create a Chart from PivotTable Data (continued)

As you learn in Chapter 9, a PivotChart, although very similar to a regular Excel chart, comes with a number of limitations on chart types, layout, and formatting; see the section "Understanding PivotChart Limitations". A PivotChart also comes with its own pivot cache, a concept you learned about in the tip on the previous page. This means that PivotCharts can use up a great deal of memory and can greatly increase the size of a workbook.

If you simply want to visualize your data, you can avoid the limitations and resource requirements of a PivotChart by creating a regular chart, instead. You do this by running the Chart Wizard on your copied PivotTable data. With a regular chart, you have access to all the available charting features, so you can use all the options presented by the Chart Wizard to construct your graph.

Create a Chart from PivotTable Data *(continued)*

7. Click the chart type you want to use.
8. Click a chart sub-type.
9. Click Next.

   The second Chart Wizard dialog box appears.

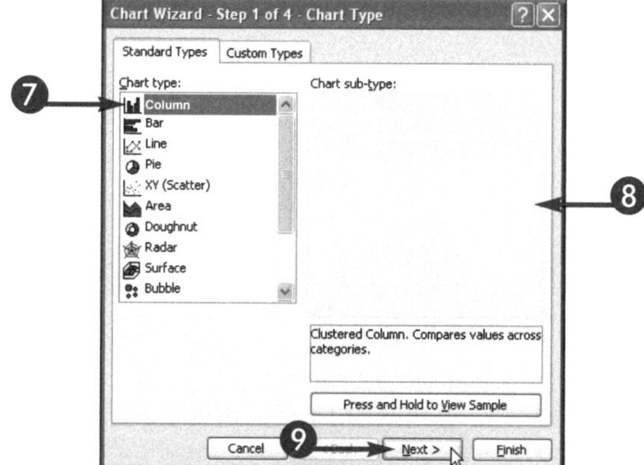

10. Click Next.

    The third Chart Wizard dialog box appears.

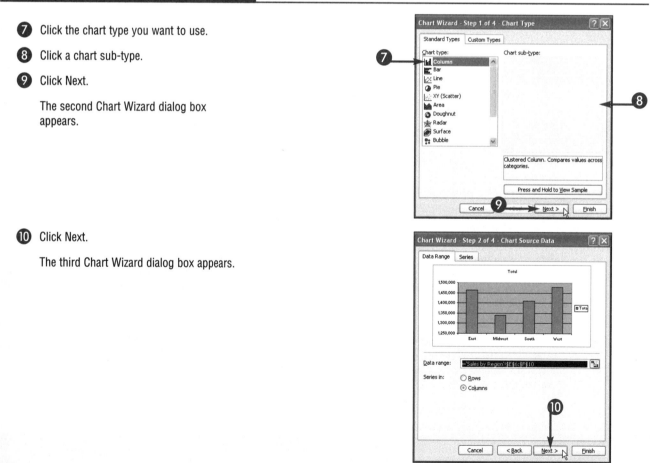

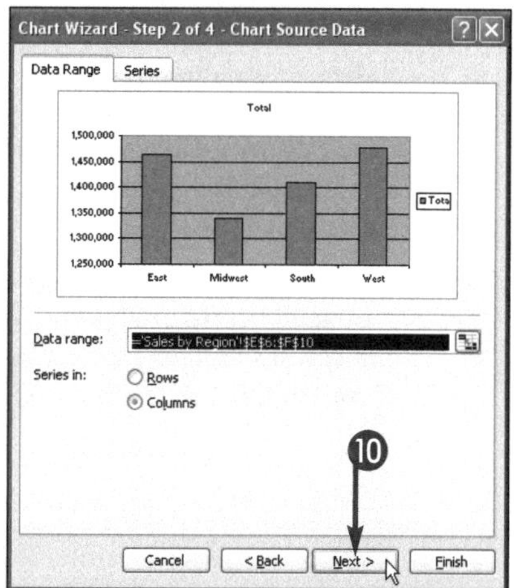

11 Select the chart options you want to use.

If you want to create the chart on a separate worksheet, click Next and then click "As new sheet."

12 Click Finish.

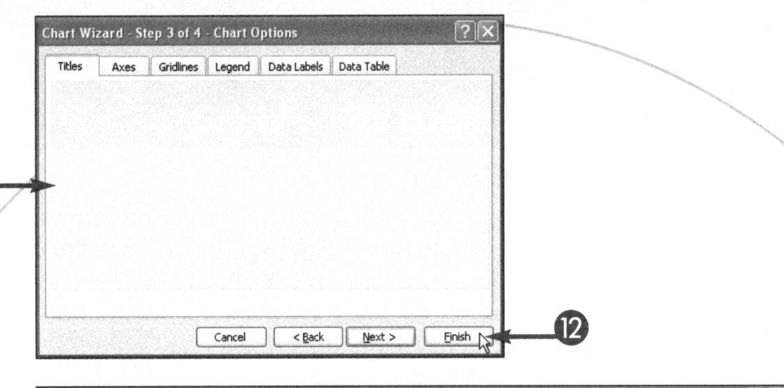

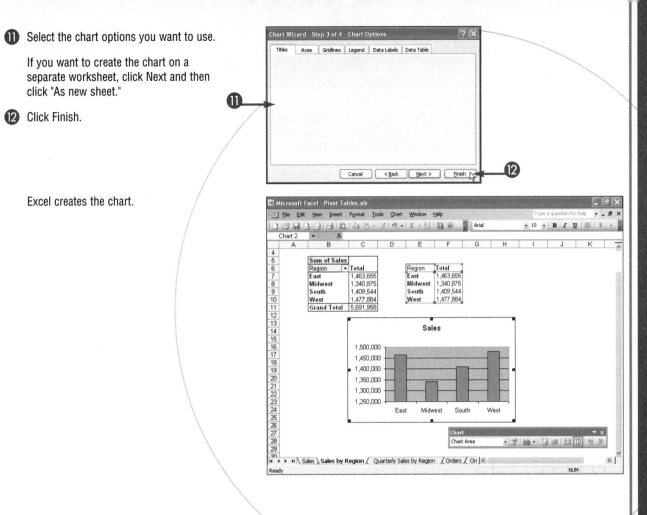

Excel creates the chart.

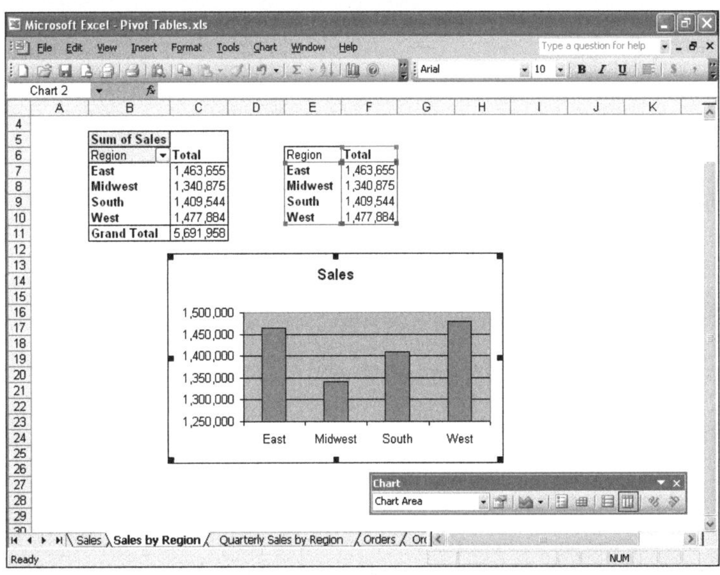

Apply It

The chart you learn how to create in this task is static, so whenever your PivotTable gets new values, you must re-create the chart from scratch. This is useful for PivotTables that do not change fields, items, or data. However, if you have a PivotTable that changes frequently, you might prefer to create a dynamic chart that updates automatically when changes occur in your PivotTable data.

To create a dynamic chart, use formulas instead of copy and paste to create a replica of the PivotTable data. That is, for each cell in the PivotTable that you want to use in your chart, create a formula in another cell that references the PivotTable cell. For example, in cell E6, enter the formula **=B6** to reference the Region label; similarly, in cell F6, enter the formula **=C6** to reference the Total label. Do the same for the data values. For example, in cell F7, enter the formula **=C7**. When you are done, you should have the same labels and values in a replica of the PivotTable. You can then base your chart on this replicated data. Because you are using formulas to reference the original data, any changes to the PivotTable will automatically be reflected in your chart.

Add Multiple Fields to the Row or Column Area

The PivotTables you have seen so far have been restricted to a single field in any of the four areas: row, column, data, and page. However, you are free to add multiple fields to any one of these areas. This is a very powerful technique because it allows you to perform further analysis of your data by viewing the data differently.

In this task you learn how to add multiple fields to a PivotTable's row and column areas. See the next tasks, "Add Multiple Fields to the Data Area" and "Add Multiple Fields to the Page Area," as well. Adding multiple fields to the row and column areas enables you to break down your data for further analysis. For example, suppose you are analyzing the results of a sales campaign that ran different promotions in several types of advertisements. A basic PivotTable might show you the sales for each Product (the row field) according to the Advertisement in which the customer reported seeing the campaign (the column field). You might also be interested in seeing, for each product, the breakdown in sales for each promotion. You can do that by adding the Promotion field to the row area, as you see in the example used in this task.

Even more powerfully, after you add a second field to the row or column area, you can change the field positions to change the view, as described in Chapter 4 in the task "Change the Order of Fields within an Area." Note that the field in the row or column area that is closest to the data area is called the *inner field* and the field furthest from the data area is called the *outer field*.

Add Multiple Fields to the Row or Column Area

USE THE PIVOTTABLE FIELD LIST

1. Click the field you want to add.
2. Click ▾ and then click either Row Area or Column Area.
3. Click Add To.

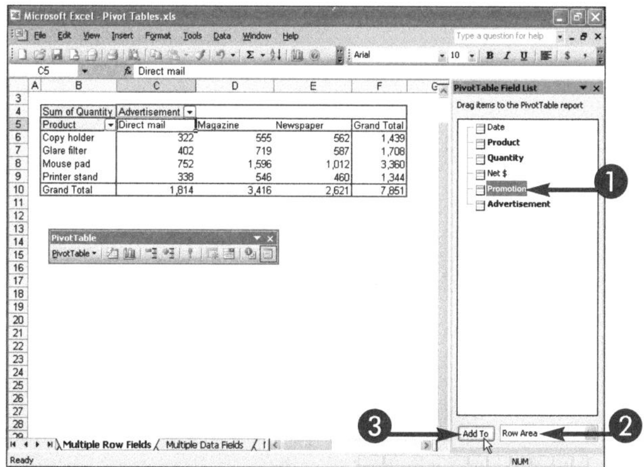

- Excel adds the field to the PivotTable. In this example, Excel adds the field to the row area.

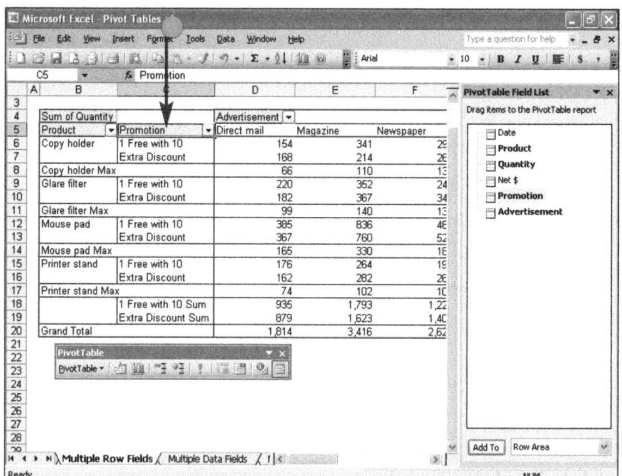

USE THE PIVOTTABLE WIZARD

1. Click PivotTable→PivotTable Wizard.

   The PivotTable and PivotChart Wizard appears.

2. Click Layout.

   The Layout dialog box appears.

3. Click and drag the field you want to add and drop the field in either the Row section or the Column section.

4. Click OK.

   Excel adds the field to the PivotTable.

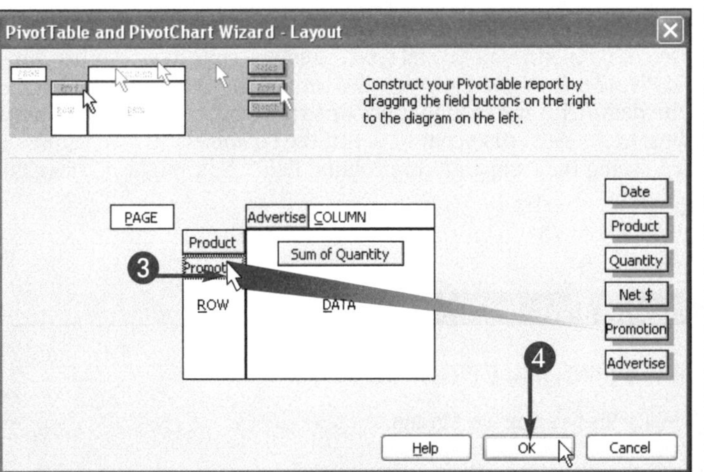

Extra

You can also add a field to the row or column area of a PivotTable by dragging. In the PivotTable Field List, click and drag the field you want to add. As you move the field into the PivotTable, the mouse pointer changes depending on the PivotTable area over which it is hovering:

BUTTON	DESCRIPTION
	Mouse pointer for the row area.
	Mouse pointer for the column area.

When you see one of these pointers, dropping the field means that Excel adds the field to that area of the PivotTable.

Note, too, that *where* you drop the field with the row or column area is significant. In the row area, for example, you can either drop the new field to the right or to the left of the existing field. If you drop it to the right, Excel displays each item in the original field broken down by the items in the new field. This is the situation in the final screen shot, above, where you see each item in the Product field broken down by the two items in the Promotion field. Conversely, if you drop the new field to the left of the existing field, Excel displays each item in the new field broken down by the items in the original field.

Add Multiple Fields to the Data Area

In this task you learn how to add multiple fields to the PivotTable's data area. See also the tasks "Add Multiple Fields to the Row and Column Area" and "Add Multiple Fields to the Page Area" in this chapter. Adding multiple fields to the data area enables you to see multiple summaries for enhancing your analysis. For example, suppose you are analyzing the results of a sales campaign that ran different promotions in several types of advertisements. A basic PivotTable might show you the sum of the Quantity sold (the data field) for each Product (the row field) according to the Advertisement in which the customer reported seeing the campaign (the column field). You might also be interested in seeing, for each product and advertisement, the net dollar amount sold. You can do that by adding the Net $ field to the data area, as you see in the example used in this task.

Even more powerfully, you are not restricted to using just sums in each data field. Excel enables you to specify a number of different summary functions in the data area, so you could apply a different function to each field. For example, you could view the sum of the Quantity field and the average of the Net $ field. You learn how to change the summary function in Chapter 7 in the task "Change the PivotTable Summary Calculation."

Add Multiple Fields to the Data Area

USE THE PIVOTTABLE FIELD LIST

1. Click the field you want to add.
2. Click ▾ and then click Data Area.
3. Click Add To.

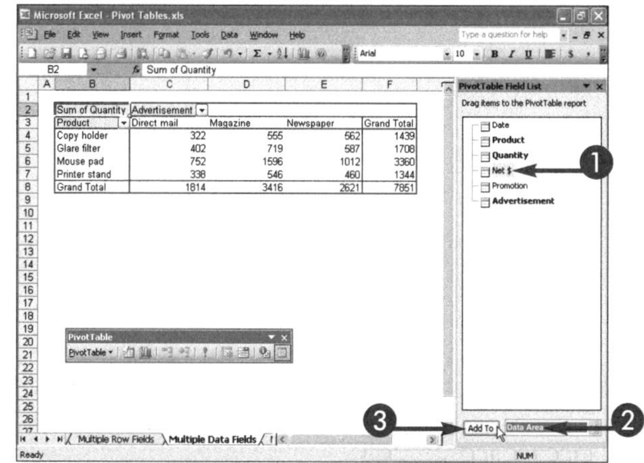

- Excel adds the field to the PivotTable's data area.

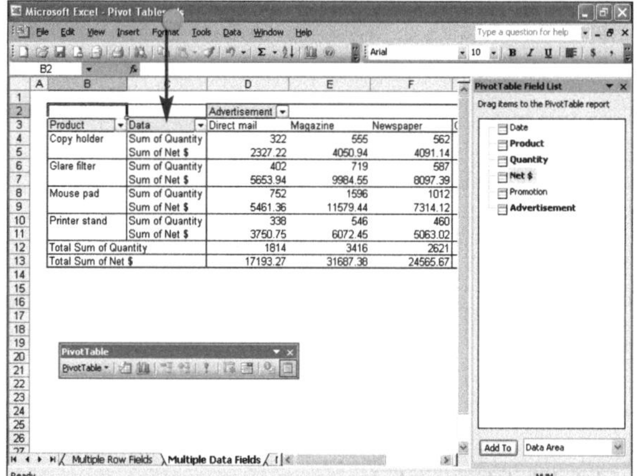

USE THE PIVOTTABLE WIZARD

1. Click PivotTable→PivotTable Wizard.

   The PivotTable and PivotChart Wizard appears.

2. Click Layout.

   The Layout dialog box appears.

3. Click and drag the field you want to add and drop the field in the Data section.

4. Click OK.

   Excel adds the field to the PivotTable's data area.

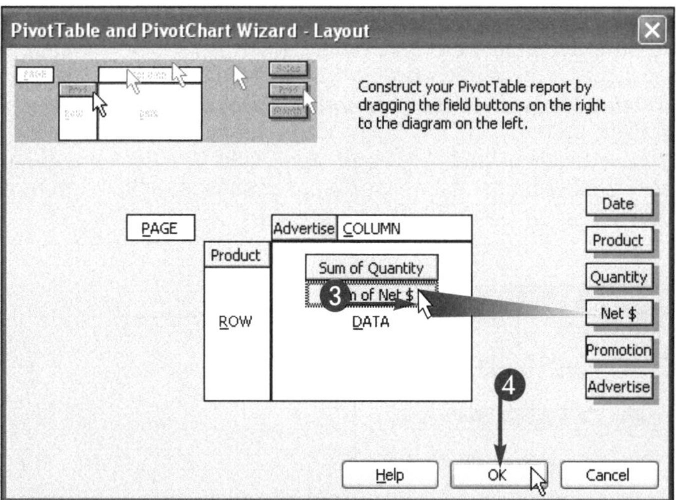

Extra

You can also add a field to the PivotTable's data area by dragging. In the PivotTable Field List, click and drag the field you want to add. As you move the field into the PivotTable's data area, the mouse pointer changes to the data area mouse pointer ( ).

When you see this pointer, drop the field to add it to the PivotTable's data area.

In the task "Remove a PivotTable Field," earlier in this chapter, you learned that you can delete a field from any PivotTable area by dragging the field's button and dropping it outside of the PivotTable. However, this technique does not work when you have multiple fields in the data area because Excel replaces the original field button with a Data button. Dragging this button off the PivotTable means that you remove all the data fields. To delete one of multiple fields in the data area, click PivotTable→PivotTable Wizard and then click Layout to display the Layout dialog box. Drag the data field you want to remove off the PivotTable diagram, and then click OK.

Add Multiple Fields to the Page Area

In this task you learn how to add multiple fields to the PivotTable's page area. See also the previous tasks, "Add Multiple Fields to the Row and Column Area" and "Add Multiple Fields to the Data Area." Adding multiple fields to the page area enables you to apply multiple filters to the PivotTable to enhance your analysis. For example, suppose you are analyzing the results of a sales campaign that ran different promotions in several types of advertisements. A basic PivotTable might show you the sum of the Quantity sold (the data field) for each Product (the column field) by Date (the row field), with a filter for the type of Advertisement (the page field). You might also be interested in filtering the data even further to show specific Promotion items. You can do that by adding the Promotion field to the page area, as you see in the example used in this task.

To get the most out of this technique, you need to know how to use a page area field to filter the data shown in a PivotTable. For example, you could use the Advertisement field to display the PivotTable results for just the Magazine item. With the Promotion field also added to the page area, you could filter the PivotTable even further to display just the results for the 1 Free with 10 item. In the Chapter 4 tasks "Display a Different Page" and "Change the Page Area Layout," you learn how to display different pages and how to reconfigure the page area layout, respectively.

Add Multiple Fields to the Page Area

USE THE PIVOTTABLE FIELD LIST

1. Click the field you want to add.
2. Click ▾ and then click Page Area.
3. Click Add To.

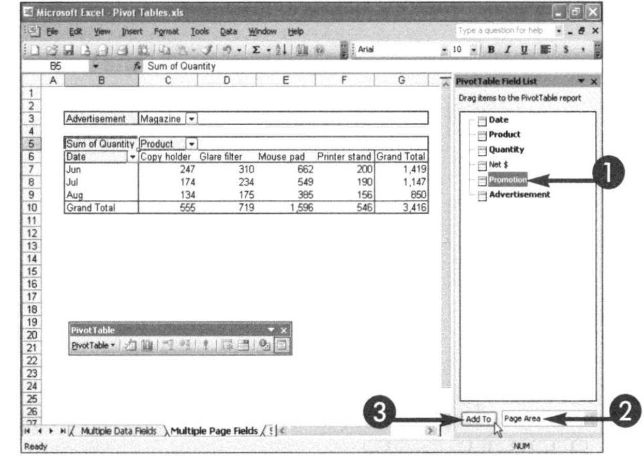

- Excel adds the field to the PivotTable's page area.

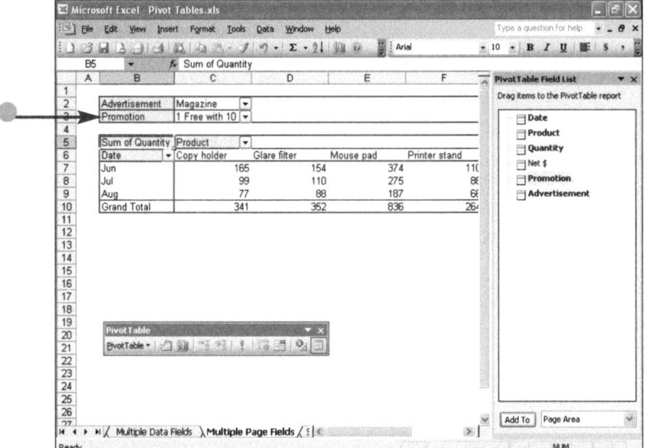

USE THE PIVOTTABLE WIZARD

1. Click PivotTable→PivotTable Wizard.

   The PivotTable and PivotChart Wizard appears.

2. Click Layout.

   The Layout dialog box appears.

3. Click and drag the field you want to add and drop the field in the Page section.

4. Click OK.

   Excel adds the field to the PivotTable's page area.

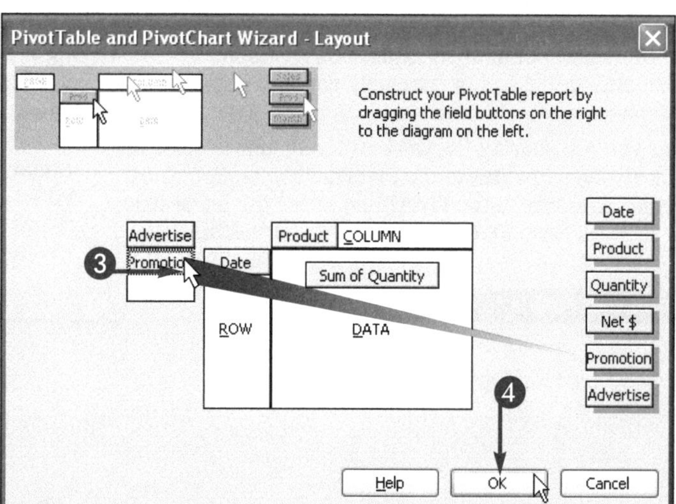

Extra

You can also add a field to the PivotTable's page area by dragging. In the PivotTable Field List, click and drag the field you want to add. As you move the field into the PivotTable's page area, the mouse pointer changes to the page area mouse pointer ( ).

When you see this pointer, drop the field to add it to the PivotTable's page area.

Earlier you learned that the order of the fields with the PivotTable's row and column areas is important because it changes how Excel breaks down the data; see the task "Add Multiple Fields to the Row and Column Area," earlier in this chapter. The order of the fields in the page area is not important because the resulting filter is the same. For example, suppose you have a collection of shirts and you want to see only those that are white and short-sleeved. You could do this by first pulling out all the white shirts and then going through those to find all the short-sleeved ones. However, you get the same result if you first take out all the short-sleeved shirts and then find all of those that are white.

Publish a PivotTable to a Web Page

When you analyze data, it is often important to involve other people in the process. For example, you might want to have other people help with some or all of the analytical tasks. Similarly, you might want to share your results with other interested parties. If the other people have Excel, you can share the workload or the results simply by sending each person a copy of the workbook that contains the PivotTable. However, although Excel is extremely popular, not everyone uses it.

Whether you are sharing the work or the results, a related problem involves updates to the PivotTable data. You know you can always refresh the PivotTable to see the latest data; see the task "Refresh PivotTable Data," earlier in this chapter. However, it is inconvenient to have to send out a new copy of the workbook each time you update the PivotTable.

You can solve both problems by placing your PivotTable on a Web page, either on the Internet or on your corporate intranet site. After the PivotTable is in Web page format, anyone — even people who do not use Excel — can view the PivotTable. It is also possible to set up the Web page version of the PivotTable to be updated automatically whenever you save the original workbook, so other people always see the latest data. Finally, you can also create interactive PivotTables, which means that other people can work with the PivotTable within the Web browser. This task shows you the steps involved in publishing a PivotTable to a Web page.

Publish a PivotTable to a Web Page

1. Select the PivotTable you want to publish.

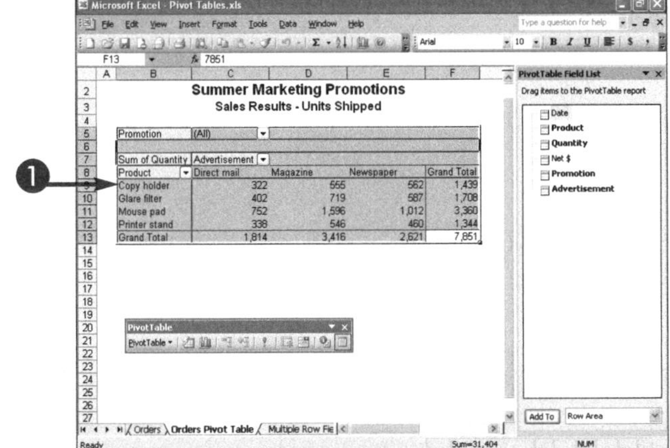

2. Click File→Save as Web Page.

   The Save As dialog box appears.

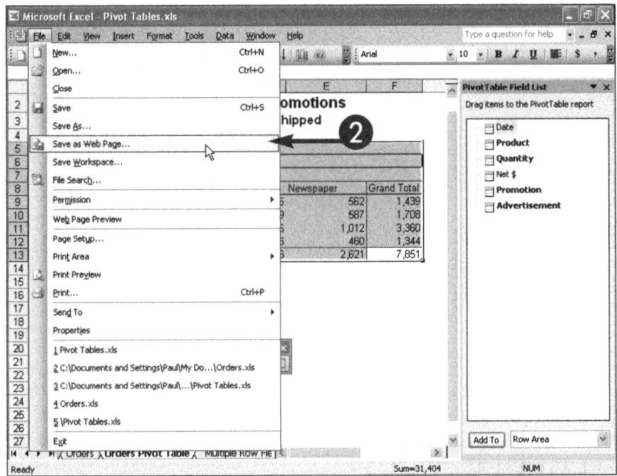

3 Click Publish.

The Publish as Web Page dialog box appears.

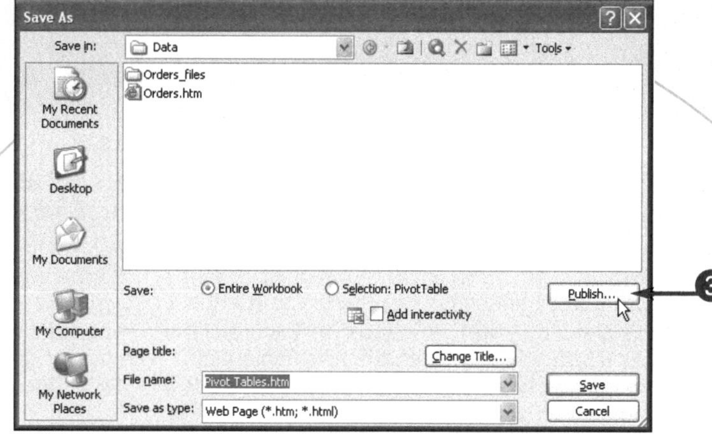

4 Click ▾ and then click the worksheet that contains the PivotTable you want to publish.

5 Click the PivotTable you want to publish.

6 Select Add interactivity with.

- Excel should automatically select PivotTable functionality in this list. If not, click ▾ and then click PivotTable functionality.

7 Click Browse.

- If you already know where you want the Web page saved, type the location and filename in this text box.

The Publish As dialog box appears.

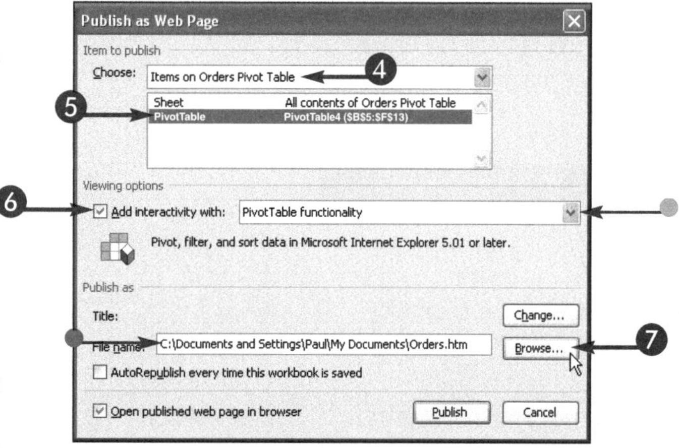

Apply It

You can tell Excel to add a title to the published PivotTable. This title appears in the Web page as text just above the PivotTable. To specify a title, click "Change in the Publish as Web Page dialog box" to display the Set Title dialog box. Type the title that you want to appear over the PivotTable and then click OK to return to the Publish as Web Page dialog box.

To ensure that the Web page version of your PivotTable is always up to date, you can tell Excel to update it for you automatically. In the Publish as Web Page dialog box, select "AutoRepublish every time this workbook is saved" (☐ changes to ☑). Unfortunately, activating this option means that every time you save the workbook, Excel displays a dialog box asking if you want to disable or enable the AutoRepublish feature. To bypass this dialog box, the next time the dialog box appears, select "Enable the AutoRepublish feature" (○ changes to ◉), select "Do not show this message again" (☐ changes to ☑), and then click OK.

continued →

Publish a PivotTable to a Web Page (continued)

When publishing a PivotTable, it is important to choose the proper location for the published Web page and its associated files. If you will be putting the PivotTable Web page on an Internet site, you should save the Web page to whatever folder you use for your other Web site files, which will likely be a subfolder of My Documents. If you will be putting the PivotTable Web page on your corporate intranet site, you should save the Web page to an appropriate network folder. Ask your system administrator for the correct folder and whether you need a username and password.

After you publish an Internet-based PivotTable Web page to your computer, you must then use an FTP utility or similar program to upload the Web page and its associated files to your directory on the Web server. You can save this extra step by specifying the particulars of your FTP sites within Excel, as described in the tip on the following page.

Publish a PivotTable to a Web Page *(continued)*

8 Click My Documents.

- To choose a different location, click ▾ in the Save in list and then click the location you want.

9 Type a name for the Web page.

Note: When typing a name for the Web page, do not use spaces and make sure the name ends with either .htm or .html.

10 Click OK.

Excel returns you to the Publish as Web Page dialog box.

11 Select this check box to open the published Web page in your Web browser.

12 Click Publish.

Excel publishes the PivotTable to the Web page.

If you are running Windows XP Service Pack 2 or later, Internet Explorer warns you that it has prevented the file from showing active content.

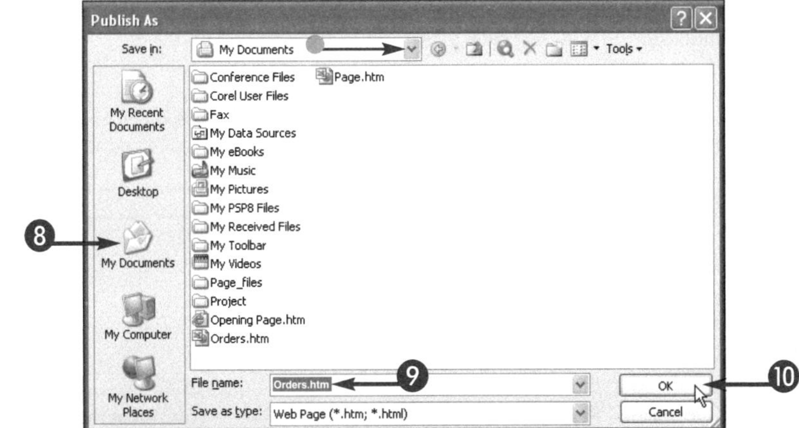

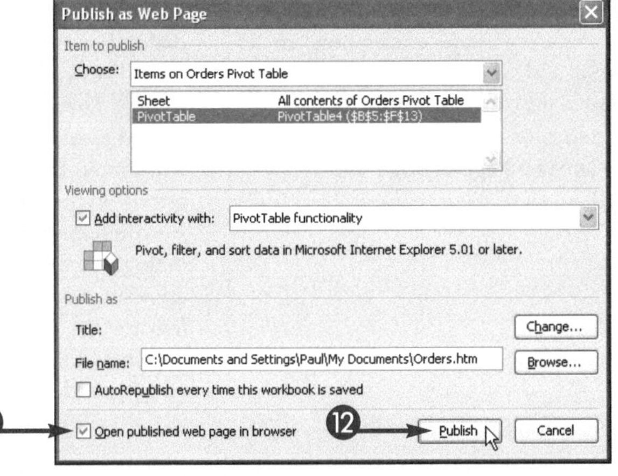

13 Click the information bar.

14 Click Allow Blocked Content.

Internet Explorer displays a dialog box asking if you are sure you want to run the active content.

15 Click Yes.

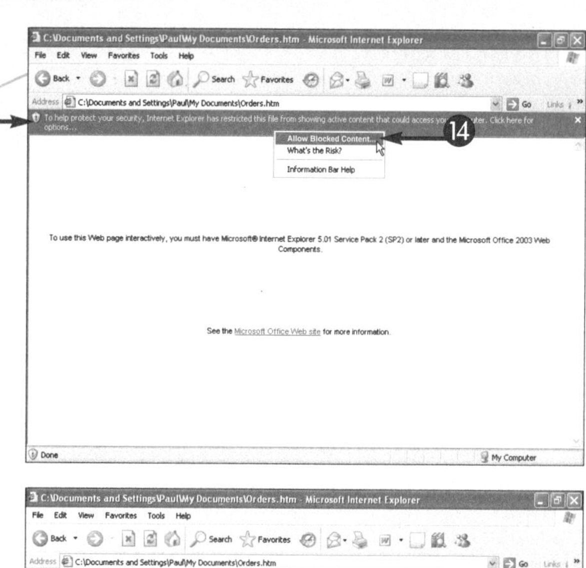

Internet Explorer displays the PivotTable on the Web page.

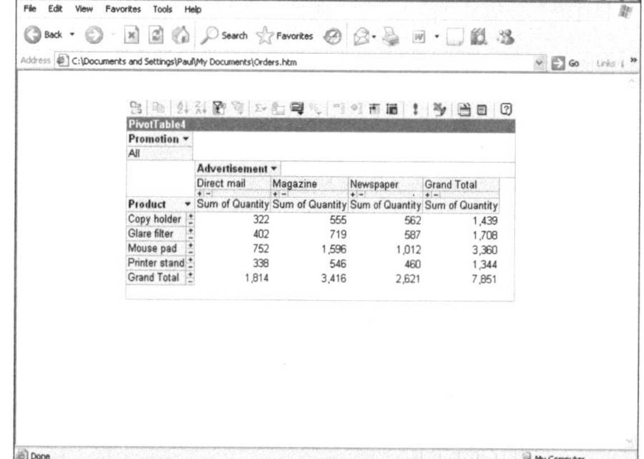

Apply It

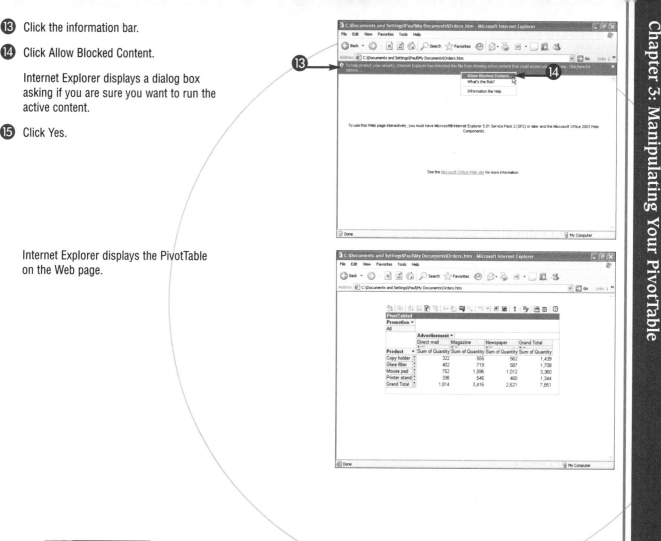

When you publish a PivotTable (or any Excel data) to a Web page, Excel creates a subfolder named *Filename*_files, where *Filename* is the name you give to the Web page file, minus the extension. Excel uses this folder to hold support files for the Web page. For a PivotTable, you see two extra files: filelist.xml and a file with the name *Filename* _ID_cachedata001.xml, where *Filename* is the name of the Web page file and ID is a random 5-digit number.

If you prefer to keep all the files in a single folder – for example, to make it easier to copy the files to your Web site – you can tell Excel not to create the subfolder. Click Tools→Options, click the General tab, click Web Options, click the Files tab, and then deselect "Organize supporting files in a folder" (☑ changes to ☐). Click OK in each open dialog box.

To specify an FTP site for uploading, display the Save As dialog box, click Add/Modify FTP Locations in the Save in list, type the site address and your username and password, and then click Add.

Convert a PivotTable to Regular Data

One of the major drawbacks of PivotTables is that they often require an inordinate amount of system resources. For example, it is not unusual to have source data that contains a large number of records or to have a PivotTable that is itself quite large and uses multiple fields in one or more areas. In such cases, the workbook containing the PivotTable can become huge and the memory used by Excel to store PivotTable data for faster performance can become excessive.

In situations where you need to manipulate the PivotTable frequently and where the source data changes, you have no choice but to put up with the burden that the PivotTable puts on your system. On the other hand, you may just be interested in the current PivotTable results and have no need to manipulate or refresh the data; similarly, you may not even need to keep the source data after you have built your PivotTable. In these scenarios, you can drastically reduce the resources used by the workbook by converting your PivotTable into regular data. When you have done that, you can delete the PivotTable — see the task "Delete a PivotTable," later in this chapter — and the source data, assuming the source data is an Excel range or list that you no longer need.

Convert a PivotTable to Regular Data

1. Select the PivotTable you want to convert to regular data.

2. Click Edit ➔Copy.

   You can also press Ctrl+C or click the Copy button ().

   Excel copies the PivotTable data.

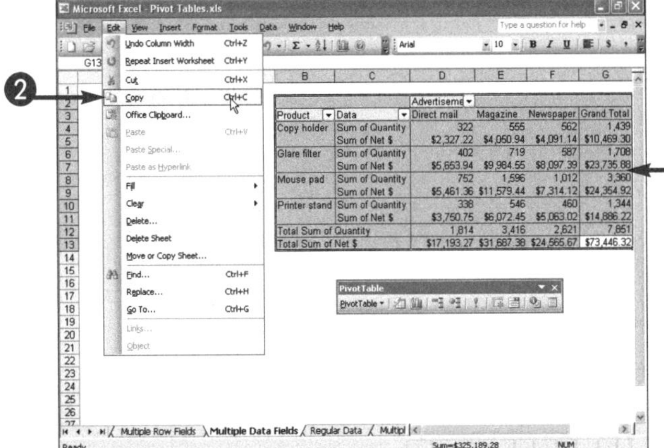

3. Click the cell where you want the regular data to appear.

4. Click Edit➔Paste Special.

   The Paste Special dialog box appears.

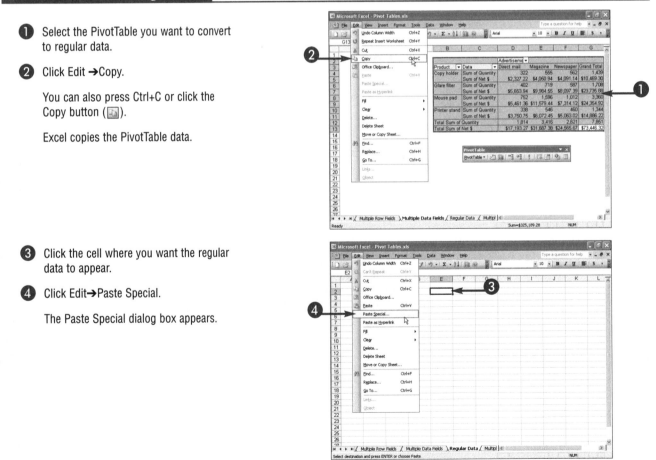

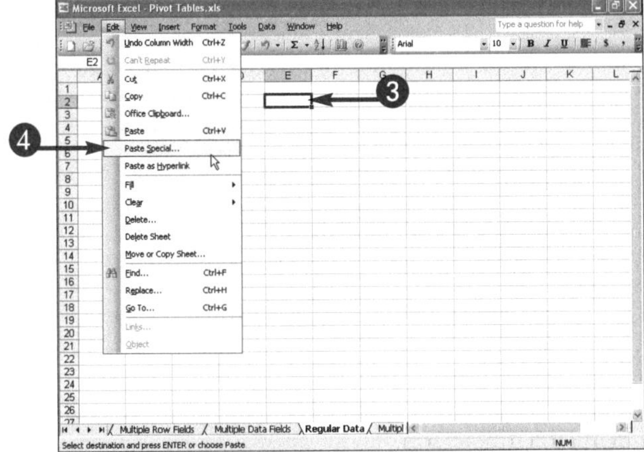

5. Click Values.
6. Click OK.

   You can also press Ctrl+V or click the Paste button ( ).

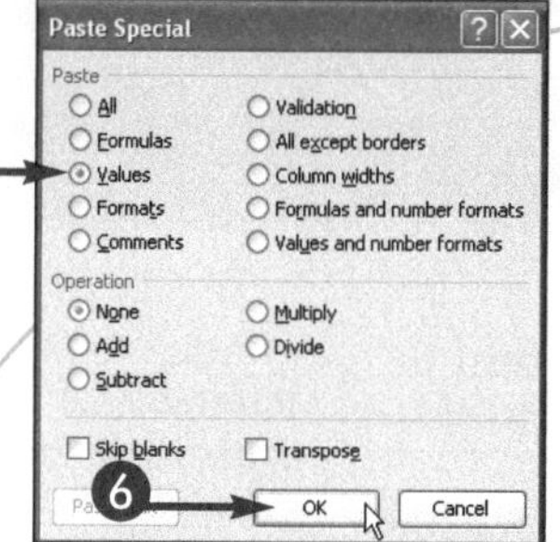

Excel pastes the PivotTable as regular data.

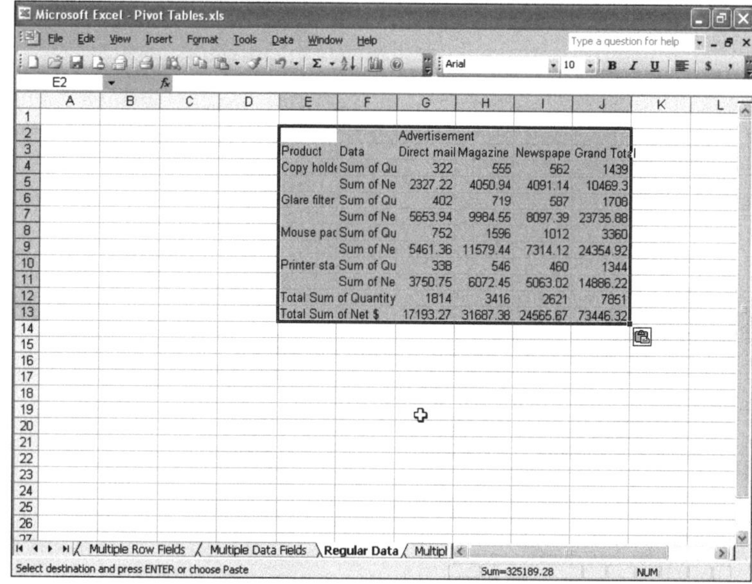

		Advertisement			
Product	Data	Direct mail	Magazine	Newspape	Grand Tota
Copy holde	Sum of Qu	322	555	562	1439
	Sum of Ne	2327.22	4050.94	4091.14	10469.3
Glare filter	Sum of Qu	402	719	587	1708
	Sum of Ne	5653.94	9984.55	8097.39	23735.88
Mouse pac	Sum of Qu	752	1596	1012	3360
	Sum of Ne	5461.36	11579.44	7314.12	24354.92
Printer sta	Sum of Qu	338	546	460	1344
	Sum of Ne	3750.75	6072.45	5063.02	14886.22
Total Sum of Quantity		1814	3416	2621	7851
Total Sum of Net $		17193.27	31687.38	24565.67	73446.32

Apply It

The biggest problem that occurs when you convert a PivotTable to regular data is that Excel does not preserve any of your PivotTable formatting. See Chapter 5 to learn how to customize PivotTable fields. If you formatted your PivotTable with one of Excel's AutoFormats, then you can easily solve the problem: select the pasted data, click Format→AutoFormat, click the AutoFormat you want, and then click OK.

If you do not want to use an AutoFormat, Excel offers a simple way to at least preserve any numeric formats you applied to the PivotTable cells. In Chapter 5, see the task "Apply a Numeric Format to PivotTable Data." In the Paste Special dialog box, select "Values and number formats" (○ changes to ◉) instead of Values.

If you just want to view the data and do not need to manipulate it in any way, you can preserve all your formatting by taking a "picture" of the PivotTable. Select the PivotTable, hold down Shift, and click Edit→Copy Picture. Select the cell where you want the picture to appear and then click Edit→Paste.

Print a PivotTable

PivotTables are mostly useful in electronic format where you can perform the manipulations that you have learned about in this chapter, as well as change the PivotTable view to enhance your analysis of the data. See Chapter 4 to learn how to change the PivotTable view.

However, after you complete the PivotTable, you might want to preserve a hard copy by printing out the PivotTable report. You can use the printout to send a copy to another person, store the report in a file, or provide a backup if you lose the original electronic report or if the original report is no longer available.

Printing the PivotTable is also useful for documenting intermediate steps in the data analysis. If your analysis consists of four or five changes to the PivotTable, you could get a printout at each stage to document what you have done.

Printouts are also useful for comparing PivotTable results side by side. For example, you could construct the PivotTable using one layout and then print it out. You could then change the PivotTable layout and get a second printout. With the two printouts beside each other, you can then quickly scan the reports to compare them.

Print a PivotTable

1. Select the PivotTable you want to print.
2. Click File→Page Setup.

   The Page Setup dialog box appears.

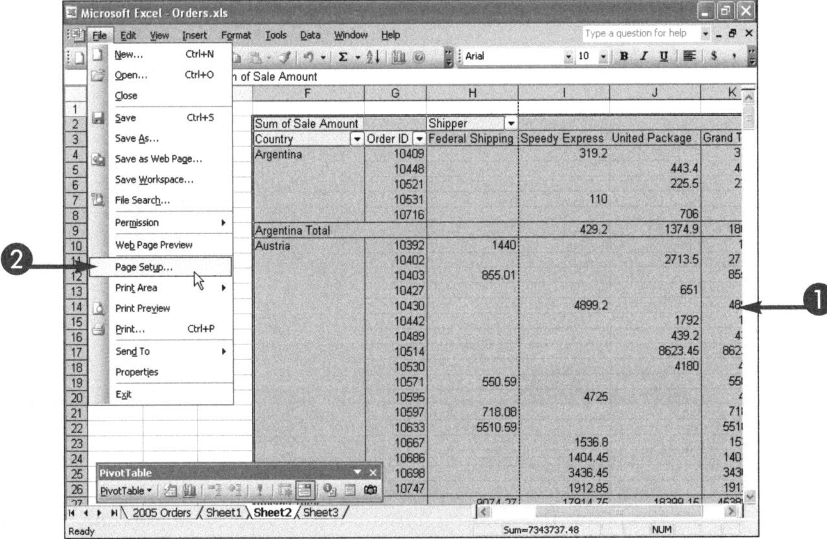

3. Set the paper type, margins, header and footer, and other page setup options.
4. Click Print.

   The Print dialog box appears.

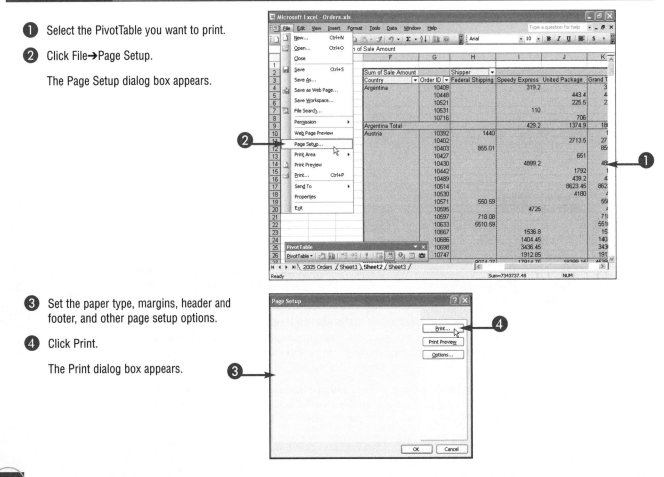

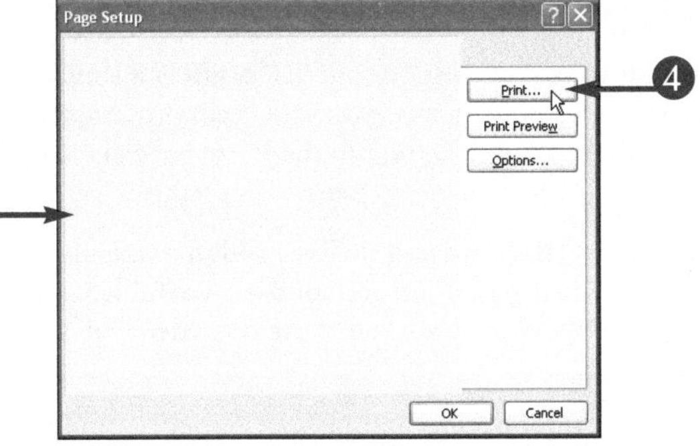

5. Select Selection.
6. Set any other print options you require.
7. Click Preview.

   The Print Preview window appears.

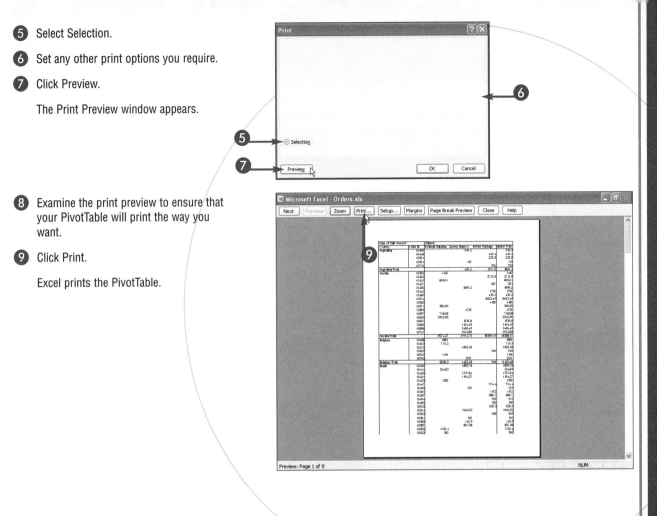

8. Examine the print preview to ensure that your PivotTable will print the way you want.
9. Click Print.

   Excel prints the PivotTable.

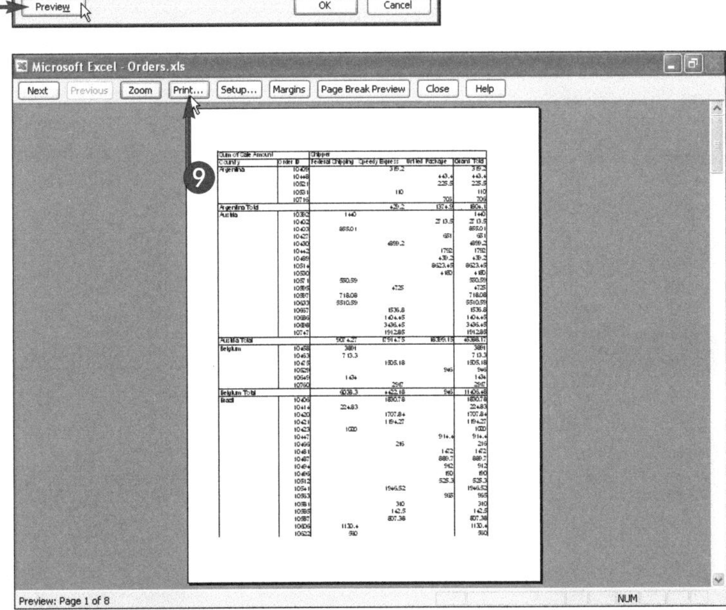

Extra

Excel offers a number of useful options for controlling the printout of a PivotTable. For example, if your PivotTable contains multiple row fields, it is often useful to display each item in the leftmost field on its own page. To set this up, right-click the leftmost field's button and then click Field Settings. Click Layout to display the PivotTable Field Layout dialog box, and then select "Insert page break after each item" (☐ changes to ☑). Click OK in each open dialog box.

Another useful printing option is to force Excel to print the row and column labels at the top of each printed page. To set this up, select the PivotTable and then click File→Print Area→Set Print Area. In the PivotTable toolbar, click PivotTable→Table Options to display the PivotTable Options dialog box. Select "Repeat item labels on each printed page" (☐ changes to ☑), select "Set print titles" (☐ changes to ☑), and then click OK.

Delete a PivotTable

PivotTables are useful data analysis tools, and now that you are becoming comfortable with them, you may find that you use them quite often. This will give you tremendous insight into your data, but that insight comes at a cost: PivotTables are very resource-intensive, so creating many PivotTable reports can lead to large workbook file sizes and less memory available for other programs. You can reduce the impact that a large number of open PivotTables have on your system by deleting those reports that you no longer need.

Even if you create just a few PivotTables, you may find that you need them only temporarily. For example, you may just want to build a quick-and-dirty report to check a few numbers. Similarly, your source data may be preliminary, so you might want to create a temporary PivotTable for now, holding off on a more permanent version until your source data is complete. Finally, you might build PivotTable reports to send them to other people. When that is done, you might no longer need the reports yourself. For all these scenarios, you need to know how to delete a PivotTable report, and this task shows you how it is done.

Delete a PivotTable

1. Click any cell within the PivotTable you want to delete.

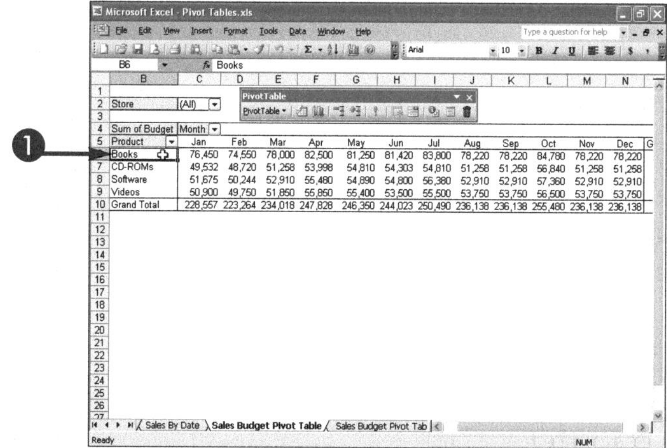

2. Click PivotTable➔Select➔Entire Table.

   Excel selects the PivotTable.

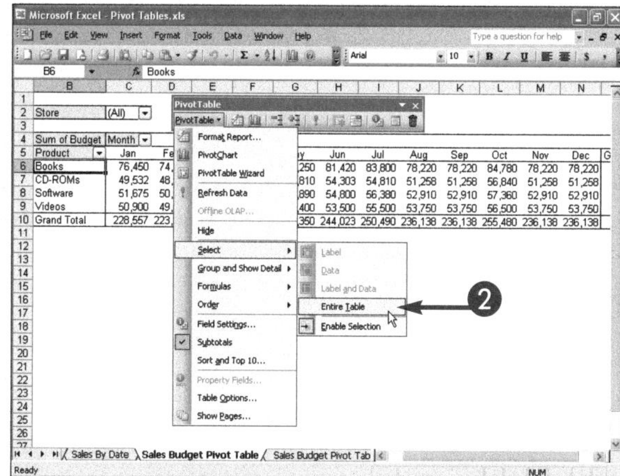

❸ Click Edit➔Clear➔All.

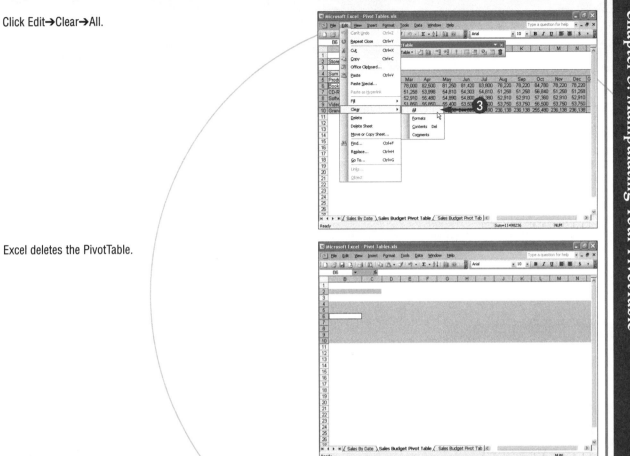

Excel deletes the PivotTable.

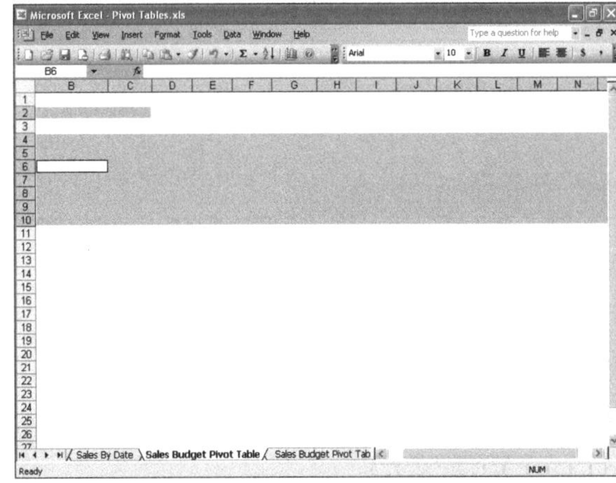

Apply It

If you create many temporary PivotTables, you should delete them to save system resources. However, this can become time-consuming if you do this quite often. To save time, use the following VBA macro (available in the sample PivotTables.xls workbook) to automatically delete the first PivotTable on the active worksheet:

```
Sub DeletePivotTable()
    Dim objPT As PivotTable, nResult As Integer
    '
    ' Work with the first PivotTable
    ' on the active worksheet
    Set objPT = ActiveSheet.PivotTables(1)
    '
    ' Confirm
    nResult = MsgBox("Are you sure you want " & _
              "to delete the PivotTable " & _
              "named " & objPT.Name & "?", vbYesNo)
    If nResult = vbYes Then
        '
        ' Select the PivotTable
        objPT.PivotSelect ""
        '
        ' Delete it
        Selection.Clear
    End If
End Sub
```

Move a Field to a Different Area

A PivotTable is a powerful data analysis tool because it can take hundreds or even thousands of records and summarize them into a compact, comprehensible report. However, unlike most of Excel's other data analysis features, a PivotTable is not a static collection of worksheet cells. Instead, you can move a PivotTable's fields from one area of the PivotTable to another. This enables you to view your data from different perspectives, which can greatly enhance the analysis of the data. Moving a field within a PivotTable is called *pivoting* the data.

The most common way to pivot the data is to move fields between the row and column areas. If your PivotTable contains just a single non-data field, moving the field between the row and column areas changes the orientation of the PivotTable between horizontal (column area) and vertical (row area). If your PivotTable contains fields in both the row and column areas, pivoting one of those fields to the other area creates multiple fields in that area. For example, pivoting a field from the column area to the row area creates two fields in the row area. This changes how the data breaks down, as described in Chapter 3; see the task "Add Multiple Fields to the Row or Column Area."

You can also pivot data by moving a row or column field to the page area, and a page field to the row or column area. This is a useful technique when you want to turn one of your existing row or column fields into a filter; see the next task, "Display a Different Page."

Move a Field to a Different Area

MOVE A FIELD BETWEEN THE ROW AND COLUMN AREAS

Note: This chapter uses the PivotTables.xls spreadsheet, available at www.wiley.com/go/pivottablesvb, or you can create your own sample database.

1. Click and drag a column field button and drop it within the PivotTable's row area.

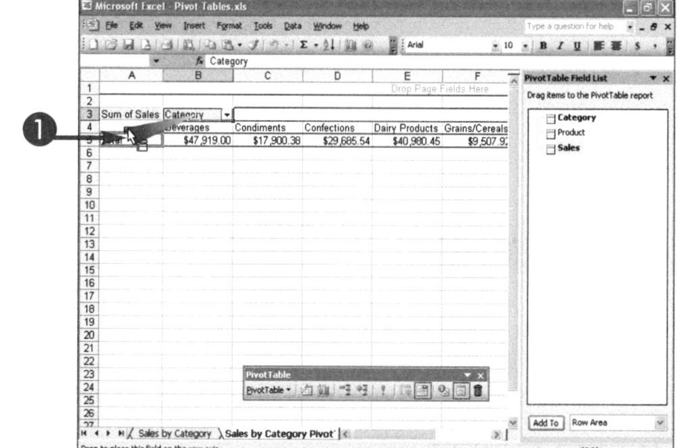

- Excel displays the field's values within the row area.

You can also drag a field button from the row area and drop it within the column area.

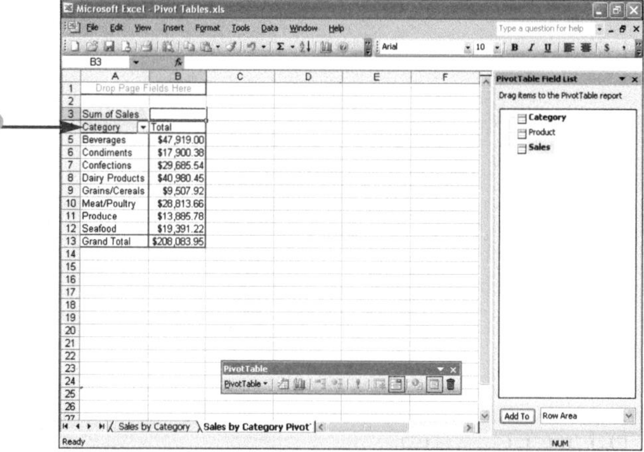

MOVE A ROW OR COLUMN FIELD TO THE PAGE AREA

1. Click and drag a row field button and drop it within the PivotTable's page area.

Note: You must display the PivotTable Field List to move a field into the page area. When the PivotTable Field List is hidden, Excel does not show the page area if it is empty.

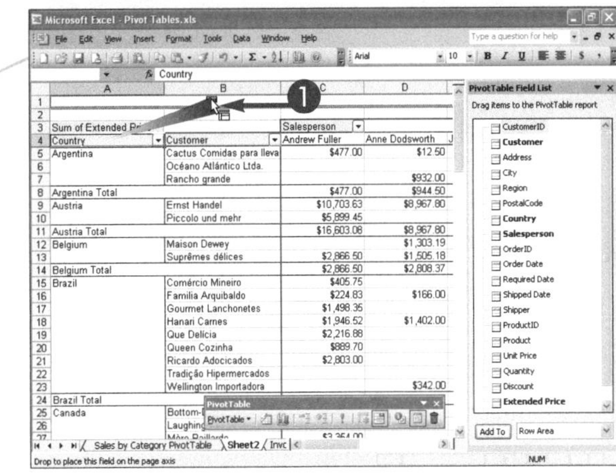

- Excel moves the field button to the page area.

You can also drag a field button from the column area and drop it within the page area.

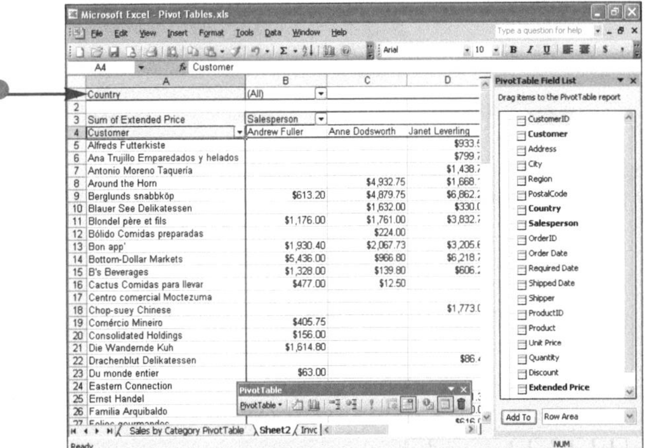

Apply It

You can also move any row, column, or page area field to the PivotTable's data area. This may seem strange because row, column, and page fields are almost always text values, and the default data area calculation is Sum. How can you sum text values? You cannot, of course. Instead, Excel's default PivotTable summary calculation for text values is Count. So, for example, if you drag the Category field and drop it inside the data area, Excel creates a second data field named Count of Category. To learn more about working with multiple data area fields, see the Chapter 3 task, "Add Multiple Fields to the Data Area."

As you move fields within the PivotTable, Excel changes the mouse pointer depending on the PivotTable area over which the pointer is hovering:

BUTTON	DESCRIPTION
	Mouse pointer for the row area.
	Mouse pointer for the column area.
	Mouse pointer for the data area.
	Mouse pointer for the page area.

Display a Different Page

By default, each PivotTable report displays a summary for all the records in your source data. This is usually what you will want to see. However, there may be situations in which you need to focus more closely on some aspect of the data. You can focus in on a specific item from one of the source data fields by taking advantage of the PivotTable's page field.

For example, suppose you are dealing with a PivotTable that summarizes data from thousands of customer invoices over some period of time. A basic PivotTable might tell you the total amount sold for each product that you carry. That is interesting, but what about if you want to see the total amount sold for each product in a specific country. If the Product field is in the PivotTable's row area, then you could add the Country field to the column area. However, there may be dozens of countries, so that is not an efficient solution. Instead, you could add the Country field to the page area. You can then tell Excel to display the total sold for each product for the specific country in which you are interested.

As another example, suppose you ran a marketing campaign in the previous quarter and you set up an incentive plan for your salespeople whereby they could earn bonuses for selling at least a specified number of units. Suppose, as well, that you have a PivotTable showing the sum of the units sold for each product. To see the numbers for a particular employee, you could add the Salesperson field to the page area, and then select the employee you want to work with.

Display a Different Page

1. Click ▾ in the page field.

   Excel displays a list of the page field values.

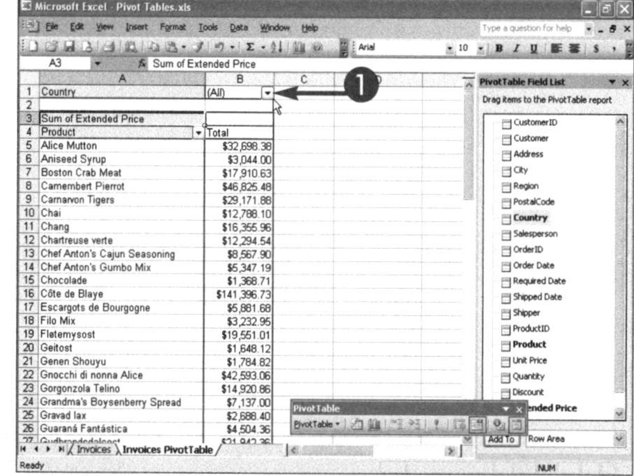

2. Click the page you want to view.
3. Click OK.

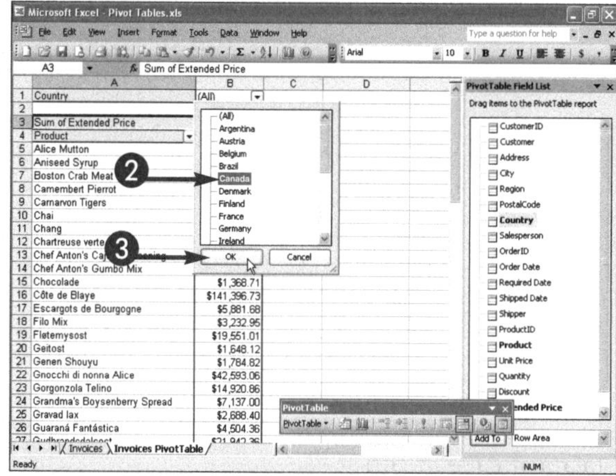

Excel filters the PivotTable to show only the data for the page you selected.

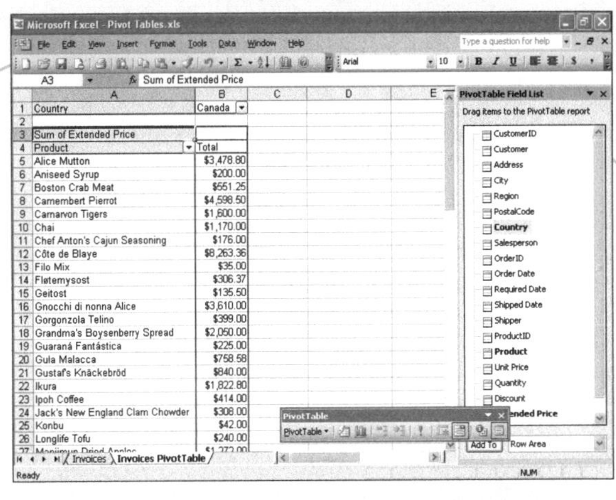

DISPLAY ALL PAGES

1. Click ▾ in the page field.

   Excel displays a list of the page field values.

2. Click All.

3. Click OK.

   Excel adjusts the PivotTable to show the data for all the pages.

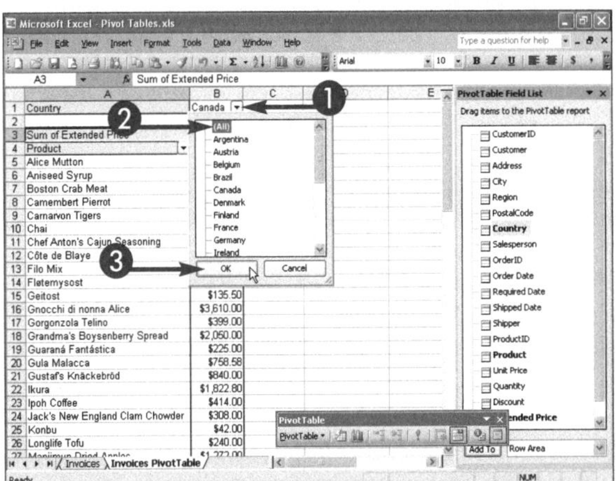

Apply It

You can add multiple fields to the page area, as described in the Chapter 3 task "Add Multiple Fields to the Page Area." This enables you to apply multiple filters to the data. For example, suppose you have a PivotTable that summarizes invoice data by showing the total amount sold for each product that you carry, and that you have a page field with Country data that enables you to isolate the sales by product for a specific country. You might then want to extend your analysis to look at the country-specific sales by product for individual salespersons.

To do this, you would add the Salesperson field as a second field in the page area. You could then use the steps shown in this task to choose a specific country and a specific salesperson. Remember that it does not matter which order the fields appear in the page area, because the filtering comes out the same in the end.

When you filter your PivotTables using multiple page fields, be aware that not all combinations of items from the fields will produce PivotTable results. For example, a particular salesperson may not have sold any products to customers in a specific country, so combining those filters produces a PivotTable without any data.

Change the Order of Fields Within an Area

You learned in the Chapter 3 task "Add Multiple Fields to the Row or Column Area," that you can add two or more fields to any area in the PivotTable. This enables you to break down the data in different ways (multiple row or column area fields), apply extra filters (multiple page area fields), or display extra summaries (multiple data area fields). After you have multiple fields in an area, Excel allows you to change the order of those fields to reconfigure your data the way you prefer. This is another example of pivoting the data.

How you pivot within a field depends on the field. For row, column, and page fields, you pivot by dragging and dropping field buttons within the same area. For example, if the row area of the PivotTable has the Product field on the outside (left) and the Promotion field on the inside (right), the PivotTable shows the sales of each product broken down by the promotion. If, instead, you prefer to see the sales of each promotion broken down by product, then you need to switch the order of the Product and Promotion fields.

If you have multiple data fields, on the other hand, Excel does not display a button for each field. In this case, you change the order of the data area fields by dragging and dropping any data field label. Note, however, that this does not change the data summaries themselves, just the order in which they appear in the PivotTable.

Change the Order of Fields Within an Area

CHANGE THE FIELD ORDER IN THE ROW, COLUMN, OR PAGE AREA

1. Click and drag the button of the field you want to move.
2. Within the row or column area, drop the field to the left or right of an existing field; within the page area, drop the file above or below an existing field.
   - Excel displays a gray bar to show you where it will position the dropped field.

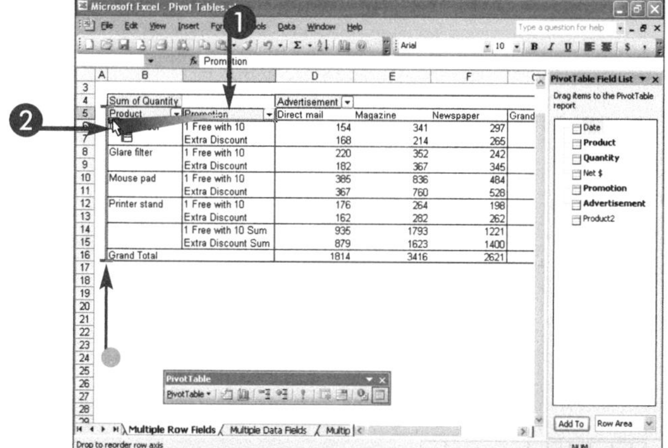

Excel reconfigures the PivotTable.

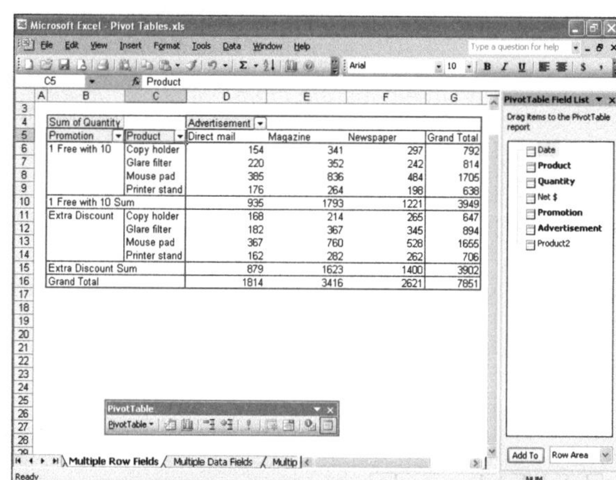

CHANGE THE FIELD ORDER IN THE DATA AREA

1. Click any label in the data field you want to move.
2. Move the mouse pointer to the top or bottom edge of the cell.
3. Click and drag the selected cell and drop it above or below a label for an existing data field.
   - Excel displays a gray bar to show you where it will position the dropped field.

Excel reconfigures the PivotTable.

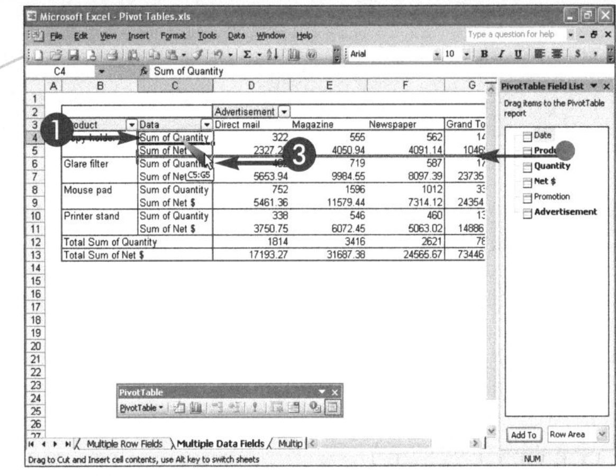

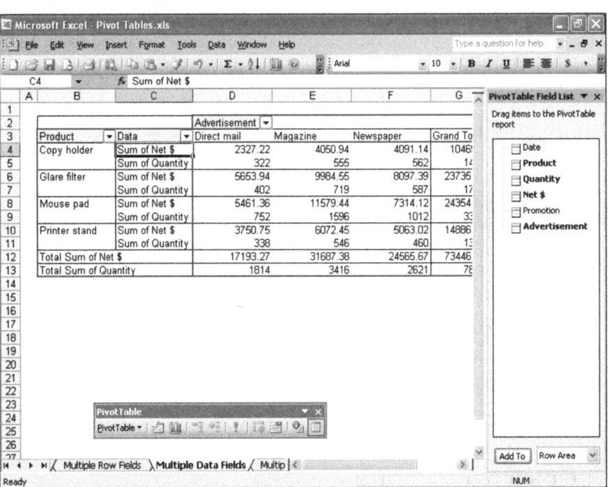

Apply It

The most common situation for changing field order is to move a row field to the outer position. Here is a VBA macro that automates this process:

```
Sub SwitchRowFields()
    Dim objPT As PivotTable
    Dim objPTField As PivotField
    ' Work with the first PivotTable on the active worksheet
    Set objPT = ActiveSheet.PivotTables(1)
    With objPT
        ' If there is just one row field, exit
        If .RowFields.Count = 1 Then Exit Sub
        ' Run through all the row fields
        For Each objPTField In .RowFields
            ' Is the current field the innermost field?
            If objPTField.Position = .RowFields.Count Then
                ' If so, make it the outer field
                objPTField.Position = 1
                ' We are done, so exit
                Exit Sub
            End If
        Next 'objPTField
    End With
End Sub
```

Sort PivotTable Data with AutoSort

When you create a PivotTable, Excel sorts the data in ascending order based on the items in the row and column fields. For example, if the row area contains the Product field, the vertical sort order of the PivotTable is ascending according to the items in the Product field. You can change this default sort order to one that suits your needs. Excel gives you two choices: you can switch between ascending and descending, or you can sort based on a data field instead of a row or column field.

Changing the sort order often comes in handy when you are working with dates or times. The default ascending sort shows the oldest items at the top of the field; if, instead, you are more interested in the most recent items, switch to a descending sort to show those items at the top of the field.

Sorting the PivotTable based on the values in a data field is useful when you want to rank the results. For example, if your PivotTable shows the sum of sales for each product, an ascending or descending sort of the product name enables you to easily find a particular product. However, if you are more interested in finding which products sold the most (or the least), then you need to sort the PivotTable on the data field.

Excel gives you two methods for sorting PivotTable items: you can have Excel sort the items automatically using the AutoSort feature, as you learn in this task; alternatively, you can create a custom sort order by manually adjusting the items; see the next task, "Move Row and Column Items."

Sort PivotTable Data with AutoSort

1. Click the button of the field you want to use for sorting.

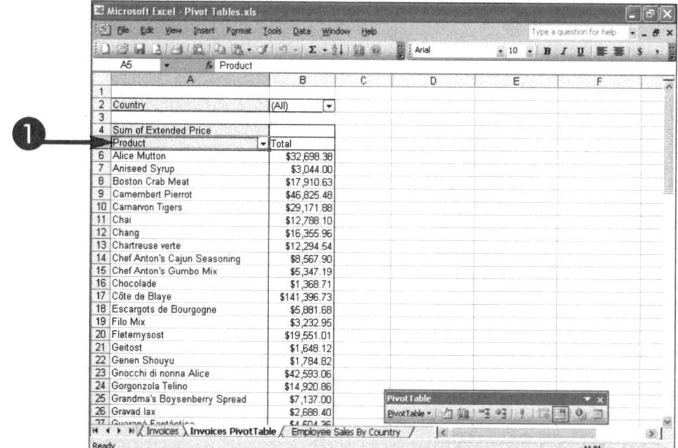

2. Click PivotTable→Sort and Top 10.

   Excel displays the PivotTable Sort and Top 10 dialog box.

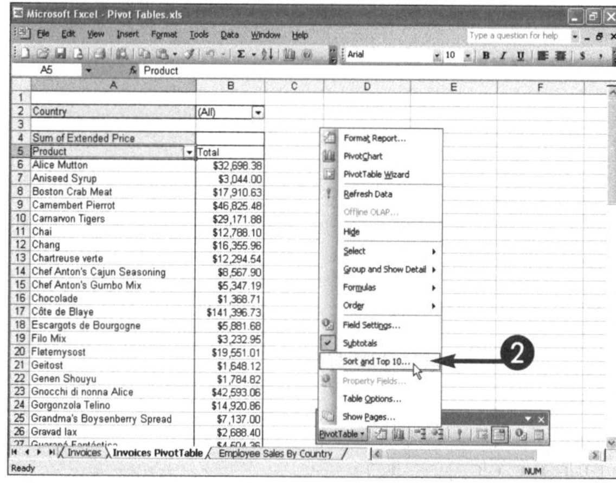

3. Select the sort order you want to use, such as Descending.

4. Click ▾ and then click the field you want to use for the sort.

5. Click OK.

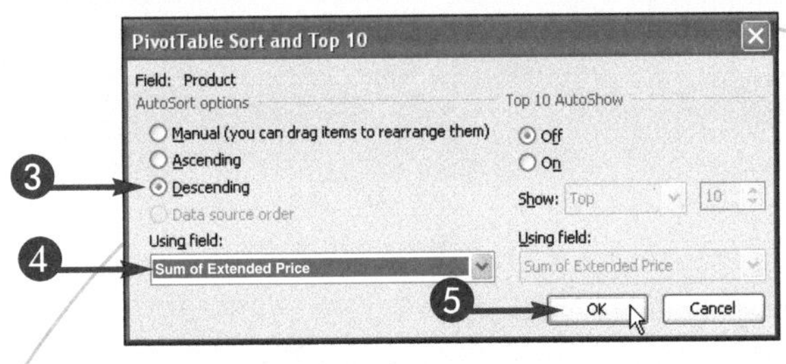

Excel sorts the PivotTable.

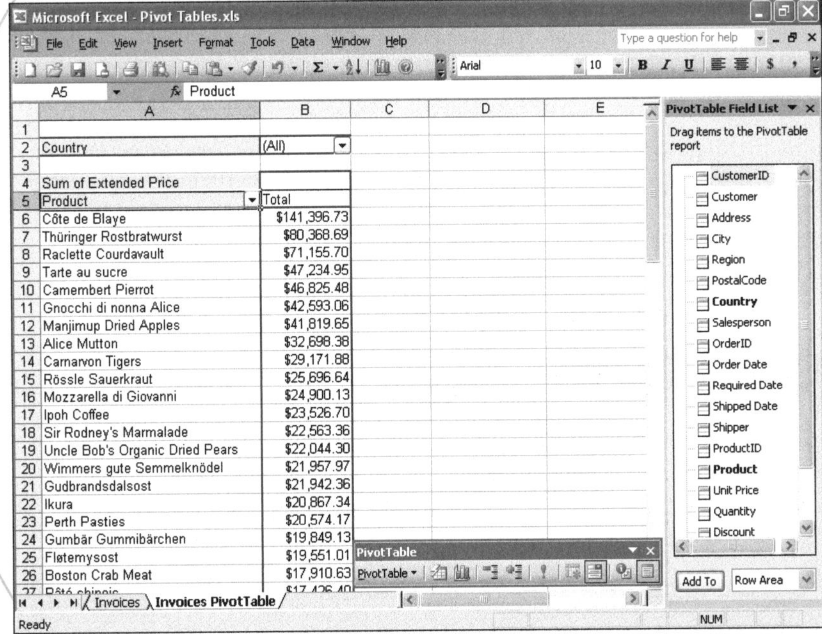

Extra

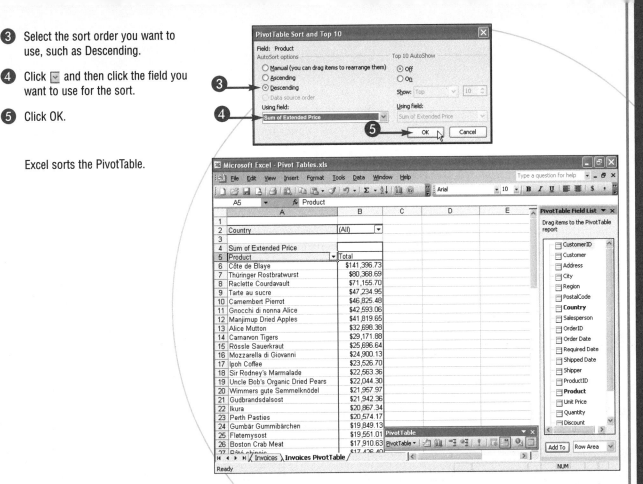

In Excel, an ascending sort means that items are arranged in the following order: numbers, text, logical values, error values (such as #REF! and #N/A), and blank cells. A descending sort reverses this order, except for blank cells: error values (such as #REF! and #N/A), logical values, text, numbers, and blank cells.

You can also sort a PivotTable using Excel's Sort feature. Click any cell in the field that you want to use for sorting: for a row or column field, click either the field button or any item within the field; for the data field, click the label or any data value within the field. Click Data→Sort to display the Sort dialog box. Select Ascending or Descending (○ changes to ◉) and then click OK.

To return the PivotTable to the default sort order, follow Steps 1 and 2 to display the PivotTable Sort and Top 10 dialog box. Select Manual (○ changes to ◉) and then click OK. Note that if you sort the PivotTable using Excel's Sort feature, as described above, Excel automatically changes the PivotTable's AutoSort setting to Manual.

Move Row and Column Items

As you saw in the previous task, Excel's AutoSort feature enables you to apply an ascending or descending sort on a row or column field, or on a data item. However, there may be situations where these basic sort options do not fit your requirements. In these cases, you can solve the problem by coming up with a custom sort order, and Excel offers a couple of methods for doing just that.

For example, suppose you have a PivotTable that shows the sales generated by each employee, broken down by country. Showing the Country field items alphabetically makes sense in most situations, but suppose you are preparing the report for managers who oversee the sales on each continent (North America, South America, Europe, and so on). In this case, it would be more convenient for those managers if you organized the PivotTable countries by continent. However, because there is no "continent" field to sort on, you need to sort the countries by hand.

To sort a PivotTable by hand, you need to move the row or column items individually. As you learn in this task, you can move individual row or column items either by using commands on the PivotTable toolbar, or by using your mouse to click and drag the items.

Move Row and Column Items

USE COMMANDS TO MOVE ROW AND COLUMN ITEMS

1. Click the row or column item you want to move.
2. Click PivotTable→Order.

   Excel displays a submenu of commands for moving the item.
3. Click the command that represents the move you want to make, such as Move Up.

   Excel moves the item.
4. Repeat Steps 2 and 3 until the item is in the position you want.

   - Excel displays the item in the position you selected.

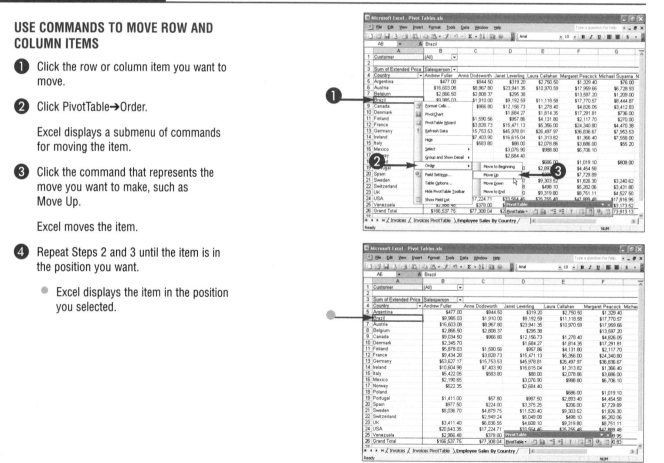

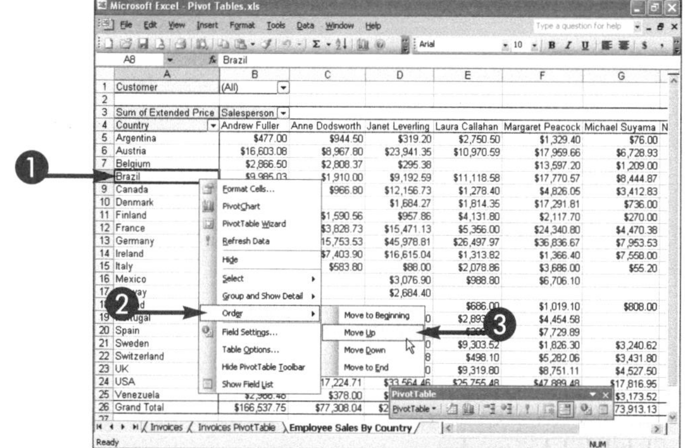

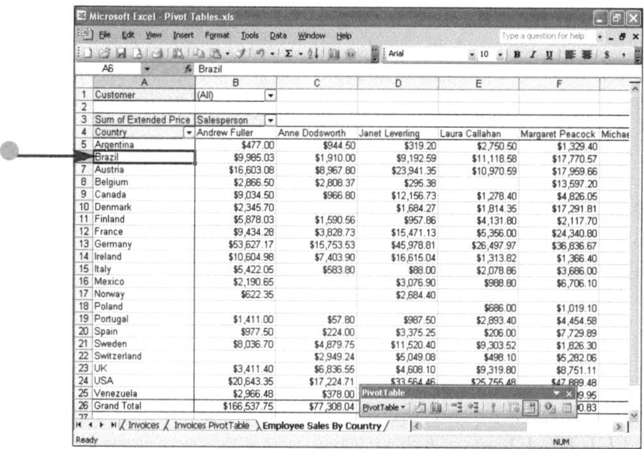

CLICK AND DRAG TO MOVE ROW AND COLUMN ITEMS

1. Click the field item you want to move.
2. Move the mouse pointer to the top or bottom edge of the cell.
3. Click and drag the item and drop it in the position you want.
   - Excel displays a gray bar to show you where it will position the dropped item.

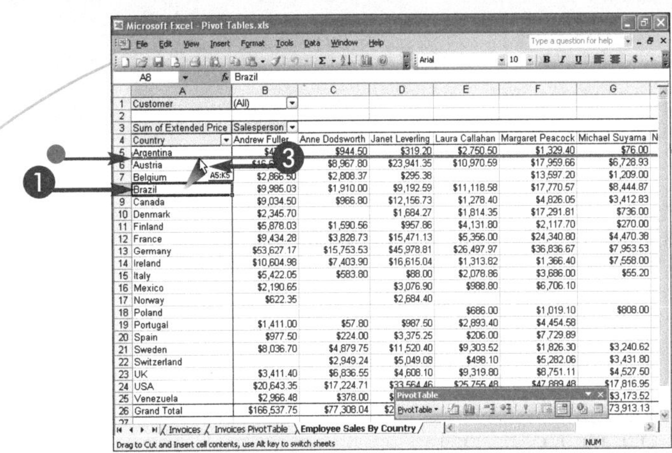

- Excel reconfigures the PivotTable.

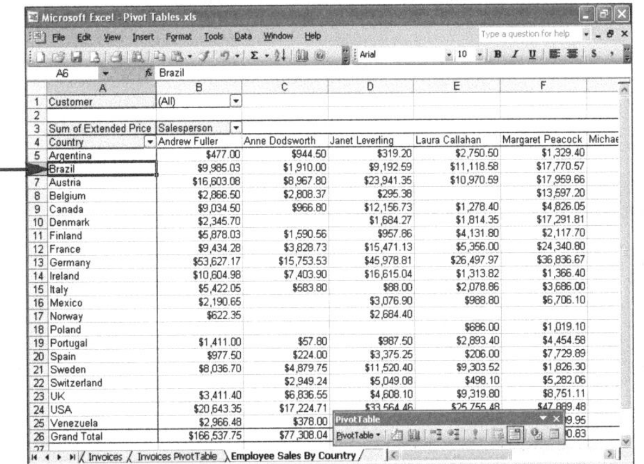

Apply It

Excel offers a third method for moving row and column items to apply a custom sort order, and this method uses a rather surprising trick. To move a particular row or column item, first click the row or column item that is currently in the position where you want the moved item to end up. For example, if you want to move the item to the top of the items in the row area, click the first item in the row area. Now type the text of the item you want Excel to move. For example, if the item you want to move is "Brazil," type **Brazil**. When you press Enter to confirm the typing, Excel switches the two items. That is, Excel moves the item you typed to the current cell, and Excel moves the item that was previously in the cell to the cell where the moved item used to appear.

What makes this technique even more convenient is that Excel monitors your typing and its AutoComplete feature should fill in the text of the item you want to move after just a few keystrokes. For example, after you type **Br**, Excel should fill in Brazil automatically.

Show Only the Top 10 Items

By default, your PivotTable shows all the items in whatever row and column fields you added to the report layout. This is usually what you want because the point of a PivotTable is to summarize all the data in the original source. However, you may not always want to see every item. In particular, you may only be interested in the top 10 items. You can generate such a report by using Excel's Top 10 AutoShow feature, which shows just the top 10 items, based on the values in the data field.

For example, suppose you have a PivotTable report based on a database of invoices that shows the total sales for each product. The basic report shows all the products, but if you are only interested in the top performers for the year, you can activate the Top 10 AutoShow feature to see the 10 products that sold the most.

Despite its name, the Top 10 AutoShow feature can display more than just the top 10 data values. You can specify any number between 1 and 255, and you can also ask Excel to show the bottommost values.

Show Only the Top 10 Items

1. Click the button of the field you want to use for sorting.

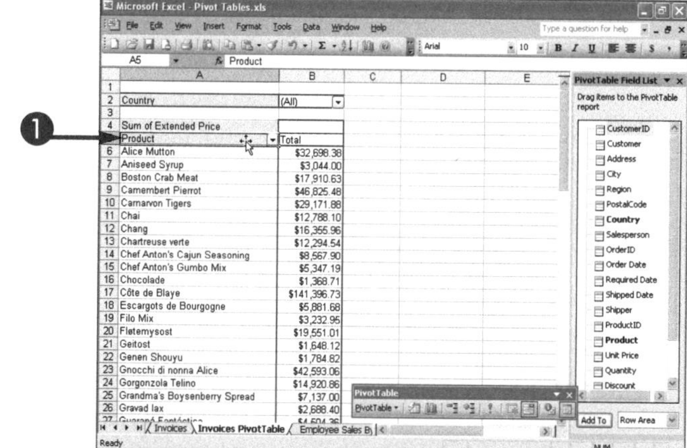

2. Click PivotTable→Sort and Top 10.

   Excel displays the PivotTable Sort and Top 10 dialog box.

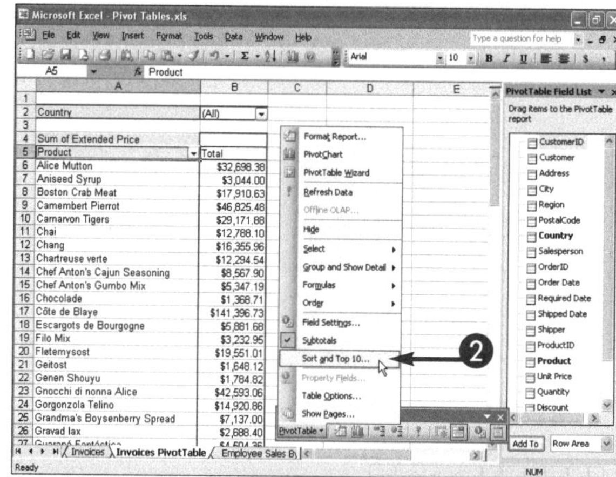

3. Select On.

4. Click ▾ and click either Top or Bottom.

5. Click ⬍ and select the number of items you want to display.

6. If you have multiple data fields, click ▾ and click the field you want to use to calculate the top 10.

7. Click OK.

   Excel displays the top 10 values for the field.

Note: To display all the items again, follow Steps 1 and 2, select Off, and then click OK.

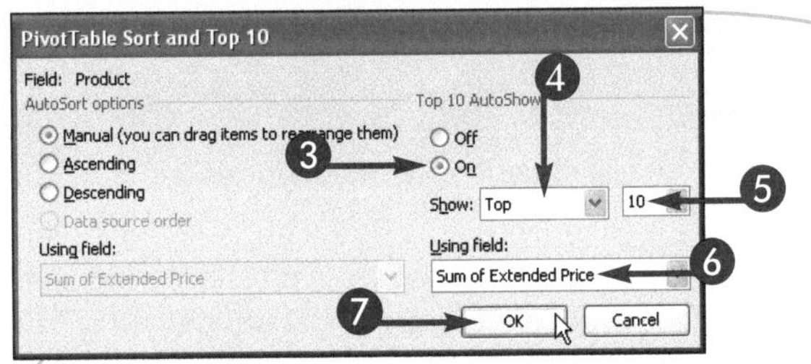

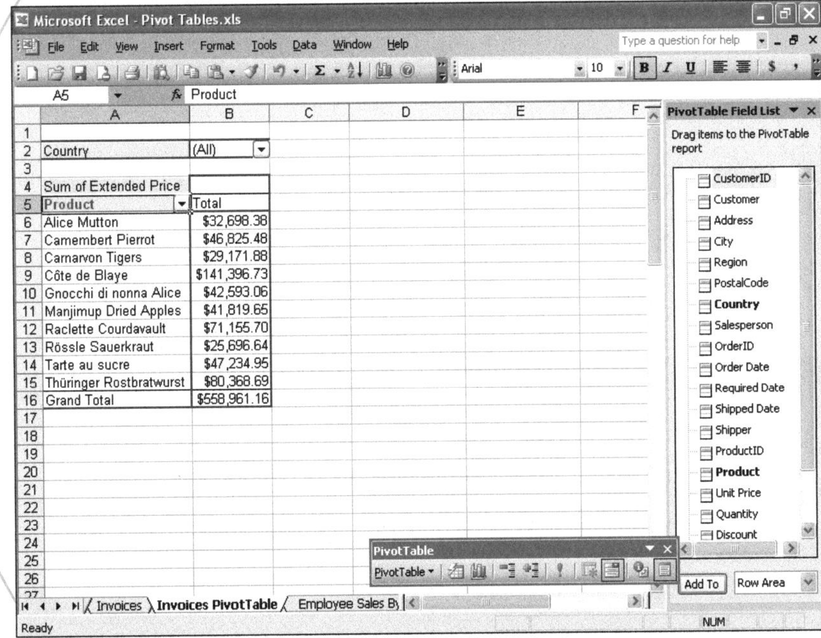

Apply It

Here is a VBA script that activates the Top 10 AutoShow feature. If you want to create a script that deactivates this features, copy the script — making sure to change the procedure name, too — and in the `AutoShow` statement, replace `xlAutomatic` with `xlManual`.

Example:

```
Sub ActivateTop10AutoShow()
    Dim objPT As PivotTable
    Dim objPTRowField As PivotField
    Dim strDataFieldName As String
    '
    ' Work with the first PivotTable on the active worksheet
    Set objPT = ActiveSheet.PivotTables(1)
    '
    ' Work with the first row field
    Set objPTRowField = objPT.RowFields(1)
    '
    ' Get the data field name
    strDataFieldName = objPT.DataFields(1).Name
    '
    ' Set the Top 10 AutoShow
    objPTRowField.AutoShow xlAutomatic, xlTop, 10, strDataFieldName
End Sub
```

Hide Items in a Row or Column Field

When you view a PivotTable report, it may contain items in a row or column field that you do not need to see. For example, in a report showing employee sales or other data, you may prefer to see only those employees that work for or with you. Similarly, if you are a product manager, you might want to customize the report to show only those items in the Product field that you are responsible for.

If you have a PivotTable that contains row or column items you do not need or want to see, you can remove those items from the report. Excel enables you to change the PivotTable view to exclude one or more items in any row or column field. After you have hidden the items, Excel reconfigures the report to display without them, and also updates the totals to reflect the excluded items. Note, too, that the items remain hidden even if you update the PivotTable, move the field to a different area, and even if you delete the field and add it back into the PivotTable.

After you have hidden one or more items, you should also know how to show them again. See the next task, "Show Hidden Items in a Row or Column Field."

Hide Items in a Row or Column Field

1. Click ▾ in the button of the field you want to work with.

   Excel displays a list of the items in the field.

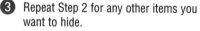

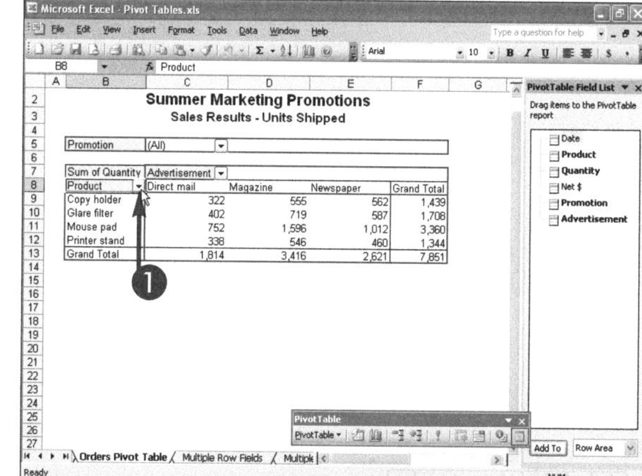

2. Deselect an item you want to hide.
3. Repeat Step 2 for any other items you want to hide.

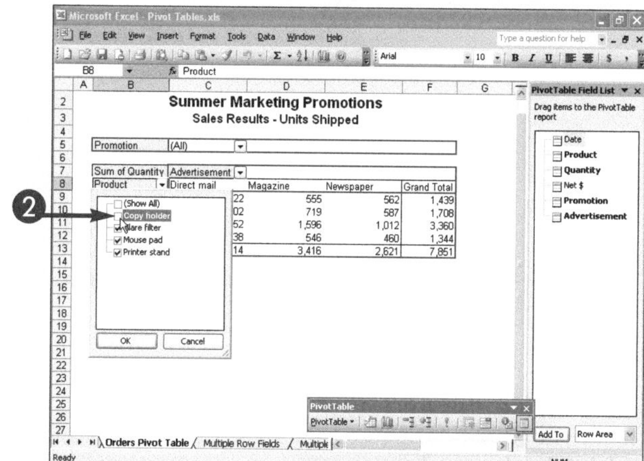

4 Click OK.

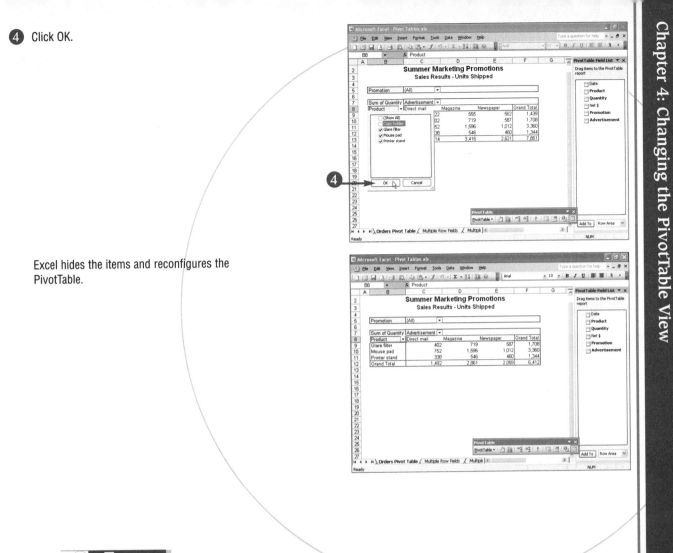

Excel hides the items and reconfigures the PivotTable.

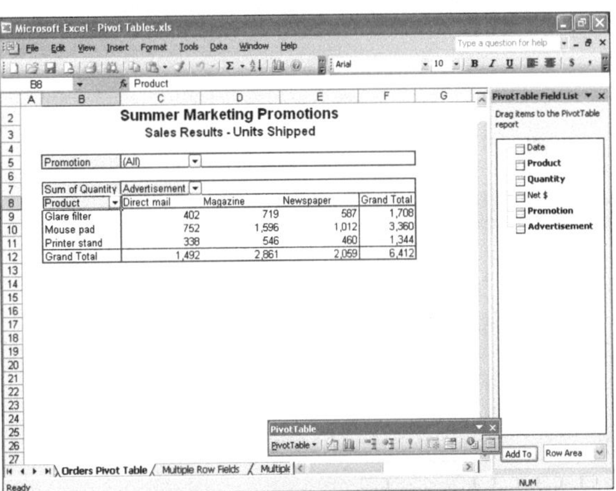

Extra

If you only want to hide a single item in a row or column field, Excel offers a more direct method: right-click the item and then click Hide. Note, however, that there is no similarly straightforward method for showing the item again. You must use the technique outlined in the next task, "Show Hidden Items in a Row or Column Field."

On the other hand, if your field has a large number of items, you may only want to show one or two of those items. Fortunately, there is a way to avoid deactivating all those check boxes. Deselect Show All (☑ changes to ☐). Excel deactivates every check box in the list. When you display the list of items, if the Show All check box is already deactivated because you have hidden one or more items, clicking Show All will activate it and activate all the check boxes in the list. In this case, click Show All again to deactivate it and deactivate all the check boxes. You can then click the check boxes for the items you want to show.

Show Hidden Items in a Row or Column Field

In the previous task, you learned how to adjust the PivotTable view by hiding one or more items in any row or column field. The opposite case is when you have one or more hidden items and you wish to show some or all of them again. For example, if you have hidden product items that are outside your division, you might want to show products from other divisions that are comparable to one or more of yours. This enables you to use the PivotTable report to compare product results between divisions.

As you see in this task, the procedure for showing hidden items is the opposite of the procedure you used to hide them in the first place.

Show Hidden Items in a Row or Column Field

1. Click ▾ in the button of the field you want to work with.

   Excel displays a list of the items in the field.

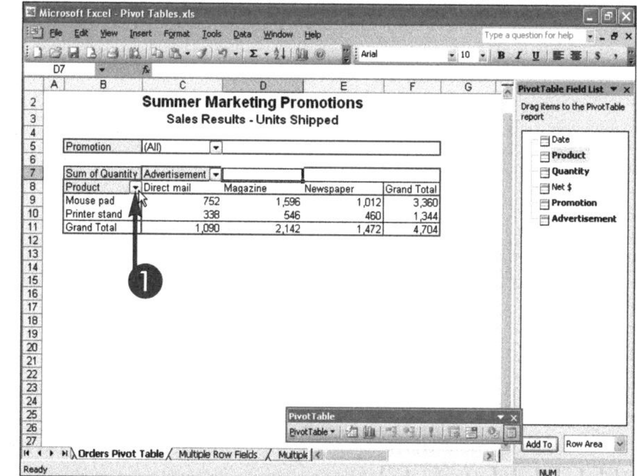

2. Select an item you want to show.
3. Repeat Step 2 for any other items you want to show.

   - If you want to show all the items in the field, you can select Show All.

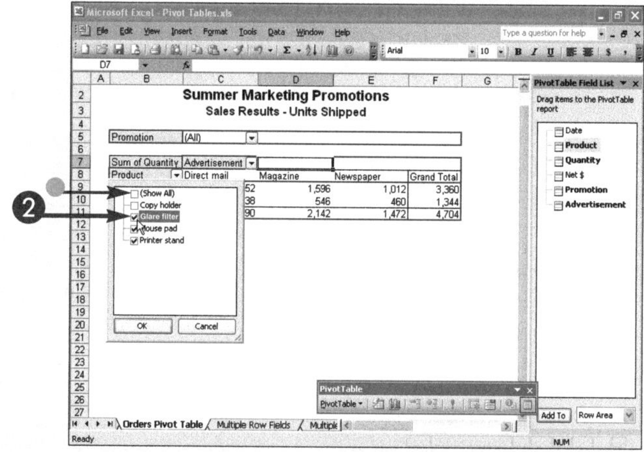

4 Click OK.

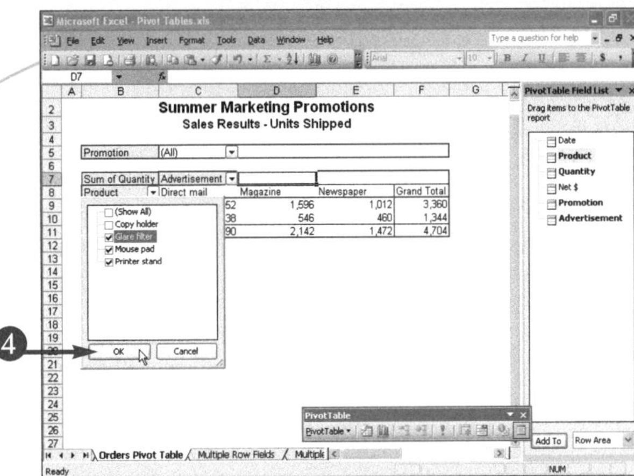

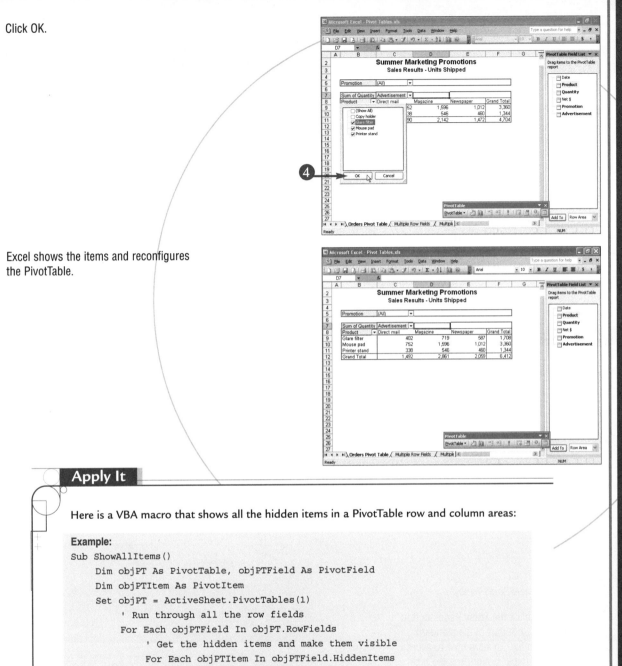

Excel shows the items and reconfigures the PivotTable.

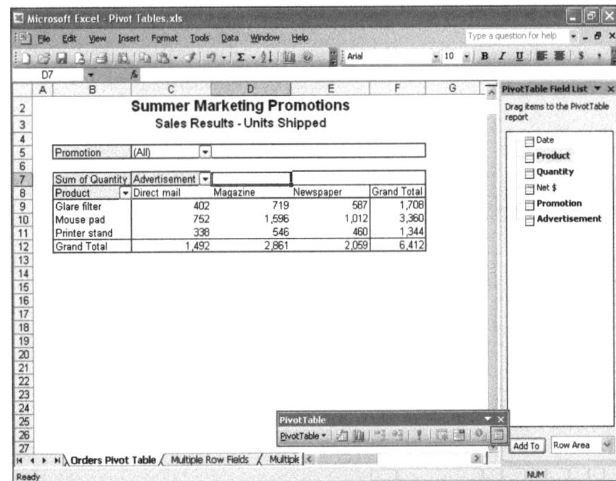

Apply It

Here is a VBA macro that shows all the hidden items in a PivotTable row and column areas:

Example:

```
Sub ShowAllItems()
    Dim objPT As PivotTable, objPTField As PivotField
    Dim objPTItem As PivotItem
    Set objPT = ActiveSheet.PivotTables(1)
        ' Run through all the row fields
        For Each objPTField In objPT.RowFields
            ' Get the hidden items and make them visible
            For Each objPTItem In objPTField.HiddenItems
                objPTItem.Visible = True
            Next 'objPTItem
        Next 'objPTField
        ' Run through all the column fields
        For Each objPTField In objPT.ColumnFields
            ' Get the hidden items and make them visible
            For Each objPTItem In objPTField.HiddenItems
                objPTItem.Visible = True
            Next 'objPTItem
        Next 'objPTField
End Sub
```

Show Pages as Worksheets

You use a page area field to act as a filter for your PivotTable data. When you select a page field item, Excel filters the PivotTable to show just the results for records that include the page item. See the task "Display a Different Page," earlier in this chapter, for details on changing PivotTable pages. This is most often useful when you want to see just a subset of data, but it can also come in handy when you want to compare the PivotTable results for two or more subsets. You configure the PivotTable for one page field item, view the results, and then repeat with a different page field item. This method works, but it is usually more efficient to compare two different PivotTables rather than switching the page items back and forth.

You can solve this problem by creating another PivotTable, but creating a replica of your PivotTable might be quite a bit of work, particularly if you are working with several pages — each of which would require its own PivotTable. Instead, Excel offers a Show Pages feature that, with just a few mouse clicks, enables you to create separate PivotTables that show the results for each item in a page field. Excel creates copies of your PivotTable in separate worksheets, one for each item in the page field. This enables you to compare the results by switching from one worksheet to another.

Show Pages as Worksheets

1. In the page field you want to work with, click ▾.
2. Click All.
3. Click OK.

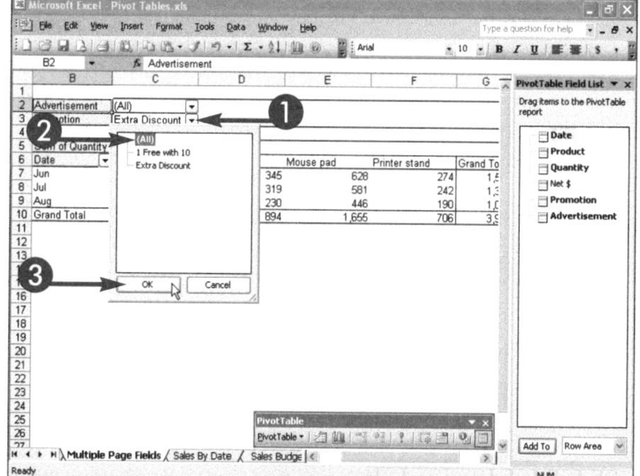

4. Click PivotTable→Show Pages.

   You can also click the Show Pages button (▦), which is not part of the standard PivotTable toolbar. To learn how to access this custom toolbar button, see the task "Customize the PivotTable Toolbar" in Chapter 3.

   Excel displays the Show Pages dialog box.

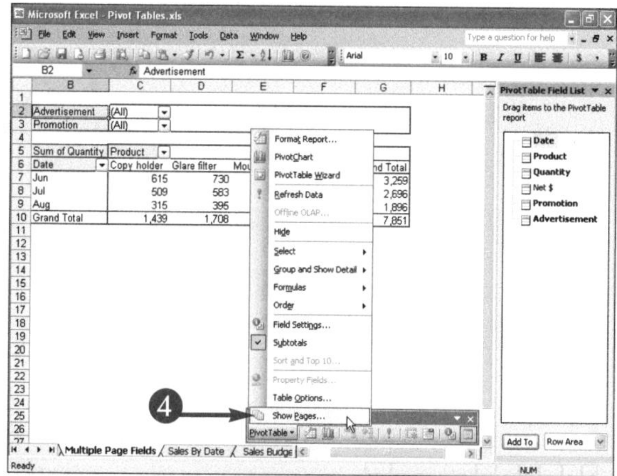

5 Click the page field you want to use.

6 Click OK.

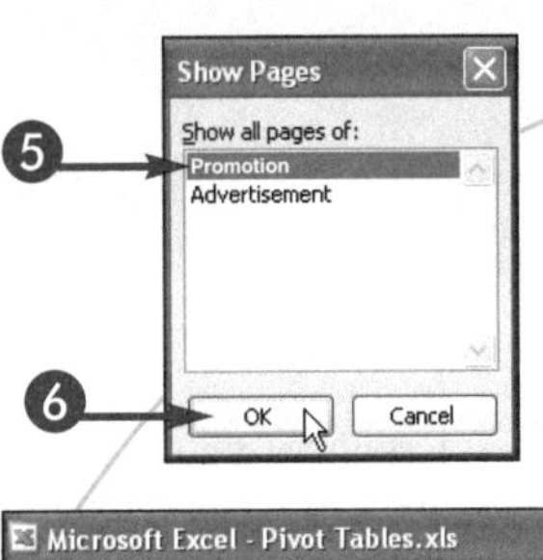

- Excel creates a new worksheet for each item in the page field.

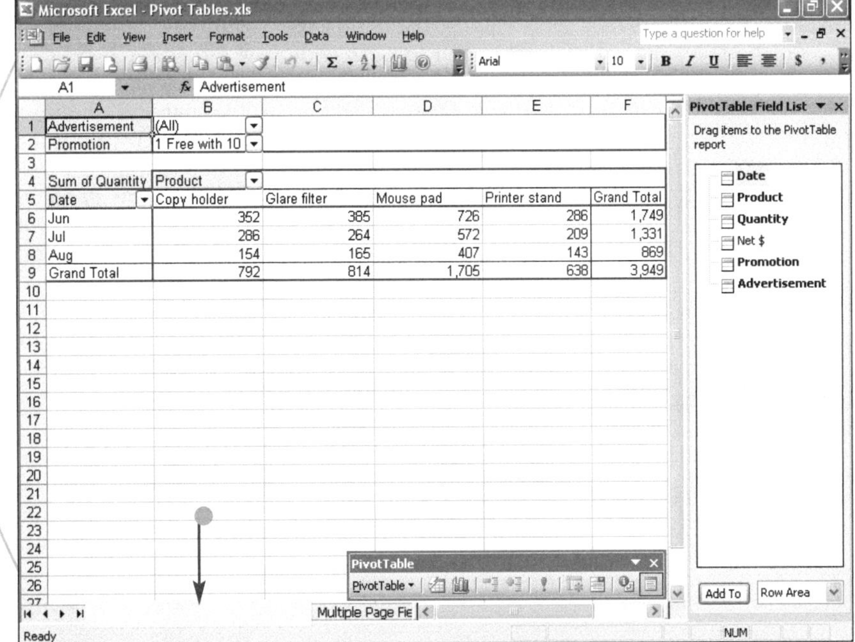

	A	B	C	D	E	F
1	Advertisement	(All)				
2	Promotion	1 Free with 10				
3						
4	Sum of Quantity	Product				
5	Date	Copy holder	Glare filter	Mouse pad	Printer stand	Grand Total
6	Jun	352	385	726	286	1,749
7	Jul	286	264	572	209	1,331
8	Aug	154	165	407	143	869
9	Grand Total	792	814	1,705	638	3,949

Apply It

If you find yourself using the Show Pages feature frequently, you may also find that you often have to delete the resulting worksheets. To help you automate this chore, here is a VBA macro that deletes the worksheets created by Show Pages:

Example:

```
Sub DeletePages()
    Dim objPT As PivotTable
    Dim objPageField As PivotField
    Dim objItem As PivotItem
    Dim strPageName As String
    ' Work with the first PivotTable on the active worksheet
    Set objPT = ActiveSheet.PivotTables(1)
    ' Work with the first page field
    Set objPageField = objPT.PageFields(1)
    ' Run through the page field items
    For Each objItem In objPageField.PivotItems
        ' Get the item value
        strPageName = objItem.Value
        ' Delete the corresponding worksheet
        ActiveWorkbook.Worksheets(strPageName).Delete
    Next 'objItem
End Sub
```

Group Numeric Values

Most PivotTable reports have just a few items in the row and column fields, which makes the report easy to read and analyze. However, it is not unusual to have row or column fields that consist of dozens of items, which makes the report much harder to work with. One solution is to cut the report down to size by hiding items; see the task "Hide Items in a Row or Column Field," earlier in this chapter. Unfortunately, this solution is not appropriate if you need to work with all the PivotTable data.

To make a report with a large number of row or column items easier to work with, you can group the items together. For example, you could group months into quarters, thus reducing the number of items from 12 to 4. Similarly, a report that lists dozens of countries could group those countries by continent, thus reducing the number of items to 4 or 5, depending on where the countries are located. Finally, if you use a numeric field in the row or column area, you may have hundreds of items, one for each numeric value. You can improve the report by creating just a few numeric ranges.

Excel enables you to group three types of data: numeric (discussed in this section), date and time (see "Group Date and Time Values"), and text (see "Group Text Values"). Grouping numeric values is useful when you use a numeric field in a row or column field. Excel enables you to specify numeric ranges into which the field items are grouped. For example, suppose you have a PivotTable of invoice data that shows the extended price (the row field) and the salesperson (the column field). It would be useful to group the extended prices into ranges and then count the number of invoices each salesperson processed in each range.

Group Numeric Values

1. Click the button of the numeric field you want to group.

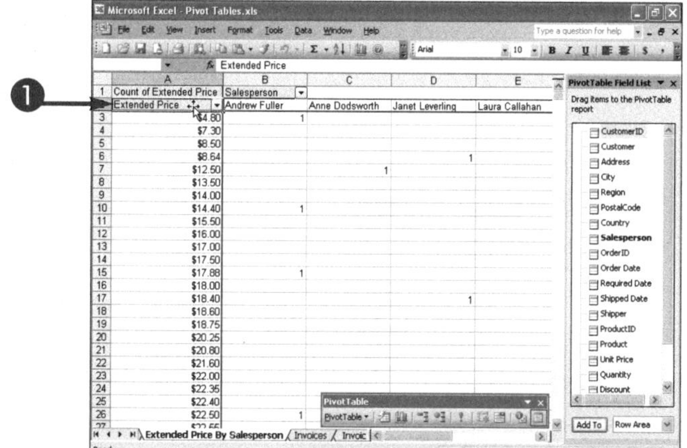

2. Click PivotTable➔Group and Show Detail➔Group.

   You can also click the Group button ( ), which is not part of the standard PivotTable toolbar. To learn how to access this custom toolbar button, see the task "Customize the PivotTable Toolbar" in Chapter 3.

   The Grouping dialog box appears.

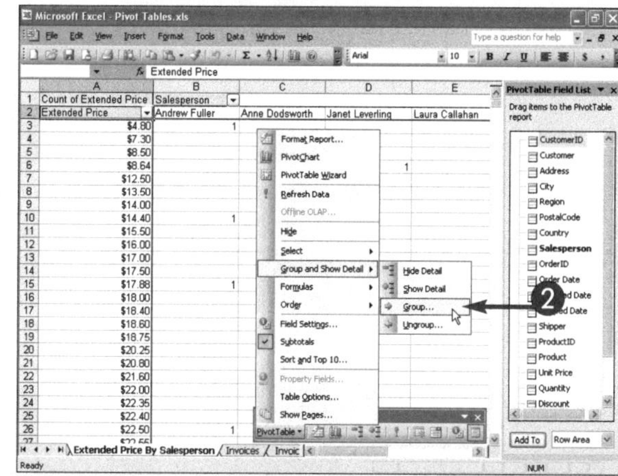

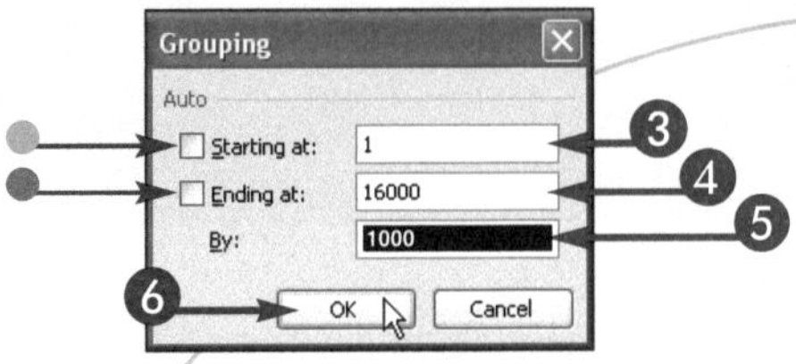

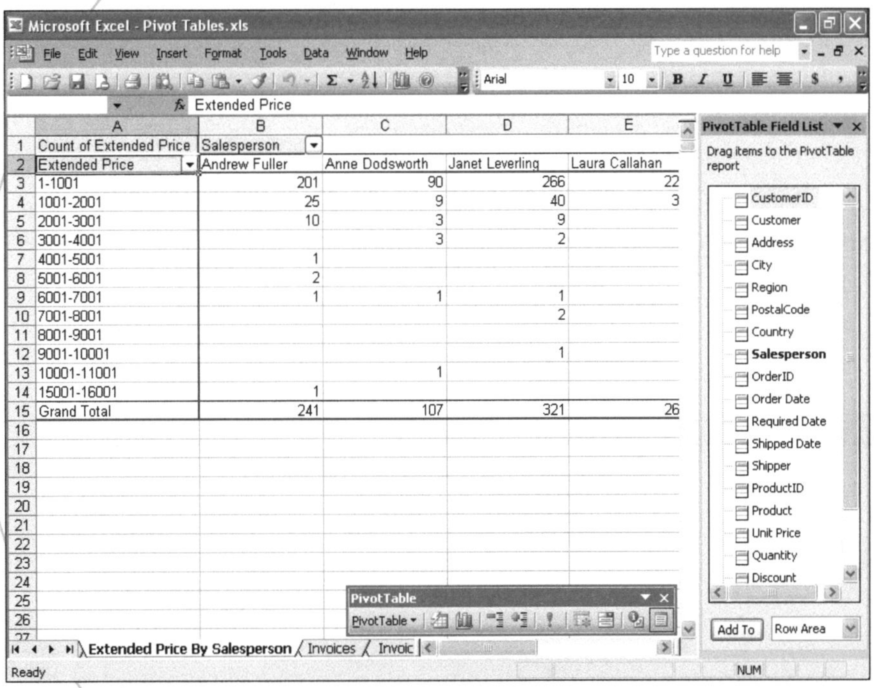

3. Type the starting numeric value.
   - Select this check box to have Excel extract the minimum value of the numeric items and place that value in the text box.
4. Type the ending numeric value.
   - Select this check box to have Excel extract the maximum value of the numeric items and place that value in the text box.
5. Type the size you want to use for each grouping.
6. Click OK.

Excel groups the numeric values.

Extra

The ranges that Excel creates after you apply the grouping to a numeric field are not themselves numeric values; they are, instead, text values. Unfortunately, this means it is not possible to use Excel's AutoSort feature to switch the ranges from ascending order to descending order; see the task "Sort PivotTable Data with AutoSort," earlier in this chapter. If you try, Excel sorts the ranges as text, which usually results in improper sort orders. For example, in a descending sort, the range 2001–3001 would come before the range 10001–11001 because 2 (the first character of the text "2001–3001") has a higher value than 1 (the first character of the text "10001–11001"). To sort the ranges, you must move the items by hand. See the task "Move Row and Column Items," earlier in this chapter.

Similarly, the text nature of the range items means that you also cannot use Excel's Top 10 AutoShow feature, which only works properly with numeric values. See the task "Show Only the Top 10 Items," earlier in this chapter. The only way to simulate this feature would be to hide those ranges you do not want to view in your report; see the task "Hide Items in a Row or Column Field," earlier in this chapter.

Group Date and Time Values

If your PivotTable includes a field with date or time data, you can use Excel's grouping feature to consolidate that data into more manageable or useful groups.

For example, a PivotTable based on a list of invoice data might show the total dollar amount, which is the Sum of Extended Price in the date area, of the orders placed on each day, which is the Date field in the row area. Tracking daily sales is useful, but a manager might need a report that shows the bigger picture. In that case, you can use the Grouping feature to consolidate the dates into weeks, months, or even quarters. Excel even allows you to choose multiple date groupings. For example, if you have several years' worth of invoice data, you could group the data into years, the years into quarters, and the quarters into months.

Excel also enables you to group time data. For example, suppose you have data that shows the time of day that an assembly line completes each operation. If you want to analyze how the time of day affects productivity, you could set up a PivotTable that groups the data into minutes — for example, 30-minute intervals — or hours.

Group Date and Time Values

1. Click the button of the date or time field you want to group.

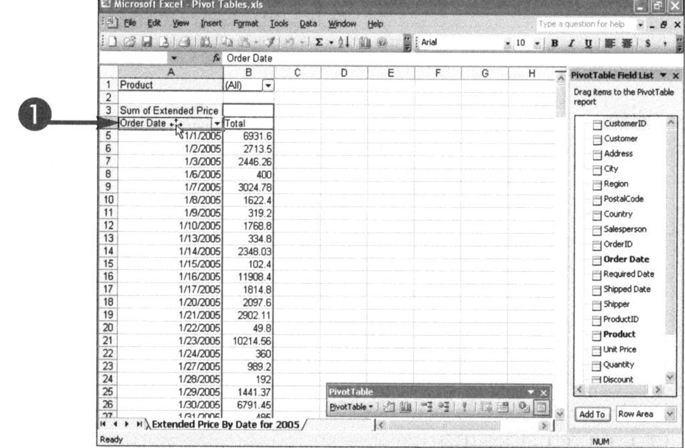

2. Click PivotTable➔Group and Show Detail➔Group.

   You can also click the Group button (), which is not part of the standard PivotTables toolbar. To learn how to access this custom toolbar button, see the task "Customize the PivotTable Toolbar" in Chapter 3.

   The Grouping dialog box appears.

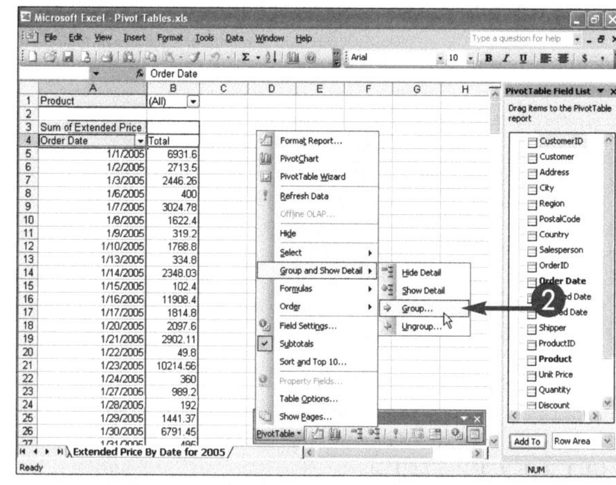

❸ Type the starting date or time.

- Select this check box to have Excel extract the earliest date or time from the data and place that value in the text box.

❹ Type the ending date or time.

- Select this option to have Excel extract the latest date or time from the data and place that value in the text box.

❺ Click the type of grouping you want.

To use multiple groupings, click each type of grouping you want to use.

- If you clicked Days in Step 5, type the number of days to use as the group interval.

❻ Click OK.

Excel groups the date or time values.

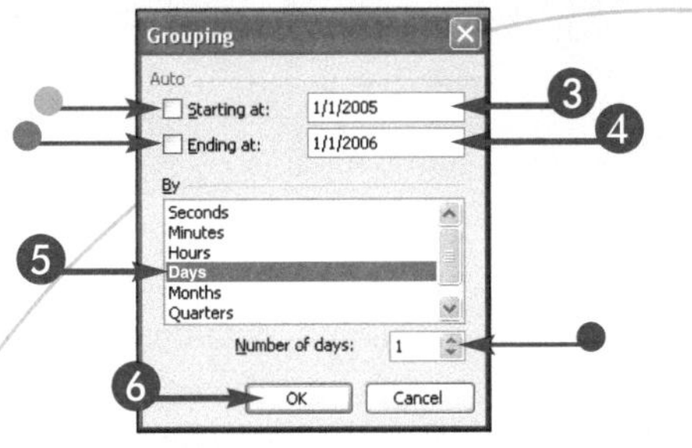

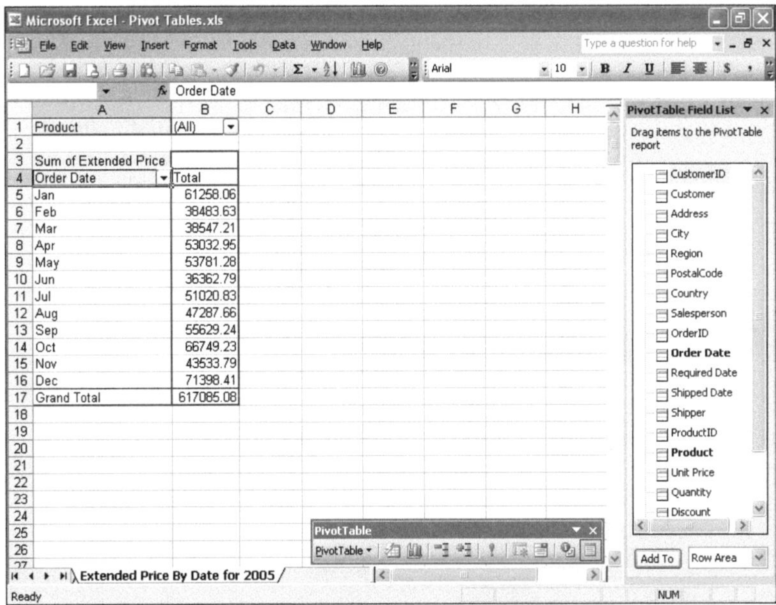

Apply It

In a factory or other manufacturing facility, it is often useful to analyze how productivity varies according to the day of the week. For example, which day of the week is the most productive? Which day is the least productive? Unfortunately, Excel does not have a "weekday" grouping type. To work around this limitation, create a new field in your source data and give it the heading Weekday. To derive the weekday for a given day, start with Excel's `WEEKDAY()` function, which returns a number from 1 to 7, where 1 corresponds to Sunday and 7 corresponds to Saturday. To convert the `WEEKDAY()` result into the day of the week, use the `CHOOSE()` function. If the cell with the date value is A1, use the following formula to derive the corresponding day of the week:

Example:

```
=CHOOSE(WEEKDAY(A1),"Sunday","Monday","Tuesday","Wednesday","Thursday","Friday",
"Saturday")
```

When you have filled this formula for all the dates in your source data, build a new PivotTable and use the Weekday field in the row or column area. Excel will automatically consolidate the Weekday items into the days of the week.

Group Text Values

You can use Excel's PivotTable Grouping feature to create custom groups from the text items in a row or column field.

One common problem that arises when you work with PivotTables is that you often need to consolidate items, but you have no corresponding field in the data. For example, the data may have a Country field, but what if you need to consolidate the PivotTable results by continent? It is unlikely that your source data includes a "Continent" field. Similarly, your source data may include employee names, but you may need to consolidate the employees according to the people they report to. What do you do if your source data does not include a "Supervisor" field?

The solution in both cases is to use the Grouping feature to create custom groups. For the country data, you could create custom groups named "North America," "South America," "Europe," and so on. For the employees, you could create a custom group for each supervisor. You select the items that you want to include in a particular group, create the custom group, and then change the new group name to reflect its content. This task shows you the steps to follow to create such a custom grouping for text values.

Group Text Values

1. Select the items that you want to include in the group.

   To select multiple cells in Excel, click the first cell, hold down Ctrl, and then click each of the other cells.

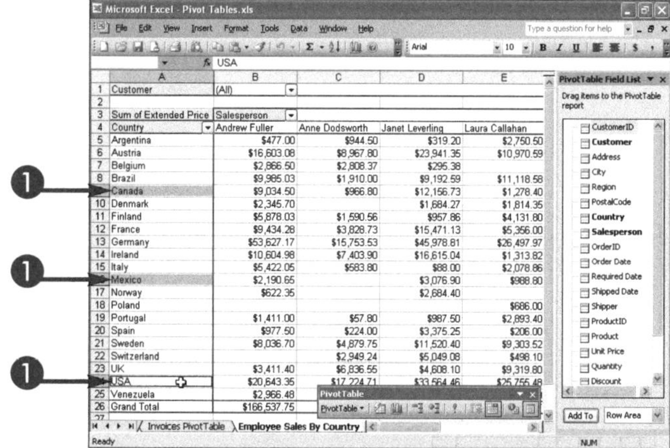

2. Click PivotTable→Group and Show Detail→Group.

   You can also click the Group button ( ), which is not part of the standard PivotTable toolbar. To learn how to access this custom toolbar button, see the task "Customize the PivotTable Toolbar" in Chapter 3.

   Excel creates a new group named Group*n* (where *n* means this is the *n*th group you have created) and restructures the PivotTable.

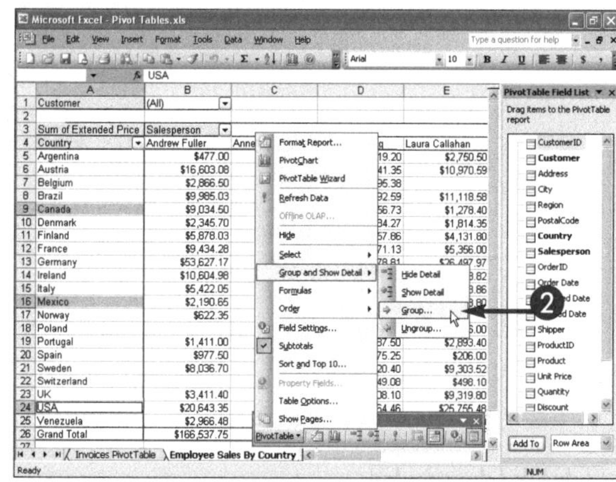

3. Double-click the group label.
4. Type a new name for the group.
5. Press Enter.

   Excel renames the group.

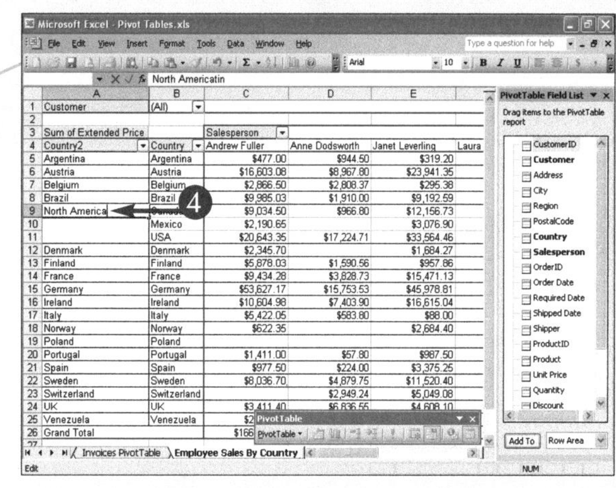

6. Repeat Steps 1 to 5 for the other items in the field until you have created all your groups.
7. Rename the field button to reflect the grouping.

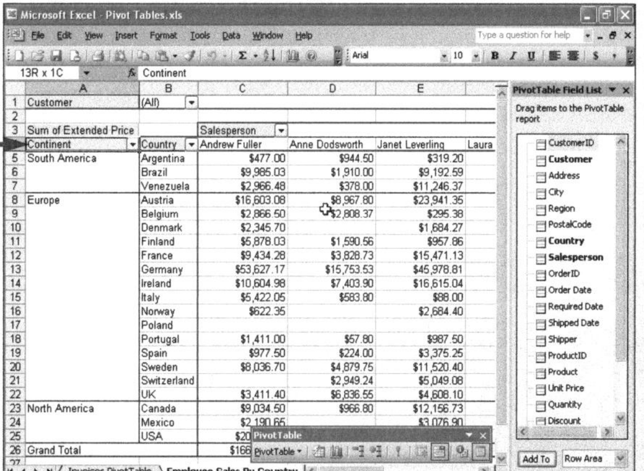

Extra

By default, Excel does not add subtotals to the bottom of each custom group. To add the subtotals, click any cell within the custom group, and then click PivotTable➔Field Settings or click . In the PivotTable Field dialog box, select Automatic (○ changes to ◉) and then click OK. This tells Excel to use the Sum function for the subtotals. If you want to use a different function, see the task "Change the PivotTable Summary Calculation," in Chapter 7.

Note, as well, that the values in the custom grouping — the group names — act as regular PivotTable text items. This means you can sort the groups either by applying an AutoSort or by moving the items by hand; see the tasks "Sort PivotTable Data with AutoSort" and "Move Row and Column Items," earlier in this chapter. You can also filter the items to hide or show only specific groups, as seen in the task "Hide Items in a Row or Column Field," earlier in this chapter.

Hide Group Details

When you consolidate a row or column field into groups, Excel reconfigures the PivotTable. For example, when you group a row field, Excel reconfigures the PivotTable to show two row fields: the groups appear in the outer row field and the items that comprise each group appear in the inner row field. The latter are called the *group details*. To make your report easier to read or manage, you can hide the details for a specific group. In this case, Excel collapses the group to a single line and displays just the group name and, in the data area, the group's subtotals. You can quickly toggle between hiding a group's details and showing them. For the latter, see the next task, "Show Group Details."

The following VBA macro hides the details for all the groups in a PivotTable's row area:

Example:

```
Sub HideAllGroupDetails()
    Dim objPT As PivotTable
    Dim objRowField As PivotField
    Dim objItem As PivotItem
    '
    ' Work with the first PivotTable on the active worksheet
    Set objPT = ActiveSheet.PivotTables(1)
    '
    ' Work with the outermost row field
    Set objRowField = objPT.RowFields(objPT.RowFields.Count)
    '
    ' Hide the details for each item
    For Each objItem In objRowField.PivotItems
        objItem.ShowDetail = False
    Next 'objItem
End Sub
```

Hide Group Details

1. Click the cell containing the name of the group.
2. Click PivotTable→Group and Show Detail→Hide Detail.

You can also click the Hide Detail button (), or double-click the group name.

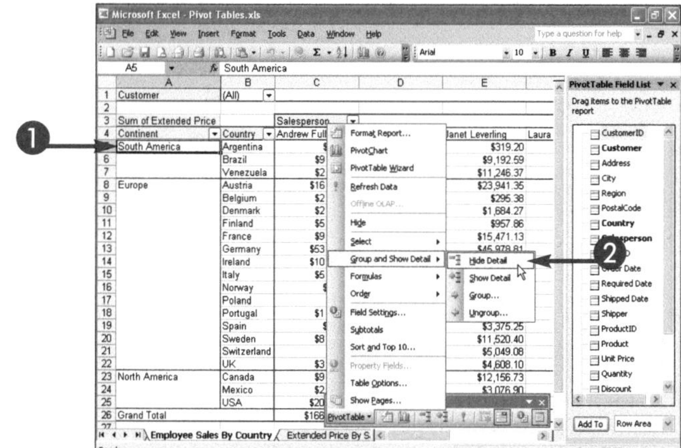

Excel hides the group's details.

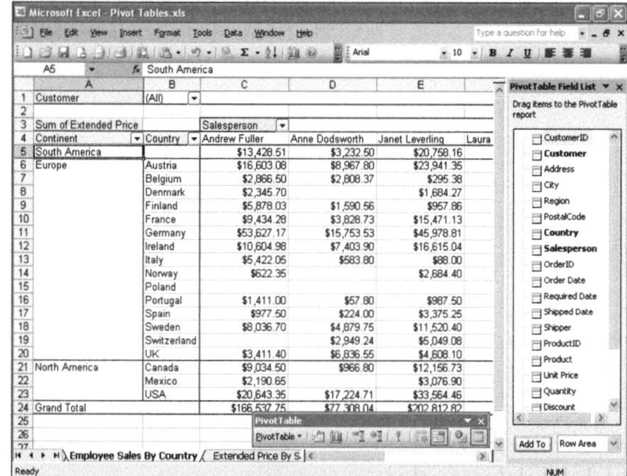

Show Group Details

If you have hidden the details for a group using the Hide Detail command — see the previous task, "Hide Group Details" — you can use the Show Detail command to redisplay the group's details. This enables you to quickly and easily display whatever level of detail you prefer in a PivotTable report.

The following VBA macro shows the details for all the groups in a PivotTable's row area:

Example:

```
Sub ShowAllGroupDetails()
    Dim objPT As PivotTable
    Dim objRowField As PivotField
    Dim objItem As PivotItem
    '
    ' Work with the first PivotTable on the active worksheet
    Set objPT = ActiveSheet.PivotTables(1)
    '
    ' Work with the outermost row field
    Set objRowField = objPT.RowFields(objPT.RowFields.Count)
    '
    ' Hide the details for each item
    For Each objItem In objRowField.PivotItems
        objItem.ShowDetail = True
    Next 'objItem
End Sub
```

Show Group Details

1. Click the cell containing the name of the group.
2. Click PivotTable➔Group and Show Detail➔Show Detail.

   You can also click the Show Detail button ( ), or double-click the group name.

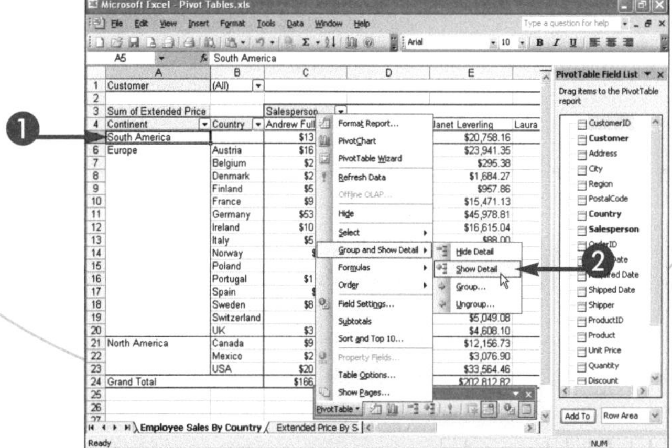

Excel shows the group's details.

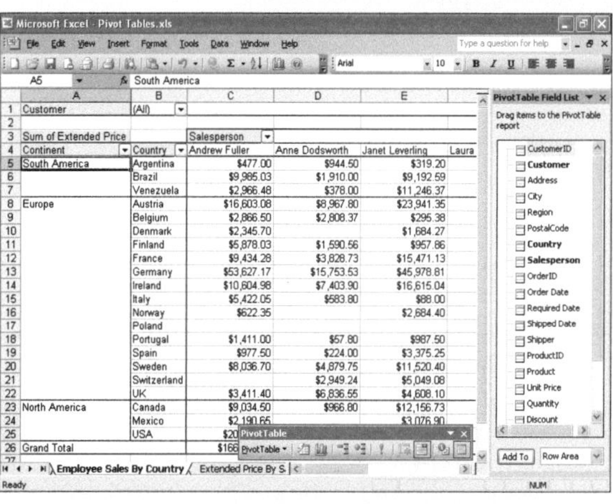

Ungroup Values

Grouping is a very useful PivotTable feature and you will likely find that you make groups a permanent part of many of your PivotTables. On the other hand, you can also use grouping as a temporary data analysis tool. That is, you build your PivotTable, organize a field into groups, and then analyze the results. At this point, if you no longer need the groupings, then you need to reverse the process. With Excel's Ungroup command, you can remove the groupings from your PivotTable.

Excel gives you two ways to use the Ungroup command. The most common method is to use the command to ungroup all the values in the row or column area, thus returning the PivotTable to its normal layout. However, if you are working with text groupings, as seen in "Group Text Values," Excel also enables you to ungroup a single grouping of values, while leaving the other text groupings intact. In this case, Excel displays the group values in both the outer and the inner fields. This can be a bit confusing, so you should only use this technique on occasion.

Ungroup Values

UNGROUP ALL VALUES

1. Click any cell within the group field.
   - If you want to ungroup all the values in a text grouping, click the group label.
2. Click PivotTable➔Group and Show Detail➔Ungroup.

   You can also click the Ungroup button (), which is not part of the standard PivotTable toolbar. To learn how to access this custom toolbar button, see the task "Customize the PivotTable Toolbar" in Chapter 3.

   Excel ungroups all the values.

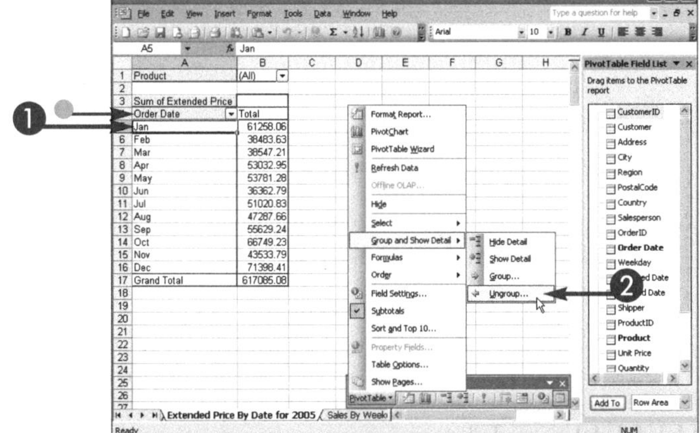

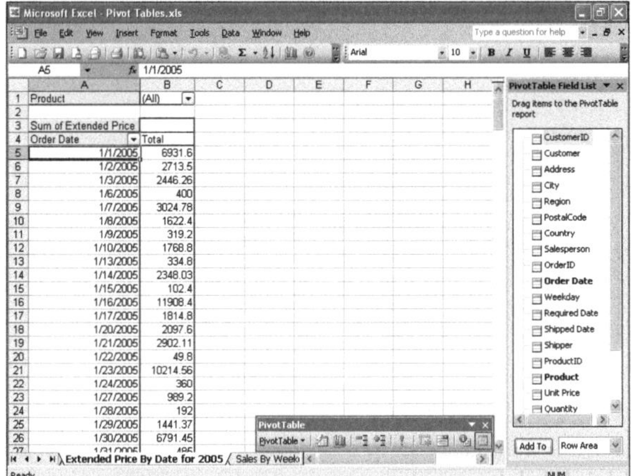

UNGROUP A TEXT GROUPING

1. Click the label of the text grouping.

2. Click PivotTable➔Group and Show Detail➔Ungroup.

   You can also click the Ungroup button (▪), which is not part of the standard PivotTable toolbar. To learn how to access this custom toolbar button, see the task "Customize the PivotTable Toolbar" in Chapter 3.

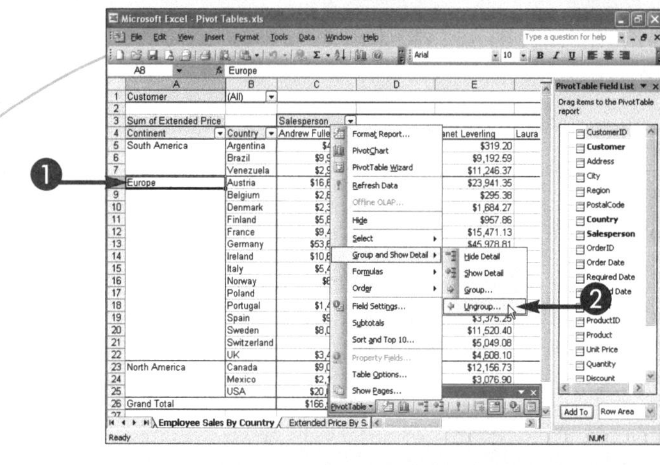

Excel ungroups all the values in the text grouping.

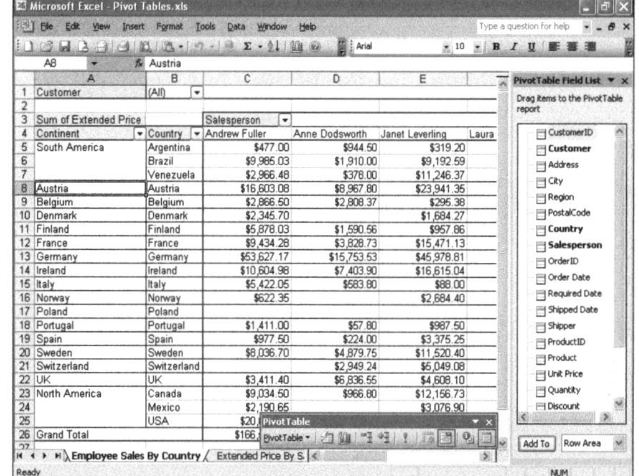

Apply It

Here is a VBA macro that ungroups the row values in a PivotTable:

Example:

```
Sub UngroupAll()
    Dim objPT As PivotTable
    Dim objRowField As PivotField
    Dim objItem As PivotItem
    '
    ' Work with the first PivotTable on the active worksheet
    Set objPT = ActiveSheet.PivotTables(1)
    '
    ' Work with the outermost row field
    Set objRowField = objPT.RowFields(objPT.RowFields.Count)
    '
    ' Select the row
    objPT.PivotSelect objRowField.Name & "[All]"
    '
    ' Ungroup it
    Selection.Ungroup
End Sub
```

Change the Page Area Layout

In Chapter 3, you learned how to add multiple fields to the PivotTable's page area; see the task "Add Multiple Fields to the Page Area." When you add a second field to the page area, Excel displays one field below the other, which is the basic page area layout. However, many PivotTable applications require a large number of page area fields, sometimes half a dozen or more. By default, Excel displays these fields vertically, one on top of another. You can alter this default configuration by changing the page area layout to one that suits the layout of the rest of the PivotTable.

Excel gives you two ways to change the page area layout. The most basic change is to reconfigure how the page area fields appear on the worksheet. The default is vertically (one on top of another), but you can also change the fields to appear horizontally (one beside another).

After you have selected the basic orientation, you can then change whether Excel displays the fields in multiple columns or rows. For example, if you choose the vertical orientation (Excel calls it Down, Then Over), you can also specify the number of fields that appear in each column. If you have, say, six page fields and you specify two columns, Excel displays the first three fields in one column and the other three fields in the next column. Similarly, if you choose the horizontal orientation (called Over, Then Down), you can also specify the number of fields that appear in each row.

Change the Page Area Layout

1 Click any cell in the PivotTable.

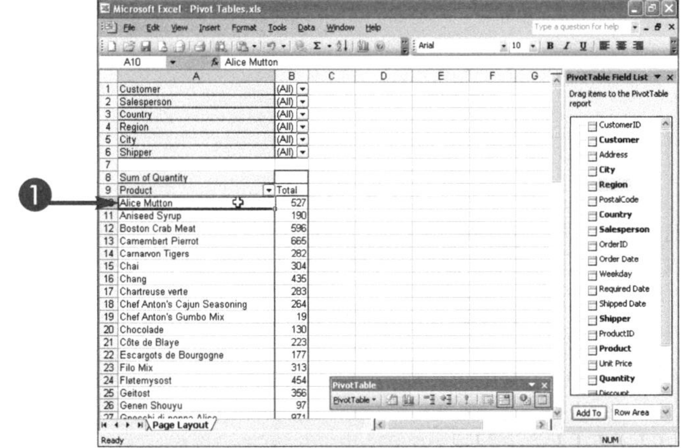

2 Click PivotTable→Table Options.

The PivotTable Options dialog box appears.

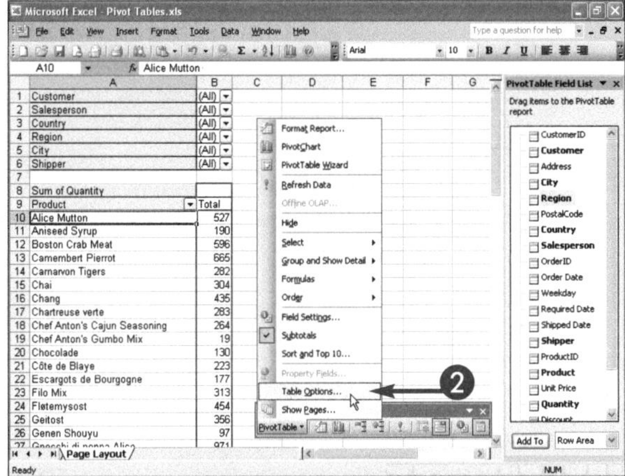

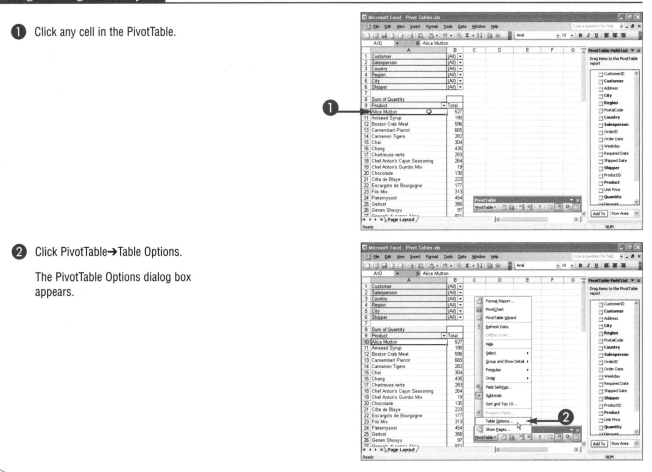

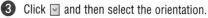

3. Click ▾ and then select the orientation.

4. Specify the maximum number of fields that you want Excel to display in each row.

   If you select the Down, Then Over page layout in Step 3, specify the maximum number of fields that you want Excel to display in each column.

Note: If you enter 0 in the Fields per row (or Fields per column) box, Excel displays the page fields in a single row (or column).

5. Click OK.

   Excel reconfigures the layout of the page area.

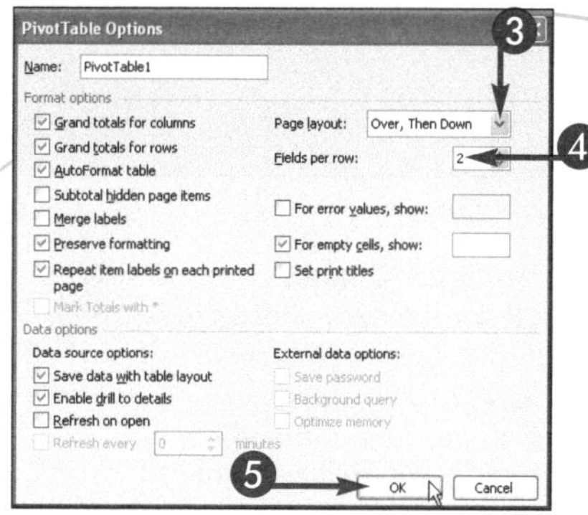

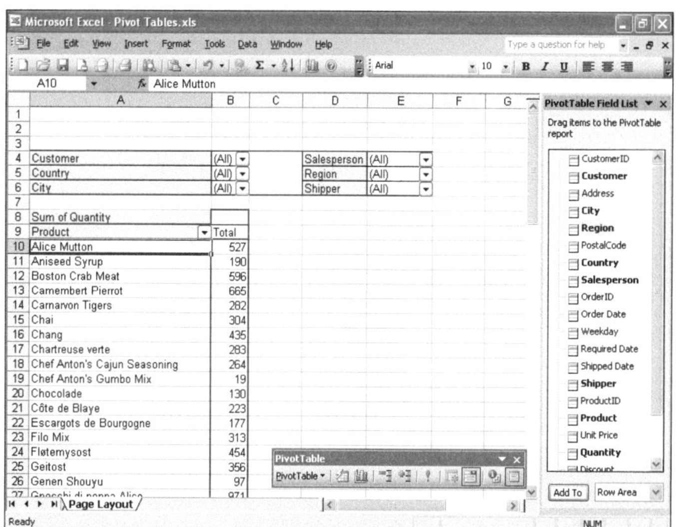

Apply It

If you want to use VBA to control the page area layout, the `PivotTable` object has two properties you can work with: `PageFieldOrder` and `PageFieldWrapCount`. Use the `PageFieldOrder` property to set the page area orientation (to either `xlDownThenOver` or `xlOverThenDown`); and use the `PageFieldWrapCount` property to set the number of rows or columns you want in the page area layout. The following code sets these properties for a `PivotTable` object:

Example:

```
Set objPT = ActiveSheet.PivotTables(1)
With objPT
    .PageFieldOrder = xlOverThenDown
    .PageFieldWrapCount = 2
End With
```

Rename a PivotTable Field

PivotTable field names come from the column headings used in the original source data. However, if you are using an external data source, the field names come from the names used in the data source's fields. If you do not like some or all of the field names in your PivotTable, you can rename them. Excel will remember the new names you specify and even preserve them when you refresh or rebuild the PivotTable. Note, however, that Excel does not change the corresponding headings in the source data.

Why rename a field? Usually because the original name is not suitable in some way. For example, many field names consist of multiple words that have been joined to avoid spaces, so you might have field names such as CustomerName and OrderDate. Renaming these fields to Customer Name and Order Date makes them easier to read. Similarly, you might have field names that are all uppercase letters and you might prefer to use title case, instead. Many PivotTable users prefer to change the name of the data field. Excel's default is "Sum of *FieldName*," where *FieldName* is the name of the field used in the summary calculation. A better name might use the form "*FieldName* Total" or something similar.

Rename a PivotTable Field

Note: This chapter uses the PivotTables.xls spreadsheet, available at www.wiley.com/go/pivottablesvb, or you can create your own sample database.

1. Click the button of the field you want to rename.

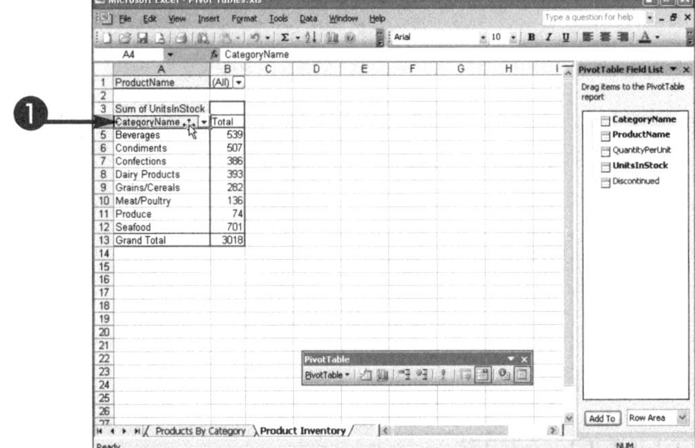

2. Click PivotTable➔Field Settings.

   You can also double-click the field button or click the Field Settings button ( ).

   The PivotTable Field dialog box appears.

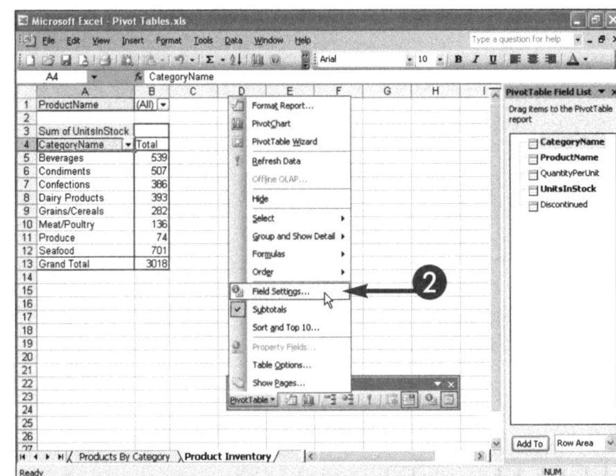

3. Change the Name text to the new field name.

Note: Make sure that the new name you use does not conflict with an existing field name.

4. Click OK.
   - Excel renames the field.
5. Click the Refresh Data button to refresh the PivotTable.
   - Excel updates the field name in the PivotTable Field List.

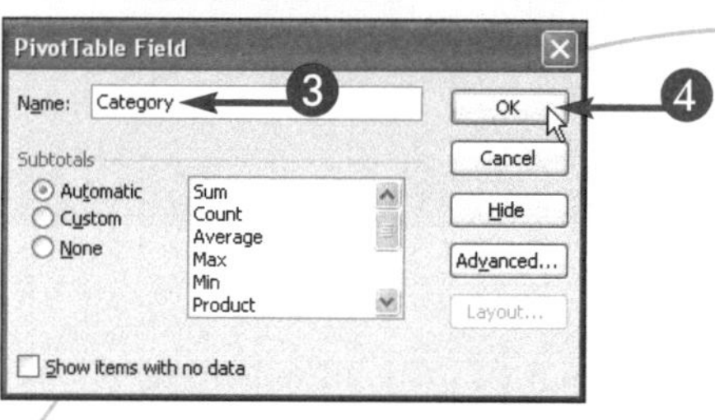

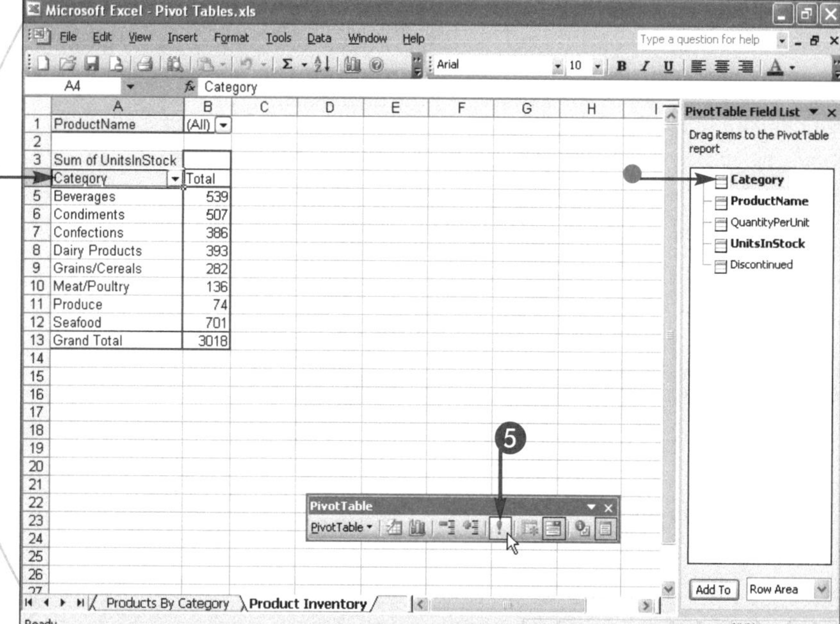

Extra

The field buttons you see in a PivotTable are not true command buttons, such as, for example, the OK and Cancel buttons in a dialog box. Instead, a PivotTable field button is really just a worksheet cell that has had special formatting applied. This means that when you click a field button, the button text appears inside Excel's formula bar. So an easier way to rename a PivotTable field is to click its button and then edit the button text that appears in the formula bar. You can also press F2 and edit the text directly in the cell. Note that when you use this method, Excel automatically updates the field name in the PivotTable Field List.

If you use this method to rename the page field, note that you will lose any text formatting that you have applied to the button text; see the task "Format a PivotTable Cell," later in this chapter. This appears to be a bug in Excel. To avoid this problem, use the PivotTable Field dialog box to rename the page field. Also, Excel does not update the PivotTable Field List when you rename a page field using the direct method. You need to click the Refresh Data button (!) to update the PivotTable Field List.

Rename a PivotTable Item

The names of the items that appear in the PivotTable's row or column area are the unique values that Excel has extracted from the source data fields you have added to each area. Therefore, because the items come from the data itself, you might think that their names would be unchangeable. That is not true, however. You can rename any field item and Excel will "remember" that the new name corresponds with the original item. Excel preserves your new names even after you refresh or rebuild the PivotTable.

As with field names, you will usually want to rename an item when its existing name is unsuitable. For example, the original name might not be very descriptive, it might be obscure, or it may come from a data source that uses all-uppercase or (more rarely) all-lowercase letters.

You should exercise a bit of caution when renaming items, however. If the people reading your report are familiar with the underlying data, they could become confused if you use names that differ significantly from the originals.

Remember, too, that renaming one or more items might cause the field to lose its current sort order. After you have finished renaming items in the field, you might need to resort the field, as described in the Chapter 4 task "Sort PivotTable Data with AutoSort."

Rename a PivotTable Item

1. Click the cell of the item you want to rename.

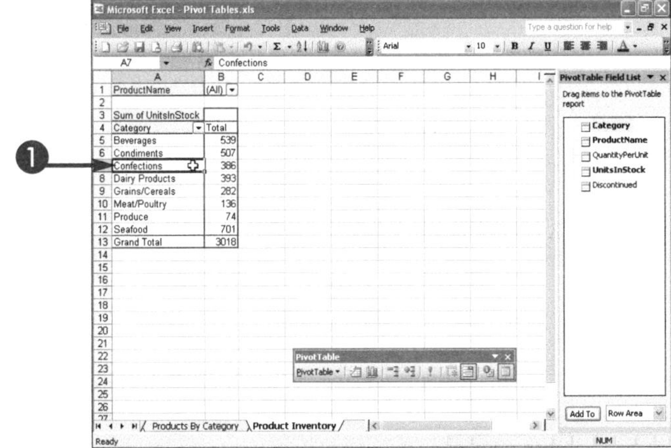

2. Press F2.

- Excel opens the cell for editing.

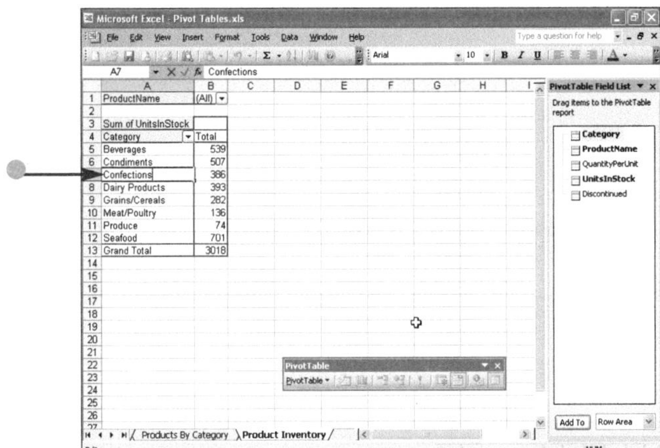

3. Type the new item name in the cell.

Note: Make sure that the new name you use does not conflict with an existing item name in the same field. If you enter an existing name, Excel switches the position of the two items. In Chapter 4, see the task "Move Row and Column Items."

4. Press Enter.

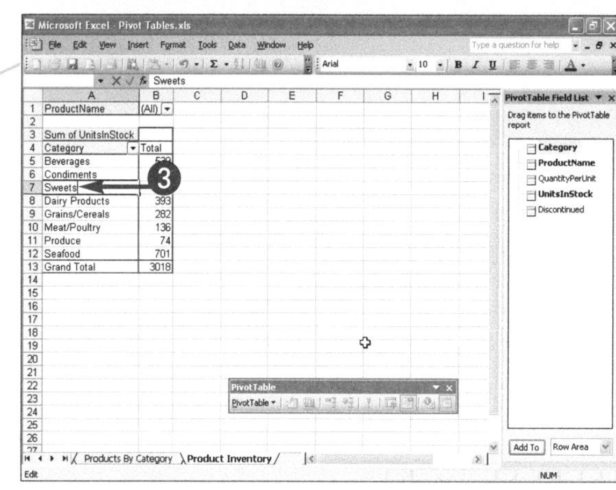

- Excel renames the item.

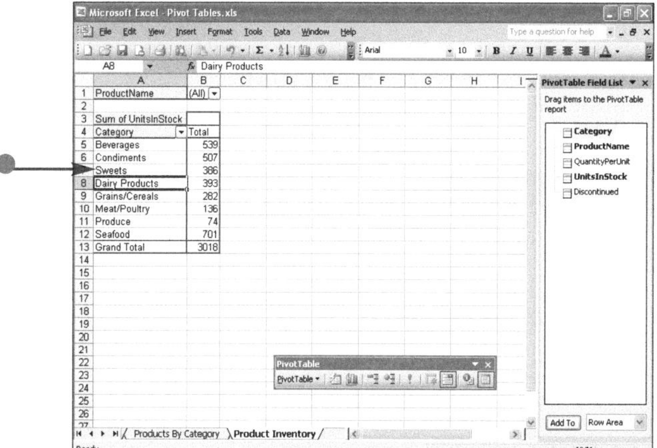

Apply It

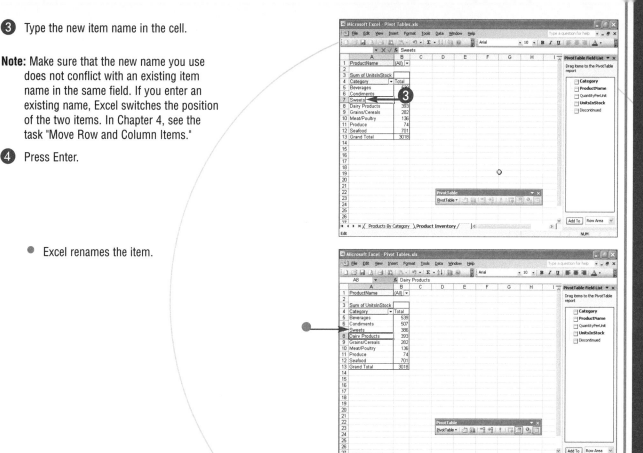

The technique you learned in this task applies to items in the row and column areas. For obvious reasons, Excel does not allow you to edit any of the cells in the data area because they are all calculated values. That leaves only the page area. So how can you rename page field items if they do not reside in worksheet cells?

The solution is to pivot the page field you want to work with over to either the row or column area. Excel displays the field's items in cells, so you can then edit the items or items you want to rename. After you have finished renaming the items, pivot the field back to the page area. Excel preserves your new names in the page field drop-down list. Moreover, Excel sets up a correspondence between your new name and the item's original name in the source data. Therefore, when you select the renamed item in the page drop-down list, Excel filters the PivotTable results appropriately.

Format a PivotTable Cell

If you will be sharing your PivotTables with other people, via a network, e-mail, the Web, or a presentation, your report will have much more impact if it is nicely formatted and presented in a readable, eye-catching layout. You can use Excel's cell-formatting tools to apply a wide variety of formats to your PivotTable cells.

By default, Excel applies almost no formatting to PivotTable labels or data. The only exceptions are the borders that separate the PivotTable areas and the Grand Totals, and the special formatting that makes the field headings look like command buttons. However, you are free to modify the formatting for any cell in the PivotTable. For example, you can apply a numeric or date format, or create a custom format, as discussed in detail in the next three tasks of this chapter. You can also change the cell alignment to the left, center, or right, or you can wrap text within the cell. For the cell font, you can change the typeface, style, size, color, and more. You can also change the cell borders and apply background shading, either as a solid color or with a fill pattern.

By the way, the default format that the PivotTable Wizard applies to a new PivotTable is an AutoFormat called PivotTable Classic. Excel offers nearly two dozen PivotTable AutoFormats that enable you to apply a uniform format to an entire PivotTable. For the details, see the Chapter 6 task "Apply an AutoFormat." Excel also has a feature that preserves your formatting when you refresh your PivotTable; see the task "Preserve PivotTable Formatting," also in Chapter 6.

Format a PivotTable Cell

1. Click the cell you want to format.

   You can also select a range or a PivotTable area.

Note: To learn how to select PivotTable areas, see the Chapter 3 task "Select PivotTable Items."

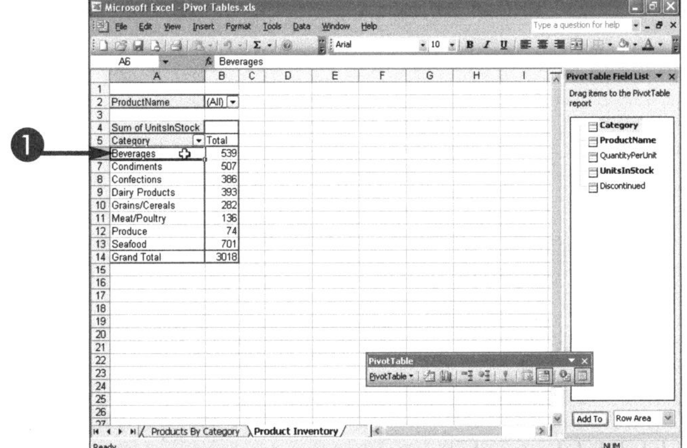

2. Click Format➔Cells.

   You can also press Ctrl+1.

   Excel displays the Format Cells dialog box.

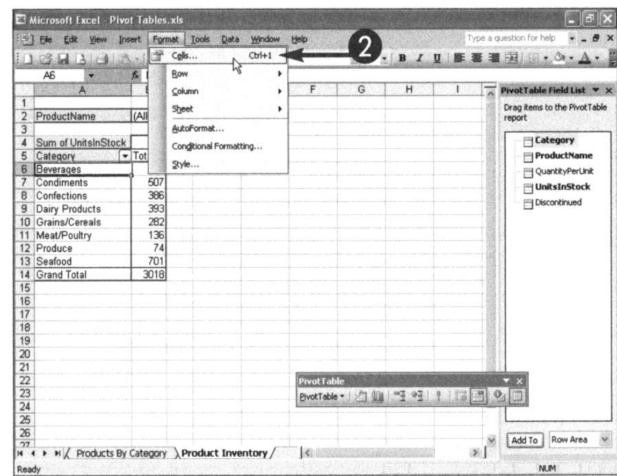

- For the details on using the Number tab, see the tasks "Apply a Numeric Format to PivotTable Data," "Apply a Date Format to PivotTable Data," and "Apply a Conditional Format to PivotTable Data," later in this chapter.

3. Use the controls in the Alignment tab to align data within the cell.

4. Use the controls in the Font tab to apply font options to the cell text.

5. Use the controls in the Border tab to apply a border to the cell.

6. Use the controls in the Patterns tab to apply a fill pattern and color to the cell background.

7. Click OK.

- Excel applies the formatting to the cell.

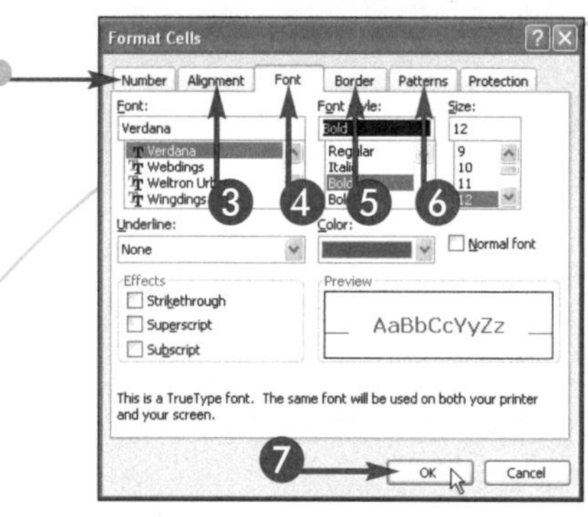

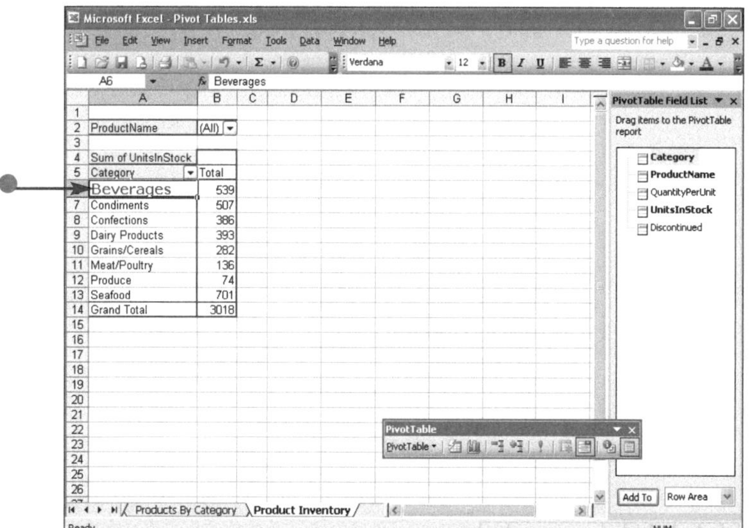

Extra

You can also format the selected cell or range using the following buttons on the Formatting toolbar:

BUTTON	DESCRIPTION
Arial	Applies a typeface.
10	Sets the font size.
B	Formats text as bold.
I	Formats text as italics.
U	Formats text as underlined.
	Left-aligns text.
	Centers text.
	Right-aligns text.
	Applies a border.
	Applies a background color.
A	Applies a text color.

Apply a Numeric Format to PivotTable Data

You can improve the readability of your PivotTable by applying the appropriate numeric formatting, such as displaying currency amounts with leading dollar signs and displaying large numbers with commas.

Excel offers six categories of numeric formats:

- **Number** — Enables you to specify three components: the number of decimal places (0 to 30), whether or not the thousands separator (,) is used, and how negative numbers are displayed. For negative numbers, you can display the number with a leading minus sign, in red, surrounded by parentheses, or in red surrounded by parentheses.
- **Currency** — This format is similar to the number format, except that the thousands separator is always used, and you have the option of displaying the numbers with a leading dollar sign ($) or other currency symbol.
- **Accounting** — Enables you to select the number of decimal places and whether to display a leading currency symbol, which Excel displays flush-left in the cell. All negative entries are displayed surrounded by parentheses.
- **Percentage** — Displays the number multiplied by 100 with a percent sign (%) to the right of the number. For example, .506 is displayed as 50.6%. You can display 0 to 30 decimal places.
- **Fraction** — Enables you to express decimal quantities as fractions. There are nine fraction formats in all, including displaying the number as halves, quarters, eighths, sixteenths, tenths, and hundredths.
- **Scientific** — Displays the most significant number to the left of the decimal, 2 to 30 decimal places to the right of the decimal, and then the exponent. For example, 123000 is displayed as 1.23E+05.

You can also create custom numeric formats. In Appendix A, see the section "Work with Custom Numeric and Date Formats."

Apply a Numeric Format to PivotTable Data

1. Click the cell or select the range you want to format.

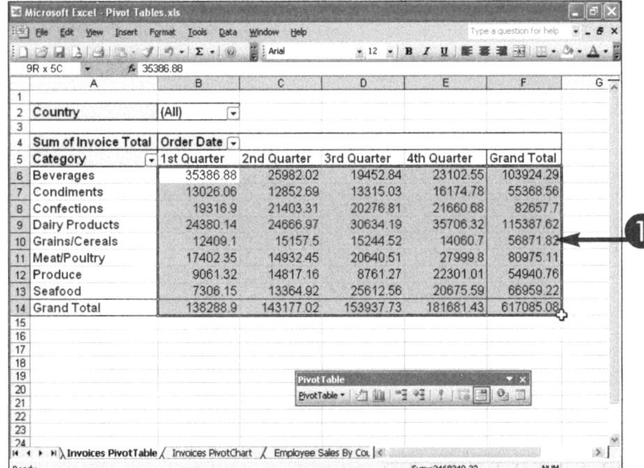

2. Click Format➔Cells.

You can also press Ctrl+1.

To apply a numeric format to an entire field, double-click the field button and then click Number.

Excel displays the Format Cells dialog box.

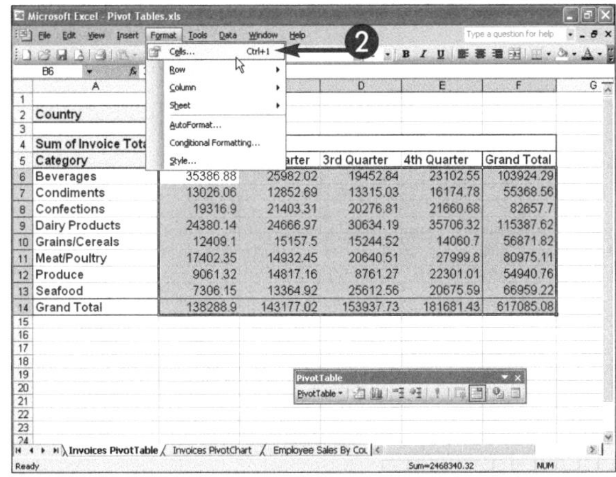

3. Click the numeric format you want to use.
4. Use the controls on the right side of the tab to select the format options.
   - The Sample area shows what your formatting will look like.
5. Click OK.

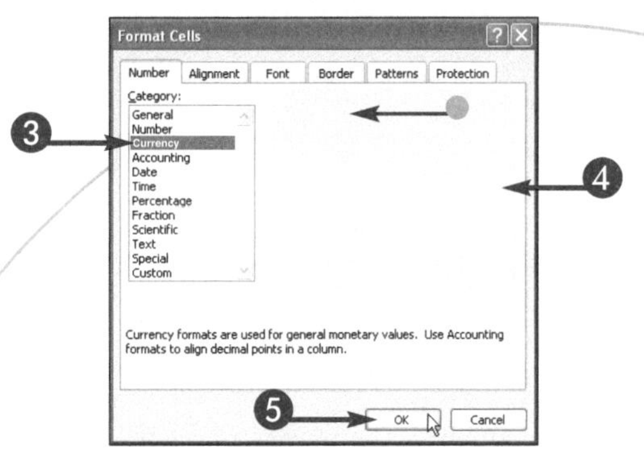

Excel applies the numeric formatting to the cell or range.

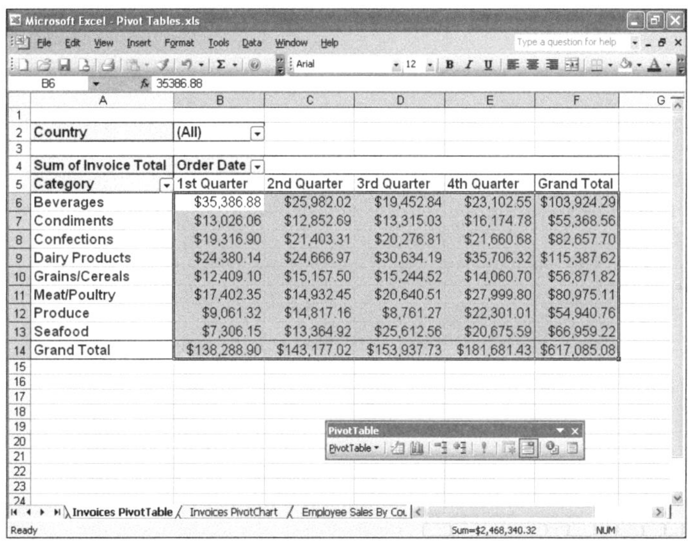

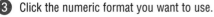

Extra

You can also set the numeric format of the selected cell or range by applying a style. Click Format➔Style and then click the numeric style you want: Comma, Currency, or Percent. You can also set the numeric format using the following buttons on the Formatting toolbar:

BUTTON	DESCRIPTION
$	Applies the Currency style.
%	Applies the Percent style.
,	Applies the Comma style.
←.0 .00	Increases the number of decimal places.
.00 →.0	Decreases the number of decimal places.

There are also a few shortcut keys you can use to set the numeric format:

PRESS	TO APPLY THE FORMAT
Ctrl+~	General
Ctrl+!	Number (2 decimal places; using the thousands separator)
Ctrl+$	Currency (2 decimal places; using the dollar sign; negative numbers surrounded by parentheses)
Ctrl+%	Percentage (0 decimal places)
Ctrl+^	Scientific (2 decimal places)

Apply a Date Format to PivotTable Data

If you include dates or times in your PivotTables, you need to make sure that they are presented in a readable, unambiguous format. For example, most people would interpret the date 8/5/06 as August 5, 2006. However, in some countries this date would mean May 8, 2006. Similarly, if you use the time 2:45, do you mean AM or PM? To avoid these kinds of problems, you can apply Excel's built-in date and time formats to a PivotTable cell or range.

The Date format specifies how Excel displays the date components — the day, month, and year — as well as which symbol to use to separate the components. For the month component of the date, Excel can display any of the following: the number (where January is 1, February is 2, and so on) with or without a leading 0; the first letter of the month name (for example, M for March); the abbreviated month name (for example, Mar for March); or the full month name. For the year component, Excel can display either the final two digits (for example, 06 for 2006) or all four digits. You can also choose either a slash (/) or a hyphen (-) to separate the date components. Depending on the location you choose, such as the United States or Canada, you may also be able to include the day of the week or use a period (.) as the date separator.

The Time format specifies which time components — hours, minutes, and seconds — Excel displays. You can also choose whether Excel uses regular time (for example, 1:30:55 PM) or military time (for example, 13:30:55). When you select a regular time format, Excel always includes either AM or PM; when you choose a military time format, Excel does not include AM or PM.

You can also create custom date formats. In Appendix A, see the section "Work with Custom Numeric and Date Formats."

Apply a Date Format to PivotTable Data

1. Click the cell or select the range you want to format.

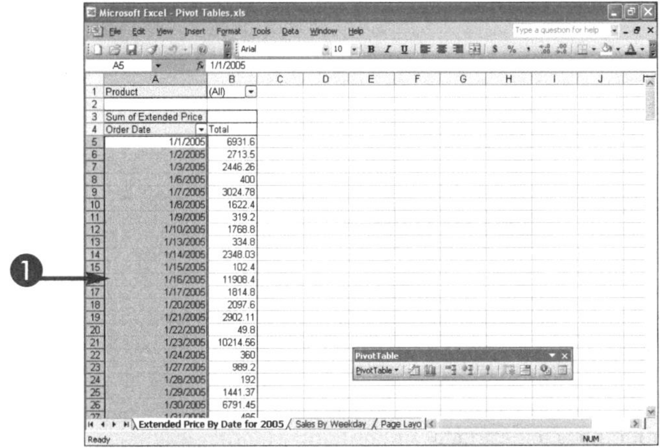

2. Click Format→Cells.

You can also press Ctrl+1.

To apply a date or time format to an entire field, double-click the field button and then click Number.

Excel displays the Format Cells dialog box.

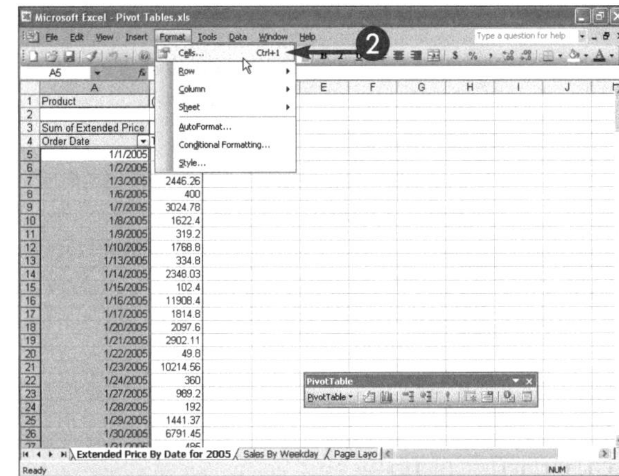

3 Click Date.

If you are formatting times, click Time, instead.

4 Click the format type you want to apply.

5 Click ▾ and click the location.

- The Sample area shows what your formatting will look like.

6 Click OK.

Excel applies the date or time formatting to the cell or range.

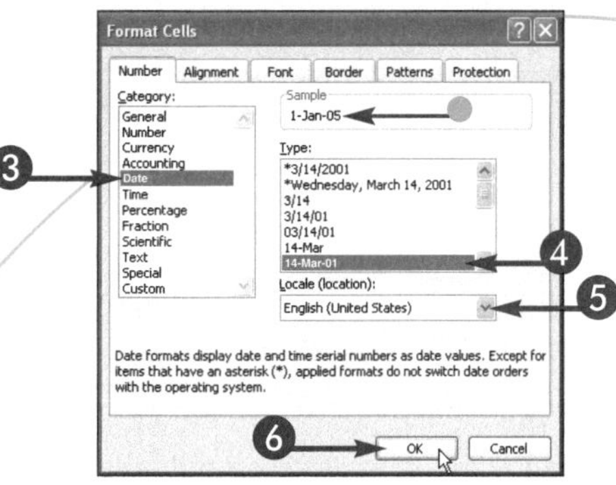

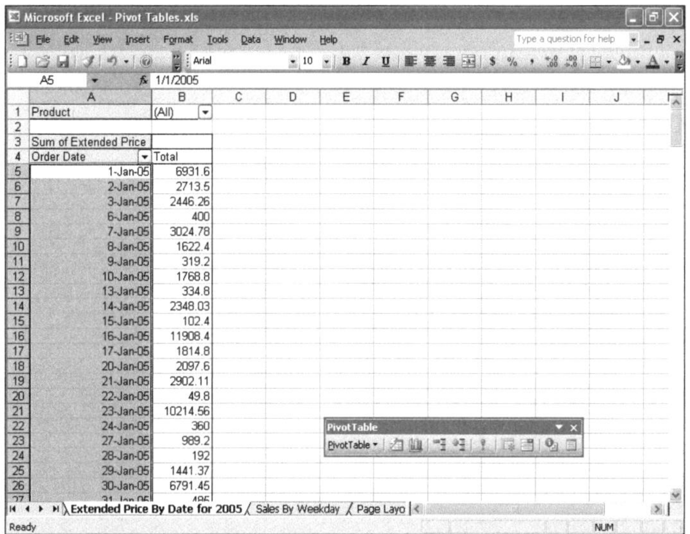

Extra

There are a few shortcut keys you can use to set the date or time format as well as to add the current date or time:

PRESS	TO
Ctrl-#	Apply the date format 14-Mar-01
Ctrl-@	Apply the time format 1:30 PM
Ctrl-;	Enter the current date using the format 3/14/2001
Ctrl-:	Enter the current time using the format 1:30 PM

In the Number tab of the Format Cells dialog box, if you click the Date format and choose English (United States) in the Locale list, Excel shows two date formats at the top of the Type list:

```
*3/14/2001
*Wednesday, March 14, 2001
```

The asterisks tell you that the order of the date components may change if someone opening the worksheet is using a different locale. For example, if you select the *3/14/2001 format, a user in the United Kingdom will likely see the date as 14/3/2001. If you want to make sure that other users always see the dates as you format them, choose a format that does not have a leading asterisk.

Apply a Conditional Format to PivotTable Data

Formatting numbers with thousands separators, decimals, or currency symbols is useful because a PivotTable is, in the end, a report, and reports should always look their best. However, the main purpose of a PivotTable is to perform data analysis, and regular numeric formatting achieves that goal only insofar as it helps you and others read and understand the report. However, if you want to extend the analytic capabilities of your PivotTables, you need to turn to a more advanced technique called *conditional formatting*.

The idea behind conditional formatting is that you want particular values in your PivotTable results to stand out from the others. For example, if your PivotTable tracks product inventory, you might want to be alerted when the inventory of any item falls below some critical value. Similarly, you might want to track the total amount sold by your salespeople and be alerted when an employee's results exceed some value so that, say, a bonus can be awarded.

Conditional formatting enables you to achieve these and similar results. With a conditional format applied to some or all of the PivotTable's data area, Excel examines the numbers and then applies formatting — a font, border, and pattern that you specify — to any cells that match your criteria. By applying, say, a bold font, thick cell border, and a background color to results that satisfy your criteria, you can find those important results with a quick glance at your PivotTable.

Note, however, that conditional formatting only works with PivotTables that have a static layout. The conditional formatting is a property of the cells to which you apply it, not of the PivotTable. So, for example, if you pivot the column field into the row area, your conditional formatting does not travel with the field.

Apply a Conditional Format to PivotTable Data

1. Select some or all of the PivotTable's data area.
2. Click Format→Conditional Formatting.

   The Conditional Formatting dialog box appears.
3. Click ▾ and click Cell Value Is in this list.
4. Click ▾ and click a comparison operator in this list.
5. Type the value you want to use with the comparison operator.
   - If you want to use another worksheet value with the comparison operator, click the Collapse Dialog button and then click the worksheet value.
6. If the comparison operator requires a second value, type or select that value.
7. Click Format.

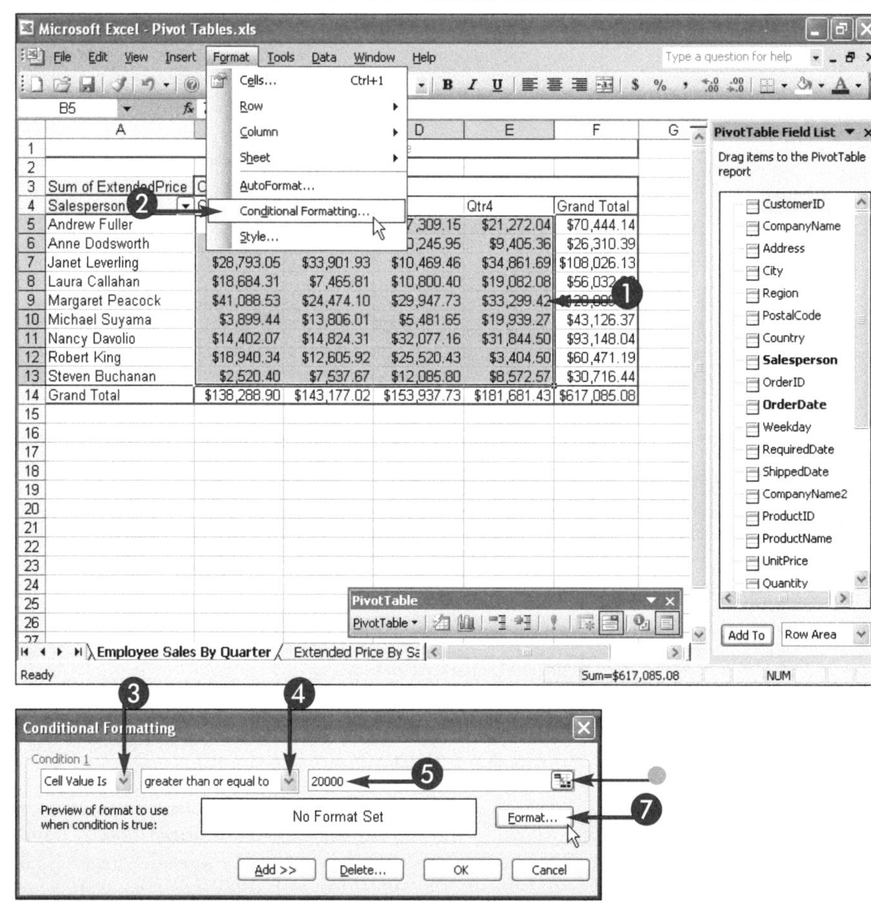

Excel displays the Format Cells dialog box.

8. Use the Font tab to apply font options to the conditional format.

9. Use the Border tab to apply a border to the conditional format.

10. Use the Patterns tab to apply a fill pattern to the conditional format.

11. Click OK.

Excel returns you to the Conditional Formatting dialog box.

12. Click OK.

Excel applies the conditional formatting to the range.

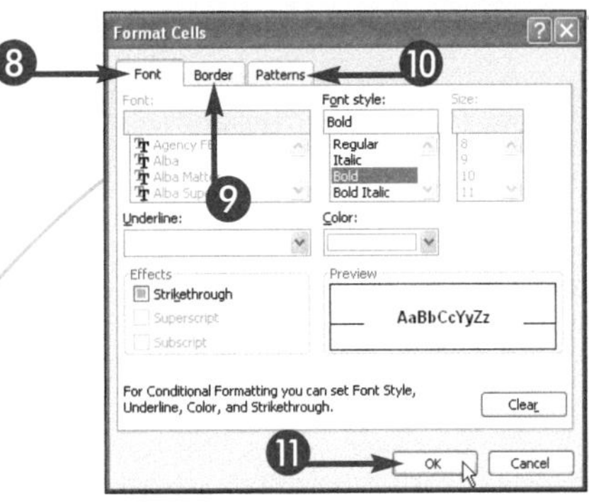

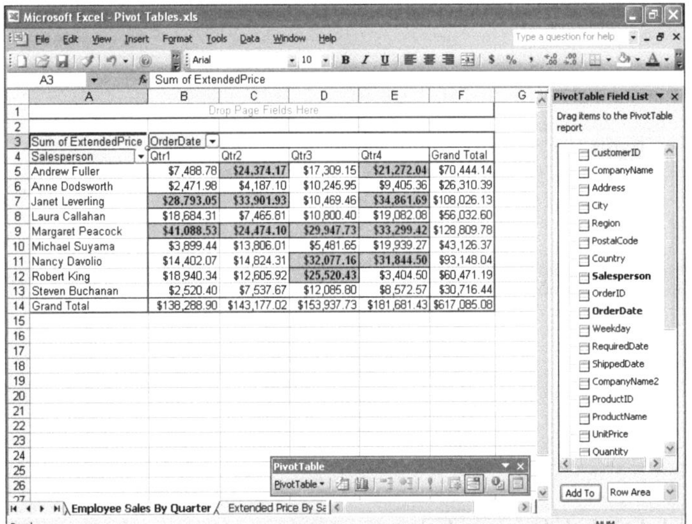

Sum of ExtendedPrice	OrderDate				
Salesperson	Qtr1	Qtr2	Qtr3	Qtr4	Grand Total
Andrew Fuller	$7,488.78	$24,374.17	$17,309.15	$21,272.04	$70,444.14
Anne Dodsworth	$2,471.98	$4,187.10	$10,245.95	$9,405.36	$26,310.39
Janet Leverling	$28,793.05	$33,901.93	$10,469.46	$34,861.69	$108,026.13
Laura Callahan	$18,684.31	$7,465.81	$10,800.40	$19,082.08	$56,032.60
Margaret Peacock	$41,088.53	$24,474.10	$29,947.73	$33,299.42	$128,809.78
Michael Suyama	$3,899.44	$13,806.01	$5,481.65	$19,939.27	$43,126.37
Nancy Davolio	$14,402.07	$14,824.31	$32,077.16	$31,844.50	$93,148.04
Robert King	$18,940.34	$12,605.92	$25,520.43	$3,404.50	$60,471.19
Steven Buchanan	$2,520.40	$7,537.67	$12,085.80	$8,572.57	$30,716.44
Grand Total	$138,288.90	$143,177.02	$153,937.73	$181,681.43	$617,085.08

Apply It

There may be times when you want to apply multiple conditional formats to your PivotTable results. For example, in an inventory report, you might want to apply one format when a product's inventory level falls below some threshold, and a second format when the inventory is zero. Similarly, for employee sales, you can establish multiple sales thresholds and assign a conditional format for each one. For these and similar situations, Excel enables you to define up to three different conditional formats — named Condition 1, Condition 2, and Condition 3.

Follow Steps 1 and 2 to display the Conditional Formatting dialog box. Enter your criteria and format options for Condition 1, and then click Add. Excel expands the dialog box to show the controls for Condition 2. You specify the criteria and formatting for Condition 2 in the same way as you did for Condition 1. If you need a third condition, click Add again to expand the dialog box to show the Condition 3 controls.

If you decide later that you no longer require one or more of these conditions, display the Conditional Formatting dialog box, click Delete, select each condition you want to remove (☐ changes to ☑), and then click OK.

Show Items with No Data

A PivotTable report is meant to be a succinct summary of a large quantity of data. One way that Excel increases the succinctness of a PivotTable is to exclude from the report any items that have no data. This is usually the behavior that you want, but it can cause some problems with certain kinds of reports.

One of the problems that comes up when some items have no data concerns filtering the report using a page field. For example, suppose there are two items in the page field, and that a particular row item has data for the first page field item, but it has no data for the second page field item. When you switch pages, your PivotTable layout will change because Excel removes the row field item from the report when you filter on the second page field.

Another problem occurs when you group the PivotTable results. If no results fall within a particular grouping, Excel does not display the grouping.

In both cases, the exclusion of a field item or grouping can be confusing and, in any case, you may be interested in seeing items or groupings that have no data.

You can work around these problems by forcing Excel to always show field items that have no data, as described in this task.

Show Items with No Data

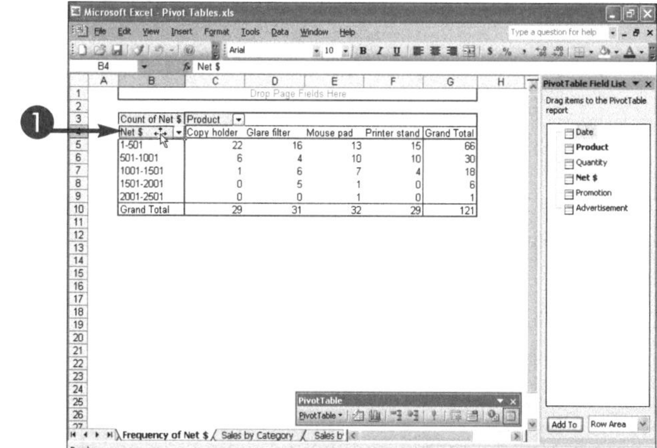

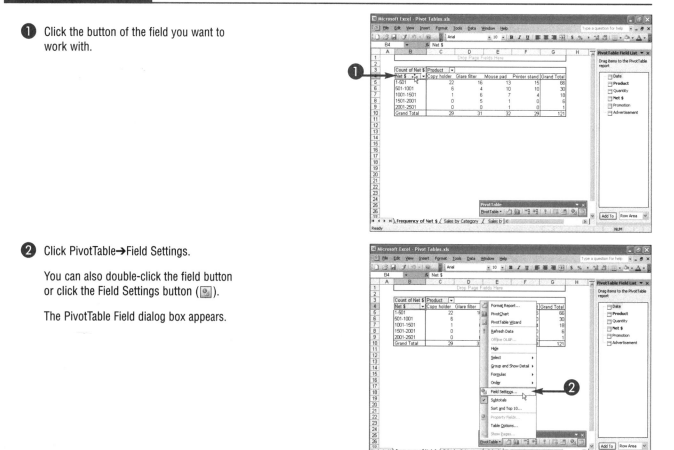

1. Click the button of the field you want to work with.

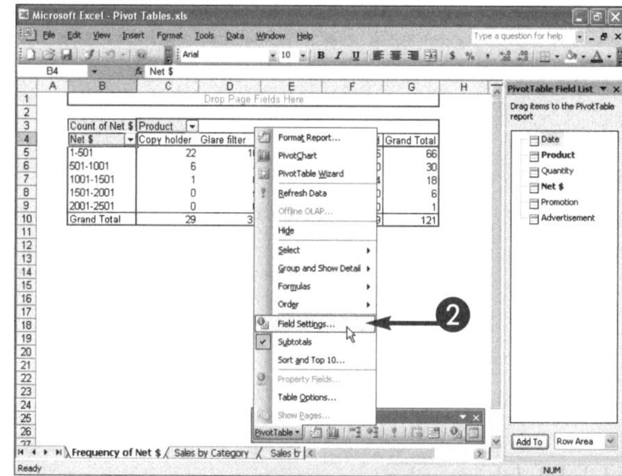

2. Click PivotTable→Field Settings.

   You can also double-click the field button or click the Field Settings button ( ).

   The PivotTable Field dialog box appears.

3 Select Show items with no data.

4 Click OK.

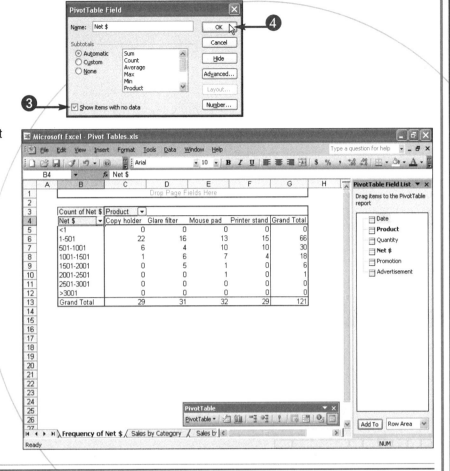

Excel displays the PivotTable report with items that have no data.

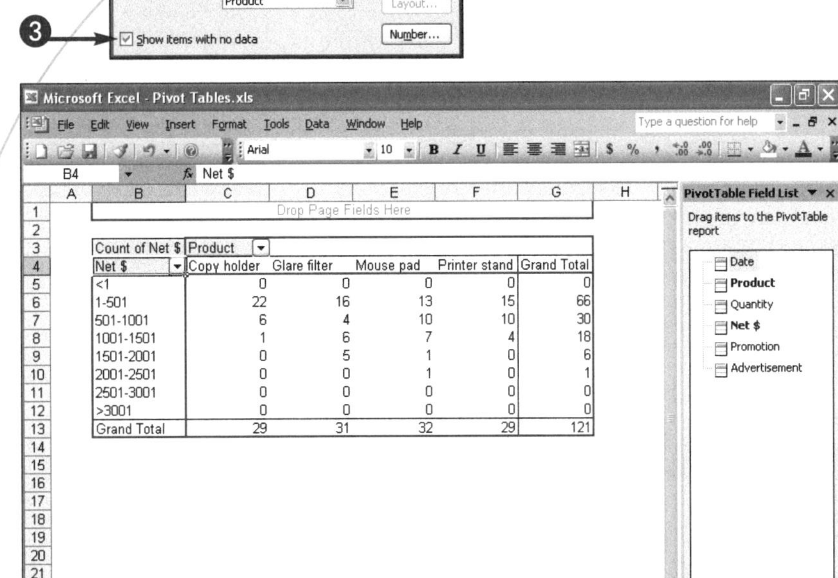

Apply It

One PivotTable problem that comes up more often than you might think is when you end up with "phantom" field items, or items that no longer exist in the source data. This occurs when an item appears originally in the source data, shows up in a PivotTable report, and is then subsequently renamed in or deleted from the source data. When you refresh the PivotTable, the item disappears. However, if you activate "Show items with no data" (☐ changes to ☑) for the field, Excel displays the item again. Even if you refresh or rebuild the PivotTable, the phantom item still appears in the report.

The only way to solve this problem is to use VBA to delete the PivotTable item. Here is a VBA macro that deletes the PivotTable item in the active worksheet cell:

Example:

```
Sub DeletePivotTableItem()
    Dim nResult As Integer
    '
    ' Work with the PivotItem object in the active cell
    With ActiveCell.PivotItem
        '
        ' Confirm the deletion
        nResult = MsgBox("Are you sure you want " & _
                  "to delete the """ & _
                  .Value & """ item?", vbYesNo)
        '
        ' If Yes, delete the PivotItem object
        If nResult = vbYes Then .Delete
    End With
End Sub
```

Exclude Items from a Page Field

You can configure your PivotTable to hide multiple page field items and thus display a subset of the pages in your PivotTable results.

In a default PivotTable that includes a page field, Excel displays the results for all items in the page field. In Chapter 4, you learned how to display the results for a single page; see the task "Display a Different Page." However, there may be times when you need to display the results for more than one page, although not all the pages. For example, you may know that the results from one or more pages are incomplete or inaccurate, and so should not be included in the report. Alternatively, your data analysis may require that you view the PivotTable results for only a subset of pages.

For these and similar situations, Excel enables you to customize the page field to exclude one or more items. Excel then redisplays the PivotTable without showing those items or including their results in the PivotTable totals. However, it is possible to include the results of hidden page fields in your PivotTable totals. In Chapter 7, see the task "Include Hidden Pages in PivotTable Results."

Exclude Items from a Page Field

1. Click the page field button.

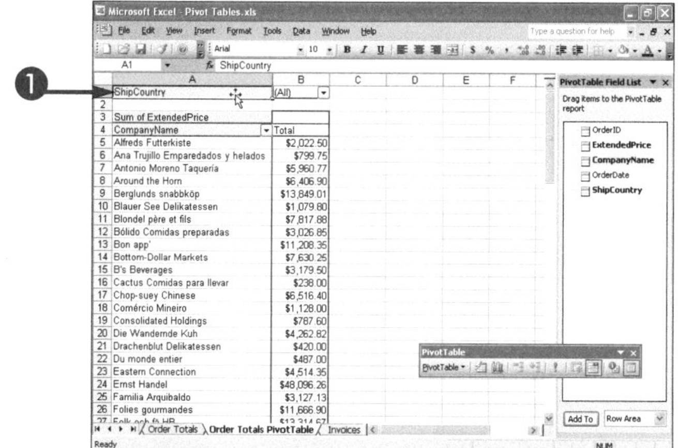

2. Click PivotTable→Field Settings.

You can also double-click the field button or click the Field Settings button ( ).

The PivotTable Field dialog box appears.

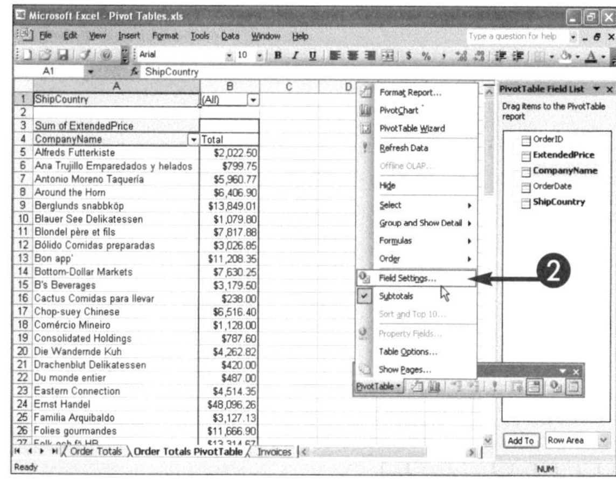

3. Click each item that you want to exclude from the PivotTable results.

4. Click OK.

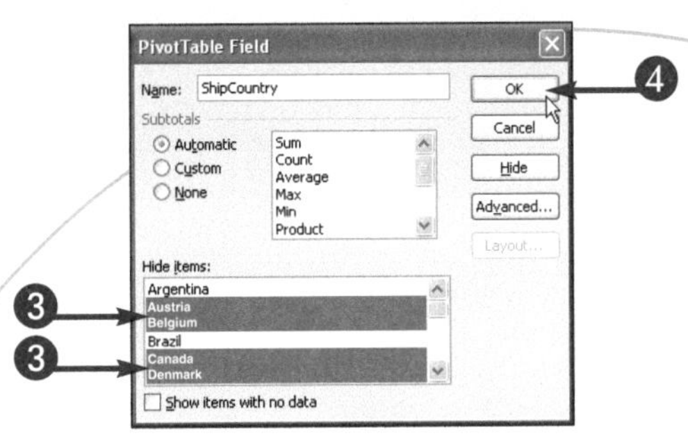

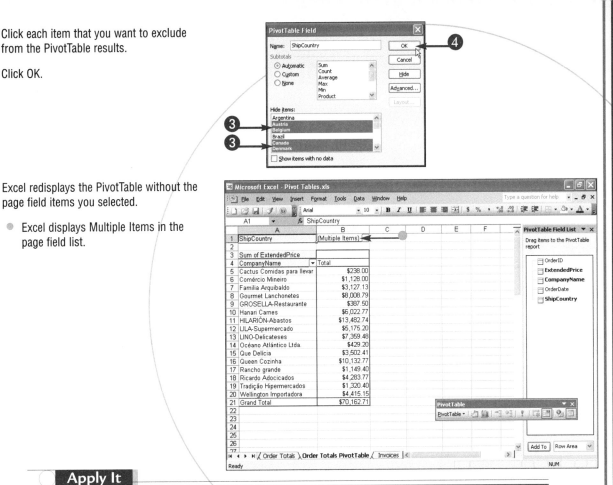

- Excel redisplays the PivotTable without the page field items you selected.

  - Excel displays Multiple Items in the page field list.

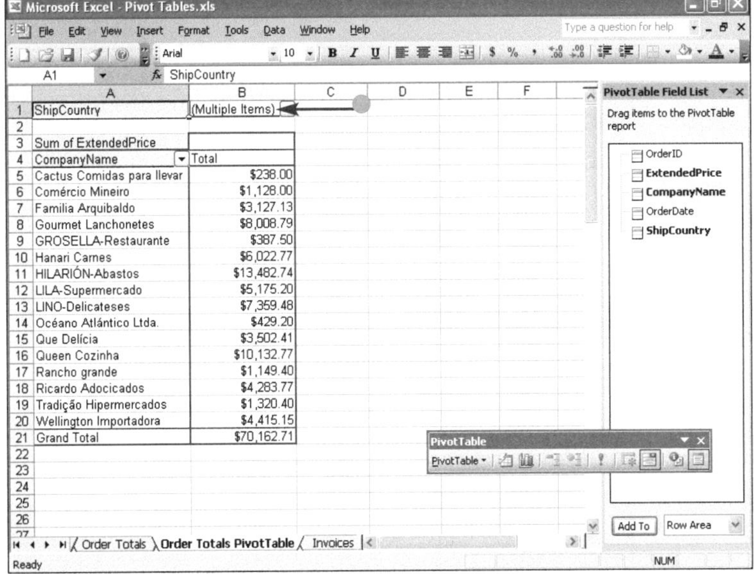

Apply It

Excel does not offer an easy way to add hidden page items back into the page field list. You need to open the PivotTable Field dialog box again and click each item that you hid earlier. To make this chore easier, you can include all page field items via VBA by setting the `Visible` property of each page field `PivotItem` object to `True`, as shown in the following macro:

Example:

```
Sub ShowAllPageFieldItems()
    Dim objPT As PivotTable
    Dim objPageField As PivotField
    Dim objPageItem As PivotItem
    '
    ' Work with the first PivotTable on the active worksheet
    Set objPT = ActiveSheet.PivotTables(1)
    '
    ' Work with the first page field
    Set objPageField = objPT.PageFields(1)
    '
    ' Run through all the page field items
    For Each objPageItem In objPageField.PivotItems
        '
        ' Display the item
        objPageItem.Visible = True
    Next 'objPageItem
End Sub
```

Apply an AutoFormat

In the Chapter 5 task "Format a PivotTable Cell," you learned how to apply formatting options such as alignments and fonts to portions of a PivotTable. This works well, particularly if you have custom formatting needs. For example, you may have in-house style guidelines that you need to follow. Unfortunately, applying formatting can be time-consuming, particularly if you are applying a number of different formatting options. And the total formatting time can become onerous if you need to apply different formatting options to different parts of the PivotTable. You can greatly reduce the time you spend formatting your PivotTables if you instead apply an AutoFormat.

An AutoFormat is a collection of formatting options — alignments, fonts, borders, and patterns — that Excel defines for different areas of a PivotTable. For example, an AutoFormat might use bold, black text on a yellow background for items, italics for grand totals and subtotals, and alternating white and gray backgrounds for columns. Defining all these formats by hand might take a half an hour to an hour. But with the AutoFormat feature, you choose the one you want to use for the PivotTable as a whole, and Excel applies the individual formatting options automatically.

Excel defines 22 AutoFormats, including PivotTable Classic, the default formatting applied to reports you create using the PivotTable Wizard, and None, which removes all formatting from the PivotTable. The other AutoFormats are named Report 1 through Report 10 and Table 1 through Table 8. Bear in mind that some AutoFormats change the layout of the PivotTable. For example, any of the "Report" AutoFormats will move the column field to the row area as the outer field. Similarly, any of the "Table" AutoFormats will move the row area's outer field to the column area.

Apply an AutoFormat

Note: This chapter uses the PivotTables.xls spreadsheet, available at www.wiley.com/go/pivottablesvb, or you can create your own sample database.

1. Click any cell within the PivotTable you want to format.

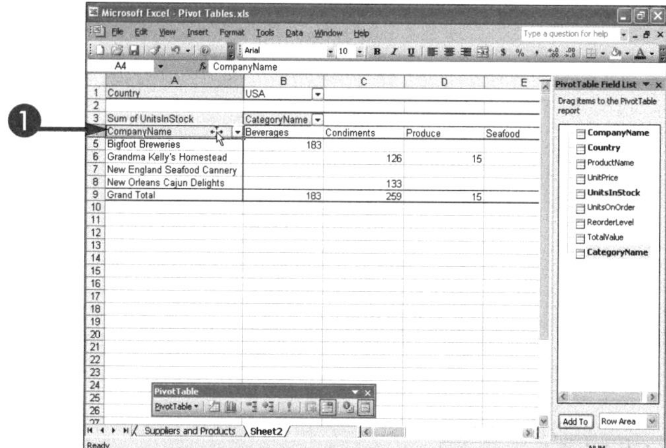

2. Click PivotTable→Format Report.

- You can also click the Format Report button in the PivotTable toolbar.

The AutoFormat dialog box appears.

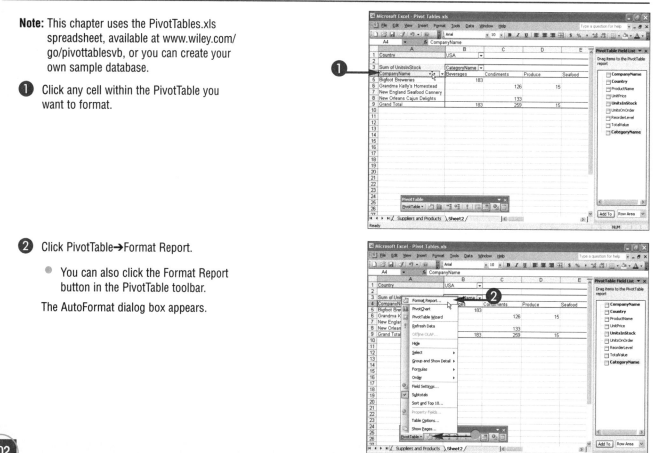

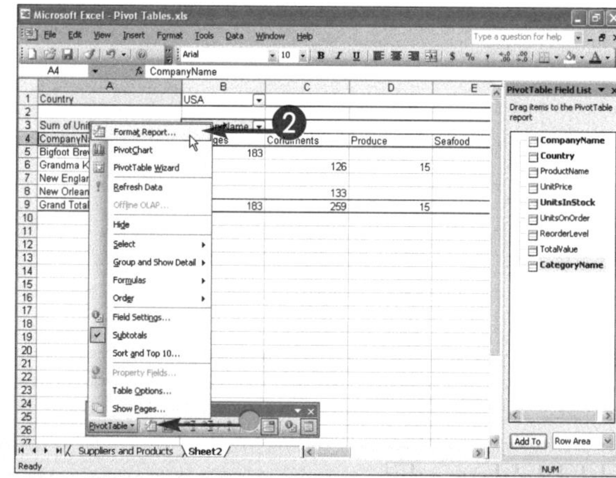

3 Click the AutoFormat you want to apply.

4 Click OK.

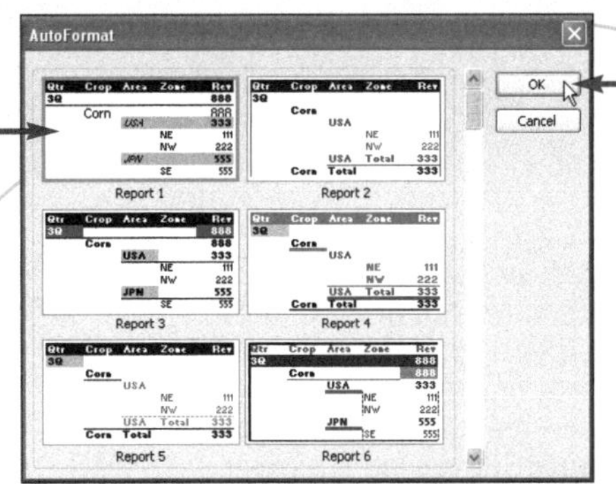

Excel applies the AutoFormat.

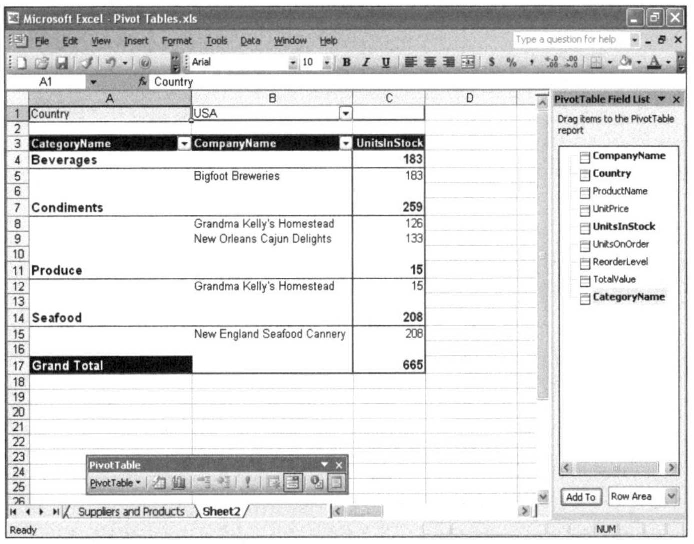

Apply It

You can use VBA to set your favorite AutoFormat. Each `PivotTable` object has a `Format` property that you can set to a constant value that corresponds to the AutoFormat you want to apply. The constants are `xlReport1` through `xlReport10`, `xlTable1` through `xlTable8`, `xlPTClassic`, and `xlPTNone`. Here is a macro that applies the Report 1 AutoFormat:

Example:

```
Sub ApplyAutoFormat()
    '
    ' Apply Report 1 AutoFormat to first PivotTable on active worksheet
    ActiveSheet.PivotTables(1).Format xlReport1
End Sub
```

Here is another macro that applies the PivotTable Classic AutoFormat:

Example:

```
Sub ApplyClassicAutoFormat()
    '
    ' Apply Classic AutoFormat to first PivotTable on active worksheet
    ActiveSheet.PivotTables(1).Format xlPTClassic
End Sub
```

Preserve PivotTable Formatting

You may find that Excel does not preserve your custom formatting when you refresh or rebuild the PivotTable. For example, if you applied a bold font to some labels, that text may revert to regular text after a refresh. Excel has a feature called Preserve Formatting that enables you to preserve such formatting during a refresh, so you can retain your custom formatting by activating this feature.

The Preserve Formatting feature is always activated in default PivotTables. However, it is possible that another user can deactivate this feature. For example, you may be working with a PivotTable created by another person and he or she deactivated the Preserve Formatting feature.

Note, however, that when you refresh or rebuild a PivotTable, Excel reapplies the report's current AutoFormat. If you have not specified an AutoFormat, Excel reapplies the default PivotTable Classic AutoFormat; if you have specified an AutoFormat — as described in the previous task, "Apply an AutoFormat" — Excel reapplies that AutoFormat.

Also, Excel always preserves your numeric formats and date formats. In Chapter 5, see the tasks "Apply a Numeric Format to PivotTable Data" and "Apply a Date Format to PivotTable Data."

Preserve PivotTable Formatting

1. Click any cell within the PivotTable you want to work with.

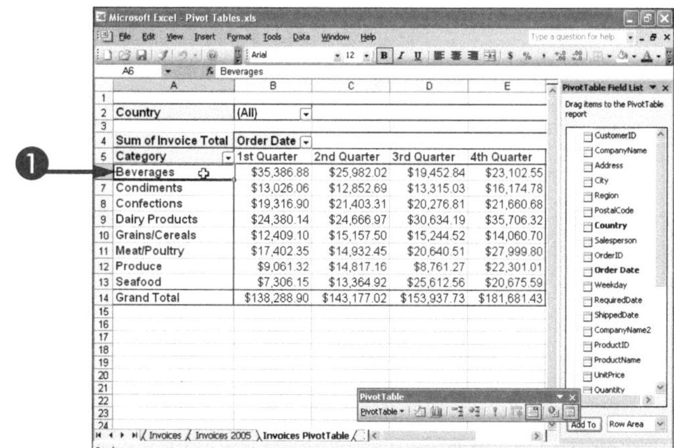

2. Click PivotTable→Table Options.

   You can also right-click any PivotTable cell and then click Table Options.

   The PivotTable Options dialog box appears.

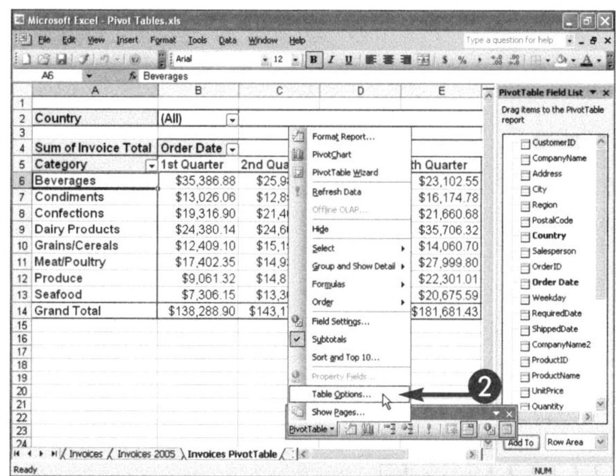

❸ Select Preserve formatting.

❹ Deselect AutoFormat table.

Note: Deselecting this check box prevents Excel from automatically formatting things such as column widths when you pivot fields.

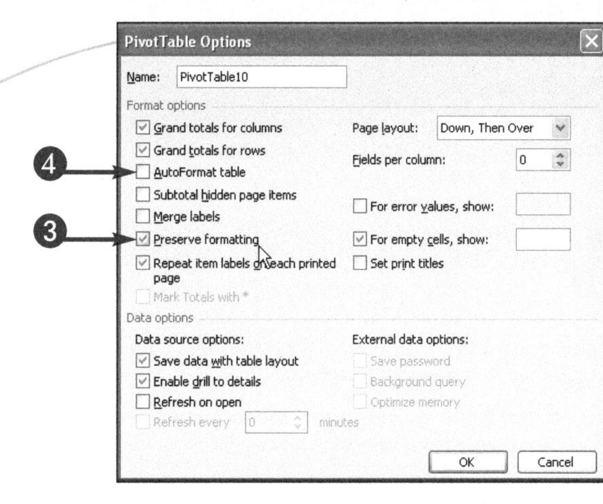

❺ Click OK.

Excel preserves your custom formatting each time you refresh the PivotTable.

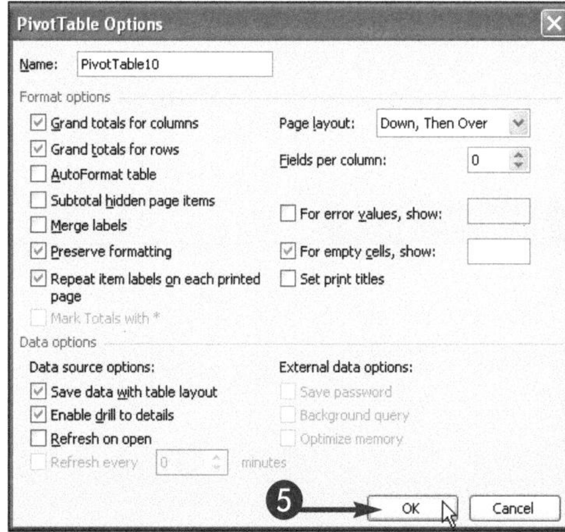

Apply It

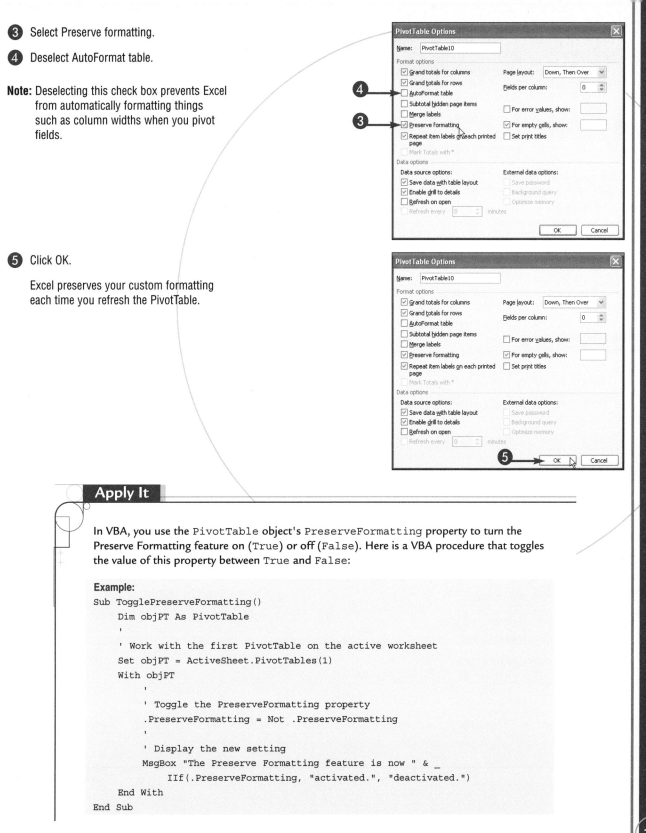

In VBA, you use the `PivotTable` object's `PreserveFormatting` property to turn the Preserve Formatting feature on (`True`) or off (`False`). Here is a VBA procedure that toggles the value of this property between `True` and `False`:

Example:

```
Sub TogglePreserveFormatting()
    Dim objPT As PivotTable
    '
    ' Work with the first PivotTable on the active worksheet
    Set objPT = ActiveSheet.PivotTables(1)
    With objPT
        '
        ' Toggle the PreserveFormatting property
        .PreserveFormatting = Not .PreserveFormatting
        '
        ' Display the new setting
        MsgBox "The Preserve Formatting feature is now " & _
            IIf(.PreserveFormatting, "activated.", "deactivated.")
    End With
End Sub
```

Rename the PivotTable

When you create the first PivotTable in a workbook, Excel gives it the default name PivotTable1. Subsequent PivotTables are named sequentially: PivotTable2, PivotTable3, and so on. If your workbook contains a number of PivotTables, you can make them easier to distinguish by giving each one a unique and descriptive name.

Why do you need to provide your PivotTables with descriptive names? The main benefit occurs after you have built a PivotTable based on a particular data source. If you then attempt to build a second PivotTable based on the same data source, Excel displays a dialog box that tells you the new report will use less memory if you base it on the first PivotTable instead of the data source itself. Recall that each PivotTable maintains a pivot cache, which is a snapshot of the data source, so your new PivotTable can share this pivot cache and your workbook will be much smaller.

However, if you elect to base your new PivotTable on an existing report, Excel asks you which report you want to use and it displays a list of the PivotTable names in the open workbooks. Excel always selects the report that it thinks you should use, but it is difficult to tell if that is the correct one if all the PivotTables use generic names such as PivotTable1 and PivotTable2. If, instead, you provide your PivotTables with descriptive names, you can easily tell them apart and select the correct report upon which to base your new PivotTable.

Rename the PivotTable

1. Click any cell within the PivotTable you want to work with.

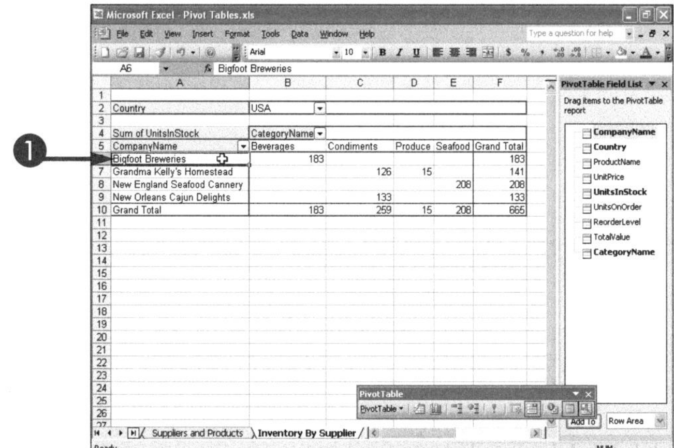

2. Click PivotTable➔Table Options.

You can also right-click any PivotTable cell and then click Table Options.

The PivotTable Options dialog box appears.

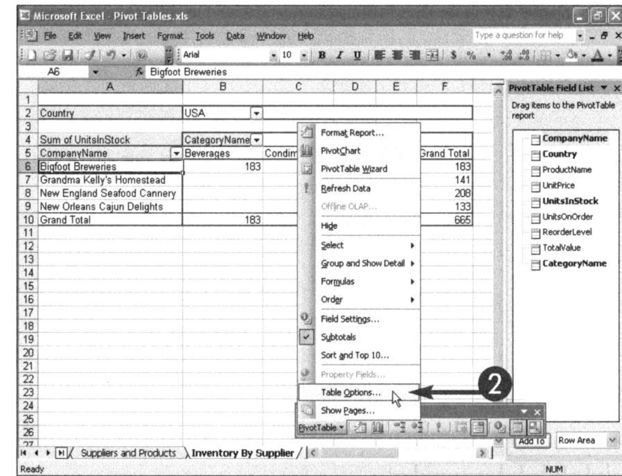

3. Type the new name for the PivotTable.

Note: The maximum length for a PivotTable name is 255 characters.

4. Click OK.

Excel renames the PivotTable.

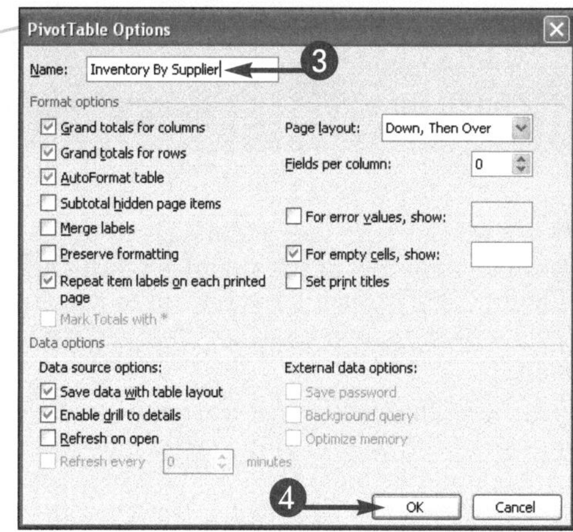

Apply It

If you use VBA to manipulate PivotTables, using unique names to reference PivotTable objects can make your code easier to read. For example, to reference a PivotTable named "Budget Summary" that exists in a worksheet named "Sheet1," you use the following statement:

```
Worksheets("Sheet1).PivotTables("Budget Summary")
```

What happens, however, if your workbook contains a large number of PivotTables? Rather than renaming each one by hand, you could use the following macro to rename each one automatically using the worksheet name:

```
Sub RenameAllPivotTables()
    Dim objWS As Worksheet
    Dim objPT As PivotTable
    Dim i As Integer
    '
    ' Run through all the worksheets
    For Each objWS In ThisWorkbook.Worksheets
        i = 1
        '
        ' Run through all the PivotTables
        For Each objPT In objWS.PivotTables
            '
            ' Rename it to the sheet name plus the value of i
            objPT.Name = objWS.Name & " " & i
            i = i + 1
        Next 'objPT
    Next 'objWS
End Sub
```

Turn Off Grand Totals

You can configure your PivotTable to not display the Grand Total row or the Grand Total column (or both). This is useful if you want to save space in the PivotTable or if the grand totals are not relevant in your data analysis.

A default PivotTable that has at least one row field contains an extra row at the bottom of the table. This row is labeled Grand Total and it includes the total of the values associated with the row field items. However, the value in the Grand Total row may not actually be a sum. For example, if the summary calculation is Average, then the Grand Total row includes the average of the values associated with the row field items. To learn how to use a different summary calculation, see the Chapter 7 task "Change the PivotTable Summary Calculation."

Similarly, a PivotTable that has at least one column field contains an extra column at the far right of the table. This column is also labeled "Grand Total" and it includes the total of the values associated with the column field items. If the PivotTable contains both a row and a column field, the Grand Total row also has the sums for each column item, and the Grand Total column also has the sums for each row item.

Besides taking up space in the PivotTable, these grand totals are often not necessary for data analysis. For example, suppose you want to examine quarterly sales for your salespeople to see which amounts were over a certain value for bonus purposes. Because your only concern is the individual summary values for each employee, the grand totals are useless. In such a case, you can tell Excel not to display the grand totals.

Turn Off Grand Totals

1. Click any cell within the PivotTable you want to work with.

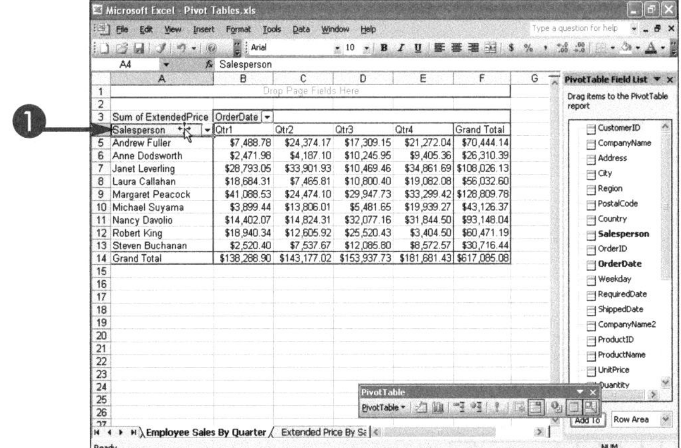

2. Click PivotTable→Table Options.

   You can also right-click any PivotTable cell and then click Table Options.

   The PivotTable Options dialog box appears.

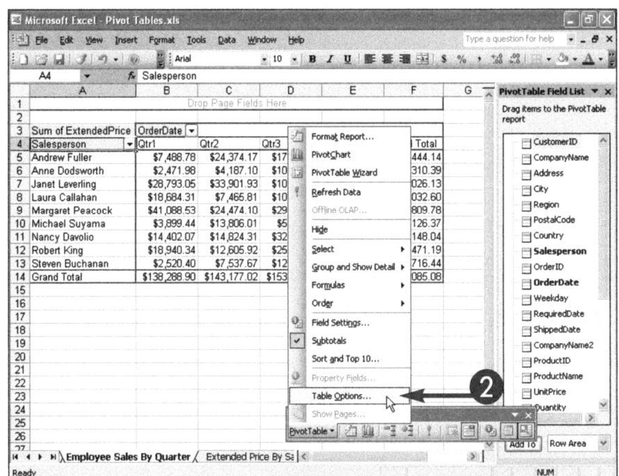

3. Deselect this check box to turn off the column grand totals.
4. Deselect this check box to turn off the row grand totals.
5. Click OK.

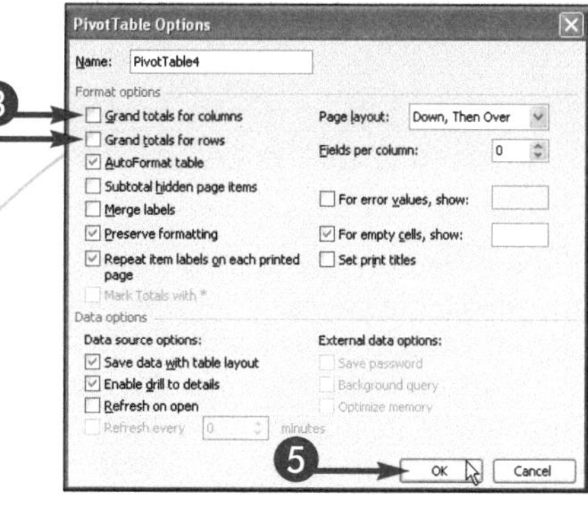

Excel displays the PivotTable without the grand totals.

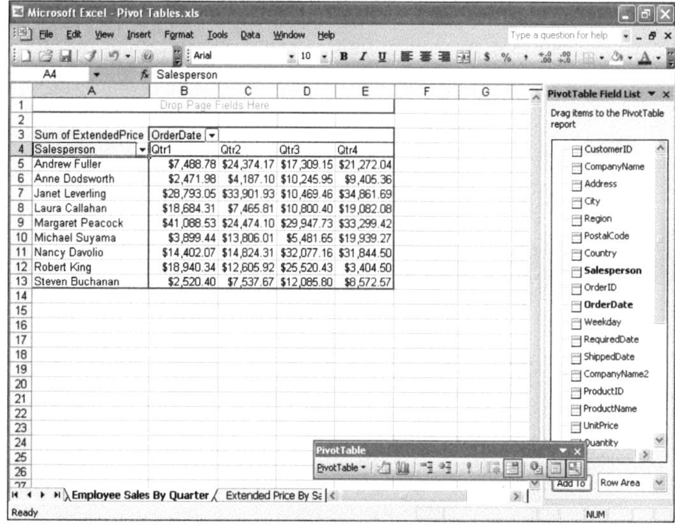

Apply It

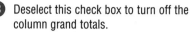

You can work with grand totals via VBA using the `PivotTable` object's `ColumnGrand` and `RowGrand` properties, which are Boolean values that hide (`False`) and display (`True`) the grand totals. The following macro toggles these properties on and off:

Example:

```
Sub ToggleGrandTotals()
    Dim objPT As PivotTable
    '
    ' Work with the first PivotTable on the active worksheet
    Set objPT = ActiveSheet.PivotTables(1)
    With objPT
        '
        ' Toggle the ColumnGrand and RowGrand properties
        .ColumnGrand = Not .ColumnGrand
        .RowGrand = Not .RowGrand
        '
        ' Display the new setting
        MsgBox "The grand totals are now " & _
            IIf(.ColumnGrand, "displayed.", "hidden.")
    End With
End Sub
```

Merge Item Labels

If you have a PivotTable with multiple fields either in the row area or the column area, you can make the outer field easier to read by merging the cells associated with each of the field's item labels.

When you configure a PivotTable with two fields in the row area, Excel displays the outer field on the left and the inner field on the right. For each item in the outer field, Excel displays the item label in the left column, and then the associated inner field items in the right column. If the inner field has two or more associated items, then there will be one or more blank cells below the outer field item. This makes the PivotTable report less attractive and harder to read because the outer field items appear just below the subtotals.

A similar problem occurs when you have multiple fields in the column area. In this case, you can end up with one or more blank cells to the right of each outer field item.

To fix these problems, you can activate a PivotTable option that tells Excel to merge the cells associated with each outer field item. Excel then displays the item label in the middle of these merged cells, which makes the PivotTable report more attractive and easier to read.

Merge Item Labels

1. Click any cell within the PivotTable you want to work with.

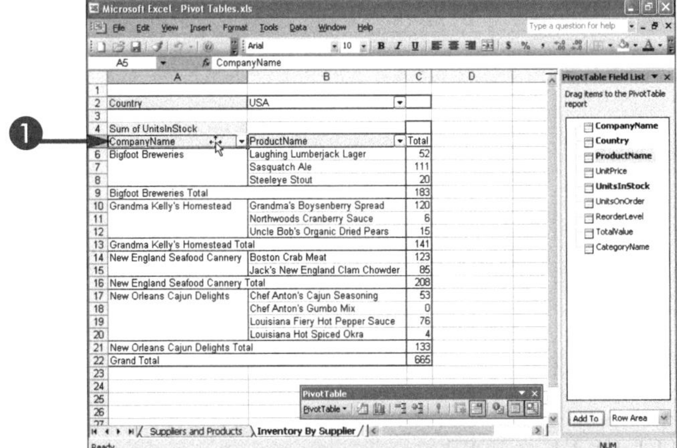

2. Click PivotTable→Table Options.

   You can also right-click any PivotTable cell and then click Table Options.

   The PivotTable Options dialog box appears.

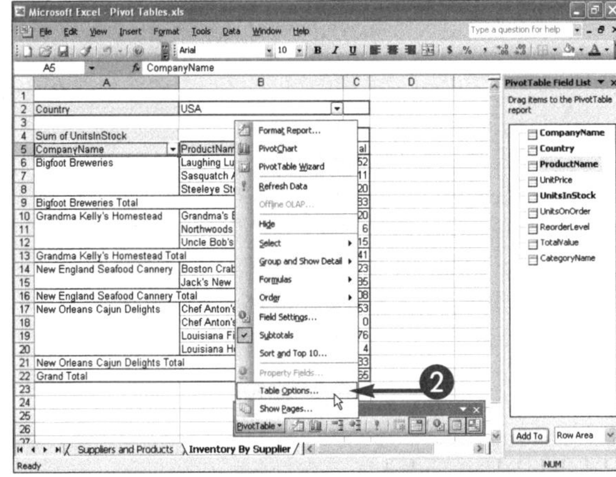

3. Select Merge labels.
4. Click OK.

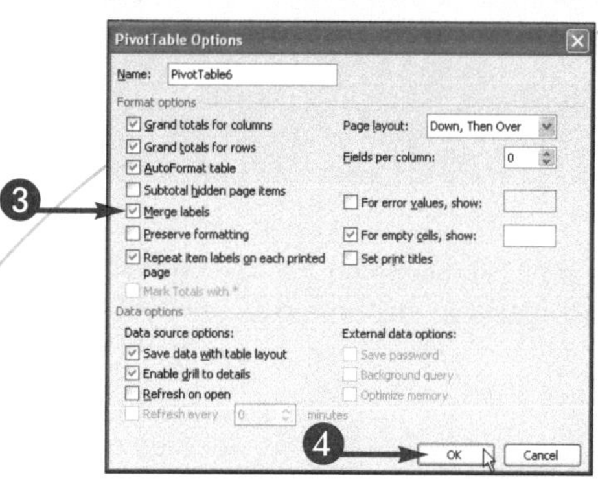

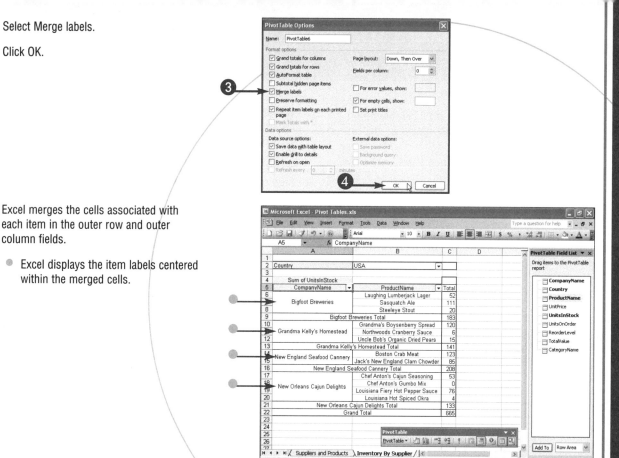

Excel merges the cells associated with each item in the outer row and outer column fields.

- Excel displays the item labels centered within the merged cells.

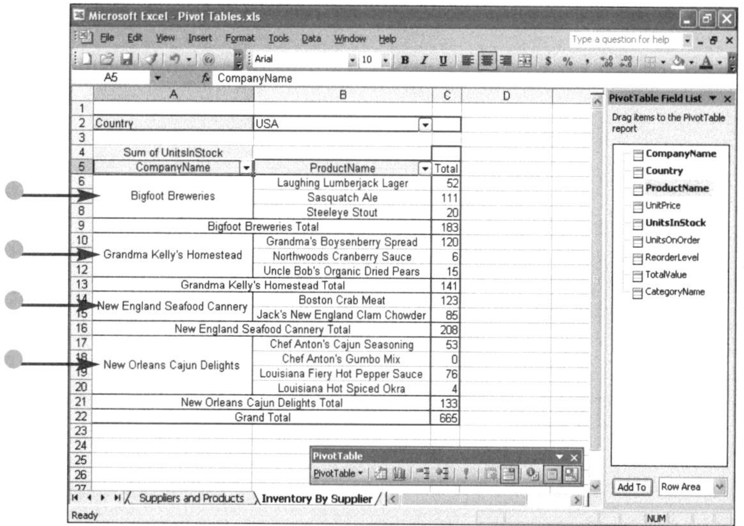

Apply It

In VBA you use the `PivotTable` object's `MergeLabels` property to turn the Merge Labels feature on (`True`) or off (`False`). Here is a VBA procedure that toggles the value of this property between `True` and `False`:

Example:

```
Sub ToggleMergeLabels()
    Dim objPT As PivotTable
    '
    ' Work with the first PivotTable on the active worksheet
    Set objPT = ActiveSheet.PivotTables(1)
    With objPT
        '
        ' Toggle the MergeLabels property
        .MergeLabels = Not .MergeLabels
        '
        ' Display the new setting
        MsgBox "The Merge Labels feature is now " & _
            IIf(.MergeLabels, "activated.", "deactivated.")
    End With
End Sub
```

Specify Characters for Errors and Empty Cells

You can improve the look of a PivotTable report by specifying alternative text to appear in place of error values and blank cells.

Excel has seven different error values: `#DIV/0!`, `#N/A`, `#NAME?`, `#NULL!`, `#NUM!`, `#REF!`, and `#VALUE!`. These errors are almost always the result of improperly constructed formulas, and because a basic PivotTable has no formulas, you rarely see error values in PivotTable results. There are two exceptions, however. First, if the source data field you are using for the PivotTable summary calculation contains an error value, then Excel reproduces that error value within the PivotTable results. Second, you can add a custom calculated field to the PivotTable, and that field's values will be based on a formula. For the details about calculated fields, see Chapter 8. If that formula generates an error, Excel displays the corresponding error value in the PivotTable results. For example, if your formula divides by 0, the `#DIV/0!` error appears. Seeing these errors is usually a good thing because it alerts you to problems in the data or the report. However, if the error is caused by something temporary, then you may prefer to hide any errors by displaying a blank or some other text, instead.

A related PivotTable concern is what to do with data area cells where the calculation results in a 0 value. By default, Excel displays nothing in the cell. This can make the report slightly easier to read, but it may also cause confusion for readers of the report. In an inventory PivotTable, for example, does an empty cell mean that the product has no stock or that it was not counted? To avoid this problem, you can specify that Excel display the number 0 or some other text instead of an empty cell.

Specify Characters for Errors and Empty Cells

1. Click any cell within the PivotTable you want to work with.
2. Click PivotTable➔Table Options.

   You can also right-click any PivotTable cell and then click Table Options.

   The PivotTable Options dialog box appears.

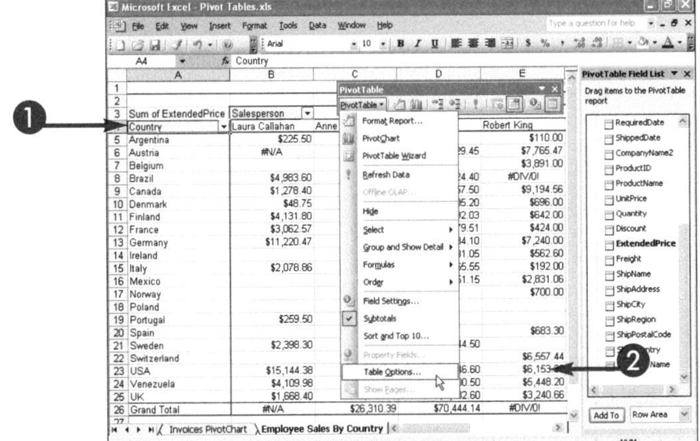

3. Select For error values, show.
4. Type the text you want Excel to show instead of errors.
5. Select For empty cells, show.
6. Type the text you want Excel to display in empty cells.
7. Click OK.

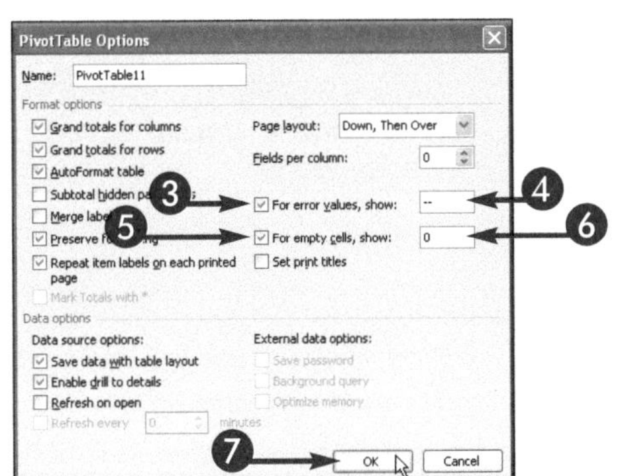

- Excel replaces the PivotTable's errors with the text you specified.
- Excel replaces the PivotTable's empty cells with the text you specified.

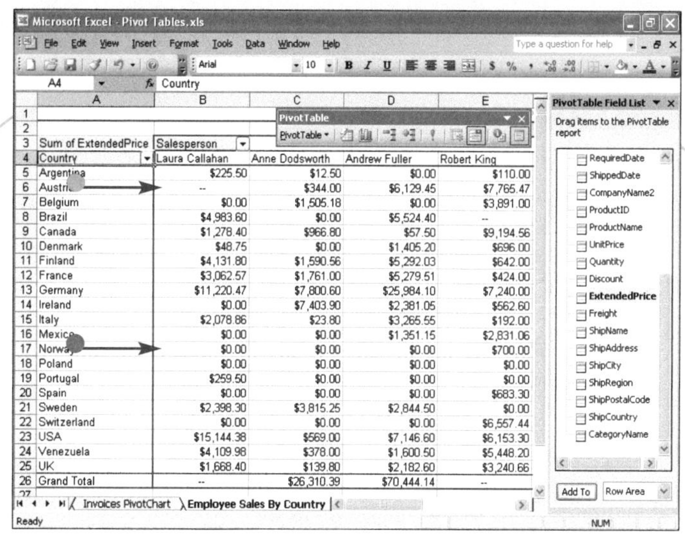

Apply It

In VBA you use the `PivotTable` object's `ErrorString` property to set the text to replace error values, and you use the `DisplayErrorString` property to turn this feature on and off. Also, you use the `PivotTable` object's `NullString` property to set the text to use in empty cells, and you use the `DisplayNullString` property to turn this feature on and off. Here is an example macro that uses these properties:

```
Sub SetTextForErrorsAndEmptyCells()
    Dim objPT As PivotTable
    '
    ' Work with the first PivotTable
    Set objPT = ActiveSheet.PivotTables(1)
    With objPT
        '
        ' Set ErrorString and activate it
        .ErrorString = "@@hy@@hy"
        .DisplayErrorString = True
        '
        ' Set NullString and activate it
        .NullString = "0"
        .DisplayNullString = True
        '
        ' Display the new settings
        MsgBox "The ErrorString text is" & _
         "now """ & .ErrorString & """" & _
         vbCrLf & _
         "The NullString text is " & _
         "now """ & .NullString & """"
    End With
End Sub
```

Protect a PivotTable

If you have a PivotTable that you will share with other people, but you do not want those people to make any changes to the report, you can activate protection for the worksheet that contains the PivotTable. This prevents unauthorized users from changing the PivotTable results.

If you have put a lot of work into the layout and formatting of a PivotTable, you most likely want to avoid having any of your work undone if you allow other people to open the PivotTable workbook. The easiest way to do this is to enable Excel's worksheet protection feature. When this feature is activated for a worksheet that contains a PivotTable, no user can modify any cells in the PivotTable. If needed, you can also apply a password to the protection, so that only authorized users can make changes to the worksheet.

Excel's default protection options affect PivotTables in two ways:

- Unauthorized users cannot edit or format PivotTable cells. However, it is possible to configure the protection to allow editing of particular cells, such as the labels of a PivotTable report. See the tip on the next page to learn how to configure protection to allow this.
- Unauthorized users cannot add, remove, pivot, filter, or group the PivotTable. However, it is possible to configure the protection to allow users to perform these PivotTable actions.

Protect a PivotTable

1. Display the worksheet that contains the PivotTable you want to protect.
2. Click Tools➔Protection➔Protect Sheet.

   The Protect Sheet dialog box appears.

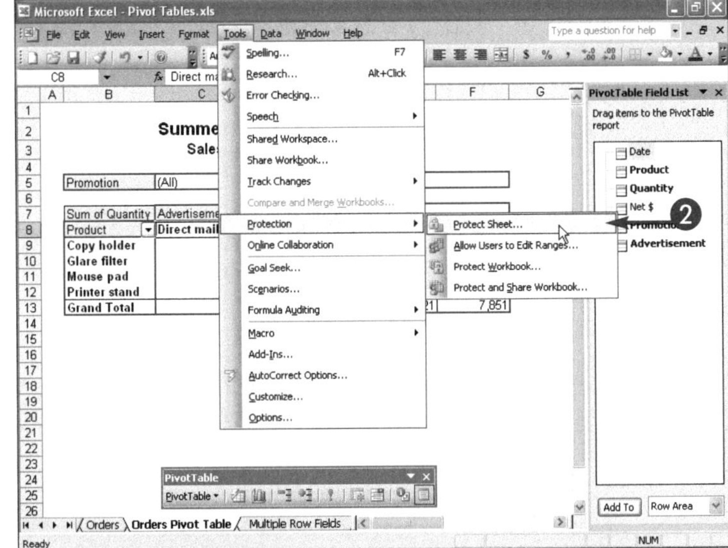

3. Select Protect worksheet and contents of locked cells.
4. Type a password that user must enter to unprotect the worksheet.

Note: Protecting the worksheet with a password is optional. However, without a password, it is very easy for a user to unprotect the worksheet.

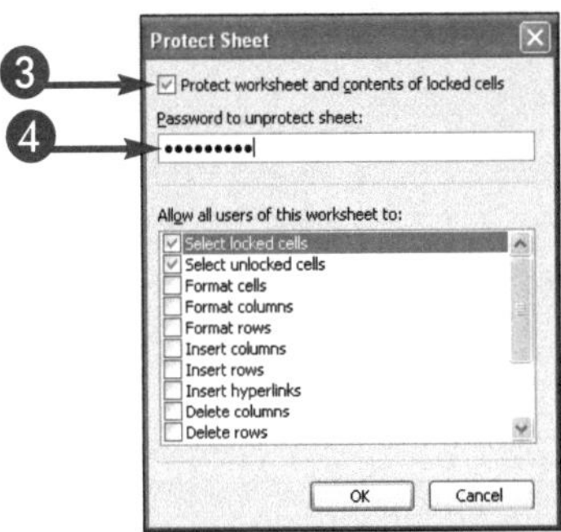

5. Select Use PivotTable reports.
6. Click OK.

   If you specified a password in Step 4, Excel asks you to confirm the password.

7. Retype the password.
8. Click OK.

   Excel protects the worksheet.

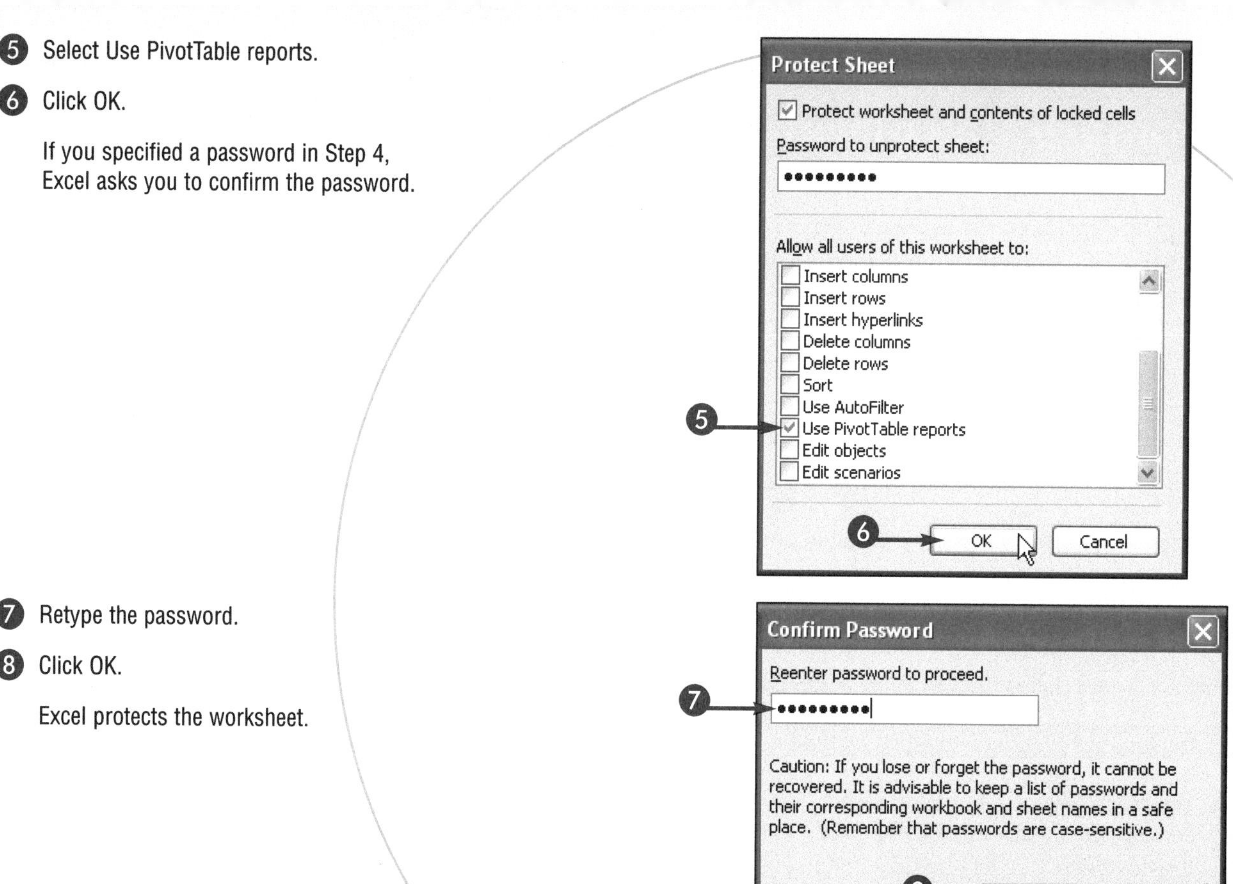

Extra

When you protect a worksheet, you may be willing to let users modify certain cells on the worksheet. In a PivotTable, for example, you may want to allow users to rename the PivotTable fields or items. You can set this up by unlocking those cells before you activate worksheet protection. Begin by selecting the cells that you will allow users to edit. Then click Format➔Cells to display the Format Cells dialog box. Click the Protection tab, deselect Locked (☑ changes to ☐), and then click OK.

When you want to make changes to a PivotTable on a protected worksheet, you must first unprotect the worksheet. Display the protected worksheet and then click Tools➔Protection➔Unprotect Sheet. If you protected the worksheet with a password, Excel displays a dialog box that asks you for the password. Type the password and then click OK. Excel unprotects the worksheet.

Change the PivotTable Summary Calculation

If you add a numeric field to the data area, Excel uses Sum as the default summary calculation. If, instead, you use a text field in the data area, Excel uses Count as the default summary calculation. If your data analysis requires a different calculation, you can configure the data field to use any one of Excel's 11 built-in summary calculations:

- **Sum** — Adds the values in a numeric field.
- **Count** — Displays the total number of cells in the source field.
- **Average** — Calculates the mean value in a numeric field.
- **Max** — Displays the largest value in a numeric field.
- **Min** — Displays the smallest value in a numeric field.
- **Product** — Multiplies the values in a numeric field.
- **Count Nums** — Displays the total number of numeric values in the source field.
- **StdDev** — Calculates the standard deviation of a population sample, which tells you how much the values in the source field vary with respect to the average.
- **StdDevp** — Calculates the standard deviation when the values in the data field represent the entire population.
- **Var** — Calculates the variance of a population sample; the variance is the square of the standard deviation.
- **Varp** — Calculates the variance when the values in the data field represent the entire population.

Change the PivotTable Summary Calculation

Note: This chapter uses the PivotTables.xls spreadsheet, available at www.wiley.com/go/pivottablesvb, or you can create your own sample database.

1. Click the data field button.

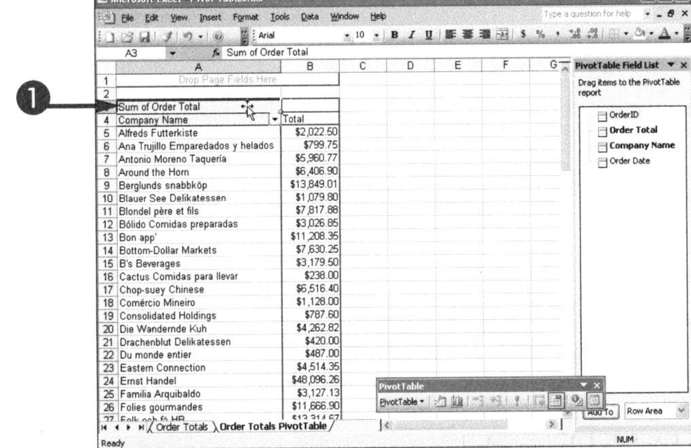

2. Click PivotTable→Field Settings.

You can also double-click the data field button or click the Field Settings button ( ).

The PivotTable Field dialog box appears.

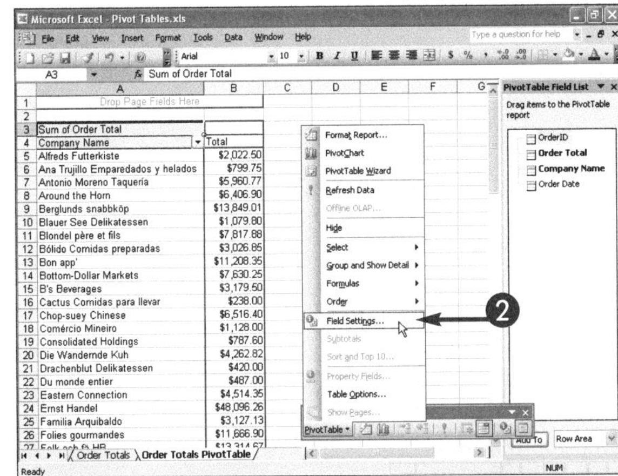

3 Click the summary calculation you want to use.

4 Click OK.

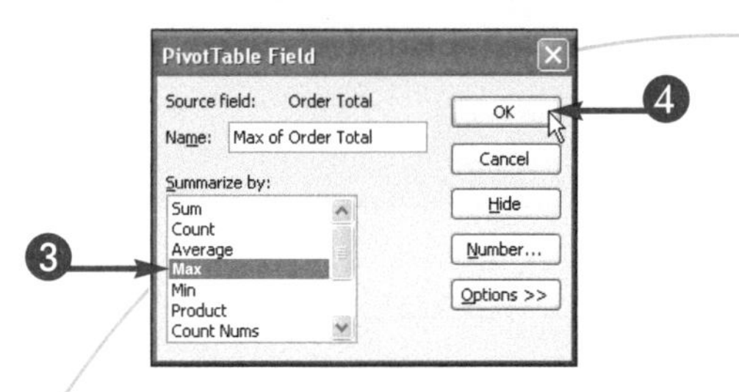

Excel recalculates the PivotTable results.

- Excel renames the data field button to reflect the new summary calculation.

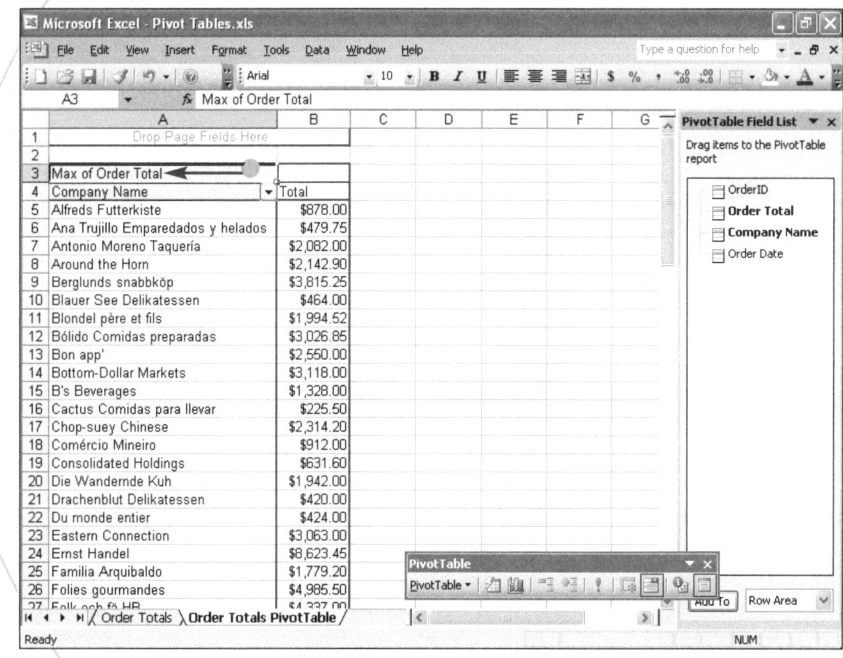

Extra

When you build your PivotTable, you may find that the results do not look correct. For example, the number may appear to be far too small. In that case, check the summary calculation that Excel has applied to the field to see if it is using Count instead of Sum. If the data field includes one or more text cells or one or more blank cells, Excel defaults to the Count summary function instead of Sum. If your field is supposed to be numeric, check the data to see if there are any text values or blank cells.

When you add a second field to the row or column area — see the Chapter 3 task "Add Multiple Fields to the Row or Column Area" — Excel displays a subtotal for each item in the outer field. By default, that subtotal shows the sum of the data results for each outer field item. However, the same 11 summary calculations — from Sum to Varp — are also available for subtotals.

To change the subtotal summary calculation for a row or column field, click the outer field button and then click PivotTable→Field Settings to display the PivotTable Field dialog box. Select Custom (○ changes to ◉), and then click the summary calculation you want to use for the subtotals. Click OK to put the new summary calculation into effect.

Create a Difference Summary Calculation

You can use Excel's difference calculations to compare the items in a numeric field and return the difference between them.

The built-in summary calculations — Sum, Count, Average, and so on — apply over an entire field. However, a major part of data analysis involves comparing one item with another. If you are analyzing sales to customers, for example, it is useful to know how much you sold this year, but it is even more useful to compare this year's sales with last year's. Are the sales up or down? By how much? Are the sales up or down with all customers or only some? These are fundamental questions that help managers run departments, divisions, and companies.

Excel offers two difference calculations that can help you perform this kind of analysis:

- **Difference From** — Compares one numeric item with another and returns the difference between them.
- **% Difference From** — Compares one numeric item with another and returns the percentage difference between them.

Before you set up a difference calculation, you need to decide which field in your PivotTable you will use as the comparison field — the *base field* — and which item within that field you will use as the basis for all the comparisons — the *base item*. For example, if you are comparing the sales in 2005 to the sales in 2004, the date field is the base field and 2004 is the base item.

Create a Difference Summary Calculation

1. Click the data field button.
2. Click PivotTable➔Field Settings.

   You can also double-click the data field button or click the Field Settings button ( ).

   The PivotTable Field dialog box appears.

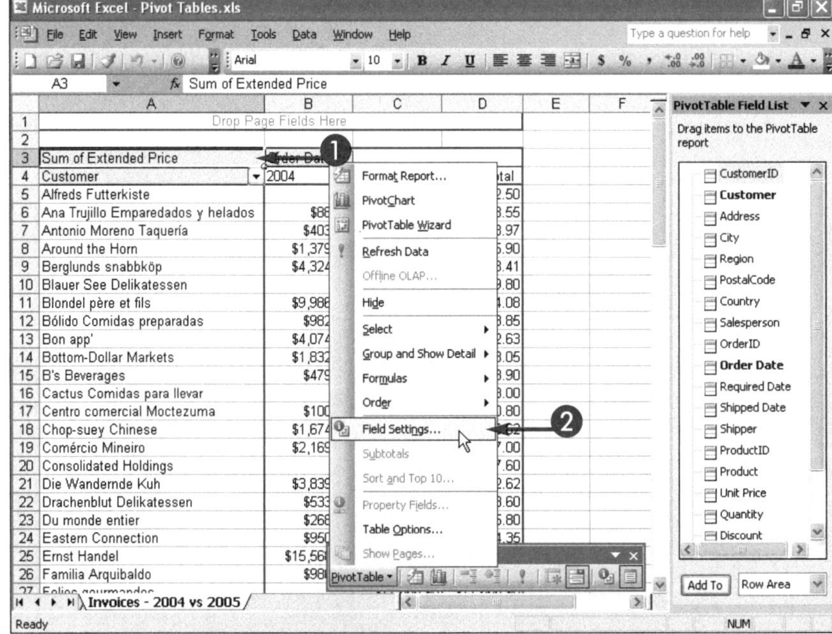

3. Click the summary calculation you want to use.
4. Click Options.

   Excel expands the dialog box.

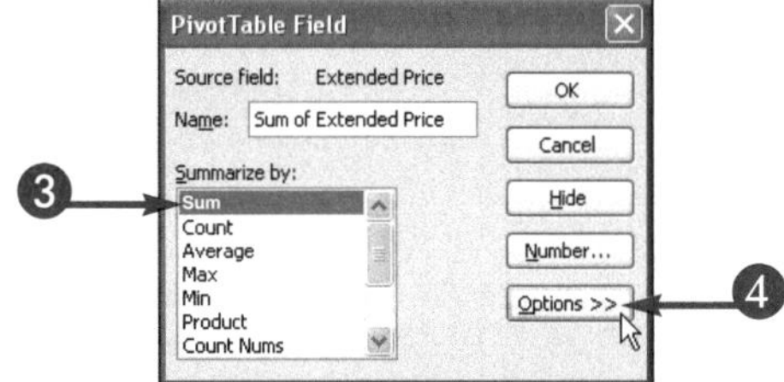

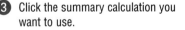

5. Click ▾ and then click Difference From.

   If you want to see the difference in percentage terms, click % Difference From, instead.

6. Click the field from which you want Excel to calculate the difference.

7. Click a Base item.

8. Click OK.

   Excel recalculates the PivotTable results.

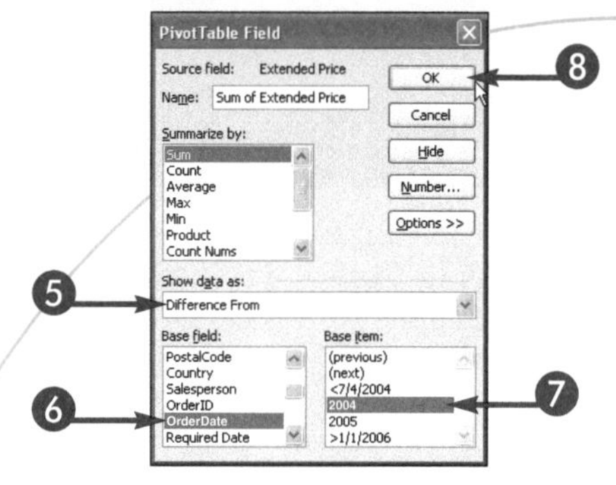

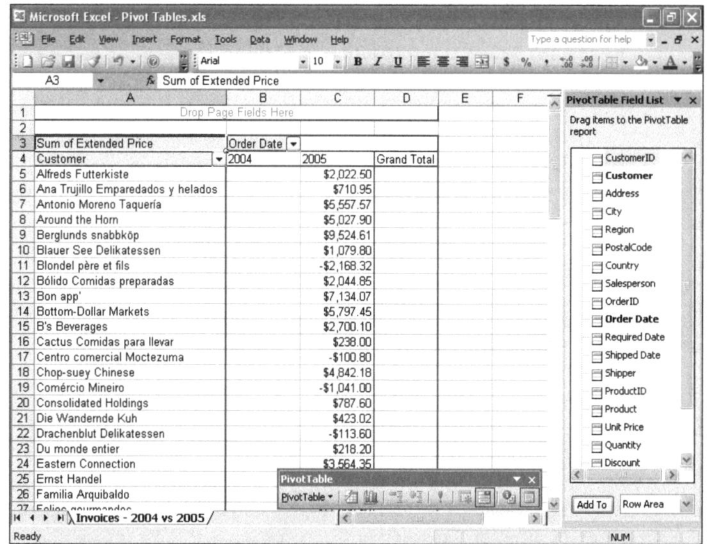

Apply It

It is sometimes handy to toggle between the Difference From and % Difference From calculations, and this is most easily handled with a macro. The following procedure uses the `PivotField` object's `Calculation` property to toggle the Sum of Extended Price field between the two calculations:

```
Sub ToggleDifferenceCalculations()
    Dim objPT As PivotTable, objDataField As PivotField
    ' Work with the first PivotTable
    Set objPT = ActiveSheet.PivotTables(1)
    ' Work with the Sum of Extended Price data field
    Set objDataField = objPT.PivotFields("Sum of Extended Price")
    ' Is the calculation currently Difference From?
    If objDataField.Calculation = xlDifferenceFrom Then
        ' If so, change it to % Difference From
        objDataField.Calculation = xlPercentDifferenceFrom
        objDataField.BaseField = "Order Date"
        objDataField.BaseItem = "2004"
        objDataField.NumberFormat = "0.00%"
    Else
        ' If not, change it to Difference From
        objDataField.Calculation = xlDifferenceFrom
        objDataField.BaseField = "Order Date"
        objDataField.BaseItem = "2004"
        objDataField.NumberFormat = "$#,##0.00"
    End If
End Sub
```

Create a Percentage Summary Calculation

You can use Excel's percentage calculations to view data items as a percentage of some other item or as a percentage of the total in the current row, column, or PivotTable.

Percentage calculations are useful data analysis tools because they enable you to make apples-to-apples comparisons between values. For example, suppose your PivotTable shows that sales to a particular customer increased by $25,000 this year. Is that good or bad? The answers depend on the total sales. If the sales last year were $25,000, then the increase is good; if the previous year's sales were $250,000, then the increase is not so good. To make this clear, you need to find out the percentage increase: a $25,000 increase on $25,000 sales is a rise of 100%, while the same increase on sales of $250,000 is only 10%.

Excel offers four percentage calculations that can help you perform this kind of analysis:

- **% Of** — Returns the percentage of each value with respect to a selected base item.
- **% of Row** — Returns the percentage that each value in a row represents of the total value of the row.
- **% of Column** — Returns the percentage that each value in a column represents of the total value of the column.
- **% of Total** — Returns the percentage that each value represents of the PivotTable grand total.

As with the difference calculations you learned about in the previous task, "Create a Difference Summary Calculation," if you use the % Of calculation, you must also choose a base field and a base item upon which Excel will calculate the percentages.

Create a Percentage Summary Calculation

1. Click the data field button.
2. Click PivotTable➔Field Settings.

   You can also double-click the data field button or click the Field Settings button ( ).

   The PivotTable Field dialog box appears.

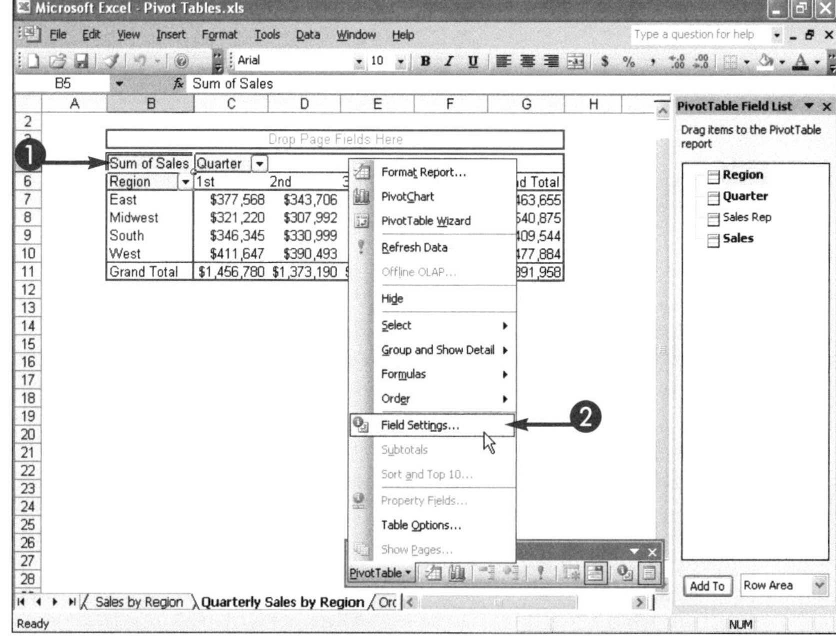

3. Click the summary calculation you want to use.
4. Click Options.

   Excel expands the dialog box.

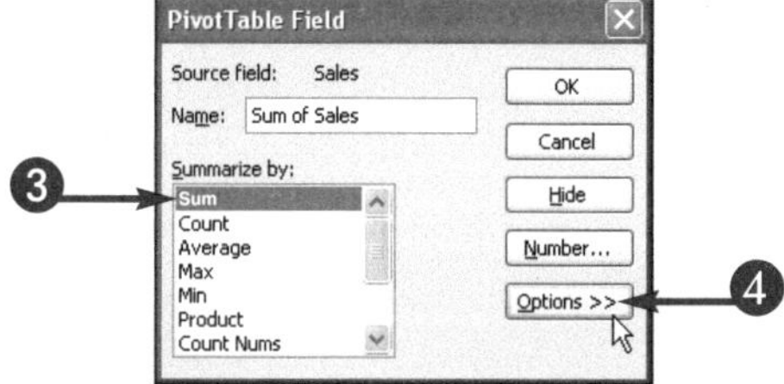

5. Click ▾ and then click the percentage calculation you want to use.
6. If you clicked % Of, click the field from which you want Excel to calculate the difference.
7. If you clicked % Of, click the Base item.
8. Click OK.

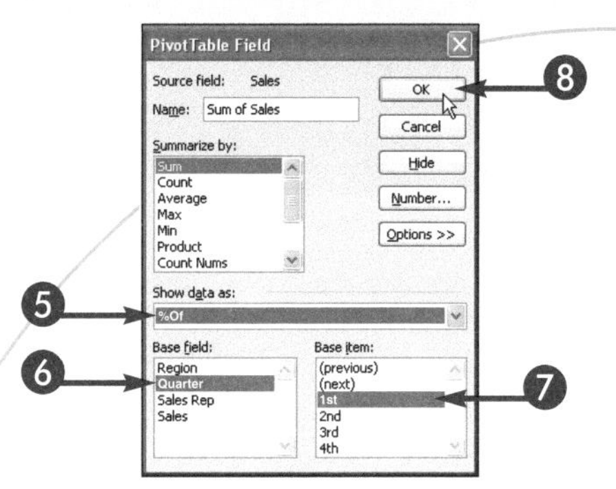

Excel recalculates the PivotTable results.

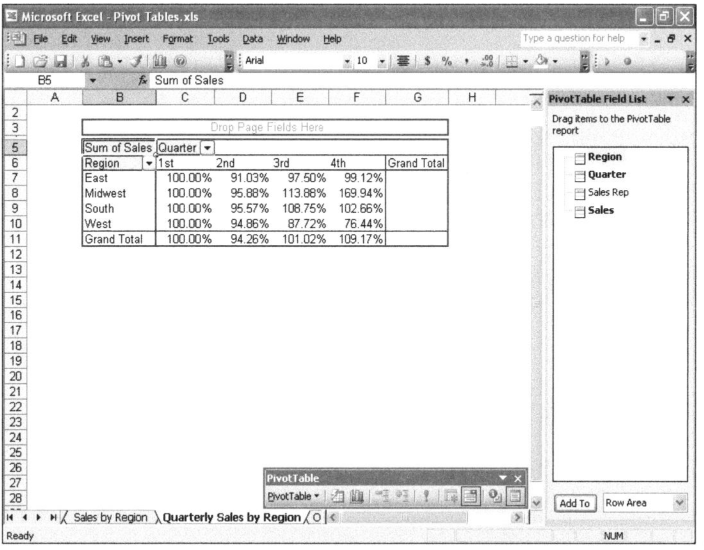

Apply It

If you want to use VBA to set the percentage calculation for a data field, set the `PivotField` object's `Calculation` property to one of the following constants: `xlPercentOf`, `xlPercentOfRow`, `xlPercentOfColumn`, or `xlPercentOfTotal`. Here is a macro that switches the Sum of Sales field between the % of Row and % of Column calculations:

```
Sub TogglePercentageCalculations()
    Dim objPT As PivotTable, objDataField As PivotField
    ' Work with the first PivotTable on the active worksheet
    Set objPT = ActiveSheet.PivotTables(1)
    With objPT
        ' Work with the Sum of Sales data field
        Set objDataField = .PivotFields("Sum of Sales")
        With objDataField
            ' Is the calculation currently % of Row?
            If .Calculation = xlPercentOfRow Then
                ' If so, change it to % of Column
                .Calculation = xlPercentOfColumn
            Else
                ' If not, change it to % of Row
                .Calculation = xlPercentOfRow
            End If
        End With
    End With
End Sub
```

Create a Running Total Summary Calculation

You can use Excel's Running Total calculation to view the PivotTable results as values that accumulate as they run through the items in a row or column field.

A *running total* is the cumulative sum of the values that appear in a given set of data. Most running totals accumulate over a period of time. For example, suppose you have 12 months of sales figures. In a running total calculation, the first value is the first month of sales, the second value is the sum of the first and second months, the third value is the sum of the first three months, and so on.

You use a running total in data analysis when you need to see a snapshot of the overall data at various points. For example, suppose you have a sales budget for each month. As the fiscal year progresses, comparing the running total of the budget figures with the running total of the actual sales tells you how your department or company is doing with respect to the budget. If sales are consistently below budget, you might consider lowering prices, offering customers extra discounts, or increasing your product advertising.

Excel offers a Running Total summary calculation that you can apply to your PivotTable results. Note, too, that the Running Total applies not just to the Sum calculation, but also to related calculations such as Count and Average. Before you configure your PivotTable to use a Running Total summary calculation, you must decide the field on which to base the accumulation, or the base field. This will most often be a date field, but you can also create running totals based on other fields, such as customer, division, product, and so on.

Create a Running Total Summary Calculation

1. Click the data field button.
2. Click PivotTable→Field Settings.

   You can also double-click the data field button or click the Field Settings button ( ).

   The PivotTable Field dialog box appears.

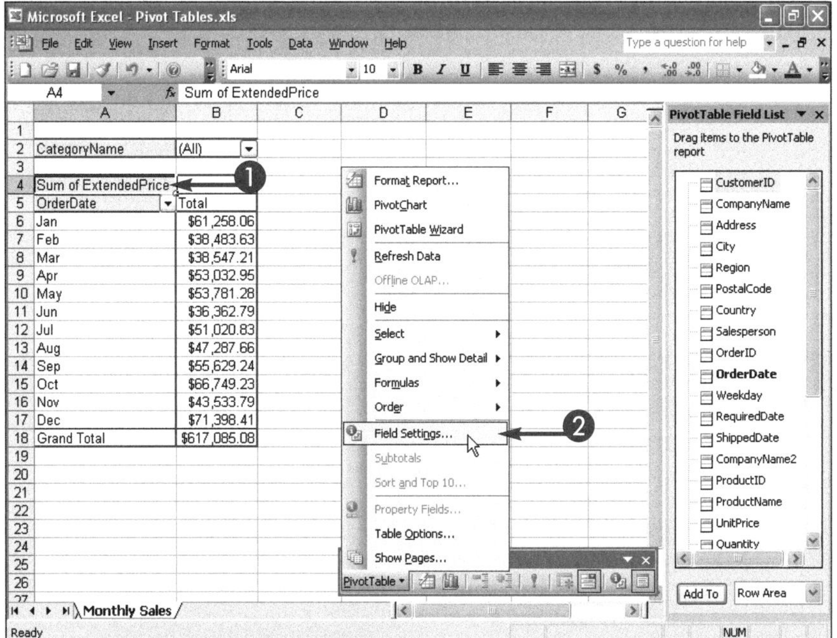

3. Click the summary calculation you want to use.
4. Click Options.

   Excel expands the dialog box.

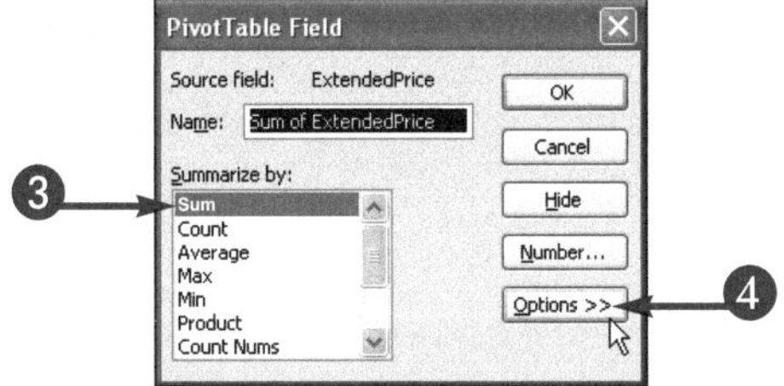

5. Click ▾ and then click Running Total in.
6. Click the base field you want to use.
7. Click OK.

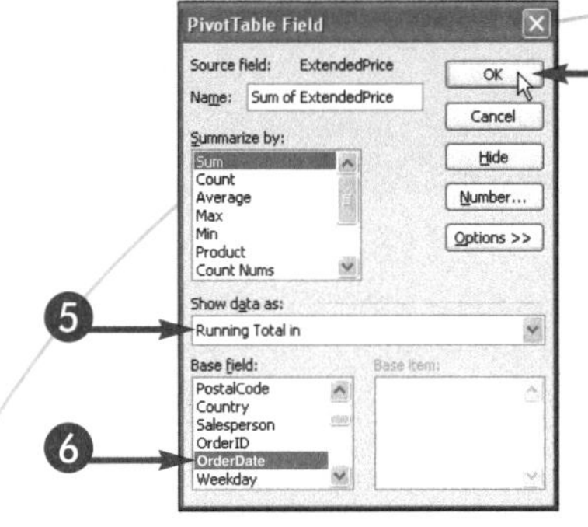

Excel recalculates the PivotTable results.

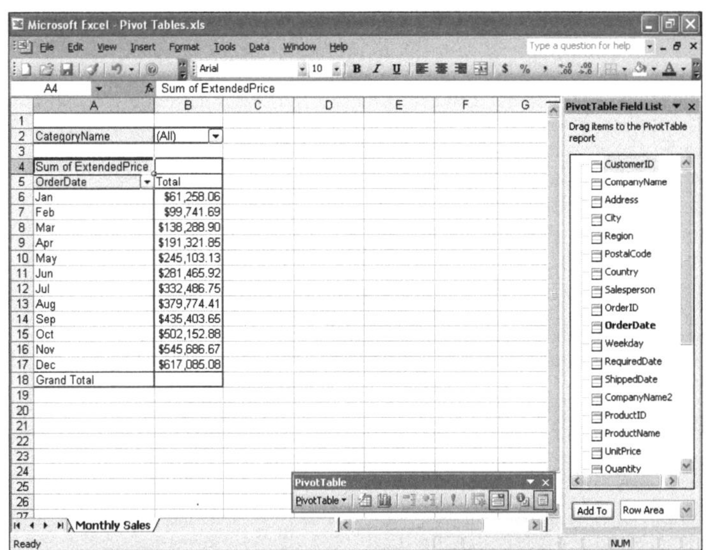

Apply It

You can use VBA to set the Running Total calculation for a data field. Set the `PivotField` object's `Calculation` property to the constant `xlRunningTotal`, and set the `BaseField` property to the name of the base field. Here is a macro that switches the Sum of ExtendedPrice field between the Running Total calculation and the normal calculation:

```
Sub ToggleRunningTotalCalculation()
    Dim objPT As PivotTable, objDataField As PivotField
    ' Work with the first PivotTable on the active worksheet
    Set objPT = ActiveSheet.PivotTables(1)
    With objPT
        ' Work with the Sum of Extended Price data field
        Set objDataField = .PivotFields("Sum of ExtendedPrice")
        With objDataField
            ' Is the calculation currently Running Total?
            If .Calculation = xlRunningTotal Then
                ' If so, turn it off
                .Calculation = xlNoAdditionalCalculation
            Else
                ' If not, change it to Running Total
                .Calculation = xlRunningTotal
                .BaseField = "OrderDate"
            End If
        End With
    End With
End Sub
```

Create an Index Summary Calculation

You can use Excel's Index calculation to determine the relative importance of the results in your PivotTable.

One of the most crucial aspects of data analysis is determining the relative importance of the results of your calculations. This is particularly true in a PivotTable, where the results summarize a large amount of data, but on the surface, provide no clue as to the relative importance of the various data area values.

For example, suppose your PivotTable shows the units sold for various product categories, broken down by state. Suppose further that in Oregon you sold 30 units of Produce and 35 units of Seafood. Does this mean that Seafood sales are relatively more important in the Oregon market than Produce sales? Not necessarily. To determine relative importance, you must take the larger picture into account. For example, you must look at the total units sold of both Produce and Seafood across all states. Suppose the Produce total is 145 units and the Seafood total is 757 units. You can see that the 30 units of Produce sold in Oregon represents a much higher portion of total Produce sales than does Oregon's 35 units of Seafood. A proper analysis would also take into account the total units sold in Oregon and the total units sold overall (the Grand Total).

This sounds complex, but Excel's Index calculation handles everything easily. The Index calculation determines the *weighted average* of each cell in the PivotTable results. Here is the formula Excel uses:

```
(Cell Value) * (Grand Total) / (Row Total) *
(Column Total)
```

In the resulting numbers, the higher the value, the more important the cell is in the overall results.

Create an Index Summary Calculation

1. Click the data field button.
2. Click PivotTable→Field Settings.

   You can also double-click the data field button or click the Field Settings button (🖼).

   The PivotTable Field dialog box appears.

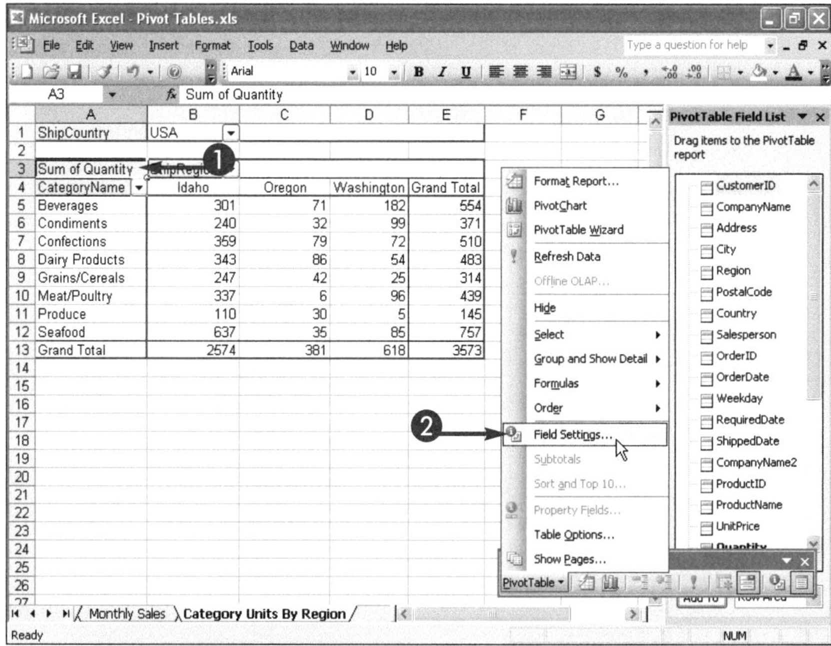

3. Click the summary calculation you want to use.
4. Click Options.

   Excel expands the dialog box.

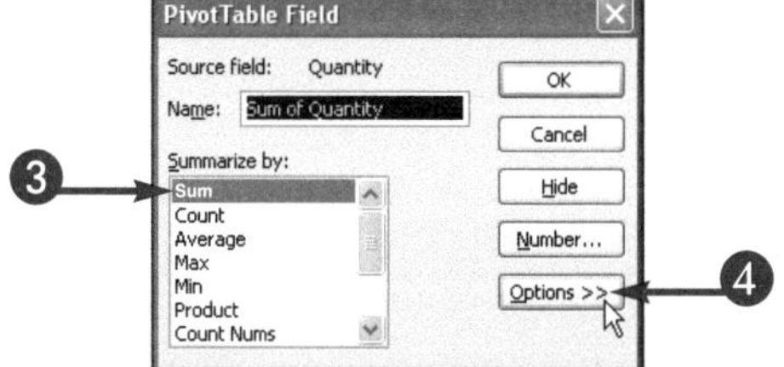

5. Click ▾ and then click Index.
6. Click Number.

   The Format Cells dialog box appears.
7. Click Number in the Category list.
8. Type **2** in the Decimal places field.
9. Click OK.

   You are returned to the PivotTable Field dialog box.
10. Click OK.

    Excel recalculates the PivotTable results.

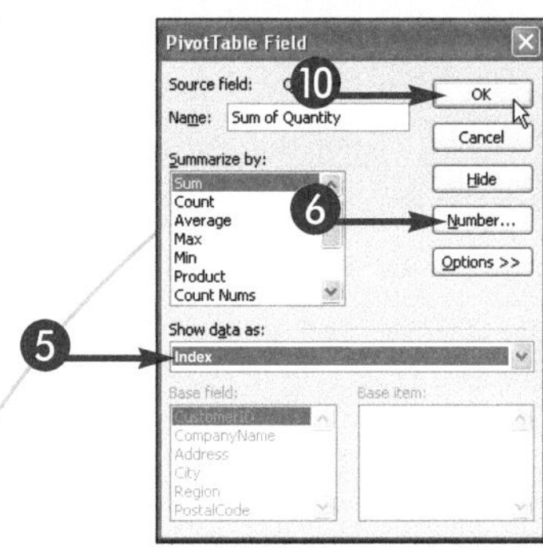
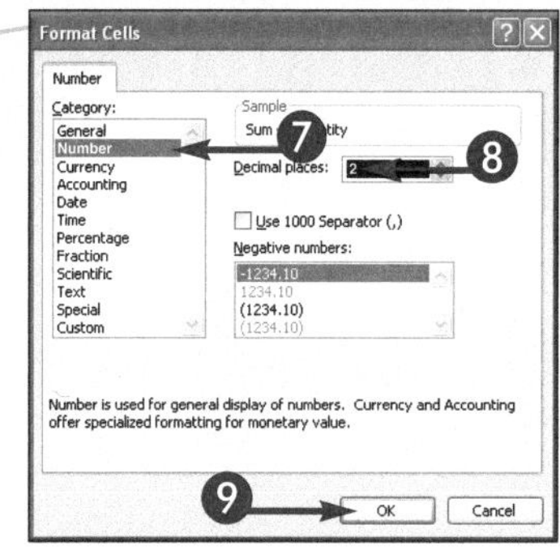
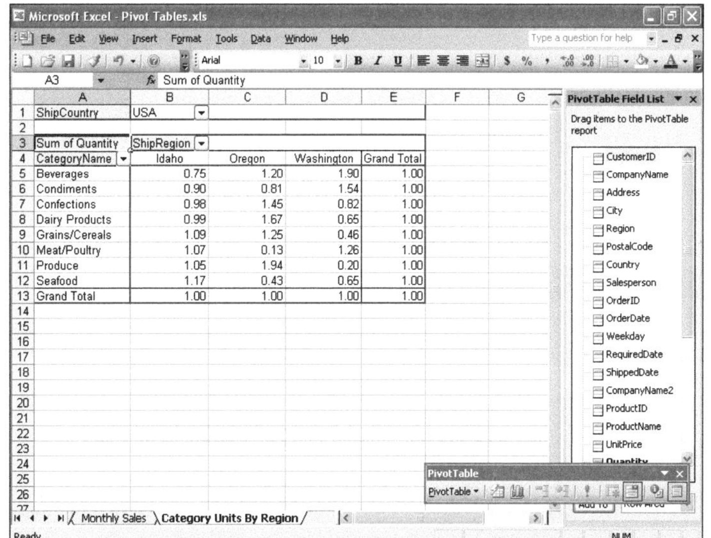

Apply It

You can use VBA to apply the Index calculation for a data field by setting the `PivotField` object's `Calculation` property to the constant `xlIndex`. Here is a macro that switches the Sum of Quantity field between the Index calculation and the normal calculation:

```
Sub ToggleIndexCalculation()
    Dim objPT As PivotTable, objDataField As PivotField
    Set objPT = ActiveSheet.PivotTables(1)
    With objPT
        ' Work with the Sum of Quantity data field
        Set objDataField = .PivotFields("Sum of Quantity")
        With objDataField
            ' Is the calculation currently Index?
            If .Calculation = xlIndex Then
                ' If so, turn it off
                .Calculation = xlNoAdditionalCalculation
                .NumberFormat = "0"
            Else
                ' If not, change it to Index
                .Calculation = xlIndex
                .NumberFormat = "0.00"
            End If
        End With
    End With
End Sub
```

Turn Off Subtotals for a Field

You can make a multiple-field row or column area easier to read by turning off the display of subtotals.

When you add a second field to the row or column area, as described in the Chapter 3 task "Add Multiple Fields to the Row or Column Area," Excel automatically displays subtotals for the items in the outer field. This is a useful component of data analysis because it shows you not only how the data breaks down according to the items in the second (inner) field, but also the total of those items for each item in the first (outer) field.

If you add a third field to the row or column area, Excel displays *two* sets of subtotals: one for the second (middle) field and one for the first (outer) field. And for every extra field you add to the row or column area, Excel adds another set of subtotals.

A PivotTable displaying two or more sets of subtotals in one area can be quite confusing to read. You can reduce the complexity of the PivotTable layout by turning off the subtotals for one or more of the fields.

Turn Off Subtotals for a Field

1. Click the button of the field you want to work with.

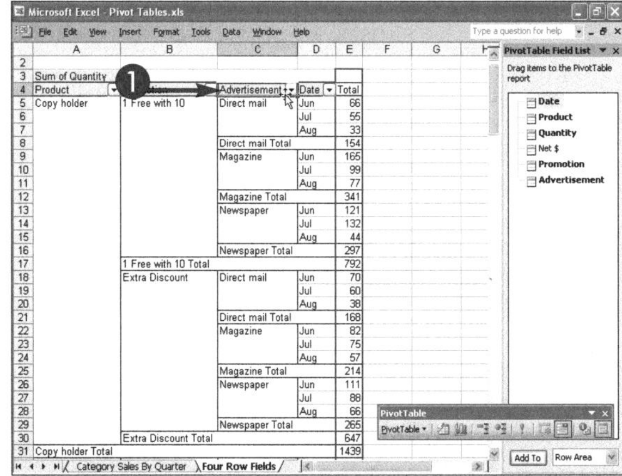

2. Click PivotTable→Field Settings.

   You can also double-click the field button or click the Field Settings button ( ).

   The PivotTable Field dialog box appears.

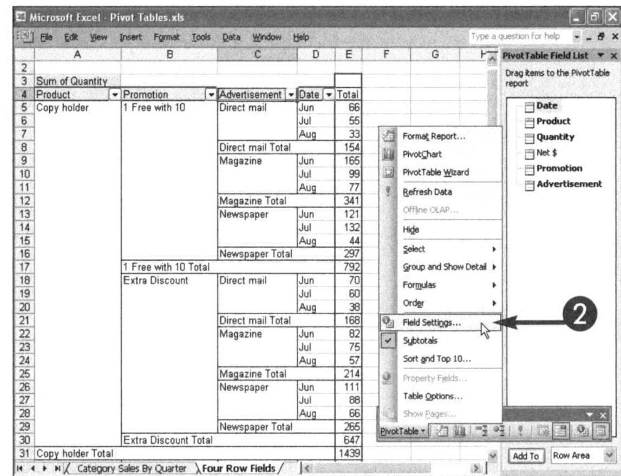

3 Select None.

4 Click OK.

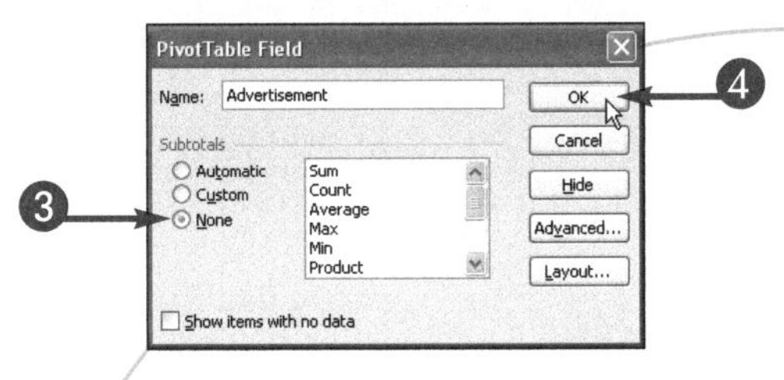

Excel hides the field's subtotals.

A faster way to toggle subtotals off and on is to click the field button and then click PivotTable➔Subtotals.

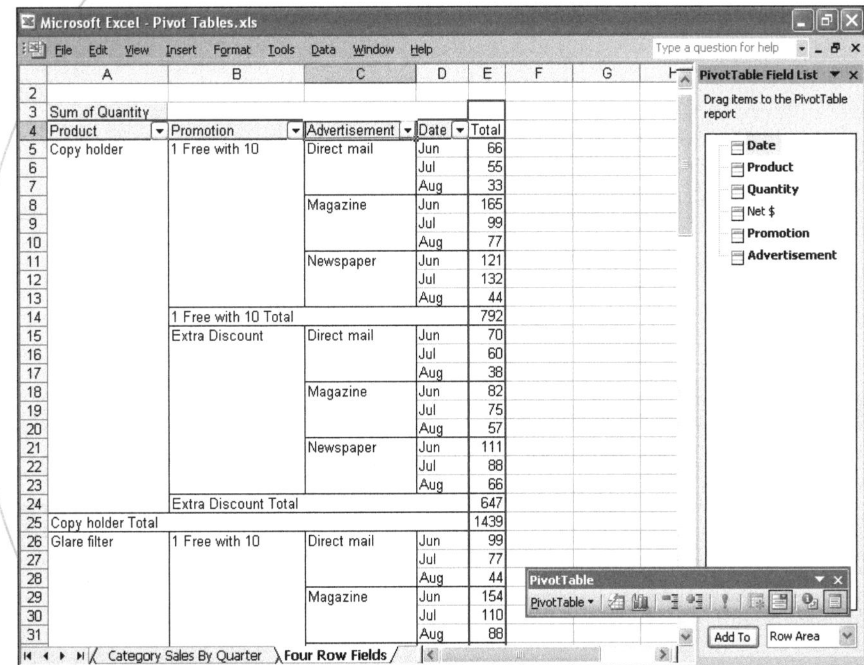

Apply It

To learn how to work with subtotals via VBA, see the tip in the next task, "Display Multiple Subtotals for a Field." The following macro uses VBA to turn a field's subtotals on and off:

```
Sub ToggleFieldSubtotals()
    Dim objPT As PivotTable, objRowField As PivotField
    Set objPT = ActiveSheet.PivotTables(1)
    Set objRowField = objPT.RowFields("Advertisement")
    With objRowField
        ' Is the Automatic subtotal option turned on?
        If .Subtotals(1) = True Then
            ' If so, turn off all subtotals
            .Subtotals = Array(False, False, False, False, _
                               False, False, False, False, _
                               False, False, False, False)
        Else
            ' If not, turn on the Automatic subtotal option
            .Subtotals = Array(True, False, False, False, _
                               False, False, False, False, _
                               False, False, False, False)
        End If
    End With
End Sub
```

Display Multiple Subtotals for a Field

You can extend your data analysis by reconfiguring your PivotTable results to show more than one type of subtotal for a given field.

When you add a second field to the row or column area, as described in the Chapter 3 task "Add Multiple Fields to the Row or Column Area," Excel displays a subtotal for each item in the outer field, and that subtotal uses the Sum calculation. If you prefer to see the Average for each item or the Count, you can change the field's summary calculation; see the task "Change the PivotTable Summary Calculation," earlier in this chapter.

However, it is a common data analysis task to view items from several different points of view. That is, you may want to study the results by seeing not just a single summary calculation, but several: Sum, Average, Count, Max, Min, and so on. Unfortunately, it is not convenient to switch from one summary calculation to another. To avoid this problem, Excel enables you to view multiple subtotals for each field, where each subtotal uses a different summary calculation. You can use as many of Excel's 11 built-in summary calculations as you need. Note, however, that it does not make sense to use StdDev and StDevp at the same time, because the former is for sample data and the later is for population data. The same is true for the Var and Varp calculations.

Display Multiple Subtotals for a Field

1. Click the button of the field you want to work with.

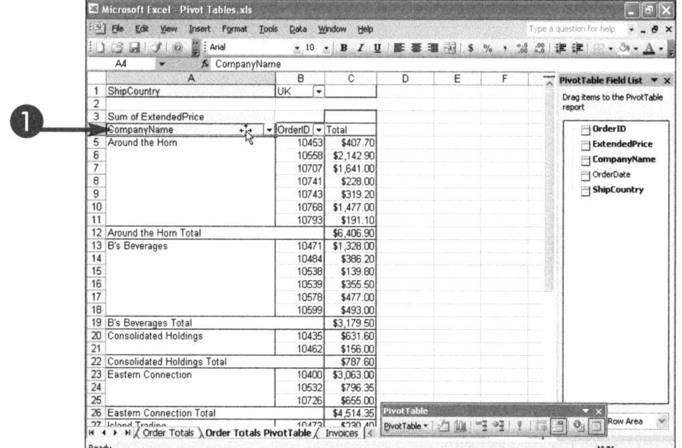

2. Click PivotTable➔Field Settings.

   You can also double-click the field button or click the Field Settings button (⊡).

   The PivotTable Field dialog box appears.

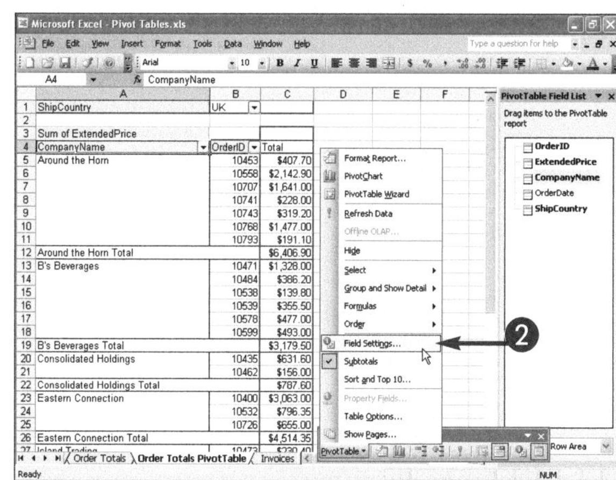

3 Select Custom.

4 Click each calculation that you want to appear as a subtotal.

5 Click OK.

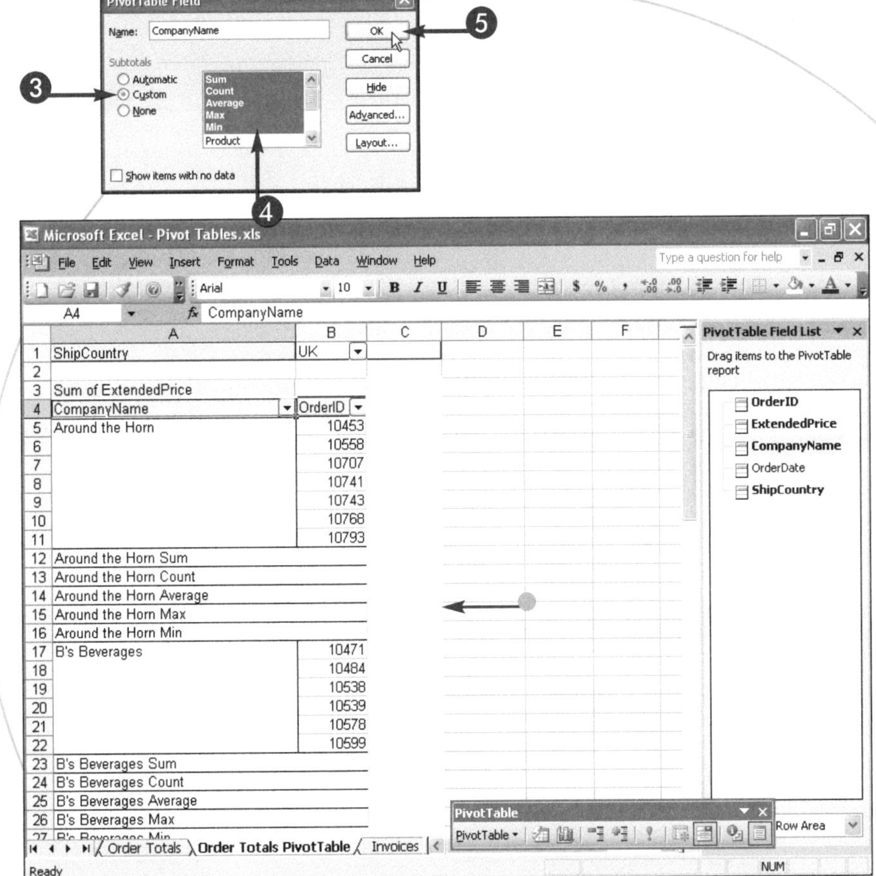

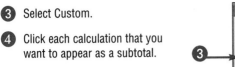

Excel recalculates the PivotTable to show the subtotals you selected.

- You may need to change the number format for some of the results.

Apply It

To work with subtotals via VBA, use the `PivotField` object's `Subtotals` property, which is a 12-item array of Boolean (`True` or `False`) values. In this array, the index numbers 1 through 12 correspond to the calculations shown in the following table:

ARRAY INDEX	CALCULATION	ARRAY INDEX	CALCULATION
1	Automatic	7	Product
2	Sum	8	Count Nums
3	Count	9	StdDev
4	Average	10	StdDevp
5	Max	11	Var
6	Min	12	Varp

The following VBA statement activates the Sum, Count, Average, Max, and Min subtotals for the field represented by the `objField` object:

Example:

```
objField.Subtotals = Array(False, True, True, True, True, True, False, False,
False, False, False, False)
```

Include Hidden Pages in PivotTable Results

If you have configured your PivotTable to hide one or more pages, you can set a PivotTable option to include the results from those hidden pages in your report totals.

When working with a page field, you can hide one or more of the pages; for the details, see the Chapter 5 task "Exclude Items from a Page Field." When you do this, Excel normally reconfigures the PivotTable report in two ways. First, it removes the hidden pages from the page field drop-down list. Second, it does not include the hidden pages in the PivotTable results. This is reasonable because in most cases you probably want those page field items completely hidden from the reader.

However, what if you only want to prevent the reader from filtering the PivotTable based on one or more page field items, while still including the data from all the pages in the PivotTable results? You can set this up in two steps. First, exclude from the page field those items you do not want the reader to use as a filter — again, see the Chapter 5 task "Exclude Items from a Page Field." Second, activate a PivotTable option that forces Excel to include all the page field items in the PivotTable results. This task shows you how to perform this second step.

Include Hidden Pages in PivotTable Results

1. Click any cell within the PivotTable.

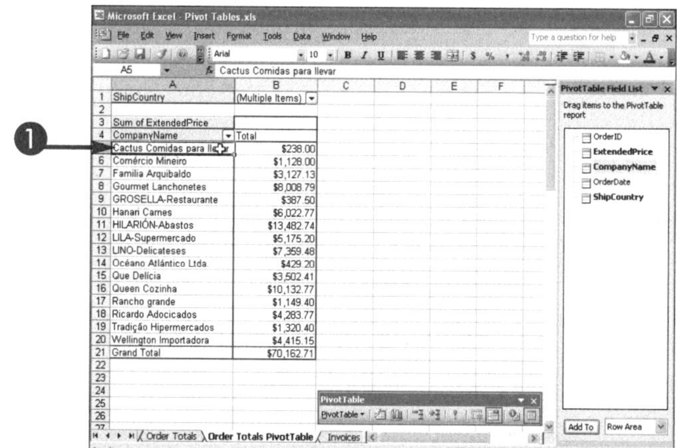

2. Click PivotTable➔Table Options.

   You can also right-click any PivotTable cell and then click Table Options.

   The PivotTable Options dialog box appears.

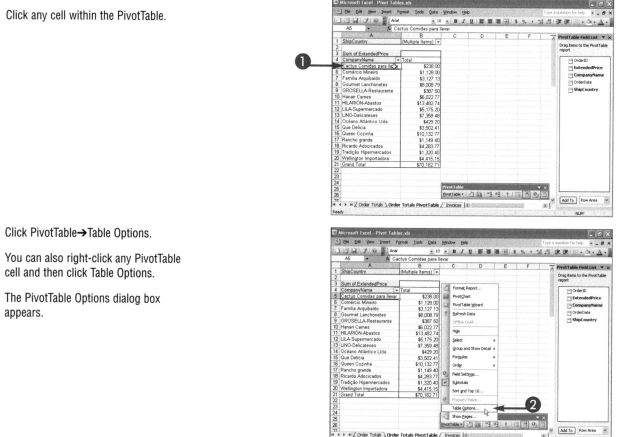

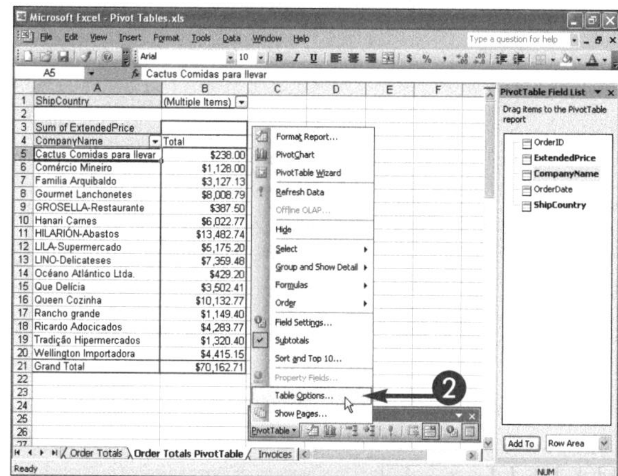

3. Select Subtotal hidden page items.
4. Click OK.

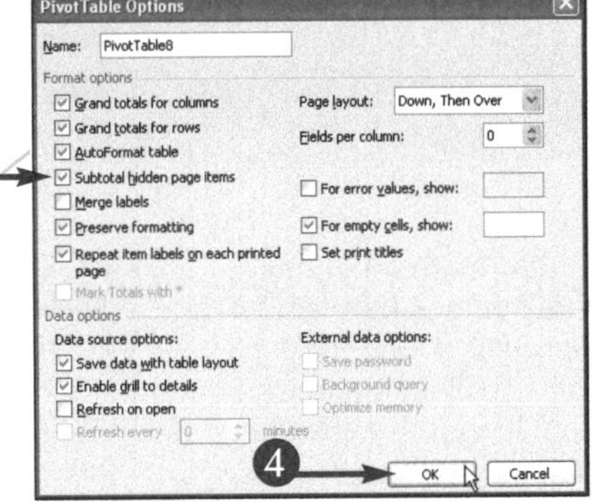

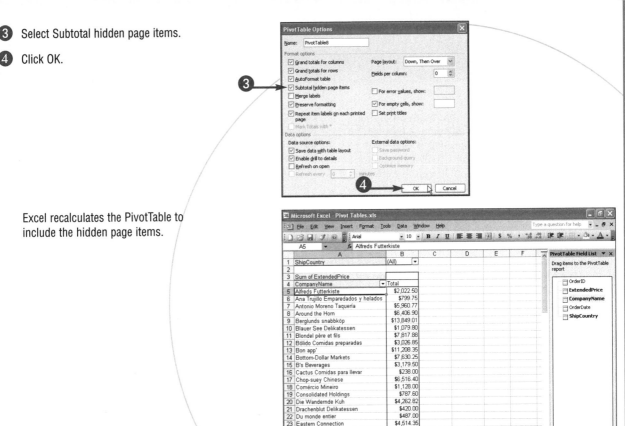

Excel recalculates the PivotTable to include the hidden page items.

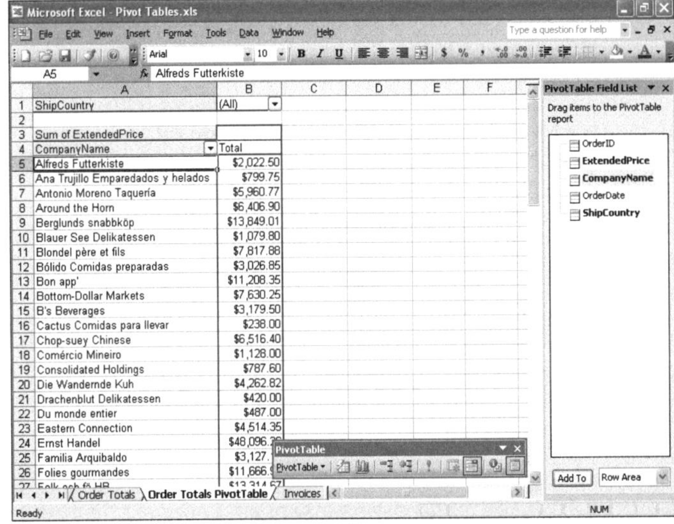

Apply It

In VBA, you use the `PivotTable` object's `SubtotalHiddenPageItems` property to turn the Subtotal hidden page option on (`True`) or off (`False`). Here is a VBA procedure that toggles the value of this property between `True` and `False`:

Example:

```
Sub ToggleSubtotalHiddenPageItems()
    Dim objPT As PivotTable
    '
    ' Work with the first PivotTable on the active worksheet
    Set objPT = ActiveSheet.PivotTables(1)
    With objPT
        '
        ' Toggle the SubtotalHiddenPageItems property
        .SubtotalHiddenPageItems = Not .SubtotalHiddenPageItems
        '
        ' Display the current setting
        MsgBox "The Subtotal Hidden Page Items option is now " & _
        IIf(.SubtotalHiddenPageItems, "on", "off") & "."
    End With
End Sub
```

Introducing Custom Calculations

A *custom calculation* is a formula that you define yourself to produce PivotTable values that would not otherwise appear in the report if you used only the source data fields and Excel's built-in summary calculations. Custom calculations enable you to extend your data analysis to include results that are specific to your needs.

For example, suppose your PivotTable shows employee sales by quarter and you want to award a 10 percent bonus to each employee with sales of more than $25,000 in any quarter. You can create a custom calculation that checks for sales greater than $25,000 and then multiplies those by 0.1 to get the bonus number.

A custom calculation is simply an Excel formula that gets applied to your source data to produce a summary result. In other words, in most cases the custom calculation is just like Excel's built-in PivotTable summary calculations, except that you define the specifics of the calculation yourself. Because you are creating a formula, you can use most of Excel's formula power, which gives you tremendous flexibility to create custom calculations that suit your data analysis needs. And by placing these calculations within the PivotTable itself — as opposed to, for example, adding the calculations to your source data — you can easily update the calculation as needed and refresh the report results.

Formula Basics

Custom calculations are formulas with certain restrictions imposed; see the next section, "Understanding Custom Calculation Limitations." You need to understand the basics of an Excel formula before you can create your own calculations. For much more detail on this topic, see Appendix A. A formula always begins with an equals sign (=), followed by one or more operands and operators.

Operands

The *operands* are the values that the formula uses as the raw material for the calculation. In a custom PivotTable calculation, the operands can be numbers, worksheet functions, or fields from your data source.

Operators

The *operators* are the symbols that the formula uses to perform the calculation. In a custom PivotTable calculation, the available operators include addition (+), subtraction (–), multiplication (*), division (/), comparison operators such as greater than (>) and less than (<) or equal to (<=), and more.

Custom Calculation Types

When building a custom calculation for a PivotTable, Excel offers two different types: a calculated field and a calculated item.

Calculated Field

A *calculated field* is a new data field in which the values are the result of a custom calculation formula. You can display the calculated field along with another data field or on its own. A calculated field is really a custom summary calculation, so in almost all cases the calculated field references one or more fields in the source data. See the task "Insert a Custom Calculated Field," later in this chapter.

Calculated Item

A *calculated item* is a new item in a row or column field in which the values are the result of a custom calculation. In this case, the calculated item's formula references one or more items in the same field. See the task "Insert a Custom Calculated Item."

Understanding Custom Calculation Limitations

Custom calculations — whether they are calculated fields or calculated items — are powerful additions to your PivotTable analysis toolbox. However, although custom calculation formulas look like regular worksheet formulas, you cannot assume that everything you do with a worksheet formula you can also do with a custom PivotTable formula. In fact, there are a number of limitations that Excel imposes on custom formulas, such as not being able to reference data outside the pivot cache, and not being able to use custom items in conjunction with grouping.

General Limitations

The major limitation inherent in custom calculations is that, with the exception of constant values, such as numbers, you cannot reference anything outside the PivotTable's source data:

- You cannot use a cell reference, range address, or range name as an operand in a custom calculation formula.
- You cannot use any worksheet function that requires a cell reference, range, or defined name. However, you can still use many of Excel's worksheet functions by substituting either a field or an item in place of a cell reference or range name. For example, if you want a calculated item that returns the average of items named Jan, Feb, and Mar, you could use the following formula:

```
=AVERAGE(Jan, Feb, Mar)
```

- You cannot use the PivotTable's subtotals, row totals, column totals, or Grand Total as an operand in a custom calculation formula.

Calculated Item Limitations

Excel imposes the following limitations on the use of calculated items:

- A formula for a calculated item cannot reference items from any field except the one in which the calculated item resides.
- You cannot insert a calculated item into a PivotTable that has at least one grouped field. You must ungroup all the PivotTable fields before you can insert a calculated item.
- You cannot group a field in a PivotTable that has at least one calculated item.
- You cannot insert a calculated item into a page field. Also, you cannot move a row or column field that has a calculated item into the page area.
- You cannot insert a calculated item into a PivotTable in which a field has been used more than once.
- You cannot insert a calculated item into a PivotTable that uses the Average, StdDev, StdDevp, Var, or Varp summary calculations.

Calculated Field Limitations

When you are working with calculated fields, it is important to understand how references to other PivotTable fields work within your calculations and what limitations you face when using field references.

Field References

It is important to understand that when you reference a field in your formula, Excel interprets this reference as the *sum* of that field's values. For example, the formula =Sales + 1 does not add 1 to each Sales value and return the sum of these results; that is, Excel does not interpret the formula as =Sum of (Sales + 1). Instead, the formula adds 1 to the sum of the Sales values — Excel interprets the formula as =(Sum of Sales) + 1.

Field Reference Problems

The fact that Excel defaults to a Sum calculation when you reference another field in your custom calculation can lead to problems. The trouble is that it does not make sense to sum certain types of data. For example, suppose you have inventory source data with UnitsInStock and UnitPrice fields. You want to calculate the total value of the inventory, so you create a custom field based on the following formula:

```
=UnitsInStock * UnitPrice
```

Unfortunately, this formula does not work because Excel treats the UnitPrice operand as Sum of UnitPrice. Of course, it does not make sense to "add" the prices together, so your formula produces an incorrect result.

Insert a Custom Calculated Field

If your data analysis requires PivotTable results that are not available using just the data source fields and Excel's built-in summary calculations, you can insert a calculated field that uses a custom formula to derive the results you need.

A custom calculated field is based on a formula that looks much like an Excel worksheet formula; see the section "Introducing Custom Calculations," earlier in this chapter. However, you do not enter the formula for a calculated field into a worksheet cell. Instead, Excel offers the Calculated Field feature which provides a dialog box for you to name the field and construct the formula. Excel then stores the formula along with the rest of the PivotTable data in the pivot cache.

Having the calculated field stored in the pivot cache is handy because the pivot cache is often shared by other PivotTables that you have built using the same source data. When you build a second PivotTable based on the same source data as the first, Excel asks if you want to reuse the original data in the new PivotTable. Therefore, you can reuse calculated fields in other PivotTable reports, which can save time.

Insert a Custom Calculated Field

Note: This chapter uses the PivotTables.xls spreadsheet, available at www.wiley.com/go/pivottablesvb, or you can create your own sample database.

1. Click any cell inside the PivotTable's data area.
2. Click PivotTable➔Formulas➔Calculated Field.

   You can also click Insert➔Calculated Field.

   The Insert Calculated Field dialog box appears.
3. Type a name for the calculated field.
4. Start the formula for the calculated field.

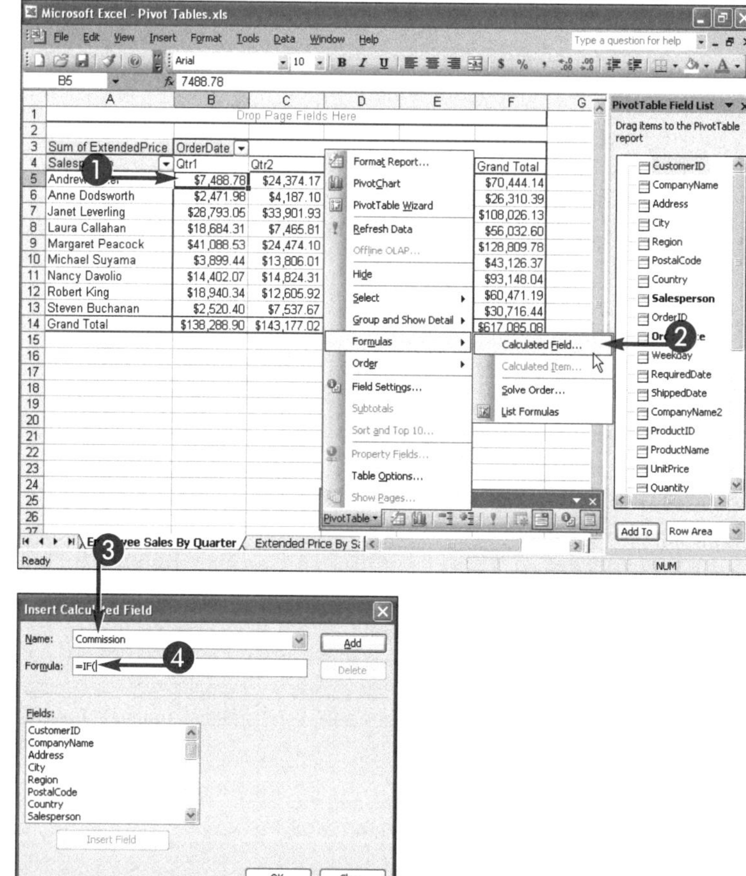

5. To insert a field into the formula at the current cursor position, click the field.
6. Click Insert Field.
7. When the formula is complete, click Add.
8. Click OK.

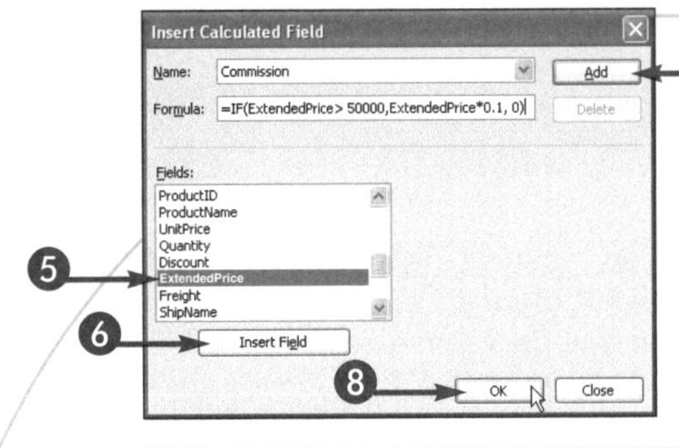

- Excel adds the calculated field to the PivotTable's data area.
- Excel adds the calculated field to the PivotTable Field List.

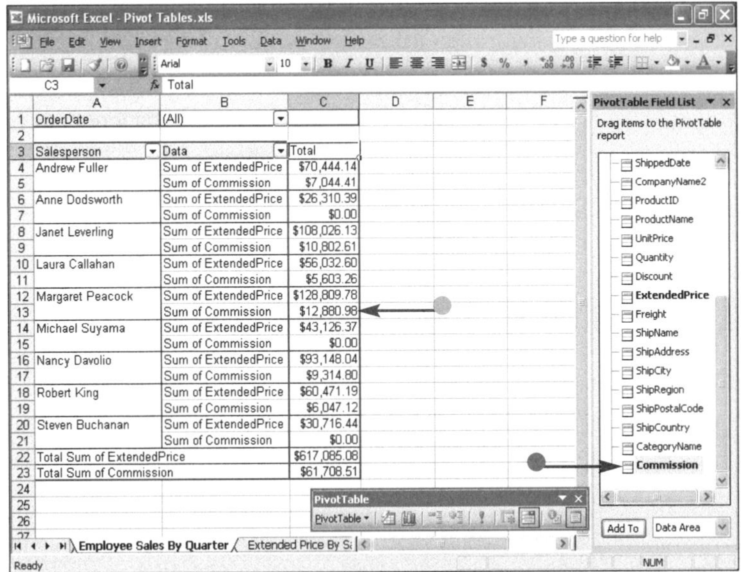

Extra

As pointed out above, the new calculated field appears in the PivotTable Field List. However, the calculated field also appears in the PivotTable Field List for *every* PivotTable that uses the same pivot cache. Therefore, you can reuse calculated fields in other PivotTable reports where the calculation makes sense. For example, you would not reuse a sales commission calculation in a PivotTable that provides an inventory summary. To do this, drag the calculated field from the PivotTable Field List and drop it inside the PivotTable's data area.

When you add a calculated field to the PivotTable, Excel also adds a new row with the label Total Sum of *FieldName*, where *FieldName* is the name you provided for the calculated field, such as Total Sum of Commission. Unfortunately, this total is often inaccurate and you should be careful not to assume that it is correct. The problem is that it is *not* a sum of the values in the calculated field. Instead, Excel applies the calculated field's formula to the sum of whatever field or fields you referenced in the formula. In the example used in this task, Excel applies the formula to the Total Sum of Extended Price value, which is not the correct way to calculate the total commission. To work around this problem, you need to set up a formula outside the PivotTable that sums the commission values.

Insert a Custom Calculated Item

If your data analysis requires PivotTable results that are not available using just the data source fields and Excel's built-in summary calculations, you can insert a calculated item that uses a custom formula to derive the results you need.

As with a calculated field, a calculated item uses a formula much like an Excel worksheet formula; see the section "Introducing Custom Calculations," earlier in this chapter. Again, however, you do not enter the formula for a calculated item into a worksheet cell. Instead, Excel offers the Calculated Item command that displays a dialog box where you name the item and construct the formula. Excel then stores the formula along with the rest of the PivotTable data in the pivot cache.

Remember that the Calculated Item feature creates just a single item in a field. However, you are free to add as many calculated items as you need. For example, suppose you want to compare the performance of male and female sales representatives. One way to do that would be to create one calculated item that returns the average sales of the men, and a second calculated item that returns the average sales of the women.

Before you create a calculated item, be sure to remove all groupings from your PivotTable; see the section "Understanding Custom Calculation Limitations," earlier in this chapter. Note that it is not enough to simply remove the grouped field from the PivotTable. Instead, you must run the Ungroup command on the field, as described in the Chapter 4 task "Ungroup Values."

Insert a Custom Calculated Item

1. Click any cell inside the field to which you want to insert the item.
2. Click PivotTable➔Formulas➔Calculated Item.

   The Insert Calculated Item dialog box appears.

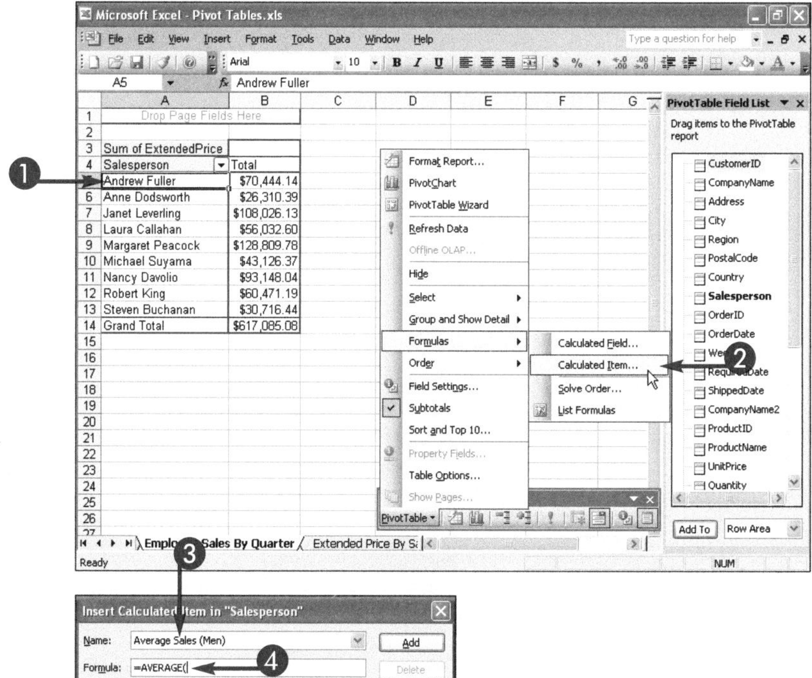

3. Type a name for the calculated item.
4. Start the formula for the calculated item.
5. To insert a field into the formula at the current cursor position, click the field.
6. Click Insert Field.

   You can also double-click the field.

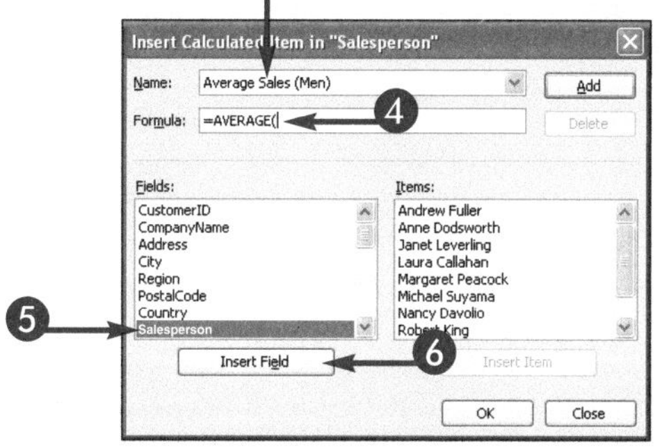

7. To insert an item into the formula at the current cursor position, click the field containing the item.
8. Click the item.
9. Click Insert Item.

   You can also double-click the item.
10. When the formula is complete, click Add.
11. Repeat Steps 3 to 10 to add other calculated items.
12. Click OK.

- Excel adds the calculated item to the field.
- The calculated item's formula appears in the formula bar when you click the result.

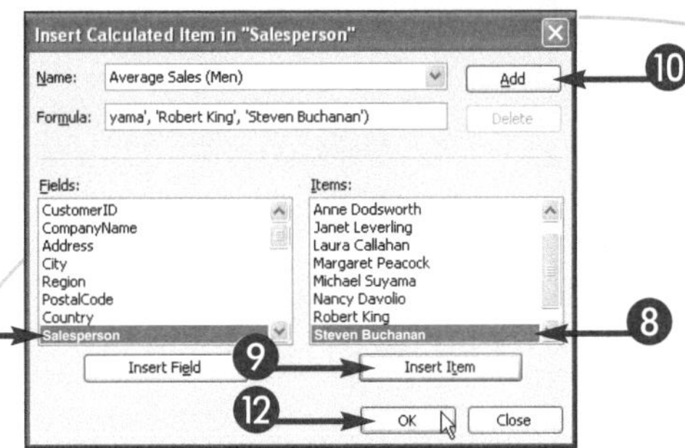

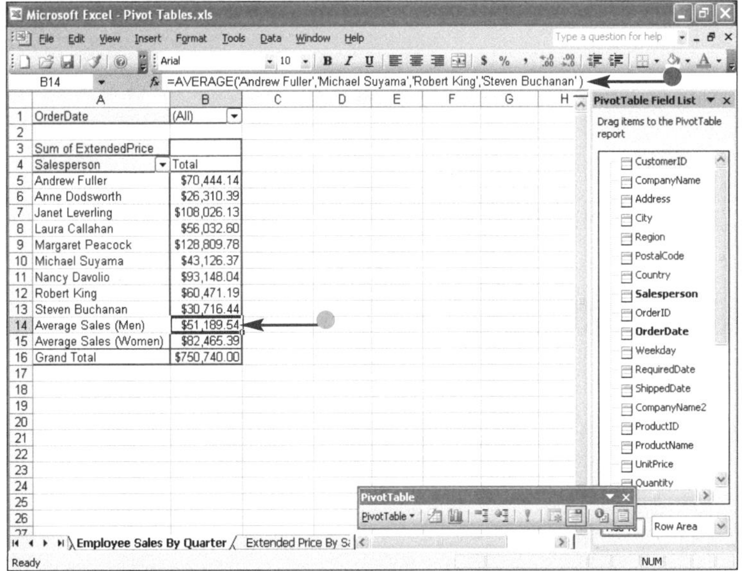

Extra

When you insert an item into a field, that item becomes part of the field within the pivot cache. For example, when you select the field in the Calculated Item dialog box, the calculated item appears in the Items list along with the regular field items. This is handy because it enables you to use the calculated item's result in other formulas.

The downside to having the calculated item become part of the field is that Excel includes the calculated item's result in the PivotTable subtotals, row or column totals, and Grand Total. This almost always causes the totals for the affected field to be inaccurate, so double-check field totals when you use a calculated item.

One way to work around this problem is to create a calculated item that uses the SUM() function to add the regular field items. Another workaround would be to hide the calculated items; see the Chapter 4 task "Hide Items in a Row or Column Field."

Edit a Custom Calculation

If you notice an error in a custom calculation, or if your data analysis needs changed, you can modify the formula used by a calculated field or calculated item.

When you add a custom calculation to a PivotTable, Excel first checks the formula to make sure that it contains no syntax errors — such as a missing comma or parenthesis — or illegal operands — such as cell addresses, unknown field or item names, or functions not supported by custom calculations. If Excel finds an error, it displays a dialog box to let you know and does not add the custom calculation to the PivotTable.

However, just because a formula contains no syntax errors or illegal operands does not necessarily mean that the formula's results are correct. In a calculated field, you may have used the wrong function for the result you are seeking. In a calculated item involving several field items, you may have accidentally missed an item.

Alternatively, your formula may be working perfectly, but it may no longer be the result you need if your data analysis needs have changed. For example, you might have a calculated field that determines whether employees get paid a bonus by looking for sales greater than $50,000. If that threshold changes to $75,000, then your calculated field will no longer produce the results you want.

Whether your custom calculation contains an error or your data analysis needs have changed, Excel enables you to edit the formula to produce the result you want.

Edit a Custom Calculation

EDIT A CALCULATED FIELD

1. Click any cell inside the PivotTable's data area.
2. Click PivotTable➔Formulas➔Calculated Field.

   You can also click Insert➔Calculated Field.

   The Insert Calculated Field dialog box appears.

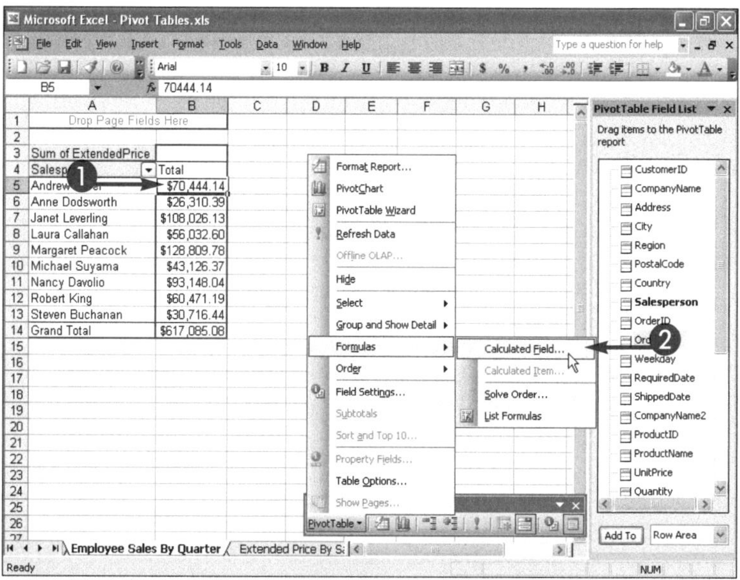

3. Click the calculated field you want to edit.
4. Edit the formula.
5. Click Modify.
6. Click OK.

   Excel updates the calculated field's results.

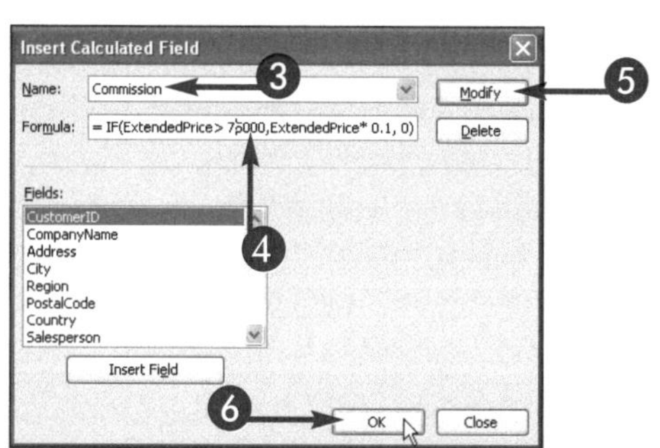

EDIT A CALCULATED ITEM

1. Click any cell inside the field that contains the calculated item.
2. Click PivotTable➔Formulas➔Calculated Item.

   The Insert Calculated Item dialog box appears.

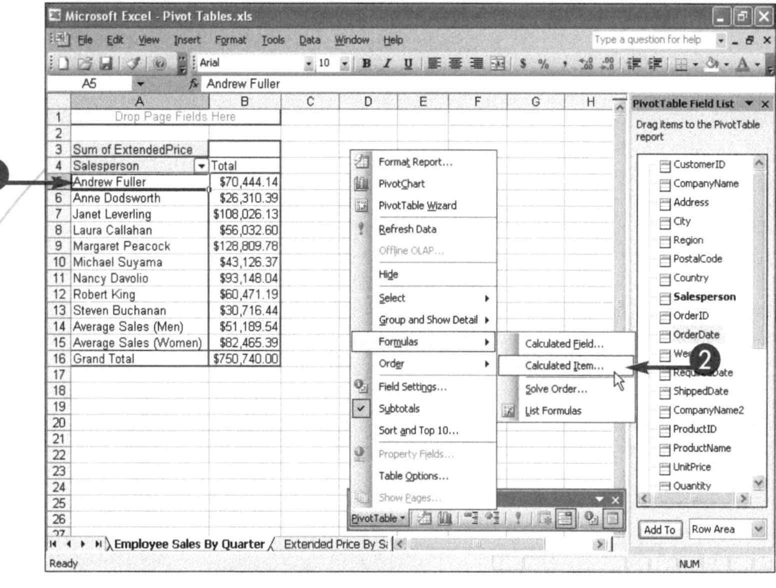

3. Click the calculated item you want to edit.
4. Edit the formula.
5. Click Modify.
6. Click OK.

   You can also edit a calculated item by clicking the item's result. The formula appears in Excel's formula bar, and you can edit it from there.

   Excel updates the calculated item's results.

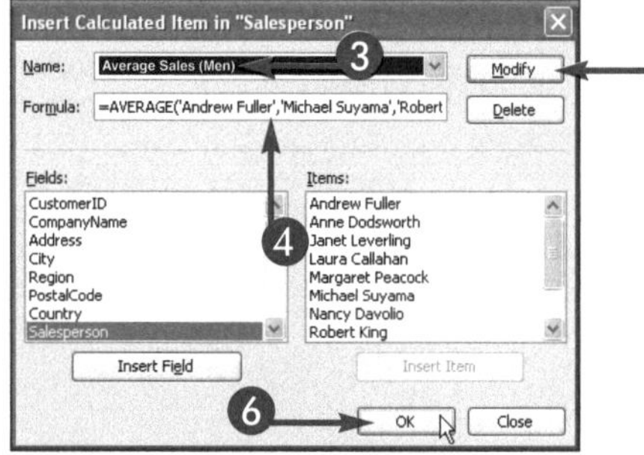

Apply It

If you use VBA to insert a calculated field or item, then you can modify the custom calculation by editing the macro.

For calculated fields, first note that each `PivotTable` object has a `CalculatedFields` collection. To insert a calculated field, use the `CalculatedField` object's `Add` method. The following statement inserts a calculated field named Commission:

Example:

```
objPT.CalculatedFields.Add _
    Name:="Commission", _
    Formula:="= IF(ExtendedPrice> 50000,ExtendedPrice* 0.1, 0)"
objPT.PivotFields("Commission").Orientation = xlDataField
```

For calculated items, note that each row and column `PivotField` object has a `CalculatedItems` collection. To insert a new calculated item, use the `CalculatedItems` object's `Add` method. The following statement inserts a calculated item named Average Sales (Men) into the Salesperson field:

Example:

```
objPT.PivotFields("Salesperson").CalculatedItems.Add _
    Name:="Average Sales (Men)", _
    Formula:="=AVERAGE('Andrew Fuller','Michael Suyama'," & _
             "'Robert King','Steven Buchanan')"
```

Change the Solve Order of Calculated Items

You can ensure that your calculated items return the correct results by adjusting the order in which Excel solves the items.

If you have multiple calculated items in a PivotTable, you may end up with cells that have values that rely on two or more formulas. For example, you may have one calculated item in a row field and another in a column field. In the PivotTable cell that lies at the intersection of these two items, the value will be the result of Excel applying one formula and then the other. The default order is the order in which you added the items to the PivotTable. Most of the time, this order does not matter. However, the order that Excel solves calculated items can make a difference.

For example, suppose you have a PivotTable that shows the number of units that customers ordered based on two different promotional offers — 1 Free with 10 and Extra Discount — broken down by advertisement — Direct Mail, Magazine, and Newspaper. Suppose further that you have added a calculated item in the row field that returns the percentage of units ordered for each promotion. For example, with the Magazine advertisement, you might find that 52.5% of units were ordered via the 1 Free with 10 promotion, and the other 47.5% were ordered via the Extra Discount promotion.

If you also want to know the overall percentages of each promotion, you run into a problem because Excel's default Grand Total calculation will add the percentages. To work around this problem, you could turn off the Grand Total calculation and create a new calculated item in the column field that adds the various Advertisement items together. If this calculated item is solved after the first one, you end up with the same problem: Excel adds the percentages. To fix this, you need to change the solve order so that Excel adds the Advertisement items first, and then calculates the percentages.

Change the Solve Order of Calculated Items

1. Click any cell in the PivotTable.
   - Calculated row items.
   - A calculated column item.
   - Incorrect results.
2. Click PivotTable➔Formulas➔Solve Order.

   The Calculated Item Solve Order dialog box appears.

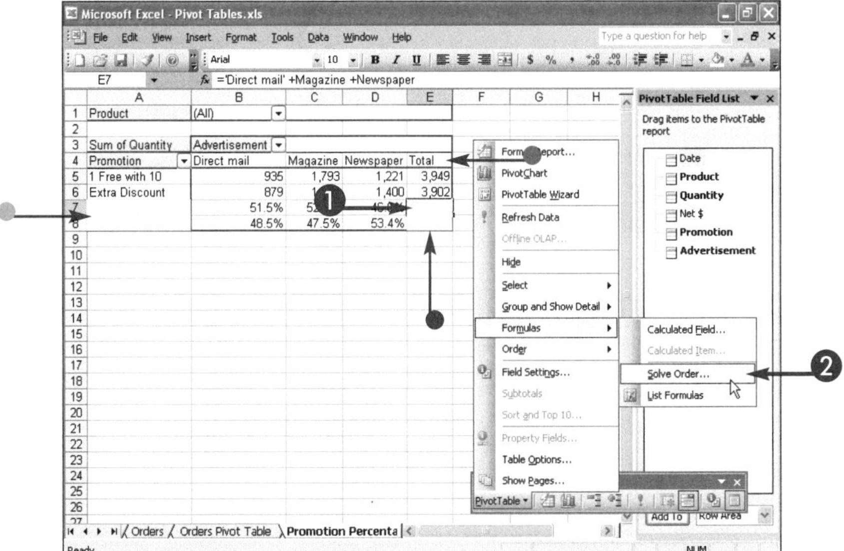

3. Click the calculated item you want to move.
4. To move the item up in the list, click Move Up.

   Excel moves the item up.

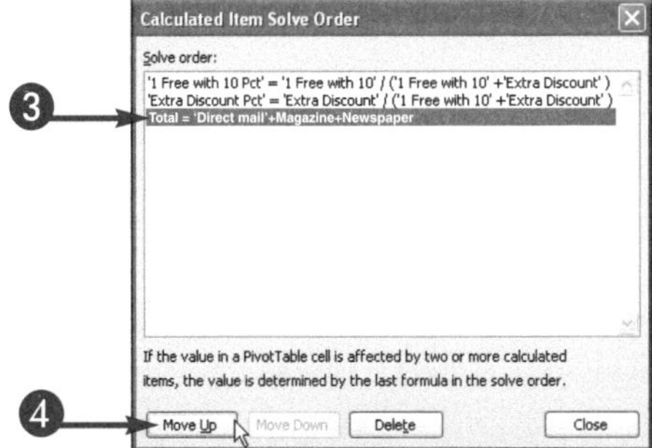

5 To move an item down in the list, click Move Down.

6 Click Close.

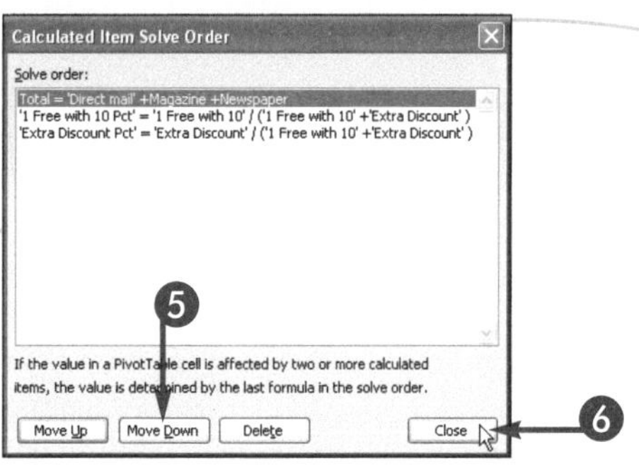

Excel adjusts the solve order and recalculates the results.

- The correct results appear.

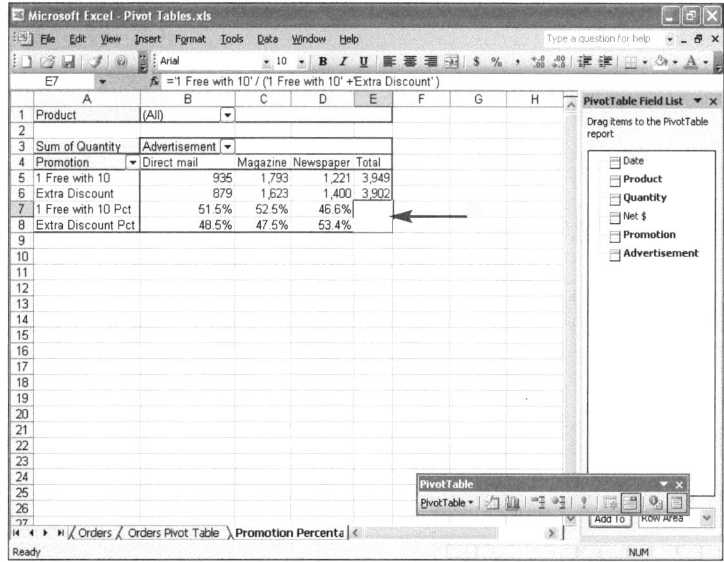

Apply It

There is another method you can often use to fix solve order problems in a PivotTable. This method relies on the fact that, in a cell that relies on multiple calculated item formulas, Excel applies the last formula in the solve order to the cell. In this task, examine the Excel formula bar in the first screen shot. This is the formula that Excel is applying to cell E7:

```
='Direct mail' + Magazine + Newspaper
```

Now examine the formula bar in the last screen shot. You can see that the formula Excel is now applying to cell E7 is the following:

```
='1 Free with 10' / ('1 Free with 10' + 'Extra Discount')
```

Therefore, in most cases you can fix the solve order problem by copying the correct formula from another cell (such as D7 in the example) and then pasting it into the problem cell.

Note, however, that Excel does not allow you to simply copy the cell and then paste it because Excel does not allow a PivotTable to be changed in this way. Instead, you must open the cell that has the formula you want, copy the cell text, open the destination cell, delete the existing formula, and then paste the copied formula.

List Your Custom Calculations

You can document your PivotTable's custom calculations by displaying the formulas for each calculated field and calculated item on a separate worksheet.

When you add several custom calculations to a PivotTable, the report can become difficult to decipher. This is particularly true with calculated fields because there is nothing in the PivotTable that shows the field's underlying formula to the reader. Calculated fields are more transparent because you can see the formula by selecting the cell, but you have no way of knowing whether there are multiple calculations that determine the cell's value.

To help the reader decipher a PivotTable's custom calculations — whether that reader is another person not familiar with the PivotTable or yourself a few months from now — Excel offers a feature that enables you to document all the custom calculations, including the formulas and solve order, in a separate worksheet.

You can use a VBA macro to list the custom calculations for a PivotTable. To do this, run the `PivotTable` object's `ListFormulas` method, as shown in the following macro:

```
Sub ListPivotTableFormulas()
    Dim objPT As PivotTable
    '
    ' Work with the first PivotTable
    Set objPT = ActiveSheet.PivotTables(1)
    '
    ' List the PivotTable's formulas
    objPT.ListFormulas
End Sub
```

List Your Custom Calculations

1. Click any cell in the PivotTable.
2. Click PivotTable➔Formulas➔List Formulas.

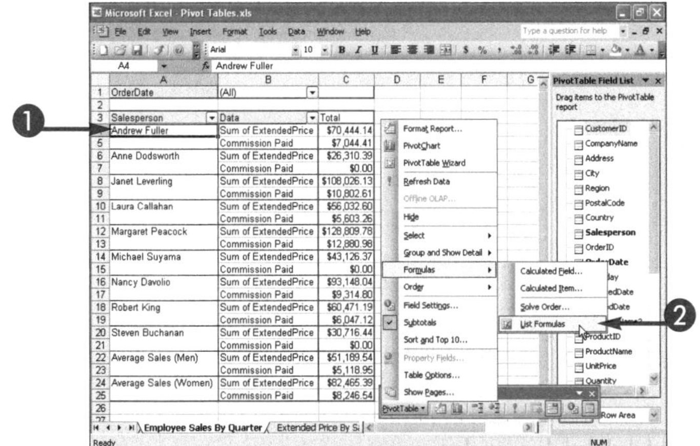

Excel inserts a new worksheet and displays the solve order, name, and formula for each calculated field and item.

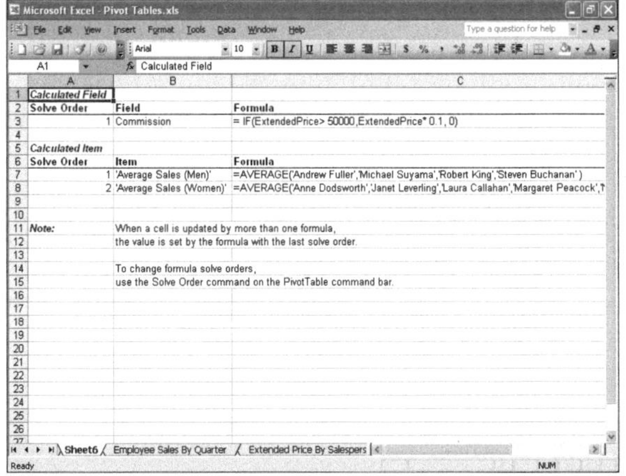

Delete a Custom Calculation

When you no longer need a calculated field or calculated item, you can delete the calculation from the PivotTable.

Custom calculations do not always remain a permanent part of a PivotTable report. For example, it is common to add a calculated field or item temporarily to the PivotTable to test the data or get a number to use elsewhere. Similarly, you may find that you create several versions of a custom calculation and you only want to keep the final version. Finally, although custom calculations are a powerful tool, they cannot do everything, so you may find that a calculation does not provide the answer you seek or help you with your data analysis.

For all these situations, Excel enables you to delete those calculated fields or items that you no longer need.

The following VBA macro deletes all the custom calculations in a PivotTable:

```
Sub DeleteAllCustomCalculations()
Dim objPF As PivotField, objCF As PivotField
Dim objCI As PivotItem
With ActiveSheet.PivotTables(1)
    For Each objCF In .CalculatedFields
        objCF.Delete
    Next 'objCF
    For Each objPF In .PivotFields
        For Each objCI In objPF.CalculatedItems
            objCI.Delete
        Next 'objCI
    Next 'objPF
End With
End Sub
```

Delete a Custom Calculation

1. Click any cell in the PivotTable.
2. To delete a calculated field, click PivotTable➔Formulas➔Calculated Field.

   To delete a calculated item, instead, click PivotTable➔Formulas➔ Calculated Item.

   The Insert Calculated Field dialog box appears.

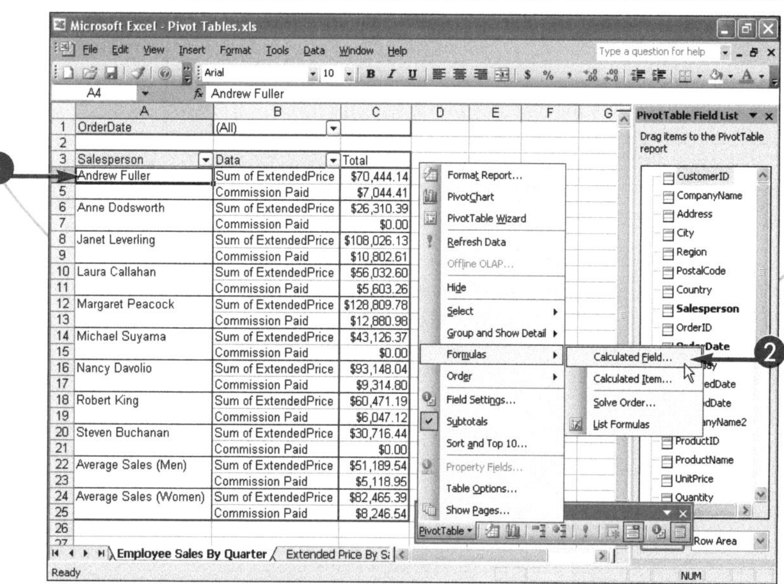

3. Click the calculation that you want to delete.
4. Click Delete.
5. Click OK.

   Excel removes the custom calculation.

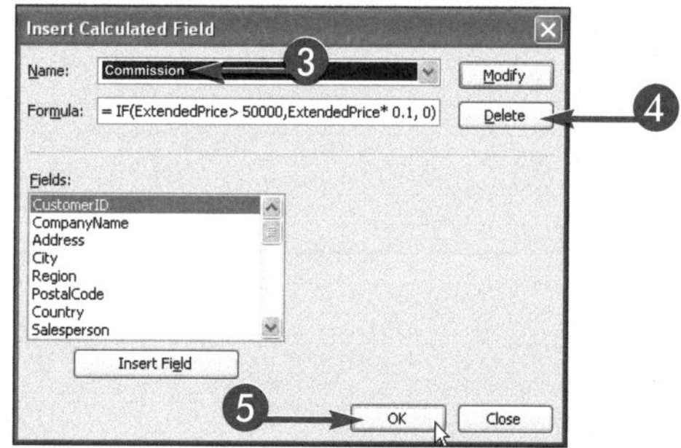

Understanding PivotChart Limitations

A PivotChart is a graphical representation of the values in a PivotTable report. However, a PivotChart goes far beyond a regular chart because a PivotChart comes with many of the same capabilities as a PivotTable. These capabilities include moving fields from one area of the chart to another, hiding items, filtering data via the page field, refreshing the PivotChart to account for changes in the underlying data, and more. You also have access to most of Excel's regular charting capabilities, so PivotCharts are a powerful addition to your data analysis toolkit.

However, PivotCharts are not a perfect solution. Excel has fairly rigid rules for which parts of a PivotTable report correspond to which parts of the PivotChart layout. Moving a field from one part of the PivotChart to another can easily result in a PivotChart layout that is either difficult to understand or that does not make any sense at all.

Similarly, you also face a number of other limitations that control the types of charts you can make and the formatting options you can apply. For example, you cannot configure a PivotChart to use the Stock chart type, which can be a significant problem for some applications. Also, Excel has a tendency to "lose" PivotChart formatting when you make certain changes to the associated PivotTable.

This section outlines these and other PivotChart limitations. Note, however, that most of these limitations are not onerous in most situations, so they should in no way dissuade you from taking advantage of the analytical and visualization power of the PivotChart.

If you have any trouble with the terminology or concepts in this chapter, be sure to refer to the Chapter 1 section "Introducing the PivotChart," for the appropriate background.

PivotTables Versus PivotCharts

One of the main sources of PivotChart confusion is the fact that Excel uses different terminology with PivotCharts and PivotTables. In both, you have a data area that contains the numeric results, and you have a page area that you can use to filter the data. However, it is important to understand how Excel maps the PivotTable's row and column areas to the PivotChart.

Row Area Versus Category Area

In a PivotTable, the row area contains the unique values — the items — that Excel has extracted from a particular field in the source data. The PivotChart equivalent is the category area, which corresponds to the chart's X-axis. That is, each unique value from the source data field has a corresponding category axis value.

Column Area Versus Series Area

In a PivotTable, the column area contains the unique values — the items — that Excel has extracted from a particular field in the source data. The PivotChart equivalent is the series area, which corresponds to the chart's Y-axis. That is, each unique value from the source data field has a corresponding data series.

Formatting Limitations

Chart Types

Excel offers a large number of chart types, and you can change the default PivotChart type to another that more closely suits your needs; see the task "Change the PivotChart Type," later in this chapter. However, there are three chart types that you cannot apply to a PivotChart: Bubble, XY (Scatter), and Stock.

Chart Formatting

Excel also allows you to format the chart using the controls in the Chart Options dialog box. However, there are a few formatting techniques that Excel disables for PivotCharts. Specifically, you cannot move or change the size of the plot area, chart title, axis titles, and legend.

Chart Customizations

Perhaps the most serious drawback of using PivotCharts is that Excel removes certain chart customizations when you refresh, rebuild, rotate, filter a PivotTable, or change the PivotTable's layout or view. Specifically, Excel removes any formatting that you have applied to data series and data points, as well as all trendlines and error bars.

Create a PivotChart from a PivotTable

You can create a PivotChart directly from an existing PivotTable. This saves times because you do not have to configure the layout of the PivotChart or any other options.

You have seen elsewhere in this book that the pivot cache that Excel maintains for each PivotTable saves time, memory, and disk space. For example, if you attempt to create a new PivotTable using the same source data as an existing PivotTable, Excel enables you to share the source data between them.

The pivot cache also comes in handy when you want to create a PivotChart. If the layout of an existing PivotTable is the same as what you want for a PivotChart, you can create the PivotChart directly from the PivotTable. Excel uses the pivot cache and the PivotTable layout to create the PivotChart immediately. You can use this method to create a PivotChart using just one or two mouse clicks or keystrokes.

You can create a chart directly from an existing PivotTable using VBA. Select the `PivotTable` object using the `PivotSelect` method and then run the `Chart` object's `Add` method, as shown in the following example:

```
Sub CreatePivotChart()
    Dim objPT As PivotTable
    ' Work with the first PivotTable
    Set objPT = ActiveSheet.PivotTables(1)
    ' Select the PivotTable
    objPT.PivotSelect ""
    ' Add the chart
    Charts.Add
End Sub
```

Create a PivotChart from a PivotTable

Note: This chapter uses the PivotTables.xls spreadsheet, available at www.wiley.com/go/pivottablesvb, or you can create your own sample database.

1. Click any cell in the PivotTable.
2. Click PivotTable➔PivotChart.

   You can also click Insert➔Chart, click the Chart Wizard button (▥) in the PivotTable toolbar, or press F11.

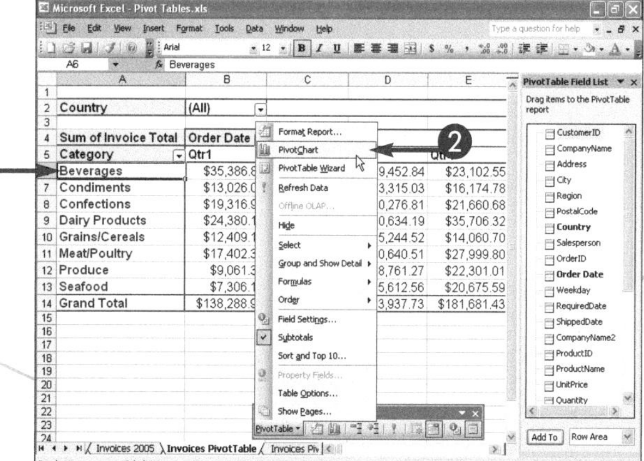

Excel creates a new chart sheet and displays the PivotChart.

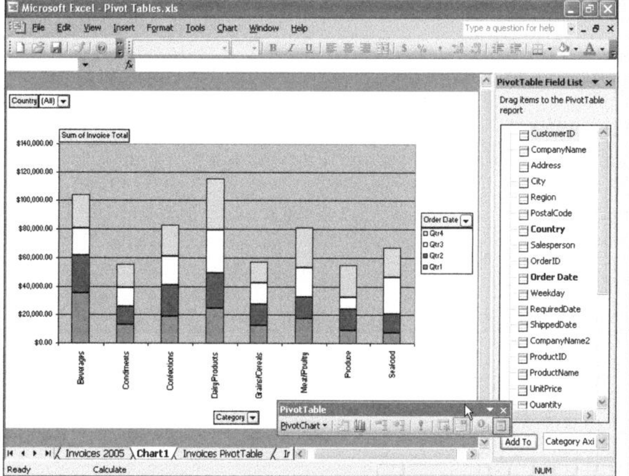

Create a PivotChart from an Excel List

If the data you want to summarize and visualize exists as an Excel range or list, you can use the PivotTable and PivotChart Wizard to build a PivotChart based on your data. The wizard takes you step by step through the process of choosing the type of report you want, specifying the location of your source data, and then choosing the location of the resulting PivotChart.

The PivotTable and PivotChart Wizard has three main steps. In the first step, you choose whether you want a PivotTable or a PivotChart. In this task you learn how to build a PivotChart. To learn how to build a PivotTable, instead, see Chapter 2. The first wizard step also enables you to specify the type of data source you are using. In this task, you learn how to build a PivotChart based on data in an Excel list or range, which is the simplest and most common type of data source. To learn how to build PivotTables from other types of data sources, see Chapters 10 and 11.

In the second step of the PivotTable and PivotChart Wizard, you specify the location of the list or range. If you choose a cell within the list or range in advance, the wizard automatically selects the surrounding list or range. Otherwise, you can click and drag with your mouse to select the data, or type the range address.

Finally, the third step of the wizard enables you to select a location for the PivotTable report that Excel constructs along with your new PivotChart, which Excel automatically places on a new chart sheet.

Create a PivotChart from an Excel List

1. Click a cell within the list or range that you want to use as the source data.
2. Click Data→PivotTable and PivotChart Report.

   The first PivotTable and PivotChart Wizard dialog box appears.

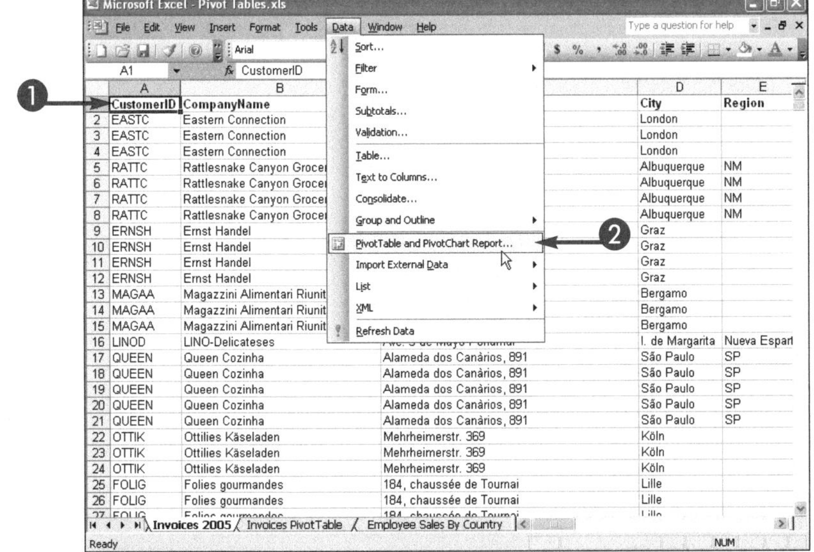

3. Select Microsoft Office Excel list or database.
4. Select PivotChart report.
5. Click Next.

   The second PivotTable and PivotChart Wizard dialog box appears.

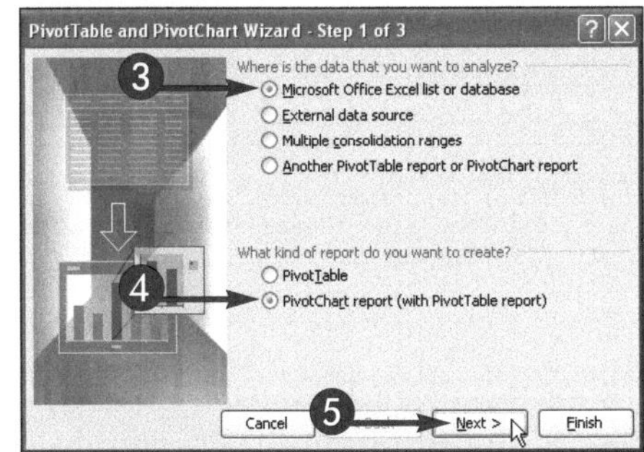

6 Ensure that the displayed range address is correct.

- If the range address is incorrect, click the Collapse Dialog button and then click and drag with your mouse to select the range.

7 Click Next.

The third PivotTable and PivotChart Wizard dialog box appears.

8 Select New worksheet to place the associated PivotTable on a new worksheet.

- If you prefer to place the PivotTable on an existing worksheet, select Existing worksheet, click the Collapse Dialog button, and then click the worksheet and cell where you want the PivotTable to appear.

9 Click Finish.

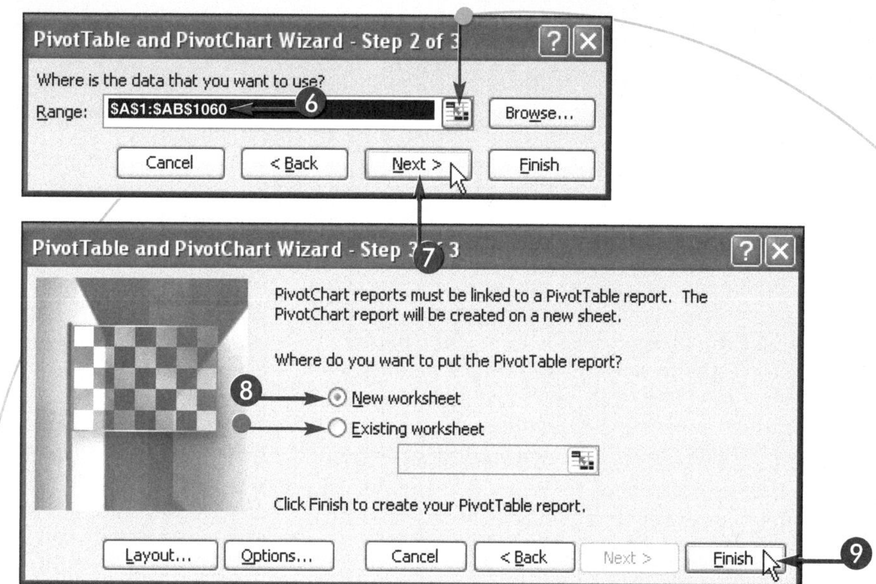

Apply It

After you click Next in the second PivotTable and PivotChart Wizard dialog box, Excel checks to see if you have already built an existing PivotTable based on the range or list you confirmed or chose in Step 6. If a PivotTable based on the same data already exists, Excel displays a dialog box that asks you if you want to base the new PivotChart and PivotTable reports on the existing report. In other words, Excel wants to know if you want the reports to share the same pivot cache.

It is always a good idea to share the pivot cache whenever possible because this greatly reduces the size of the workbook — the bigger the source data, the more space you save. This also reduces the amount of memory the workbook requires, which speeds up your PivotChart and PivotTable operations.

Therefore, be sure to click Yes in the dialog box. Excel then displays a list of the existing PivotTables. This list can be daunting if you have several PivotTables in the workbook and they all have cryptic names such as PivotTable1 and PivotTable2. For this reason, it is a good idea to rename all your PivotTables. In Chapter 6, see the task "Rename the PivotTable." However, Excel automatically selects the PivotTable it thinks you ought to use, so just click Next to move on to the next wizard dialog box.

continued →

Create a PivotChart from an Excel List (continued)

When you click Finish in the third PivotTable and PivotChart Wizard dialog box, Excel creates an empty PivotChart in a new chart sheet. It also creates a PivotTable in a new worksheet or in a location you specify. The empty PivotChart displays four areas with the following labels: Drop Category Fields Here, Drop Series Fields Here, Drop Data Items Here, and Drop Page Fields Here. To complete the PivotTable, you must populate some or all of these areas with one or more fields from your data.

When you add a field to the category, series, or page area, Excel extracts the unique values from the field and displays them in the area. For example, if you add the Salesperson field to the category area, Excel displays the unique salesperson names as categories that run along the X-axis of the chart. Similarly, if you add the Shipper field to the series area, Excel displays the unique shipper names as a separate chart data series. Finally, if you add, say, the Country field to the page area, Excel displays the unique country names in a drop-down list above the PivotChart.

When you add a field to the data area, Excel performs calculations based on the numeric data in the field. The default calculation is sum, so if you add, for example, the Quantity field to the data area, Excel sums the Quantity values. How Excel calculates these sums depends on the fields you have added to the other areas. For example, if you add just the Salesperson field to the row area, Excel displays the sum of the QuantitySale Amount values for each salesperson. You can also use other calculations such as Average and Count; see Chapter 7 to learn how to change the summary calculation.

Create a PivotChart from an Excel List *(continued)*

- Excel creates the empty PivotChart.
- Excel creates the associated PivotTable on a separate worksheet.
- The PivotTable toolbar appears.
- The PivotTable Field List appears.

10 Click and drag a field from the PivotTable Field List and drop it inside the category area.

Excel displays the field's unique values in the PivotChart's category area.

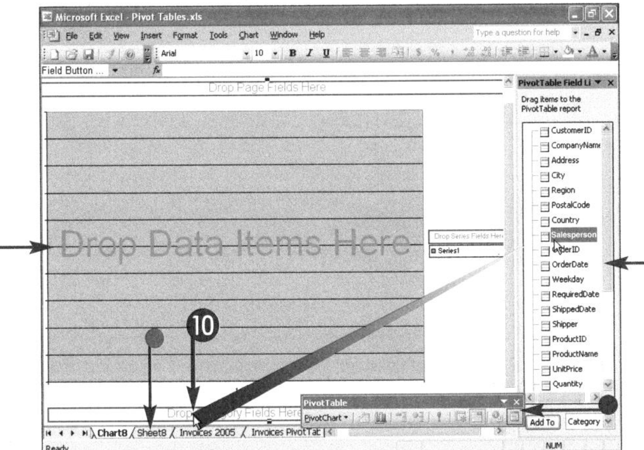

- Excel displays the field's unique values in the PivotChart's category area.

11 Click and drag a numeric field from the PivotTable Field List and drop it inside the data area.

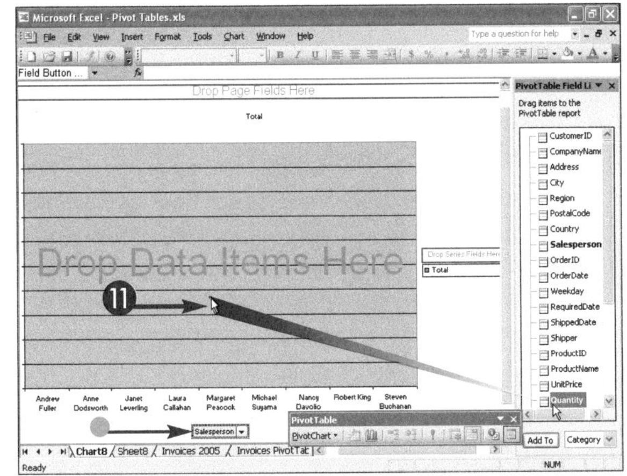

- Excel displays the summary results in the PivotChart plot area.

⓬ If required for your PivotTable, click and drag a field from the PivotTable Field List and drop it inside the series area.

⓭ If required for your PivotTable, click and drag a field from the PivotTable Field List and drop it inside the page area.

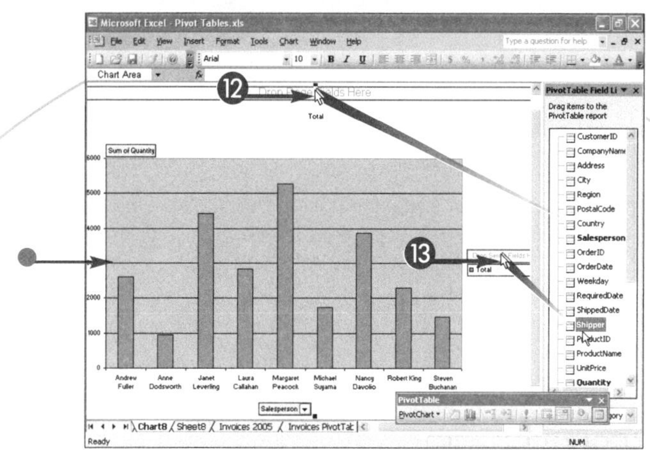

- Excel displays the field's unique values as PivotChart data series.
- Excel displays the field's unique values in the PivotChart's page drop-down list.

The basic PivotChart is complete.

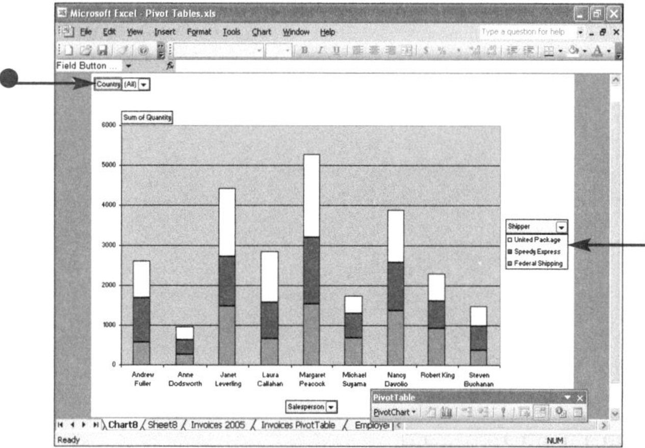

Extra

If your PivotChart includes just a category field, then Excel displays the results using a standard bar chart. If the PivotChart includes both a category field and a series field, then Excel displays the results using a stacked column chart. To learn how to view the PivotChart using a different type of chart, see the task "Change the PivotChart Type," later in this chapter.

The stacked column chart is a great way to visualize two-dimensional PivotTable results, but it is not always easy to decipher the chart. This is particularly true if you have a large number of data series, which usually means that most of the columns in each category are quite small. To help get a better understanding of the chart, you might want to know what data is represented by specific columns.

You can find the specifics related to each column by moving the mouse pointer over the column in the plot area. Excel then displays a banner with data in the following format:

```
Series "SeriesItem" Point "CategoryItem" Value: Value
```

Here, *SeriesItem* is an item from the series field, *CategoryItem* is an item from the category field, and *Value* is the value of the data point. For example, if the Shipper field has an item named United Package, the Salesperson field has an item named Steven Buchanan, and the value is 488, the banner shows the following:

```
Series "United Package" Point "Steven Buchanan" Value: 488
```

Create a PivotChart Beside a PivotTable

You can create a PivotChart on the same worksheet as its associated PivotTable. This enables you to easily compare the PivotTable and the PivotChart.

Whether you create a PivotChart directly from an existing PivotTable — see the task "Create a PivotChart from a PivotTable" — or use the PivotTable and PivotChart Wizard — see the task "Create a PivotChart from an Excel List," — Excel places the chart on a new chart sheet. This is usually the best solution because it gives you the most room to view and manipulate the PivotChart. However, it is often useful to view the PivotChart together with its associated PivotTable. For example, when you change the PivotTable view, Excel automatically changes the PivotChart view in the same way. Rather than switching from one sheet to another to compare the results, having the PivotChart on the same worksheet enables you to compare the PivotChart and PivotTable immediately.

This task shows you how to create a new PivotChart on the same worksheet as an existing PivotTable. This is called *embedding* the PivotChart on the worksheet. If you already have a PivotChart, you can move it to the PivotTable's worksheet; see the next task, "Move a PivotChart to Another Sheet."

Create a PivotChart Beside a PivotTable

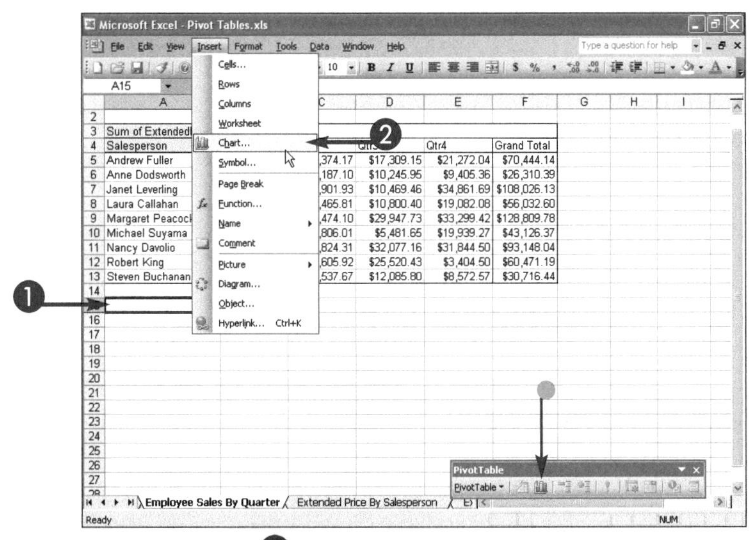

1. Click any cell in the PivotTable's worksheet.

Note: Make sure the cell you click is not within the PivotTable itself.

2. Click Insert➔Chart.

   - You can also click the Chart Wizard button in the Standard toolbar.

   The first Chart Wizard dialog box appears.

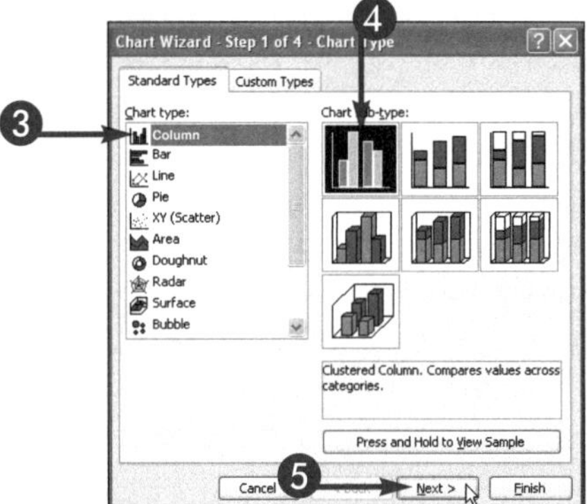

3. Click the chart type you want.

Note: You cannot use the XY (scatter), Bubble, or Stock chart type with a PivotChart.

4. Click the Chart sub-type you want.
5. Click Next.

   The second Chart Wizard dialog box appears.

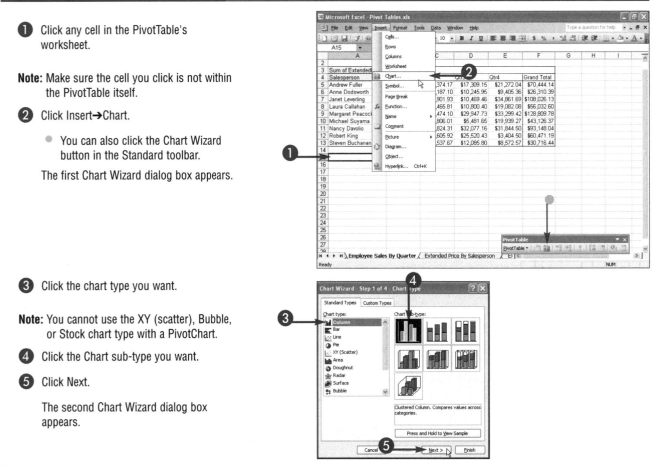

6 Click any cell in the PivotTable.

- Excel adds the PivotTable range to the Data range text box.

7 Click Finish.

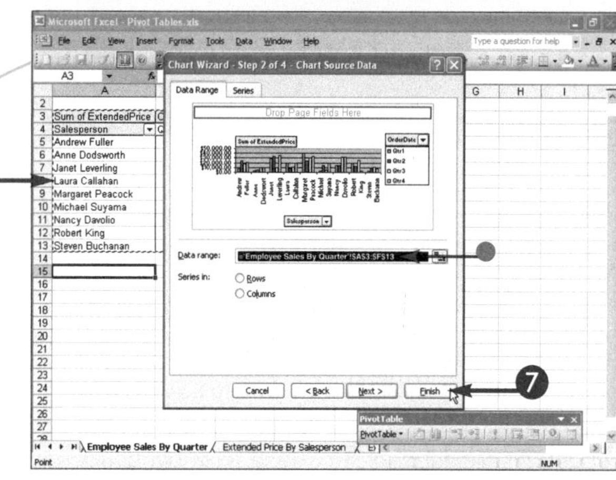

Excel embeds the PivotChart on the PivotTable's worksheet.

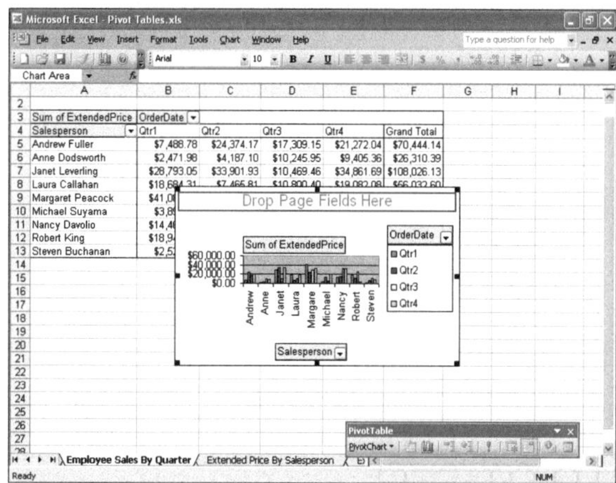

Apply It

Excel embeds the PivotChart in the center of the visible worksheet area. In most cases, this means the new PivotChart overlaps your existing PivotTable, which makes it more difficult to compare them. To fix this problem, you can move or resize the PivotChart. To move the PivotChart, move the mouse pointer over an empty part of the chart area, and then click and drag the chart object to the new position. To resize the PivotChart, first click the chart to select it. Then move the mouse pointer over any one of the black selection handles that appear on the chart area's corners and sides. Click and drag a handle to the size you require.

In the task "Create a PivotChart from a PivotTable," earlier in this chapter, you saw a macro that created a new PivotChart from a PivotTable. You can modify that macro to embed the PivotChart on the PivotTable's worksheet by using the `Chart` object's `Location` property to specify the worksheet name. Specifically, you can add the following statement after the `Charts.Add` method:

Example:

```
ActiveChart.Location _
    Where:=xlLocationAsObject, _
    Name:=objPT.Parent.Name
```

Move a PivotChart to Another Sheet

If you have an existing PivotChart that resides in a separate chart sheet, you can move the PivotChart to a worksheet. This reduces the number of sheets in the workbook and, if you move the chart to the PivotTable's worksheet, it makes it easier to compare the PivotChart with its associated PivotTable.

In the task "Create a PivotChart Beside a PivotTable," earlier in this chapter, you learned how to create a new PivotChart on a worksheet instead of in the default location, which is a separate chart sheet. However, there may be situations where this separate chart sheet is not convenient. For example, if you want to compare the PivotChart and its associated PivotTable, that comparison is more difficult if the PivotChart and PivotTable reside in separate sheets. Similarly, you may prefer to place all your PivotCharts on a single sheet so that you can compare them or so that they are easy to find. Finally, if you plan on creating a number of PivotCharts, you might not want to clutter your workbook with separate chart sheets.

The solution in all these cases is to move your PivotChart or PivotCharts to the sheet you prefer. This task shows you how to move a PivotChart to a new location.

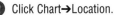

Move a PivotChart to Another Sheet

1. Click the PivotChart you want to move.

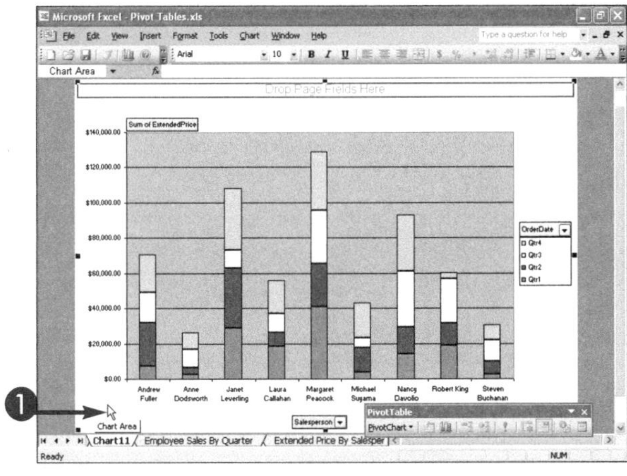

2. Click Chart➔Location.

   You can also right-click the chart area or plot area and then click Location.

   The Chart Location dialog box appears.

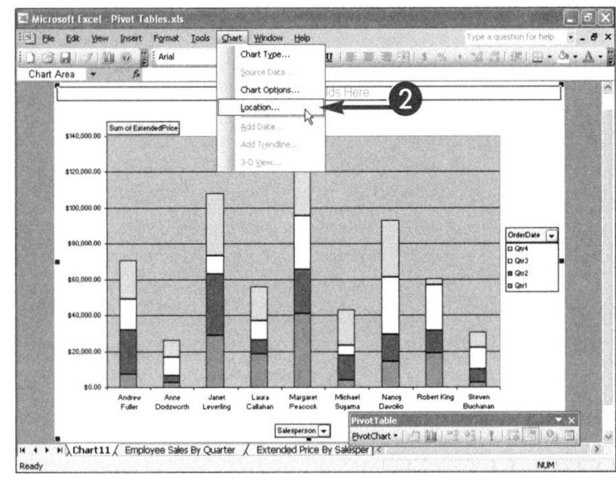

3. Select As object in.
4. Click ▾ and then click the sheet to which you want to move the PivotChart.
5. Click OK.

Excel moves the PivotChart to the location you specified.

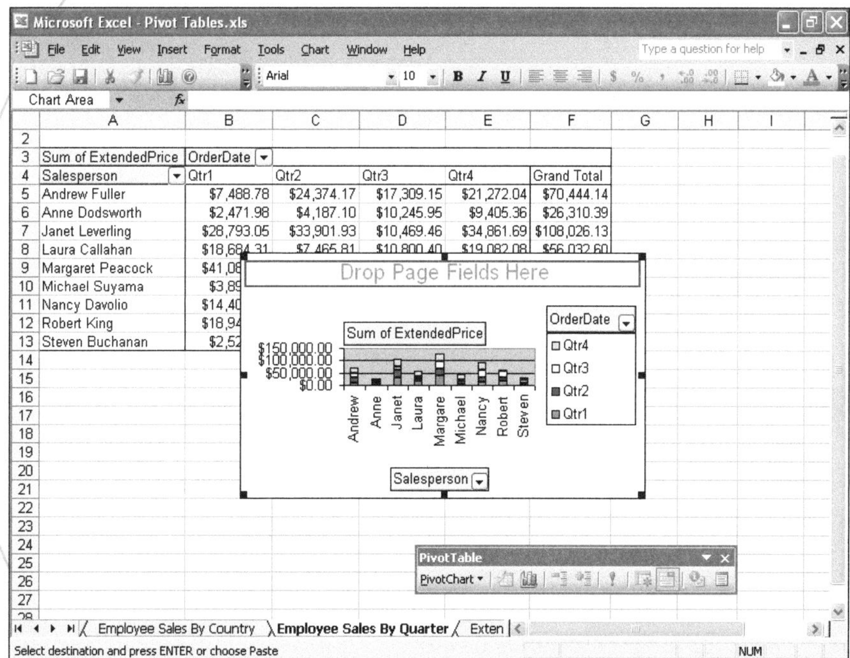

Extra

The steps you learned in this task apply both to PivotCharts embedded in separate chart sheets and to PivotChart objects floating on worksheets. For the latter, however, there is a second technique you can use. First, click the PivotChart object to select it. Then click Edit→Cut, click the Cut button ( ), or press Ctrl+X. Display the sheet to which you want to move the PivotChart. If you are moving the PivotChart to a worksheet, click the cell where you want the upper-left corner of the chart to appear. Click Edit→Paste, click the Paste button ( ), or press Ctrl+V. Excel pastes the PivotChart object to the sheet. Move and resize the PivotChart object as needed.

Hide or Show PivotChart Field Buttons

You can toggle off and on the buttons that Excel displays for each field you have added to a PivotChart. Hiding the field buttons is useful if you need more room to display the PivotChart results or if you do not want others to change the PivotChart layout.

When you add a field to the PivotChart's category, series, data, or page area, Excel displays a button for the field. In the category and series areas, you can use the field button to display a list of items in the field, and you can then hide or display the items you want to include in the PivotChart. In the page area, the field button is a drop-down list that enables you to filter the PivotChart data based on the selected page field item. For all four PivotChart areas, you can also use the field buttons to change the layout of the PivotChart by moving a field from one area to another.

However, there may be times when you do not want to include the field buttons in the PivotChart view. For example, the field buttons take up a significant amount of room within the chart area. If the entire chart does not fit onscreen, or if you want to increase the size of the PivotChart to fit the screen, hiding the field buttons can give you extra room. Alternatively, you may prefer not to allow other users to manipulate the PivotChart layout: moving fields, hiding items, or filtering the data. You can prevent this by hiding the field buttons.

Hide or Show PivotChart Field Buttons

HIDE PIVOTCHART FIELD BUTTONS

1. Click the PivotChart.
2. Click PivotChart→Hide PivotChart Field Buttons.

   Excel displays a check mark beside the Hide PivotChart Field Buttons command.

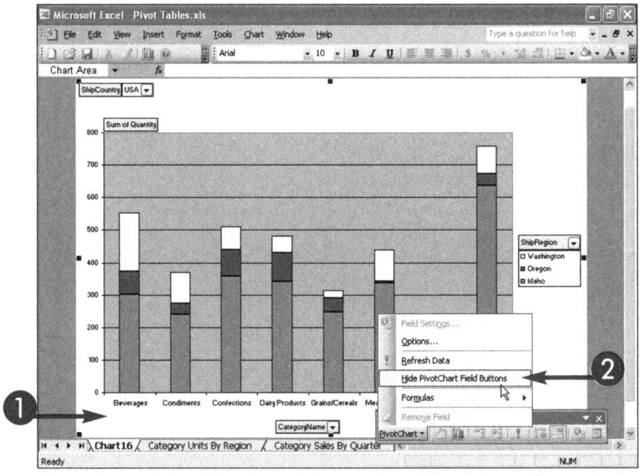

Excel hides the field buttons.

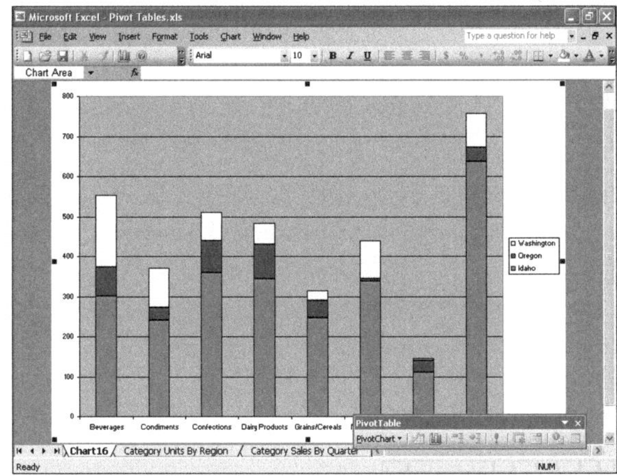

SHOW PIVOTCHART FIELD BUTTONS

1. Click the PivotChart.

2. Click PivotChart→Hide PivotChart Field Buttons.

   Excel removes the check mark from beside the Hide PivotChart Field Buttons command.

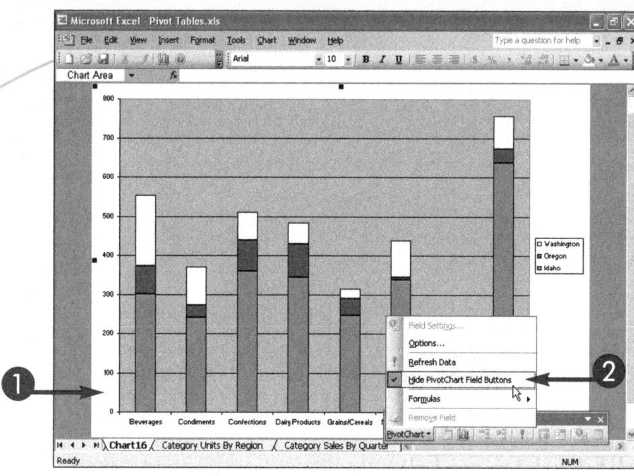

Excel shows the field buttons.

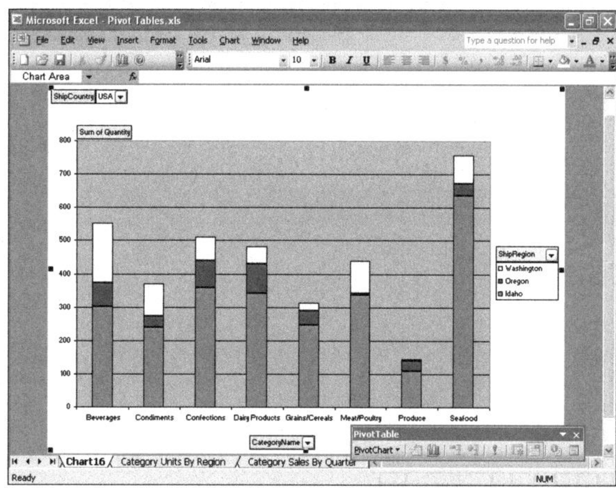

Apply It

You can use a VBA macro to control the display of a PivotChart's field buttons. You can do this by setting the `Chart` object's `HasPivotFields` property to `True`, with the buttons displayed, or `False`, with the buttons hidden. The following macro toggles the field buttons on and off for the active PivotChart:

Example:

```
Sub TogglePivotChartFieldButtons()
    '
    ' Work with the active chart
    With ActiveChart
        '
        ' Toggle the HasPivotFields property
        .HasPivotFields = Not .HasPivotFields
        '
        ' Display the current state
        MsgBox "The PivotChart's field buttons are now " & _
               IIf(.HasPivotFields, "visible.", "hidden.")
    End With
End Sub
```

Change the PivotChart Type

You can modify your PivotChart to use a chart type that is more suitable for displaying the report data.

When you create a PivotChart, by default, Excel uses a stacked column chart. If you do not include a series field in the PivotChart, Excel displays the report using regular columns, which is useful for comparing the values across the category field's items. If you include a series field in the PivotChart, Excel displays the report using stacked columns, where each category shows several different-colored columns stacked on top of each other, one for each item in the series field. This is useful for comparing the contribution each series item has on the category totals.

Although this default chart type is fine for many applications, it is not always the best choice. For example, if you do not have a series field and you want to see the relative contribution of each category item to the total, a pie chart would be a better choice. If you are more interested in showing how the results trend over time, then a line chart is usually the ideal type.

Whatever your needs, Excel enables you to change the default PivotChart type to any of the following types: Column, Bar, Line, Pie, Area, Doughnut, Radar, Surface, Cylinder, Cone, or Pyramid. Remember that Excel does not allow you to use the following chart types with a PivotChart: XY (Scatter), Bubble, or Stock.

Change the PivotChart Type

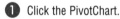

1. Click the PivotChart.
2. Click Chart→Chart Type.

   The Chart Type dialog box appears.

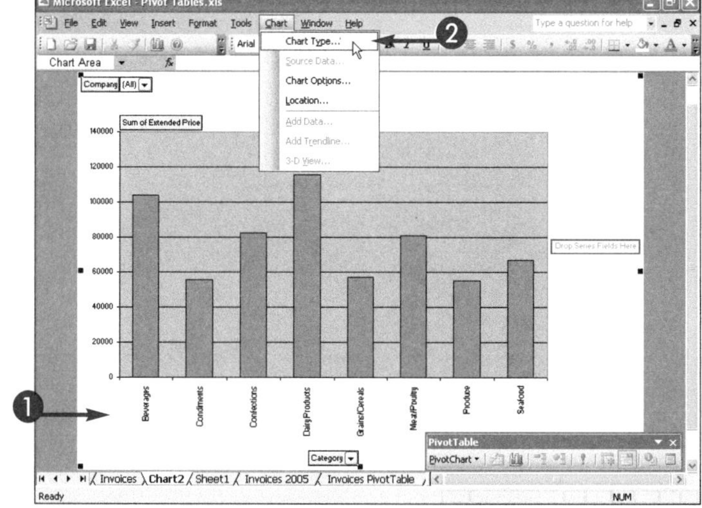

3. Click the chart type you want to use.

   Excel displays the available chart sub-types.

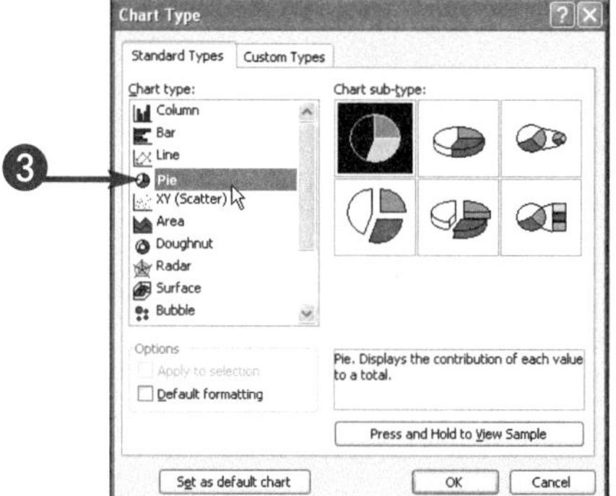

4 Click the Chart sub-type you want to use.

5 Click OK.

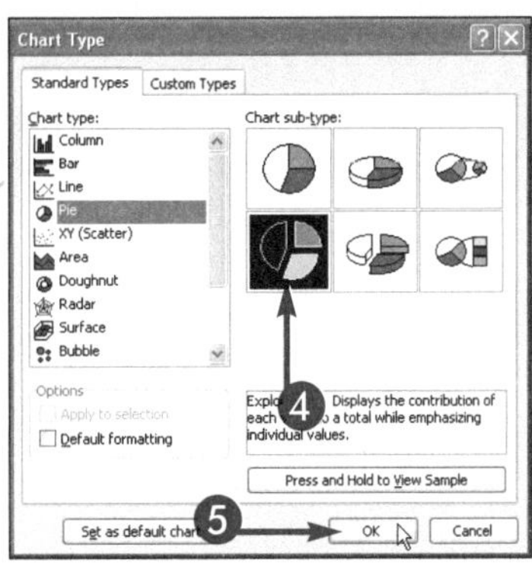

Excel redisplays the PivotChart with the new chart type.

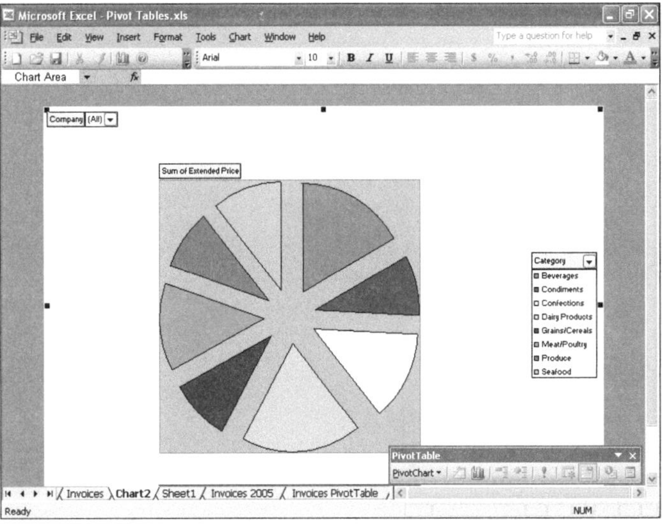

Extra

Depending on the chart type you choose, it is often useful to augment the chart with the actual values from the report. For example, with a pie chart, you can add to each slice the value as well as the percentage the value represents of the grand total. In most cases you can also add the series name and the category name.

To add these data labels to your PivotChart, click the chart and then click Chart→Chart Options. In the Chart Options dialog box, click the Data Labels tab, and then activate the Value check box (☐ changes to ☑). Depending on the data, you may also be able to activate the Series name, Category name, and Percentage check boxes (☐ changes to ☑).

If there is a particular chart type that you would prefer to use for all your future PivotCharts, you can set that chart type as the default. Follow Steps 1 to 4 in this task to open the Chart Type dialog box and choose your chart type and sub-type. Then click the "Set as default chart" button. When Excel asks you to confirm that you want to use this chart type as the default, click Yes. Click OK to close the Chart Type dialog box.

Change the PivotChart Series Order

You can customize the PivotChart to display the data series in a different order.

When you create a PivotChart and include a series field, Excel displays the data series based on the order of the field's items as they appear in the PivotTable. That is, as you move left to right through the items in the PivotTable's category field, the data series moves bottom to top in the PivotChart's series field. This default series order is fine in most applications, but you may prefer to change the order. In the default stacked column chart, for example, you may prefer to reverse the data series so that they appear from top to bottom.

In other cases, you may prefer to display the data series in some custom order. For example, you may want to rearrange employee names so that those who have the same supervisor or who work in the same division appear together. It is possible to sort the data series items, but Excel also gives you the option of rearranging the series order by hand, as described in this task. See the tip on the next page for more about sorting data series items.

Change the PivotChart Series Order

1. Right-click any data series and then click Format Data Series.

   The Format Data Series dialog box appears.

2. Click the Series Order tab.

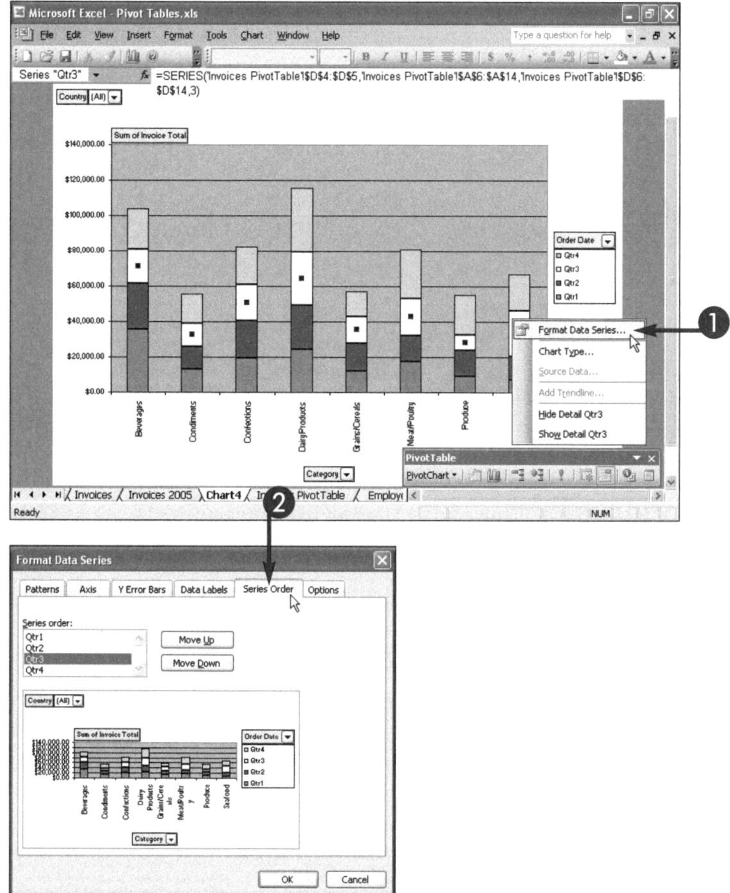

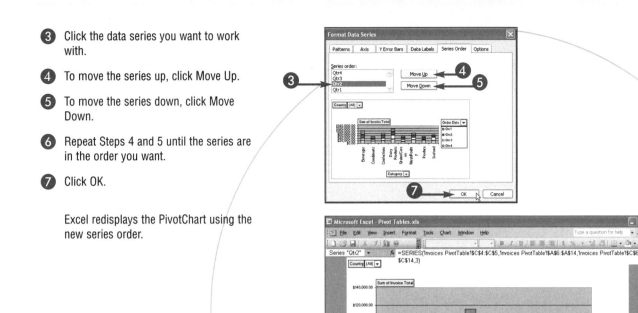

3 Click the data series you want to work with.

4 To move the series up, click Move Up.

5 To move the series down, click Move Down.

6 Repeat Steps 4 and 5 until the series are in the order you want.

7 Click OK.

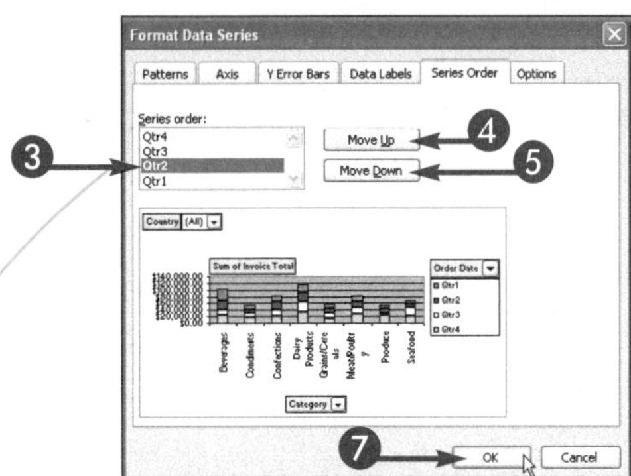

Excel redisplays the PivotChart using the new series order.

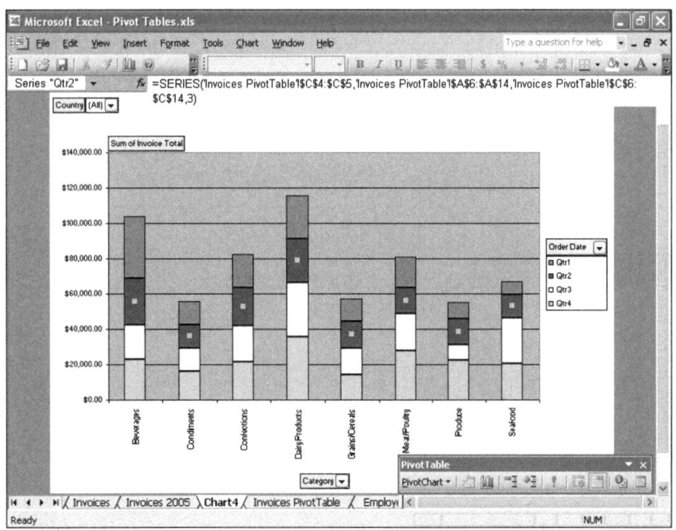

Extra

Besides changing the series order by moving data series by hand, Excel also enables you to sort the PivotChart's data using the AutoSort feature. To learn more about this feature, see the task "Sort PivotTable Data with AutoSort" in Chapter 4.

Click the data series field button and then click PivotChart→Field Settings to display the PivotTable Field dialog box. Click Advanced to display the PivotTable Field Advanced Options dialog box. Select Ascending (○ changes to ◉) or Descending (○ changes to ◉) and then click the field upon which you want to base the sort. Note that this field is almost always the same as the field used for the data series items. Then click OK to return to the PivotTable Field dialog box, and click OK again to sort the data series items.

Note, as well, that you can apply the same technique to the items in the category field and the page field.

Add PivotChart Titles

You can add one or more titles to your PivotChart to make the report easier to understand.

By default, Excel does not add any titles to your PivotChart. This is not a concern for most PivotCharts because the field names and item labels often provide enough context to understand the report. However, the data you are using may have cryptic field names or it may have coded item names, so the default PivotChart may be difficult to decipher. In that case, you can add titles to the PivotChart that make the report more comprehensible.

Excel offers three PivotChart titles: an overall chart title that sits above the chart's plot area; a title for the category (X) axis that sits between the category items and the category field button; and a title for the value (Y) axis that sits to the left of the value axis labels. You can add one or more of these titles to your PivotChart. And although Excel does not allow you to move these titles to a different location, you can adjust the font, border, background, and text alignment.

The downside to adding PivotChart titles is that each one takes up some space within the chart area, which means there is less space to display the PivotChart itself. This is not usually a problem with a simple PivotChart, but if you have a complex chart — particularly if you have a large number of category items — then you may prefer not to display titles at all, or you may prefer to display only one or two.

Add PivotChart Titles

1. Click the PivotChart.
2. Click Chart➔Chart Options.

   The Chart Options dialog box appears.

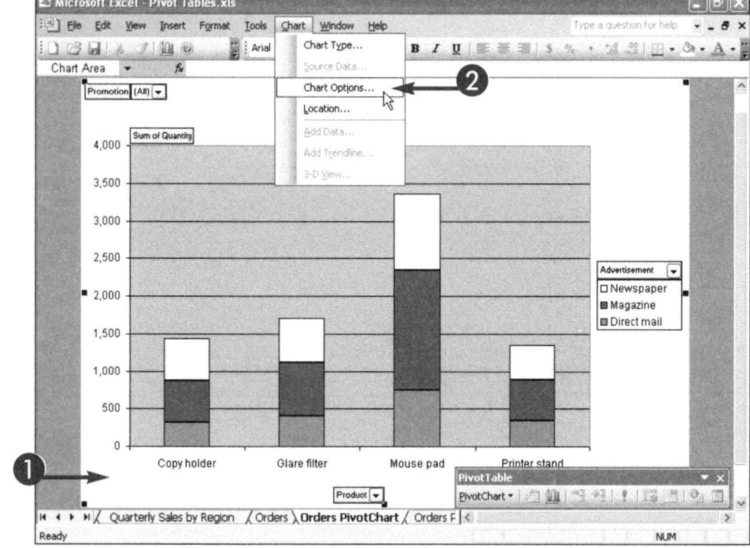

3. Click the Titles tab.

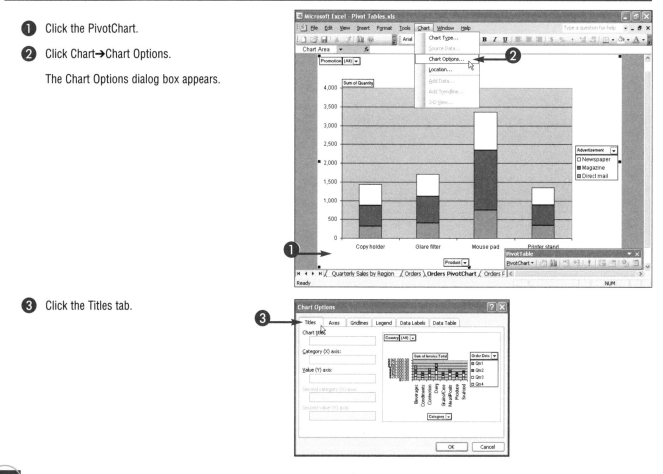

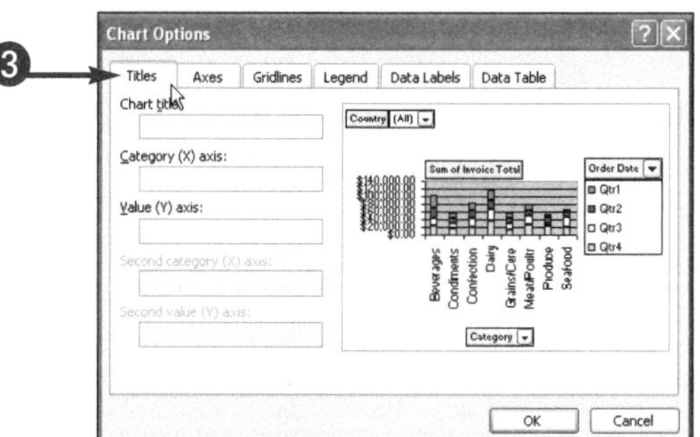

4. Type the Chart title.
5. Type the Category (X) axis title.
6. Type the Value (Y) axis title.
7. Click OK.

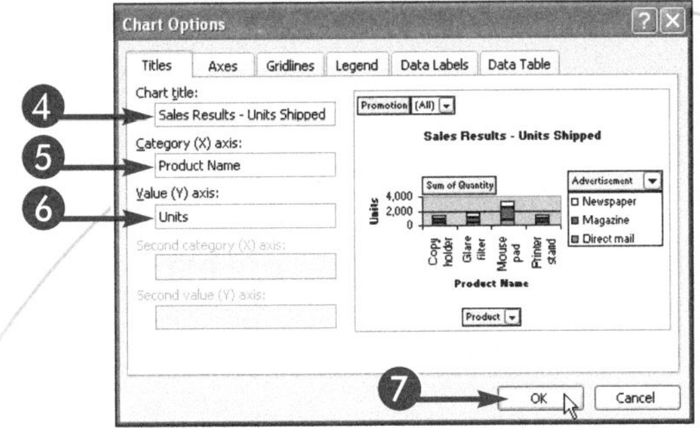

Excel displays the titles in the PivotChart.

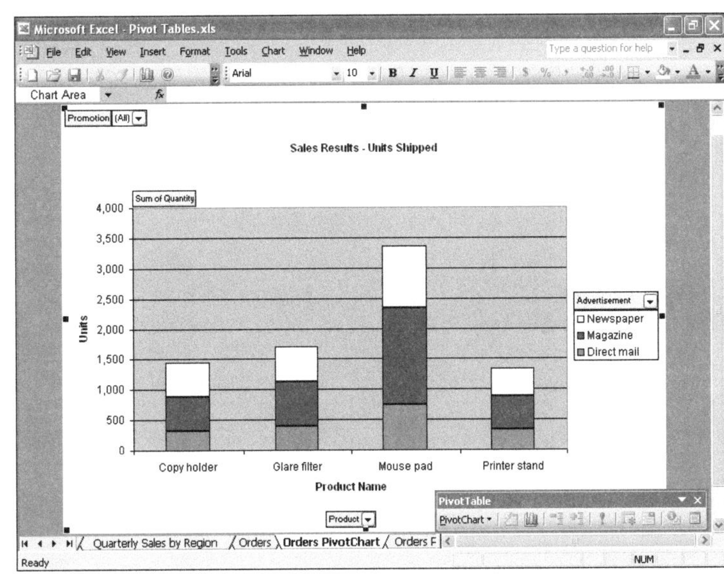

Apply It

To format the chart title, right-click the title and then click Format Chart Title. To format an axis title, right-click the title and then click Format Axis Title. Or, you can also double-click a title. In the dialog box that appears, use the Patterns tab to apply a border or shadow effect, as well as a background color or fill effect. You can use the Font tab to specify the typeface, style, size, color, and effects for the title text. You can use the Alignment tab to configure the alignment and orientation of the text within the title. Click OK when you are done. Note, too, that you can also format a title by clicking it and then clicking the buttons in Excel's Formatting toolbar.

To edit a title, either follow the steps in this task and change the text in the Titles tab, or click the title once to select it, and then click the text to open the title for editing. Excel gives you three methods for removing a title from a PivotChart:

- Follow the steps in this task and, in the Titles tab, delete the text for the title you want to remove.
- Right-click the title you want to remove and then click Clear.
- Click the title you want to remove and then press Delete.

Move the PivotChart Legend

You can change the placement of the PivotChart legend to give the chart more room or to better display the data series within the legend.

The PivotChart legend appears below the series field button and it displays the series field items along with a colored box that tells you which series belongs to which item. By default, Excel displays the legend to the right of the plot area. This is usually the best position because it does not interfere with other chart elements such as titles — see the previous task, "Add PivotChart Titles" — or the value (Y) axis labels.

However, displaying the legend on the right does mean that it takes up space that would otherwise be used by your PivotChart. If you have a number of category items in your PivotChart report, you may prefer to display the legend above or below the plot area to give the PivotChart more horizontal room.

Excel enables you to move the legend to one of five positions with respect to the chart area: right, left, bottom, top, and upper right corner. Bear in mind that Excel always displays the series field button with the legend, so if you move the legend you also move the field button.

Move the PivotChart Legend

1. Click the PivotChart.
2. Click Chart➔Chart Options.

   The Chart Options dialog box appears.

3. Click the Legend tab.

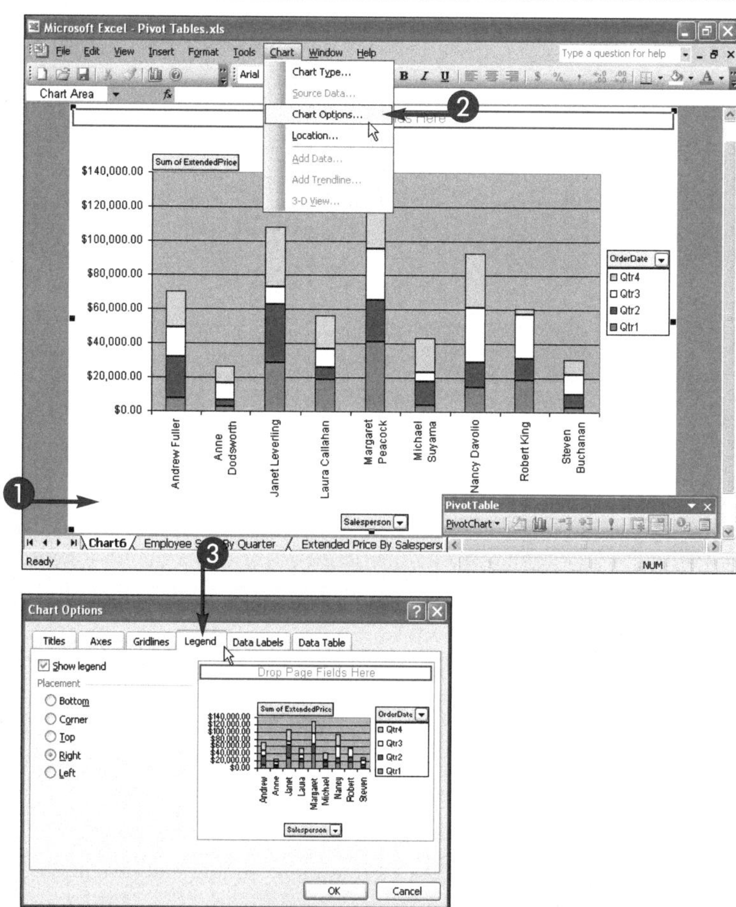

4 Select the placement option you want.

5 Click OK.

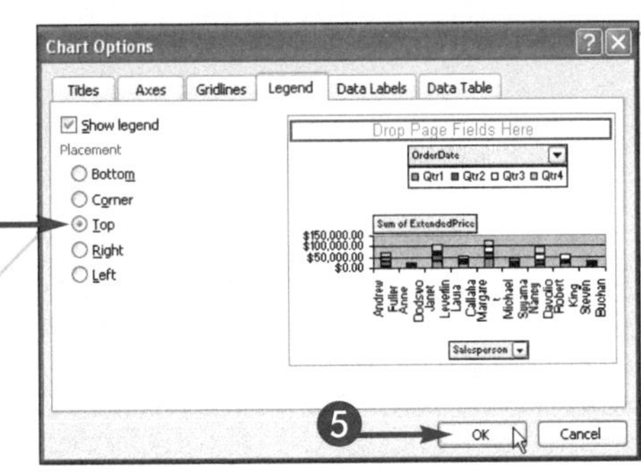

Excel displays the legend in the new position.

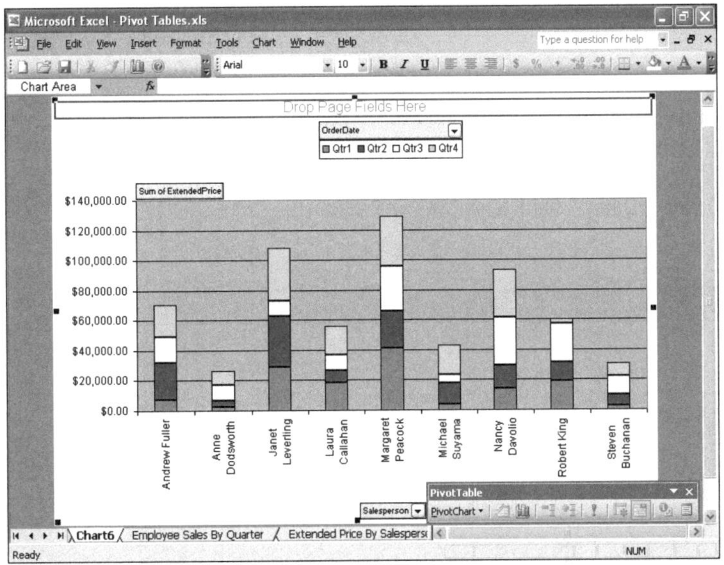

Extra

In some cases, you might prefer to not display the legend at all. For example, if your PivotChart does not have a series field, Excel still displays a legend for the default "series" named Total. This is not particularly useful, so you can gain some extra chart space by hiding the legend. To do this, follow Steps 1 to 3 to display the Legend tab. Deselect "Show legend" (☑ changes to ☐) and then click OK. Alternatively, right-click the legend and then click Clear.

To format the legend, right-click the legend and then click Format Legend; you can also double-click the legend. In the Format Legend dialog box, use the Patterns tab to apply a border or shadow effect, as well as a background color or fill effect. Use the Font tab to specify the typeface, style, size, color, and effects for the title text. Note, too, that you can also format a legend by clicking it and then clicking the buttons in Excel's Formatting toolbar.

You can also change the font of individual legend entries. Click the legend to select it, and then click the legend entry you want to work with. Right-click the entry, click Format Legend Entry, and then, in the dialog box that appears, use the Font tab to set the entry font.

Display a Data Table with the PivotChart

To augment your PivotChart and make the chart report easier to understand and analyze, you can display a data table that provides the values underlying each category and data series.

The point of a PivotChart is to combine the visualization effects of an Excel chart with the pivoting and filtering capabilities of a PivotTable. The visualization part helps your data analysis because it enables you to make at-a-glance comparisons between series and categories, and it enables you to view data points relative to other parts of the report.

However, while visualizing the data is often useful, it lacks a certain precision because you do not see the underlying data. Excel offers several ways to overcome this including creating the PivotChart on the same worksheet as the PivotTable, see the task "Create a PivotChart Beside a PivotTable;" moving a chart to the PivotTable worksheet, see the task "Move a PivotChart to Another Sheet;" and displaying data labels, see the tip in the task "Change the PivotChart Type," all earlier in this chapter.

Yet another method is to display a data table along with the PivotChart. A PivotChart data table is a table that displays the chart's categories as columns and its data series as rows, with the cells filled with the actual data values. Because these values appear directly below the chart, the data table gives you an easy way to combine a visual report with the specifics of the underlying data.

Display a Data Table with the PivotChart

1. Click the PivotChart.
2. Click Chart→Chart Options.

   The Chart Options dialog box appears.

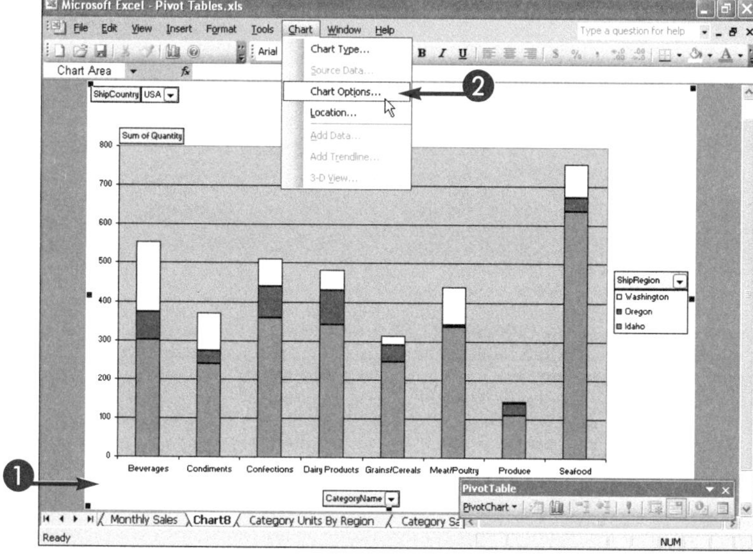

3. Click the Data Table tab.

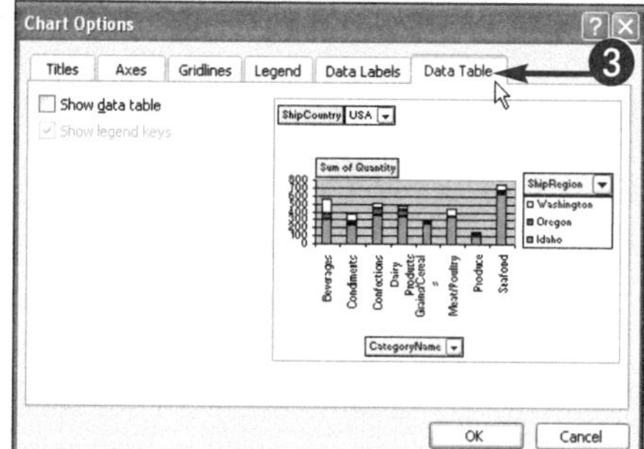

4 Select Show data table.

5 Click OK.

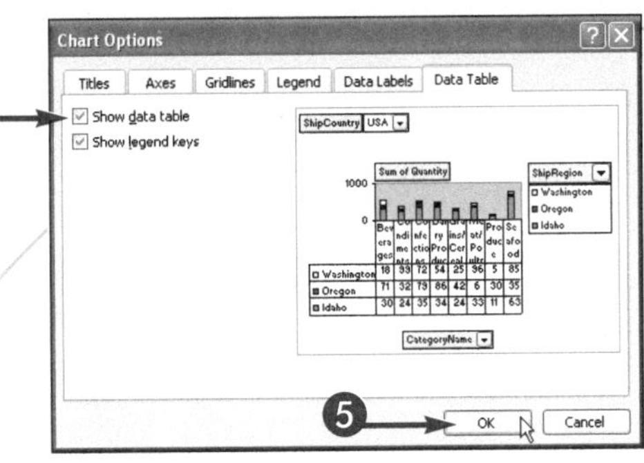

Excel displays the data table below the PivotChart.

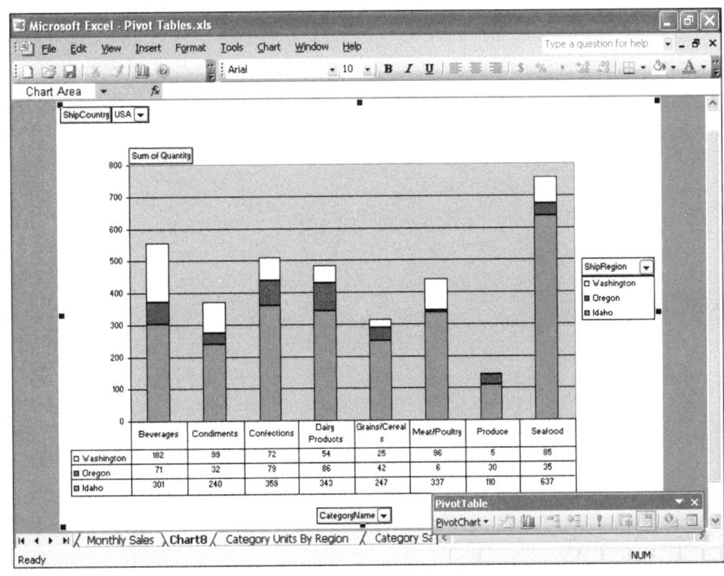

Apply It

You can use a VBA macro to control the display of a PivotChart's data table. You do this by setting the `Chart` object's `HasDataTable` property to `True`, with the data table displayed, or `False` with the data table hidden. The following macro toggles the data table on and off for the active PivotChart:

Example:

```
Sub TogglePivotChartDataTable()
    '
    ' Work with the active chart
    With ActiveChart
        '
        ' Toggle the HasDataTable property
        .HasDataTable = Not .HasDataTable
        '
        ' Display the current state
        MsgBox "The PivotChart's data table is " & _
               IIf(.HasDataTable, "visible.", "hidden.")
    End With
End Sub
```

Print a PivotChart

You can print your PivotChart if you require a hard copy for mailing, faxing, or filing, if you want to document changes, or if you want to compare PivotCharts.

Like a PivotTable, a PivotChart is most useful in electronic form where you can format it, change the layout, and perform the other manipulations that you have learned about in this chapter to enhance your analysis of the data.

However, after you have completed the PivotChart, you might want to preserve a hard copy by printing out the PivotChart report. You can use the printout to send a copy to another person, store the report in a file, or provide a backup if you lose the original electronic report or if the original report is no longer available.

Printing the PivotChart is also useful for documenting intermediate steps in the data analysis. If your analysis consists of four or five changes to the PivotChart, you could get a printout at each stage to document what you have done.

Printouts are also useful for comparing PivotChart results side by side. For example, you could construct the PivotChart using one layout and then print it out. You could then change the PivotChart layout and get a second printout. With the two printouts beside each other, you can then quickly scan the reports to compare them.

Print a PivotChart

1. Click the chart sheet containing the PivotChart you want to print.

   If the PivotChart you want to print is embedded on a worksheet, click the chart object.

2. Click File➔Page Setup.

   The Page Setup dialog box appears.

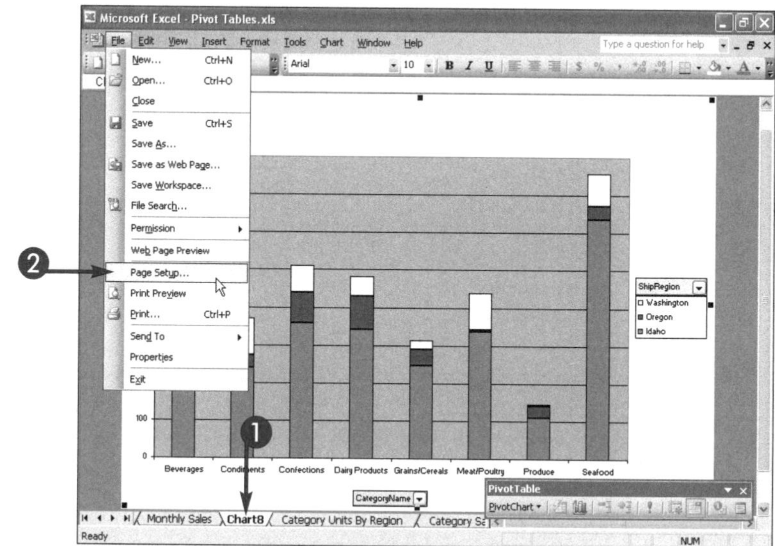

3. Set the paper type, margins, header and footer, and other page setup options.

4. Click Print.

   The Print dialog box appears.

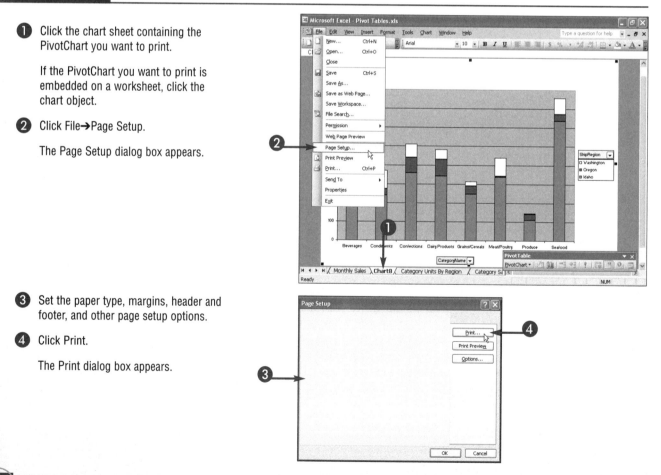

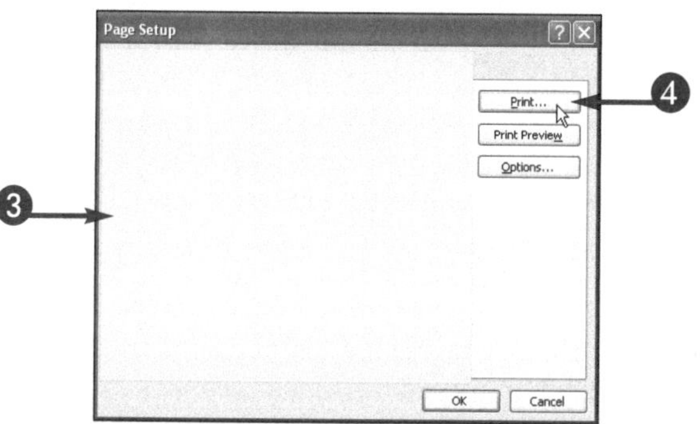

5 Select Active sheet(s).

If the PivotChart you want to print is embedded on a worksheet, select Selected Chart, instead.

6 Set any other print options you require.

7 Click Preview.

The Preview window appears.

8 Examine the print preview to ensure that your PivotChart prints the way you want.

9 Click Print.

Excel prints the PivotChart.

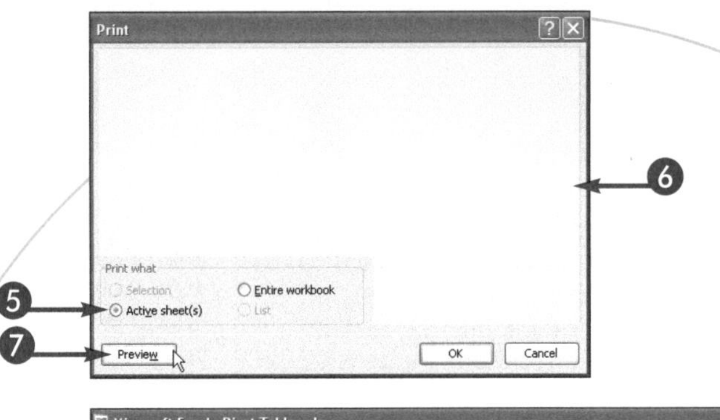

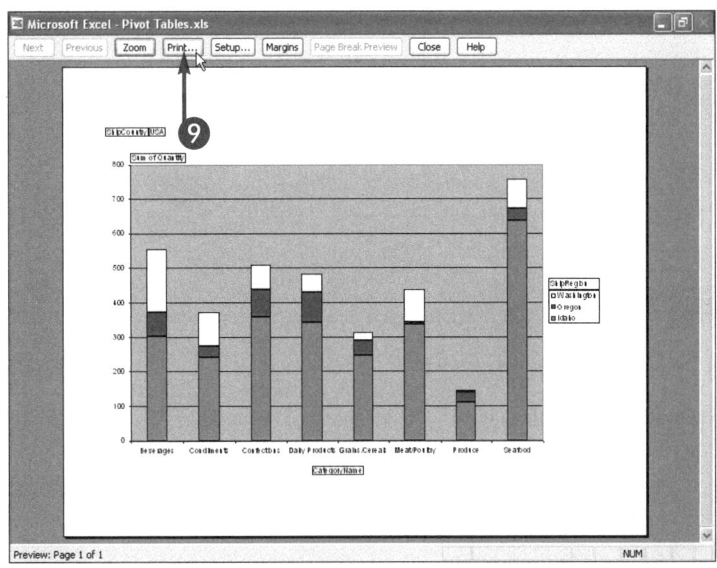

Extra

Excel gives you several options for controlling the size of the PivotChart printout. To see these options, follow Steps 1 and 2 to display the Page Setup dialog box, and then click the Chart tab. The options appear in the Printed chart size group.

If you have a small PivotChart and you want the maximum print size to make the chart easier to read, select the "Use full page" option (◯ changes to ⦿). Excel increases the PivotChart width and height so that it uses the entire page, up to but not including the margins.

If you have a large PivotChart that does not print on a single page, select the "Scale to fit page" option (◯ changes to ⦿). Excel scales the PivotChart dimensions so that it fits onto a single printed page.

If you would rather set the size of the PivotChart printout by hand, select the Custom option, instead (◯ changes to ⦿). In this case, after you click OK, Excel displays a sizing border around the PivotChart. Click and drag the edges or corners of the border to set the size of the PivotChart printout you want.

Delete a PivotChart

PivotCharts are useful data analysis tools, and now that you are becoming comfortable with them, you may find that you use them quite often. This gives you tremendous insight into your data, but that insight comes at a cost: PivotCharts are very resource-intensive, so creating many PivotChart reports can lead to large workbook file sizes and less memory available for other programs. You can reduce the impact that a large number of open PivotCharts have on your system by deleting those reports that you no longer need.

Even if you create just a few PivotCharts, you may find that you need them only temporarily. For example, you may just want to build a quick-and-dirty report to check a few numbers. Similarly, your source data may be preliminary, so you might want to create a temporary PivotChart for now, holding off on a more permanent version until your source data is complete. Finally, you might build a PivotChart report to send to other people. When that is done, you might no longer need the reports yourself. For all these scenarios, you need to know how to delete a PivotChart report, and this task shows you how it is done.

Delete a PivotChart

DELETE A PIVOTCHART SHEET

1. Right-click the tab of the PivotChart sheet.
2. Click Delete.

   Excel asks you to confirm the deletion.

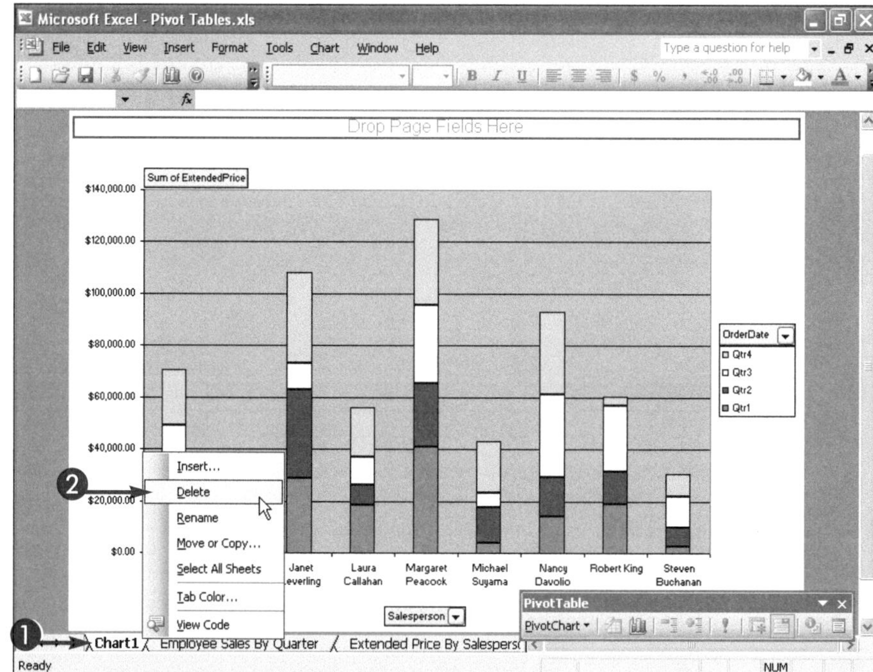

3. Click Delete.

   Excel deletes the PivotChart sheet.

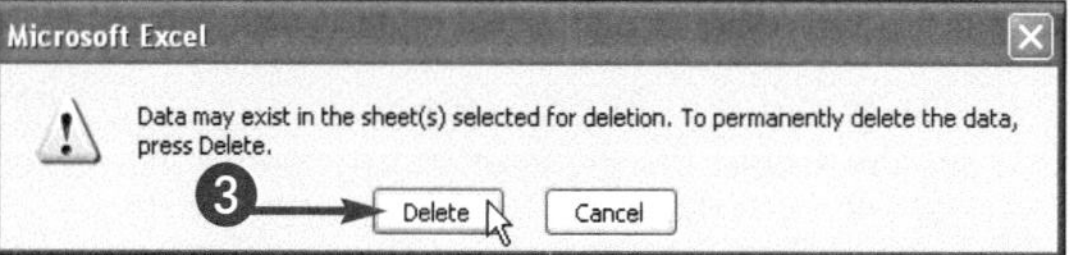

DELETE AN EMBEDDED PIVOTCHART

1. Click the embedded PivotChart.

2. Press Delete.

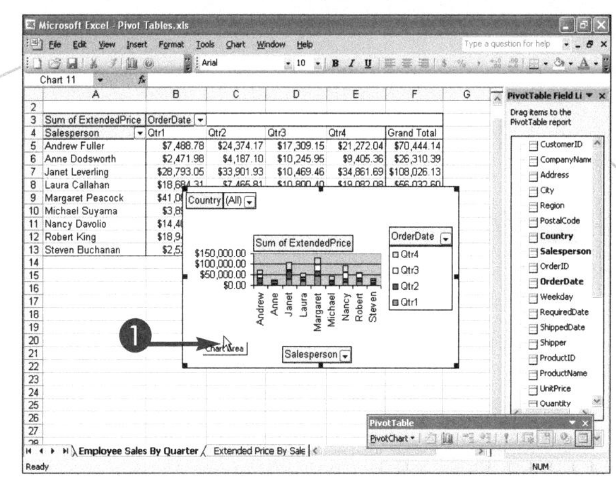

Excel deletes the PivotChart.

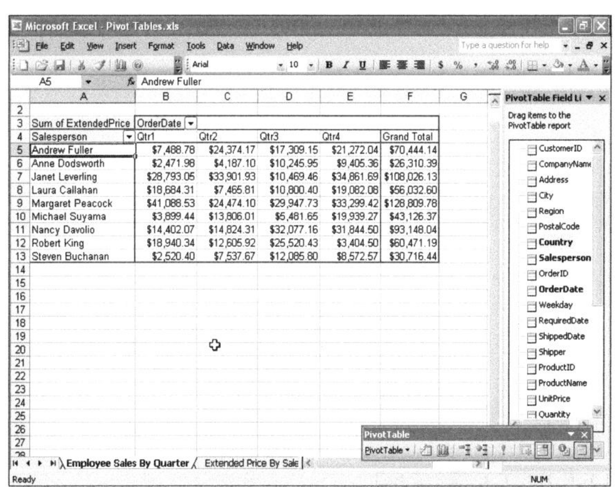

Apply It

If you create many temporary PivotCharts, you should delete them to save system resources. However, this can become time-consuming if you do it quite often. To save time, use the following VBA macro to run through all the `Chart` objects (chart sheets) and prompt for deletion:

Example:

```
Sub DeletePivotCharts()
    Dim objChart As Chart, nResult As Integer
    ' Run through all the chart sheets
    For Each objChart In ActiveWorkbook.Charts
        ' Activate the chart
        objChart.Activate
        ' Confirm the deletion
        nResult = MsgBox("Do you want to " & _
                  "delete the chart named " & _
                  objChart.Name & "?", vbYesNo)
        If nResult = vbYes Then
            ' Select the chart
            objChart.Select
            ' Delete it
            objChart.Delete
        End If
    Next 'objChart
End Sub
```

Create a PivotTable from Multiple Consolidation Ranges

If your source data exists in two or more ranges, Excel can consolidate all the ranges and then produce a PivotTable report based on the consolidated data.

Many businesses create worksheets for a specific task and then distribute them to various departments. The most common example is budgeting. Accounting might create a generic "budget" template that each department or division in the company must fill out and return. Similarly, you often see worksheets distributed for inventory requirements, sales forecasting, survey data, experiment results, and more.

Creating these worksheets, distributing them, and filling them in are all straightforward operations. The tricky part, however, comes when the sheets are returned to the originating department where all the new data must be combined into a summary report showing company-wide totals. This task is called *consolidating* the data, and it is often difficult and time-consuming, especially for large worksheets. However, Excel has a powerful PivotTable feature that can make it easy to consolidate the data and summarize it into a simple report.

Create a PivotTable from Multiple Consolidation Ranges

Note: This chapter uses the spreadsheets Division_I_Budget.xls, Division_II_Budget.xls, Division_III_Budget.xls, and PivotTables.xls, and the Web page Orders.htm, available at www.wiley.com/go/pivottablesvb. You can also create your own sample database.

1. Click Data➔PivotTable and PivotChart Report.

   The PivotTable and PivotChart Wizard appears.

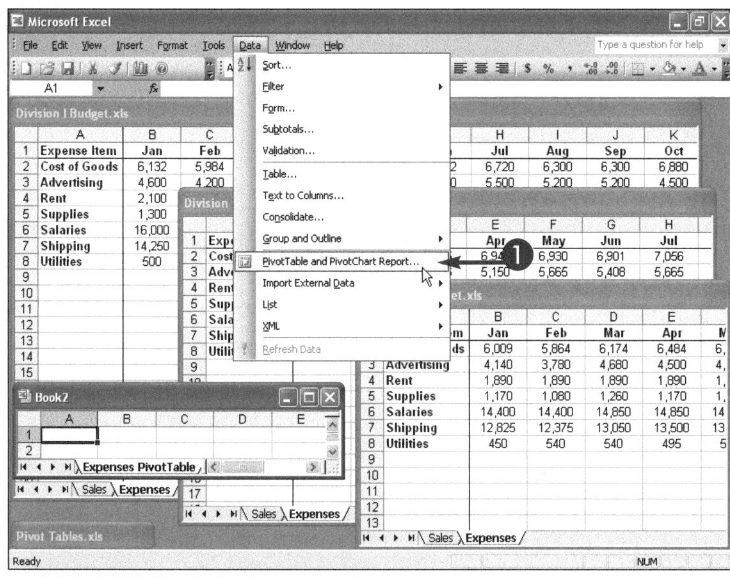

2. Select Multiple consolidation ranges.
3. Select PivotTable.
4. Click Next.

   The next PivotTable and PivotChart Wizard dialog box appears.

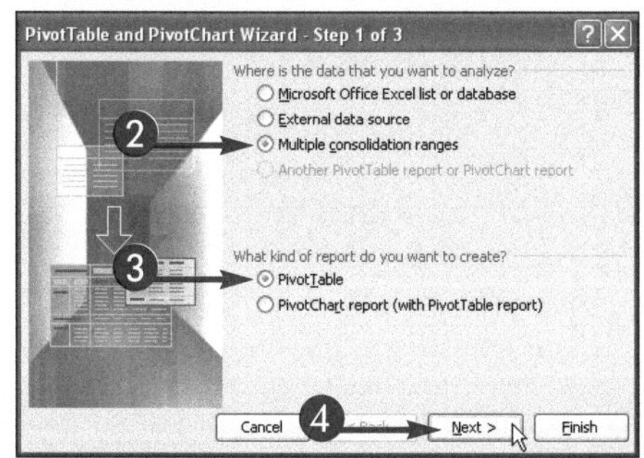

5 Select I will create the page fields.

6 Click Next.

The next PivotTable and PivotChart Wizard dialog box appears.

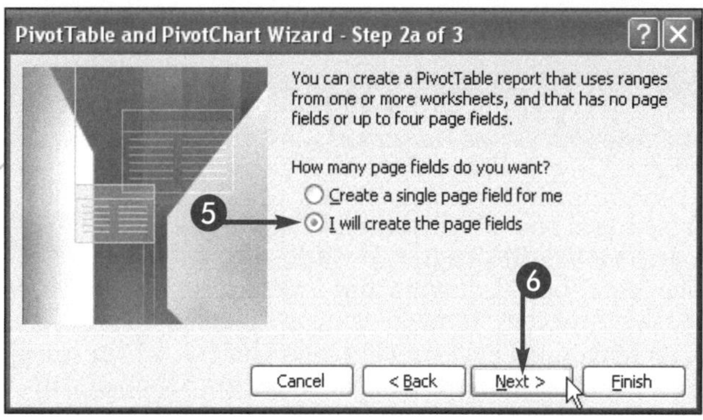

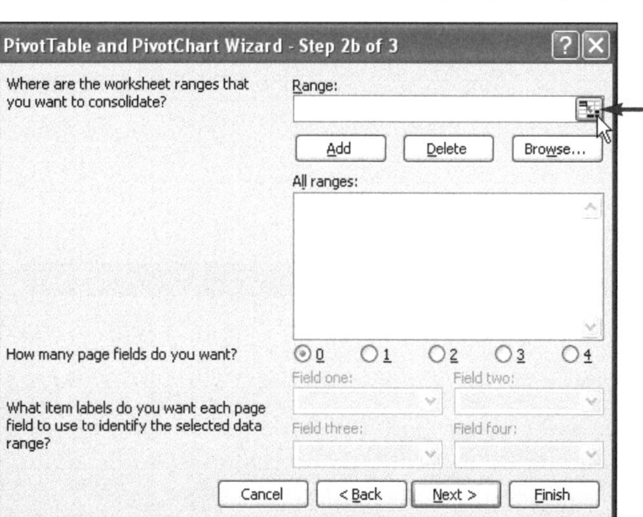

7 Click the Collapse Dialog button.

Excel collapses the dialog box to show just the Range input box.

Apply It

Another way to summarize data that exists in multiple ranges is to use Excel's Consolidate feature. With this feature, Excel can consolidate your data using one of two methods:

- **Consolidate by position** — Excel consolidates the data from several worksheets using the same range coordinates on each sheet. You can use this method if the worksheets you are consolidating have an identical layout.
- **Consolidate by category** — Excel consolidates the data by looking for identical row and column labels in each sheet. So, for example, if one worksheet lists monthly Gizmo sales in row 1 and another lists monthly Gizmo sales in row 5, you can still consolidate as long as both sheets have a "Gizmo" label at the beginning of these rows.

To use this feature, select Data→Consolidate to display the Consolidate dialog box. Click the summary Function you want to use, such as Sum or Count, enter the range references for the source data, and then click OK.

continued →

Create a PivotTable from Multiple Consolidation Ranges (continued)

In a PivotTable based on multiple consolidation ranges, Excel only offers a limited layout: a row field, a column field, a value (data) field, and up to four page fields. The items in the row field come from the leftmost columns of the source data ranges; the items in the column field come from the topmost row in the source data ranges; and the items in the value field come from the rest of the source data ranges.

For the page field, Excel sets up the report so that you can display the data from all the ranges or just the data from one of the ranges. In other words, Excel enables you to filter the PivotTable report based on the source ranges, and it uses the page field to do this.

However, if you let Excel set up this page field for you, it uses generic item names such as Item1, Item2, and Item3. To avoid the hassle of renaming these items after you create the PivotTable, you can specify them as you work with the PivotTable and PivotChart Wizard. That is why you selected the "I will create the page fields" option in Step 5. In Steps 12 to 15 of this task, you define the page field item names yourself.

Create a PivotTable from Multiple Consolidation Ranges *(continued)*

8. Select the range you want to include in the PivotTable report.
9. Click the Restore Dialog button.

   Excel restores the PivotTable and PivotChart Wizard.

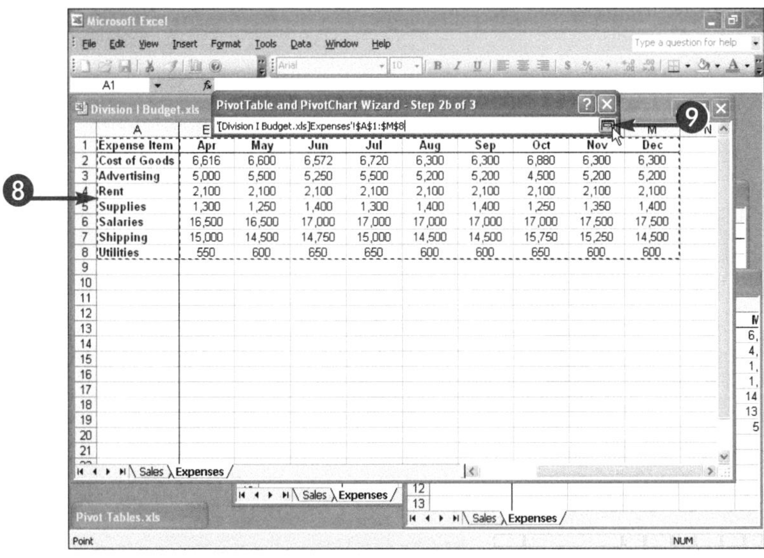

10. Click Add.
11. Repeat Steps 7 to 10 to add the other ranges you want to consolidate.
12. Select 1.
13. Click the range you want to work with.
14. Type a label that identifies the range.
15. Repeat Steps 13 and 14 for each range.
16. Click Next.

   The final PivotTable and PivotChart Wizard dialog box appears.

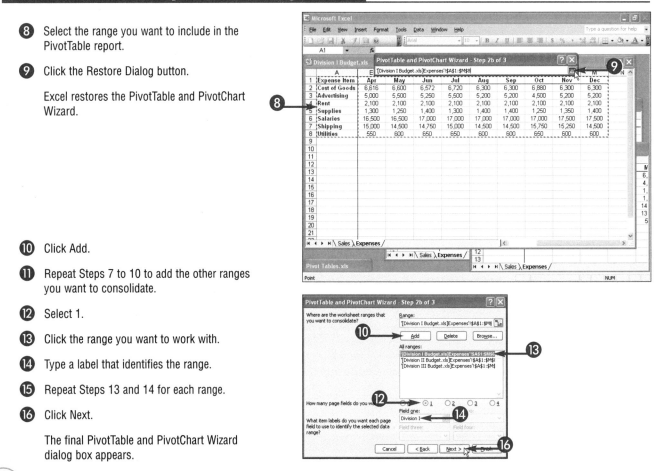

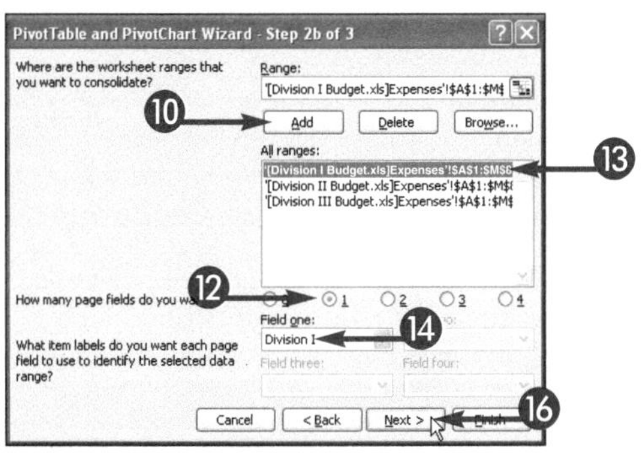

⑰ Select New worksheet to place the PivotTable on a new worksheet.

- If you prefer to place the PivotTable on an existing worksheet, select Existing worksheet, click the Collapse Dialog button, and then click the worksheet and cell where you want the PivotTable to appear.

⑱ Click Finish.

Excel consolidates the ranges and creates the PivotTable.

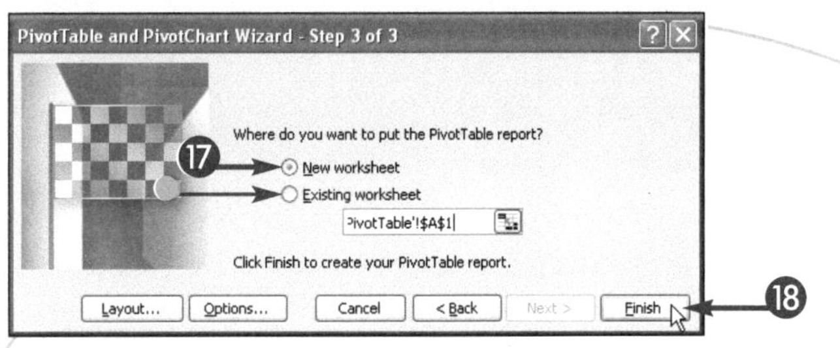

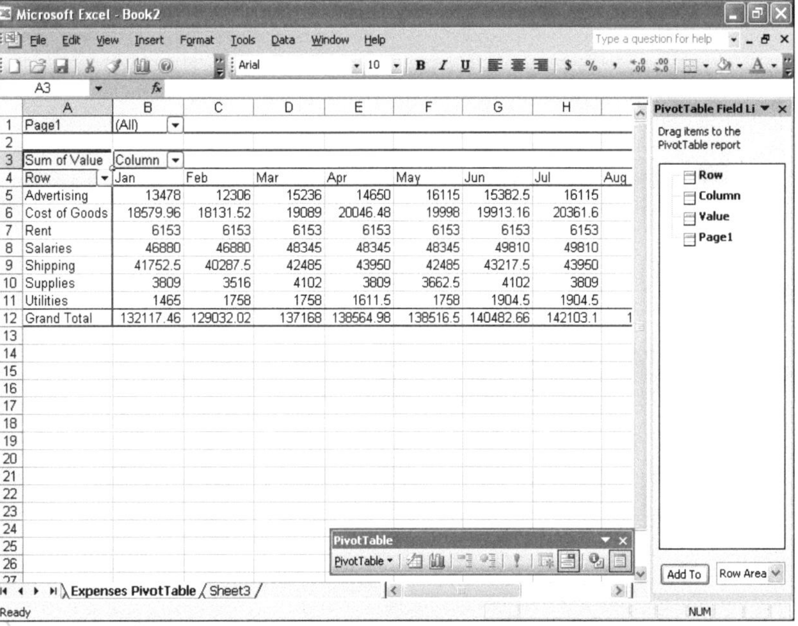

Extra

When you complete the wizard, the PivotTable Field List shows only four items: Row, Column, Value, and Page1. You can add up to three more page fields, but other than that you cannot add any other fields to the Field List. However, you are free to rename the fields to provide more meaningful names; in Chapter 5, see the task "Rename a PivotTable Field." You can also perform most other PivotTable tasks, including pivoting the fields and changing the summary calculation.

To create more page fields, click PivotTable→PivotTable Wizard and then click Back to display the PivotTable and PivotChart Wizard's Step 2b of 3 dialog box. Select the number of page fields you want: 2, 3, or 4 (◯ changes to ◉). Then perform Steps 13 to 15 to define the item names for each page field. For Step 14, be sure to use the appropriate text box (Field two, Field three, or Field four).

If you allowed Excel to create the page field automatically, you need to rename the page field items to give them more meaningful names. Pivot the page field into the row area so that the items are visible. Rename each item, and then pivot the field back into the page area.

Create a PivotTable from an Existing PivotTable

You can save time and effort by creating a new PivotTable based on the data in an existing PivotTable.

You learned in several places throughout this book that Excel maintains a pivot cache for each PivotTable. This pivot cache is a memory location that holds the source data and other information relating to the PivotTable. Keeping this data in memory means that your PivotTable recalculates quickly when you change the layout, grouping, filtering, or summary calculation. The price you pay for having the pivot cache is extra workbook size and less memory available for other tasks, but the tradeoff is usually worth it.

You can minimize the downside of the pivot cache by building new PivotTables based on existing PivotTables wherever possible. If you build a new PivotTable using the same data source as an existing PivotTable, Excel asks if you want to base the new report on the existing report. However, you can also build a new PivotTable from an existing PivotTable on purpose. Doing this not only means that the two PivotTables share the same pivot cache, but it also takes less time and effort to build the new PivotTable.

Create a PivotTable from an Existing PivotTable

1. Click Data→PivotTable and PivotChart Report.

   The PivotTable and PivotChart Wizard appears.

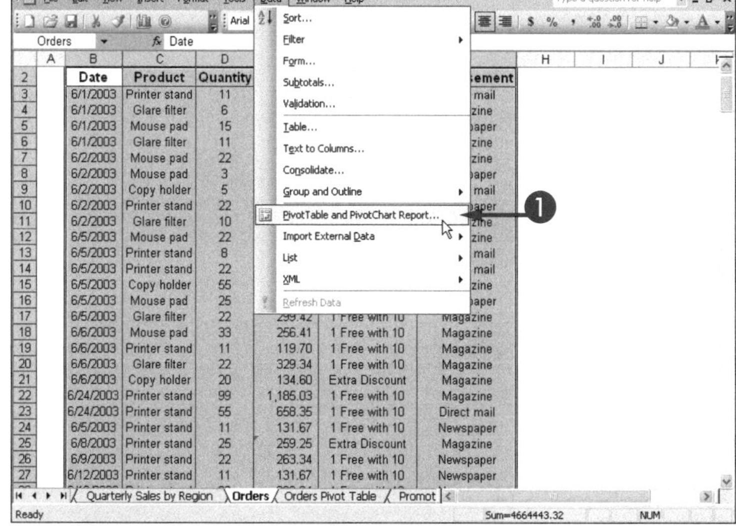

2. Select Another PivotTable report or PivotChart report.
3. Select PivotTable.
4. Click Next.

   The second PivotTable and PivotChart Wizard dialog box appears.

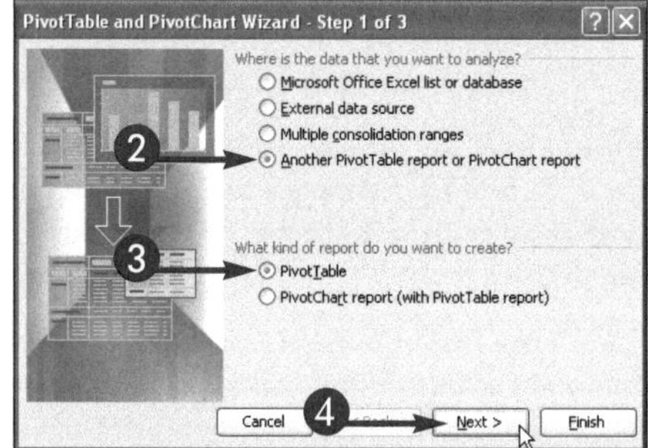

5. Click the PivotTable upon which you want to base the new PivotTable.

6. Click Finish.

Excel creates an empty PivotTable.

- The fields available in the PivotTable that you choose in Step 5 appear in the PivotTable Field List.

7. Click and drag fields from the PivotTable Field List and drop them in the PivotTable areas.

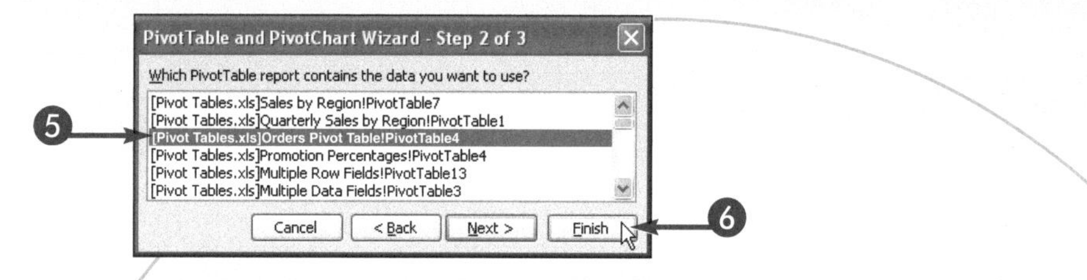

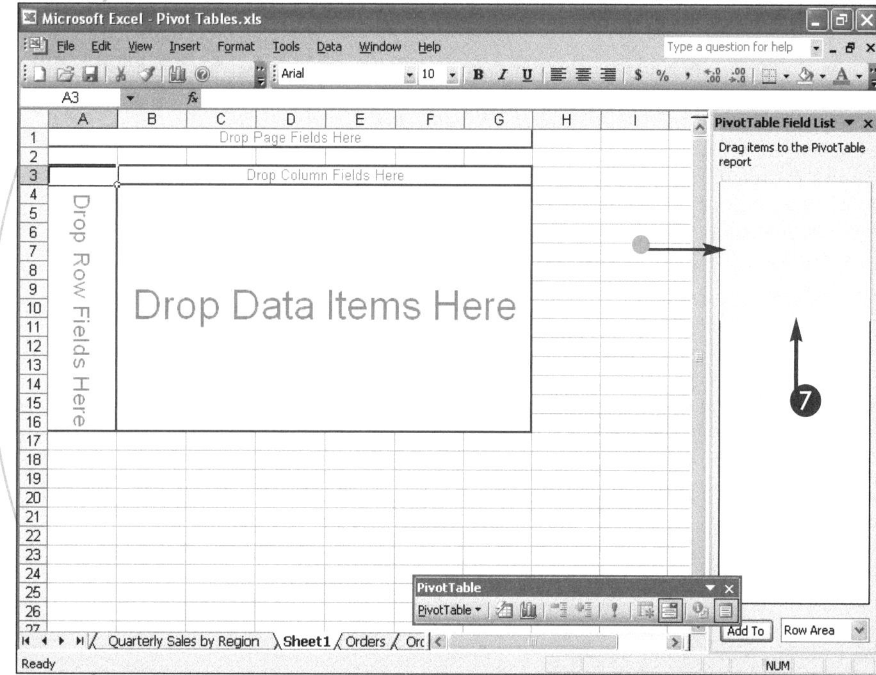

Apply It

If you know the name of the PivotTable report from which you want to create your new PivotTable, you can use the Worksheet object's `PivotTableWizard` method to create the new PivotTable. Set the `SourceType` parameter to `xlPivotTable` and set the `SourceData` parameter to the name of the existing PivotTable, including the workbook name — enclosed in square brackets [] — worksheet name, and PivotTable name, as shown in the following example:

Example:

```
ActiveSheet.PivotTableWizard _
    SourceType:=xlPivotTable, _
    SourceData:="[Pivot Tables.xls]Orders Pivot Table!PivotTable4"
```

Create a PivotTable from External Data

You can create a PivotTable using an external data source, which enables you to build reports from extremely large datasets and from relational database systems.

So far in this book you have learned about data sources that reside on Excel worksheets as ranges or lists. This is a convenient way to work with PivotTables because you have access to the source data, enabling you to easily change field names, add and delete fields, insert records, and so on. However, working with data in Excel suffers from two major drawbacks:

- Excel offers only simple row-and-column database management. You cannot use Excel to perform relational database management where, when two or more datasets are related on a common field, you can combine those datasets in powerful ways.
- Excel worksheets are limited to 65,536 rows, so that is the maximum number of records you can have in a range or list data source.

To overcome these limitations, you need to use a relational database management system (RDBMS) such as Microsoft Access or SQL Server. With these programs, you can set up a table, query, or other object that defines the data you want to work with. In most cases, the data object can be as complex and as large as you need. You can then build your PivotTable based on this *external data source.*

Create a PivotTable from External Data

1. Click Data➔PivotTable and PivotChart Report.

   The PivotTable and PivotChart Wizard appears.

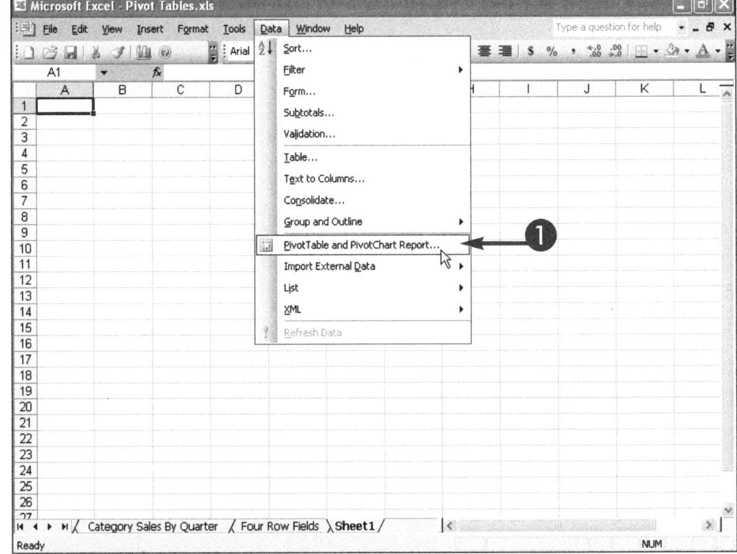

2. Select External data source.
3. Select PivotTable.
4. Click Next.

   The second PivotTable and PivotChart Wizard dialog box appears.

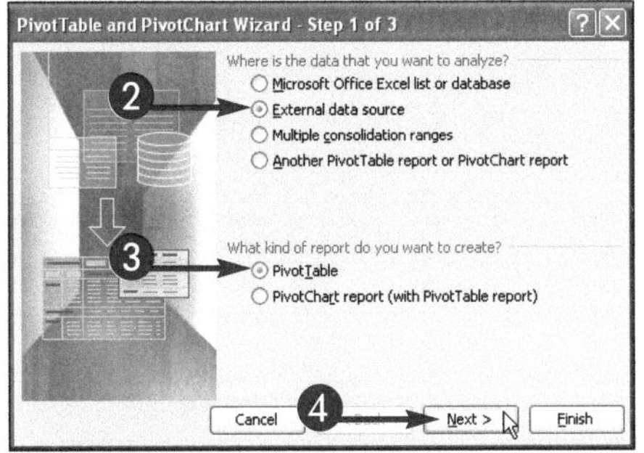

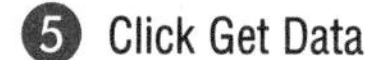

5 Click Get Data.

The Choose Data Source dialog box appears.

6 Click the data source you want to use.

Note: To learn how to create data sources, see the Appendix B task "Define a Data Source."

7 Click OK.

The Query Wizard's Choose Columns dialog box appears.

8 Click the table or column you want to use as the source data for your PivotTable.

9 Click >.

- The table's fields or the columns appear in this list.

10 Click Next.

The Query Wizard's Filter Data dialog box appears.

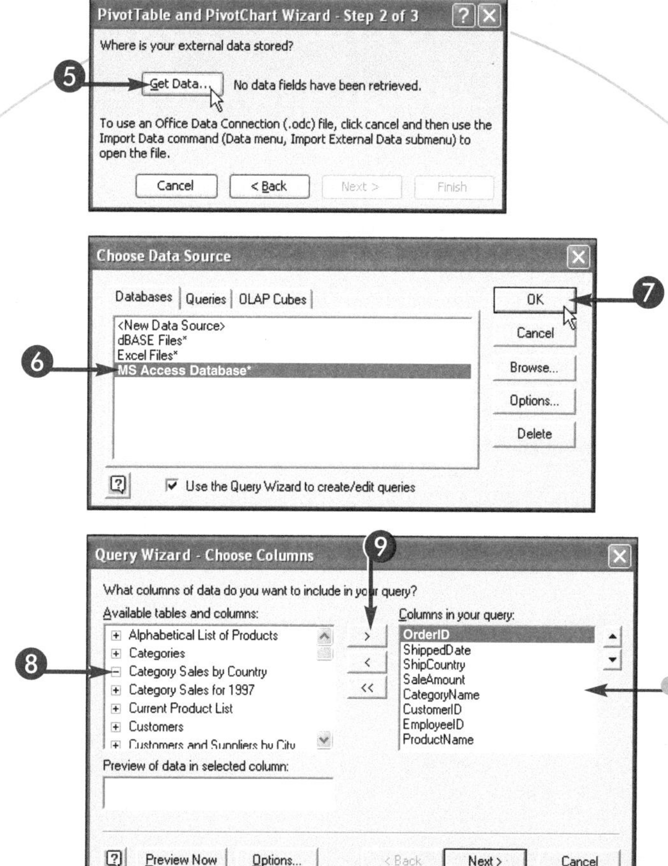

Extra

You can reduce the size of the new PivotTable's pivot cache by including only those fields that you need for your PivotTable. In the Query Wizard's Choose Columns dialog box, each table has a plus sign (+) beside it. Click a table's plus sign to display a list of that object's fields, or columns, as the Query Wizard calls them. You can then click a field and click the > button to add it to the list of fields to be used with your PivotTable. You can also double-click the field.

If you are not sure what items a field contains, click the field in either list and then click Preview Now. The Query Wizard displays the field's items in the "Preview of data in selected column" list.

If you add a table, query, or field by mistake, click the item in the "Columns in your query" list, and then click the < button to remove it. If you want to start over, click the << button to remove everything from the "Columns in your query" list.

continued →

Create a PivotTable from External Data (continued)

The Choose Data Source dialog box and the various Query Wizard dialog boxes are not part of Excel. Instead, they are components of a program called Microsoft Query. You can use this program to work with external data. For more detail on how this program works, see Appendix B. For the purposes of this task, I assume that you have already defined the appropriate data source, as shown in the Appendix B task "Define a Data Source," and that you do not want to work with Microsoft Query directly; see the Appendix B task "Start Microsoft Query." Note, too, that Steps 10 and 11 essentially skip over the Query Wizard dialog boxes that enable you to filter and sort the external data, because this is not usually pertinent for a PivotTable report. For the details of these steps, in Appendix B, see the task "Define a Data Source."

The other assumption I made in this task is that you do not want the external data imported to Excel. Rather, in this task the external data resides only in the new PivotTable's pivot cache; you do not see the data itself in your workbook. This is particularly useful if the external data contains more than 65,536 records, because otherwise Excel would not allow you to import so much data. However, you can still easily refresh and rebuild your PivotTable, just like you can with a report based on a local range or list. If you want to learn how to import external data into Excel, see Appendix C.

Create a PivotTable from External Data *(continued)*

11. Click Next.

    The Query Wizard's Sort Order dialog box appears.

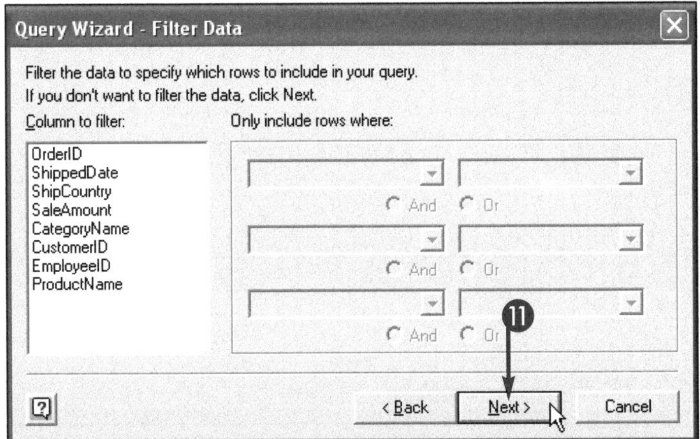

12. Click Next.

    The Query Wizard's Finish dialog box appears.

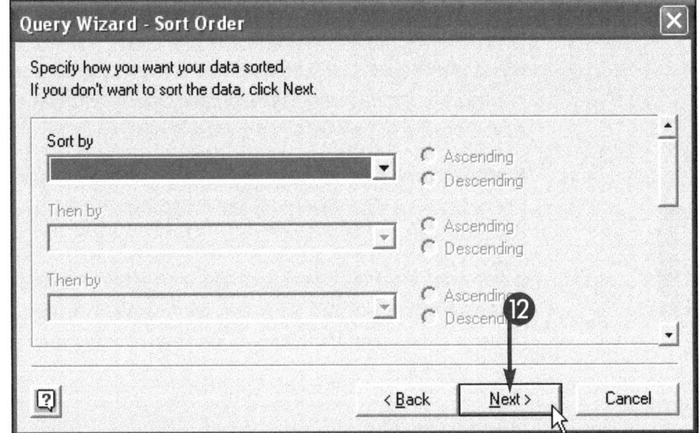

13 Select Return Data to Microsoft Office Excel.

14 Click Finish.

The second PivotTable and PivotChart Wizard dialog box appears.

15 Click Finish.

Excel creates an empty PivotTable.

- The fields available in the table or query that you chose in Step 8 appear in the PivotTable Field List.

16 Click and drag fields from the PivotTable Field List and drop them in the PivotTable areas.

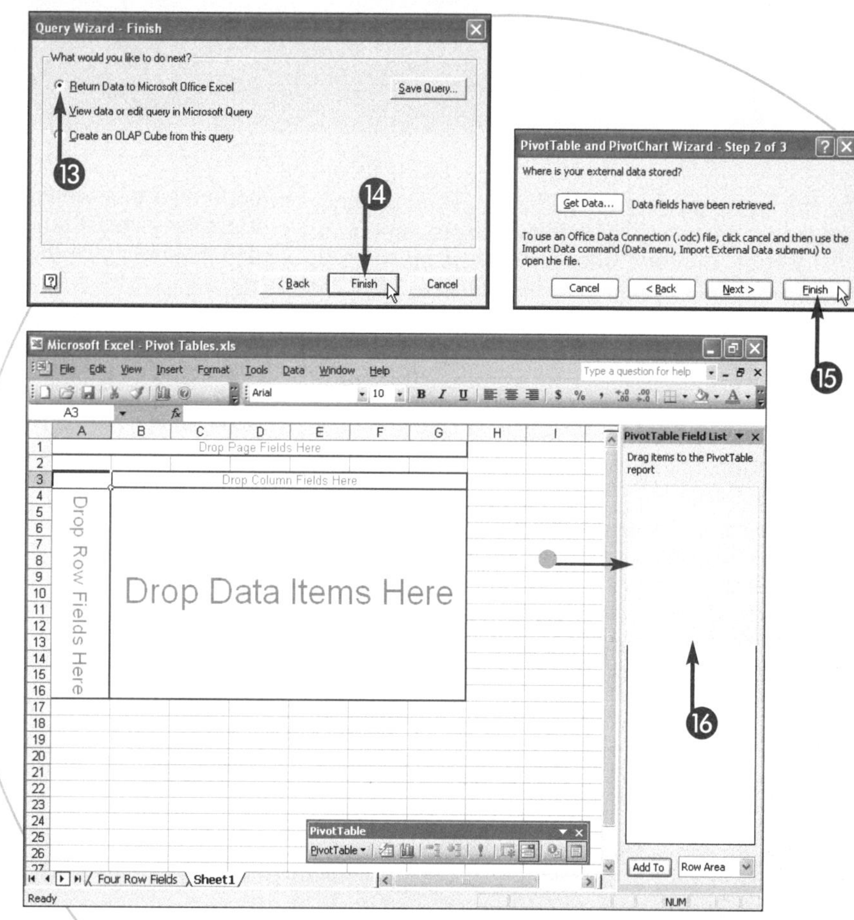

Extra

The most common drawback to using an external data source is that you often have no control over the external file itself. This may mean that the database login data changes, or that the file might get moved to a new location, renamed, or even deleted. If this happens and you attempt to refresh the PivotTable, Excel displays an error message. For example, if the external data source is an Access database, Excel displays an error dialog box telling you that, for example, it cannot find the external database file. In this case, click OK to close the dialog box and display the Login dialog box.

If you suspect the problem is a change to the login data, find out the correct login name and password from the database administrator, enter the new data in the Login dialog box, and then click OK.

If you suspect the problem is that the database file has been moved or renamed, click Database in the Login dialog box. You can use the Select Database dialog box to find and click the database file, and then click OK to return to the Login dialog box. Click OK to return to Excel.

Set Up a Server-Based Page Field

If the external source contains a large amount of data, Excel may run very slowly or it may display an out of memory error. You can work around these problems by setting up a server-based page field that retrieves page data only when you request it from the server.

When you connect to an external data source, and when you refresh a PivotTable based on an external data source, Excel retrieves all the data from the external file. If you are dealing with a database on a remote server, or if the source contains a large amount of data, retrieving all the data may take a very long time.

Part of the problem is that Excel retrieves all the data even if you are currently displaying the results for just a single page field: Excel still retrieves the data for those page fields that are not currently displayed. This increases the performance of the PivotTable when you switch pages, but it greatly increases the amount of memory that Excel uses and it slows down the refreshing of the PivotTable.

To overcome these problems, you can configure the page field as a *server page field*. This means that Excel only retrieves the data for the currently displayed page field. When you display a different page, Excel queries the server and retrieves the new data — this is called *querying page-by-page*. This means it takes longer to switch pages, but it greatly reduces the amount of memory used by Excel, and it speeds up the refreshing of the PivotTable.

Note that querying page-by-page is only available for certain types of external data, such as SQL Server data sources. This technique is unreliable when used with Access databases.

Set Up a Server-Based Page Field

1. Click the page field button.
2. Click PivotTable→Field Settings.

   You can also double-click the page field button.

   The PivotTable Field dialog box appears.

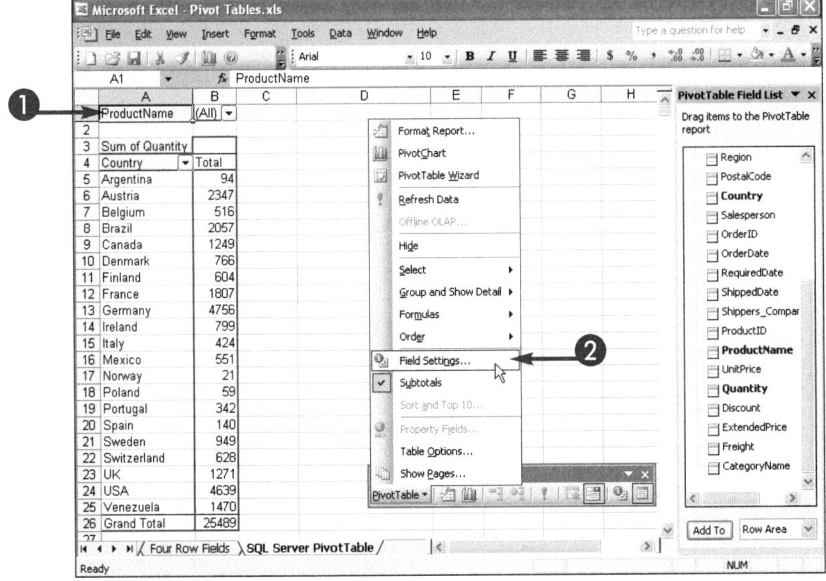

3. Click Advanced.

   The PivotTable Field Advanced Options dialog box appears.

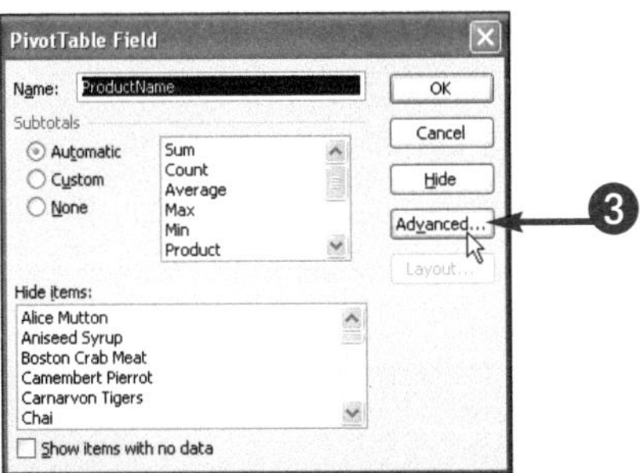

4. Select this option to retrieve data page-by-page.
5. Click OK.

   Excel returns you to the PivotTable Field dialog box.
6. Click OK.

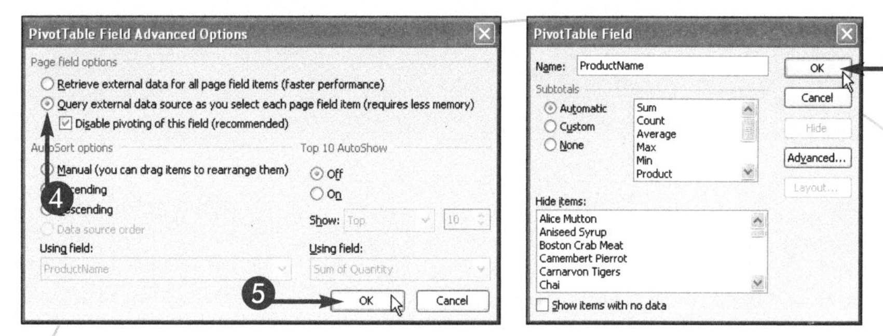

- Excel queries the external data source to return the data for just a single page.

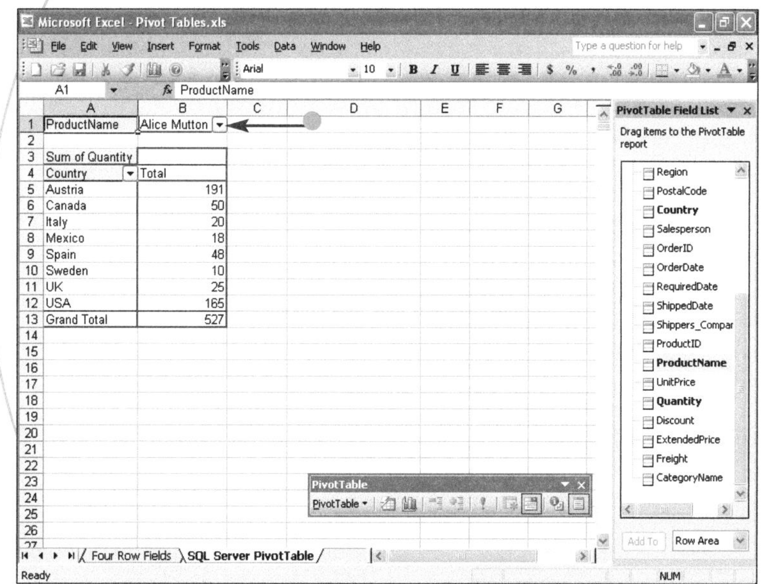

Extra

If you find that the "Query external data source" option is unavailable, check to see if your page field items are grouped. You cannot query page-by-page using grouped pages, so ungroup the page field before following the steps in this task.

In the PivotTable Field Advanced Options dialog box, after you select "Query external data source" (○ changes to ⦿), be sure to leave the "Disable pivoting of this field" check box activated. If you deactivate this check box and then pivot the page field to the row or column area, Excel attempts to retrieve the data for all the items in the page field. Depending on the size of the data source, this could overwhelm your system and cause memory errors.

When you set up a server page field, Excel disables the All item in the page field drop-down list. If you have the All item displayed prior to setting up the server page field, Excel always displays the first item in the page field after you set up page-by-page querying. Note, too, that Excel also disables the Show Pages command in the PivotTable toolbar.

Set External Data Options

Excel offers several options related to PivotTables built using external data sources. You can use these options to save time and effort and to reduce the amount of memory used by these PivotTables. In the PivotTable Options dialog box, there are three check boxes related to external data sources:

- **Save password** — Some external data sources require a login name and password to access the data. By default, Excel does not save the login password in the pivot cache. If you close the workbook, reopen it, and then refresh the PivotTable, you must log in again to the external data source. To prevent this, activate the "Save password" check box, and Excel saves the login data with the PivotTable.
- **Background query** — When you refresh the PivotTable, Excel queries the external data source to retrieve the latest data. While the query is in progress, you cannot do anything else in Excel. This is fine if the query takes only a few seconds, but it can be a problem for queries that take a very long time. If you activate the "Background query" check box, Excel continues the query in the background and allows you to perform other work in Excel.
- **Optimize memory** — When Excel retrieves data from an external source, it stores the data in the pivot cache. By default, Excel adds each record to the cache as it is retrieved, and the size of the cache grows accordingly. However, Excel has the ability to reduce the size of the cache, but only if it knows in advance how many records the query is going to return. If you activate the "Optimize memory" check box, Excel interrogates the external data source to determine how many records the query retrieves, and uses that information to reduce the pivot cache size as much as possible. Note, however, that it takes Excel extra time to interrogate the external data source, so activating this option may slow down the PivotTable's performance.

Set External Data Options

1 Click any cell in the PivotTable.

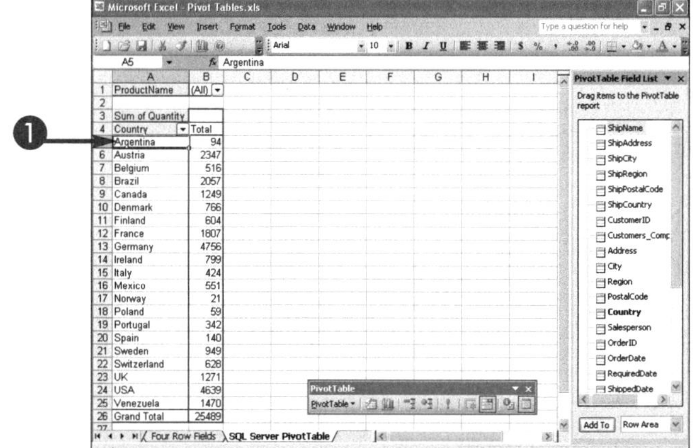

2 Click PivotTable➔Table Options.

The PivotTable Options dialog box appears.

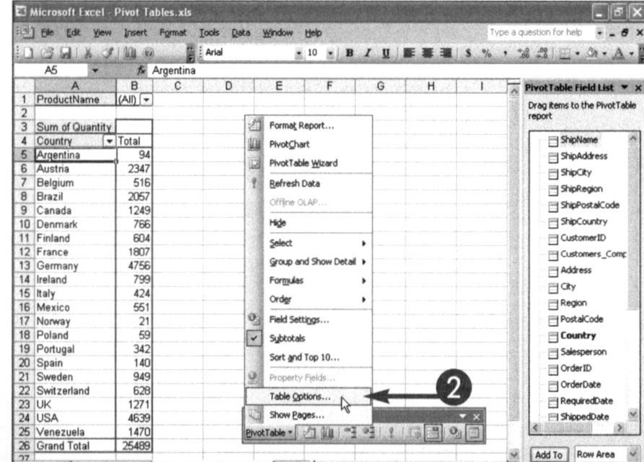

3 Select Save password.

4 Select Background query.

5 Select Optimize memory.

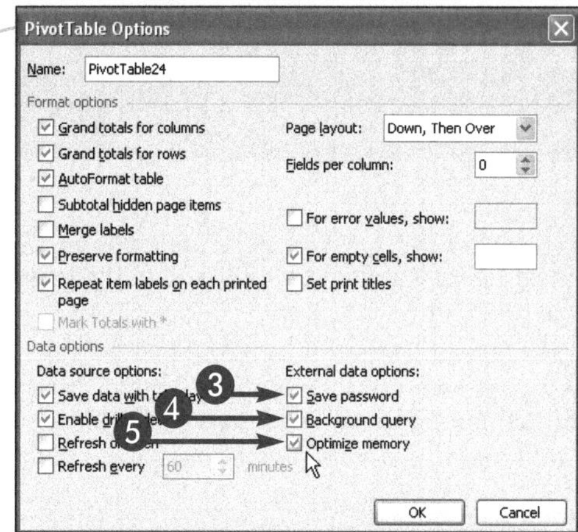

6 Click OK.

Excel puts the external data source options into effect.

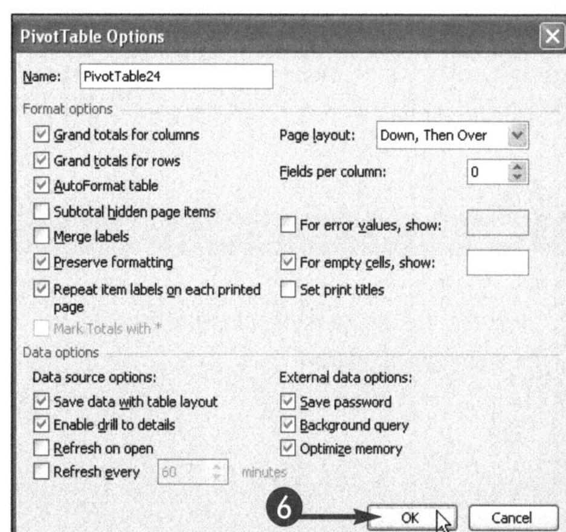

Apply It

You can control the external data source options using VBA. You can use the `PivotTable` object's `PivotCache` property, which is itself an object with three properties that correspond to the three check boxes: `SavePassword`, `BackgroundQuery`, and `OptimizeCache`. The following macro toggles these three properties on and off:

Example:

```
Sub ToggleExternalDataOptions()
    Dim objPT As PivotTable
    Set objPT = ActiveSheet.PivotTables(1)
    With objPT.PivotCache
        .SavePassword = Not .SavePassword
        .BackgroundQuery = Not .BackgroundQuery
        .OptimizeCache = Not .OptimizeCache
    End With
End Sub
```

Export PivotTable Data from a Web Page to Excel

If you are working with a PivotTable list on a Web page, you can export that PivotTable's data from the Web page to Excel.

In Chapter 3, you learned how to publish a PivotTable to a Web page; see the task "Publish a PivotTable to a Web Page." The resulting Web page-based PivotTable is displayed using an Office Web component called a *PivotTable list*. If you are working with a PivotTable list on a Web page, you can also perform the opposite technique and export the PivotTable list to Excel. This gives you a regular Excel PivotTable in a read-only file, which you can then save to your computer.

Export PivotTable Data from a Web Page to Excel

1. Open the Web page containing the PivotTable list you want to export.

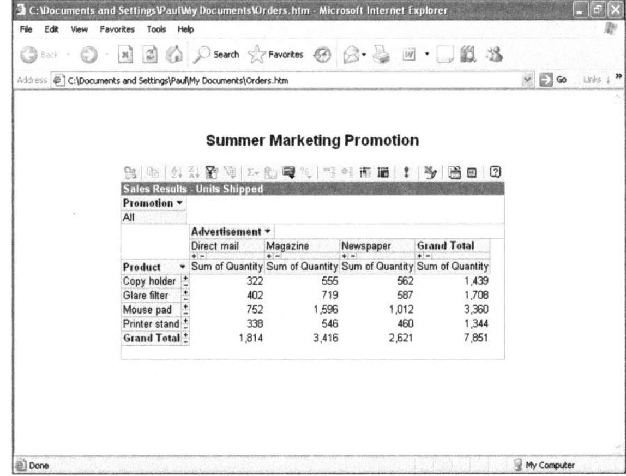

2. Click the Export to Microsoft Office Excel button.

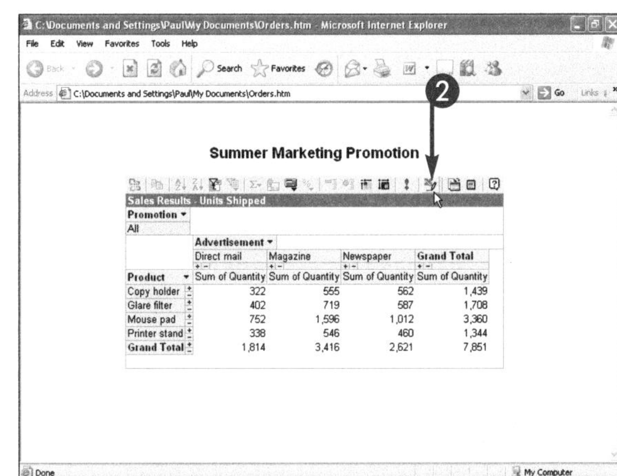

If the PivotTable list contains features not supported by PivotTable reports, a warning dialog box appears.

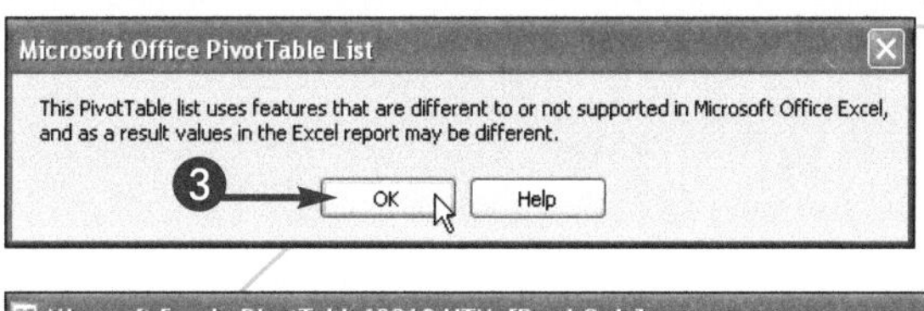

3 Click OK.

The PivotTable appears in a temporary Excel worksheet.

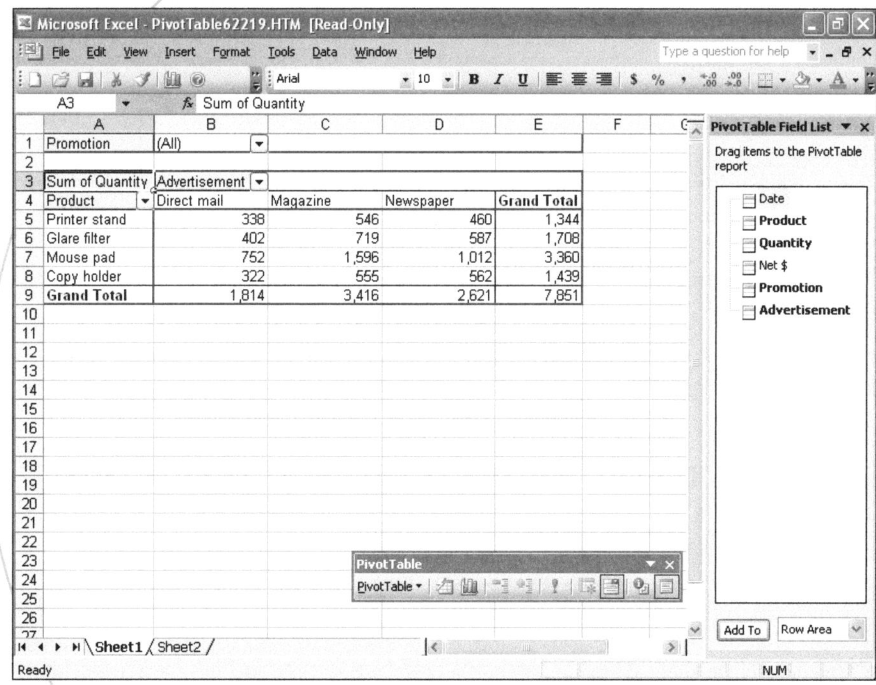

Extra

A PivotTable list looks and operates much like a PivotTable report, but there are a few differences that affect how the PivotTable list gets imported into Excel. This is why you see a warning dialog box if the PivotTable list contains features not supported by Excel's PivotTable reports.

For example, PivotTable lists enable you to display summary detail and underlying detail simultaneously, but PivotTable reports do not. Therefore, calculated fields in the PivotTable list detail area are not exported to Excel. Similarly, PivotTable lists support hyperlinks, but PivotTable reports do not, so hyperlinks are not exported. Finally, you can group items in a PivotTable list by text, such as the first few characters, and by week – neither of which is available in PivotTable reports, so these groupings are not exported.

Reduce the Size of PivotTable Workbooks

You can reduce the size of your Excel workbooks by not saving the PivotTable source data in the pivot cache.

If you build a PivotTable from data that resides in a different workbook or in an external data source, Excel stores the source data in the pivot cache. This greatly reduces the time it takes to refresh and recalculate the PivotTable. The downside is that it can increase both the size of the workbook and the amount of time it takes Excel to save the workbook. If your workbook has become too large or it takes too long to save, you can tell Excel not to save the source data in the pivot cache.

You can control whether Excel uses the pivot cache via VBA. To do this, set the `PivotTable` object's `SaveData` property to `True`, with the pivot cache on, or to `False`, with the pivot cache off, as shown in the following macro:

```
Sub TogglePivotCache()
    Dim objPT As PivotTable
    ' Work with the first PivotTable on the active worksheet
    Set objPT = ActiveSheet.PivotTables(1)
    ' Toggle the SaveData property
    objPT.SaveData = Not objPT.SaveData
    ' Display the current state
    MsgBox "The PivotTable's pivot cache is now " & _
           IIf(obj.SaveData, "on.", "off.")
End Sub
```

Reduce the Size of PivotTable Workbooks

1. Click any cell in the PivotTable.
2. Click PivotTable➔Table Options.

   The PivotTable Options dialog box appears.

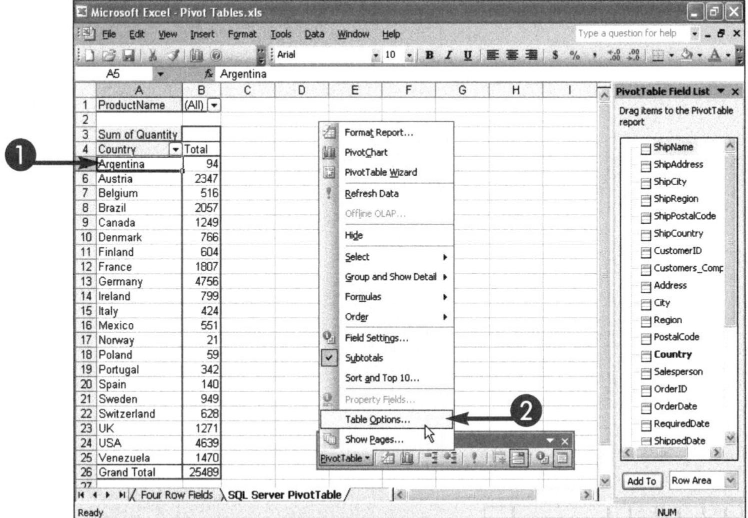

3. Deselect Save data with table layout.
4. Click OK.

   Excel puts the external data source options into effect.

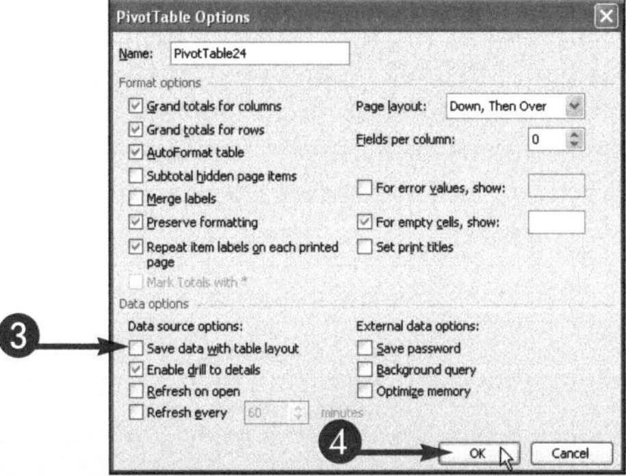

Use a PivotTable Value in a Formula

When you reference a PivotTable report value in a formula, you can ensure that the reference remains accurate by using a special Excel worksheet function.

As part of your data analysis, you may need to use a value from a PivotTable report in a worksheet formula that resides outside the PivotTable. You normally reference a cell in a formula by using the cell's address. However, this does not work with PivotTables because the addresses of the report values change as you pivot, filter, group, and refresh the PivotTable.

To ensure accurate PivotTable references, use Excel's GETPIVOTDATA worksheet function. This function uses the data field, PivotTable location, and one or more (row or column) field/item pairs that specify the exact value you want to use. This way, no matter what the PivotTable layout, as long as the value remains visible in the report, your formula reference remains accurate.

If you want to reference a PivotTable value only temporarily, you might prefer that Excel not generate the GETPIVOTDATA function. To turn off this feature, click the Generate GetPivotData toolbar button ( ). See the Chapter 3 task "Customize the PivotTable Toolbar" to learn how to add this button to the PivotTable toolbar. You can also control whether Excel generates the GETPIVOTDATA function using VBA. Set the `Application` object's `GenerateGetPivotData` property to `True`, which generates the GETPIVOTDATA function, or to `False`, which does not generate the GETPIVOTDATA function. The complete code for this macro is available at www.wiley.com/go/pivottablesvb.

Use a PivotTable Value in a Formula

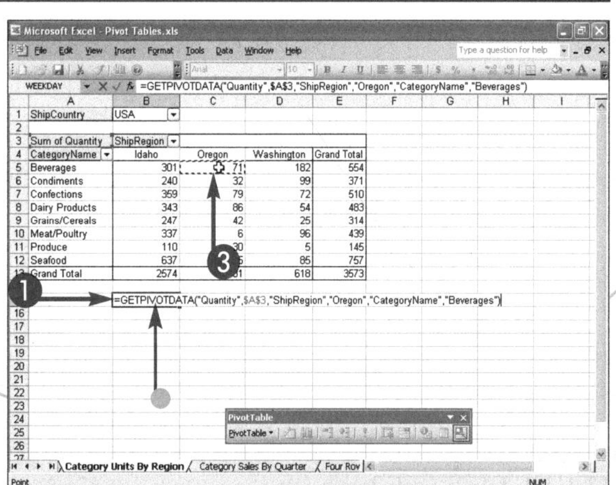

1. Click the cell in which you want to build your formula.
2. Type =.
3. Click the PivotTable cell containing the value you want to include in your formula.
   - Excel generates a GETPIVOTDATA function for the PivotTable value.
4. Complete the formula and press Enter.

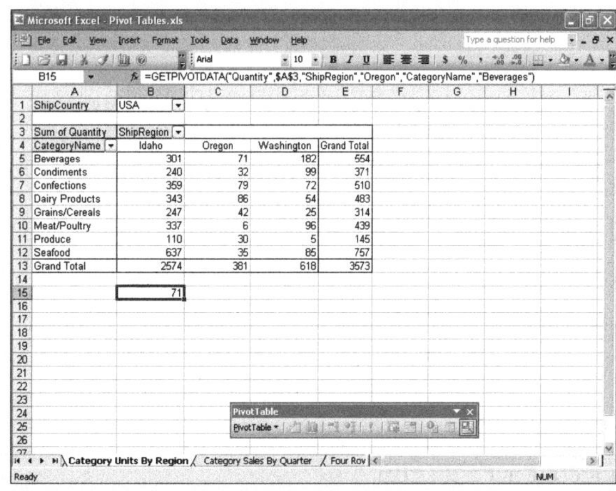

Excel includes the PivotTable value in the formula result.

Note: The GETPIVOTDATA function looks complicated, but it really only contains a few parameters. The first parameter is the name of the data field ("Quantity" in the example); the second parameter is the location of the PivotTable ("$A$3"); subsequent parameters come in pairs: a field name ("ShipRegion") and an item in that field ("Oregon").

Understanding OLAP

So far in this book you have worked with relatively small data sources such as the Northwind sample database that comes with Microsoft Access. In the business world, however, it is common to work with data sources that are much larger: from hundreds of thousands of records to millions, even billions of records. You cannot place such a huge data source on a worksheet, and even trying to manipulate all that data via a regular external data source is extremely time consuming and resource intensive. Fortunately, such huge data sources often reside on special servers that use a technology called *online analytical processing*, or *OLAP*. OLAP enables you to retrieve and summarize immense and complex data sources. When combined with Excel, OLAP enables you to view the data in a PivotTable or PivotChart report and manipulate the data quickly and easily.

Data Warehouse

In a traditional relational database management system, or RDBMS, such as Access, multiple tables are related using common fields. In the Northwind sample database, for example, the Customers table is related to the Orders table based on the common CustomerID field, and the Orders table is related to the Order Details table on the common OrderID field. You can use a query to pick and choose fields from each table and return them in a dataset. However, this can be a very slow process with a massive data source, so OLAP uses a different concept called the *data warehouse*. This is a data structure — called a *star schema* — with a central fact table that contains the numeric data you want to summarize and pointers to surrounding related tables.

Fact Table

A *fact table* is the primary table in a data warehouse and it contains data on events or processes — the facts — within a business, such as sales transactions or company expenses. Each record in the fact table contains two types of data: measures and dimensions.

Measure

A *measure* is column of numeric values within the fact table and it represents the data that you want to summarize. In a data warehouse of sales transactions, for example, there might be one measure for units sold and another for dollars sold. An OLAP measure is analogous to a data field in a regular data source.

Dimension

A *dimension* is a category of data, so it is analogous to a row, column, or page field in an ordinary data source. However, dimensions often contain hierarchical groupings called *levels*. For example, a Store dimension may have a hierarchy of location levels, such as Country, State, and City. Similarly, a Time dimension may have Year, Quarter, and Month levels. Each level has its own set of items, called *members*. For example, the Month level has the items January, February, and so on. Because most fact tables contain keys to multiple dimension tables, OLAP data is often called *multidimensional data.*

OLAP Cube

An *OLAP cube* is a data structure that takes the information in a data warehouse and summarizes each measure by every dimension, level, and member. For example, a three-dimensional cube might summarize sales based on the dimensions of Time, Product, and Store. The cube could then tell you, say, the units sold of rye bread at store #6 in January, or the dollars worth of scissors sold in California in the second quarter. All the measures come pre-calculated in the cube, so Excel does not have to perform any calculations when you use an OLAP cube as a source for a PivotTable.

OLAP PivotTable Limitations

NonOLAP and OLAP PivotTables look and operate much the same. However, OLAP PivotTables have a number of limitations and differences of which to be aware:

Calculations

- You cannot change the summary function in the OLAP PivotTable data area. The summary function used by a measure is defined in advance and the calculations are performed on the OLAP server.
- You cannot change the summary function for PivotTable subtotals.
- You cannot create calculated fields or calculated items. However, there may be calculated members that are defined on the OLAP server.

Other Differences

- You cannot enable the Background query or the Optimize memory option; see the Chapter 10 task, "Set External Data Options."
- Excel does not save the external data with the PivotTable layout. Only the data used in the PivotTable report is returned from the OLAP server or cube file.
- Excel can only work with OLAP data in a PivotTable or PivotChart report. You cannot save OLAP data to a worksheet.
- You cannot set up a server-based page field with an OLAP PivotTable; see the Chapter 10 task, "Set Up a Server-Based Page Field."

Layout

- In the PivotTable Field List, dimensions appear with the Cube dimension icon ( ) and measures appear with the Cube measure icon ( ).
- Dimensions can only be used in the PivotTable's row, column, and page areas.
- Measures can only be used in the PivotTable's data area.
- You cannot display the underlying detail for an OLAP summary value.
- Items initially appear in the sort order defined by the OLAP server. However, you can sort the PivotTable results yourself; see the Chapter 4 task, "Sort PivotTable Data with AutoSort."
- You cannot use the Show Pages command to display each PivotTable page on a separate worksheet.
- If you rename a dimension or member, hide it, and then add it back into the PivotTable, Excel displays the dimension or member using its original name.

Create an OLAP Cube Data Source

Before you can use an OLAP cube as the underlying data for a PivotTable, you must first create a data source that points to either a database on an OLAP server or to an offline cube file.

If you are on a network that runs an OLAP server — such as Microsoft SQL Server with Analysis Services, SAS OLAP Server, or Oracle OLAP Server — then you can get the most flexibility by connecting to the server and working with a database that has one or more OLAP cubes defined. This ensures that you are always working with the most recent data. Check with your database administrator to learn how to find the OLAP server and whether you need a separate login username and password to access the server.

Create an OLAP Cube Data Source

START THE DATA SOURCE

Note: Portions of this chapter use the SalesCube.cub offline cube file, available at www.wiley.com/go/pivottablesvb, or you can create your own sample database.

1. Click Data➔Import External Data➔New Database Query.

   The Choose Data Source dialog box appears.

2. Click the OLAP Cubes tab.
3. Click New Data Source.
4. Click OK.

   The Create New Data Source dialog box appears.

5. Type a name for the OLAP cube.
6. Click ▾ and select the OLAP provider that you use to connect to the OLAP server or cube file.
7. Click Connect.

   The Multidimensional Connection dialog box appears.

Note: If you want to use an OLAP server, follow the steps in the section "Connect to an OLAP Server." If you want to use a cube file, follow the steps in the section "Connect to a Cube File."

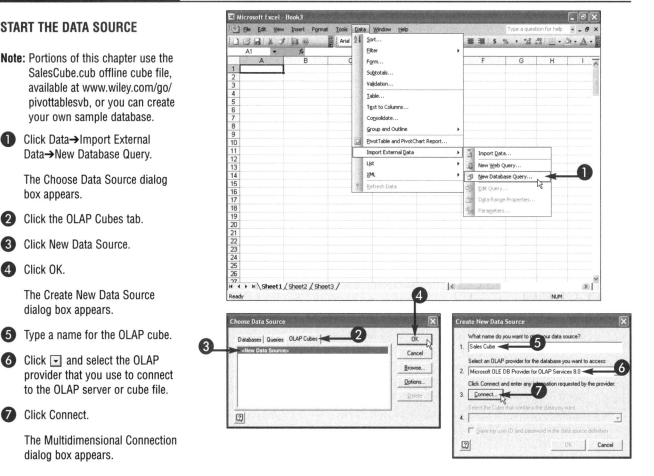

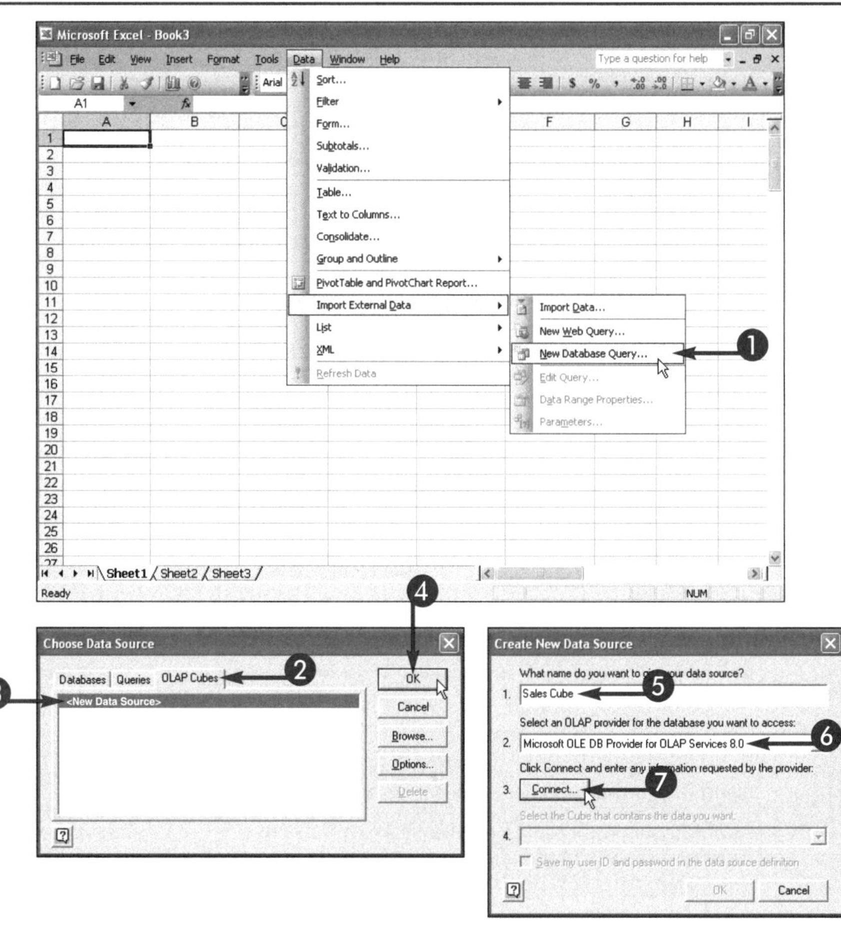

CONNECT TO AN OLAP SERVER

1. Select Analysis server.
2. Type the server name or address.
3. If you are connecting to the server via the Internet, type the User ID and Password, if required.
4. Click Next.

   A list of databases on the OLAP server appears.

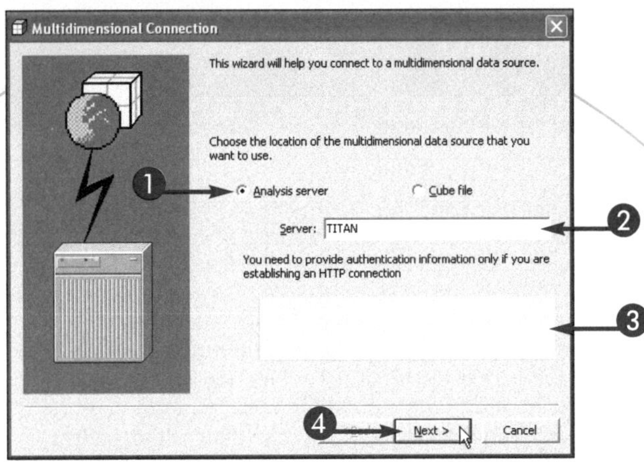

5. Click the database that contains the OLAP cube you want to use.
6. Click Finish.

   The Create New Data Source dialog box appears.

Note: To finish the data source, follow the steps in the section "Complete the Data Source."

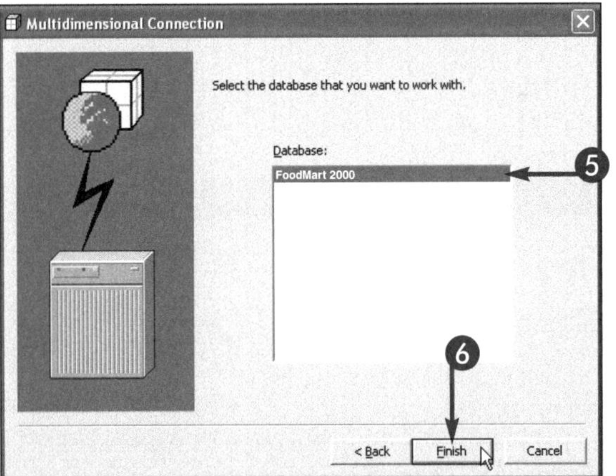

Apply It

You can also create OLAP cubes from relational data by creating a query for, say, an Access object, and then saving it as an OLAP cube. First set up a data source that points to the Access database; see the Appendix B task, "Define a Data Source." Then select the data source using the Query Wizard; see the Appendix B task, "Select a Data Source." In the final Query Wizard dialog box, select "Create an OLAP Cube from the query" (○ changes to ◉) and then click Finish to launch the OLAP Cube Wizard.

The OLAP Cube Wizard has three steps. In the first step, you can select the measures you want to include in the cube. In the second step, you can specify the dimensions and levels you want to include in the cube – drag a dimension field and then drag its levels onto it. In the third step, you can either create a cube file or you can create an online cube.

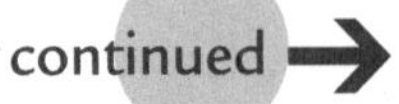
continued

Create an OLAP Cube Data Source (continued)

Instead of connecting to an OLAP server, you may have access to a *cube file*, which is a version of an OLAP cube that has been saved to a local or network folder. A cube file is "offline" in the sense that the data is not connected to an OLAP server, so it is a static snapshot of the data. This is useful if you are working out of the office and do not have access to the OLAP server. However, you may also want to work with a cube file while you are connected to the network. If you know the data is not going to change soon, working with a cube file tends to be faster than working online with a server because network traffic may slow down the server connection.

Your database administrator may be able to create a cube file for you. Alternatively, you can use the OLAP Cube Wizard to create a cube file, as described in the tip on the previous page. See also the task "Create an Offline OLAP Cube," later in this chapter.

Create an OLAP Cube Data Source *(continued)*

CONNECT TO A CUBE FILE

1. Click Cube file.
2. Click this button to specify the cube file you want to use.

   The Open dialog box appears.

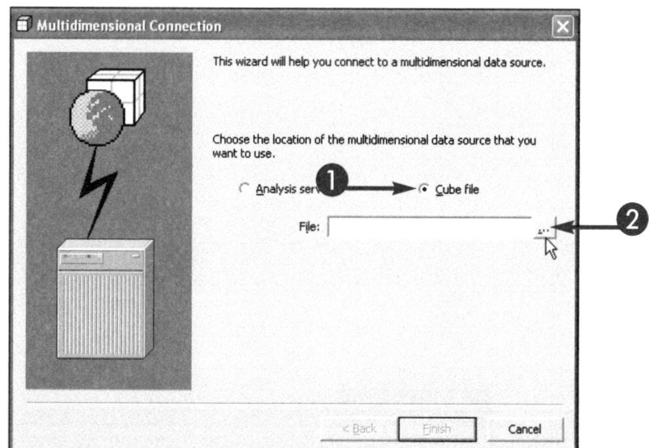

3. Click the cube file you want to use.
4. Click Open.

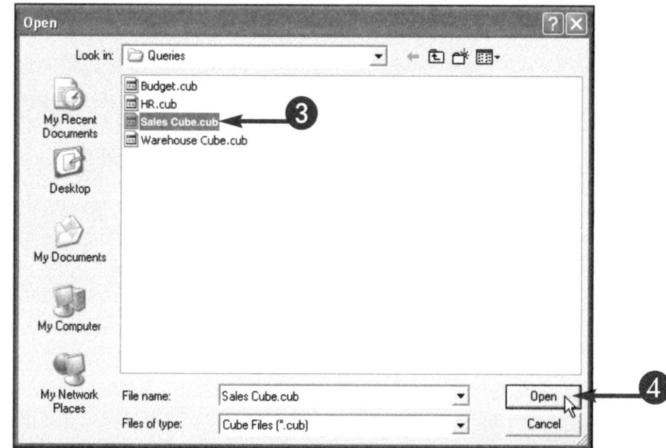

❺ Click Finish.

The Create New Data Source dialog box appears.

Note: To finish the data source, follow the steps in the section "Complete the Data Source."

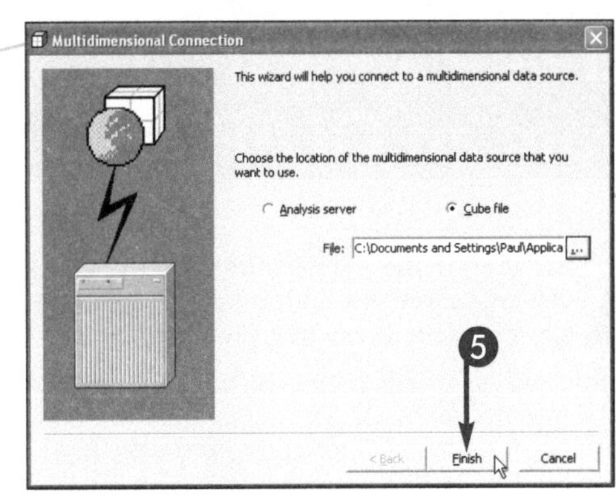

COMPLETE THE DATA SOURCE

❶ Click ▾ and select the cube you want to work with.

❷ Click OK.

The Choose Data Source dialog box appears.

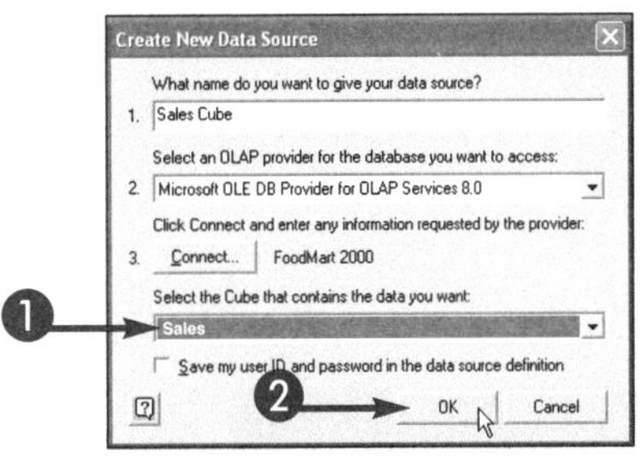

- The cube data source appears in the OLAP Cubes tab.

❸ Click Cancel.

You can now use the cube data source to create a PivotTable.

Note: If you want to create the PivotTable right away, click OK instead of Cancel in the Choose Data Source dialog box.

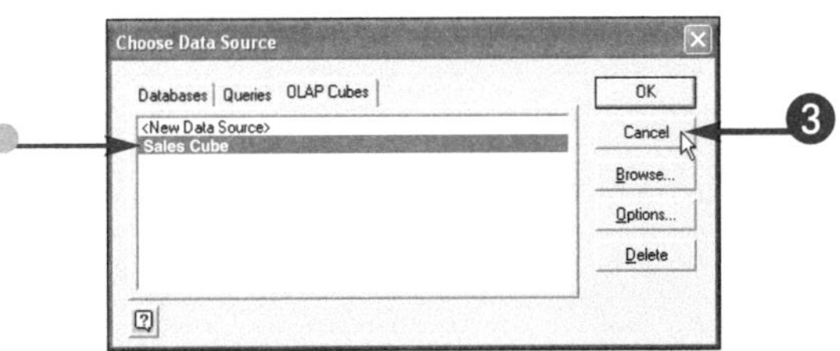

Apply It

If your network uses SQL Server with Analysis Services as its OLAP server, then you should also have access to the sample Foodmart database. This is a relatively large database of transactions based on a fictional grocery store chain. The OLAP database is based on an Access database named Foodmart 2000.mdb, which is normally stored in the following folder:

```
C:\Program Files\Microsoft Analysis Services\Samples
```

The database includes a number of fact tables, such as sales_fact_1998, which contains more than 160,000 records. On the OLAP server, there are several built-in cubes, including Sales, HR, and Budget. If you do not see the Foodmart database when you access your OLAP server, ask your database administrator whether the Foodmart sample can be made available.

Create a PivotTable from an OLAP Cube

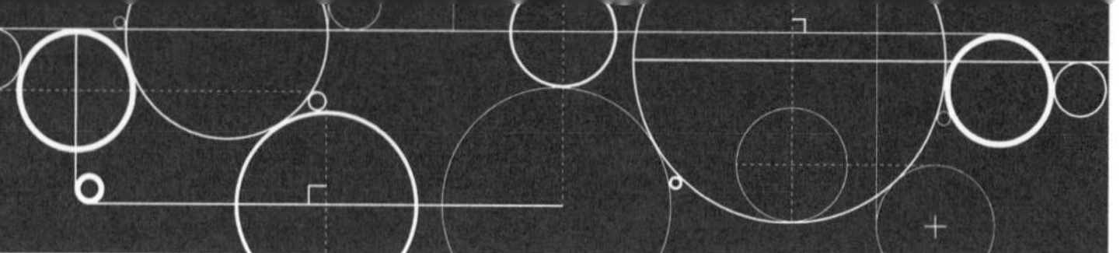

After you define a data source for the OLAP cube you want to work with, you can then use that data source as the basis of a PivotTable.

By definition, an OLAP cube is already a summary of the underlying data in the OLAP database. When creating an OLAP cube, the database administrator specifies one or more measures, and then the OLAP server applies those measures to every dimension, level, and member. So every possible combination of measure and dimension is already part of the cube. This is what makes cubes so powerful. Because all the summarizing work has already been done and the results are part of the cube, Excel requires very little processing power to pivot, filter, and summarize the data.

Because the OLAP cube is already a summary of data, it can only appear in Excel as part of a PivotTable or a PivotChart. So if you want to work with an OLAP cube within Excel, you must do it as part of a PivotTable.

Create a PivotTable from an OLAP Cube

1. Click Data→Import External Data→ New Database Query.

   The Choose Data Source dialog box appears.

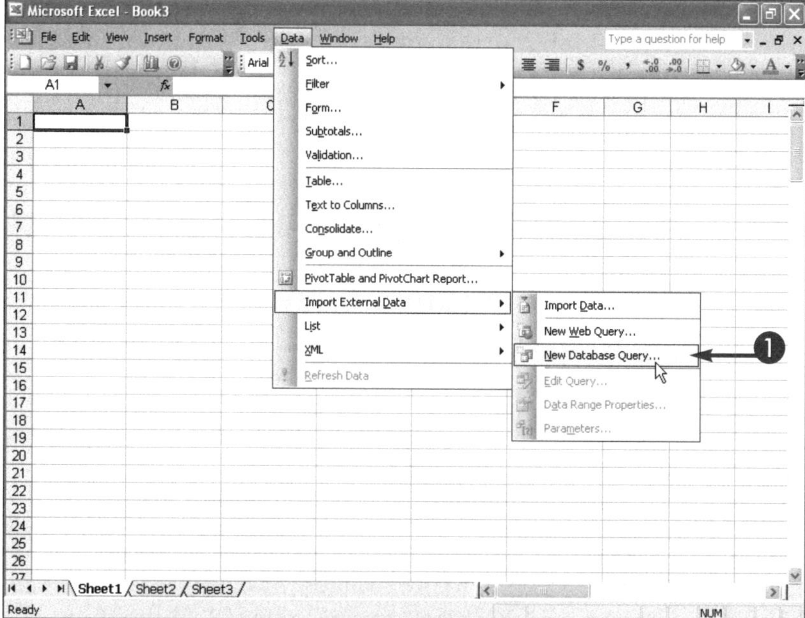

2. Click the OLAP Cubes tab.
3. Click the OLAP cube you want to work with.
4. Click OK.

   The PivotTable and PivotChart Wizard - Step 3 of 3 dialog box appears.

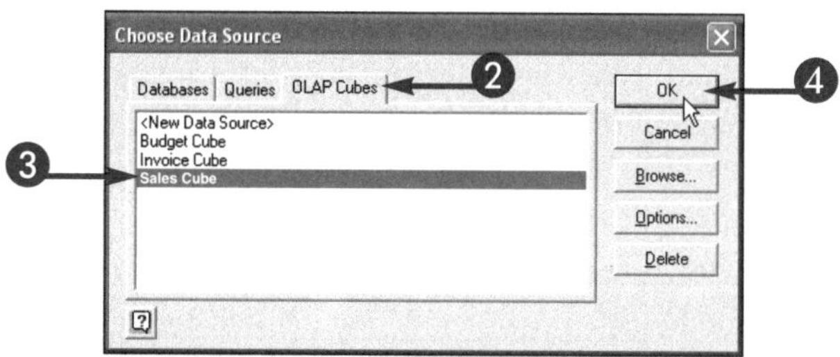

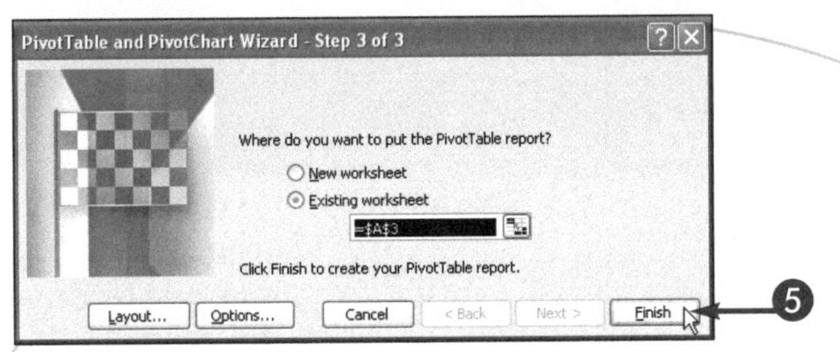

5 Click Finish.

Excel creates an empty PivotTable and displays the PivotTable toolbar and the PivotTable Field List.

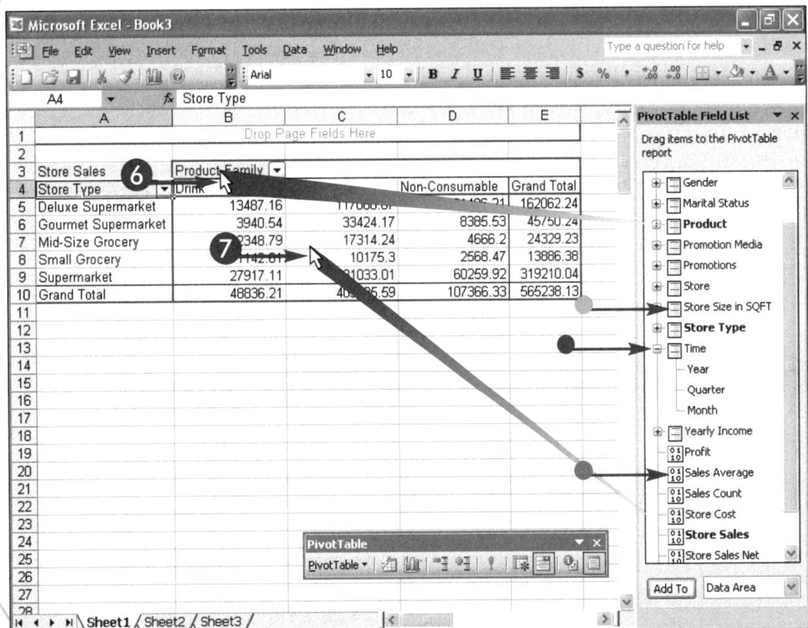

- Cube dimensions appear with the Cube dimension icon.
- Cube measures appear with the Cube measure icon.
- To display a dimension's levels, click the plus sign.

6 Click and drag one or more dimensions to the row, column, or page area.

7 Click and drag a measure to the data area.

Excel displays the completed PivotTable.

Extra

If your network uses SQL Server Analysis Services and you are working with OLAP cubes extensively, consider downloading and installing the Excel 2002/2003 Add-in for SQL Server Analysis Services from www.microsoft.com/office/solutions/accelerators/exceladdin/default.mspx.

After you install this add-in, restart Excel and you will see a new Cube Analysis menu. You can use the options on this menu to connect to a cube and to build special reports that enable you to analyze the data in more detail than you can with a PivotTable report. For example, you can use the Drillthrough command to drill down into the measure values to see the underlying data. There is also a What-If Analysis feature that enables you to perform what-if analysis on the report data.

Show and Hide Details for Dimensions and Levels

You can enhance your data analysis by displaying the details for one or more of the dimensions and levels in an OLAP PivotTable.

When you add a dimension to an OLAP PivotTable, Excel shows the members that comprise the top level of the dimension's hierarchy. For example, if you add the Product dimension in the Foodmart Sales cube, Excel displays the members of the Product Family level: Drink, Food, and Non-Consumable. However, the dimension hierarchy may have more levels. For example, in the Foodmart Sales cube, the Product Family's Drink member has another level that includes the items Alcoholic Beverages, Beverages, and Dairy. Similarly, the Beverages member has another level that includes Carbonated Beverages, Drinks, and Hot Beverages.

Some dimensions have only a single level, but others can have four or five. For these multilevel dimension hierarchies, you can drill down into the dimension's details to see more specific slices of the cube data.

In this task, you learn how to move up and down through a dimension's hierarchy one level at a time. An OLAP PivotTable also enables you to display only selected levels and members, and you learn how to do that in the task "Display Selected Levels and Members," later in this chapter.

Show and Hide Details for Dimensions and Levels

SHOW DETAILS

1. Click the dimension button or level item you want to work with.
2. Click PivotTable→Group and Show Detail→Show Detail.

   You can also click the Show Detail button ( ) or, for an item, double-click the item's cell.

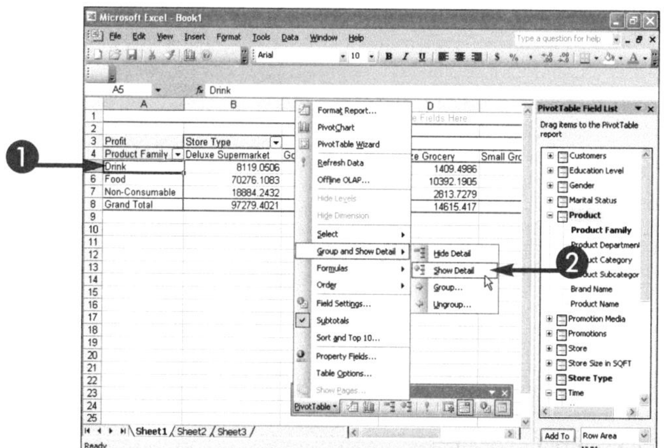

- Excel shows the detail.

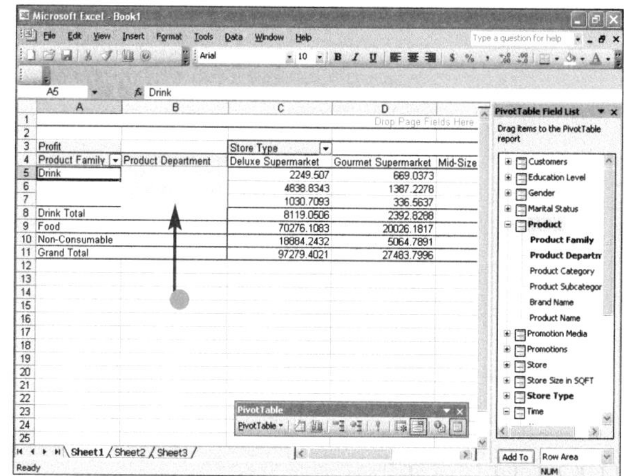

HIDE DETAILS

1. Click the dimension button or level item you want to work with.

2. Click PivotTable➔Group and Show Detail➔Hide Detail.

   You can also click the Hide Detail button (
) or, for an item, double-click the item's cell.

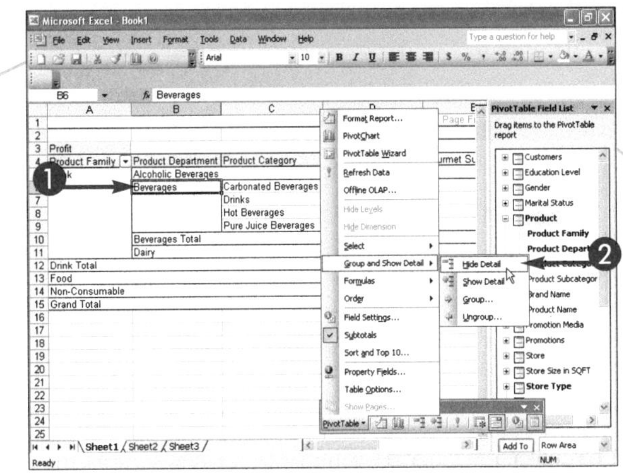

Excel hides the detail.

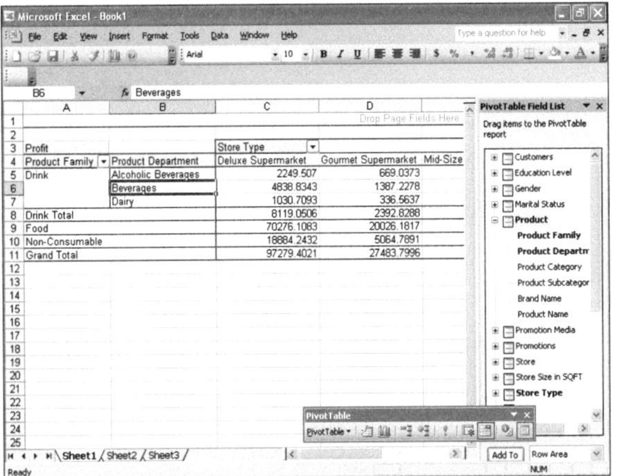

Apply It

You can use VBA to control whether a cube field displays details by setting the `PivotField` object's `DrilledDown` property to `True`. You can access all the members in a cube field by using the `PivotField` object's `CubeField.PivotFields` collection, as shown in the following macro, which shows details for up to five levels of the cube field in the active cell:

Example:

```
Sub ShowAllDetails()
    Dim objPF1 As PivotField, objPF2 As PivotField
    Dim objPF3 As PivotField, objPF4 As PivotField, objPF5 As PivotField
    On Error Resume Next
    Set objPF1 = ActiveCell.PivotField
    For Each objPF2 In objPF1.CubeField.PivotFields
        objPF2.DrilledDown = True
        For Each objPF3 In objPF2.CubeField.PivotFields
            objPF3.DrilledDown = True
            For Each objPF4 In objPF3.CubeField.PivotFields
                objPF4.DrilledDown = True
                For Each objPF5 In objPF4.CubeField.PivotFields
                    objPF5.DrilledDown = True
                Next 'objPF5
            Next 'objPF4
        Next 'objPF3
    Next 'objPF2
End Sub
```

Hide Levels

After you show the details for one or more levels in a hierarchical cube field, you can reconfigure the PivotTable to hide all the levels above a specified level in the hierarchy.

Displaying details is useful because it enables you to see more specific slices of the OLAP cube data. However, the extra levels can sometimes make the PivotTable more difficult to read. You can work around that problem by hiding the levels you do not want to see. For example, in the Foodmart Sales cube, the Product dimension has six levels: Product Family, Product Department, Product Category, Product Subcategory, Brand Name, and Product Name. If you want to view some measure with respect to the Product Name level, you must display details for all the upper levels. The resulting PivotTable is difficult to read and cumbersome to navigate, but you can make it easier by hiding the upper levels — the ones from Product Family to Brand Name.

You can control the number of levels a cube field displays by setting the `HiddenLevels` property. For example, if you set this property to 5, Excel hides the five top levels in the cube field hierarchy:

```
ActiveCell.PivotField.CubeField.
HiddenLevels = 5
```

To show all levels, set `HiddenLevels` to 0:

```
ActiveCell.PivotField.CubeField.
HiddenLevels = 0
```

Hide Levels

1. Click the field button for the bottommost level that you want to hide.
2. Click PivotTable→Hide Levels.

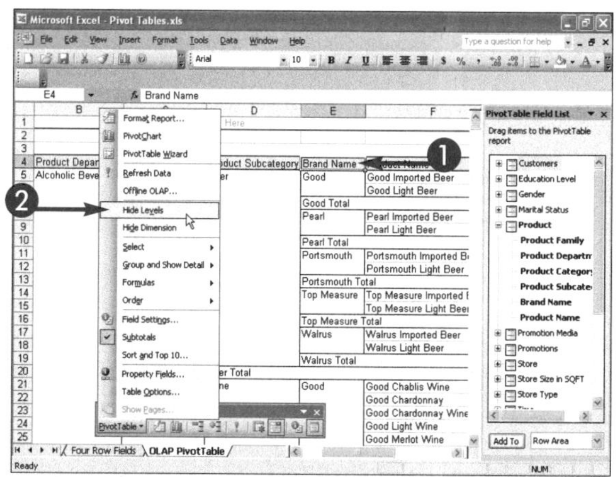

Excel hides the levels above and including the level that you clicked.

To show the levels again, click the field button for any remaining level and then click PivotTable→Show Levels.

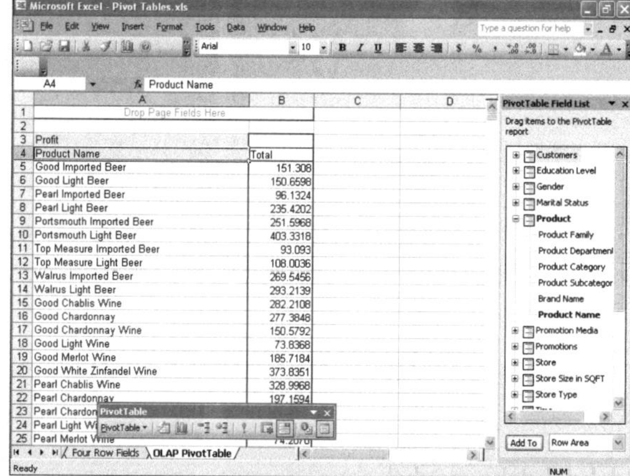

Display Selected Levels and Members

You can control exactly which levels and members Excel displays for a dimension that you have added to a PivotTable.

By default, Excel displays all the members of the top level when you add a dimension to the PivotTable. If you click the level button and then run the Show Details command, Excel displays all the members of the next level. If, on the other hand, you only want to display the members associated with a particular item in a level, then you can click the item and run the Show Details command.

However, your data analysis might require even more control over the display of levels and members. Excel enables you to hide members of any level, and this task shows you how to do that.

Extra

When you are working in the dimension drop-down list, you see the following check box states:

BUTTON	DESCRIPTION
☑	The level or member is displayed; for a level, none of its lower levels or members are displayed.
☐	The level or member is not displayed; for a level, none of its lower levels or members are displayed.
☑ (shaded)	The level or member is displayed; for a level, some or all of its lower levels or members are displayed.

Display Selected Levels and Members

1. Click the drop-down arrow in the dimension you want to work with.

   Excel displays a hierarchical list of the levels and members in the dimension.

2. Click the plus sign to open a level and see its members.

3. Deselect the check box of any level or member that you do not want to display.

4. Repeat Steps 2 and 3 to set the levels and members you want to display.

5. Click OK.

   Excel displays just the levels and members that you selected.

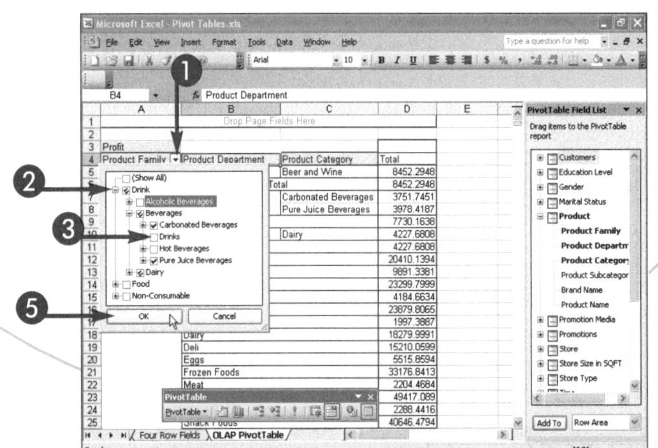

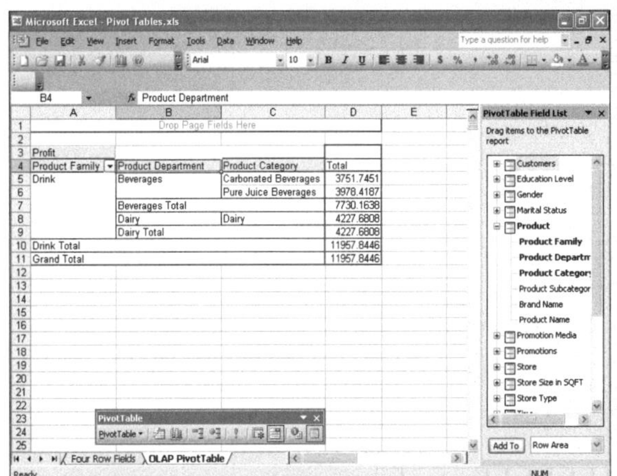

Display Multiple Page Field Items

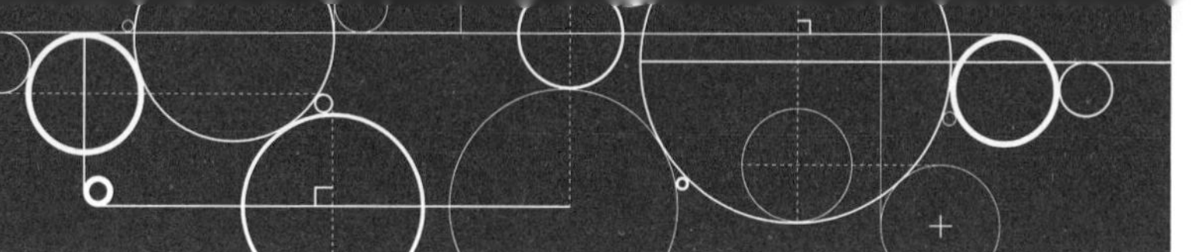

With an OLAP PivotTable, you can filter the report using two or more items in the page field.

A major component of good PivotTable-based data analysis is the ability to filter the report so that you see only the data you want to work with. In a regular PivotTable, you can filter the report by selecting an item from the page field. However, filtering on a single item is often not exactly what you want. For example, suppose your report shows the store sales of beverages to consumers in various income groups and you want to filter that report based on the education level of the consumers. Filtering the report to show just those consumers with a bachelor's degree or a graduate degree is useful, but your analysis may require that you examine both types of consumers together. In a regular PivotTable, it is possible to filter on multiple page field items, but it requires hiding all the items you do not want to include in the report. In an OLAP PivotTable, you can do this more directly by selecting just the items you want to include in the report filter.

Display Multiple Page Field Items

1. Click the page field's drop-down arrow.

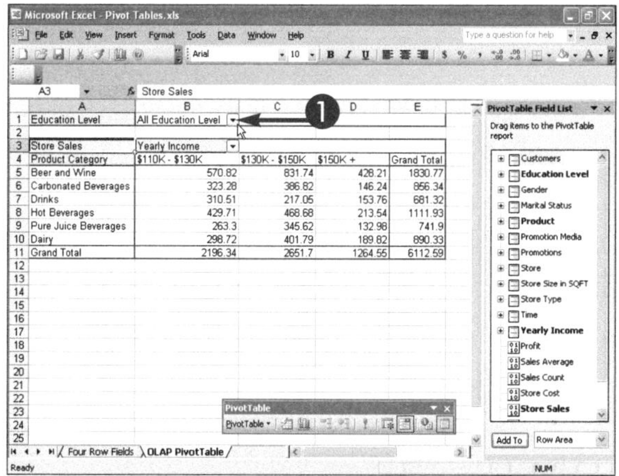

2. Check Select multiple items.
3. Click the plus sign to open the dimension and see the top level members.

   Excel displays a hierarchical list of the levels and members in the dimension.

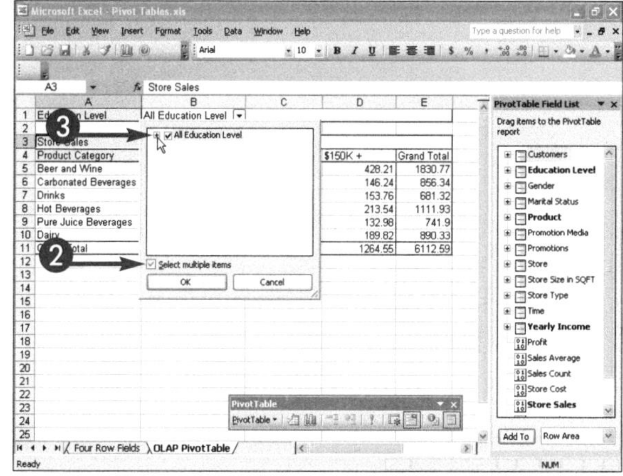

4. Click the plus sign to open a level and see its members.

5. Deselect the check box of any level or member that you do not want to display.

6. Repeat Steps 4 and 5 to set the levels and members you want to display.

7. Click OK.

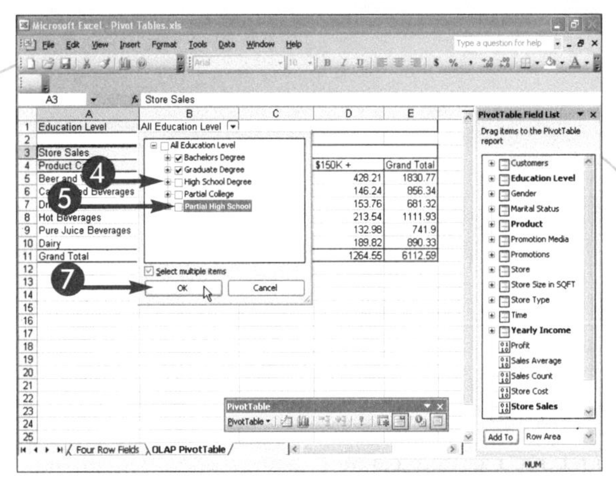

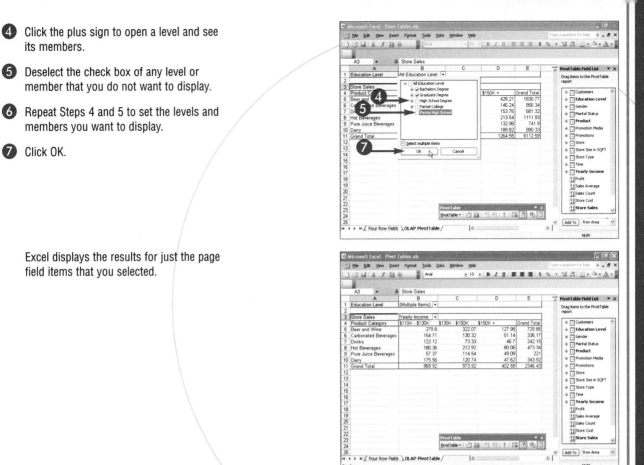

Excel displays the results for just the page field items that you selected.

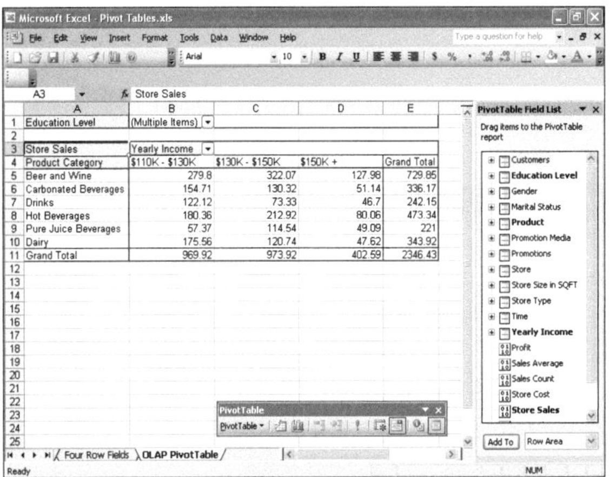

Apply It

A quick way to reset the report to display the data for all the page field items is to use the drop-down page field list and check "Select multiple items" (☐ changes to ☑). When you deactivate this check box, Excel automatically selects the "All" item in the list. Click OK to reset the report.

You can also do this via VBA by setting the `CubeField` object's `EnableMultiplePageItems` property to `True`. The following macro toggles this property on and off:

Example:

```
Sub ToggleMultiplePageFieldItems()
    Dim objPF As PivotField
    ' Work with the first page field in the active PivotTable
    Set objPF = ActiveCell.PivotTable.PageFields(1)
    ' Work with the CubeField object
    With objPF.CubeField
        ' Toggle the EnableMultiplePageItems property
        .EnableMultiplePageItems = Not .EnableMultiplePageItems
    End With
End Sub
```

Create an Offline OLAP Cube

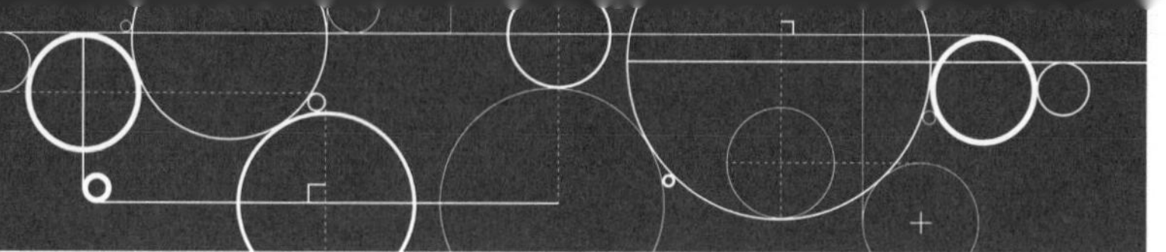

You can work with an OLAP PivotTable while your computer is not connected to the network by creating and using an offline version of the cube that includes some or all of the data stored on the OLAP server.

We live in a world of mobile computing where the "desktop" is any reasonably flat surface upon which you can balance your notebook or handheld computer. Unfortunately, although your computer may be quite portable, your data is not always so prepared to travel. This is particularly true when that data resides on a network server. After you disconnect from the network, you lose access to the server and, hence, to your data.

Many solutions exist that enable a roaming computer to make a remote connection to the network. But technologies such as Virtual Private Networking and dial-up connections are often expensive, difficult to set up, and too slow for heavy-duty data work.

A better solution is to take some or all the data on the road with you. By storing a version of the data on your traveling computer, you can work with the data at any time and without needing a remote connection. For most OLAP data, Excel offers the Create Cube File Wizard, which takes you step by step through the process of creating an offline cube file. Note, however, that this wizard does not work with all data warehouse software. You can then take that cube file with you when you travel and work with the cube's associated OLAP PivotTable, just as though it resided on an OLAP server.

Create an Offline OLAP Cube

1. Click any cell in the OLAP PivotTable you want to work with.

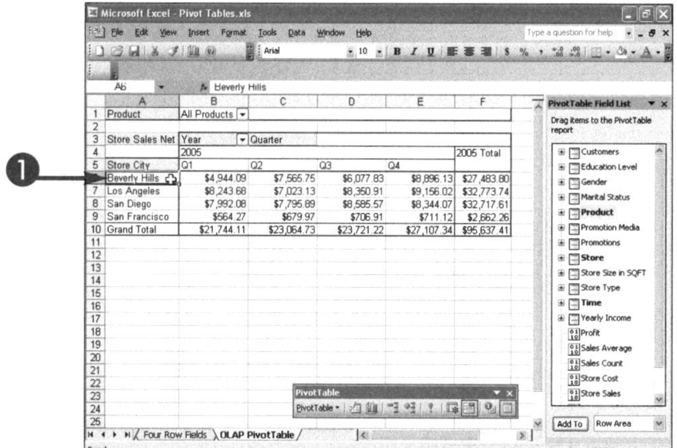

2. Click PivotTable→Offline OLAP.

The Offline OLAP Settings dialog box appears.

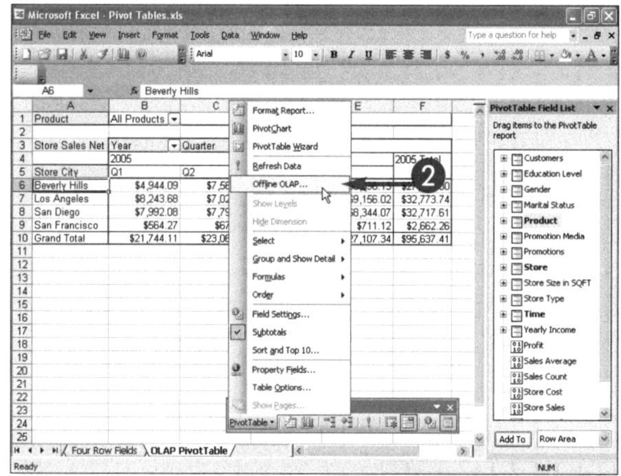

3. Click Create offline data file.

   The Create Cube File Wizard appears.

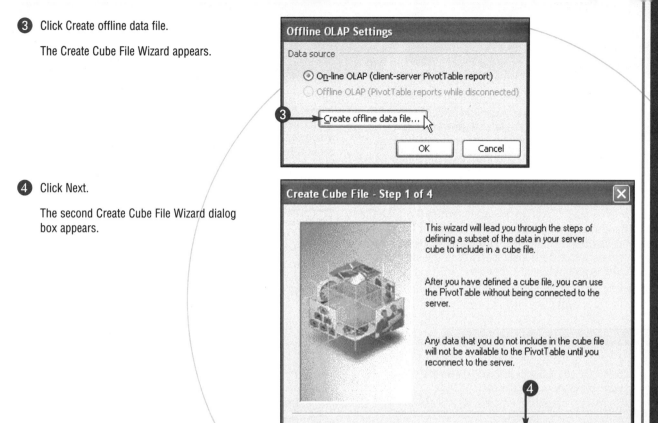

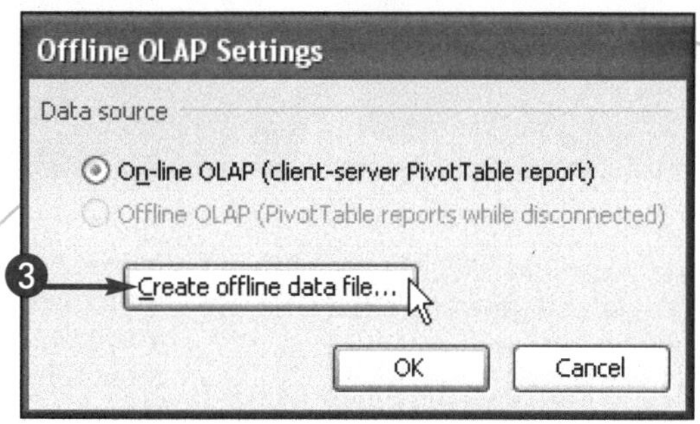
Offline OLAP Settings
Data source
On-line OLAP (client-server PivotTable report)
Offline OLAP (PivotTable reports while disconnected)
3
Create offline data file...
OK
Cancel

4. Click Next.

   The second Create Cube File Wizard dialog box appears.

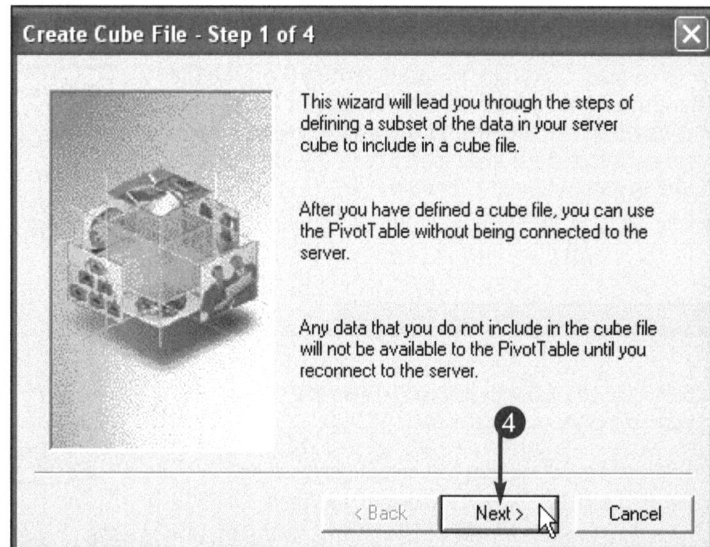
Create Cube File - Step 1 of 4
This wizard will lead you through the steps of defining a subset of the data in your server cube to include in a cube file.
After you have defined a cube file, you can use the PivotTable without being connected to the server.
Any data that you do not include in the cube file will not be available to the PivotTable until you reconnect to the server.
4
< Back
Next >
Cancel

Apply It

If you simply want to create a cube file that uses the same dimensions, levels, members, and measures that are in the current PivotTable, VBA gives you an easy way to do it. You can use the `PivotTable` object's `CreateCubeFile` method and specify only the File parameter, which is a string that specifies the location and name of the cube file. The following macro prompts the user for a file path and name and then uses the active PivotTable to create just such a cube file:

Example:

```
Sub CreateDefaultCubeFile()
    Dim strFilePath As String
    ' Build the default path from the USERPROFILE environment variable
    strFilePath = Environ("USERPROFILE") & "\My Documents\"
    ' Get the user's file path and name
    strFilePath = InputBox("Type the location of the cube (.cub) file:", _
                           "Create Default Cube File", _
                           strFilePath)
    ' Did the user click Cancel?
    If strFilePath <> "" Then
        ' If not, create the cube file with the specified pathname
        ActiveCell.PivotTable.CreateCubeFile _
            File:=strFilePath
    End If
End Sub
```

continued →

Create an Offline OLAP Cube (continued)

You can use the Create Cube File Wizard to specify exactly the data that you require while you work with the OLAP PivotTable offline.

Depending on how much data is stored in the online OLAP cube, the offline version could be massive. In fact, most OLAP cubes contain enough multidimensional data to create offline cube files that are dozens or even hundreds of megabytes in size. If you are not transferring the cube file to a different computer, such as your notebook PC, if you are not e-mailing the cube file, and if your computer contains lots of free hard disk space, then the size of the OLAP cube is probably not a concern.

However, it is common to require a cube file transfer — either to a portable machine or via e-mail. Alternatively, you may be running low on hard disk space and cannot store a huge file. For these situations, you need to restrict the size of the offline cube file. You can do this in the Create Cube File Wizard by specifying the data that you are certain you need while disconnected from the network. The wizard gives you two ways to do this. First, you can select for inclusion in the cube file just those dimensions that you want to work with. Second, you can select just those top level items that you want to work with. These top level items include all the measures in the OLAP cube and all the items in the dimensions that you selected for inclusion in the cube file.

Create an Offline OLAP Cube *(continued)*

5. Select the check box beside each dimension you want to include in the cube file.
6. To include lower levels of a dimension in the cube file, first click the plus sign to display the levels.
7. Select the check box beside each level you want to include in the cube file.
8. Repeat Steps 5 to 7, as needed.
9. Click Next.

   The third Create Cube File Wizard dialog box appears.

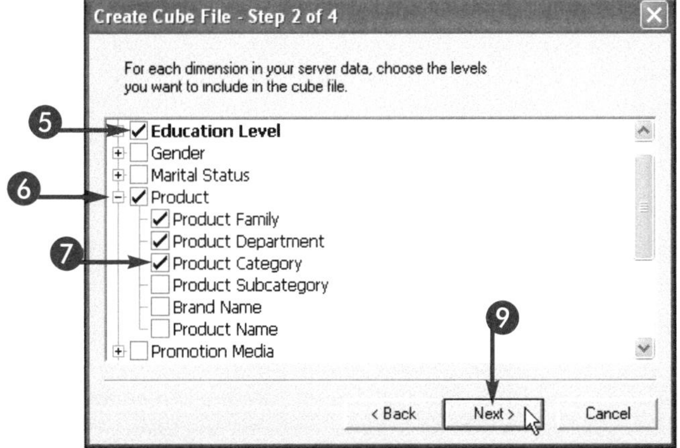

10. To include items from a top level in the cube file, first click the plus sign to display the items.
11. Select the check box beside each item you want to include in the cube file.
12. Repeat Steps 10 and 11 to specify all the top level items you want in the cube file.
13. Click Next.

    The fourth Create Cube File Wizard dialog box appears.

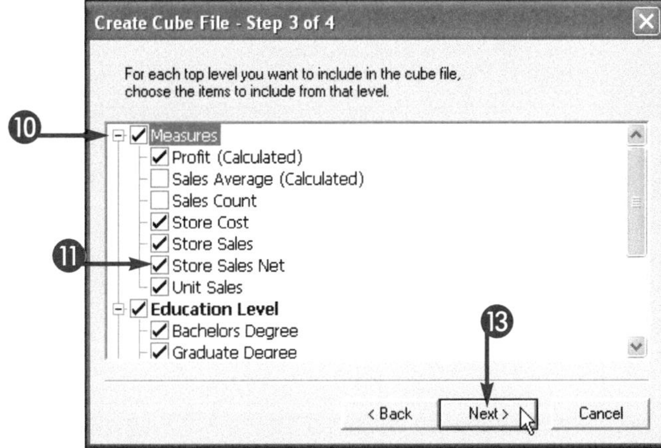

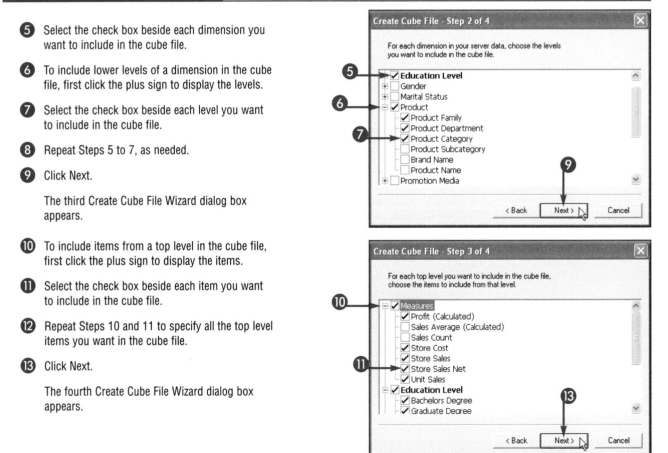

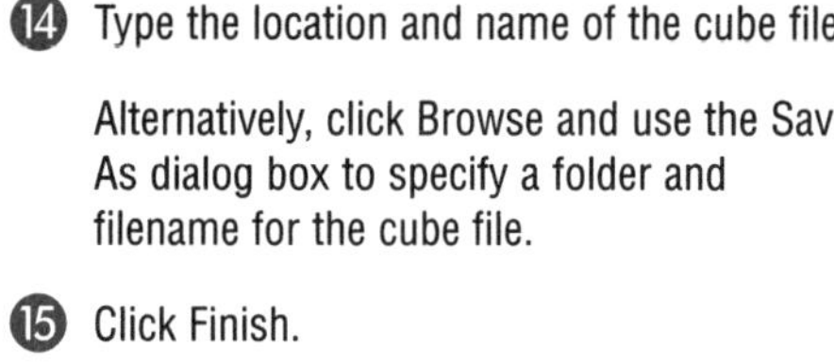

14. Type the location and name of the cube file.

    Alternatively, click Browse and use the Save As dialog box to specify a folder and filename for the cube file.

15. Click Finish.

    Excel creates the cube file and returns you to the Offline OLAP Settings dialog box.

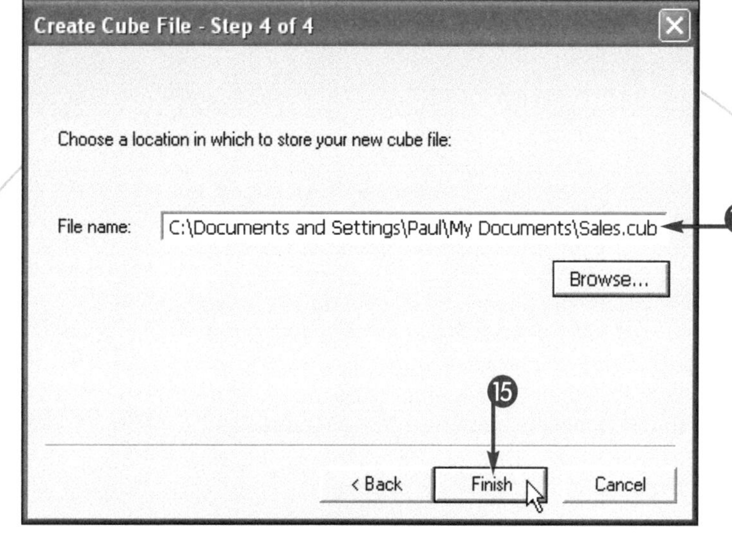

16. Select Offline OLAP.

17. Click OK.

    You can now use the OLAP PivotTable while disconnected from the network.

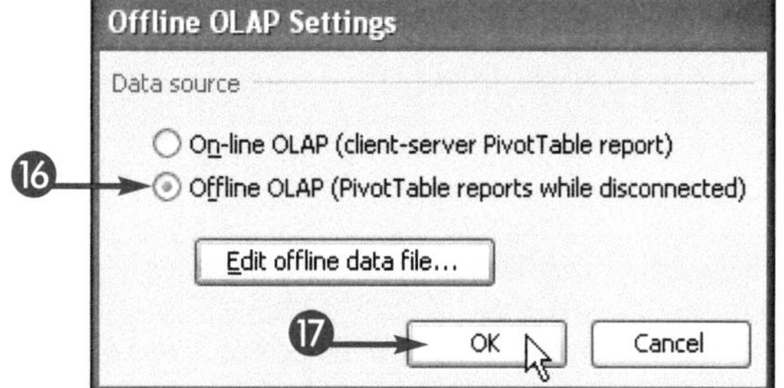

Extra

When you are offline and using the cube file for your PivotTable, you are free to create other PivotTables using the same cube file. First, you need to create a data source that connects to the cube file. In the task "Create an OLAP Cube Data Source," see the section "Connect to a Cube File." When that is done, you can then create the new PivotTable using the cube file data source; see the task "Create a PivotTable from an OLAP Cube."

When you reconnect to the network, you should switch to using the online OLAP data so that you can refresh the PivotTable report to get the latest data. To switch from the offline OLAP cube, click any cell in the PivotTable report and then click PivotTable→Offline OLAP. In the Offline OLAP Settings dialog box, select On-line OLAP (○ changes to ◉) and then click OK.

Introducing Formulas

One of the most powerful techniques you can use to enhance PivotTable-based data analysis is custom calculations in your reports. Whether you create a new calculated field or one or more new calculated items within a field, custom calculations enable you to interrogate your data and return the exact information that you require.

To get the most out of custom calculations, you need to understand formulas: their components, types, and how to build them. In this appendix, you learn how to understand and work with formulas and functions. However, the formulas you use with a PivotTable differ in important ways from regular Excel worksheet formulas. This appendix highlights the differences and focuses on formula ideas and techniques that apply to PivotTable calculations. This section gets you started by showing you the basics of the two major formula components: operands and operators.

For the specifics of implementing custom calculations in your PivotTable reports, see Chapter 8.

Operands

Operands are the values that the formula uses as the raw material for the calculation. In a custom PivotTable calculation, the operands can be constants, worksheet functions, fields from your data source, or items within a data source field. Note that you cannot use cell references or defined names as operands in the PivotTable formula.

Constants

A *constant* is a fixed value that you insert into a formula and use as is. For example, suppose you want a calculated item to return a result that is 10 percent greater than the value of the Beverages item. In that case, you create a formula that multiplies the Beverages item by the constant 110 percent, as shown here:

```
=Beverages * 110%
```

In PivotTable formulas, the constant values are almost always numbers, although when using comparison formulas you may occasionally use a string — text surrounded by double quotation marks, such as "January" — as a constant. Note that custom PivotTable formulas do not support constant date values.

Worksheet Functions

You can use many of Excel's built-in worksheet functions as operands in a custom PivotTable formula. For example, you can use the AVERAGE function to compute the average of two or more items in a field, or you can use logic functions such as IF and OR to create complex formulas that make decisions. The major restriction when it comes to worksheet functions is that you cannot use cell addresses or range references in PivotTable formulas, so functions that require such parameters — such as the lookup and reference functions — are off limits. See the section "Introducing Worksheet Functions," later in this appendix, for more details.

PivotTable Fields

The third type of operand that you can use in a formula for a calculated field is a PivotTable field. Remember, however, that when you reference a field, Excel uses the sum over all the records in that field, not the individual records in that field. This does not matter for operations such as multiplication and division, because the result is the same either way. However, it can make a big difference with operations such as addition and subtraction. For example, the formula =Condiments + 10 does not add 10 to each Condiments value and return the sum of these results; that is, Excel does not interpret the formula as =Sum of (Condiments + 10). Instead, the formula adds 10 to the sum of the Condiments values; that is, Excel interprets the formula as =(Sum of Condiments) + 10.

Operands (continued)

PivotTable Items

The fourth and final type of operand that you can use in a formula is a PivotTable field item, which you can only use as part of a calculated item. In the Insert Calculated Item dialog box, click the field, click the item, and then click Insert Item; see the Chapter 8 task, "Insert a Custom Calculated Item." You can also augment the item reference by including the field name along with the item name. With this method, you can either use the item name directly or refer to the item by its absolute or relative position within the field.

DIRECT REFERENCE

To reference a field and one of its items directly, type the field name followed by square brackets that enclose the item name — surrounded by single quotation marks if the item name includes spaces. For example, in a field named Salesperson, you can reference the Robert King item as follows:

```
Salesperson['Robert King']
```

You can use the field name in this way to make your formulas a bit easier to read and to avoid errors when two fields have items with the same name. For example, a report may have a Country field and a ShipCountry field, both of which might include an item named USA. To differentiate between them, you can use ShipCountry[USA] and Country[USA].

POSITIONAL REFERENCE

To reference a field and one of its items by position, type the field name followed by square brackets that enclose the position of the item within the field. For example, to reference the first item in the ProductName field, you can use the following:

```
ProductName[1]
```

This ensures that your formula always references the first item, no matter the sort order you use in the report.

You can also reference a field and one of its items by the position relative to the calculated item that you create. A positive number references items later in the field, and a negative number references items earlier in the field. For example, if the calculated item is the second item in the ProductName field, then ProductName[-1] refers to the first item in the field and ProductName[+1] refers to the third item in the field.

Operators

It is possible to use only an operand in a PivotTable formula. For example, in a calculated field, if you reference just a field name after the opening equals sign (=), then the values in the calculated field are identical to the values in the referenced field.

A calculated field that is equal to an existing field is not particularly useful in data analysis. To create PivotTable formulas that perform more interesting calculations, you need to include one or more operators. The operators are the symbols that the formula uses to perform the calculation.

In a custom PivotTable calculation, the available operators are much more limited than they are with a regular worksheet formula. In fact, Excel only allows two types of operators in PivotTable formulas: arithmetic operators — such as addition (+), subtraction (-), multiplication (*), and division (/) — and comparison operators — such as greater than (>) and less than or equal to (<=). See the next section, "Understanding Formula Types," for a complete list of available operators in these two categories.

Understanding Formula Types

Although a worksheet formula can be one of many different types, the formulas you can use in calculated fields and items are more restricted. In fact, there are only two types of formulas that make sense in a PivotTable context: arithmetic formulas for computing numeric results, and comparison formulas for comparing one numeric value with another.

Because you almost always deal with numeric values within a PivotTable report, the type of formula is determined by the operators you use: arithmetic formulas use arithmetic operators and comparison formulas use comparison operators. This section shows you the operators that define both types. Note, however, that the two types are not mutually exclusive and can be combined to create formulas as complex as your data analysis needs require. For example, the IF worksheet function uses a comparison formula to return a result, and you can then use that result as an operand in a larger arithmetic formula.

Arithmetic Formulas

An arithmetic formula combines numeric operands — numeric constants, functions that return numeric results, and fields or items that contain numeric values — with mathematical operators to perform a calculation. Because PivotTables primarily deal with numeric data, arithmetic formulas are by far the most common formulas used in custom PivotTable calculations.

The following table lists the seven arithmetic operators that you can use to construct arithmetic formulas in your calculated fields or items:

OPERATOR	NAME	EXAMPLE	RESULT
+	Addition	=10 + 5	15
-	Subtraction	=10 - 5	5
-	Negation	=-10	-10
*	Multiplication	=10 * 5	50
/	Division	=10 / 5	2
%	Percentage	=10%	0.1
^	Exponentiation	=10 ^ 5	100000

Comparison Formulas

A comparison formula combines numeric operands — numeric constants, functions that return numeric results, and fields or items that contain numeric values — with special operators to compare one operand with another. A comparison formula always returns a logical result. This means that if the comparison is true, then the formula returns the value 1, which is equivalent to the logical value TRUE; if the comparison is false, instead, then the formula returns the value 0, which is equivalent to the logical value FALSE.

The following table lists the six operators that you can use to construct comparison formulas in your calculated fields or items:

OPERATOR	NAME	EXAMPLE	RESULT
=	Equal to	=10 = 5	0
<	Less than	=10 < 5	0
<=	Less than or equal to	=10 <= 5	0
>	Greater than	=10 > 5	1
>=	Greater than or equal to	=10 >= 5	1
<>	Not equal to	=10 <> 5	1

Operator Precedence

Most of your formulas include multiple operands and operators. In many cases, the order in which Excel performs the calculations is crucial. For example, consider the following formula:

```
=3 + 5 ^ 2
```

If you calculate from left to right, the answer you get is 64 (3 + 5 equals 8, and 8 ^ 2 equals 64). However, if you perform the exponentiation first and then the addition, the result is 28 (5 ^ 2 equals 25, and 3 + 25 equals 28). Therefore, a single formula can produce multiple answers, depending on the order in which you perform the calculations.

To control this problem, Excel evaluates a formula according to a predefined order of precedence. You can also control the order of precedence yourself. See the tip in the task "Build a Formula," later in this appendix. This order of precedence enables Excel to calculate a formula unambiguously by determining which part of the formula it calculates first, which part second, and so on. The order of precedence is determined by the formula operators, as shown in the following table:

OPERATOR	OPERATION	ORDER OF PRECEDENCE
-	Negation	1st
%	Percentage	2nd
^	Exponentiation	3rd
* and /	Multiplication and division	4th
+ and -	Addition and subtraction	5th
= < <= > >= <>	Comparison	6th

Introducing Worksheet Functions

A *function* is a predefined formula that accepts one or more inputs and then calculates a result. In Excel, a function is often called a *worksheet function* because you normally use it as part of a formula that you type in a worksheet cell. However, Excel enables you to use many of its worksheet functions in the PivotTable formulas you create for calculated fields and items.

This section introduces you to worksheet functions by showing you their advantages and structure and by examining a few other worksheet ideas that you should know. The next section, "Understanding Function Types," takes you through the various types of functions that you can use in custom PivotTable calculations, and the task "Build a Function," later in this appendix, shows you a technique for building foolproof functions that you can paste into your custom formulas.

Function Advantages

Functions are designed to take you beyond the basic arithmetic and comparison formulas that you learned about in the previous section. Functions do this in three ways:

- Functions make simple but cumbersome formulas easier to use. For example, suppose that you have a PivotTable report showing average house prices in various neighborhoods and you want to calculate the monthly mortgage payment for each price. Given a fixed monthly interest rate and a term in months, here is the general formula for calculating the monthly payment:

```
House Price*Interest Rate/(1-(1+Interest Rate)^-Term)
```

  Fortunately, Excel offers an alternative to this intimidating formula — the PMT function:

```
PMT(Interest Rate, Term, House Price)
```

- Functions enable you to include complex mathematical expressions in your worksheets that otherwise are difficult or impossible to construct using simple arithmetic operators. For example, you can calculate a PivotTable's average value using the Average summary function, but what if you prefer to know the *median* — the value that falls in the middle when all the values are sorted numerically — or the *mode* — the value that occurs most frequently? Either value may be time-consuming to calculate by hand, but they are easy to calculate using Excel's MEDIAN and MODE worksheet functions.
- Functions enable you to include data in your applications that you could not access otherwise. For example, the powerful IF function enables you to test the value of a field item — for example, to see whether it contains a particular value — and then return another value, depending on the result.

Function Structure

Every worksheet function has the same basic structure:

```
NAME(Argument1, Argument2, ...)
```

Function Name

The NAME part identifies the function. In worksheet formulas and custom PivotTable formulas, the function name always appears in uppercase letters: PMT, SUM, AVERAGE, and so on.

No matter how you type a function name, Excel always converts the name to all-uppercase letters. Therefore, when you type the name of a function that you want to use in a formula, always type the name using lowercase letters. This way, if you find that Excel does not convert the function name to uppercase characters, it likely means you misspelled the name, because Excel does not recognize it.

Arguments

The items that appear within the parentheses are the functions' *arguments*. The arguments are the inputs that functions use to perform calculations. For example, the SUM function adds its arguments and the PMT function calculates the loan payment based on arguments that include the interest rate, term, and present value of the loan. Some functions do not require any arguments at all, but most require at least 1 argument, and some as many as 9 or 10. If a function uses two or more arguments, be sure to separate each argument with a comma, and be sure to enter the arguments in the order specified by the function.

Function arguments fall into two categories: required and optional. A *required argument* is one that must appear between the function's parentheses in the specified position; if you omit a required argument, Excel generates an error. An *optional argument* is one that you are free to use or omit, depending on your needs. If you omit an optional argument, Excel uses the argument's default value in the function. For example, the PMT function has an optional "future value" argument with which you can specify the value of the loan at the end of the term. The default future value is 0, so you need only specify this argument if your loan's future value is something other than 0.

In the task "Build a Function," later in this appendix, you see that Excel uses two methods for differentiating between required and optional arguments. When you enter a function in a cell, the optional arguments are shown surrounded by square brackets: [and]; when you build a function using the Insert Function dialog box, or if you look up a function in the Excel Help system, required arguments are shown in bold text and optional arguments are shown in regular text.

If a function has multiple optional arguments, you may need to skip one or more of these arguments. If you do this, be sure to include the comma that would normally follow each missing argument. For example, here is the full PMT function syntax — the required arguments are shown in bold text:

PMT(**rate**, **nper**, **pv**, fv, type)

Here is an example PMT function that uses the *type* argument but not the *fv* argument:

```
PMT(0.05, 25, 100000, ,1)
```

Understanding Function Types

Excel comes with hundreds of worksheet functions, and they are divided into various categories or types. These function types include Text, Information, Lookup and Reference, Date and Time, and Database. However, none of these categories are particularly useful in a PivotTable context where you mostly deal with aggregate values: sums, counts, averages, and so on. Therefore, there are only four function types that you will likely use in your custom PivotTable formulas: Math, Statistical, Financial, and Logical. This section introduces you to these four function types and lists the most popular and useful functions in each category. Note that for each function the required arguments are shown in bold type.

Mathematical Functions

PivotTables deal with numbers derived by summary operations such as sum, count, average, max, and min. In the formulas for your calculated fields and calculated items, you can often use mathematical worksheet functions to manipulate those numbers. The following table lists a few of the most useful mathematical functions:

FUNCTION	DESCRIPTION
CEILING(***number***,***significance***)	Rounds *number* up to the nearest integer
EVEN(***number***)	Rounds *number* up to the nearest even integer
FACT(***number***)	Returns the factorial of *number*
FLOOR(***number***,***significance***)	Rounds *number* down to the nearest multiple of *significance*
INT(***number***)	Rounds *number* down to the nearest integer
MOD(***number***,***divisor***)	Returns the remainder of *number* after dividing by *divisor*
ODD(***number***)	Rounds *number* up to the nearest odd integer
PI()	Returns the value Pi
PRODUCT(***number1***,*number2*,...)	Multiplies the specified numbers
RAND()	Returns a random number between 0 and 1
ROUND(***number***,***digits***)	Rounds *number* to a specified number of *digits*
ROUNDDOWN(***number***,***digits***)	Rounds *number* down, toward 0
ROUNDUP(***number***,***digits***)	Rounds *number* up, away from 0
SIGN(***number***)	Returns the sign of *number* (1 = positive; 0 = zero; -1 = negative)
SQRT(***number***)	Returns the positive square root of *number*
SUM(***number1***,*number2*,...)	Adds the arguments
TRUNC(***number***,*digits*)	Truncates *number* to an integer

Statistical Functions

Excel's statistical functions calculate a wide variety of highly technical statistical measures. For PivotTable calculations, however, you can only use the basic statistical operations, such as calculating the average, maximum, minimum, and standard deviation. The following table lists the worksheet functions that perform these basic statistical operations:

FUNCTION	DESCRIPTION
AVERAGE(***number1***,*number2*,...)	Returns the average of the arguments
COUNT(***number1***,*number2*,...)	Counts the numbers in the argument list

Statistical Functions (continued)

FUNCTION	DESCRIPTION
MAX(***number1***,*number2*,...)	Returns the maximum value of the arguments
MEDIAN(***number1***,*number2*,...)	Returns the median value of the arguments
MIN(***number1***,*number2*,...)	Returns the minimum value of the arguments
MODE(***number1***,*number2*,...)	Returns the most common value of the arguments
STDEV(***number1***,*number2*,...)	Returns the standard deviation based on a sample
STDEVP(***number1***,*number2*,...)	Returns the standard deviation based on an entire population
VAR(***number1***,[*number2*,...])	Returns the variance based on a sample
VARP(***number1***,[*number2*,...])	Returns the variance based on an entire population

Financial Functions

Excel's financial functions offer you powerful tools for calculating such things as the future value of an annuity and the periodic payment for a loan. The financial functions that you can use within a PivotTable use the following arguments:

rate	The fixed rate of interest over the term of the loan or investment
nper	The number of payments or deposit periods over the term of the loan or investment
pmt	The periodic payment or deposit
pv	The present value of the loan (the principal) or the initial deposit in an investment
fv	The future value of the loan or investment
type	The type of payment or deposit: 0 (the default) for end-of-period payments or deposits; 1 for beginning-of-period payments or deposits

FUNCTION	DESCRIPTION
FV(***rate***,***nper***,***pmt***,*pv*,*type*)	Returns the future value of an investment or loan
IPMT(***rate***,***per***,***nper***,***pv***,*fv*,*type*)	Returns the interest payment for a specified period of a loan
NPER(***rate***,***pmt***,***pv***,*fv*,*type*)	Returns the number of periods for an investment or loan
PMT(***rate***,***nper***,***pv***,*fv*,*type*)	Returns the periodic payment for a loan or investment
PPMT(***rate***,***per***,***nper***,***pv***,*fv*,*type*)	Returns the principal payment for a specified period of a loan
PV(***rate***,***nper***,***pmt***,*fv*,*type*)	Returns the present value of an investment
RATE(***nper***,***pmt***,***pv***,*fv*,*type*,*guess*)	Returns the periodic interest rate for a loan or investment

Logical Functions

The logical functions operate with the logical values TRUE and FALSE, which in your PivotTable calculations are interpreted as 1 and 0, respectively. In most cases, the logical values used as arguments are expressions that make use of comparison operators such as equal to (=) and greater than (>). The following table lists the logical functions that you can use in your custom PivotTable formulas:

FUNCTION	DESCRIPTION
AND(***logical1***,*logical2*,...)	Returns 1 if all the arguments are true; returns 0, otherwise
IF(***logical_test***,***true_expr***,*false_expr*)	Performs a logical test; returns *true_expr* if the result is 1 (true); returns *false_expr* if the result is 0 (false)
NOT(***logical***)	Reverses the logical value of the argument
OR(***logical1***,*logical2*,...)	Returns 1 if any argument is true; returns 0, otherwise

Build a Function

If you are not sure how to construct a particular function, you can build it within a worksheet cell to ensure that the syntax is correct and that all the required arguments are in place and in the correct order.

When you need to use a function within a custom PivotTable formula, it is common to not know or remember the correct structure of the function. For example, you may not know which arguments are required or what order to enter the arguments. Unfortunately, if you build the function within either the Insert Calculated Field or the Insert Calculated Item dialog box, Excel does not offer any help with the function syntax.

However, when you build a function within a worksheet cell, Excel displays a pop-up banner that shows the correct syntax for the function. This is very useful, so it pays to take advantage of this feature when building your PivotTable formulas. That is, before you display either the Insert Calculated Field or the Insert Calculated Item dialog box, build the function — or even the entire formula — you want in a worksheet cell. You can then copy the function or formula and paste it into the Insert Calculated Field or the Insert Calculated Item dialog box.

Build a Function

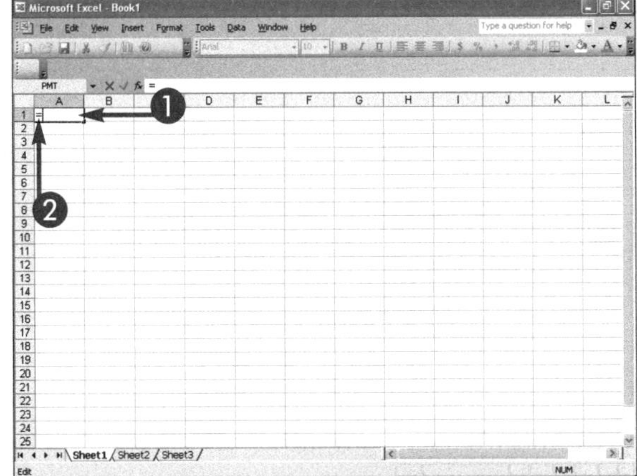

1. Click the worksheet cell in which you want to build your function.
2. Type = to start a formula.

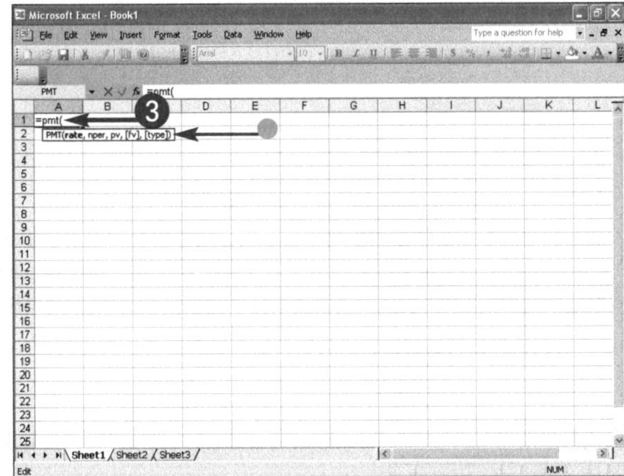

3. Type the function name and then the left parenthesis.
   - Excel displays a pop-banner showing the function syntax.

- The current argument is bold.
- Optional arguments are surrounded by square brackets ([and]).

4 Type the argument values you want to use.

Note: If you plan on using the names of PivotTable fields or items as function arguments, enter the name of some other placeholder.

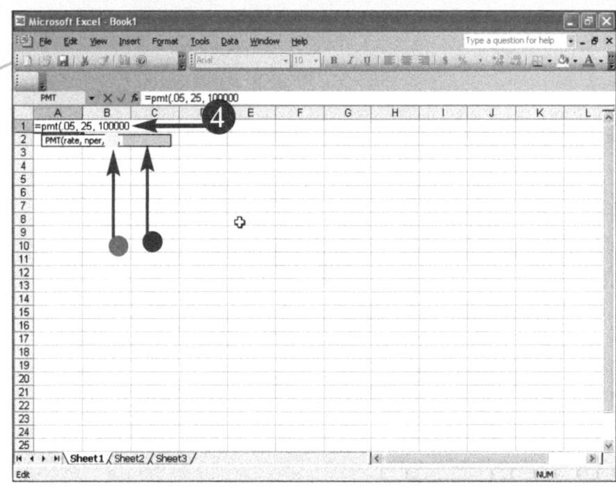

5 Type the right parenthesis to complete the function.

6 Press Enter to finish editing the cell.

Note: If you have a PivotTable field or item name in your function, Excel displays a #NAME? error in the cell because it does not recognize the name outside the PivotTable. You can ignore this error.

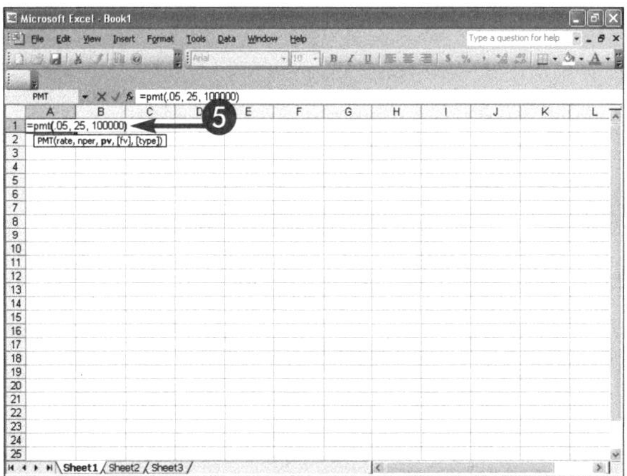

Extra

If you are not sure which function to use, or if you are not sure how to spell the function name, Excel offers an alternative method for building a function: the Insert Function feature. To use this feature, click an empty cell, type an equals sign (=), and then click Insert→Function or click the Insert Function button (fx) in the formula bar. Excel displays the Insert Function dialog box.

You can use the "Or select a category" list to click the function category you want to use: Math & Trig, Statistical, Financial, or Logical. Then you can use the "Select a function" list to click the function you want to use. Click OK to display the Function Arguments dialog box, which offers text boxes for each argument used by the function. Type the argument values you want to use and then click OK to insert the function into the cell.

If you know the name of the function you want to use, but you want to use the Function Arguments dialog box to type your argument values, type an equals sign (=) and then the function name in an empty cell. Then either press Ctrl+A or click the Insert Function button (fx). Excel displays the Function Arguments dialog box for the function you typed.

Build a Formula

You are now ready to build a custom formula for a calculated field or a calculated item. You learned in the previous task, "Build a Function," that it is helpful to first create a function in a worksheet cell because Excel displays pop-up text that helps you use the correct structure and arguments for the function. Unfortunately, no such help is available when you build a formula in a worksheet cell. Therefore, you will be building your formulas in either the Calculated Field dialog box or the Calculated Item dialog box.

One way to reduce errors when building a custom PivotTable formula is to avoid typing field or item names when you need to use them as operands in your formula. If you are creating a calculated field, for example, it is likely that it will use at least one PivotTable field as an operand. Rather than type the field name and introduce the risk of misspelling the name, you can ask Excel to insert the name for you. You learned how to do this in Chapter 8 in the task "Insert a Custom Calculated Field." Similarly, you can also ask Excel to insert field items in a formula for a calculated item, as described in Chapter 8's "Insert a Custom Calculated Item" task.

Build a Formula

Note: This appendix uses the PivotTables.xls spreadsheet, available at www.wiley.com/go/pivottablesvb, or you can create your own sample database.

1. Display the Insert Calculated Field dialog box or the Insert Calculated Item dialog box.

Note: See the tasks "Insert a Custom Calculated Field" and "Insert a Custom Calculated Item" in Chapter 8.

2. Type a name for the formula.
3. Type =.

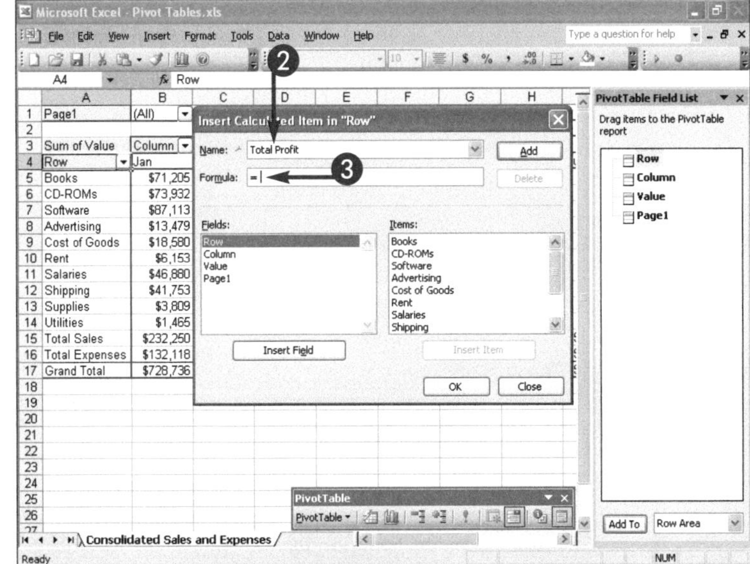

4. Insert an operand.

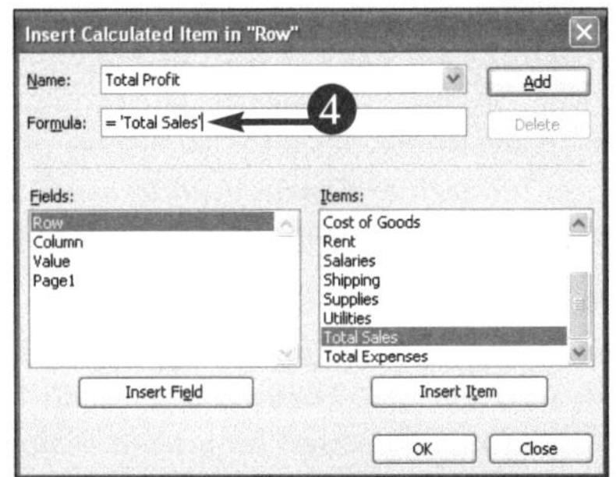

5. Type an operator.

6. Repeat Steps 4 and 5 until the formula is complete.

7. Click Add.

8. Click OK.

- Excel uses the formula to create the new calculated field or item.

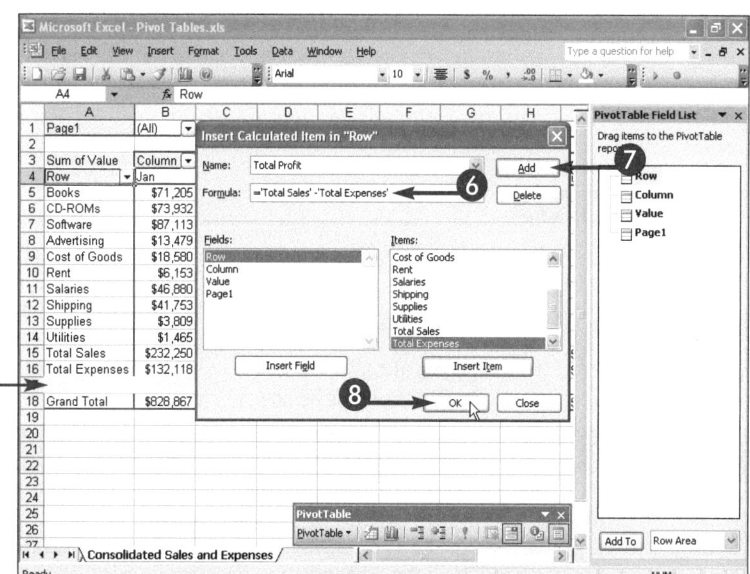

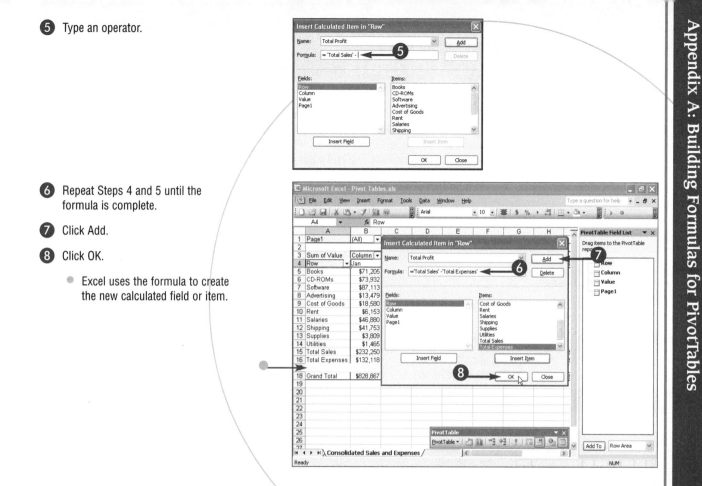

Apply It

In the section "Understanding Formula Types," earlier in this appendix, you learn about operator precedence — the default order that Excel uses to process the operators in a formula. For example, Excel performs multiplication and division before it performs addition and subtraction. This seems harmless, but it can lead to errors in your formula results. Consider a formula that calculates the gross margin for a business. Gross margin is profit — sales minus expenses — divided by expenses. Therefore, you might start with the following formula:

```
=Profit - Expenses \ Expenses
```

However, when Excel processes this formula, operator precedence tells it to perform the division first, so the formula becomes this:

```
=Profit - 1
```

This is clearly incorrect. To force Excel to perform a particular operation first, surround the expression with parentheses. For example, to force Excel to perform the subtraction first in the gross margin calculation, you can surround the expression Profit - Expenses with parentheses, as shown here:

```
=(Profit - Expenses) \ Expenses
```

Work with Custom Numeric and Date Formats

You can display your PivotTable results exactly the way you want by applying a custom numeric to the values. If your PivotTable includes dates or times, you can also control their display by applying a custom date or time format.

In Chapter 5, you learn how to apply formats to the numbers and dates in your PivotTable. These are predefined Excel formats that enable you to display numbers with thousands of separators, currency symbols, or percentage signs, as well as dates and times using various combinations of days, months, and years or seconds, minutes, and hours.

Excel's list of format categories also includes a Custom category that enables you to create your own formats and display your numbers or dates precisely the way you want. This section shows you the special symbols that you can use to construct these custom numeric and date formats.

Custom Numeric Formats

Every Excel numeric format, whether built-in or customized, has the following syntax:

positive format;negative format;zero format;text format

The four parts, separated by semicolons, determine how various numbers are presented. The first part defines how a positive number is displayed, the second part defines how a negative number is displayed, the third part defines how zero is displayed, and the fourth part defines how text is displayed. If you leave out one or more of these parts, numbers are controlled as shown here:

NUMBER OF PARTS USED	FORMAT SYNTAX
Three	positive format;negative format;zero format
Two	positive and zero format; negative format
One	positive, negative, and zero format

The following table lists the special symbols you can use to define each of these parts:

SYMBOL	DESCRIPTION
#	Holds a place for a digit and displays the digit exactly as typed. Displays nothing if no number is entered.
0	Holds a place for a digit and displays the digit exactly as typed. Displays 0 if no number is entered.
?	Holds a place for a digit and displays the digit exactly as typed. Displays a space if no number is entered.
. (period)	Sets the location of the decimal point.
, (comma)	Sets the location of the thousands separator. Marks only the location of the first thousand.
%	Multiplies the number by 100 (for display only) and adds the percent (%) character.
E+ e+ E- e-	Displays the number in scientific format. E- and e- place a minus sign in the exponent; E+ and e+ place a plus sign in the exponent.
/ (slash)	Sets the location of the fraction separator.
$ ( ) : - + <space>	Displays the character.
*	Repeats whatever character immediately follows the asterisk until the cell is full.
_ (underscore)	Inserts a blank space the width of whatever character follows the underscore.
\ (backslash)	Inserts the character that follows the backslash.
"text"	Inserts the text that appears within the quotation marks.

Custom Date and Time Formats

Custom date and time formats generally are simpler to create than custom numeric formats. There are fewer formatting symbols, and you usually do not need to specify different formats for different conditions. The following table lists the date formatting symbols:

SYMBOL	DESCRIPTION
d	Day number without a leading zero (1 to 31)
dd	Day number with a leading zero (01 to 31)
ddd	Three-letter day abbreviation (Mon, for example)
dddd	Full day name (Monday, for example)
m	Month number without a leading zero (1 to 12)
mm	Month number with a leading zero (01 to 12)
mmm	Three-letter month abbreviation (Aug, for example)
mmmm	Full month name (August, for example)
yy	Two-digit year (00 to 99)
yyyy	Full year (1900 to 2078)
/ -	Symbols used to separate parts of dates

The following table lists the time formatting symbols:

SYMBOL	DESCRIPTION
h	Hour without a leading zero (0 to 24)
hh	Hour with a leading zero (00 to 24)
m	Minute without a leading zero (0 to 59)
mm	Minute with a leading zero (00 to 59)
s	Second without a leading zero (0 to 59)
ss	Second with a leading zero (00 to 59)
AM/PM, am/pm, A/P	Displays the time using a 12-hour clock
: .	Symbols used to separate parts of times

Examples

The following table lists a few examples of custom numeric, date, and time formats:

VALUE	CUSTOM FORMAT	DISPLAYED VALUE
.5	#.##	.5
12500	0,.0	12.5
1234	#,##0;-#,##0;0;"Enter a number"	1,234
-1234	#,##0;-#,##0;0;"Enter a number"	-1,234
text	#,##0;-#,##0;0;"Enter a number"	Enter a number
98.6	#,##0.0°F	98.6°F
8/23/2006	dddd, mmmm d, yyyy	Wednesday, August 23, 2006
8/23/2006	mm.dd.yy	08.23.06
3:10 PM	hhmm "hours"	1510 hours
3:10 PM	hh"h" mm"m"	15h 10m

Understanding Microsoft Query

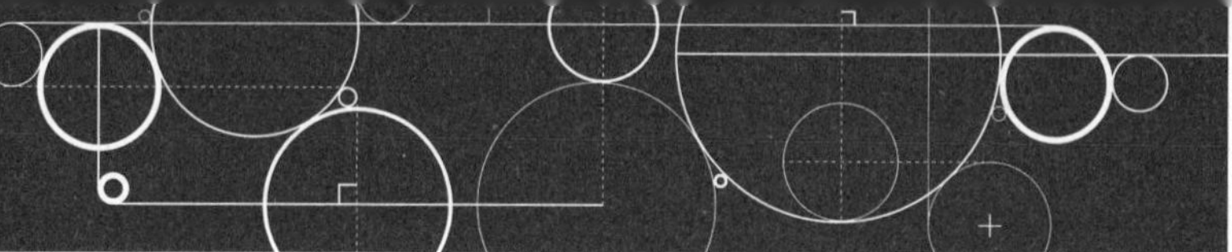

If you want to build a PivotTable using a sorted, filtered, subset of an external data source, you must use Microsoft Query to specify the sorting and filtering options and the subset of the source data that you want to work with.

Databases such as those used in Microsoft Access and SQL Server are often very large and contain a wide variety of data scattered over many different tables. When your data analysis requires a PivotTable, you can never use an entire database as the source for the report. Instead, you can extract a subset of the database: a table or perhaps two or three related tables. You may also require the data to be sorted in a certain way and you may also need to filter the data so that you only work with certain records.

You can accomplish all three operations — extracting a subset, sorting, and filtering — by creating a database query. In Excel, the program that you use to create and run database queries is Microsoft Query. You learn how to use Microsoft Query in this appendix. This section gets you started by introducing you to various query concepts and how they fit into Microsoft Query.

Data Source

All database queries require two things at the very beginning: access to a database and an *Open Database Connectivity*, or *ODBC*, data source for the database installed on your computer. ODBC is a database standard that enables a program to connect to and manipulate a data source. An ODBC data source contains three things: a pointer to the file or server where the database resides; a driver that enables Microsoft Query to connect to, manipulate, and return data from the database; and the login information that you require to access the database.

You learn how to create a new data source in the next task, "Define a Data Source."

Database Query

Database queries knock a large database down to a more manageable size by enabling you to perform three tasks: selecting the tables and fields you want to work with, filtering the records, and sorting the records.

Select Tables and Fields

The first task you perform when you define a query is to select the table or tables that you want to work with. After you have done that, you then select the fields from those tables that you want to use in your PivotTable. Because external databases often contain a large amount of data, you can speed up your queries and reduce the amount of memory Excel uses by returning only those fields that you know you need for your PivotTable.

Filter Records

You may not require all a table's records in your PivotTable report. For example, if a table contains invoice data from several years, you may only want to work with records from a particular year. Similarly, you may be interested in records for a particular product, country, or employee. In each case, you can configure the database query to *filter* the records so that you only get the records you want.

Sort Records

A database query also enables you to sort the data that you are extracting. This does not matter too much with a PivotTable because Excel sorts the field items in ascending alphabetical order by default. However, the sorting option is important if you import the data into your Excel worksheet; as described in Appendix C.

Query Criteria

You can specify the filtering portion of a database query by specifying one or more *criteria*. These are usually logical expressions that, when applied to each record in the query's underlying table, return either a true or false result. Every record that returns a true result is included in the query, and every record that returns a false result is filtered out of the query. For example, if you only want to work with records where the Country field is USA, then you would set up criteria to handle this, and the query would discard all records where the Country field is not equal to USA. The following table lists the operators you can use to build your criteria expressions:

OPERATOR	VALUE IN THE FIELD
Equals	Is equal to a specified value
Does not equal	Is not equal to a specified value
Is greater than	Is greater than a specified value
Is greater than or equal to	Is greater than or equal to a specified value
Is less than	Is less than a specified value
Is less than or equal to	Is less than or equal to a specified value
Is one of	Is included in a group of values
Is not one of	Is not included in a group of values
Is between	Is between (and including) one value and another
Is not between	Is not between one value and another
Begins with	Begins with the specified characters
Does not begin with	Does not begin with the specified characters
Ends with	Ends with the specified characters
Does not end with	Does not end with the specified characters
Contains	Contains the specified characters
Does not contain	Does not contain the specified characters
Like	Matches a specified pattern
Not like	Does not match a specified pattern
Is Null	Is empty
Is Not Null	Is not empty

Microsoft Query

Microsoft Query is a special program that you can use to perform all the database query tasks mentioned in this section. You can use Microsoft Query to create data sources, add tables to the query, specify fields, filter records using criteria, and sort records. You can also save your queries as query files so that you can reuse them later. If you start Microsoft Query from within Excel, you can return the query records to Excel and use them in a PivotTable.

Define a Data Source

Before you can do any work in Microsoft Query, you must select the data source that you want to use. If you have a particular database that you want to query, you can define a new data source that points to the appropriate file or server.

As you learned in the previous section, "Understanding Microsoft Query," an ODBC data source contains: a pointer to the file or server where the database resides; a software driver that enables Microsoft Query to connect to, query, and return data from the database; and the login information that you require to access the database.

Most data sources point to database files. For example, the relational database management programs Access, Visual FoxPro, Paradox, and dBase all use file-based databases.

You can also create data sources based on text files and Excel workbooks. However, some data sources point to server-based databases. For example, SQL Server and Oracle run their databases on special servers.

As part of the data source definition, you need to include the software driver that Microsoft Query uses to communicate with the database. An Access database requires an Access driver; a SQL Server database requires a SQL Server driver, and so on.

Finally, you must include in the data source any information that you require to access the database. Most file-based databases do not require a login, but some are protected with a password. For server-based data, you are almost certainly required to provide a username and password.

Define a Data Source

Note: This appendix uses the Northwind.mdb database, which comes with Microsoft Access, or you can create your own sample database.

1. Click Data➔Import External Data➔New Database Query.

   The Choose Data Source dialog box appears.

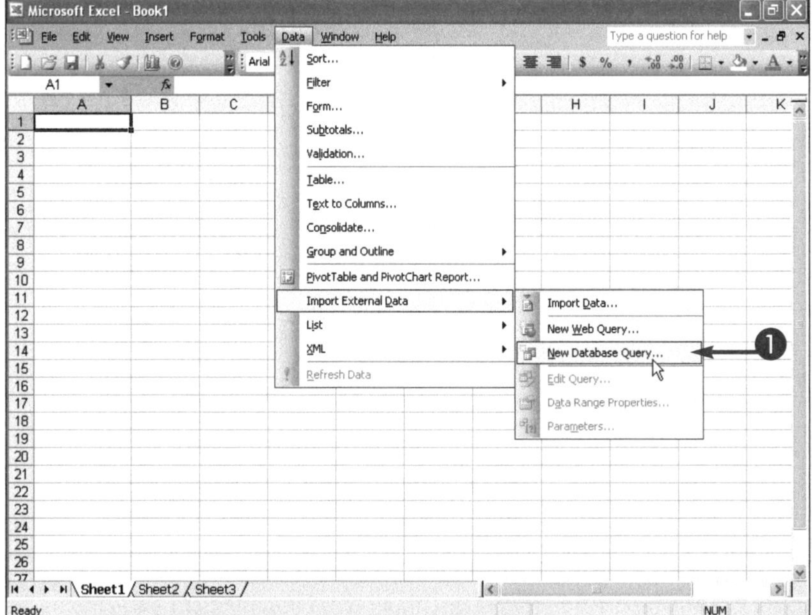

2. Click New Data Source.
3. Deselect Use the Query Wizard to create/edit queries.
4. Click OK.

   The Create New Data Source dialog box appears.

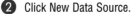

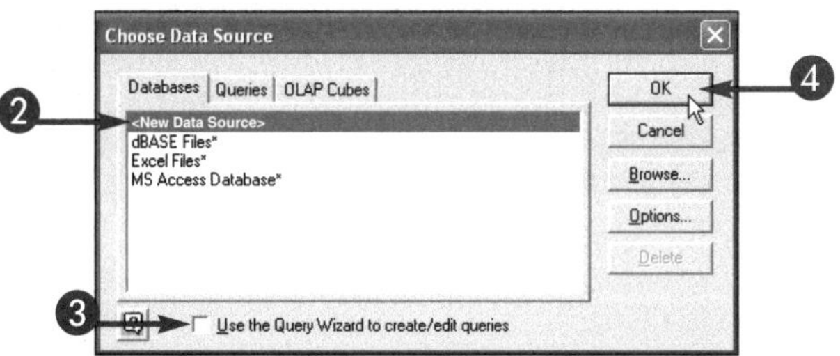

5. Type a name for your data source.
6. Click ▾ and select the database driver that your data source requires.
7. Click Connect.

   The dialog box for the database driver appears.

Note: The steps that follow show you how to set up a data source for a Microsoft Access database.

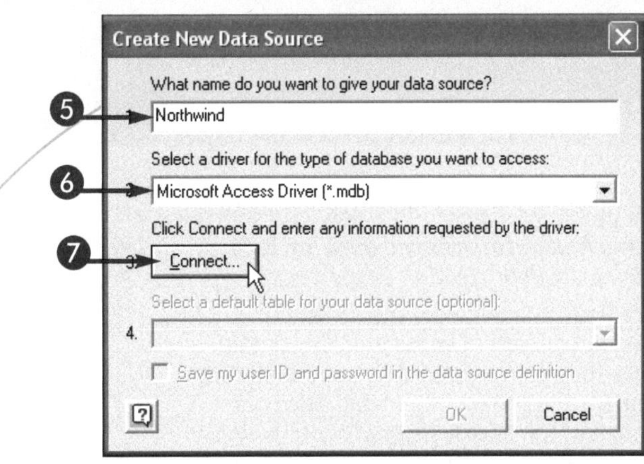

8. Click Select.

   The Select Database dialog box appears.

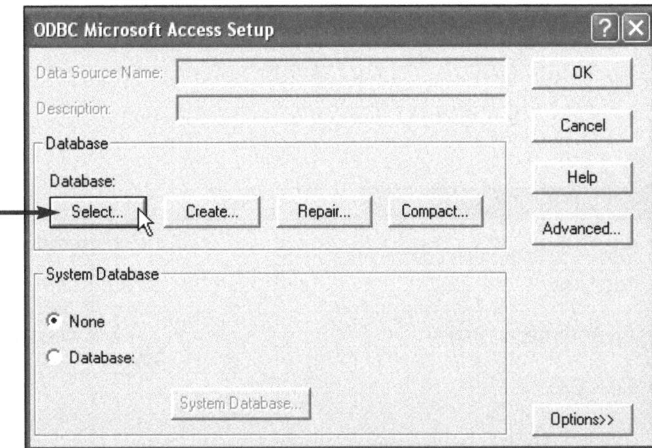

Apply It

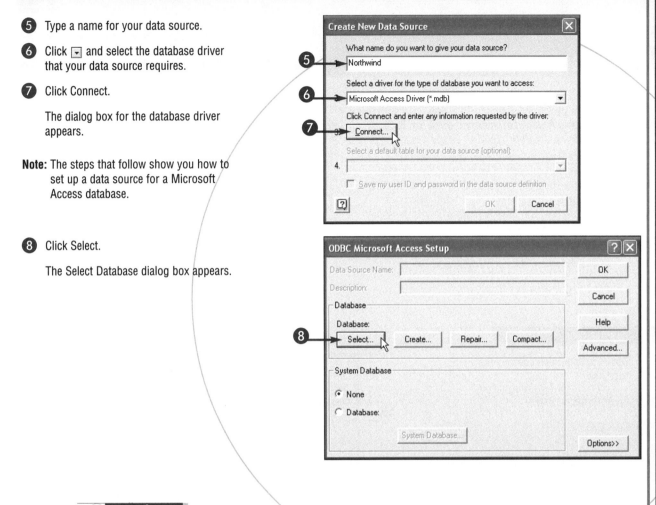

Many medium- and large-sized businesses store their data on Microsoft's SQL Server database system. This is a robust and powerful server-based system that can handle the largest databases and hundreds or thousands of users. If you need to define a data source for a SQL Server installation on your network or some other remote location, first follow Steps 1 to 4 to get to the Create New Data Source dialog box.

Type a name for the data source and then, in the list of database drivers, click SQL Server. Click Connect to display the SQL Server Login dialog box. Your SQL Server database administrator should have given you the information you require to complete this dialog box.

Type the name or remote address of the SQL Server in the Server text box. If the SQL Server administrator has associated your Windows login data with the SQL Server login, then you do not need to specify login data, so click OK. Otherwise, deselect Use Trusted Connection (☑ changes to ☐), type your SQL Server login ID and password, and then click OK.

Perform Steps 13 to 15 later in this task to complete the SQL Server data source.

continued →

Define a Data Source (continued)

Your system probably comes with a few data sources already defined, and you can use these predefined data sources instead of creating new ones.

In the Choose Data Source dialog box, the list in the Databases tab often shows one or more predefined data sources. These data sources are created by programs that you install on your system. When you install Microsoft Office and, in particular, the Microsoft Query component, the installation program creates three default data sources: dBase Files, Excel Files, and MS Access Database. These are incomplete data sources in the sense that they do not point to a specific file. Instead, when you click one of these data sources and then click OK, Microsoft Query prompts you for the name and location of the file. For example, if you use the dBase Files data source, Microsoft Query prompts you to specify a dBase (.dbf) database file. These data sources are useful if you often switch the files that you are using. However, if you want a data source that always points to a specific file, use the steps outlined in this task.

Define a Data Source *(continued)*

9 Open the folder that contains the database.

10 Click the database file.

11 Click OK.

You are returned to the database driver's dialog box.

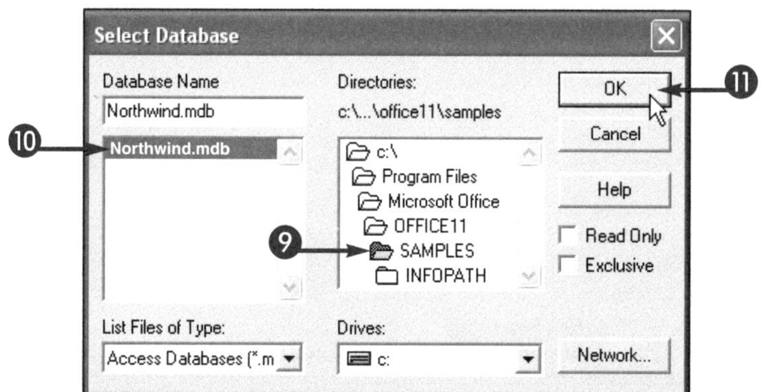

- If you must provide a login name and password to access the database, click Advanced to display the Set Advanced Options dialog box. Type the login name and password and then click OK.

12 Click OK.

You are returned to the Create New Data Source dialog box.

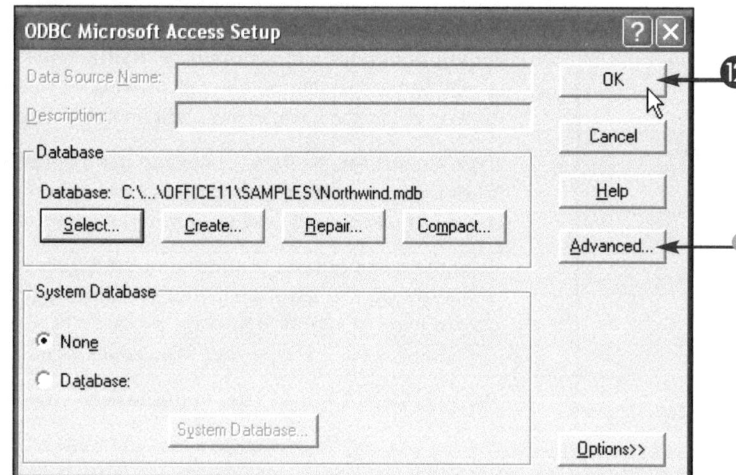

- If you specified a login name and password as part of the data source, select this check box to save the login data.

13 Click OK.

You are returned to the Choose Data Source dialog box.

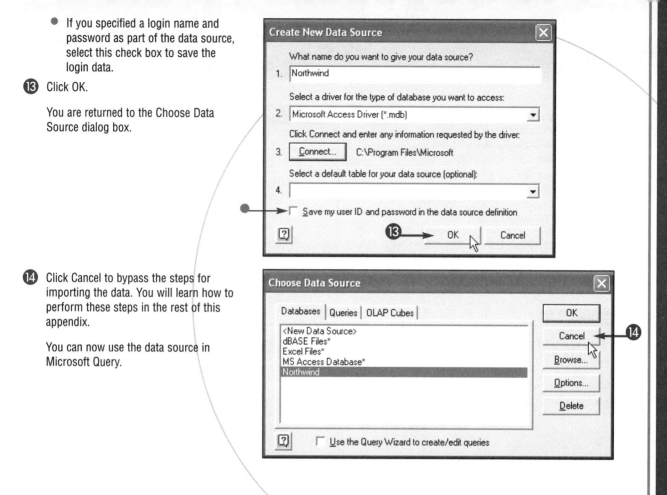

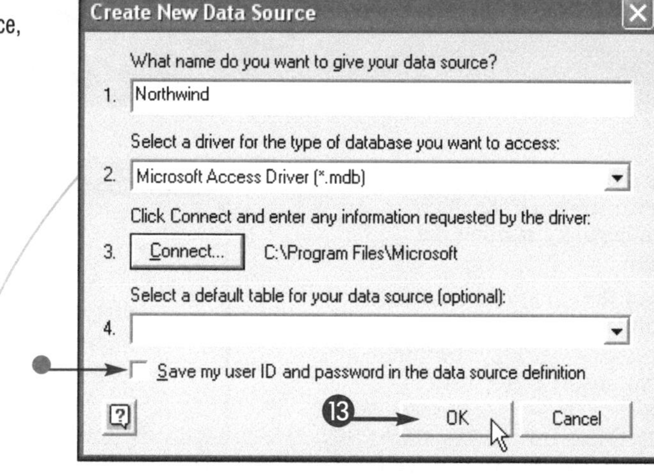

14 Click Cancel to bypass the steps for importing the data. You will learn how to perform these steps in the rest of this appendix.

You can now use the data source in Microsoft Query.

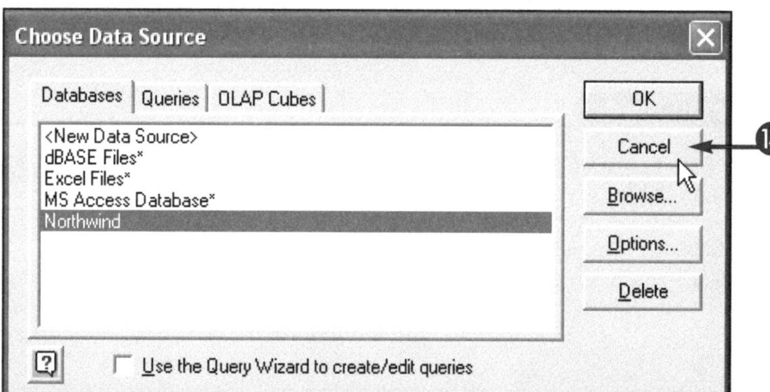

Apply It

If you have a data source that you no longer use, you should delete it to ensure that only usable data sources appear in the Choose Data Source dialog box. Click Data→Import External Data→New Database Query to display the Choose Data Source dialog box. Click the data source and then click Delete. When Microsoft Query asks you to confirm the deletion, click Yes.

Unfortunately, the Choose Data Source dialog box does not enable you to reconfigure or rename a data source. To reconfigure a data source, click Start→Run to open the Run dialog box, type **odbcad32**, and then click OK. In the ODBC Data Source Administrator dialog box that appears, click the File DSN tab. Click the data source you want to work with and then click Configure to open the Setup dialog box for the database driver.

To rename a data source, use My Computer to open the following folder:

```
C:\Program Files\Common Files\ODBC\Data Sources
```

Click the data source file, press F2, type the new name, and then press Enter.

Start Microsoft Query

To create a query that defines the fields and records that appear in your PivotTable report, you must begin by starting the Microsoft Query program.

Microsoft Query is part of the Office Tools collection that ships with Microsoft Office. Although you can start the program on its own — click Start→Run, type **c:\program files\microsoft office\office11\msqry32.exe**, and then click OK — you can almost always start it from within Excel. That way, the data you configure with the query is automatically returned to Excel so that you can build your PivotTable report.

Extra

If you cannot follow the steps in this task, you may not have Microsoft Query installed on your computer. Select Start→Control Panel and double-click Add or Remove Programs. In the Add or Remove Programs window, click Microsoft Office and then click Change. Click Add or Remove Features (○ changes to ◉) and then click Next. Click "Choose advanced customization of applications" (☐ changes to ☑) and then click Next. Click the plus sign (⊞) to open the Office Tools branch, click Microsoft Query, and then click Run from My Computer. Click Update to install the program.

Start Microsoft Query

1. Click Data→Import External Data→New Database Query.

   The Choose Data Source dialog box appears.

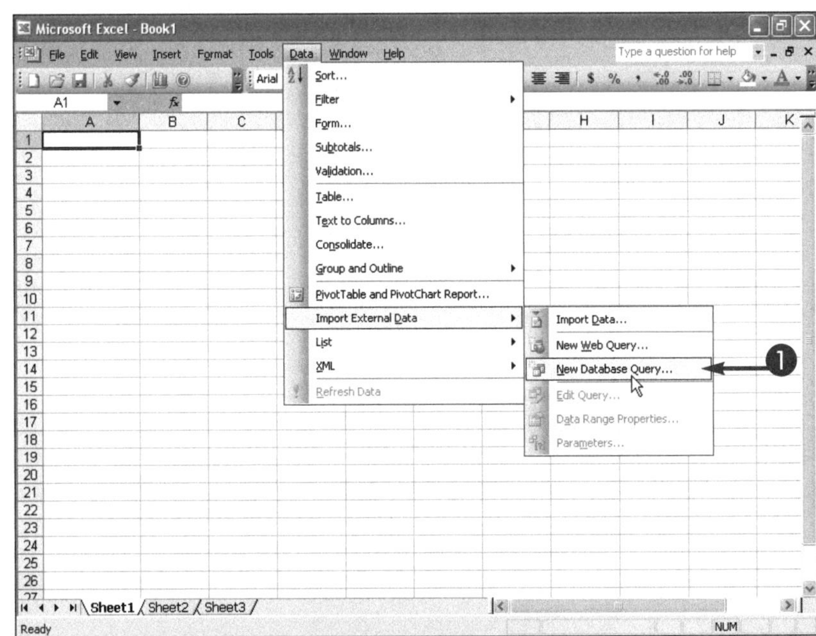

2. Click the data source you want to work with.
3. Deselect Use the Query Wizard to create/edit queries.
4. Click OK.

   The Microsoft Query window and the Add Tables dialog box appear.

Note: To learn how to use the Add Tables dialog box, see the task "Add a Table to the Query," later in this appendix.

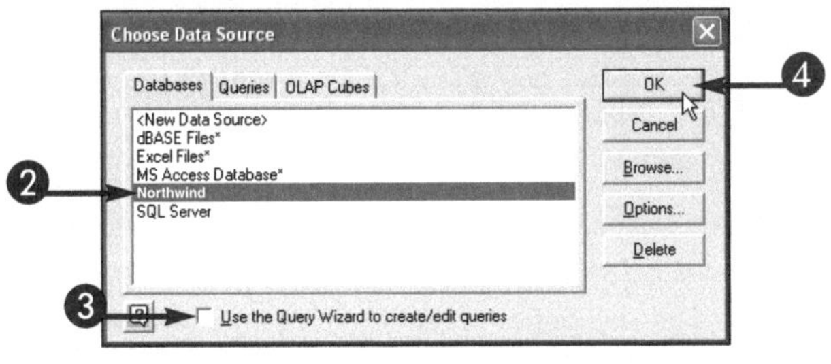

Tour the Microsoft Query Window

You can get the most out of Microsoft Query if you understand the layout of the screen and what each part of the Microsoft Query window represents. Although you have not yet created a query using the Microsoft Query program, it is worthwhile to pause now and take a look at the various elements that make up the Microsoft Query window. Do not worry if what you currently see on your screen does not look like the window shown in this section. By the time you finish this appendix, you will see and work with all the elements shown here.

A QUERY WINDOW

This window is where you create and edit, as well as preview the results. The query window is divided into three panes: the table pane, the criteria pane, and the results pane.

B TOOLBAR

This toolbar contains buttons that give you one-click access to many of Microsoft Query's most useful features.

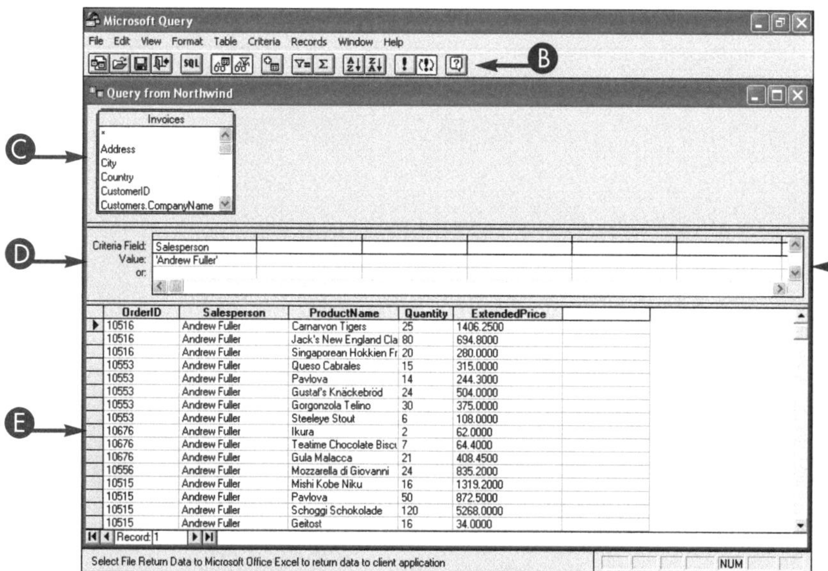

C TABLE PANE

This pane displays one list for each table that you add to the query; see the task "Add a Table to the Query," later in this appendix. Each list shows the fields that are part of the table. Click View→Tables to toggle this pane on and off.

D CRITERIA PANE

This pane is where you define the criteria that filter the records you want to return to Excel. See the task "Filter the Records with Query Criteria," later in this appendix. Click View→Criteria to toggle this pane on and off.

E QUERY RESULTS

This pane gives you a preview of the fields and records that your query will return to Excel. As you add fields to the query, change the query criteria, and sort the query (see the task "Sort the Query Records," later in this appendix), Microsoft Query updates the results pane, also called the data grid, automatically to show you what effect your changes will have.

Add a Table to the Query

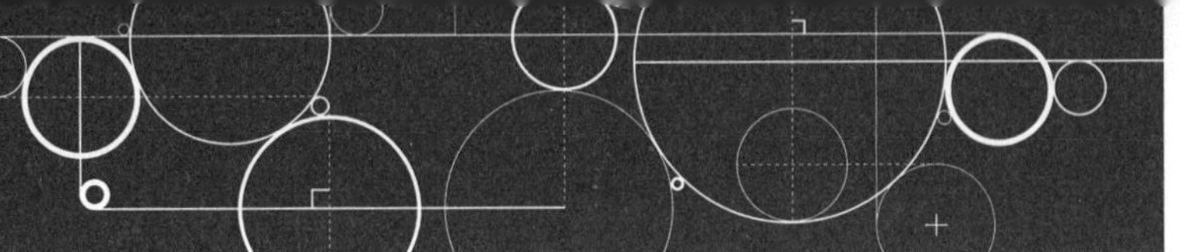

With your data source running and Microsoft Query started, the next step you must take is to add a table to the query.

In a database, a *table* is a two-dimensional arrangement of rows and columns that contains data. The columns are *fields* that represent distinct categories of data, and the rows are *records* that represent individual sets of field data. In some database management systems, the database files themselves are tables. However, in most systems, each database contains a number of tables. Therefore, your first Microsoft Query task in most cases is to select which table you want to work with.

Note, too, that many database systems also enable you to filter and sort data using their own versions of the querying process. Creating a query in Microsoft Access, for example, is similar to creating one in Microsoft Query. By default, when Microsoft Query shows you a list of the tables in the database, it also includes any queries — or *views*, as Microsoft Query calls them — that are defined in the database, so you can add these objects to your query, if required.

However, if the query is based on multiple, related tables, then for best results you may also need to add all the related tables to your query. For example, if you are using the Northwind sample database and you add the Invoices view to your query, it includes the field Customers.CompanyName. This tells you that you should also add the Customers table to your query.

Add a Table to the Query

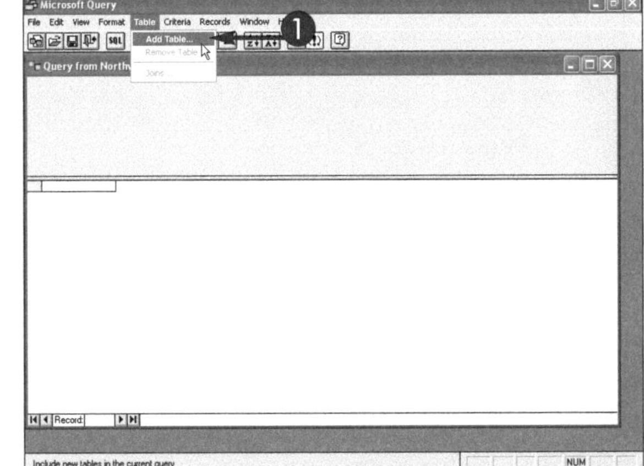

1 Click Table→Add Tables.

You can also click the Add Tables toolbar button ( ).

The Add Tables dialog box appears.

Note: When you start Microsoft Query from Excel, the Add Tables dialog box appears automatically, so you can skip Step 1.

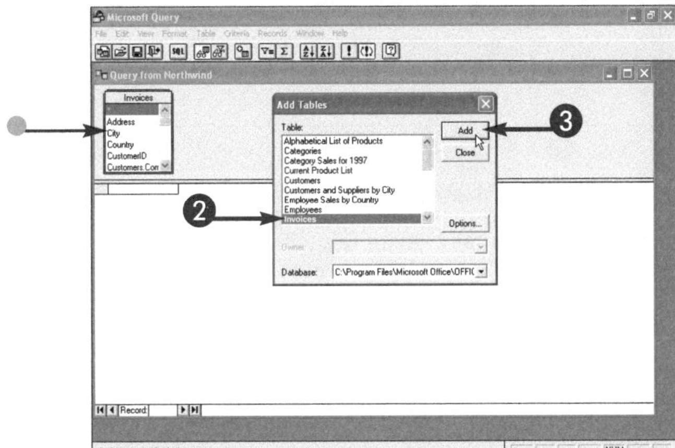

2 Click the table you want to add.

3 Click Add.

- Microsoft Query adds the table to the table pane.

4 Repeat Steps 2 and 3 if you want to add multiple, related tables to the query.

- If the tables are related, Microsoft Query displays a join line that connects the common fields.

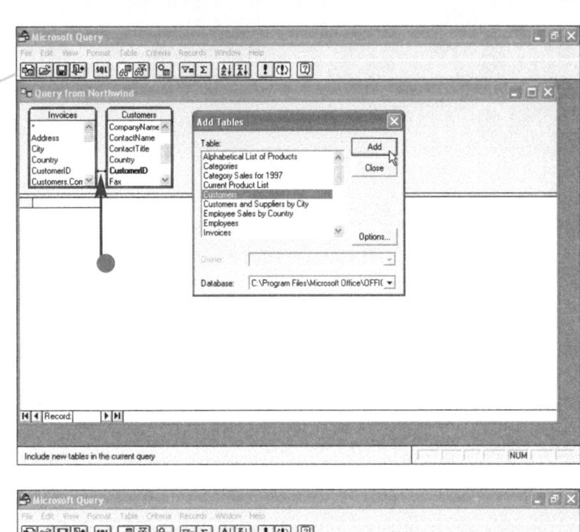

5 Click Close.

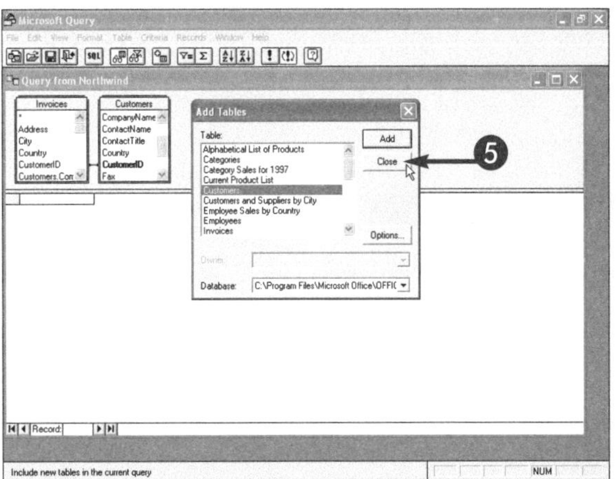

Extra

If two tables are related, they are joined to each other using a common field. These joins are almost always defined in the original database, so you should not have to worry about creating or editing the joins. However, if you come across two tables that you know are related, but no join line appears when you add them to your query, you can create the join yourself.

After you add the two tables to your query, click Table➔Joins to display the Joins dialog box. In the Left list, click the common field from one of your tables. In the Right list, click the common field from the other table. In the Operator list, click = (equals). Click Add to add the join to the query, and then click Close.

To remove a table from the query, first click the table in the table pane. Then click Table➔Remove Table. Alternatively, click the table and then press Delete. Microsoft Query deletes the table list. If you added fields from the table to the criteria pane or the results pane, Microsoft Query removes those fields as well.

Add Fields to the Query

To display records in the query's results pane, you must first add one or more fields to the query.

After you add one or more tables to the query, your next step is to filter the resulting records so that you return to Excel only the data you need for your PivotTable. Filtering the records involves two tasks: specifying the fields you want to work with and specifying the criteria you want to apply to records. This task shows you how to add fields — or *columns*, as Microsoft Query calls them — to the query. See the next task, "Filter the Records with Query Criteria," to learn how to add criteria to the query.

In the query window's table pane, you see a list for each table in the query. Each list contains an item for each field in the table. At the top of each list, you also see an asterisk (*) item. The asterisk item represents *all* the fields in the table. So if you know that you want to include in your query every field from a particular table, you can do this easily by adding the asterisk "field" to the query.

As you add fields to the query, Microsoft Query automatically shows the corresponding records in the results pane. If you would rather control the display of the results, click the Auto Query toolbar button ([icon]) to turn off this feature. Then when you are ready to view the results, click the Query Now toolbar button ([!]).

Add Fields to the Query

1. Click Records→Add Column.

   The Add Column dialog box appears.

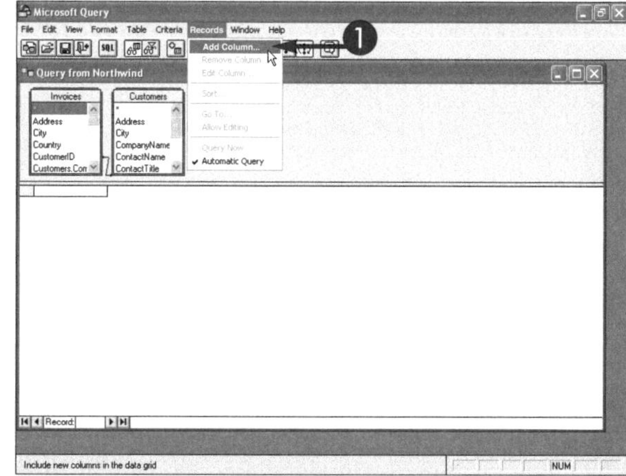

2. In the Field list, click the field you want to add.

3. If you want to use a different field name, type the new name here.

4. Click Add.

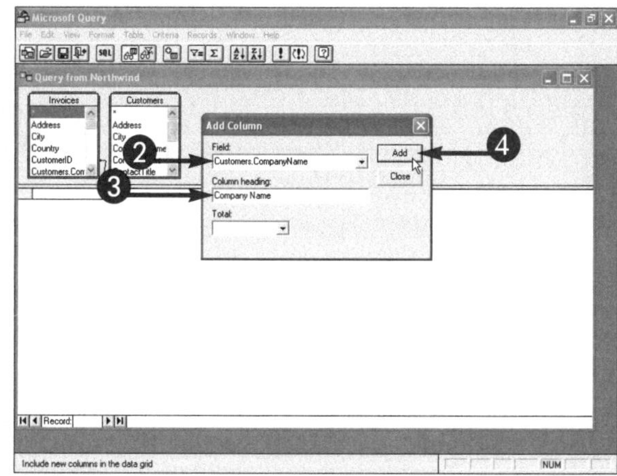

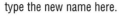

- Microsoft Query adds the field to the results pane.

5. Repeat Steps 2 to 4 until you have added all the fields that you want to appear in the query.

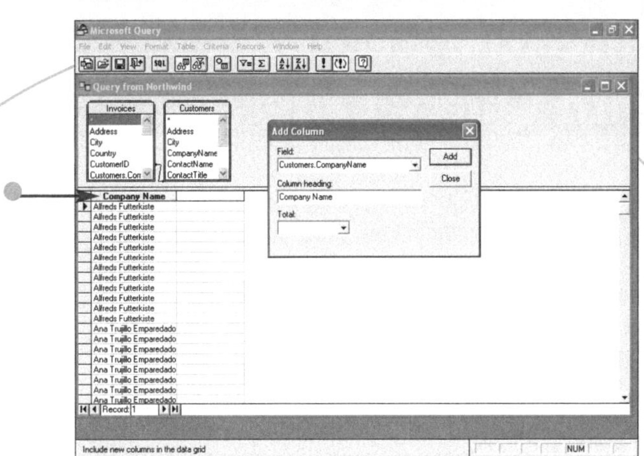

6. Click Close.

You can also either double-click a field name in a table list, or click and drag a field name in a table list and drop it inside the results pane.

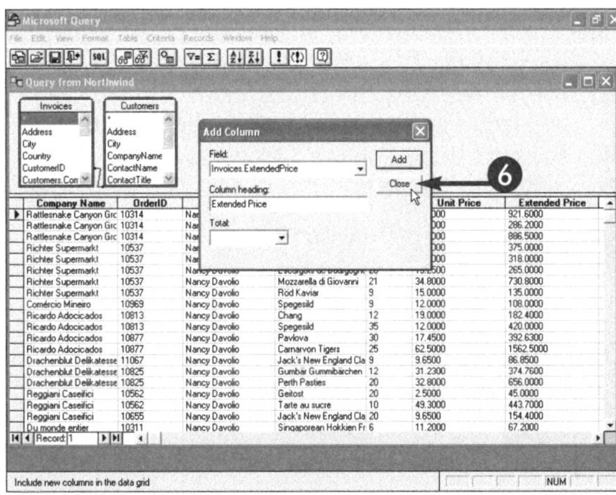

Extra

The order of the fields in the results pane is not fixed. To change where a field appears in the data grid, first click the field heading to select the entire field. Then click and drag the field heading to the left or right and drop the field into the new position.

If you want to make changes to a field — that is, you want to change to a different field or edit the name displayed in the field header — click the field heading or click any cell in the field, and then click Records➔Edit Column. You can also double-click the field heading. You can use the Edit Column dialog box to change the field or edit the field heading, and then click OK.

If you no longer need a field in the query, you should delete it from the data grid. Click the field heading or click any cell in the field; note that Microsoft Query does not ask for confirmation when you delete a field, so be sure you click the correct field. Then either click Records➔Remove Column, or press Delete.

Filter the Records with Query Criteria

To display specific records that you want to return to Excel for your PivotTable, you must use criteria to filter the records.

After you add your fields to the data grid, your next step is to specify which records you want to include in the results. You can do this by specifying the conditions that each record must meet to be included in the results. If you are working with invoice data, for example, you may only want to see those orders where the customer name begins with R, the order quantity is greater than 10, the unit price is between $10 and $40, and so on.

In each case, you specify a *criteria*, which is an expression — an operator and one or more values — applied to a specific field. Only those records for which the expression returns a true answer are included in the query results.

You can enter just a single criteria — the plural word is used even if you are talking about just one expression — or you can enter two or more. If you use multiple criteria, you must decide if you want Microsoft Query to include in the results those records that match *all* the criteria, or those records that match *any one* of the criteria.

You learned the various criteria operators in the section "Understanding Microsoft Query," earlier in this appendix. Operators such as "equals" and "is one of" are English language equivalents of the actual operators that Microsoft Query uses. These actual operators include the comparison operators (=, <>, >, >=, <, and <=) as well as keywords such as Between x And y, In, and Like. However, if you use the Add Criteria dialog box, as shown in this task, you do not need to use the actual operators directly.

Filter the Records with Query Criteria

1. Click Criteria➔Add Criteria.

   The Add Criteria dialog box appears.

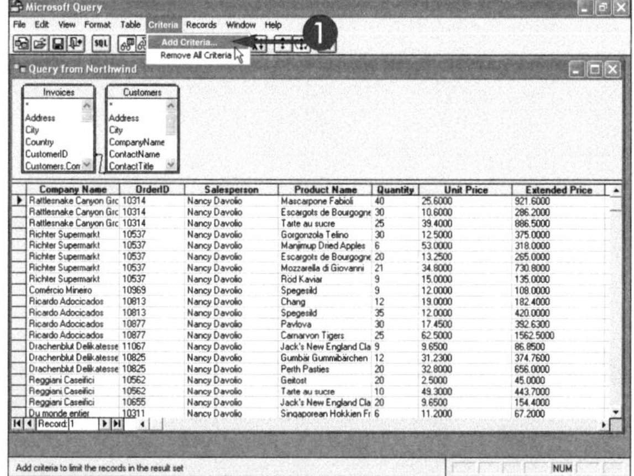

2. In the Field list, click ▾ and then click the field to which you want the criteria applied.
3. In the Operator list, click ▾ and then click the operator you want to use.
4. Type the value or values for the criteria.
   - To use a value from the selected field, click Values, click the value you want to use, and then click OK.
5. Click Add.

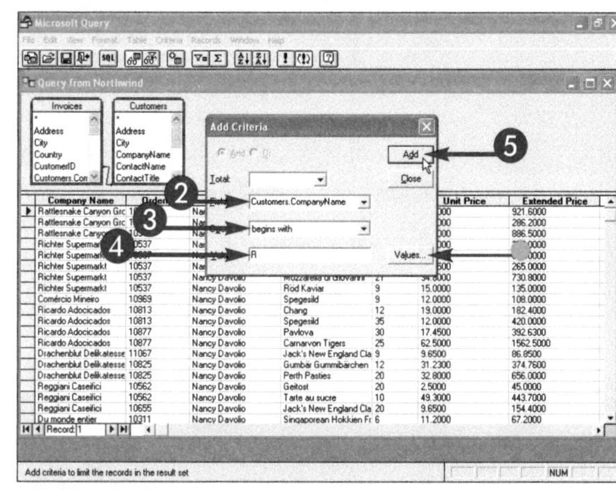

- Microsoft Query displays the criteria pane and adds the criteria.
- Select Or to add another criteria, and Microsoft Query matches records that meet one criteria or the other.

6 If you select And, Microsoft Query matches records that meet all the criteria.

7 Repeat Steps 2 to 6 until you have added all the criteria that you want to appear in the query.

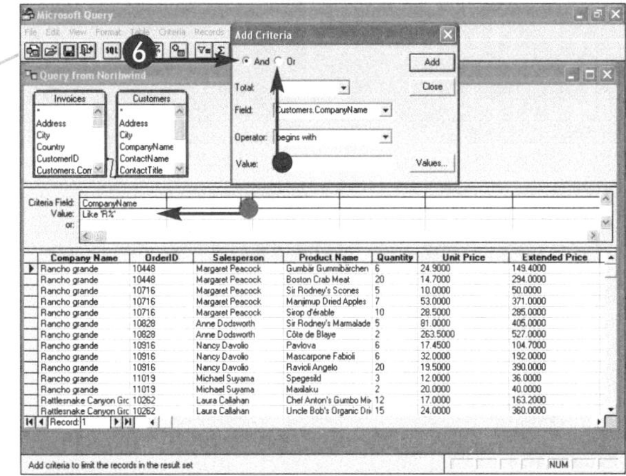

8 Click Close.

Microsoft Query filters the records to show just those that match your criteria.

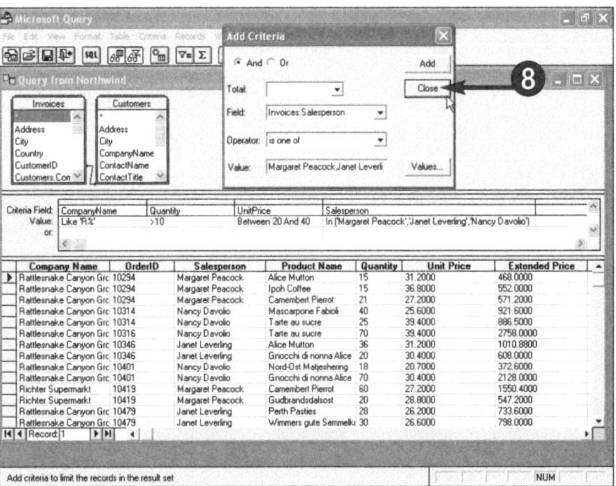

Extra

If you want to change the field to which a criteria expression applies, there are two methods you can use within the criteria pane:

- Double-click the field name to display the Edit Criteria dialog box. You can use the Field list to click a different field, and then click OK.
- Click the field name. Microsoft Query adds a drop-down arrow to the right of the field cell. Click the arrow to display the Field list, and then click the field you want to use.

If you want to change the criteria expression, again there are two methods you can use with the criteria pane:

- Double-click the expression to display the Edit Criteria dialog box. You can use the Operator list and Value text box to specify a different expression, and then click OK.
- Edit the expression directly in the criteria pane.

If you no longer need a criteria in the query, you should delete it from the criteria grid. Click the bar just above the field name to select the entire criteria; note that Microsoft Query does not ask for confirmation when you delete a criteria, so be sure you click the correct one. Then press Delete. If you want to remove all the criteria and start over, click Criteria→Remove All Criteria.

Sort the Query Records

You can sort the query results on one or more fields to get a good look at your data.

If you are using the query results within a PivotTable, it does not matter if the results are sorted, because Excel uses a default ascending alphabetical sort when it displays the unique values from a field in the PivotTable report. However, there are two reasons why you might want to sort the records that appear in Microsoft Query's results pane:

- You want to be sure that you are returning the correct records, and the records are often easier to examine if they are sorted.
- You are importing the query results to Excel instead of applying them directly to a PivotTable; see Appendix C. In this case, the sort order you apply in Microsoft Query is the order that the records will appear in Excel.

You can sort the records either in ascending order (0 to 9, A to Z) or descending order (Z to A, 9 to 0). You can also sort the records based on more than one field. In this case, Microsoft Query sorts the records using the first field, and then sorts within those results on the second field. For example, in the invoice data, suppose you are sorting first on the OrderID field and then on the Quantity field. Microsoft Query first orders the records by OrderID. Then, within each OrderID value, Microsoft Query sorts the Quantity field values.

Sort the Query Records

1. Click Records➔Sort.

   The Sort dialog box appears.

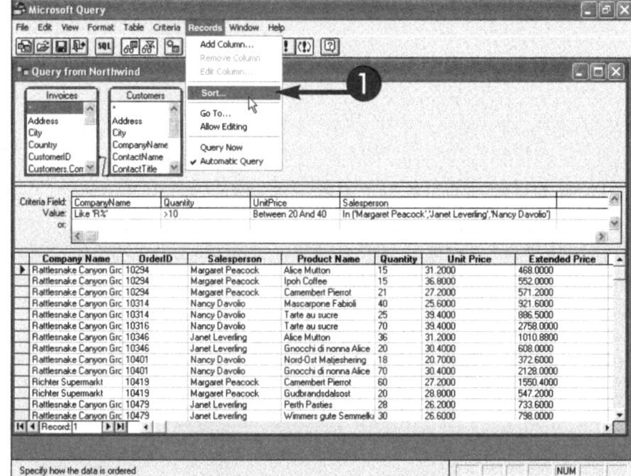

2. In the Column list, click the field you want to sort.
3. Select a sort order, Ascending or Descending.
4. Click Add.

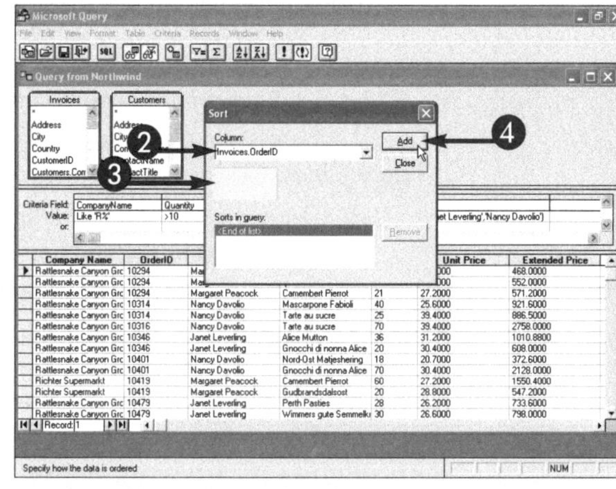

- Microsoft Query sorts the records in the results pane.
- Microsoft Query adds the sort to the Sorts in query list.

5 Repeat Steps 2 to 4 until you have added all the sorts that you want to use in the query.

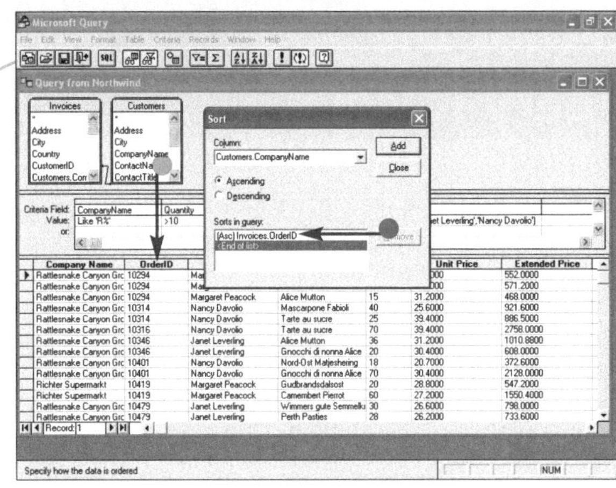

6 Click Close.

Microsoft Query sorts the records.

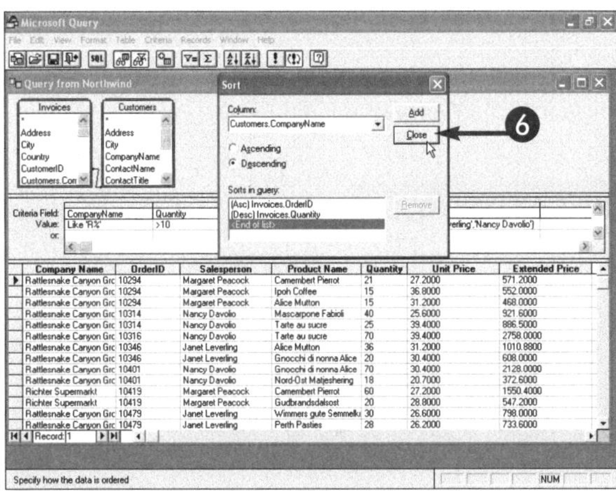

Extra

If you only want to sort the query results on a single field, you can perform the sort much faster by using the toolbar. First, in the results pane, click any cell in the field you want to sort. Then click one of the following buttons:

BUTTON	DESCRIPTION
A↓Z	Sorts the field in ascending order
Z↓A	Sorts the field in descending order

If you want to sort on multiple fields, you can still use the toolbar, but it takes a bit more work. First, organize the fields in the results pane so that all the fields you want to use in the sort are side by side, in the order you want to apply the sort. Click and drag the mouse pointer from the heading of the first sort field to the heading of the last sort field. You should now have all the sort fields selected. Finally, click either sort button, A↓Z or Z↓A.

If you have applied a sort that you no longer want to use, you should remove it from the query. Click Records→Sort to display the Sort dialog box. In the "Sort in query" list, click the sort that you want to delete, and then click Remove.

Return the Query Results

After you finish adding fields to the query, filtering the data using criteria, and sorting the data, you are ready to return the results to Excel for use in your PivotTable.

Microsoft Query is just a helper application, so the data that resides in the query results does not really "exist" anywhere. To manipulate or analyze that data, you must store it in a different application. In your case, you are interested in using the query results as the source data for a PivotTable report. Therefore, you need to return the query results to Excel, and then start a new PivotTable based on those results.

If you think you will reuse the query at a later date, you should save the query before returning the results. See the tip on the next page to learn how to save and open Microsoft Query files.

Return the Query Results

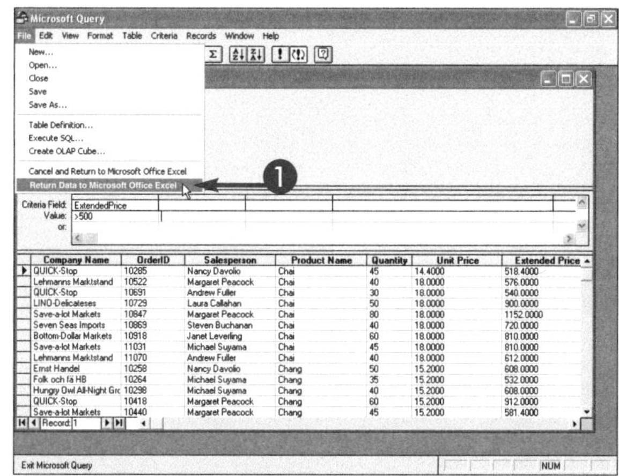

1. Click File→Return Data to Microsoft Office Excel.

   You can also click the Return Data toolbar button ( ).

   Microsoft Query closes, and Microsoft Excel displays the Import Data dialog box.

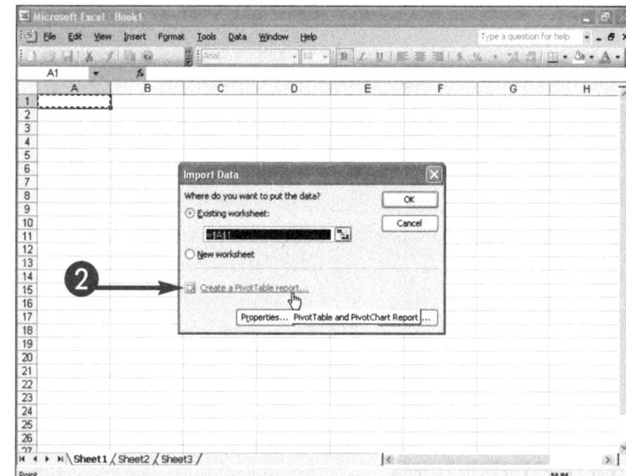

2. Click Create a PivotTable report.

   The PivotTable and PivotChart Wizard appears.

3. Click Finish.

Excel builds an empty PivotTable report based on the data returned from Microsoft Query.

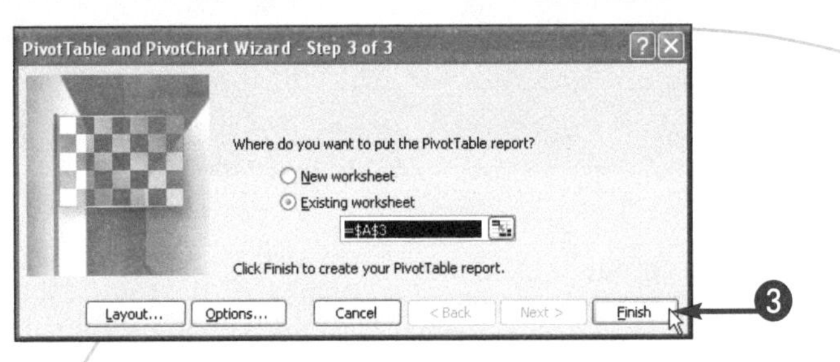

4. Drag fields to the PivotTable drop areas to complete the report.

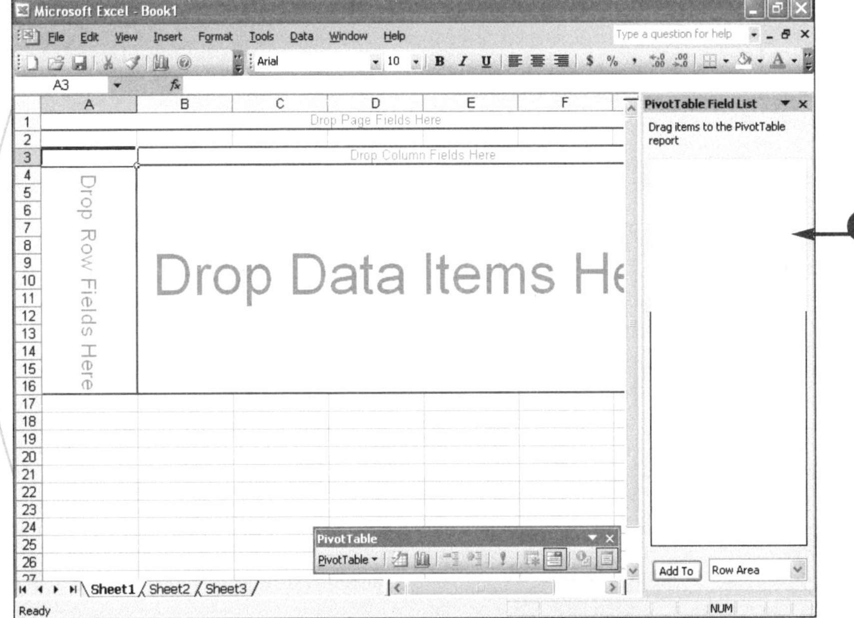

Extra

If you want to make changes to your query, you need to edit the results in Microsoft Query. Click any cell in the PivotTable report that you built from the returned data. Then click PivotTable➔PivotTable Wizard to launch the PivotTable and PivotChart Wizard. Click Back to display the second Wizard dialog box, and then click Get Data. This starts Microsoft Query and loads the query results. Make your changes and then return the data to Excel.

If your query includes a complex combination of tables, fields, criteria, and sorting, it can be dismaying to realize that you have to start from scratch if you want to use a similar query for a different PivotTable report. To avoid this extra work, you should save your queries as you work on them, which enables you to reopen the queries any time you need them.

To save a query using Microsoft Query, click File➔Save to display the Save As dialog box. Click the folder in which you want to store the query file, type a filename, and then click Save. To use the query file: start Microsoft Query, click File➔Open to display the Open Query dialog box, click the query file, and then click Open.

Understanding External Data

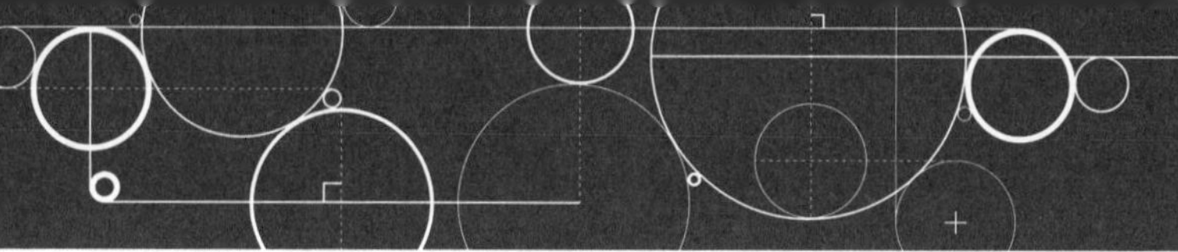

External data is data that resides outside of Excel in a file, database, server, or Web site. You can import external data into Excel either directly into a PivotTable or into a worksheet for additional types of data analysis.

A vast amount of data exists in the world, and most of it resides in some kind of nonworkbook format. Some data exists in simple text files, perhaps as comma-separated lists of items. Other data resides in tables, either in Word documents or, more likely, in Access databases. There is also an increasing amount of data that resides in Web pages and in XML files.

By definition, all this data is not directly available to you via Excel. However, Excel offers a number of tools that enable you to import external data into the program. Depending on your needs and on the type of data, you can either import the data directly into a PivotTable report, or you can store the data on a worksheet and then build your PivotTable from the resulting worksheet range. In most cases, Excel also enables you to refresh the data so that you are always working with the most up-to-date version of the data.

External Data Types

Excel can access a wide variety of external data types. However, in this appendix you only learn about six of them: data source files, Access tables, Word tables, text files, Web pages, and XML files.

Data Source File

In Appendix B, you learned about ODBC data sources, which give you access to data residing in databases such as Access or dBase or on servers such as SQL Server and Oracle; see the Appendix B section "Understanding Microsoft Query." However, there are many other data source types, including data connection files — which connect to specific objects in a data source, such as an Access table — Web queries, OLAP cubes, query files — saved via Microsoft Query; see Appendix B — Web-based data retrieval services, and XML files. See also the next task, "Import Data from a Data Source."

Access Table

Microsoft Access is the Office suite's relational database management system, so it is often used to store and manage the bulk of the data used by a person, team, department, or company. You can connect to Access tables either via Microsoft Query or by importing table data directly into Excel. See the task "Import Data from an Access Table," later in this appendix.

Word Table

Simple nuggets of nonrelational data are often stored in a table embedded in a Word document. You can only perform so much analysis on that data within Word, so it is often useful to import the data from the Word table into an Excel worksheet. See the task "Import Data from a Word Table," later in this appendix.

Text File

Text files often contain useful data. If that data is formatted properly — for example, each line has the same number of items, all separated by spaces, commas, or tabs — then it is possible to import that data into Excel for further analysis. See the task "Import Data from a Text File," later in this appendix.

Web Page

People and companies are storing useful data on Web pages that reside either on the Internet or the company's intranet. This data is often a combination of text and tables, but you cannot analyze Web-based data in any meaningful way in your Web browser. Fortunately, Excel enables you to create a Web query that lets you import text and/or tables from a Web page. See the task "Import Data from a Web Page," later in this appendix.

XML

XML — eXtensible Markup Language — is redefining how data is stored. This is reflected in the large number of tools that Excel now has for dealing with XML data, particularly tools for importing XML data into Excel. See the task "Import Data from an XML File," later in this appendix.

Access to External Data

To use external data, you must have access to it. This usually means knowing at least one of the following: the location of the data or the login information required to authorize your use of the data.

Location

By definition, external data resides somewhere other than in an Excel worksheet on your system. Therefore, to access external data, you must at least know where it is located. Here are some of the possibilities:

- **On your computer** — The data may reside in a file in your hard disk, on a CD or DVD disc, or on a memory card or other removable storage medium.
- **On your network** — The data may reside in a folder on a computer that is part of your local or wide area network. If that folder has been shared with the network, and if you have the appropriate permissions to view files in that folder, then you can access the data within the files.
- **On a server** — Some data is part of a large, server-based database management system, such as SQL Server or Oracle. In this case, you need to know the name or network address of the server.
- **On a Web page** — If the data resides on a Web page, either as text or as a table, you need to know the address of the Web page.
- **On a Web server** — Some data resides on special Web servers that run data retrieval services such as Windows SharePoint Services. In this case, you need to know the address of the server and the location of the data on that server.

Login

Knowing where the data is located is probably all that is required if you are dealing with a local file or database or, usually, a Web page. However, after you start accessing data remotely — on a network, database server, or Web server — authorization will usually also be required to secure that access. See the administrator of the resource to obtain a username or login ID as well as a password.

Import Data

After you have access to the data, your next step is to import it into Excel for analysis and manipulation. You have two choices:

Import to PivotTable

If you are building a PivotTable using the external data as the source, then in most cases Excel enables you to import the data directly into a PivotTable. The advantage here is that Excel does not have to store two copies of the data: one on a worksheet and another in the pivot cache. The disadvantage is that you can only analyze the data using the PivotTable report. Other types of data analysis that require direct access to worksheet data are not possible.

Import to Worksheet

In all cases, you can also import the data directly into an Excel worksheet. Depending on the amount of data, this can make your worksheet quite large. However, having direct access to the data gives you maximum flexibility when it comes to analyzing the data. Not only can you create a PivotTable from the worksheet data, but you can also use Excel with other data analysis tools: lists, database functions, scenarios, and what-if analysis.

Import Data from a Data Source

You can quickly import data into just about any format by importing the data from a defined data source file.

You learned how to create data source files in several places in this book. For OLAP queries, see the Chapter 11 task, "Create an OLAP Cube Data Source;" for OLAP cube files, see the Chapter 11 task, "Create an Offline OLAP Cube;" for ODBC data sources, see the Appendix B task, "Define a Data Source;" for Microsoft Query files, see Appendix B, the tip in the task "Return the Query Results." You can also create data connection files that point to specific objects in a database, such as an Access table. Excel also considers file types such as Access databases and projects, dBase files, Web pages, text files, and Lotus 1-2-3 spreadsheets to be data sources.

In this task, you learn how to import data from a *data connection file*, which uses the .odc extension. This is a data source that connects you to a wide variety of data, including ODBC, SQL Server, SQL Server OLAP Services, Oracle, and Web-based data retrieval services. See the tip on the following page to learn how to create a data connection file. Note, however, that not all data connection file types support direct import into a PivotTable. For example, if you use a data retrieval service such as MSN MoneyCentral, you cannot import that data directly to a PivotTable.

Import Data from a Data Source

1. Click the cell where you want the PivotTable or imported data to appear.
2. Click Data→Import External Data→Import Data.

   The Select Data Source dialog box appears.

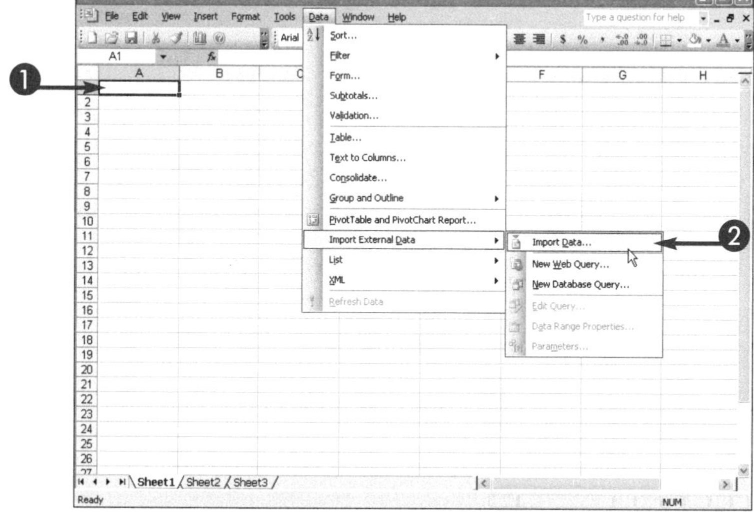

3. Click ▾ and select the My Data Sources folder.
4. Click the data source you want to import.
5. Click Open.

   Excel displays the Import Data dialog box.

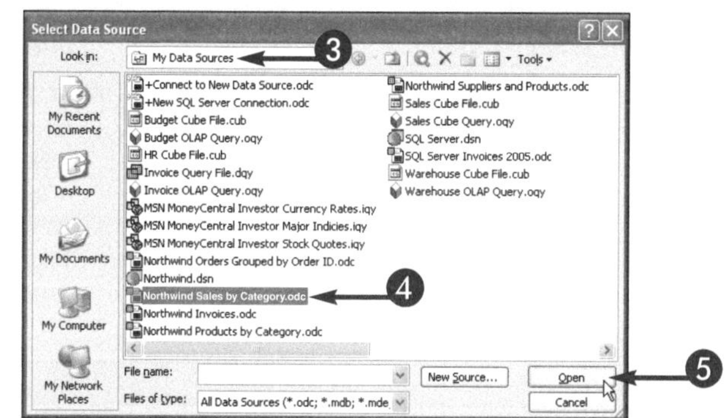

6 Select Existing worksheet.

7 Click OK.

- If you want to import the data into a PivotTable, click Create a PivotTable report. When the PivotTable and PivotChart Wizard appears, click Finish.

Excel imports the data into the worksheet.

- The External Data toolbar appears.

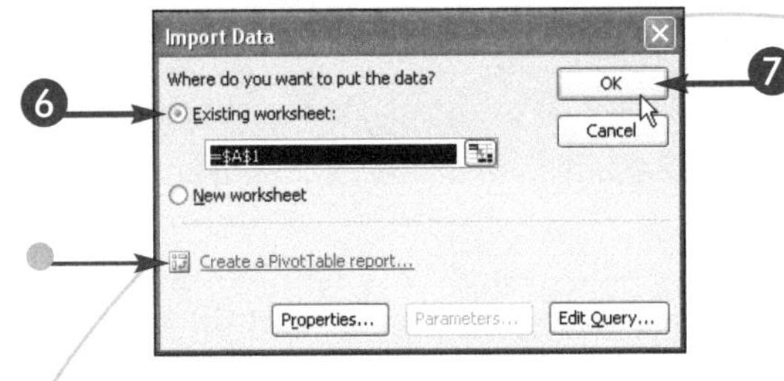

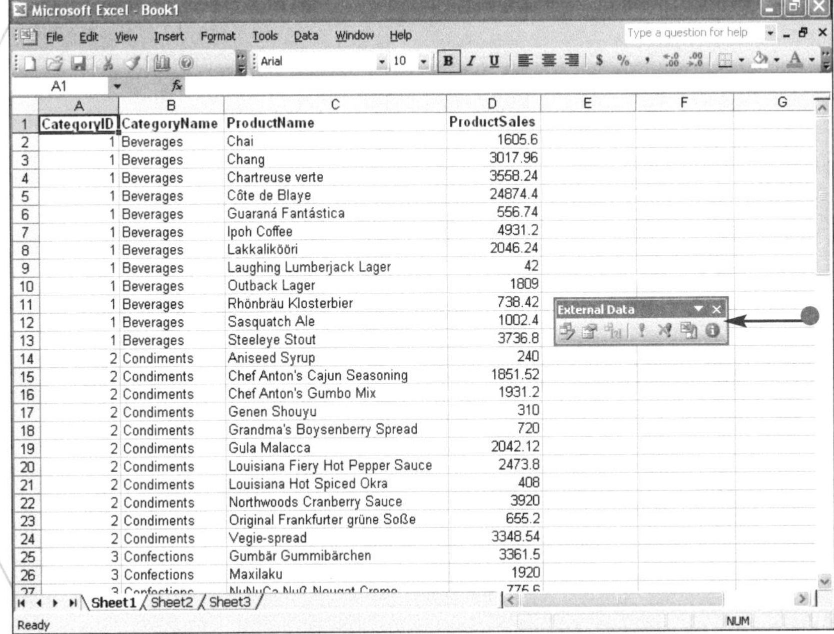

Apply It

If you do not see the data source you want in the My Data Sources folder, you can create one yourself. In most cases, you will want to create a data connection file. To create your own data connection (.odc) file, click Data→Import External Data→Import Data to display the Select Data Source dialog box. Click the New Source button to display the Data Connection Wizard. Click the data source you want and then click Next.

The next wizard step depends on the data source you choose:

- For Microsoft SQL Server or Oracle, you specify the server name or address and your server login data.
- For ODBC DSN, you choose the ODBC data source, and then specify the location of the file and the specific table you want to connect to.
- For data retrieval services — including Microsoft Business Solutions — you specify the network name or Web address of the data retrieval server.

Follow the rest of the wizard's steps and then choose your new data source in the Select Data Source dialog box. Note that the Data Connection Wizard stores all new data source files in the My Data Sources folder, which is a subfolder of My Documents.

Import Data from an Access Table

If you want to use Excel to analyze data from a table within an Access database, you can import the table to an Excel worksheet.

In Appendix B, you learned how to use Microsoft Query to create a database query to extract records from a database, filter and sort the records, and return the results to Excel. You learned that you can create a database query for any ODBC data source, including an Access database.

If you simply want the raw data from an Access table, you can still use Microsoft Query. That is, you add the table to the query, add the asterisk (*) "field" — representing all the table's fields — to the data grid, and then return the results without adding any criteria to filter the records.

However, Excel gives you an easier way to do this: you can import the table directly from the Access database. To make this technique even easier, Excel automatically creates a data connection file for the database and table that you import. Therefore, you can import the same table in the future simply by opening the data connection file.

Note, too, that you can also use the steps in this task to import data from any query that is already defined in the Access database.

Import Data from an Access Table

Note: This task uses the Northwind.mdb database that comes with Microsoft Access, or you can create your own sample database.

1. Click the cell where you want the PivotTable or imported data to appear.
2. Click Data→Import External Data→Import Data.

   The Select Data Source dialog box appears.

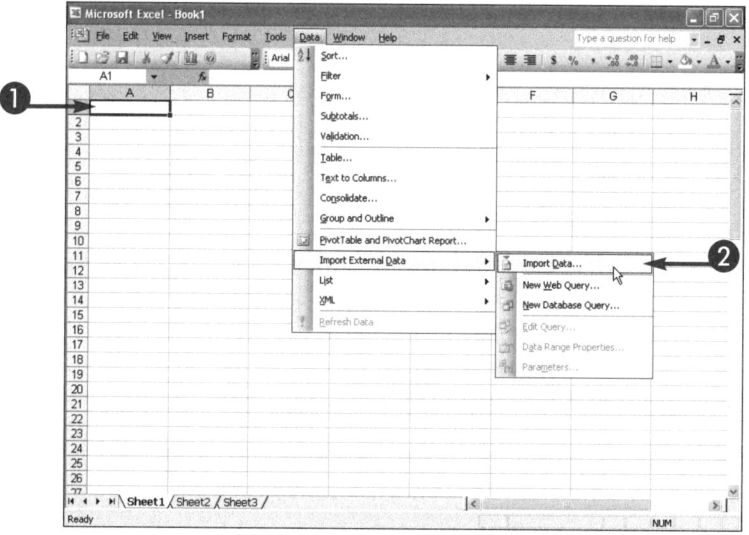

3. Open the folder that contains the Access database.
4. Click the Access database file.
5. Click Open.

Note: If another user has the database open, you may see the Data Link Properties dialog box. If so, make sure the login information is correct and then click Test Connection until you are able to connect successfully. Then click OK.

Microsoft Excel displays the Select Table dialog box.

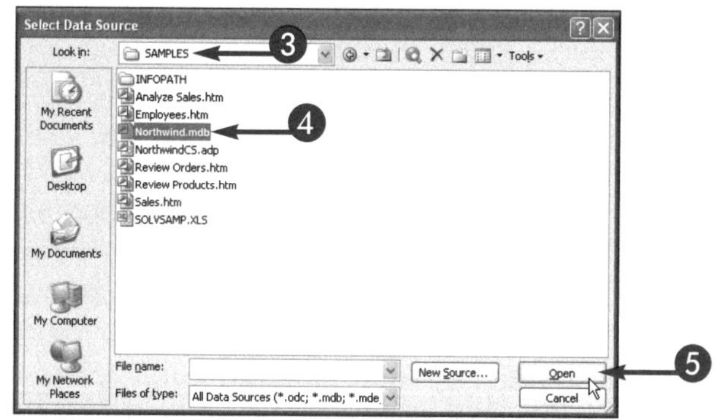

6 Click the table or query you want to import.

7 Click OK.

Microsoft Excel displays the Import Data dialog box.

8 Select Existing worksheet.

9 Click OK.

- If you want to import the data into a PivotTable, click Create a PivotTable report. When the PivotTable and PivotChart Wizard appears, click Finish.

Excel imports the data to the worksheet.

- The External Data toolbar appears.

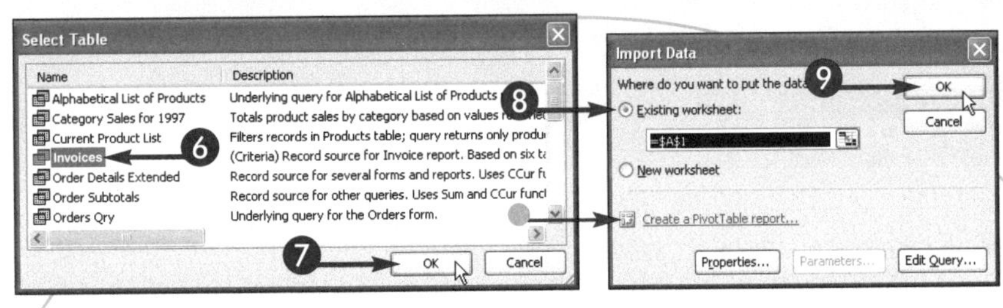

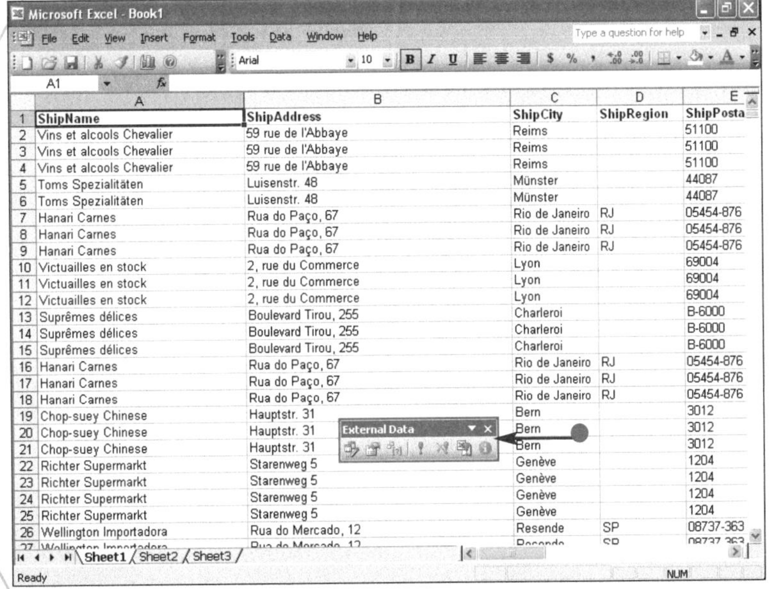

Extra

Excel automatically creates a new data connection file for the Access table and stores the .odc file in the My Data Sources folder. The name of the data connection file depends on the table name and database name. For example, if you select the Invoices query from the Northwind sample database, the new data connection file is named Northwind Invoices.odc.

If you want to import the same table in the future, you need only click the data connection file in the Select Data Source dialog box, and then click Open.

If the Access database requires you to log in with a password, you may need to type the password again when you refresh the imported data. To avoid this extra step, you can tell Excel to save the database password along with the external data. If you have the Import Data dialog box onscreen, click Properties; if you have already imported the data, click the Data Range Properties button ( ) in the External Data toolbar, instead. In the External Data Range Properties dialog box, click Save password (☐ changes to ☑), and then click OK.

Import Data from a Word Table

You can improve your analysis of Word table data by importing the table into an Excel worksheet.

Word tables are collections of rows and columns and cells, which means they look something like Excel ranges. Moreover, you can insert fields into Word table cells to perform calculations. In fact, Word fields support cell references such as B1 — the cell in the second column and first row of the table — and you can use cell references, built-in functions such as SUM and AVERAGE, and operators such as addition (+), multiplication (*), and greater than (>), to build formulas that calculate results based on the table data.

However, even the most powerful Word field formula is a far cry from what you can do in Excel, which offers far more sophisticated data analysis tools. Therefore, to analyze your Word table data properly, you should import the table into an Excel worksheet.

Import Data from a Word Table

Note: This task uses the 2006Budget.doc Word file, available at www.wiley.com/go/pivotablesvb, or you can create your own sample Word table.

1. Select the Word table you want to import.

   A quick way to select a table in Word is to click any cell in the table and then press Alt+Shift+5.

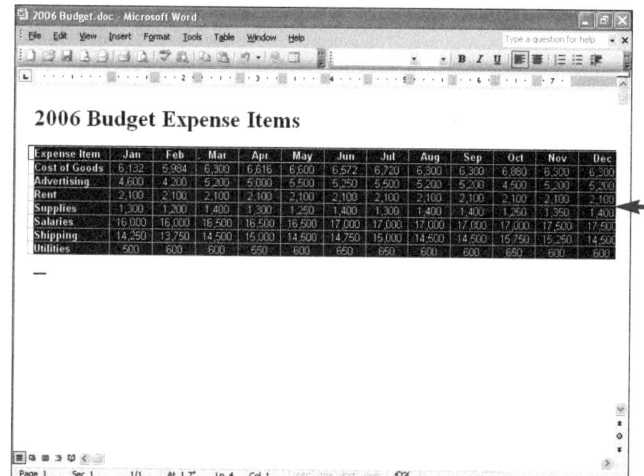

2. Click Edit→Copy.

   You can also click the Copy button ( ) or press Ctrl+C.

   Word copies the table to the Clipboard.

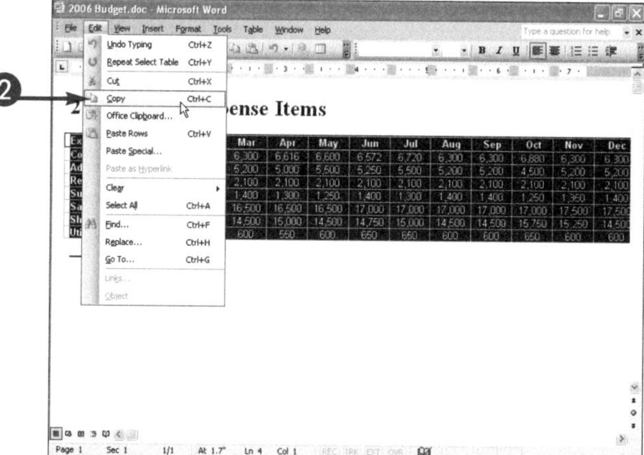

3. Switch to the Excel workbook into which you want to import the table.

4. Click the cell where you want the table to appear.

5. Click Edit→Paste.

   You can also click the Paste button (icon) or press Ctrl+V.

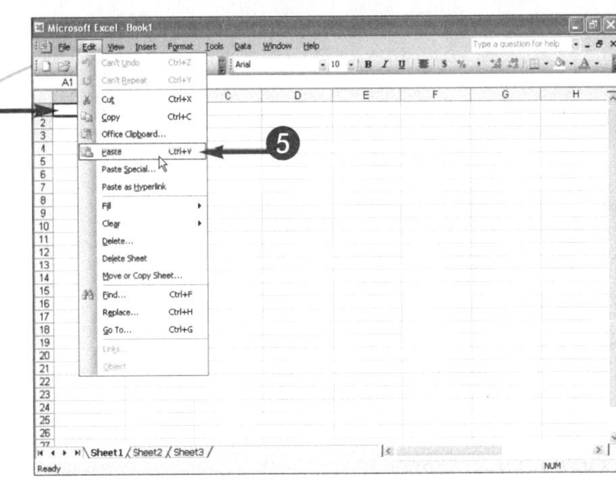

Excel pastes the Word table data.

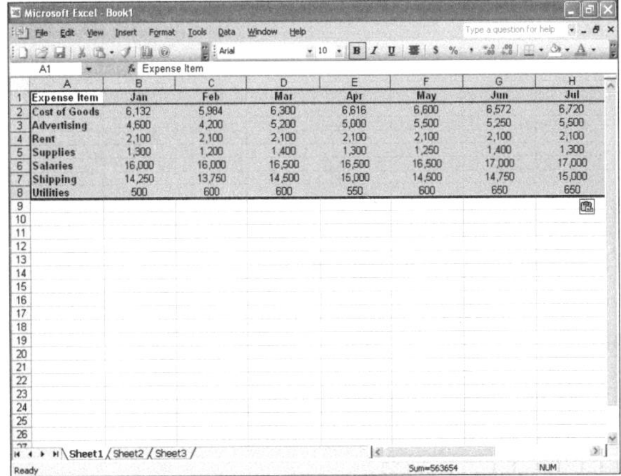

Apply It

The problem with this copy-and-paste method is that there is no connection between the data in Word and the data in Excel. If you make changes to one set of data, those changes are not automatically reflected in the other set of data. You can paste the Word data into Excel as a linked Word object, but you are not able to manipulate the data in Excel.

A better approach is to shift the data's container application from Word to Excel. That is, after you paste the table data into Excel, copy the Excel range, switch to Word, and then select Edit→Paste Special. In the Paste Special dialog box, click HTML Format in the As list, select "Paste link" (○ changes to ◉), and then click OK. The resulting table is linked to the Excel data, which means that any changes you make to the data in Excel automatically appear in the Word table. Note, however, that the link does not work the other way. That is, if you change the data in Word, you cannot update the original data in Excel.

Import Data from a Text File

You can analyze the data contained in certain text files by importing some or all the data into an Excel worksheet.

Nowadays, most data resides in some kind of special format: database object, XML file, Excel workbook, and so on. However, it is still relatively common to come across data stored in simple text files because text is a universal format that users can work with on any system and in a wide variety of programs, including Excel.

Note, however, that you cannot import just any text files into Excel. Some or all the files must use one of these two structures:

- **Delimited** — This is a text structure in which each item on a line of text is separated by a character, called a *delimiter*. The most common text delimiter is the comma (,), and there is even a special text format called *Comma Separated Values* (*CSV*) that uses the comma delimiter. A delimited text file is imported into Excel by placing each line of text on a separate row and each item between the delimiter in a separate cell.
- **Fixed width** — This is a text structure in which all the items on a line of text use up a set amount of space — say, 10 characters or 20 characters — and these fixed widths are the same on every line of text. For example, the first item on every line might use 5 characters, the second item on every line might use 15 characters, and so on. A fixed-width text file is imported into Excel by placing each line of text on a separate row and each fixed-width item in a separate cell.

The importing of text files into Excel is handled by the Text Import Wizard, the steps for which vary depending on whether you are importing a delimited or fixed-width text file.

Import Data from a Text File

START THE TEXT IMPORT WIZARD

Note: This task uses the StockPrices.csv text file, available at www.wiley.com/go/pivottablesvb, or you can create your own sample text file.

1. Click the cell where you want the PivotTable or imported data to appear.
2. Click Data➔Import External Data➔Import Data.

   The Select Data Source dialog box appears.

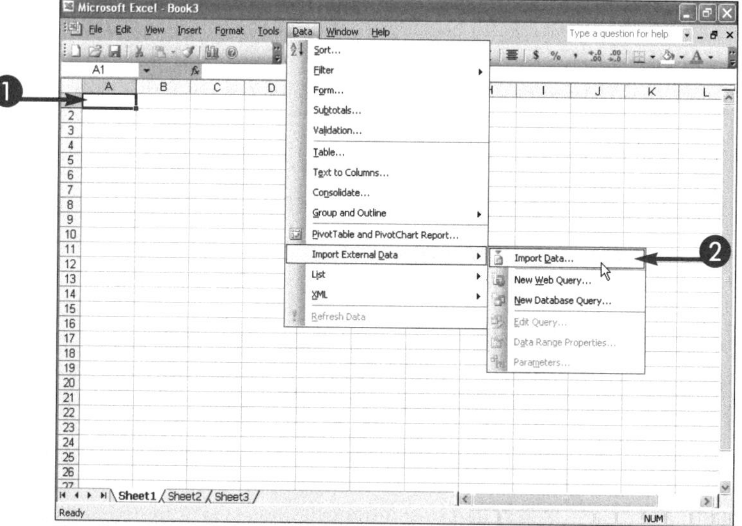

3. Open the folder that contains the text file.
4. Click the text file.
5. Click Open.

   The Text Import Wizard appears.

Note: For delimited text, continue with "Import Delimited Data." For fixed-width text, skip to "Import Fixed-Width Data."

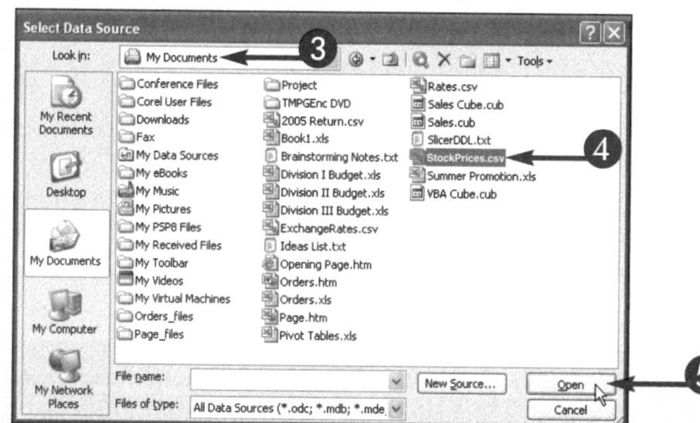

IMPORT DELIMITED DATA

1. Select Delimited.
2. Click here to set the first row you want to import.
3. Click Next.

   The second Text Import Wizard dialog box appears.

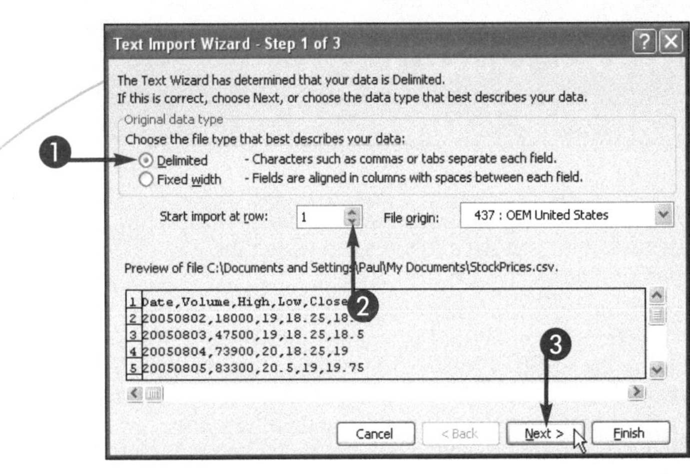

Text Import Wizard - Step 1 of 3
The Text Wizard has determined that your data is Delimited.
If this is correct, choose Next, or choose the data type that best describes your data.
Original data type
Choose the file type that best describes your data:
Delimited - Characters such as commas or tabs separate each field.
Fixed width - Fields are aligned in columns with spaces between each field.
Start import at row: 1
File origin: 437 : OEM United States
Preview of file C:\Documents and Settings\Paul\My Documents\StockPrices.csv.
1 Date,Volume,High,Low,Close
2 20050802,18000,19,18.25,18.
3 20050803,47500,19,18.25,18.5
4 20050804,73900,20,18.25,19
5 20050805,83300,20.5,19,19.75
Cancel
< Back
Next >
Finish

4. Select the delimiter character that your text data uses.
   - If you choose the correct delimiter, the data should appear in separate columns.
5. Click Next.

   The third Text Import Wizard dialog box appears.

Note: To complete this task, see "Finish the Text Import Wizard."

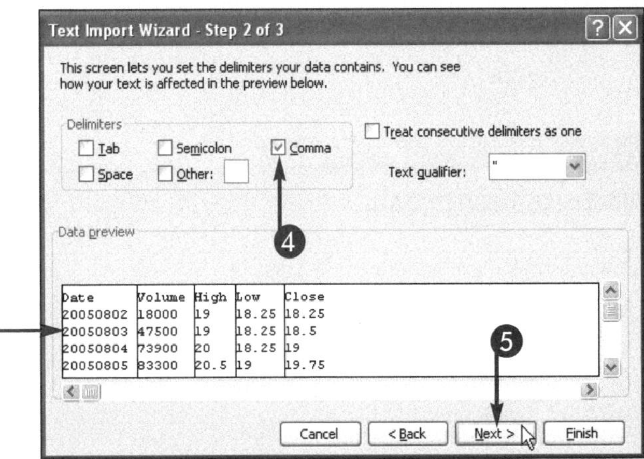

Text Import Wizard - Step 2 of 3
This screen lets you set the delimiters your data contains. You can see how your text is affected in the preview below.
Delimiters
Tab
Semicolon
Comma
Treat consecutive delimiters as one
Space
Other:
Text qualifier: "
Data preview
Date Volume High Low Close
20050802 18000 19 18.25 18.25
20050803 47500 19 18.25 18.5
20050804 73900 20 18.25 19
20050805 83300 20.5 19 19.75
Cancel
< Back
Next >
Finish

Extra

It is common for text files to include a title or one or more lines of explanatory text at the top of the document. In this case, you probably do not want to import this introductory text into Excel. The exception to this would be if the text file has a line of column headings. In that case, you should import the headings so that Excel includes them at the top of the range of imported data. To skip text at the beginning of the text file, use the "Start import at row" spin box in the first Text Import Wizard dialog box. Set the value of this control to the row number where the data starts. For example, if you have 4 lines of introductory text that you want to skip over, set the spin box value to 5.

If your text file originated from a system that is different from the one you are running, then the text may not display properly. To fix this, use the "File origin" list in the first Text Import Wizard dialog box. For example, if the text file originated on a Macintosh system, click Macintosh in the list. Similarly, if the text file was created in a language that uses different characters or accents, click the appropriate alphabet — such as Cyrillic or Greek — in the list.

continued →

Import Data from a Text File (continued)

If you are importing data that uses the fixed-width structure, then you need to tell Excel where the separation between each field occurs.

In a fixed-width text file, each column of data is a constant width. The Text Import Wizard is usually quite good at determining the width of each column of data, and in most cases the wizard automatically sets up *column break lines*, which are vertical lines that separate one field from the next. However, titles or introductory text at the beginning of the file can throw off the wizard's calculations, so you should check carefully that the proposed break lines are accurate. In the second Text Import Wizard dialog box, you can scroll through all the data to see if any break line is improperly positioned for the data in a particular field. If you find a break line in the wrong position, you can move it to the correct position before importing the text.

Note, too, that in some cases the Text Import Wizard adds an extra break line. For example, if the text file has three columns of data, the wizard may suggest three break lines, which divide the data into four columns. In this case, you can delete the extra break line.

IMPORT FIXED-WIDTH DATA

Note: You need to have performed the steps in "Start the Text Import Wizard" before continuing with this section.

1. Select Fixed width.
2. Click here to set the first row you want to import.
3. Click Next.

   The second Text Import Wizard dialog box appears.

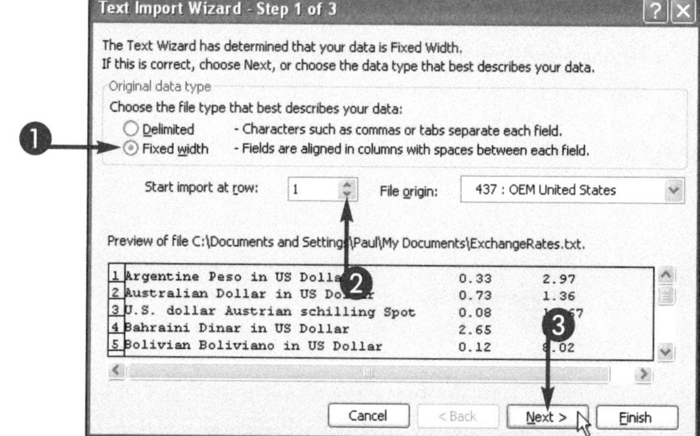
Text Import Wizard - Step 1 of 3
The Text Wizard has determined that your data is Fixed Width.
If this is correct, choose Next, or choose the data type that best describes your data.
Original data type
Choose the file type that best describes your data:
Delimited - Characters such as commas or tabs separate each field.
Fixed width - Fields are aligned in columns with spaces between each field.
Start import at row: 1
File origin: 437 : OEM United States
Preview of file C:\Documents and Settings\Paul\My Documents\ExchangeRates.txt.
Cancel
< Back
Next >
Finish

4. Click and drag a break line to set the width of each column.

   To create a break line, click the ruler at the point where you want the break to appear.

   To delete a break line, double-click it.
5. Click Next.

   The third Text Import Wizard dialog box appears.

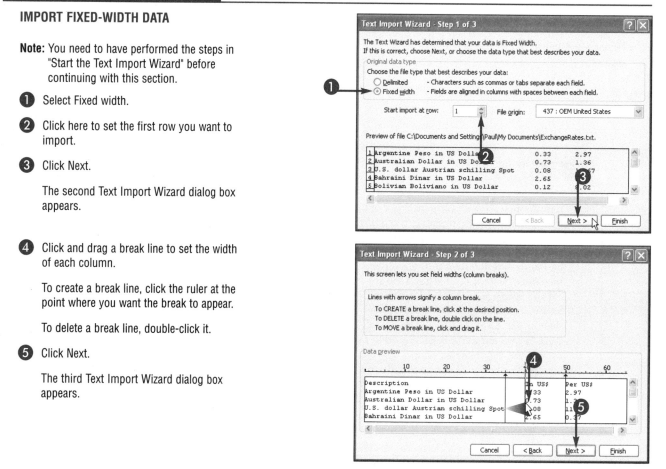

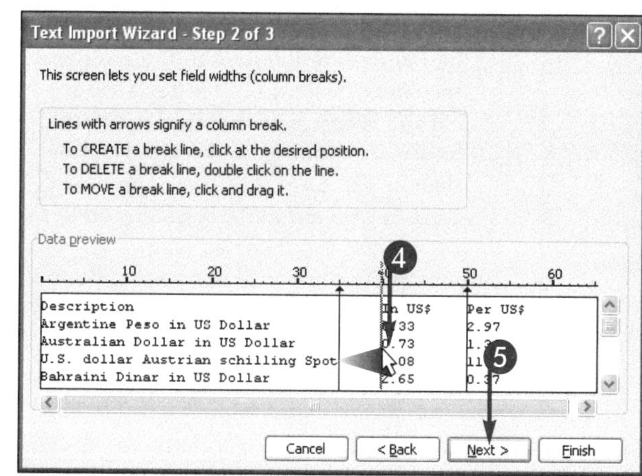
Text Import Wizard - Step 2 of 3
This screen lets you set field widths (column breaks).
Lines with arrows signify a column break.
To CREATE a break line, click at the desired position.
To DELETE a break line, double click on the line.
To MOVE a break line, click and drag it.
Data preview
Cancel
< Back
Next >
Finish

FINISH THE TEXT IMPORT WIZARD

1. Click a column.
2. Select the data format you want Excel to apply to the column.
3. If you select Date, use this list to click the date format your data uses.
4. Repeat Steps 1 to 3 to set the data format for all the columns.
5. Click Finish.

   Excel displays the Import Data dialog box.

6. Select Existing worksheet.
7. Click OK.

   - If you want to import the data into a PivotTable, click Create a PivotTable report. When the PivotTable and PivotChart Wizard appears, click Finish.

   Excel imports the data to the worksheet.

   - The External Data toolbar appears.

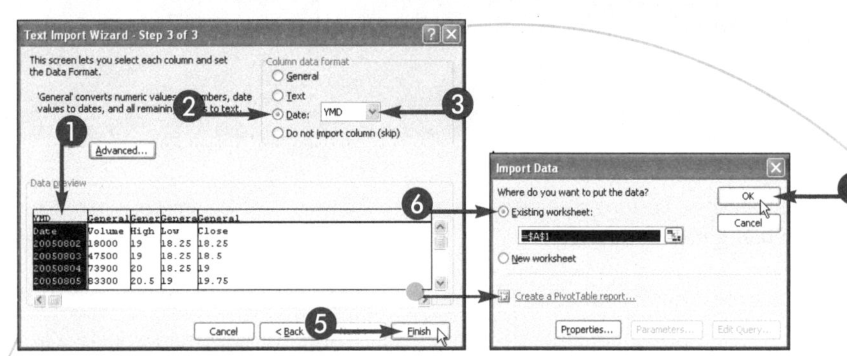

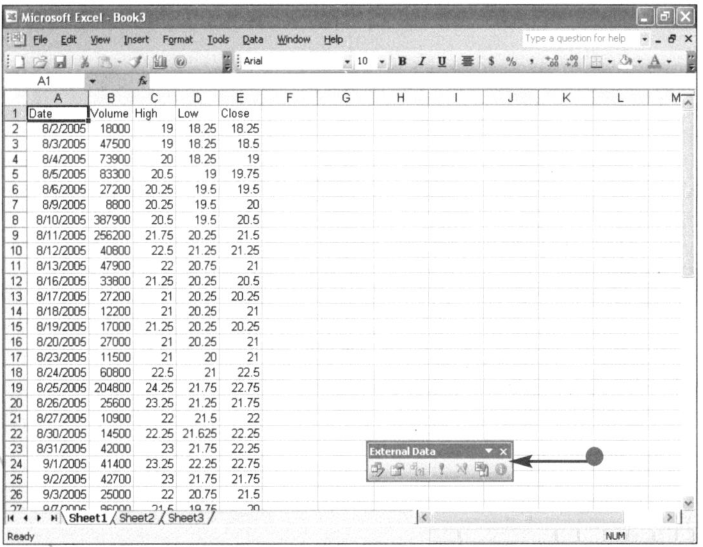

Extra

Some text files may contain numbers that use a comma instead of a dot as the decimal separator, or a dot instead of a comma as the thousands separator. To ensure that Excel imports such numeric data correctly, click Advanced in the third Text Import Wizard dialog box to display the Advanced Text Import Settings dialog box. You can use the "Decimal separator" list to click the decimal separator used by the text, and use the "Thousands separator" list to click the thousands separator used by the text. Click OK to put the settings into effect.

If you make a mistake when importing a text file, you do not need to start the import from scratch. Click any cell in the imported data and then click the Edit Text Import button ( ) in the External Data toolbar. Excel displays the Import Text File dialog box. Click the file you want to import and then click Import. Excel launches the Import Text Wizard to enable you to run through the wizard's options again.

Import Data from a Web Page

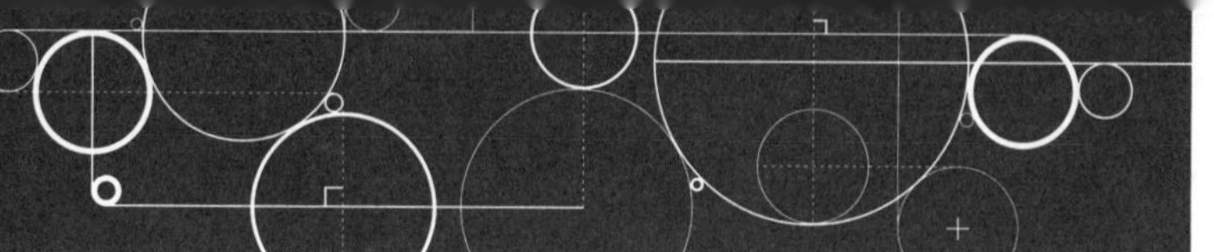

You can analyze Web page data by importing it into Excel using a Web Query.

To make data more readily available to a wide variety of users, many people are placing data on Web pages that are accessible via the Internet or a corporate *intranet* — a local network that uses Web servers and similar technologies to implement Web sites and pages that are accessible only to network users. Although this data is often text, most Web page data comes in one of two formats:

- **Table** — This is a rectangular array of rows and columns, with data values in the cells created by the intersection of the rows and columns.
- **Preformatted text** — This is text that has been structured with predefined spacing. In many cases, this spacing is used to organize data into columns with fixed widths.

Both types of data are suitable for import into Excel, which enables you to perform more extensive data analysis using Excel's tools. To import Web page data into Excel, you must create a *Web query* — a data request that specifies the page address and the table or preformatted text that you want to import.

Import Data from a Web Page

Note: This task uses the products.html Web page, available at www.wiley.com/go/pivottablesvb, or you can create your own sample Web page.

1. Click the cell where you want the PivotTable or imported data to appear.
2. Click Data→Import External Data→New Web Query.

   The New Web Query dialog box appears.
3. Type the address of the Web page that contains the data you want to import.
   - Excel loads the page into the dialog box.
4. Click [➡] beside the table that you want to import.

   [➡] changes to [✓].
   - Excel selects the table.
5. If the page has other tables that you want to import, repeat Step 4 for each table.
6. Click Import.

   Excel displays the Import Data dialog box.

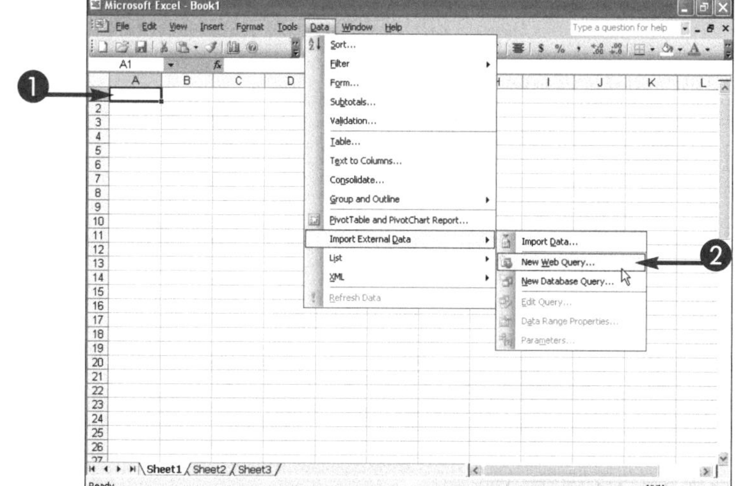

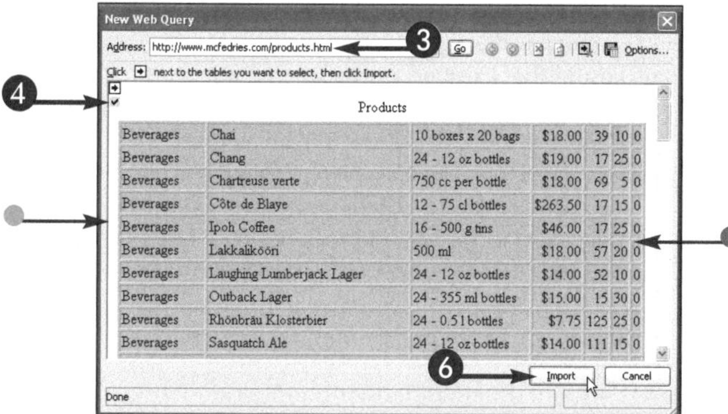

7. Select Existing worksheet.
8. Click OK.
   - If you want to import the data into a PivotTable, click Create a PivotTable report. When the PivotTable and PivotChart Wizard appears, click Finish.

Excel imports the data to the worksheet.

- The External Data toolbar appears.

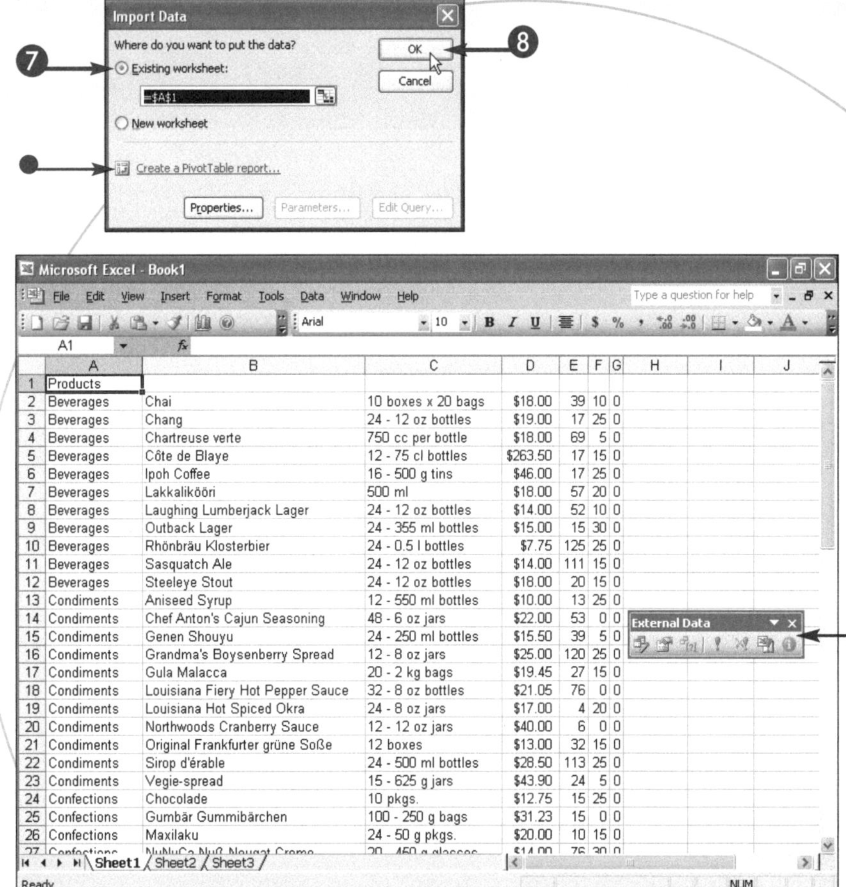

Import Data
Where do you want to put the data?
Existing worksheet:
=$A$1
New worksheet
Create a PivotTable report...
OK
Cancel
Properties...
Parameters...
Edit Query...
7
8
Microsoft Excel - Book1
File Edit View Insert Format Tools Data Window Help
Type a question for help
Arial
10
A1
Products
Beverages Chai 10 boxes x 20 bags $18.00 39 10 0
Beverages Chang 24 - 12 oz bottles $19.00 17 25 0
Beverages Chartreuse verte 750 cc per bottle $18.00 69 5 0
Beverages Côte de Blaye 12 - 75 cl bottles $263.50 17 15 0
Beverages Ipoh Coffee 16 - 500 g tins $46.00 17 25 0
Beverages Lakkalikööri 500 ml $18.00 57 20 0
Beverages Laughing Lumberjack Lager 24 - 12 oz bottles $14.00 52 10 0
Beverages Outback Lager 24 - 355 ml bottles $15.00 15 30 0
Beverages Rhönbräu Klosterbier 24 - 0.5 l bottles $7.75 125 25 0
Beverages Sasquatch Ale 24 - 12 oz bottles $14.00 111 15 0
Beverages Steeleye Stout 24 - 12 oz bottles $18.00 20 15 0
Condiments Aniseed Syrup 12 - 550 ml bottles $10.00 13 25 0
Condiments Chef Anton's Cajun Seasoning 48 - 6 oz jars $22.00 53 0 0
Condiments Genen Shouyu 24 - 250 ml bottles $15.50 39 5 0
Condiments Grandma's Boysenberry Spread 12 - 8 oz jars $25.00 120 25 0
Condiments Gula Malacca 20 - 2 kg bags $19.45 27 15 0
Condiments Louisiana Fiery Hot Pepper Sauce 32 - 8 oz bottles $21.05 76 0 0
Condiments Louisiana Hot Spiced Okra 24 - 8 oz jars $17.00 4 20 0
Condiments Northwoods Cranberry Sauce 12 - 12 oz jars $40.00 6 0 0
Condiments Original Frankfurter grüne Soße 12 boxes $13.00 32 15 0
Condiments Sirop d'érable 24 - 500 ml bottles $28.50 113 25 0
Condiments Vegie-spread 15 - 625 g jars $43.90 24 5 0
Confections Chocolade 10 pkgs. $12.75 15 25 0
Confections Gumbär Gummibärchen 100 - 250 g bags $31.23 15 0 0
Confections Maxilaku 24 - 50 g pkgs. $20.00 10 15 0
External Data
Sheet1 Sheet2 Sheet3
Ready
NUM

Apply It

Besides the steps you learned in this task, Excel gives you several other methods for creating Web queries. All these alternative methods assume that you already have the Web page open in Internet Explorer:

- In the Internet Explorer toolbar, pull down the Edit With toolbar list and click Edit with Microsoft Office Excel.
- Right-click the page and then click Export to Microsoft Excel.
- Copy the Web page text, switch to Excel, and then paste the text. When the Paste Options smart tag appears, click the button and then click Create Refreshable Web Query.

Each of these methods opens the New Web Query dialog box and automatically loads the Web page.

If you want to save the Web query for future use in other workbooks, click the Web Query Save Query button ( ) in the New Web Query dialog box and then use the Save Workspace dialog box to save the query file.

Import Data from an XML File

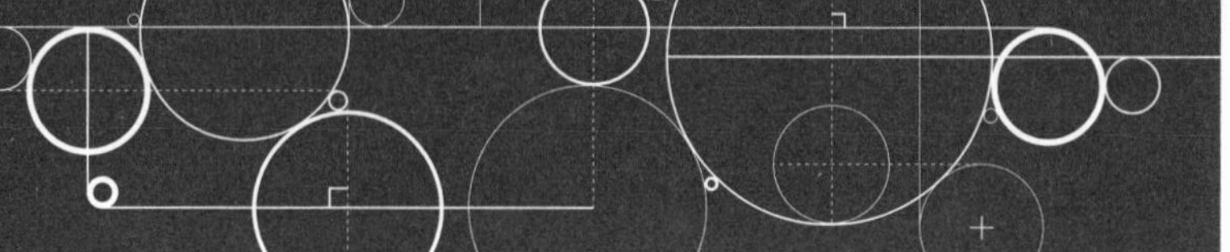

You can analyze data that currently resides in XML format by importing that data into Excel and then manipulating and analyzing the resulting XML list.

XML — eXtensible Markup Language — is a standard that enables the management and sharing of structured data using simple text files. These XML files organize data using tags, among other elements, that specify the equivalent of a table name and field names. Here is a simple XML example that constitutes a single record in a table named "Products":

```
<Products>

<ProductName>Chai</ProductName>

<CompanyName>Exotic Liquids</CompanyName>

<ContactName>Charlotte Cooper</ContactName>

</Products>
```

These XML files are readable by a wide variety of database programs and other applications, including Excel 2003. Because the XML is just text, if you want to work with the data, you must import the XML file into another application. If you want to perform data analysis on the XML file, for example, then you must import the XML data into Excel.

Excel usually stores imported XML data in an *XML list*, a range that looks and operates much like a regular Excel list, except that it has a few XML-specific features.

Import Data from an XML File

Note: This task uses the Suppliers.xml file, available at www.wiley.com/go/pivottablesvb, or you can create your own sample XML file.

1. Click the cell where you want the PivotTable or imported data to appear.
2. Click Data➔XML➔Import.

   The Import XML dialog box appears.

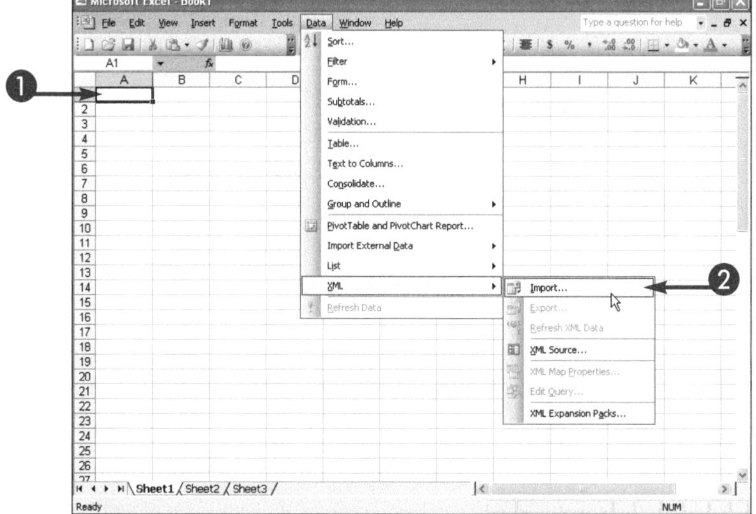

3. Click ▾ and select the folder that contains the XML file.
4. Click the XML file you want to import.
5. Click Import.

   Excel displays the Import Data dialog box.

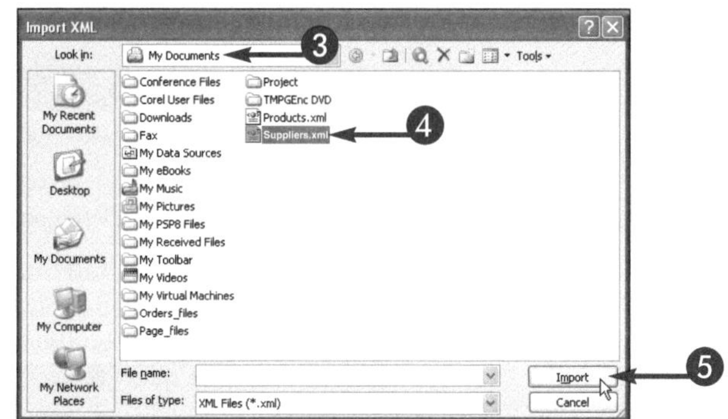

6. Select XML list in existing worksheet.
7. Click OK.

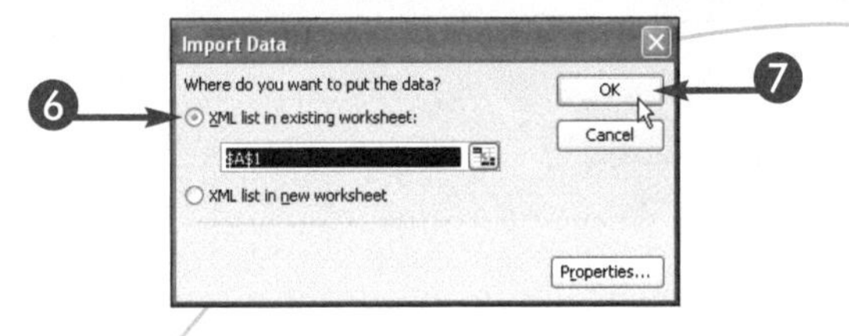

Excel imports the data into the worksheet as an XML list.

- The List toolbar appears.

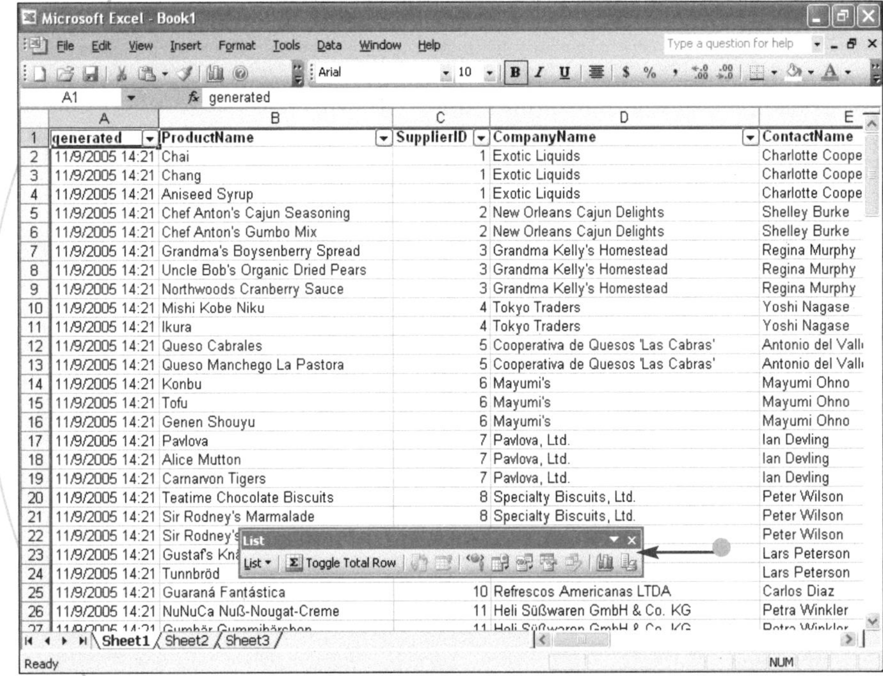

	A	B	C	D	E
1	generated	ProductName	SupplierID	CompanyName	ContactName
2	11/9/2005 14:21	Chai	1	Exotic Liquids	Charlotte Coope
3	11/9/2005 14:21	Chang	1	Exotic Liquids	Charlotte Coope
4	11/9/2005 14:21	Aniseed Syrup	1	Exotic Liquids	Charlotte Coope
5	11/9/2005 14:21	Chef Anton's Cajun Seasoning	2	New Orleans Cajun Delights	Shelley Burke
6	11/9/2005 14:21	Chef Anton's Gumbo Mix	2	New Orleans Cajun Delights	Shelley Burke
7	11/9/2005 14:21	Grandma's Boysenberry Spread	3	Grandma Kelly's Homestead	Regina Murphy
8	11/9/2005 14:21	Uncle Bob's Organic Dried Pears	3	Grandma Kelly's Homestead	Regina Murphy
9	11/9/2005 14:21	Northwoods Cranberry Sauce	3	Grandma Kelly's Homestead	Regina Murphy
10	11/9/2005 14:21	Mishi Kobe Niku	4	Tokyo Traders	Yoshi Nagase
11	11/9/2005 14:21	Ikura	4	Tokyo Traders	Yoshi Nagase
12	11/9/2005 14:21	Queso Cabrales	5	Cooperativa de Quesos 'Las Cabras'	Antonio del Vall
13	11/9/2005 14:21	Queso Manchego La Pastora	5	Cooperativa de Quesos 'Las Cabras'	Antonio del Vall
14	11/9/2005 14:21	Konbu	6	Mayumi's	Mayumi Ohno
15	11/9/2005 14:21	Tofu	6	Mayumi's	Mayumi Ohno
16	11/9/2005 14:21	Genen Shouyu	6	Mayumi's	Mayumi Ohno
17	11/9/2005 14:21	Pavlova	7	Pavlova, Ltd.	Ian Devling
18	11/9/2005 14:21	Alice Mutton	7	Pavlova, Ltd.	Ian Devling
19	11/9/2005 14:21	Carnarvon Tigers	7	Pavlova, Ltd.	Ian Devling
20	11/9/2005 14:21	Teatime Chocolate Biscuits	8	Specialty Biscuits, Ltd.	Peter Wilson
21	11/9/2005 14:21	Sir Rodney's Marmalade	8	Specialty Biscuits, Ltd.	Peter Wilson
22	11/9/2005 14:21	Sir Rodney's			Peter Wilson
23	11/9/2005 14:21	Gustaf's Kn			Lars Peterson
24	11/9/2005 14:21	Tunnbröd			Lars Peterson
25	11/9/2005 14:21	Guaraná Fantástica	10	Refrescos Americanas LTDA	Carlos Diaz
26	11/9/2005 14:21	NuNuCa Nuß-Nougat-Creme	11	Heli Süßwaren GmbH & Co. KG	Petra Winkler

Extra

If there are fields in the XML list that you do not want to use, you can remove them. First display the XML Source pane by clicking Data➔XML➔XML Source. The XML Source pane displays a list of the fields — called *elements* — including the "generated" field that tells when you imported the data. To remove an element, right-click it and then click Remove element. To add an element back into the XML list, right-click the element and then click Map element.

You can also use the XML Source pane to map the XML elements that you want on your worksheet before importing the data. Click the XML Maps button to display the XML Maps dialog box, and then click Add. In the Select XML Source dialog box, click the XML file you want to import, and then click Open. If the XML data source has multiple roots, Excel prompts you to select one. Click dataroot and then click OK to return to the XML Maps dialog box, and then click OK. You should now see the XML field elements in the XML Source pane. To add an element to the worksheet, either right-click it and then click Map element, or drag the element and drop it on the worksheet. When you are done, import the XML data.

Refresh Imported Data

External data often changes, and you can ensure that you are working with the most up-to-date version of the information by refreshing the imported data.

Refreshing the imported data means retrieving the most current version of the source data. This is a straightforward operation most of the time. However, it is possible to construct a query that accesses confidential information or destroys some or all the external data. Therefore, when you refresh imported data, Excel always lets you know the potential risks and asks if you are sure the query is safe.

Remember, as well, that most external data resides on servers or in remote network locations. Therefore, the refresh may take some time, depending on the amount of data, the load on the server, and the amount of traffic on the network.

Refresh Imported Data

REFRESH NON-XML DATA

1. Click any cell inside the imported data.
2. Click Data➔Refresh Data.
   - You can also click the Refresh Data button.
   - To refresh all the imported data in the current workbook, click the Refresh All button.

   Excel asks if you trust the data source.

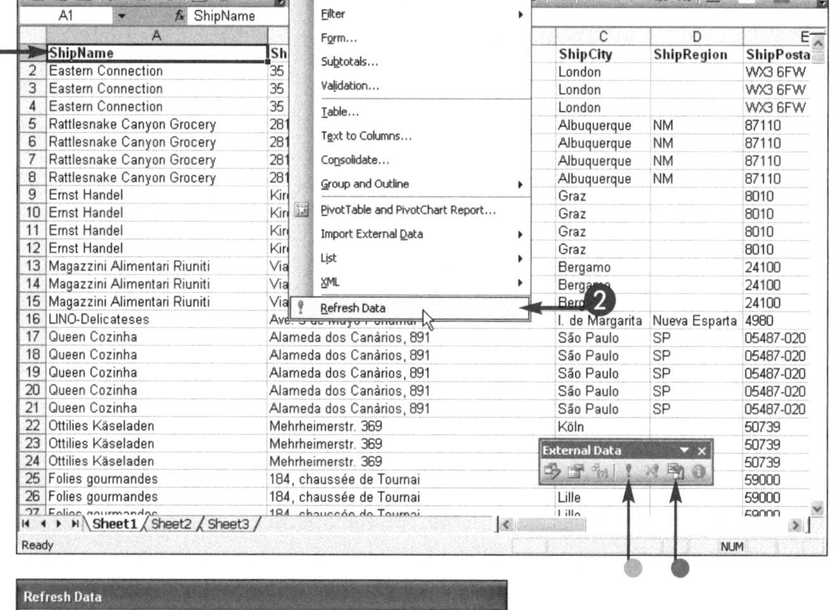

3. Click OK.

   Excel refreshes the imported data.

   The refresh may take a long time. To check the status of the refresh, click the Refresh Status button ( ) to display the External Data Refresh Status dialog box. Click Close to continue the refresh.

   If the refresh is taking too long, click the Cancel Refresh button ( ) to cancel it.

REFRESH XML DATA

❶ Click any cell inside the imported XML data.

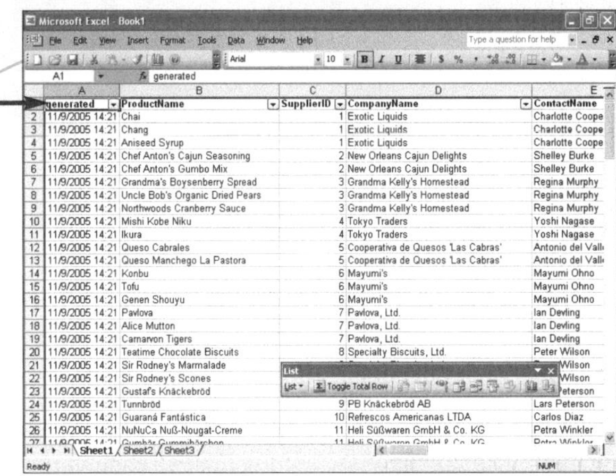

❷ Click Data➔XML➔Refresh XML Data.

You can also click XML Refresh button (![icon]) in the List toolbar.

Excel refreshes the imported XML data.

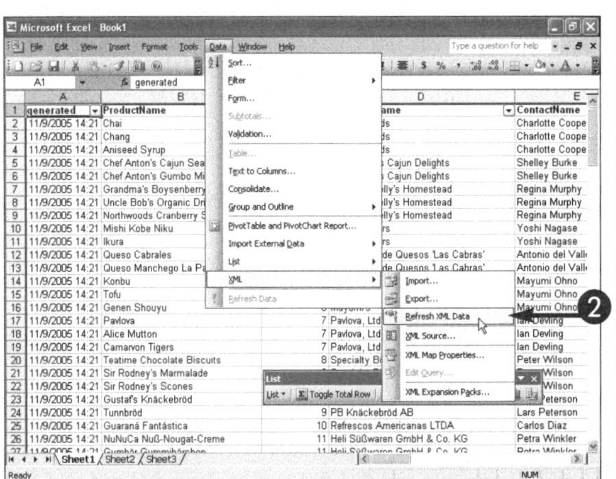

Apply It

For certain types of external data, you can set up a schedule that automatically refreshes the data at a specified interval. This is useful when you know that the source data changes frequently and you do not want to be bothered with constant manual refreshes.

Click any cell inside the imported data, and then click the Data Range Properties button (![icon]) in the External Data toolbar. In the External Data Range Properties dialog box, select "Refresh every" (☐ changes to ☑) and then use the spin box to specify the refresh interval, in minutes.

Note, however, that you might prefer not to have the source data updated too frequently. Depending on where the data resides and how much data you are working with, the refresh could take some time, which will slow down the rest of your work.

You can also tell Excel to automatically refresh the imported data when you open the workbook. In the External Data Range Properties dialog box, select "Refresh data on file open" (☐ changes to ☑).

Record a Macro

You can save time and make the process of creating a macro easier by recording some or all the actions you want your macro to perform.

A *macro* is a sequence of actions, commands, and statements that are executed one after another to perform a specific task. In Excel, as in all the other Office programs that support macros, the macro programming language is called *Visual Basic for Applications*, or *VBA*.

VBA is a powerful language that can perform a wide variety of tasks. However, VBA's main task is to operate on the application in which it is running. With Excel VBA, for example, you can create macros that add text and formulas to cells, format ranges, insert or delete worksheets, create and manipulate PivotTables, and much more.

Unfortunately, it can sometimes take a while to build and test a macro, and it is often difficult to remember the objects, properties, and methods that you are required to use to perform a task. Fortunately, when you want to build a macro that manipulates Excel in some way, VBA gives you an alternative method that is faster and easier: the macro recorder. After you activate this tool, you only need to use Excel to perform the action or actions that you want in the macro. All the text or formulas you insert in cells, all the formatting you apply, all the commands and buttons that you click, are recorded, translated into the equivalent VBA statements, and then stored as a macro for later use. You can store your recorded macros in any workbook, but Excel provides a special workbook for this purpose: the Personal Macro Workbook.

Record a Macro

1. Click Tools→Macro→Record New Macro.
   - You can also click the VBA Record New Macro button in the Visual Basic toolbar.

   The Record Macro dialog box appears.

2. Type a name for the macro.
3. Type a shortcut character.
4. Click ▾ and select the workbook in which you want to store the macro.
5. Click OK.

Note: If the macro name already exists, Excel displays a warning. Click Yes to replace the existing macro; click No to return to the Record Macro dialog box; click Cancel to stop the recording.

Excel starts the macro recorder.

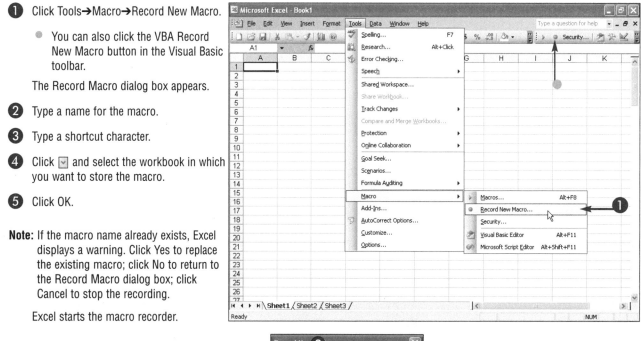

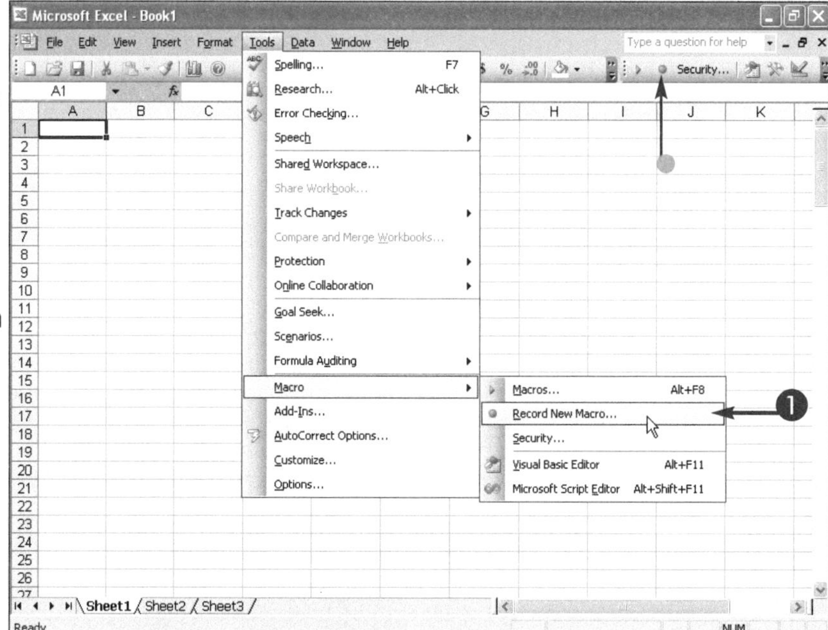

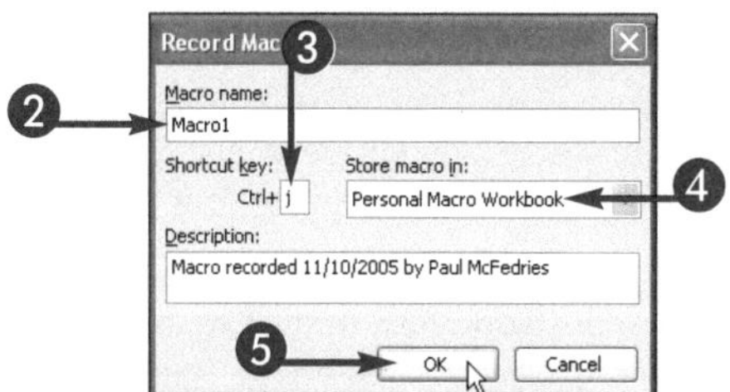

- The Stop Recording toolbar appears.
- The word Recording appears in the status bar.

6. Perform the Excel steps you want to record.

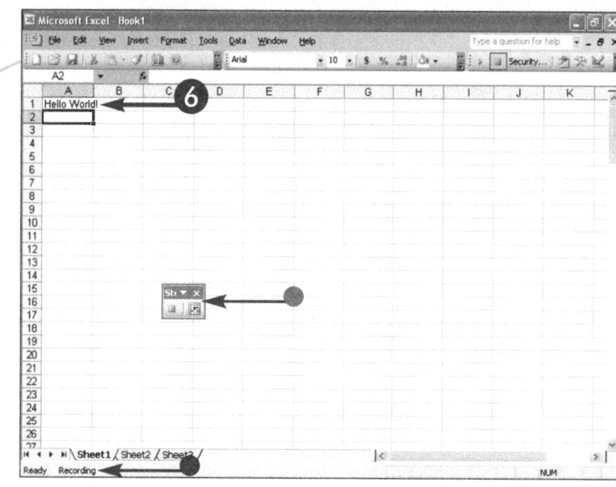

7. Click the VBA Stop Recording button.

   Excel stops the macro recorder and saves the macro in the workbook.

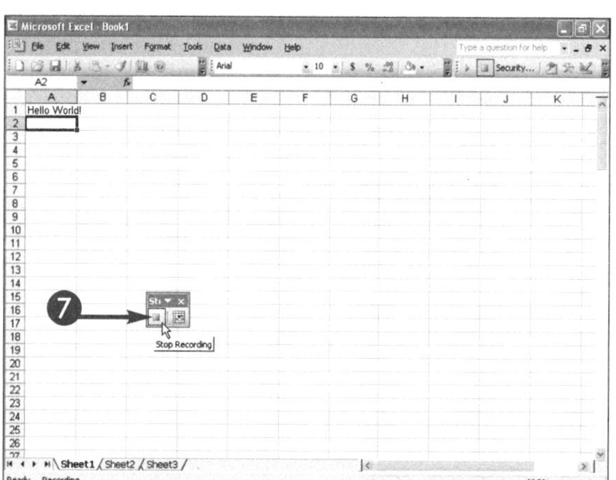

Extra

The shortcut key you specify in Step 3 is case sensitive, meaning you can create separate shortcuts with uppercase and lowercase letters. For example, if you type **e** into the Ctrl+ text box, you have to press Ctrl+E to run the macro. However, if you type **E** into the Ctrl+ text box, you have to press Ctrl+Shift+E to run the macro.

Make sure you do not specify a shortcut key that conflicts with Excel's built-in shortcuts — such as Ctrl+B for Bold or Ctrl+C for Copy. If you use a key that clashes with an Excel shortcut, Excel overrides its own shortcut and runs your macro instead, provided that the workbook containing the macro is open.

There are only five letters not assigned to Excel commands that you can use with your macros: e, j, m, q, and t. You can get extra shortcut keys by using uppercase letters. For example, Excel differentiates between Ctrl+b and Ctrl+B, or more explicitly, Ctrl+Shift+b. Note, however, that Excel uses four built-in Ctrl+Shift shortcuts: A, F, O, and P.

Finally note that you can assign a shortcut key to a macro after you create it. Click Tools➔Macro➔Macros, or press Alt+F8. In the Macro dialog box, click the macro and then click Options. In the Macro Options dialog box, type the shortcut character in the Ctrl+ text box, and then click OK.

Open the Visual Basic Editor

If you want to view or make changes to your recorded macro, or if you want to create macros from scratch, you need to open the Visual Basic Editor.

After you finish recording your actions, Excel translates them into VBA statements and stores them as a complete macro. Excel then saves the macro in a *module*, a special window in which you can view, edit, and run macros. If you are satisfied that your recording is accurate and properly executed, then you may never need to view the module in which it was stored. You can run the macro from Excel any time you want; see the task "Run a Macro," later in this appendix.

However, if you make mistakes during the recording, or if you want to augment the recorded macro with other VBA statements, then you need to view the module to work with the macro. Similarly, you also require access to the module if you want to create new macros from scratch.

In both cases, you access the module using the Visual Basic Editor, a program that enables you to view, create, edit, and run VBA macros. This task shows you how to start the Visual Basic Editor and how to open a module, such as one that contains a recorded macro.

Open the Visual Basic Editor

1. Click Tools➔Macro➔Visual Basic Editor.

   You can also press Alt+F11 or click the VBA Editor button in the Visual Basic toolbar.

   The Visual Basic Editor window appears.

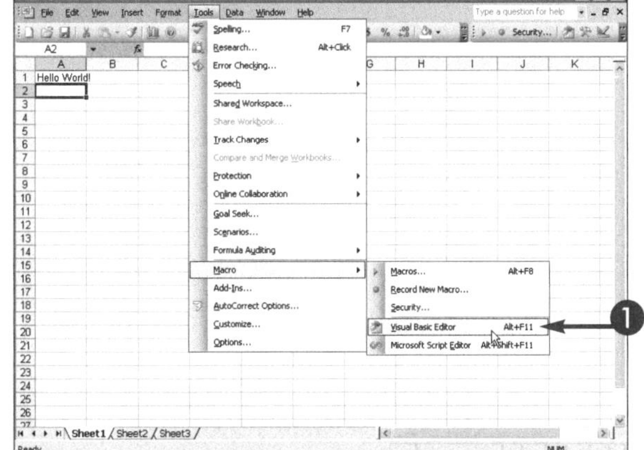

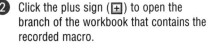

2. Click the plus sign (⊞) to open the branch of the workbook that contains the recorded macro.

Note: If you do not see the Project pane, click View➔Project Explorer, or press Ctrl+R.

3. Click the plus sign (⊞) to open the Modules branch.

   Excel displays the workbook's modules.

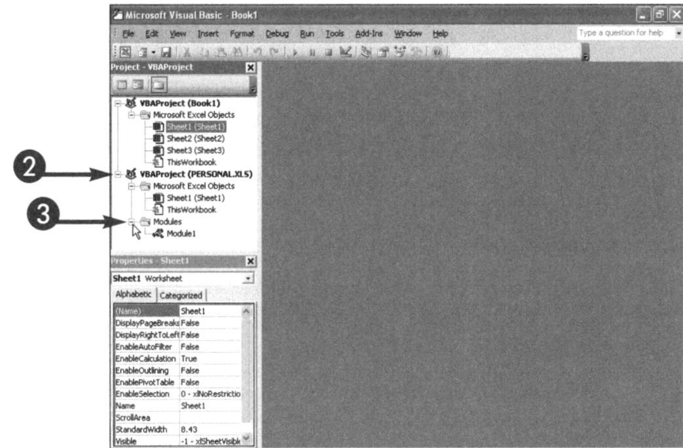

4 Double-click the module.

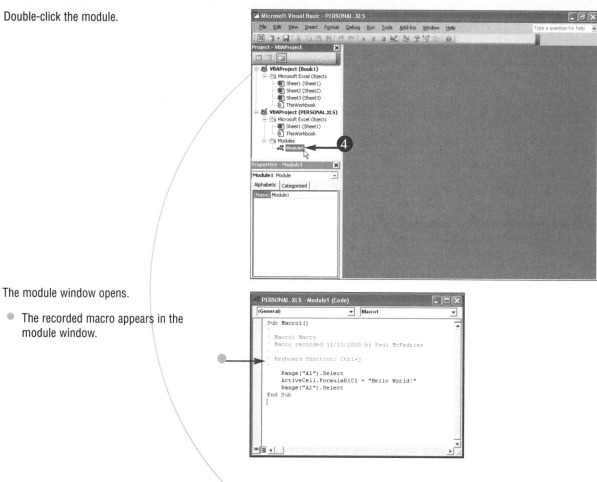

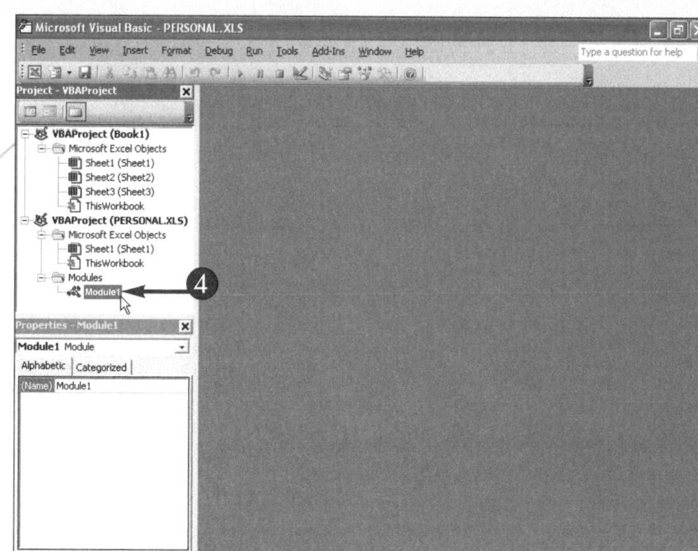

The module window opens.

- The recorded macro appears in the module window.

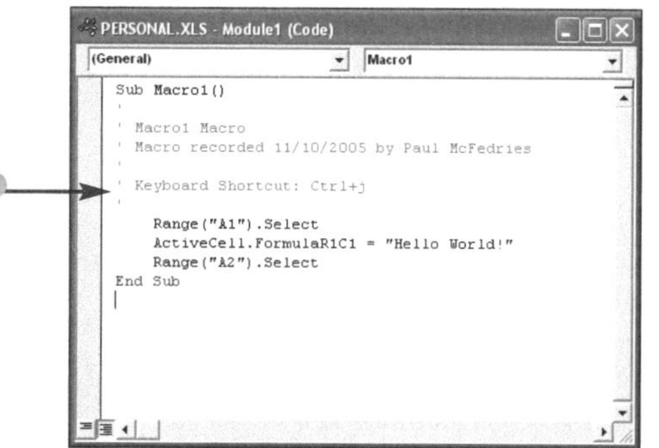

Apply It

It is a good idea to store all your macros in the Personal Macro Workbook. Excel keeps this workbook open all the time, so the macros you store in it are always available to you. Note, however, that Excel keeps the Personal Macro Workbook hidden, which is why you do not see it when you are working in Excel.

If you want to see the Personal Macro Workbook, you need to unhide it. Switch to Excel and click Window→Unhide to display the Unhide dialog box. Click Personal.xls and then click OK.

If the Unhide command is disabled, or if you do not see the Personal Macro Workbook in the Unhide dialog box, then it is likely that the Personal Macro Workbook does not exist. In most cases, Excel only creates this workbook after you use it to store a recorded macro for the first time. Follow the steps in the previous task, "Record a Macro," and be sure to click Personal Macro Workbook in the Record Macro dialog box.

Explore the PivotTable Object Model

To program PivotTables with VBA, you need to understand Excel's PivotTable object model.

You can build and manipulate a PivotTable using Excel commands, buttons, and dialog boxes. Therefore, many of Excel's PivotTable features are recordable, so you can create PivotTable-related macros by recording the appropriate PivotTable actions.

However, PivotTables are relatively complex features, so it is not always possible to record a PivotTable macro exactly the way you want. Therefore, most recorded PivotTable macros require a few adjustments to get them to work properly. This means that you need at least a basic understanding of how Excel translates PivotTable actions into VBA code. In other words, you need some understanding of the PivotTable object model.

In the programming lexicon, an *object model* is a complete summary of the objects associated with a particular program or feature, the hierarchy used by those objects, and the properties and methods supported by each object. Here an *object* is a distinct, manipulable item such as a PivotTable, a PivotTable field, or a value within a PivotTable field; a *property* is a programmable characteristic of an object such as a PivotTable's name or whether the PivotTable is displaying grand totals; and a *method* is an action you can perform on an object, such as refreshing or applying an AutoFormat to a PivotTable.

PivotTable Object

The top object in the PivotTable hierarchy is the `PivotTable` object, which represents an entire PivotTable report. You can reference a specific PivotTable either by using the `PivotTables` collection — which represents all the `PivotTable` objects on a specified worksheet, or by using the `Range` object's `PivotTable` property — which represents the PivotTable of which the range is a part. Here are some examples:

```
Worksheets("Budget").PivotTable("Sales")

ActiveSheet.PivotTables(1)

ActiveCell.PivotTable
```

PivotTable Properties

PROPERTY	DESCRIPTION
`ColumnGrand`	Toggles column grand totals on and off.
`Name`	The name of the PivotTable.
`RowGrand`	Toggles row grand totals on and off.
`HasAutoFormat`	Returns `True` if the report has an AutoFormat applied.
`SaveData`	Toggles whether source data is saved with the report.

PivotTable Methods

METHOD	DESCRIPTION
`Format`	Applies an AutoFormat to the report.
`PivotSelect`	Selects all or part of the report.
`PivotTableWizard`	Runs the PivotTable and PivotChart Wizard.
`ShowPages`	Shows each page item in a separate report.
`Update`	Refreshes the report.

PivotField Object

The `PivotField` object represents a row, column, page, or data field in a `PivotTable` object. You can reference a specific `PivotField` object using the `PivotFields` collection, which represents all the `PivotField` objects in a PivotTable report. Here is an example:

```
Worksheets("Budget").PivotTable("Sales").
PivotFields("Division")
```

Alternatively, you can use one of the following `PivotTable` object collections: `RowFields`, `ColumnFields`, `PageFields`, or `DataFields`.

PivotField Properties

PROPERTY	DESCRIPTION
`DrilledDown`	Toggles whether you can drill down to the field's details.
`Name`	The name of the field.
`Orientation`	Where the field resides in the PivotTable layout (row, column, and so on).
`SourceName`	The name of the field in the source data.
`Subtotals`	Sets the subtotals displayed with a row or column field.

PivotField Methods

METHOD	DESCRIPTION
`AutoShow`	Applies a Top 10 AutoShow to the field.
`AutoSort`	Applies an AutoSort to the field.
`Delete`	Removes the field from the report.

PivotItem Object

The `PivotItem` object represents an item in a row, column, or page `PivotField` object. You can reference a specific `PivotItem` object using the `PivotItems` collection, which represents all the `PivotItem` objects in a field. Here is an example:

```
Worksheets("Budget").PivotTable("Sales").
PivotFields("Division").PivotItems("East")
```

PivotItem Properties

PROPERTY	DESCRIPTION
`IsCalculated`	Returns `True` if the item is a calculated item.
`Name`	The name of the item.
`Position`	The item's position within its field.
`SourceName`	The name of the item in the source data.
`Visible`	Toggles the item between visible and hidden.

PivotItem Method

METHOD	DESCRIPTION
`Delete`	Removes the item from the report.

Add a Macro to a Module

If you have a macro that you want to create or copy, you need to add the VBA code for the macro to a module in the Visual Basic Editor.

As you become familiar with manipulating PivotTables using VBA, you will likely come up with many macro ideas for simplifying complex tasks and automating routine and repetitive chores. To implement these macro ideas, you need to type your code into an existing module in the Visual Basic Editor.

Similarly, you may run across a macro that you want to use for your own work, either as-is or by modifying the code to suit your needs. For example, you have seen many PivotTable macro examples throughout this book, and these examples are available on the Web; see www.wiley.com/go/pivottablesvb. You can either transcribe these macros into a module on your system or, better yet, copy the macros and then paste them into a module.

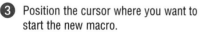

Add a Macro to a Module

1. Start the Visual Basic Editor.

Note: See the task "Open the Visual Basic Editor," earlier in this appendix.

2. Double-click the module into which you want to add the macro.

   If you prefer to add your code to a new module, click Insert➔Module, instead.

   Excel opens the module window.

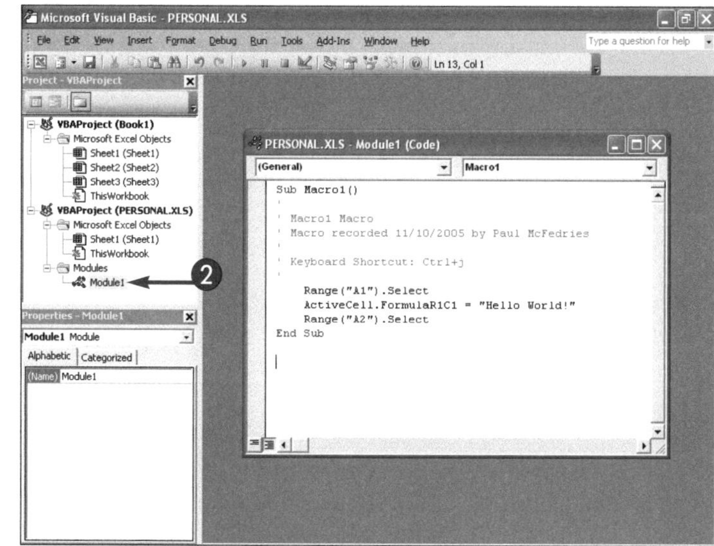
Microsoft Visual Basic - PERSONAL.XLS
Project - VBAProject
VBAProject (Book1)
Microsoft Excel Objects
Sheet1 (Sheet1)
Sheet2 (Sheet2)
Sheet3 (Sheet3)
ThisWorkbook
VBAProject (PERSONAL.XLS)
Microsoft Excel Objects
Sheet1 (Sheet1)
ThisWorkbook
Modules
Module1
2
Properties - Module1
Module1 Module
Alphabetic
Categorized
(Name) Module1
PERSONAL.XLS - Module1 (Code)
(General)
Macro1
Sub Macro1()
' Macro1 Macro
' Macro recorded 11/10/2005 by Paul McFedries
' Keyboard Shortcut: Ctrl+j
Range("A1").Select
ActiveCell.FormulaR1C1 = "Hello World!"
Range("A2").Select
End Sub

3. Position the cursor where you want to start the new macro.

Note: You must add the new macro either before or after an existing macro.

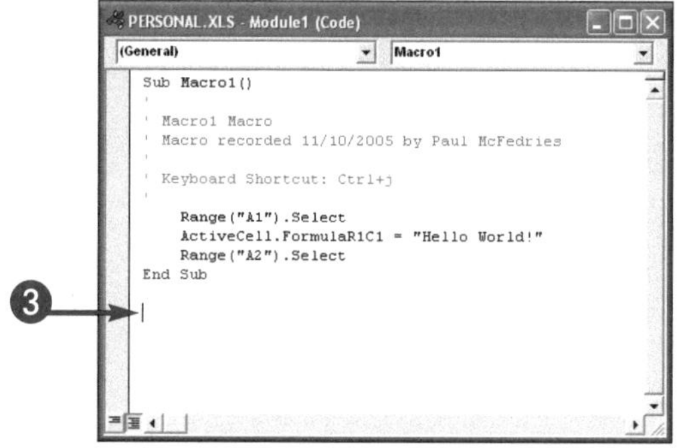
PERSONAL.XLS - Module1 (Code)
(General)
Macro1
Sub Macro1()
' Macro1 Macro
' Macro recorded 11/10/2005 by Paul McFedries
' Keyboard Shortcut: Ctrl+j
Range("A1").Select
ActiveCell.FormulaR1C1 = "Hello World!"
Range("A2").Select
End Sub
3

❹ Type **sub**, a space, and then type the name of the new macro.

Note: Make sure the name you use is not the same as any existing macro name in the module.

❺ Press Enter.

The Visual Basic Editor adds the line `End Sub` to denote the end of the macro.

If you copied the macro code from another source, click Edit➔Paste, instead.

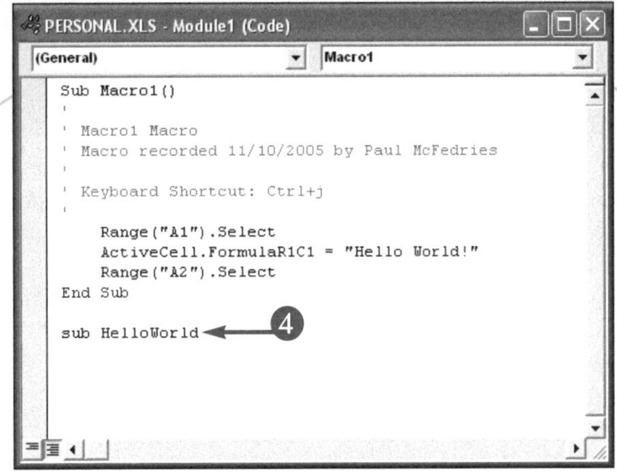

PERSONAL.XLS - Module1 (Code)
(General)
Macro1
Sub Macro1()
' Macro1 Macro
' Macro recorded 11/10/2005 by Paul McFedries
' Keyboard Shortcut: Ctrl+j
Range("A1").Select
ActiveCell.FormulaR1C1 = "Hello World!"
Range("A2").Select
End Sub
sub HelloWorld
4

❻ Type the macro statements between the `Sub` and `End Sub` lines.

- As you type a VBA function, object, property, or method, the Visual Basic Editor displays the syntax in a pop-up box.

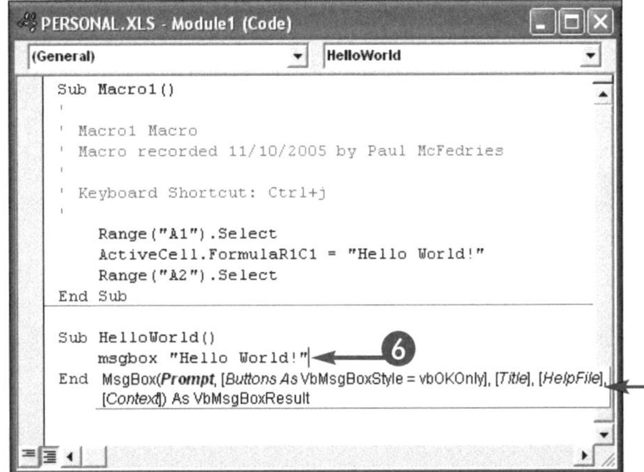

PERSONAL.XLS - Module1 (Code)
(General)
HelloWorld
Sub Macro1()
' Macro1 Macro
' Macro recorded 11/10/2005 by Paul McFedries
' Keyboard Shortcut: Ctrl+j
Range("A1").Select
ActiveCell.FormulaR1C1 = "Hello World!"
Range("A2").Select
End Sub
Sub HelloWorld()
msgbox "Hello World!"
6
End
MsgBox(Prompt, [Buttons As VbMsgBoxStyle = vbOKOnly], [Title], [HelpFile], [Context]) As VbMsgBoxResult

Extra

Here are some notes to bear in mind as you create your macros:

- If you want to begin your macro with a few comments — notes that describe what the macro does — type an apostrophe (') at the beginning of each comment line.
- To make your code easier to read, indent each statement by pressing the Tab key at the beginning of the line — you do not need to do this for the `Sub` and `End Sub` lines. VBA preserves the indentation on subsequent lines, so you only have to indent the first line.
- After you enter a statement, VBA formats the color of each word in the line. By default, VBA keywords are blue, comments are green, errors are red, and all other text is black.
- After you enter a statement, VBA converts keywords to their proper case. For example, if you type **msgbox**, VBA converts it to `MsgBox` when you press Enter.
- By always entering VBA keywords in lowercase letters, you can catch typing errors by looking for those keywords that VBA does not recognize; in other words, the ones that remain in lowercase.
- Click Tools➔Options and then the Editor tab. Select Require Variable Declaration (☐ changes to ☑) and click OK. This adds `Option Explicit` to the top of all modules, which requires you to declare all variables to avoid errors.
- After you enter a statement, VBA checks for syntax errors, which are errors when a word is misspelled, a function is entered incorrectly, and so on. VBA signifies a syntax error either by displaying a dialog box to let you know what the problem is, or by not converting a word to its proper case or color.

Run a Macro

You can run a macro from any open workbook. You have the option of running the macro from the Visual Basic Editor or from Excel.

Excel maintains a list of the macros that are stored in each open workbook. When you want to run a macro, you can either open the module that contains the macro or display Excel's list of available macros. Either way, to run a macro, you must first open the workbook in which the macro is stored.

Note, however, that Excel's default macro security settings may prevent you from running any macros stored outside the Personal Macro Workbook. If you cannot perform the steps in this task — particularly after you create one or more macros and then close and restart Excel — then you either need to lower Excel's macro security settings or "self-sign" your own macros. See the next task, "Set Macro Security," for the details.

After you open a workbook, you then have two ways to run one of its macros:

- From the Visual Basic Editor
- From Excel

It is best to use the Visual Basic Editor if you are testing the macro, because although VBA switches to Excel to execute the code, it drops you back at the Visual Basic Editor when it is done. Therefore, you can run the code, see whether it works properly, and then adjust the code as necessary. When your code is working properly, you can run it from Excel without having to load the Visual Basic Editor.

Run a Macro

RUN A MACRO FROM THE VISUAL BASIC EDITOR

1. Open the module that contains the macro.
2. Click any statement within the macro you want to run.
   - The macro name appears in the list of macros.
3. Click Run➔Run Sub/UserForm.

   You can also press F5 or click the VBA Run button (▶).

   The Visual Basic Editor runs the macro.

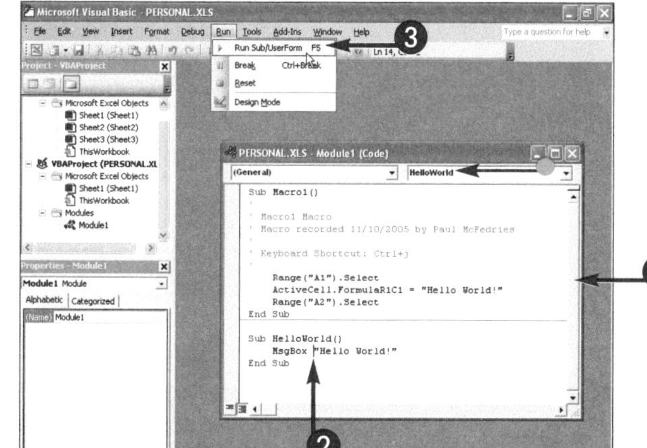

RUN A MACRO FROM EXCEL

1. Open the workbook that contains the macro.

   You can skip Step 1 if the macro is stored in the Personal Macro Workbook.

2. Click Tools➔Macro➔Macros.

   You can also press Alt+F8 or click the VBA Run button (▶) in the Visual Basic toolbar.

   The Macro dialog box appears.

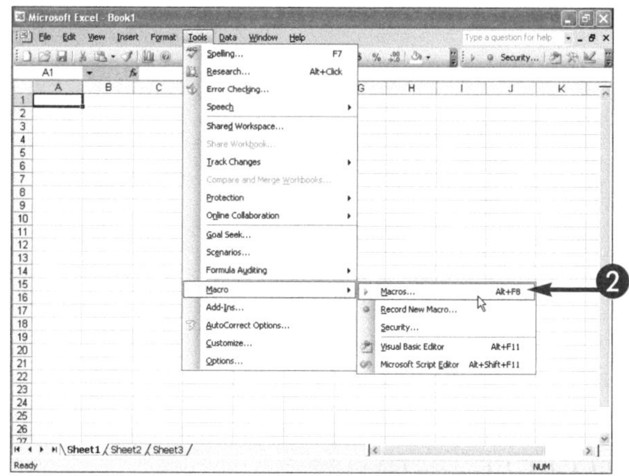

❸ Click [▾] and select the workbook that contains the macro you want to run.

If you are not sure which workbook contains the macro, select All Open Workbooks, instead.

- Excel displays a list of macros in the workbook.

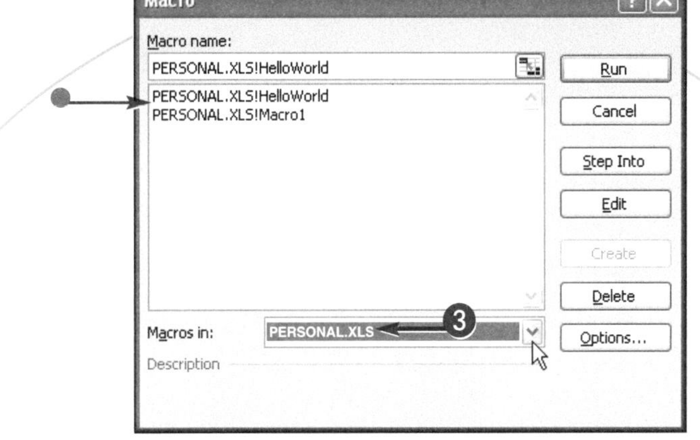

❹ Click the macro you want to run.

❺ Click Run.

If you assigned a shortcut key to the macro, you can avoid Steps 1 to 4 by pressing the shortcut key.

Excel runs the macro.

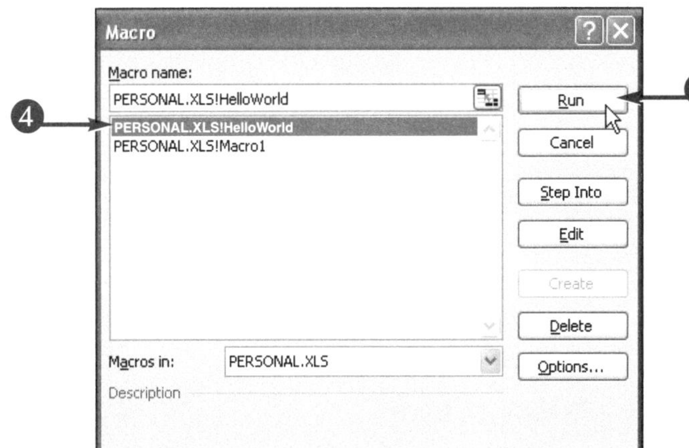

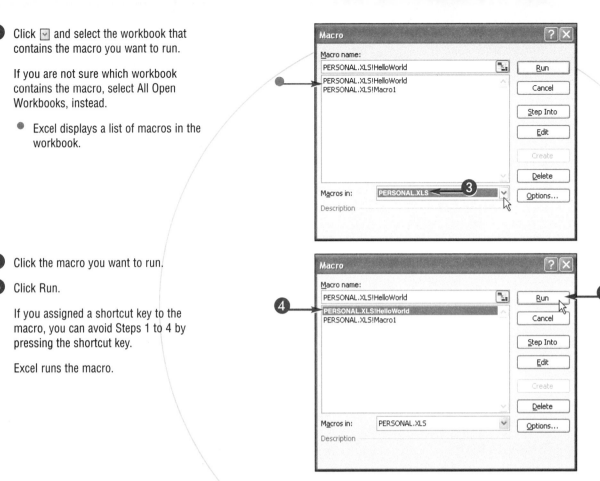

Extra

Some macros expect a particular workbook, worksheet, or cell to be active. You can tell this if you see the following in your code:

- `ActiveWorkbook` — This keyword references the active workbook.
- `ActiveSheet` — This keyword references the active worksheet.
- `ActiveCell` — This keyword references the active cell.

In each case, "active" means that the object — the workbook, worksheet, or cell — has the focus. That is, the active workbook or active worksheet is the one that is displayed in Excel, while the active cell is the one that is currently selected.

If your code uses any of these keywords, make sure that the appropriate workbook, worksheet, or cell is active. For example, it is common to generalize a PivotTable macro to work with any PivotTable by using the `PivotTable` object referenced by the following code:

```
ActiveCell.PivotTable
```

This is convenient, but it means that before you run the macro, you must select a cell in the PivotTable report that you want the macro to work with.

Set Macro Security

VBA is a powerful programming language that can make your life easier and more efficient. Unfortunately, VBA's power is all too often used for nefarious ends—such as viruses that can trash entire systems—so Microsoft Office comes with VBA macros disabled as a security precaution. The exception is macros stored in Excel's Personal Macro Workbook, which you can always run.

Therefore, to run macros — even macros you create yourself — you need to adjust Excel's macro security setting to one of the following values:

- **Very High** — Excel only enables macros if they are installed in a trusted folder on your hard disk. This gives you near-total macro safety, but it is overkill for most people.
- **High** — Excel only enables macros if they come from a trusted source — that is, a source that has digitally signed the VBA project using a trusted code-signing certificate. Macros from any other source are automatically disabled. This is Excel's default security level and it gives you almost total macro safety. However, you need to self-sign your own macros, as described later in this task.
- **Medium** — Excel warns you when a document you are about to open contains macros and asks if you want to enable or disable them. This is a useful option if you often open third-party documents. If you are expecting the document to contain macros, enable them; if you are not expecting macros, disable them and then check for malicious code.
- **Low** — Excel runs all macros without prompting. If you do not have a virus scanner installed, use this level if you only run your own macros and you never open documents created by a third-party. If you do have a virus scanner, this level is probably safe if you only open third-party documents from people or sources you know.

Set Macro Security

SET THE MACRO SECURITY LEVEL

1. Click Tools➔Macro➔Security.

   The Security dialog box appears.

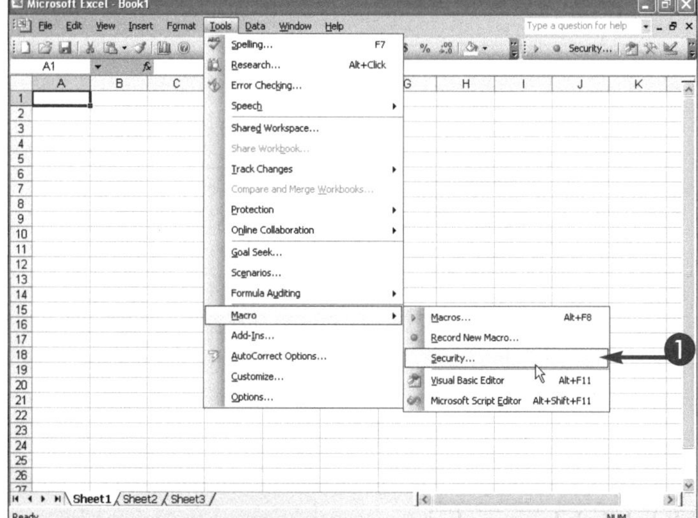

2. Select the security level you want to use.
3. Click OK.

   Excel puts the new security level into effect.

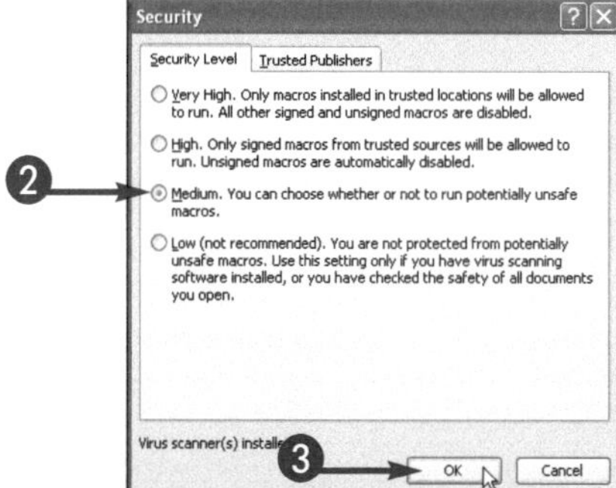

CREATE A DIGITAL CERTIFICATE FOR YOUR MACROS

1. Click Start→My Computer.
2. Open the folder where you installed Microsoft Office.

Note: The default folder for Microsoft Office is C:\Program Files\Microsoft Office.

3. If you have Office 2003, open the Office 11 subfolder.

   For Office XP, open the Office 10 subfolder, instead.

4. Double-click the SelfCert.exe file.

   The Create Digital Certificate dialog box appears.

5. Type your name.
6. Click OK.

   Excel creates a digital certificate in your name and displays a dialog box when it is done.

7. Click OK.

   You can now use the digital certificate to sign your VBA code.

Note: See the next page to learn how to apply the digital certificate to your VBA projects.

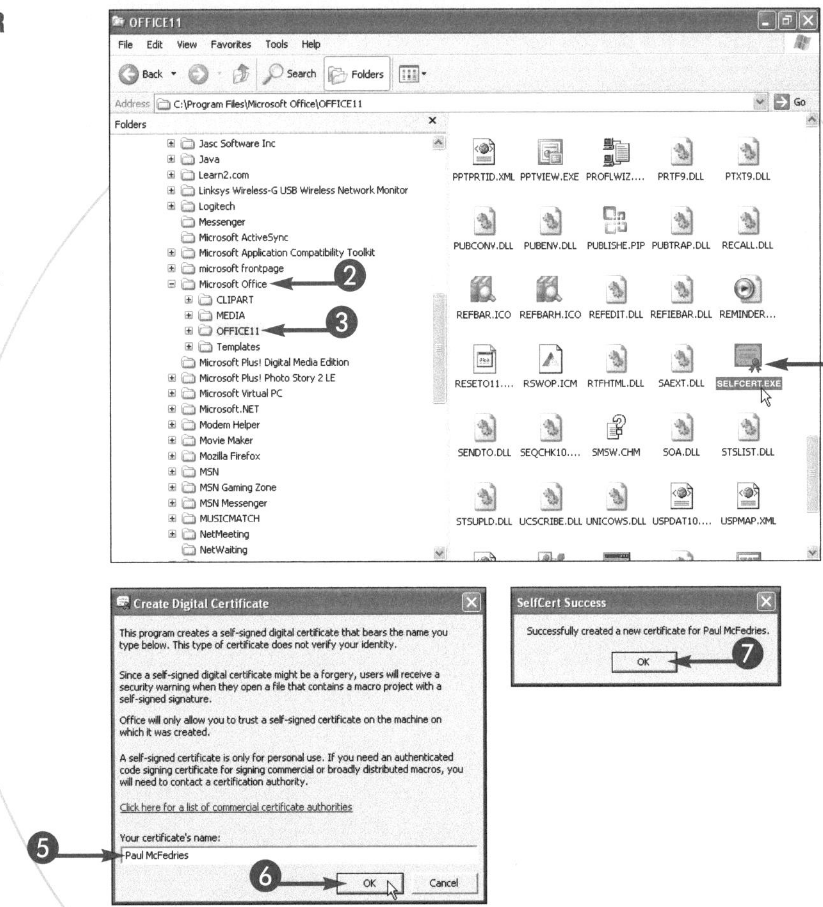

Apply It

If you do not see the SelfCert.exe file, then it is not installed on your system. Click Start→Control Panel, and then click Add or Remove Programs. In the list of installed programs, click Microsoft Office and then click Change to start the Office Setup program. Select Add or Remove Features (○ changes to ◉) and then click Next. Select "Choose advanced customization of applications" (☐ changes to ☑) and then click Next. Click the plus sign (⊞) to open the Office Shared Features branch. Click Digital Certificate for VBA Projects and then click Run from My Computer. Click Update to install the program.

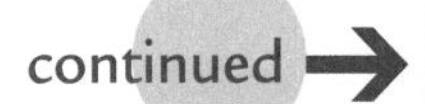
continued →

Set Macro Security (continued)

If you are a VBA programmer and you set Excel's macro security level to High, you immediately run into a problem: Excel does not allow you to run any of your own macros that reside outside the Personal Macro Workbook. This seems like overkill at first, but this stringent security policy is not without its fair share of common sense. That is, Excel has no way to tell whether you are the author of such macros. By definition, macros in the Personal Macro Workbook are yours, but code in any other file could have come from a third party, which makes that code a potential security risk.

Does this mean that you have to store *all* your macros in the Personal Macro Workbook? That would make it difficult to distribute your macros to other people, so fortunately the answer is "no." That is, because it is possible to "prove" that you are the author of your own macros. You can do that by *self-certifying*, which creates a trust certificate that applies only to your own work and to using that work on your own computer. The certificate is not valid on any other computer, so it is not a substitute for getting a proper code-signing digital certificate. However, if all you want to do is run your own macros, then self-certifying enables you to do that while still using the High macro security level.

After you run the SelfCert.exe program to create your personal digital certificate, the next step is to assign that certificate to a VBA project. Note that you need to assign the certificate to each project that contains macros you want to run.

Set Macro Security *(continued)*

ASSIGN A DIGITIAL CERTIFICATE

1. In the Visual Basic Editor, click the project to which you want to assign the certificate.
2. Click Tools➔Digital Signature.

   The Digital Signature dialog box appears.

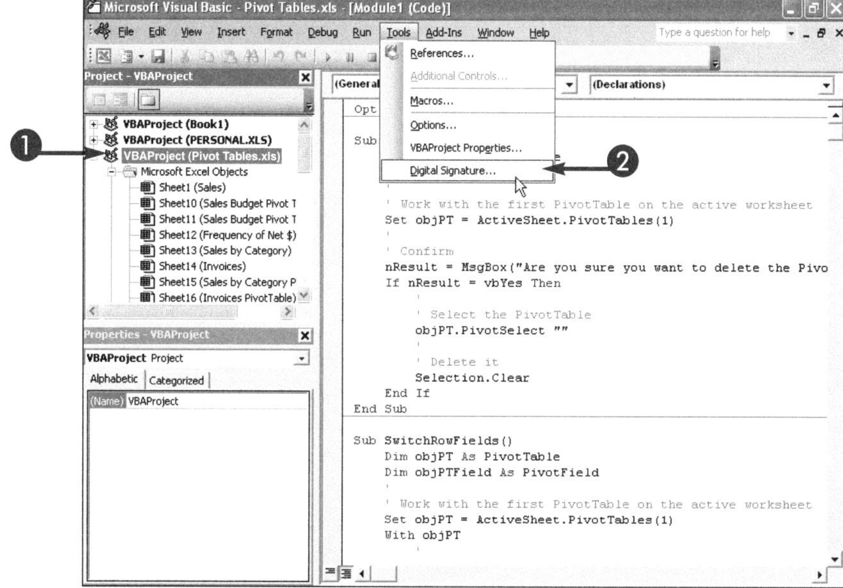

3. Click Choose.

   The Select Certificate dialog box appears.

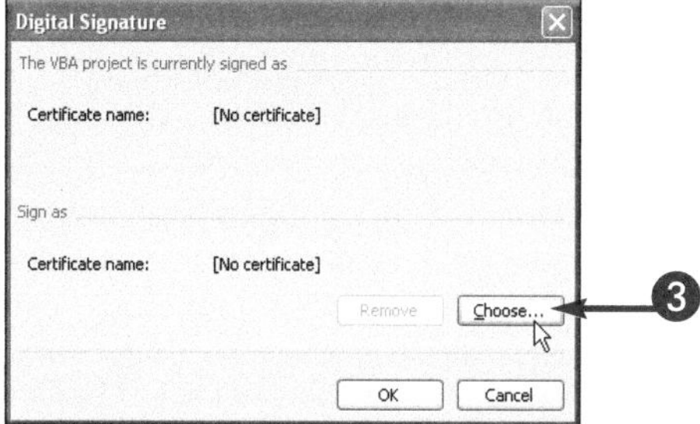

4. Click the certificate that was issued in your name.

5. Click OK.

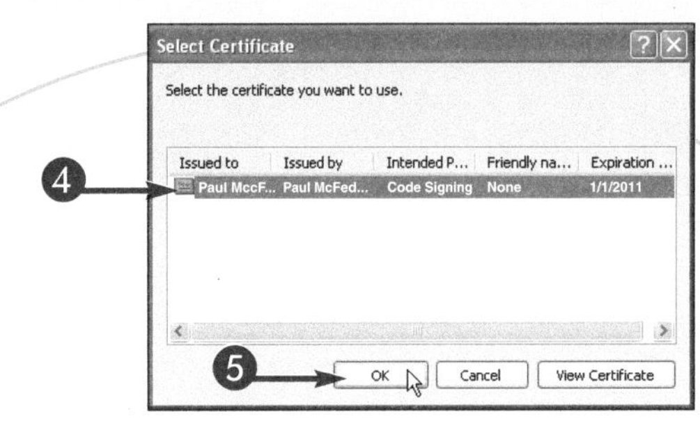

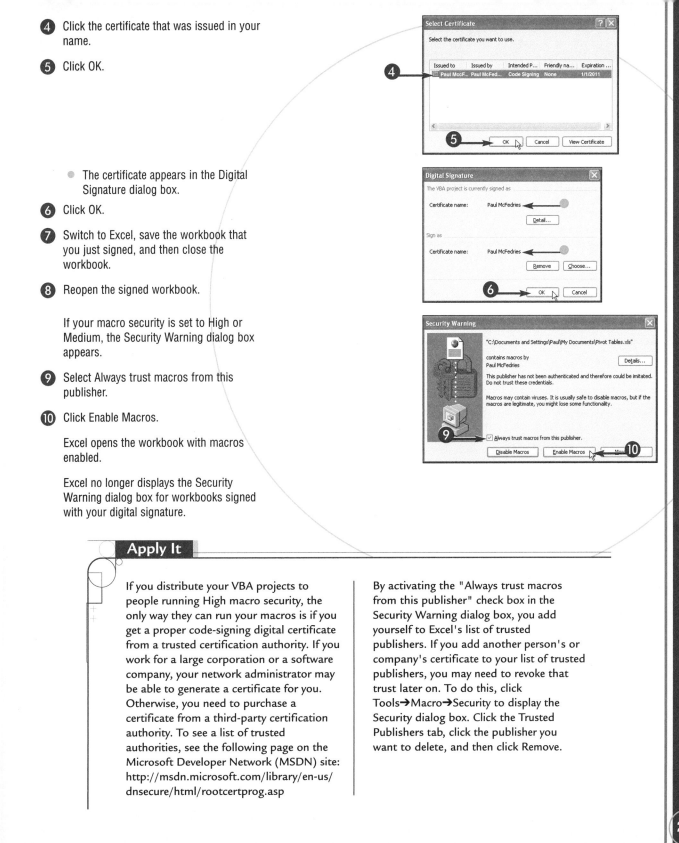

- The certificate appears in the Digital Signature dialog box.

6. Click OK.

7. Switch to Excel, save the workbook that you just signed, and then close the workbook.

8. Reopen the signed workbook.

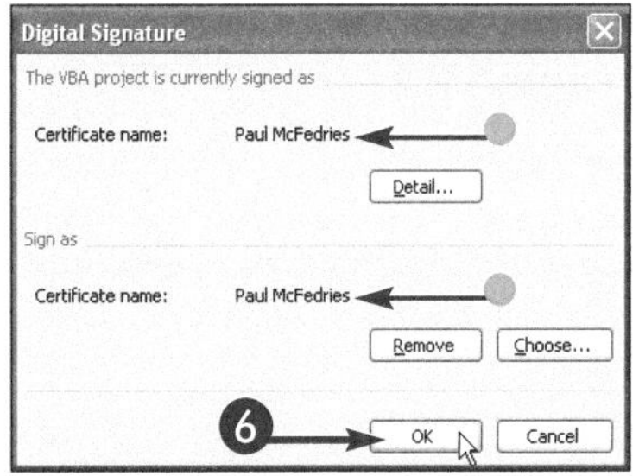

If your macro security is set to High or Medium, the Security Warning dialog box appears.

9. Select Always trust macros from this publisher.

10. Click Enable Macros.

Excel opens the workbook with macros enabled.

Excel no longer displays the Security Warning dialog box for workbooks signed with your digital signature.

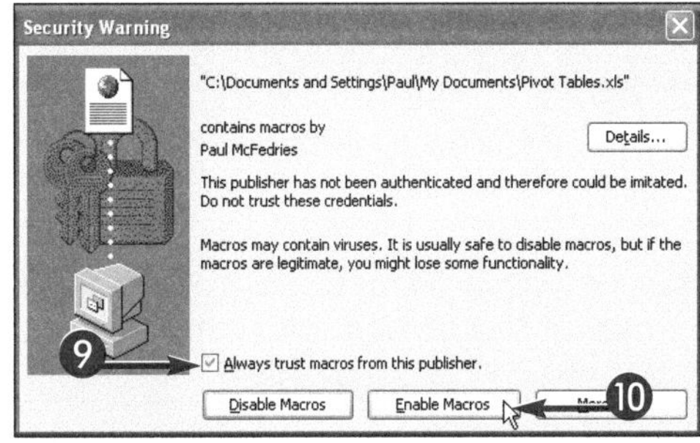

Apply It

If you distribute your VBA projects to people running High macro security, the only way they can run your macros is if you get a proper code-signing digital certificate from a trusted certification authority. If you work for a large corporation or a software company, your network administrator may be able to generate a certificate for you. Otherwise, you need to purchase a certificate from a third-party certification authority. To see a list of trusted authorities, see the following page on the Microsoft Developer Network (MSDN) site: http://msdn.microsoft.com/library/en-us/dnsecure/html/rootcertprog.asp

By activating the "Always trust macros from this publisher" check box in the Security Warning dialog box, you add yourself to Excel's list of trusted publishers. If you add another person's or company's certificate to your list of trusted publishers, you may need to revoke that trust later on. To do this, click Tools→Macro→Security to display the Security dialog box. Click the Trusted Publishers tab, click the publisher you want to delete, and then click Remove.

Assign a Macro to a Toolbar Button

If you have a VBA macro that you use frequently, you can give yourself one-click access to the code by assigning that macro to an Excel toolbar.

A macro saves time by combining several actions into a single procedure. The more often you perform those actions in your day-to-day work, the more time you save by running the macro instead of doing the task by hand. However, the more macros you have, the longer it can take to run the macro you want because you have to scroll through a long list of macros. Assigning a shortcut key can help, but Excel only has a limited number of macro shortcut keys to go around.

A better solution is to create a new toolbar button and assign the macro to that button. As long as you leave the toolbar visible and as long as you leave open the workbook in which the macro is stored, you have one-click access to the macro. Because you must have the macro's workbook open, it is a good idea to only create toolbar buttons for macros in your Personal Macro Workbook, which is always open.

Note, too, that you can assign the macro to a button on an existing toolbar or to a button on a custom toolbar that you create yourself. The custom toolbar is often a better choice because it avoids cluttering existing toolbars with macro buttons. See the tip on the next page to learn how to create a custom toolbar.

Assign a Macro to a Toolbar Button

1. Display the toolbar into which you want to add the macro button.

Note: A quick way to display a toolbar is to right-click any visible toolbar or menu and then click the toolbar name.

2. Click Tools➔Customize.

   You can also right-click any visible toolbar or menu and then click Customize.

   The Customize dialog box appears.

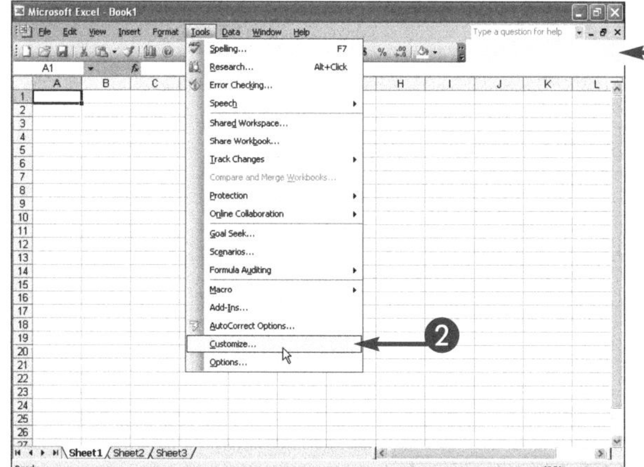

3. Click the Commands tab.
4. Click Macros.
5. Click and drag the Custom Button command and drop it on the toolbar you want to customize.

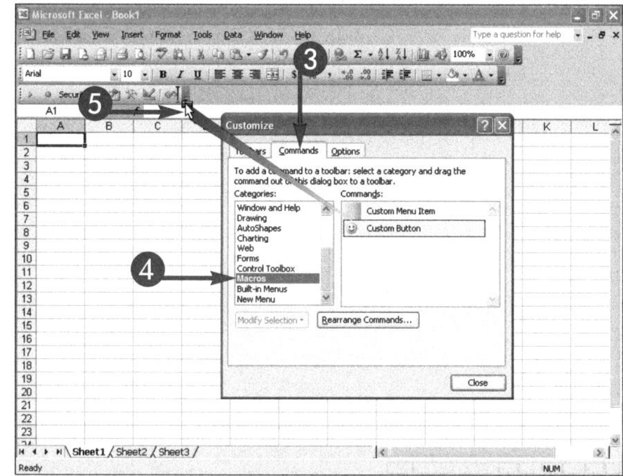

- A new button appears on the toolbar.

6. Click Modify Selection→Assign Macro.

   The Assign Macro dialog box appears.

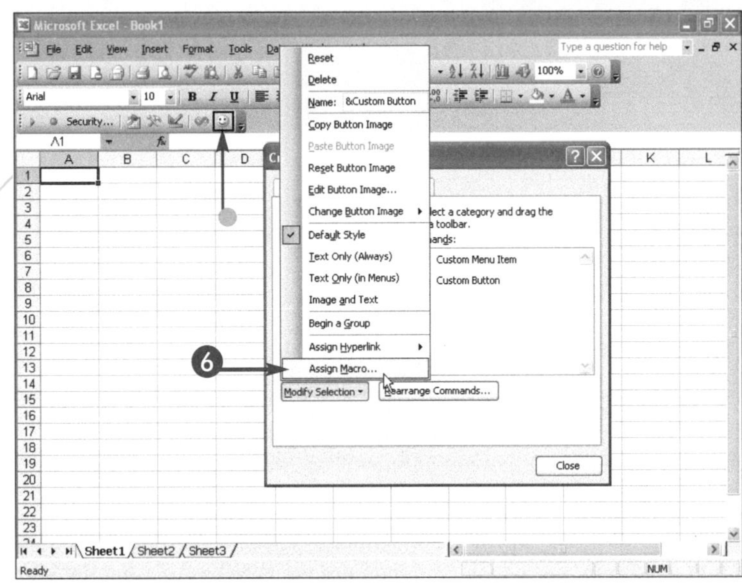

7. Click the macro you want to assign to the new button.

8. Click OK.

   Excel assigns the macro to the toolbar button.

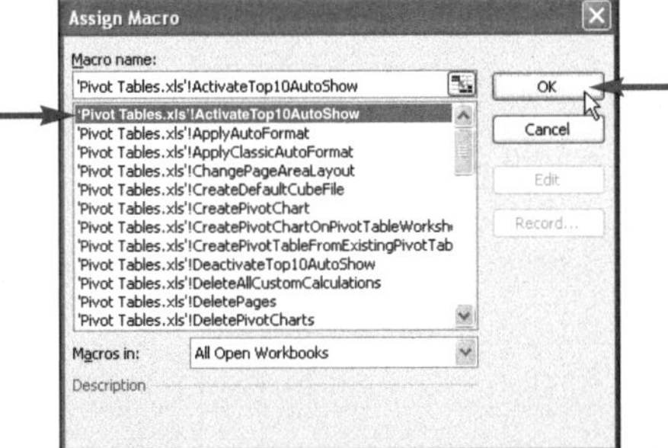

Apply It

You can customize your new toolbar button in a number of ways. With the Customize dialog box open to the Commands tab, click the new toolbar button to select it. Click Modify Selection and then click the button style you want: Default Style — for toolbar buttons, this style shows just the image; Text Only (Always); or Image and Text. If you opt to include text on the button, you can customize the text by editing the contents of the Name text box. If you show an image on the button, you can customize the image by clicking Change Button Image and then clicking the image you want. You can also click Edit Button Image to create a custom image by hand.

If you want to create a new toolbar to hold your macro buttons, display the Customize dialog box and click the Toolbars tab. Click New to display the New Toolbar dialog box. Type the name of your toolbar and then click OK.

Assign a Macro to a Menu Command

If you have a large number of VBA macros, you can give yourself easier access to your most common macros by creating new menu commands that run the macros.

When you learn VBA and, in particular, VBA techniques for manipulating PivotTables, you may find that you end up with several dozen PivotTable-related macros on your system. It is likely that you run most of these macros only occasionally. However, it is common to have a few macros that you use a few times a week, or even every day. When you use a macro regularly, you do not want to waste time scrolling through a long list in the Macros dialog box, or worse, finding and running the macro in the Visual Basic Editor. On the other hand, you may not run the macro frequently enough to justify assigning it to a new toolbar button; see the previous task, "Assign a Macro to a Toolbar Button."

The middle ground here is to create a new command on a menu and then assign the macro to that command. When you pull down the menu and click the new command, Excel runs the macro automatically, which is quite a bit easier than using the Macros dialog box or the Visual Basic Editor. As with macro toolbar buttons, note that you must have the macro's workbook open, so it is a good idea to only create menu commands for macros in your Personal Macro Workbook, which is always open.

Note, too, that you can assign the macro to a command on an existing menu or on a custom menu that you create yourself. The custom menu is often a better choice because it avoids cluttering existing menus with macro commands. See the tip on the next page to learn how to create a custom menu.

Assign a Macro to a Menu Command

1. Click Tools➔Customize.

   You can also right-click any visible toolbar or menu and then click Customize.

   The Customize dialog box appears.

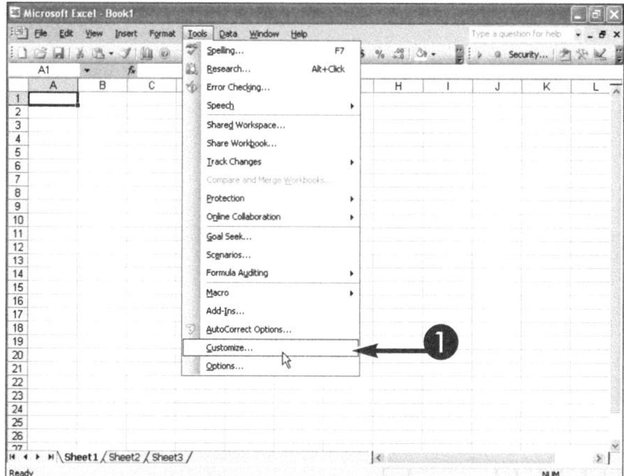

2. Click the Commands tab.
3. Click Macros.
4. Click and drag the Custom Menu Item command and drop it on the menu you want to customize.

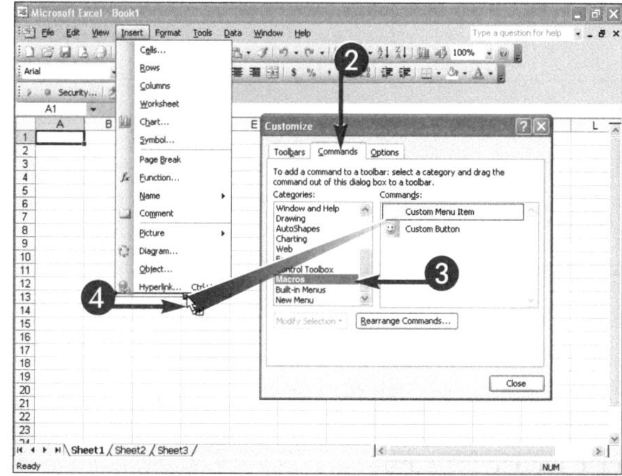

- A new command appears on the menu.

5 Click Modify Selection➔Assign Macro.

The Assign Macro dialog box appears.

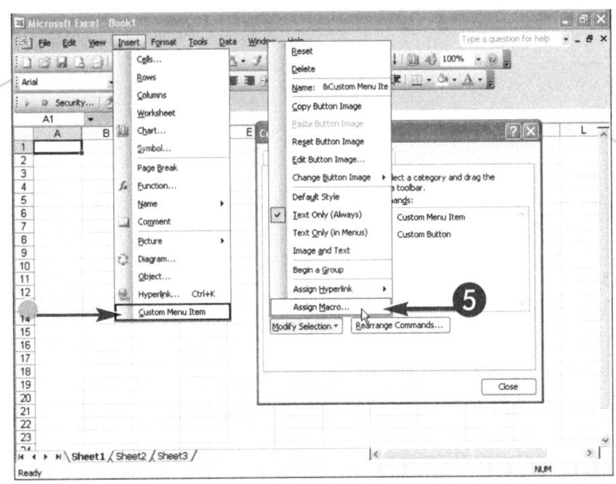

6 Click the macro you want to assign to the new command.

7 Click OK.

Excel assigns the macro to the menu command.

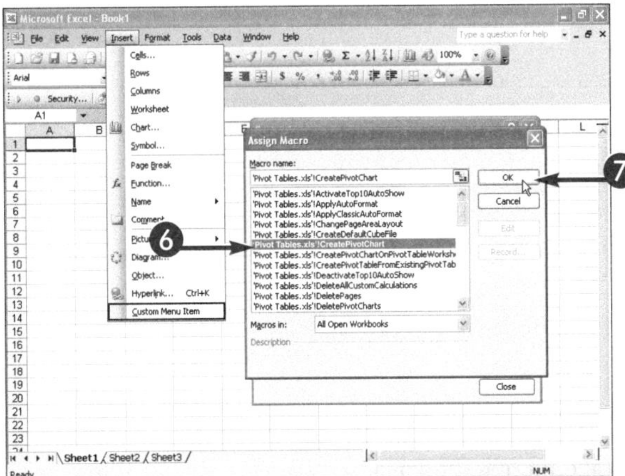

Apply It

You can customize your new menu command in a number of ways. With the Customize dialog box open, click the new menu command to select it. Click Modify Selection and then click the command style you want: Text Only (Always) or Image and Text. To customize the command text, edit the contents of the Name text box. If you show an image along with the command name, you can customize the image by clicking Change Button Image and then clicking the image you want. You can also click Edit Button Image to create a custom image by hand. Finally, you can add a separator bar above the command by clicking the Begin a Group command.

If you want to create a new menu to hold your macro buttons, display the Customize dialog box and click the Commands tab. In the Categories list, click New Menu. In the Commands list, click and drag the New Menu item and then drop it on Excel's menu bar. Click Modify Selection and then type the menu name in the Name text box. You can now use the technique in this task to add macro commands to this new menu.

Glossary of PivotTable Terms

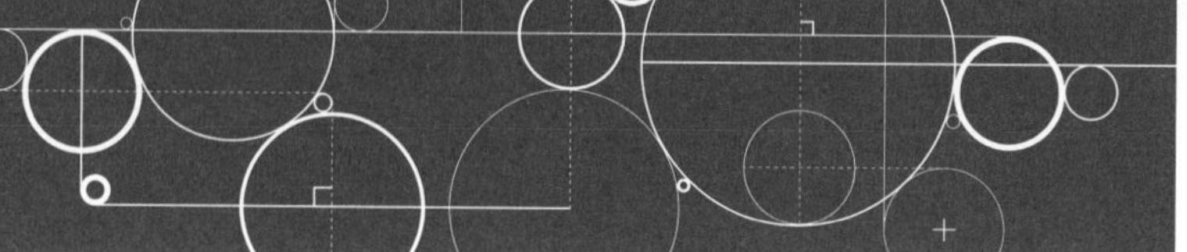

Argument

A value that is used as an input for a function and which the function uses to calculate a result. The arguments of a function must correspond to the function's parameters.

Arithmetic Formula

A formula that combines numeric operands — numeric constants, functions that return numeric results, and fields or items that contain numeric values — with mathematical operators to perform a calculation.

AutoFormat

A collection of formatting options — alignments, fonts, borders, and patterns — that Excel defines for different areas of a PivotTable.

Background Query

A query that Excel executes behind the scenes so that you can continue to perform other work in Excel.

Base Field

In a running total summary calculation, the field on which to base the accumulation.

Break-Even Analysis

The number of units of a product that you must sell for the profit to be 0.

Calculated Field

A new data field in which the values are the result of a custom calculation formula.

Calculated Item

A new item in a row or column field in which the values are the result of a custom calculation.

Category Area

The PivotChart drop area in which the category field appears.

Category Field

A source data field added to the PivotChart's category area; the field's items form the chart's X-axis values.

Column Area

The PivotTable drop area in which the column field appears.

Column Field

A source data field added to a PivotTable's column area; the field's items form the report's columns.

Comma Separated Values

A type of text file in which the items on each line are separated by commas.

Comparison Formula

A formula that combines numeric operands — numeric constants, functions that return numeric results, and fields or items that contain numeric values — with special operators to compare one operand with another.

Conditional Formatting

Formatting — a custom font, border, and pattern — applied to any cells that match criteria that you specify.

Consolidation

Data that is combined from two or more ranges but have a similar structure.

Constant

A fixed value that you insert into a formula and use as-is.

Criteria

One or more expressions that filter a query by specifying the conditions that each record must meet to be included in the results.

Custom Calculation

A formula that you define to produce PivotTable values that otherwise do not appear in the report if you use only the source data fields and Excel's built-in summary calculations.

Data

The calculated values that appear within the data area.

Data Analysis

The application of tools and techniques to organize, study, reach conclusions about, and sometimes also make predictions about, a specific collection of information.

Data Area

The PivotTable drop area in which the data field appears.

Data Connection File

A data source that connects to a wide variety of data, including ODBC, SQL Server, SQL Server OLAP Services, Oracle, and Web-based data retrieval services.

Data Field

A source data field added to a PivotTable's data area; Excel uses the field's numeric data to perform the report's summary calculations.

Data Model

A collection of cells designed as a worksheet version of some real-world concept or scenario. The model includes not only the raw data, but also one or more cells that represent some analysis of the data.

Data Source

A file, database, or server that contains data.

Data Table

A range of cells where one column consists of a series of input cells. You can then apply each of those inputs to a single formula, and Excel displays the results for each case.

Data Warehouse

A data structure with a central fact table that contains the numeric data you want to summarize and pointers to surrounding related tables.

Delimited Text File

A text file that contains data and each line item is separated by a delimiter.

Delimiter

The character used to separate items on each line in a text file.

Dimension

A category of data in a data warehouse. A dimension is analogous to a row, column, or page field in an ordinary data source.

Drill Down

View the details that underlie a specific data value in a PivotTable.

Drop Area

A region of the PivotTable onto which you can drop a field from the source data or from another area of the PivotTable.

External Data

Source data that comes from a nonExcel file or database, or from a remote source such as a server or Web page.

Fact Table

The primary table in a data warehouse. The fact table contains data on events or processes — the *facts* — within a business, such as sales transactions or company expenses.

Field

A distinct category of data in a PivotTable or a database table.

Fixed-Width Text File

A text file containing data where the items on each line use up a set amount of space.

Formula

A set of symbols and values that perform some kind of calculation and produce a result. All Excel formulas have the same general structure: an equals sign (=) followed by one or more operands separated by one or more operators.

Function

A predefined formula that is built-into Excel.

continued

Glossary of PivotTable Terms (continued)

Grand Totals

The totals that appear in a PivotTable for each row and column item.

Inner Field

The field that is closest to the data area in the row or column area.

Input Cells

The cells used as input values by a data table.

Item

A unique value from a row, column, or page field.

Labels

The nondata area elements of a PivotTable. The labels include the field buttons, field items, and page area drop-down list.

Levels

A collection of hierarchical groupings in a data warehouse dimension.

List

A worksheet collection of related information with an organizational structure that makes it easy to add, edit, and sort data. A list is a type of database where the data is organized into rows and columns, with each column representing a database field and with each row representing a database record.

Measure

A column of numeric values within a data warehouse fact table. A measure represents the data that you want to summarize.

Member

The items that appear within each level in a data warehouse dimension.

Method

An action you can perform on an object.

Module

A special window in which you can view, edit, and run VBA macros.

Multidimensional Data

OLAP data in which the fact table contains keys to multiple dimension tables.

Object

A distinct item that is manipulable via VBA code.

Object Model

A complete summary of the objects associated with a particular program or feature, the hierarchy used by those objects, and the properties and methods supported by each object.

ODBC

Open Database Connectivity. A database standard that enables a program to connect to and manipulate a data source.

OLAP

Online analytical processing. A database technology that enables you to quickly retrieve and summarize immense and complex data sources.

OLAP Cube

A data structure that takes the information in a data warehouse and summarizes each measure by every dimension, level, and member.

OLAP Cube File

A version of an OLAP cube that has been saved to a local or network folder. A cube file is "offline" in the sense that the data is not connected to an OLAP server, so it is a static snapshot of the data.

Operand

In a worksheet formula, a literal value, cell reference, range, range name, or worksheet function. In a custom calculation formula, a literal value, worksheet function, PivotTable field, or PivotTable item.

Operator

In a formula, a symbol that combines operands in some way, such as the plus sign (+) and the multiplication sign (*).

Operator Precedence

The order in which Excel processes operands in a formula.

Optional Argument

A function argument that you are free to use or omit, depending on your needs.

Outer Field

In the row or column area, the field that is farthest from the data area.

Page Area

The PivotTable drop area in which the page field appears.

Page Field

A source data field added to a PivotTable's page area; you use the field's items to filter the report.

Parameter

A placeholder in a function that specifies the type of argument value.

Phantom Field Item

A PivotTable field item that no longer exists in the source data.

Pivot

Move a field from one drop area of a PivotTable to another.

Pivot Cache

Source data that Excel keeps in memory to improve PivotTable performance.

Property

A programmable characteristic of an object.

Query

Retrieves data from an external data source, particularly by specifying the tables and fields you want to work with, filtering the records using criteria, and sorting the results.

Query Page-By-Page

Queries the server for new data each time you change the page field item; used with a server page field.

Record

An individual set of field data in a database table.

Refresh

Rebuild a PivotTable report using the most current version of the source data.

Required Argument

A function argument that must appear between the function's parentheses in the specified position.

Row Area

The PivotTable drop area in which the row field appears.

Row Field

A source data field added to a PivotTable's row area; the field's items form the report's rows.

Running Total

A type of summary calculation that returns the cumulative sum of the values that appear in a given set of data. Most running totals accumulate over a period of time.

Scenario

A collection of input values that you plug into formulas within a model to produce a result.

Self-Certify

Create a trust certificate that applies only to your own VBA projects and only to those projects on your own computer.

continued →

Series Area

The PivotChart drop area in which the series field appears.

Series Field

A source data field added to the PivotChart's series area; the field's items form the chart's data series.

Server Page Field

A page field in which Excel only retrieves the data for the currently displayed page item. When you display a different page, Excel queries the server and retrieves the new data.

Solve Order

The order in which Excel solves the calculated items in a PivotTable.

Source Data

The original data from which you built your PivotTable. The source data can be an Excel range or list, an Access table, a Word table, a text file, a Web page, an XML file, SQL Server data, or OLAP server data, among others.

Star Schema

A type of data warehouse.

Summary Calculation

The mathematical operation that Excel applies to the values in a numeric field to yield the summary that appears in the data area. Excel offers 11 built-in summary calculations: Sum, Count, Average, Maximum, Minimum, Product, Count Numbers, Standard Deviation (sample), Standard Deviation (population), Variance (sample), and Variance (population).

Table

A two-dimensional arrangement of rows and columns that contains data in a database.

What-If Analysis

The creation of worksheet models designed to analyze hypothetical situations.

XML

eXtensible Markup Language. A standard that enables the management and sharing of structured data using simple text files.

INDEX

Symbols

A

B

C

D

INDEX

E

F

INDEX

G

H

I

L

M

INDEX

N

O

P

INDEX

INDEX

T

U

V

W

X

Y

Z

For more professional instruction in a visual format, try these.

All designed for visual learners—just like you!

Read Less–Learn More®

Visual®

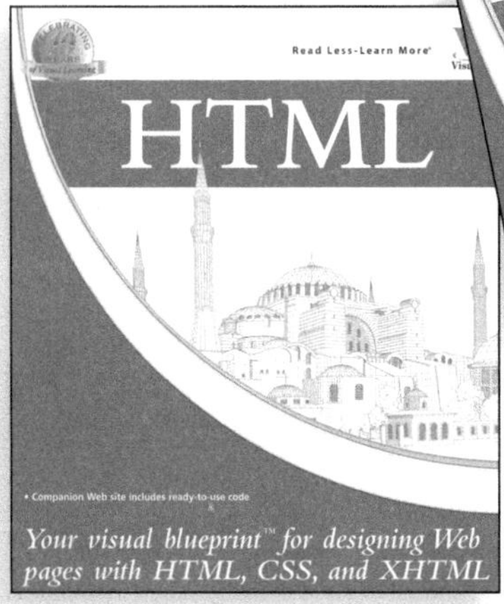

0-7645-8331-X

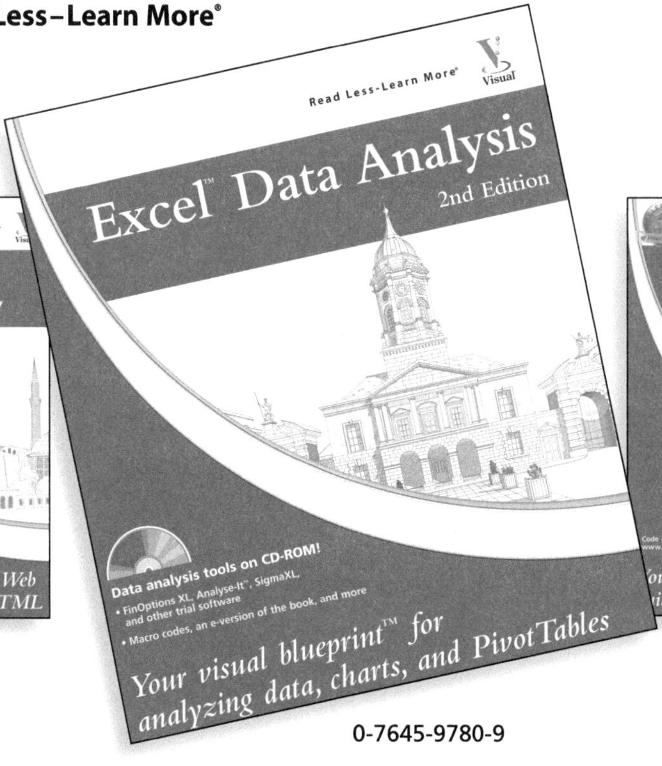

0-7645-9780-9

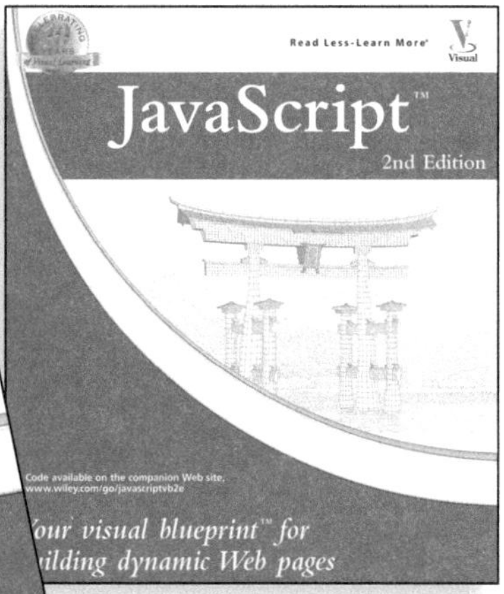

0-7645-7497-3

For a complete listing of *Visual Blueprint*™ titles and other Visual books, go to wiley.com/go/visualtech

Visual®
An Imprint of WILEY
Now you know.